Racism at Work

Racism at Work

Bobby Siu

UNIVERSITY OF TORONTO PRESS
Toronto Buffalo London

Racism at Work

Irwin Law
An imprint of University of Toronto Press
Toronto Buffalo London
utppublishing.com
Printed in Canada

ISBN 978-1-0498-0021-9 (paper) ISBN 978-1-0498-0022-6 (PDF)
ISBN 978-1-0498-0023-3 (EPUB)

Library and Archives Canada Cataloguing in Publication

Title: Racism at work / Bobby Siu.
Names: Siu, Bobby, 1948- author
Description: Includes bibliographical references and index.
Identifiers: Canadiana (print) 20250255677 | Canadiana (ebook) 20250255731 | ISBN 9781049800219 (softcover) | ISBN 9781049800233 (EPUB) | ISBN 9781049800226 (PDF)
Subjects: LCSH: Discrimination in employment—Law and legislation—Canada. | LCSH: Racism in the workplace—Canada.
Classification: LCC KE3254 .S58 2026 | LCC KF3464 .S58 2026 kfmod | DDC 344.7101/133—dc23

Cover design: Greg Jorss
Cover image: James Lee/"Close-Up Photo of Feathers"

We wish to acknowledge the land on which the University of Toronto Press operates. This land is the traditional territory of the Wendat, the Anishnaabeg, the Haudenosaunee, the Métis, and the Mississaugas of the Credit First Nation.

University of Toronto Press acknowledges the financial support of the Government of Canada, the Canada Council for the Arts, and the Ontario Arts Council, an agency of the Government of Ontario, for its publishing activities.

Canada Council for the Arts Conseil des Arts du Canada

Funded by the Government of Canada Financé par le gouvernement du Canada

To
Forrest
with
Love

Summary Table of Contents

Detailed Table of Contents

List of Tables

Preface

Not many people like to talk about racism publicly. The concept triggers negative and uncomfortable feelings among people.

Racism, as a baggage of human thoughts and practices, violates one of the core values in Western cultures—that every individual is born equal and should not be treated unfairly. Hence, at an individual level, some feel offended when accused of being racist. The term itself triggers an immediate negative reaction. For some people, it is difficult to accept the notion that racism exists on a collective and societal scale. For others, racism at an individual personal level is even more problematic. Accordingly, the common ways in which to bypass these uncomfortable feelings is for people to view racism as only a subjective perception as a result of poor communication and misunderstanding and to believe that there are a few "bad apples" around or that racialized people are "too sensitive" about how they have been treated and how they are more than ready to label others as racially biased, prejudiced, or discriminatory.

Overall, there are many opinions about racism and why it exists. This book does not pretend to foster a consensus on this concept because it seems rather futile to do so. Often, emotions take over reasons, and biases take over facts. However, by using research studies, statistical data, and personal observations and experiences of racialized minorities, the book aims to show how extensively, deeply, and persistently racism has permeated our society, in general, and our workplaces, in particular.

Why should we pay attention to workplace racism now?

It must be acknowledged upfront that there are many empirical studies done on the topic of racism. However, only certain aspects of racism have been focused on in these studies, and other aspects have been relatively neglected in the past. In English-speaking countries, due to their countries' history with slavery, American scholars have concentrated almost exclusively on anti-Black racism and have not focused on other racialized groups, including Indigenous peoples. Due to their countries' colonial past, English scholars have focused on racism involving people from their former colonized countries. In contrast to other English-speaking countries, Canadian studies on racism are relatively under-developed considering Canada's long history with Indigenous peoples and the arrival of racialized minorities with Black and Asian backgrounds in the past decades.

A significant portion of these studies on racism in English-speaking countries has focused largely on law enforcement (primarily on policing and incarceration). Only in recent years has there been an emerging interest in knowing more about the racial issues in health care, housing, education, and employment. While studies of racism in these emerging fields are desperately needed for their contributions to a better understanding of racism, they remain sporadic and unsystematic, and concerned researchers are yearning for more.

Racism in employment is the field designated for analysis in this book largely because work is an integral part of our lives. It provides financial resources, social identities, and the potential for self-actualization in each of us. As this book will discuss later, workplace racism plays a critical role in the life chances of every individual as well as in the future of the country.

PURPOSES OF WRITING THIS BOOK

The first purpose of this book is to meet the challenge of filling in the knowledge gap in racism studies. Racism has been studied in many ways through time. Traditionally, studies of racialized people and Indigenous people have largely dwelled on the topic of unemployment and employment in low-status jobs with low income, prestige, and power. In Canada, in very broad strokes, racialized people and Indigenous peoples have been clustered, in a disproportional manner, in the low end of the occupational structure. And Canada, as a whole, is like a "vertical mosaic," as coined by John Porter (1965). According to him, elites are disproportionately dominated by White English Canadians, with multiple ethnic and racialized groups concentrated in different segments and strata below them. Exactly how such a mosaic is formed in the larger society remains a mystery, and whether such a hierarchical pattern is evident in the workplace is also unclear.

There are many aspects of employment that could be studied but which have not yet been considered. With this in mind, this book aims to fill in the knowledge gap by breaking down employment into smaller components and examining the different stages of an employee's career. These stages of work cover individuals as they go through their "life cycle" of employment, including recruitment, selection, hiring, onboarding, training, development, promotion, succession, retention, and termination. In this manner, racism is analyzed in a systematic manner. The core question posed is how human resources mechanisms work to perpetuate the unequal status of racialized people and Indigenous peoples.

The second purpose of the book is to examine the loopholes and blind spots in our current legislation, regulations, policies, programs, and practices in the areas of anti-racism. For many years, we have had numerous employment laws and practices that purport to be fair to all people. The federal and provincial laws in human rights, employment equity, health and safety, and leadership diversity have been enacted with the goal of instilling fairness, equity, and equality in the workplace. Moreover, for decades, business practices in diversity, equity, and inclusiveness and equality of opportunities have been marketed and put into operation. And, with the recent addition of environmental, social, and governance guiding principles and measurement in business practices, one would wonder why progress in eradicating racism has been so slow and, in some instances, reversed in momentum. Should we look at all these measures with a critical lens and see why they have failed? To what extent does legislation end racism at work, or is the failure a function of policy focus or program design, the manner of execution and management, the allocation of resources, the degree of law enforcement, or other factors that have yet to be discovered? Is it safe to say that workplace racism is such a huge monster that no amount of effort can wrestle it to the ground, or are there so many factors at work that persistently keep workplace racism alive and well?

The third purpose of this book is to provide recommendations for change. Once we realize the overwhelming, persistent, and penetrating nature of racism at work and the weaknesses of the current legal system and business practices in eradicating racism, it is hard to shake off the idea of inaction on our part. This book will ask the following questions: is there anything that the government, businesses, and workers can do to end racism; which aspects of the legislation and law enforcement could be changed; what strategies can organizations develop to redirect anti-racism work; and what can workers do inside and outside their workplaces?

SEQUENCE OF PRESENTATION

To accomplish these three purposes, this book approaches racism in a holistic and contextual manner. It views racism as an overwhelming force that permeates the livelihoods of racialized and Indigenous peoples and the human resources management of organizations in the public, private, and non-profit sectors. The book is divided into four parts: Part 1 examines the social context of racism as it has developed in the twentieth century; Part 2 exposes racism in the workplace as it manifested in the employment field, people's stereotypes and prejudice, hiring, promotion and retention domains; Part 3 discusses the roles of change agents – governments, employers, and labour unions; and Part 4 is an examination of both the internal and external forces which are shaping racism and how that could be tackled.

PART 1: SOCIAL CONTEXT OF RACISM

In Chapter 1, we will examine the historical context of our times around the COVID-19 pandemic and explain why, at that historical juncture, our traditional and comfortable world-views had shattered. The configuration of the pandemic, economic forces, political directions, and social protests/movements became fertile ground for examining the work environment critically and exploring how social justice issues are getting more attention.

In Chapter 2, the concept of racism will be examined with a focus on how different schools of thought have shed light on the functions of racism. These schools elaborated their arguments on why racism exists. Along with these schools are the government perspectives upon which public policies, strategies, and programs have been developed and implemented. They represent the pragmatic side of tackling racism—namely, what it is rather than why it is. A pragmatic working definition of racism is proposed for this book that guides our inquiry on workplace racism.

Chapter 3 presents a bigger picture of what it is like to be an Indigenous and racialized person living in Canada with all the embedded racial biases in our society. Every domain of individual lives is saturated with racial disparities when compared with non-Indigenous and non-racialized groups. This chapter includes examples of people at different stages of life, including childhood and adulthood, and from all walks of life, ranging from the school system and mass media to recreation, sports, and the criminal justice system. In each of these spheres, racism manifests itself in different forms. The idea is to show how prevalent racism is in our society and how encompassing it is in its affect on people.

PART 2: WORKPLACE RACISM

As the book continues, starting in Chapter 4 and ending in Chapter 8, workplace racism is seen as an extension of the racism that is found in the larger social context outside the work environment. Racism is analyzed in the context of the "life cycle" of individuals going through different stages of employment: job application, hiring, job advancement/movement, and their exit from the work organization. Using this "life cycle" approach, readers may relate to, and reflect on, the progression of their own careers and see how racial biases are embedded in organizational policies and programs, work arrangements, culture, and ideology. They may see how the stereotyping and prejudice of people that has played out in the larger society are now at play in the workplace. It is through these discussions of the multiple forms of racism found in different stages of employment that various pieces of laws and practices of employers, employees, and unions are examined critically in order to assess how to end racism effectively.

Throughout these chapters, racialized and Indigenous peoples share many similar aspects of racialization at work, and they are often discussed as a collective entity. However, there are situations where Indigenous peoples' issues are different from those of racialized minorities (such as Blacks and Asians). In those cases, they are discussed separately for clarity purposes.

PART 3: CHANGE AGENTS

In light of the identified problems inherent in the legislation, the ways in which laws are enforced, and the misplaced attention on some business policies, programs, and initiatives, Chapters 9, 10, and 11 shift their focus to the question of the alternative ways in which government, employers, and unions could end racism at work. In terms of legislative changes, these chapters focus on creating a new focus on how best to revamp legislation, shift the direction and resources of law enforcement, and strengthen public education and skills development in order to be stricter in imposing penalties and more resourceful for smaller employers.

In terms of employers' focus, Part 3 emphasizes the structural modification to, or changes in, policy and program work, an increase in resource allocation, an increase in the accountability of executives and managers in social justice, an extensive education and training campaign for middle-level managers and employees, and a cultural shift in the workplace.

In terms of unions' initiatives, Part 3 emphasizes consultation and joint responsibilities, human right education and training, and the removal of seniority rights, supportive networks of employees, and negotiation on social justice matters. In one way or another, these recommendations could be embedded in amendments to existing legislation, corporate policies, and collective agreements.

PART 4: NEW CHALLENGES, NEW DIRECTIONS

In Chapters 12, this book wraps up the discussion on racism and anti-racism by showing the power dynamics of the work environment and what employees can and cannot do. It points out the restraining forces within the workplace for both employers and employees as well as some plausible solutions. Chapter 13 considers the historical juncture and puts racism and anti-racism in the larger context beyond the workplace, showing how emerging and persistent political, social, and technological forces have given rise to authoritarianism, illiberalism, and populism; hate speech, hate crimes, and violence; anti-wokeism and its institutionalization; and challenges on the bias of artificial intelligence, which are impacting on the workplace. It demonstrates how government, employers, unions, and racialized and Indigenous peoples must keep in mind how they navigate this new world order in order to eradicate racism. Chapter 14 summarizes the importance of government actions, partnership with employers and labour unions, and the urgency of racism eradication at this historical juncture.

SOURCES OF INFORMATION

To write a book of this nature, I depended on both primary and secondary sources. Information on employers and employees and their experiences come from the author's interviews and consultations, focus groups, surveys, and observations over the past thirty years of consulting experiences in the private, broader public, public, and non-profit sectors, community work on social justice projects, and academic research on issues related to human rights, race relations, employment equity, diversity, and inclusiveness.

Secondary sources came from statistical data on race, population, and the labour force taken from Statistics Canada as well as from many other research studies on race and employment. Most information is taken from Canadian sources, while some is based on international sources. This book utilizes many academic findings and research reports from governments, think tanks, and consulting firms. Human right tribunal decisions and human right policy papers, white papers, and position papers have also been used.

TERMINOLOGY

The term "Indigenous Peoples" or "Indigenous people" is used in this book. They are preferred by the people who used to be called "Aboriginal peoples" by the federal government. The latter is a term used in the *Employment Equity Act* to mean "persons who are Indians, Inuit or Metis."[1] Statistics Canada uses "Indigenous people" (with the word "people" spelled without an "s" and the "p" not capitalized) to mean First Nations, Metis, and Inuit.

"Racialized people" is broadly used in this book, along with "racialized population" or "racialized groups," "racialized persons," or "racialized communities." Often, in Canada, the term "Black, Indigenous, and People of Colour" (BIPOC) is used to mean "racialized people." This term represents a mix of American ("people of colour" and "Black") and Canadian usages ("Indigenous"). When the data sources, especially those from government publications (such as Statistics Canada) are cited, the term "visible minority" is used. This term is seen as being out of date by some scholars and institutions (such as the

1 *Employment Equity Act*, SC 1995, c 44.

United Nations), but the federal government of Canada continues to use it in the federal *Employment Equity Act* as well as elsewhere. This term defines visible minorities as "persons, other than Aboriginal peoples, who are non-Caucasian in race or non-white in colour." Following the categories used in the Canadian Census for communication and analytical products, the visible minority population consists of South Asian, Chinese, Black, Filipino, Arab, Latin American, Southeast Asian, West Asian, Korean, and Japanese.

"Diversity, equity and inclusiveness" is a term that will be broadly used in this book. It is still evolving in its usage both in the United States and Canada. Often, this term refers to a school of management thought that pays special attention to the value of incorporating and celebrating differences among people in the workplace and a focus on equitable representation of diverse populations and their acceptance and inclusion in workplace practices.

PART ONE

SOCIAL CONTEXT OF RACISM

While this book focuses specifically on how racism operates in the workplace, it seems reasonable to expand our horizon broader to the outside perimeter of the workplace so that we can see the social changes that are taking place in Canada and the larger world and the forms of racism that are in action outside of employment in Canada. The social context largely focuses on the impact of COVID-19 on people and the workplace, the political direction of the federal government, and social justice protests/movements. It proves to be useful when we try to understand racism and how to combat it better in a specific historical period in which many of our traditional thoughts about the workplace, the economy, and the world have been shattered and potential alternatives in work arrangement and human resources management are visible as a result.

In this part, we will review different schools of thoughts on racism—what it means and why it exists. There have been many articles and books written on this concept, but, in this instance, it will be examined briefly and compared with how governments define the concept. Such a contrast allows us to understand the focus of the government in tackling racism and the boundaries of its definitions. In addition, based on scholarly research and government documents as well as statistical data, the experiences of racialized and Indigenous peoples throughout their lives are summarized, giving readers a broad spectrum of their racial encounters and observations. Evidence has shown that, compared with their counterparts, racialized and Indigenous peoples are disadvantaged in every aspect of their lives from birth to death.

CHAPTER 1

Disruptive Forces

INTRODUCTION

We are at a historical juncture in which several macroscopic challenges are coming together affecting the economic, political, and social aspects of Canada. These challenges come from the top, the bottom, and anywhere in between. They are political ideologies, utopian ideas, geopolitical forces, and public health, labour force, and economic changes. In itself, each one of these challenges may not be strong enough to advance social justice; however, when they come together, they force people to ask critical questions and cast doubt on the status quo of how things have been conventionally done:

- economic: the emergence and prevalence of the COVID-19 pandemic and inflation and their disruptive impacts on work and the Canadian economy;
- political: the political messages and public policies declared from above; and
- social: the rise of social justice protests and movements representing the voices from below.

These challenges have signalled a shift in the political and economic climate and the uncertainty of the future. In this chapter, we will examine how the configuration of these challenges constitutes the background of why racism has emerged as a topical public discussion. Now is the time for us to ask more probing questions on racism related to the workplace and a more diligent search for viable solutions. They are the catalysts for us to think about racism.

We are currently going through a unique time in Canadian history. The disruptions posed for our economy, politics, and social life has driven us to give more thought to what has happened to our physical and mental health and well-being, our organizational arrangements and social hierarchy, and the future of our country. The COVID-19 pandemic came as a surprise to many people, institutions, and power structures as it demanded us to make drastic changes to our lives and social systems. The traditional ways of how we organize our lives and work, how we relate and interact with other people, how we deal with crises and "life and death" issues, and how we run this country and prepare it for our future are all on the table for assessment, evaluation, design, and planning. The COVID-19 pandemic affected racialized and Indigenous peoples adversely in a disproportionate manner: it harmed more of them, made life harder for them, and left them largely unsupported. Worse still, they experienced more racial harassment and discrimination, and their voices were largely unheard. However, such negative impacts were reported in the media and made people realize the disproportionate harms that racialized and Indigenous peoples have to endure, thus raising their awareness of racism. These pandemic disruptions have given rise to an unusual window of opportunity for social changes or even transformation. We may be seeing a paradigm shake-up in which opportunities to build a more visionary, functional, equitable, and fairer framework of work life is possible.

This book is a call for evaluating workplace racism with the objective of ending it under a mix of "moving parts" as people, organizations, institutions, and the larger society undergo small and large shifts due to the disruptions imposed by the pandemic. As our history of new perspectives and innovations (such as the new world-views of the Copernicus Revolution some five hundred years ago), new transportation machinery (such as motor cars 140 years ago and airplanes about 120 years ago), new electronic inventions (such as computers around eighty years ago), new information networks (such as the Internet about fifty years ago), and new communication tools (such as smartphones around thirty years ago) has suggested, new ideas and things emerge when old ones no longer function well, when organizational and government policies or regulations are no longer relevant or applicable, and when the existing ways of doing things no longer make sense. The social environment is in need of change and is conducive to alternative ideas and competitions, and people are being bold and vocal enough to challenge the status quo. Unless there are obstructions from the top (that is, from chief executive officers [CEOs] and executives in the private/non-profit sectors and/or different levels of the government), the voices and actions of the people below may have a chance to prevail and effect such changes.

ECONOMIC DISRUPTION AND CHALLENGES ALL OVER

Canada, along with other countries, went through the COVID-19 pandemic from 2019 onwards. Although the pandemic went through several waves of virus variants during this period, it seems that Canada has not been able to shake it off completely, even at the time of writing this book. While its origins remain contentious, its impacts on the country are undeniable. The Canadian economy has gone through major changes since the COVID-19 pandemic emerged, and these changes have introduced new options and alternatives for people, organizations, and society as a whole to accept, negotiate, or reject. These alternatives are opportunities to consider new options and to cast off old ways of doing things or living our lives. In other words, the routine that people have grown up with is now shattered. In times like these, people can think or dream of the future, which is yet to be defined.

Workplace Disruptions

The Canadian economy went through many challenges as the contagiousness of the corona virus caught many Canadians by surprise. Since the ascendency of the pandemic, the lack of knowledge of scientists, governments, businesses, and the public about the virus revealed how unprepared Canadians were for such a crisis. In its early stages, medical and health-care professionals did not know how best to respond to the virus or contain its spread of infection as they were still trying to understand how the corona virus worked. Government officials were unsure about what public policies should be developed to deal with the multiple and interlocking implications of the spread of the virus. Private sector employers were unable to rely on the traditional on-site face-to-face work arrangement to manage their employees, and their organizational support systems had to undergo some drastic changes as it was not safe enough for employees to work on site and normal work processes had to be truncated and adjusted.

The emergence and spread of the corona virus in Canada disrupted many aspects of our organizations and people's lives, making it very risky for people to concentrate in one location and to be in close proximity to each other since the virus could spread among them even if they had no symptoms. Traditional work sites and meeting places with their concentration of employees, customers, and participants were no longer safe, and employers were forced to make some changes and let employees do work remotely if that was possible (Mayer and Willis 2022). Public sector and non-profit sector employers and employees followed suit with some variations.

However, this remote work arrangement was generally only feasible for knowledge-based workers who utilized computer and telecommunication technology to the largest extent possible. In spite of this change, there was still a sizeable work force who had to go outside their homes to do their paid work. These workers were usually front-line workers in construction, food processing, personal care, health care, law enforcement, emergency services, retail, manufacturing, public transportation, pharmaceutical and grocery stores, and many other occupations and industries. Due to the anxiety and uncertainty as well as the resulting business restrictions and lockdowns and school closures created by COVID-19, a segment of the workforce took early retirement, resigned, or were (temporarily or permanently) laid off. As a result, employers have had problems finding qualified employees to fill their positions even when the restrictions and lockdowns were eventually lifted. These organizational changes on such a large scale were unprecedented, and it provided an opportunity for people to assess their situations and see whether some modified or abrupt changes were warranted or not. This moment in time was precious because the COVID-19 outbreak enabled many people to pause and consider their next move and if it was warranted. The same applied to corporate executives, directors, and managers; they were also given a moment to rethink the old ways of doing things and working with people, and they reassessed whether there might be new ways to run their organizations in a different way.

Service Disruptions

Meanwhile, the federal and provincial governments worked hard to find the safest possible way to regulate the work arrangements in various industries so as to contain the spread of the virus and, at the same time, keep the economy going. For this reason, the economy was divided into two major types of services: essential and non-essential services. "Essential services," at one point in Ontario during the pandemic in 2020, included selected businesses in the supply chains, food industry, services affecting the daily lives of people (such as pharmacies and security), financial services, telecommunication and information technology infrastructure and service providers, maintenance, manufacturing, agriculture and food production, construction, resources and energy, community services, and research. Other businesses or services not included in these industries were considered to be "non-essential services" (*CTVNews* 2020).

Such a dichotomy of services mandated by the provincial governments necessitated a major disruption in the smooth functioning of the Canadian economy. The conventional time-tested "just-in-time" model of running the economy based on a careful well-calculated and coordinated process of moving people, goods, and services within the Canadian economy and around the world was no longer functional during the pandemic. One of the sources of the problem was that employers could not depend on the full mobilization of their workforces: some workers were sick with the virus, hospitalized or not; a segment of the workforce (known as non-essential service workers) was required by the government to stay at home, working or not working, lest the virus spread to more people unchecked and uncontained; another segment of the workforce (known as essential service workers) was required by the government to work only with safety precautions (such as face masks and physical distancing); and yet another segment of the workforce was unable to work because their children were not able to attend school (as physical distancing proved to be difficult to arrange in the early days of the pandemic) and they had to take care of them at home. This unprecedented shortage of workers, vehicles, facilities, and operational supports paralyzed production, processing, and delivery systems, created broken supply chains of consumer goods, building materials, and other goods and services, and made the movement of people and services difficult (Mayer and Willis 2022).

These disruptions in the production and service delivery of goods certainly made life inconvenient for many people, but they also revealed that the traditional ways of getting the economy moving no longer applied. This phenomenon provided a good opportunity for people to get by with less than the adequate number of goods and services and shattered the traditional world-view of how countries should be run. It was a situation in which employers had to work with a much smaller workforce and to find ways to get through the COVID-19 ordeal. A disruption of this nature triggered a reassessment process of what it meant to run a business and how best to avoid or tackle the kinds of problems that have implications on human resources, infrastructure, supply chains, service delivery, and the entire process of running a business.

Financial Disruptions

In addition, during this pandemic period, there were personal and household financial disruptions of various degrees across the board that could only be resolved partially through special government emergency payments and benefits designed and developed to support people who had experienced financial difficulty. They could not work, even if they wanted to, due to the collapse of the support systems discussed above. People in "non-essential services" either worked at home or were temporary or permanently out of work, and they had to live on federal government benefits (such as the Canada Emergency Response Benefit), which was available for eligible persons between 15 March 2020 and 7 May 2022 (Statistics Canada 2022b). This "life-boat" type of financial support did ease the difficult situation for a while, but it was not seen as a long-term solution for such structural interruptions as a pandemic.

The conventional model of earning a living before the pandemic no longer applied for many people. Those people who were self-employed or running a small business experienced increased uncertainty as the previous flow of customers and earnings could no longer be counted on. These entrepreneurs had to consider finding other sources of income or creating new businesses to make money; however, not all people were dislocated in the same way. Knowledge-based workers could easily continue in their same jobs as they could work at home because technology had advanced to the point where they could utilize computers and communications to get work done, at least on an individual basis.

While the pre-pandemic "team-work" environment and the corporate culture were somehow disjointed or diminished for these employees, their general performance was still acceptable.

Small- and medium-sized Canadian businesses constituted 98.1 percent of employer businesses in 2021. Small businesses employed 9.7 million individuals, which was about two-thirds of the total labour force in 2020, medium-sized businesses employed 3.2 million individuals (21.2 percent of the labour force), and large businesses employed 2.3 million individuals (14.8 percent of the labour force). Overall, businesses of all sizes expected greater financial hardships, but the smaller ones were more pessimistic: small businesses were more pessimistic about their business future than their larger counterparts. They were not sure about the sales in the next three months. One-third of them expected a decrease in profitability. Compared with their larger counterparts, small businesses were more inclined to expect rising cost of inputs, insufficient demand for goods and services, fluctuations in consumer demands, more challenges in getting financing, maintaining sufficient cash flow, and managing debt.

The federal government set up the Canada Emergency Business Account, which acted as a "lifeline" loan program for businesses. Almost nine hundred thousand businesses participated in this program. Many of them were also concerned about repaying these "lifeline" loans as well as their business future in the absence of government financial supports, especially when some of them were not able to take on more debt (Li, Soods, and Johnston 2022). In 2023, paying back the financial supports had made many businesses "panicked," and the Canadian Federation of Independent Businesses urged the federal government to extend the loan repayment, which was ultimately confirmed by the federal government, extending the loan to 2026 (Cousins 2023). On a broader level, the business sector experienced a huge financial setback. Since the pandemic began in 2020, all provinces mandated the closure of schools and businesses to some extent. As a result, about 3.1 million Canadians were impacted through reduction in work hours or job loss. An estimated 41 percent of jobs were done remotely. Approximately, 60 percent of small businesses suffered a loss of 20 percent or more in revenues (Statistics Canada 2020). The Canadian Federation of Independent Business (2020) reported that the revenues of 70 percent of small businesses in Canada have declined by 30 percent or more since the start of the pandemic (Mo et al. 2020).

These financial disruptions for people and businesses were wake-up calls as the government benefits were not adequate for them to run businesses or for them to support themselves or their families as they once had been. They were "stop-gap" measures to bridge difficult and abnormal situations. However, when people and businesses must go through difficult times, the experiences often make them think how they will move forward once the crisis subsides. It was this opportunity to reflect and recalibrate that may have proven useful for businesses and people.

Pandemic Disparities

Health Disparities

During the pandemic period, it also became obvious that some segments of the population suffered more than others due to their age, race, ability, gender, income level, housing status, and geographic location. Examples of disproportionate misery due to the spread of the virus was found among older persons in long-term care homes, immigrant or racialized workers working in close proximity in factories, health-care front-line service providers in health clinics and hospitals, persons with disabilities and those with chronic health issues (who did not get timely and appropriate health-care services), and Indigenous peoples and low-income persons living in close proximity with members of their families or other people in dwellings with core housing needs.

As far as racialized people are concerned, during a period in 2020 when the pandemic was observed, at the aggregated level, neighbourhoods with 25 percent of racialized peoples had two times the mortality rate than those with less than 1 percent. This pattern of disparity of higher mortality rates based on the concentration of racialized people was further accentuated in Ontario and Quebec neighbourhoods (two times the rate) and especially in neighourhoods in British Columbia (ten times the rate) (Subedi, Greenberg, and Turcotte 2020). These examples illustrate the widespread systemic health inequities for people with cumulative racial disadvantages due largely to poor residential or workplace conditions (Government of Canada 2022c, 2022f; Hahmann and Kumar 2022; Kemei et al. 2023). Evidence on the health inequities posed by the pandemic, in one form or another, were broadcast in electronic and print media and were widely publicized among Canadians (Bascarramurty, Weeks, and Andrew-Gee 2020; Rodriguez 2021a). Some business people recognized and acknowledged these health disparities along social identity and demographic lines. For them, they showed that there were deep cleavages in Canada that must be addressed by politicians, policy developers, and those decision makers in the business and non-profit sectors.

In a press release issued by the Conference Board of the United States (2021), Dr. Richard Besser, president and CEO of Robert Wood Johnson Foundation—an organization aimed at improving the health and well-being of everyone in the United States—stated:

> What we mean by equity is opportunity. That everyone in America should have a fair and just opportunity for health and well-being. That different people will require different things to achieve health. And that if you're not looking at removing barriers—barriers that people face due to racism, and sexism, and classism, barriers due to where they may live—if you're not addressing these barriers, you're going to end up with major health disparities like we have in our country. The health disparities that have been made so clear this past year with the COVID pandemic.

McKinsey & Company, a global consulting firm, advised the business sector to pay attention to "inclusive growth" in light of female workers' burnout in the workplace during the COVID-19 period: "Sustainable, inclusive growth will require changing the workplace to maximize the contributions of all people" (McLaughlin 2022).

Economic Disparities

In addition to health inequities, marginalized groups also suffered economically in a disproportionate manner. Due to the fact that they were often clustered in precarious jobs, women's job loss and income loss during the pandemic was disproportionate. Most women were in front-line work in the health-care and social services sector, which made their work more prone to infection, less safe, and more stressful during this period. The Canadian Women's Chamber of Commerce and Dream Legacy Foundation (2020) reported that 61 percent of women business founders lost their contracts, clients, or customers during the pandemic. Similarly, racialized people and recent immigrants tended to cluster in precarious and low-paying jobs, and the job loss and financial insecurity that came with COVID-19 also affected them adversely. Businesses owned by Indigenous peoples, racialized people, immigrants, persons with disabilities, and women reported revenue declines of 20 percent or more compared with the overall average of businesses in general. Moreover, while 20 percent of all businesses that paid rent actually deferred rent during the pandemic period, businesses owned by racialized people (23.7 percent), immigrants (26.8 percent), Indigenous peoples (22.3 percent), and women (25.6 percent) had their rents deferred more often. This suggests that the businesses of diverse groups went through a tougher time during the pandemic period (Mo et al. 2020).

Going forward, based on these research findings, political and corporate decision makers increasingly realized that, to address the damages done to the Canadian economy as a result of the pandemic, health inequities, financial difficulties, and bleak business situations were compounding the long-term structural problems that marginalized segments of the population faced. These issues had to be rectified in order to prepare for a full economic recovery after the pandemic.

Economic Uncertainty and Hardship

As COVID-19 vaccination began to show its effectiveness in containing the threat of the pandemic's spread, the Canadian economy, which had been formally paralyzed by the contagion, began to show some signs of recovery: school children were going back to schools, vehicles were appearing on the roads, pedestrians were found walking on sidewalks, travellers were going places, and consumers were shopping and eating in restaurants. But these activities had still not reached their pre-pandemic level in 2023. The workplace is one of the areas that is still struggling to become "normal" again as employees are reluctant to go back to their offices to work. This may explain why some commercial buildings have remained largely unoccupied since employees are still not going to their offices. Remote work is widely popular. While the norm seems to be moving from a full "remote-working" pattern to a "hybrid-working" mode, structured or unstructured, the work arrangement still appears to be fluid and flexible to the extent that it is still difficult for many human resources functions to operate smoothly (such as onboarding, teamwork, employee engagement, performance, and retention) and for workplace culture rebuilding to consolidate. We are in a "new normal" in the work environment, especially for knowledge-based employees.

Meanwhile, even when the economy was struggling to recover, labour shortage in some industries has remained a persistent problem. Some hospitals, long-term care homes, emergency services, childcare facilities, schools, and public transit (including airlines) are experiencing labour shortages, and some have been forced to "stretch" their workforce so that their services can be made available at the expense of increasing employee stress and compromising the quality of work, without getting into the realm of work stoppage. It is a prevalent problem in some workplaces (such as in health care and hospitality sectors). It has created a massive problem in human resources management, work arrangements, supply chain disruptions, and, needless to say, economic disruptions and human misery.

On top of these human resources and business operation problems, inflation on a massive scale has grown across Canada. There are multiple sources of the current inflation: the demand for goods and services from industries and consumers is higher than the supply; the geopolitical tensions generated through military turmoil in Europe and the Middle East; the growing conflict between the United States (and its allies) and China over global supremacy and economic might; the developing grievances among Asian countries, Australia, and China; and various natural disasters (such as wildfires, floods, and hurricanes) generated by climate change. When these forces combined, as they are doing now, they gave rise to persistent "sticky" inflation and economic uncertainty that refuses to go away. The economic fallouts of inflation in the Canadian economy are many. Chief among them are high mortgage rates, high grocery and energy bills, high cost of housing, great economic uncertainty, and growing lack of confidence in economic recovery. Under these circumstances, businesses are curtailing their investment and expansion and are cutting down the costs of doing business as much as possible. At the human level, employees are being laid off, cash flow for paying mortgages and running households are shrinking, borrowing loans has become more difficult, and raising children and being secure about food has become an issue.

These problems have increased the overall hardship of many people, especially for younger generations who have to chase after precarious jobs and those with low or fixed incomes who do not see any alternatives (Lenarduzzi 2023). They also cause headaches for politicians in terms of their public policy development and the allocation of financial resources to fix the problems and for businesses and employers in terms of the militant work actions and high wage demands of their employees.

Disruptions, Challenges, and Opportunities

Overall, these economic forces—inflation, high interest rates, low confidence, housing crisis, low consumer demands, and uncertain employment opportunities—are compounding on each other, making their adverse impacts on government, businesses, and people much more severe than during the pre-COVID period. None of these issues are easy to resolve, and the economic situation elsewhere is not much better. The real gross domestic product is expected to drop from 3.7 percent in 2022 to 1.4 percent in 2023 and 0.9 percent in 2024, based on a forecase from GlobalData (2023). In their own ways, government, businesses, and people have spent many hours finding alternative or innovative means to resolve the issues facing them and trying to minimize the economic risks that they have to face. There are still many uncertainties and instabilities in the Canadian economy and other parts of the world, and it is in this environment that we must all rethink how we live our daily lives, increase our productivity, grow our industries and trades, and hold steady stewardship in our economy in a fragile geopolitical world.

Collectively, employers have experienced multiple unprecedented challenges that came with the widespread disruptions in the work environment, such as the absence of a stable and well-coordinated workforce, the uncertainty of business revenues due to changes in work and consumer behaviours, the additional expences in making the workplace safe for workers who came to work, the unpredictability of government financial supports throughout the pandemic period, the unreliable dependency of trading partners and their responses, and the overall global economic instability (Statistics Canada 2023k). Overall, there were a lot of unknowns and no readily available solutions to the national and international problems during the pandemic period. At the same time, alternative and innovative ways had to be developed to meet all sorts of challenges just to keep business alive (Mayer and Willis 2022).

How different stakeholder groups in Canada met these challenges during the pandemic period suggests that their resilience and adaptation have been the hallmarks even though there was no prior learning on their part on how best to resolve these unprecedented issues. Their experience also suggests that new ideas and innovative ways of resolving problems did emerge during the times of uncertain conditions and financial difficulties when the corona virus posed a "life-and-death" decision for many people. In some unchartered territories, often due to labour shortage and the reallocation of staff resources, people had to learn new knowledge and skills just to get the work done and keep their companies afloat during an emergency situation. There were many incidents where people had to use their talents to meet new challenges, and many corporate CEOs, politicians, public policy developers, educators, and decision makers in a broad range of industrial sectors (primary, secondary, and tertiary) had to develop innovative strategies to meet the challenges posed by the pandemic.

At that stage, it was unclear whether our economy could emerge from the pandemic with a full economic recovery. Currently, we are at this historical juncture where moving forward in economic terms requires new visions and perspectives, public policies and strategies, and corporate approaches, programs, and initiatives in the economic arena. It is also at this stage that we are seeing opportunities emerge, and those who have made use of these opportunities to turn things around have been rewarded. Vaccines to fight against the coronavirus were developed by various global pharmaceutical companies in an unusually short time frame to meet global demands. Steve Mayer and Andrew Willis (2022) documented the many ways in which Canadian corporations (such as Air Canada, Canadian Tire, Four Seasons Hotels and Resorts, and Maple Leaf Canada) met their management challenges imposed by the pandemic. Various levels of government, along with the private and non-profit sectors, came together to address multiple strategic and operational issues related to the unprecedented public health hazards and contagions, finance, food security, supply chains, transportation, education, and other domains related to the daily lives of people. While the new solutions in health-care services, medical surgery, government emergency benefits, food supplies, movement of manufactured goods, wait times and lost luggage, school attendance and online learning, and logistic problems may not be satisfactory to everyone, they nevertheless kept the economy going under pandemic conditions. And some of these new solutions, such as remote work, virtual medical counselling, and online shopping, have become more prevalently adopted since the end of the pandemic.

It was in the depth of the pandemic period when public policy developers and decision makers, city planners, corporate heads, and human resources professionals began to realize that COVID-19 had impacted on marginalized groups more severely than other segments of the population. Without racialized people as a significant segment of the population working on the front line in the health-care sector, working on the production line, and playing a key role in essential services moving people and goods as expeditiously as possible, it was difficult to get the battered economy going under these trying times. Their contributions and value-added efforts in keeping the essential services going have been noticed by people in positions of power as well as by the general public. It was at this time that people finally recognized the importance of historically marginalized groups and how crucial their roles were during that period.

POLITICAL MESSAGES AND CHALLENGES FROM ABOVE

When the Liberal government under Prime Minister Justin Trudeau first assumed power after the defeat of the Conservative government under Stephen Harper, it was determined to declare one of its political priorities as social justice and to lead by example. The government initiated several new policy directions and created a new and rejuvenated momentum in rectifying the historical social injustice system associated with women, Indigenous peoples, racialized people, and, to some extent, persons with disabilities. These are the four employment equity-designated groups under the 1986 federal legislation on employment equity. This political momentum was focused on the Canadian political agenda to address the structural inequalities that had been experienced by newthese population segments for decades and even centuries, which is well documented in the literature (Abella 1984, 1985). This momentum persisted throughout Justin Trudeau's regime through laws, policies, and programs: the announcement of the Cabinet's composition of 50 percent women in 2015; the amendment to the *Canada Business Corporations Act* in 2020; the establishment of the National Inquiry into Missing and Murdered Indigenous Women and Girls in 2016–19; the acceptance of the Final Report of the Truth and Reconciliation Commission and the federal government's commitment to reconcile in 2015; and the announcement of the anti-racism strategy and its related programs in 2018–19.[1] These declarations signalled a new beginning of addressing the negative impacts of past inequalities. Underling all of them was a commitment to steer the country, its institutions, and its

1 *Canada Business Corporations Act*, RSC 1985, c C-44.

people in the direction of social justice through what the government was able to do within its jurisdiction.

Gender Equity

The *Employment Equity Act* was passed in 1986 by the thirty-third Canadian Parliament under the Mulroney government; since then, the legislation has been enforced, but it has been applicable only to federally regulated industries and federal contractors and, later, to crown corporations.[2] Progress toward employment equity for the four designated groups in the workplace has been slow over the twenty-nine years from 1986 to 2015. The concept of employment equity was elevated to a new significance when the Liberal party came to power on 14 November 2015. The government's immediate policy change announcement was to ensure gender balance in the composition of the Cabinet—at least 50 percent of the Cabinet posts were to be occupied by women. The first Cabinet was made up of fifteen women and fifteen men. It was the first gender-balanced Cabinet in Canadian history (Murphy 2015). Trudeau's new Cabinet in 2021 was also gender balanced with nineteen men and nineteen women. Women in Cabinet also commanded important posts such as finance, defence, and foreign affairs (Fillion 2021).

Enhanced Employment Equity

While this was largely a political and symbolic initiative, it sent out a political message from the top that gender equity was a political priority for the government. Such priority was further reinforced by an amendment to the *Canada Business Corporations Act*, which received royal assent on 1 May 2018. The amendment came into effect on 1 January 2020 and required federally regulated companies to diversify their boards of directors and executive teams to include a representative share of Indigenous people, persons with disabilities, racialized people, and women. This amendment included the scope of designated groups in equitable representation and is not limited only to women, as was previously enacted. It remains to be seen whether this government effort (which uses a "comply-or-explain" approach to ensure compliance) works or not. At a minimum, the Liberal party sent out a political

---

2 *Employment Equity Act*, SC 1995, c 44.

message to the private sector, especially to those individuals on corporate boards of directors, CEOs, and senior executives that Indigenous peoples, persons with disabilities, racialized people, and women must have equitable representation in corporate decision-making positions. This is because, over the past three decades prior to the passing of this amendment in 2018, the *Employment Equity Act* had seemed to be rather ineffective in making meaningful changes for these designated groups at the decision-making level.

National Inquiry into Missing and Murdered Indigenous Women and Girls

In addition, the federal government in power pushed for equity as a political priority for Indigenous peoples and racialized people. The first Cabinet of Justin Trudeau also included two Indigenous persons and three South Asian men. It sent a signal to the Western world (Murphy 2015). When the Liberal party had assumed power in 2015, the government had made it clear that it intended to improve the relationship between the Crown and Indigenous communities. The newly appointed minister of Indigenous Affairs, Carolyn Bennett, took on the responsibility of establishing a national inquiry into the issue of missing and murdered Indigenous women and girls, which began in 2016 (Murphy 2015). While this national inquiry had its "ups and downs" in terms of the Crown-Indigenous relationship, it did unearth, with the participation of 2,386 participants including survivors, family members, artists, experts, and knowledge keepers, an extensive amount of critical information that illustrated the plights of Indigenous women and girls. After two years of public hearings and evidence gathering, the inquiry ended in 2019. With the release of the final report, with its 231 calls for justice directed at all stakeholder groups (including businesses) and plans of action, the mass media provided an extensive coverage of how historical colonial oppression (including poverty, housing insecurity, homelessness, educational underfunding, unemployment and under-employment, poor health-care services, and inappropriate cultural supports), intertwined with sexism and racism, had resulted in disproportionate rates of mortality.

There was an immense collection of evidence of marginalization and trauma, both personal and collective. As a result, the public got a better view of why Indigenous death has been defined as a form of genocide—including killing, bodily/mental harm, physical destruction, preventing births, and the forced transfer of children—a strongly loaded word endorsed by Trudeau. This perspective reflects an aspect of Indigenous experience not broadly known or acknowledged by non-Indigenous Canadians until now. The final report also vindicated Indigenous peoples' belief that Indigenous women and girls had been killed disproportionately (National Inquiry into Missing and Murdered Indigenous Women and Girls 2019a, 2019b).

Truth and Reconciliation Commission

The Government of Canada under Prime Minister Stephen Harper established the Truth and Reconciliation Commission in 2007. Indigenous peoples have been vocal about their relationship with Europeans as being that of the colonizers and the colonized. The forced assimilation of Indigenous children under the Indian Residential School System across Canada has been described as cultural genocide by Indigenous peoples. Over 150,000 Indigenous children were taken away from their parents and placed in different residential schools under the management of religious organizations. Under this government arrangement, which was managed by religious organizations, Indigenous languages, traditional cultures, and ways of life were intentionally suppressed and eradicated.

The Truth and Reconciliation Commission, with the collaboration of Indigenous peoples, documented the history of the Indian Residential School System. The goal of this school system was to eradicate their Indian identity and culture and assimilate Indigenous children into the European culture. This process lasted over a century from the 1870s to the 1990s. What made this commission's work more prominent and striking was the discovery of the dead bodies of Indigenous children on the grounds where some residential schools were located. Indigenous peoples have long believed that these children were killed and buried. The Government of Canada and Indigenous peoples worked together on this commission with the objective of rebuilding and renewing Indigenous relationships and the relationship between Indigenous and non-Indigenous Canadians. The commission focused on finding truth, enabling healing, and committing to reconciliation through a joint effort of First Nations, Metis, and Inuit former Indian Residential School students, family members, communities, religious groups, and formal school employees, government, and the people of Canada. Between 2007 and 2015, the Harper government provided seventy-two million dollars to support the commission's activities, and the commission spent six years travelling around Canada, hearing from over sixty-five hundred witnesses and engaging the public in seven national events. The commission issued ninety-four "calls for action" to the Government of Canada for addressing the legacy of the residential schools.

In December 2015, Prime Minister Justin Trudeau accepted the final report of the commission on behalf of Canada and declared his commitment to work with national Indigenous organizations to implement the recommendations and advance reconciliation. This would include the implementation of the *United Nations Declaration on the Rights of Indigenous Peoples* (*UNDRIP*).[3] Furthermore, the Liberal government is working with Indigenous leaders and parties to the *Indian Residential School Settlement Agreement* to develop a national engagement strategy for a national reconciliation framework (Government of Canada 2022g).[4]

Anti-Racism Strategy

On the racial equality front, the federal government has established an anti-racism strategy as a model for combating racism. This strategy is consistent with the federal government's former promise of what they will do in the report entitled *Taking Action against Systemic Racism and Religious Discrimination*, which was published in 2018 by the Standing Committee on Canadian Heritage (2008), including action to combat Islamophobia (Souissi 2021). This strategy was the result of a comprehensive process of consultation with racialized communities and Indigenous communities from October 2018 to March 2019. A series of forums were organized to engage these communities in discussion on racism and anti-racism. In light of the prevalent systemic anti-Indigenous, anti-Semitic, anti-Asian, anti-Black, anti-Muslim, and other hateful sentiments that occur in every corner of Canada, the federal government believes that a strong and prominent strategy to combat these sentiments is a way to move forward. As the national leader

---

3 *United Nations Declaration on the Rights of Indigenous Peoples*, UN Doc A/61/49, 13 September 2007.

4 *Indian Residential Schools Settlement Agreement*, Schedule N, 8 May 2006.

in fighting racism, the federal government also wants to set an example for Canadians. As the title of the strategy document states, it is meant to be "a Foundation for Change." In the words of the Honourable Pablo Rodriguez, minister of Canadian heritage and multiculturalism, "the Government of Canada is committed to building a foundation for change by removing barriers and promoting a country where every person is able to fully participate and have an equal opportunity to succeed" (Government of Canada 2023a).

Accordingly, the federal government has created an Anti-Racism Secretariat to coordinate actions through community engagement with "communities and Indigenous Peoples, Stakeholders, and other levels of government, ... empowering them, ... and building and changing attitudes." The ultimate goal is to enable "corrective action toward the elimination of racism and discrimination" (Government of Canada 2023a). One of the effects of this strategy has been the federal government's efforts in engaging the provinces and territories in anti-racism actions through the existing federal-provincial-territorial networks. From 2019 to 2022, the federal government allocated thirty million dollars to support community-based anti-racism projects and additional funds for integrating the federal government's projects on missing and murdered Indigenous women and girls, truth and reconciliation efforts, and anti-hate programs (especially online hate and violent extremism). The federal government has committed to reporting the progress and accomplishments of this strategy to the public on a yearly basis (Government of Canada 2021). All these initiatives by the federal government under the banner of social justice rallied Canadians and Canadian institutions to prioritize combating sexism, racism, anti-Indigenous, and other hate sentiments. The federal government can only effect change with its own jurisdiction and provide the necessary resources, tools, and models for institutions and people to utilize. But these initiatives began a national conversation on Indigenous peoples, racism and anti-racism, and women.

PEOPLE'S VOICES AND CHALLENGES FROM BELOW

Social protests and movements are created to raise public awareness of issues and concerns to some segments of the population. These segments use such protests/movements to build up their capabilities and effect the social changes that they have envisioned. Their rise and fall depend on many factors, including how authorities respond to them, how they are organized and sustained in the public arena, and how their concerns are promoted, neutralized, suppressed, distracted, or institutionalized. In this section, we focus on how three protest movements for social justice—#MeToo movement, the Black Lives Matter movement, and the Anti-Asian Hate movement—constitute a disruptive force that pushes businesses, governments, and the public to ask critical questions about the status quo and its impact on racism. These social actions often utilize the coverage of the media, especially social media, to disseminate their political messages and proposed solutions. Given that their political messages have seldom been publicized until now, issues related to racism and sexism are now being exposed publicly and are often stimulating public dialogues among decision makers and people in general. Despite this exposure, the messages of these movements do not necessarily influence public opinion to the point of toleration or acceptance, but their social actions can be publicly broadcast and amplified, which means that racist or sexist beliefs or activities can be publically challenged and condemned. This is what Indigenous peoples, racialized people, and women from these groups want.

The following sections provide an overview of these protests/movements, highlighting a few key messages that are impactful to the rethinking of racism, sexism, and their intersectionality with the public, public policy decision makers, and corporate CEOs and executives. They highlight the undercurrents of society that impact on our relationships with each other in the workplace and outside. Given that the federal government has been quite vocal in supporting social justice, these protests/movements have been encouraged, in one way or another, by the messages from above. The signal has been clear: the government supports causes for social justice.

#MeToo Movement

The movement that galvanized women to share their experiences of sexual harassment and assaults worldwide was started in 2006 by Tarana Burke, a Black female activist, who focused on gathering supports and resources for all women, especially those who are racialized, young, and poor. The movement was invigorated with the hashtag #MeToo in 2017 as allegations of sexual harassment and assaults were made against Harvey Weinstein, a well-known film producer in Hollywood. With the energy from the entertainment industry and Hollywood celebrities, the movement made international headlines immediately. From that year on, the #MeToo movement has been largely claimed as the brainchild of White feminists and not of Black women. Indigenous and racialized women are not happy about this because the movement essentially ignores their own calling out on sexual harassment and assaults and has highlighted, once again, the marginalization of Indigenous and racialized women by White women. White women have problems in acknowledging the unique harassment experiences of Black women due to the intersectionality of race and sex. The #MeToo movement also does not acknowledge the intersectionality of other factors including age, religion, disability, gender identity, citizenship, and socio-economic status when it comes to the analysis of harassment and discrimination (Onwuachi-Willig 2018). This schism in the movement highlights the critical issue of race in daily dialogues of employees in the workplace.

In spite of this serious defect, the movement has signalled a new wave of protests by women on sexual harassment, discrimination, and assaults in Canada with the help of social media and printed/electronic media. The *Globe and Mail* carried stories on sexism in government institutions (for example, the Royal Canadian Mounted Police), and the court case on Jian Ghomeshi's alleged sexual assaults was widely broadcasted (LeBlanc 2015; Hasham 2017). The movement has also organized #MeToo marches and forums to publicize the issue since 2017. Indigenous women are more likely to be the victims of sexual victimization and violence, and their likelihood of being sexually assaulted is higher than non-Indigenous women (Perreault 2015; Sutton 2023). With this understanding, the #MeToo movement means more to Indigenous women than White women because their victimization is much more frequent and deadly. Indigenous women's focus is on racism, sexism, and colonization combined. As Tess Ryan (2019) of the Learning and Teaching Centre at the Australian Catholic University has pointed out, the personal experiences of Indigenous women are different from those of White women. "#MeToo is more than just person-to-person abuse," it is a collective fight against the abusive and controlling relationships imposed by White colonizers and oppressors. Their core issues involve the power imbalance with colonial power. Indigenous women may not subsume their organizing efforts for justice for missing women and girls as part of a #MeToo movement, but their efforts have been witnessed in the truth-gathering process and in the analysis of the National Inquiry into Missing and Murdered Indigenous Women and Girls and the resulting reports in 2015–19 (National Inquiry into Missing and Murdered Indigenous Women and Girls, n.d.). Their works were broadcasted broadly during this period and drummed into the minds of people who were making public policy and those in program design on addressing this social injustice.

Plan International Canada did a survey and found that two-thirds of Canadians believed the #MeToo movement helps women to share their experiences, and one-third agreed that the movement has changed their views on sexual assault (Canadian Women's Foundation 2021). The movement has encouraged more reporting of sexual harassment and assaults from women across Canada, irrespective of their race. Moreover, some police services have taken up the challenge of reviewing and changing their intake and investigation procedures and have also been investigating more cases since 2017 (Allen 2018; Cloubrough 2018; Doolittle 2018). Overall, the movement has been quite effective in raising consciousness on sexual harassment and assault. It has shown that women must speak up on social injustice in order to effect social changes, including those in the workplace. It has raised the level of assertiveness and confidence that women have in claiming their rights in leadership positions. This is not to say that the #MeToo movement has created a new battle cry for rights in leadership, but it provides the same kind of feeling of "me too" when women have been unsuccessful in getting promoted to leadership positions in the workplace. Women have noticed for many years that they are largely under-represented or even unrepresented among board directors, executives, and managers in the public and private sectors. Leadership has been and remains homogenously White and male. Indigenous and racialized women have an even harder time accessing leadership positions (Siu 2021). Equally important to acknowledge is the fact that, even within the Indigenous communities, women are not represented equitably in leadership (Pugliese 2020).

The #MeToo movement heightens the awareness of White women in recognizing the gender-based nature of institutional and cultural barriers that women face in seeking access to leadership. Similar to sexual harassment and assault, it boils down to the power imbalance between the male gatekeepers and women seeking entry to the "old boys' networks" (Macnab 2022). For Indigenous and racialized women, propelled by the sensitivity generated by the movement, they have realized that their gatekeepers are not only male but also White, which means that their barriers to leadership are gendered racism or racist sexism. The #MeToo movement has created a momentum in questioning the nature of male/female relationship in all aspects of social life, including the power imbalance and sexual norms often taken for granted by men, irrespective of their sex, role, and position in the workplace. It has called into question the stereotypes and prejudice toward women and Indigenous and racialized peoples. It has also raised the awareness of people to the biases embedded in the status quo and, for some organizations, the process of review, evaluation, and adjustment on what has been taken for granted in human resources policies, procedures, and practices. It has called for changes that are necessary for organizations to align with contemporary values and standards.

Indigenous Movement

There is a multifaceted Indigenous movement going on in Canada. It is made up of numerous issues pertinent to Indigenous peoples that have existed ever since the early encounters between Indigenous peoples and Europeans. There are important milestones in the relationship between Indigenous peoples and Europeans: the *Guswenta/Two Row Wampum Treaty* of 1613, the *Royal Proclamation* of 1763, the *British North American Act* of 1867, and the *Indian Act* of 1876. These legal documents and subsequent actions of Europeans (largely British and French) fermented the ongoing conflicts and tension that we are now witnessing. Organized Indigenous protests have been persistent on land and self-determination rights, school underfunding, lack of drinking water, poverty, skewed incarceration, unemployment, malnutrition, and other issues affecting Indigenous peoples both on and off reserves. All these are increasingly viewed by Indigenous peoples as the result of centuries of colonization.

With the institutionalized efforts of the federal government, there have been two relatively recent movements in Indigenous communities that have raised public awareness to a higher level seldom seen in recent history—the Truth and Reconciliation Commission, which was created in reaction to the residential school issue, and the inquiry on missing and murdered Indigenous females. The recent discovery of the bodies of dead children on the grounds of former Indian residential schools and the alarming stories of violence on Indigenous women in the media and public events have elevated public consciousness and conversation. When these two issues are placed in context with centuries of social injustice and the mistreatment of Indigenous people, more people are beginning to reassess their traditional perspectives and conducts, social processes and structures, and visions for the future of this country.

Anti-Black Racism Movement

Black Lives Matter Canada

The Anti-Black racism movement in Canada consists of multiple local initiatives with the key objective of eradicating systemic racism against Black people. In this section, we will take a look at one social protest—namely, Black Lives Matter Canada (BLMC)—and one bottom-up organization, known as BlackNorth. The BLMC has several regional and local branches. It is affiliated with an international network and appears to be modelled after its counterpart in the United States that focused on fighting against racism, primarily on the police's treatment of Black people. Its first protest caught media attention following a police shooting of two Black men and managed to shut down a roadway leading to a major express highway in Toronto in 2015. Since then, the BLMC has taken several civic actions to call attention to police racial injustice and LGBTQIA+ issues. One key feature of the BLMC is its solidarity with Indigenous peoples and identification with the injustice that they experience. In addition to fighting against police brutality and other forms of state-sanctioned injustice, the BLMC educates people, builds Black culture, and urges the state to disinvest in law enforcement agencies and diverge its funding to community services instead (Black Lives Matter Canada 2023).

One central theme of the BLMC is its focus on anti-Black racism. This is different from the conventional belief that racism is homogenous without any distinctions among racialized groups. Calling out anti-Blackness is a way in which to point out how combating racism has to be strategic and focused because being Black is different from being Brown (South Asian) or Yellow (Chinese and other East Asian).

BlackNorth

BlackNorth is an organization that aims at fighting anti-Black systemic racism and creating opportunities for Black people with the support of five hundred companies in Canada. It was founded by Wes Hall, a

Black Canadian businessman, who was triggered to take on anti-Black racism actions by the news of the killing of George Floyd, a Black man, by the police on a Minneapolis street in 2020. CEOs of these five hundred companies have pledged to establish goals and timetables for hiring Black students in their workforces and appointing Black people on their boards and executive teams. BlackNorth has also collected corporate donations to establish a homeownership program, a business development hub, and a mental health service for Blacks. These are just the beginning of initiatives for Black people to overcome systemic racism (Hall 2022, 262–84). BlackNorth's actions are not so much a protest as a pragmatic response to the institutions that created obstacles for Blacks in Canada in order to maintain their human dignity and equitable share of economic lifelines.

Anti-Asian Racism and Anti-Islamophobia Movements

Anti-Asian Hate

Hatred toward Asians has been in Canada since the arrival of Chinese immigrants in Canada in the nineteenth century. The influx of Chinese to Canada induced a fear in the White inhabitants, for which the term "yellow peril" was invented. It reflects the collective phobia in White people about the growing risks of having an influx of Chinese people in Canada, inclluding the damage and contamination of White culture. Flash forward to the COVID-19 pandemic in 2019, and mounting anger against Asians, especially the Chinese, grew as a result of the suspicion that the virus had originated in China. Allegations of the origin of the virus from Wuhan, China, gained momentum as the pandemic spread. The COVID-19 pandemic has solidified White people's anxiety and hostility toward Asians in Canada ever since Chinese landed in Canada more than a century ago. They have been subjected to increased racial harassment (such as slurs), assaults (such as spitting and exerting physical harm), and discrimination in jobs and services. The rise in the frequency of anti-Asian hate incidents is documented in a 2021 survey launched by the Toronto chapter of the Chinese Canadian National Council (Balintec 2022). In response, Asian people have organized counter-measures to address the issue. While some levels of the government and the public have acknowledged anti-Asian hate as sentiments similar to anti-Islamophobia, anti-Asian hate does not command the same level of public attention and is not thoroughly understood. As such, the anti-Asian hate movement is now focusing on raising public awareness and educating people regarding its nature.

The Chinese Canadian National Council Toronto chapter has worked with the Tamil Canadian Centre for Civic Action to created resource materials, artwork, and workshops on anti-Asian racism, white privilege, micro-aggression, class and racial justice, online hate and media, oppression and intersectionality, cultural appropriation, and other pertinent topics. Getting media outlets, front-line workers, seniors, youths, and other community organizations in various fields involved in this educational process is their top priority. Similarly, there are numerous Canadian organizations (which include the Asian Canadian Labour Alliance, the Asian Canadian Women's Alliance, the Stand with Asians Coalition, the Chinese Canadian National Council on Social Justice, the National Association of Japanese Canadians, and Scholar Strike Canada) that work tirelessly against Asian racism. These organizations have increasingly joined forces with Indigenous, Black, and other racialized communities, along with migrant workers, LGBTQIA+, and sex workers to bring attention to the plights of Asian Canadians.

Anti-Islamophobia

The fateful "9/11" plane attacks on the Twin Towers of the World Trade Centers in New York City and the Pentagon in Arlington, Virginia, on 11 September 2001, stirred up strong suspicion and hatred toward Muslims, and this is when the term "Islamophobia" first originated. Although Muslims in Canada came from all over the world, they have a large population from the "Middle East." These "Middle Easterners" in Canada are subject to a mix of Islamophobia and anti-Asian hate. A combination of the historical events of the "9/11" attacks and the rise of the COVID-19 pandemic intensified this sentiment.

The 2021 survey of the Chinese Canadian National Council Toronto chapter also showed that there was a large increase in violent incidents toward South Asians (318 percent) and Southeastern Asians (121 percent). Many of the people from these regions are Muslim, and Islamophobia appears to be the driving force in anti-Asian violence (Balintec 2022). These violent incidents included the killing of six Muslim men in Quebec City in January 2017, the killing of a Muslim individual outside a mosque in Toronto in September 2020, and the death of several Muslims from one family when a vehicle drove into them in London,

Ontario, which left four dead and one injured in June 2021. In addition, there have also been police reports of hate crimes against Muslims and unreported incidents of anti-Muslim harassment and assaults.

There have been community protests against Islamophobia throughout several major cities in Canada (Azpiri and Dooley 2017; Cheung, Bridge and Nasser 2017; Green 2021). Often these protests joined hands with other anti-racism groups aimed at combating White supremacy messages preached by far-right movements (Reynolds 2016; Moore 2019). Joining in the fight against Islamophobia and advocating for social justice are the National Council of Canadian Muslims, the Islamic Social Services Association, the Canadian Council of Muslim Women, the South Asian Legal Clinic, the Metropolitan Action Committee on Violence against Women and Children, the Noor Cultural Centre, and many local mosques and community/service organizations. In July 2021, the National Summit on Islamophobia put forward sixty-one recommendations for the federal, provincial, and municipal governments to take more anti-Islamophobia actions (National Council of Canadian Muslims 2021).

Challenges and Opportunities

Each of the movements just discussed have their own characteristics: the #MeToo movement has galvanized many women's actions, mainly at the White professional women level, to expose sexual harassment and assaults mainly in the workplace and businesses; the Indigenous movement has joined force with the federal government in collecting evidence, raising public awareness on the legacy of residential schools and missing and murdered women and girls, and implementing reconciliation recommendations; the anti-Black racism movement has combined both grassroots protests and corporate drives to combat anti-Black systemic racism; and anti-Asian hate racism and anti-Islamophobia are largely community based, and they draw public attention to hate messages against ethnic, racial, and religious groups. These protests/movements often have joined hands together to raise public consciousness on racism and sexism, which, in turn, has called for actions from businesses and governments. Their views of past injustice and their visions of the proper domains for women, racialized people (Blacks, Asians, and Muslims), and Indigenous peoples have presented alternative views. These views are critical for the current situation of marginalized groups, and they pose challenges to the status quo. Consider the current trend of focusing on diversity in corporations and the pressure from social protests on justice issues that provides an impetus for finding new ways to address the marginalization and traumas of Indigenous and racialized segments of people.

DISRUPTIONS, CHALLENGES, AND SOCIAL CHANGE

Throughout Canadian history and, as a matter of fact, in many parts of the world, major disruptions have turned the status quo upside down. In the economic sphere, when domestic companies are not able to compete with international companies, supplies and demands are not in equilibrium, wage increases are not catching up with rising inflation rates, and investment capital or labour are in short supply, a series of economic problems emerge including factory or office shutdowns, increased lay-offs, rising unemployment, supply chain breakdown, and stock and real estate market collapse. The economy may even spiral down. During the COVID-19 pandemic, Canada experienced an almost complete shutdown where only essential services were carried out, and a broad range of economic activities slowed down (including transportation and even health care and medical services). People felt insecure and unsafe and were uncertain about the future of their lives, their families, and their countries. Institutions became dysfunctional or had reduced capacities.

In the political sphere, it is obvious that, when civil wars break out, external military forces invade, or coups and political assassinations take place, countries are likely to be in an emergency or wartime mode, and many normal social activities are curtailed or ceased. When the Front de Liberation du Quebec kidnapped James Richard Cross, the British trade commissioner, on 5 October 1970 and, a few days later, Pierre Laporte, the Quebec minister of labour, Prime Minister Pierre Trudeau invoked the *War Measure Act* on 16 October of that same year. It allowed police searches and arrests without warrants and suspended basic civil rights and liberties. On 17 October, the police found the strangled body of Pierre Laporte. It was a political assassination. The current escalation of the war between Russia and Ukraine in the eastern part of Ukraine and that between Israel and Hamas in Gaza and the West Bank are examples of military conflicts. Many local people in these parts of the world are fleeing as refugees from these war zones.

In contemporary Canada, such intensive political scenarios are almost non-existent. Instead, what we are witnessing in the years since Justin Trudeau assumed power in 2015 is a political system in which one of the political agenda items is diversity and equity with a focus on Indigeneity, race, and gender. Unlike the examples of political assassination and military attacks mentioned above, it is a milder, but more significant, form of political change. It is significant because, when the *UNDRIP* was adopted on 13 September 2007 by the majority of 144 states in favour, eleven countries abstained, and Canada was one of the four countries that voted against the declaration. The *UNDRIP* is a framework of human rights standards and fundamental freedoms for Indigenous Peoples. Canada finally adopted the *UNDRIP* in 2016 (Fontaine 2016), and, on 21 June 2021, the *Act Respecting the United Nations Declaration of the Rights of Indigenous Peoples* became law in Canada.[5]

This further reinforced the Government of Canada's commitment to abide by the universal framework on the rights of Indigenous peoples and to collaborate with them to implement an action plan for the betterment of Indigenous peoples (Native Women's Association of Canada 2023). It is also a political message that the federal government intends to transmit to all people and to pose a challenge to all institutions, municipalities, provinces, and territories in Canada to follow suit. The commitment to work with Indigenous organizations toward truth and reconciliation and to eliminate racial barriers that give rise to disproportionately high missing and murder rates of Indigenous girls and women are two examples of this political message. On the anti-racism front, not only has the federal government announced its anti-racism strategy, as discussed earlier, but it has also created the Anti-Racism Secretariat whose mandate is to lead a government-wide approach to identify systemic racial barriers and gaps and develop policies, services, and programs for Indigenous, racialized, and religious minorities (Government of Canada, n.d.). It also created a national action plan on combating hate (including online hate) under the auspices of the federal anti-racism strategy.

In the social sphere, community organizing and the grassroots mobilization of people in protests and anti-establishment movements

---

5 *Act Respecting the United Nations Declaration of the Rights of Indigenous Peoples*, SC 2021, c 14.

have been conducive in raising public awareness of various social issues. Throughout history, these kinds of activities by ordinary people may produce an immense impact. Compounded by the power of social media, messages from these movements could reach far and wide. Historically, small protests and demonstrations have been shown to be powerful enough to create social movements, as witnessed with the environmental (climate change) movement, the waves of suffragists and feminist movements, and the abortion and anti-abortion movements in the United States and Canada. Protests against racism that have been organized by racialized people, including anti-Black racism, anti-Asian hate, and anti-Islamophobia, have noticeably emerged in Canada over the past few decades. In spite of some sporadic militancy exhibited by Black Lives Matter, anti-racism protests have not quite mushroomed into a full-blown organized movement or even as a united front made up of Asians, Blacks, Indigenous peoples, and Muslims until now. There have been signs in the last few years that some of these groups have formed partnerships and have even teamed up with LGBTQIA+ groups. The political and economic gains that have been achieved by women fighting for their rights since the 1960s have been noteworthy. While it is still too early to predict what these anti-racism "movements" could do, the current collaboration of anti-racism activists may be able to forge some political and economic gains in the future. Nevertheless, in their current forms, these protests are raising public awareness of racism issues, even among corporate executives, as witnessed in BlackNorth's recent pledge to support Black youths in education and employment.

Canada is at a historical juncture of economic, political, and social forces. These three forces have converged while the economy has been teetering in downturns, slow growth, inflation, and labour unrest as a result of the COVID-19 pandemic, and the national political leadership has been steering the country in the direction of redress of past inequality and genocide, healing and reconciliation to advance rights for Indigenous peoples, and marginalized people—Indigenous peoples and racialized people—are rising up and demanding for social justice. These are encompassing economic disruptions and human pains, political shifts from the top, and rising voices from the historically disenfranchised. As history has demonstrated, this social context is conducive to an acceleration of further disruptive forces or trends that often emerge before the disruptions, the gradual disappearance of old ways of doing things, more economic adjustments or monetary/fiscal policy changes, an increase in political conflict/tension as powers seize opportunities for advantage, and the ascendency of new perspectives, paradigm shifts, innovative technology, and new ways of human adaptation.

This changing context in Canada and other parts of the world is global in scale, drastic in speed, and massive in impact. Each country is figuring out how best to tackle these economic, political, and social changes—some seem to be better in working through the transition, but others are experiencing more radical changes. Overall, this is a time in which we see both challenges and opportunities. It also offers us a glimpse of hope to make the world a better place. In essence, the disruptions of the pandemic and its related fallouts in the last few years offer an opportunity for us to do some rethinking of what could be done better in the area of race and racism in the workplace. The "good old days" of work arrangements, workplace hierarchy and culture, and employment policies and practices before the disruption of COVID-19 may not return, and the disruptions that we have been experiencing are not making it easy for us. The health and mortality disparities noted among racial groups are hard to ignore, and the desperation of the public health sector in stabilizing and reducing human suffering are to be remembered. In order to move forward, we may have no choice but to learn from the mistakes of the past and to prepare for a new future.

The economic, political, and social challenges in Canada identified in this chapter have created an environment in which we can ask deeper and more comprehensive questions about how our workplaces are organized and managed. There are employment policies and practices, workplace culture, and leadership and management styles that we have taken for granted all our lives, but now the COVID-19 pandemic has shown us a few work-related problems that could mushroom to a crisis situation that may be unrepairable and unmanageable. We can use this pandemic-induced destabilized work environment to act as a catalyst for deeper critical thinking on how best to recruit, hire, promote, and retain people, to innovate and provide services more effectively and efficiently, and to enhance employee engagement, creativity, productivity, collaboration, inclusiveness, and accountability. These are just a few areas in the workplace that could be transformed when we look at them with a critical mind through the lens of race and how to eradicate systemic racism in the workplace as a prerequisite for redesigning and restructuring the work environment.

While not all of us share the same degree of urgency on racial justice, work, and the economy, the pandemic disruptions and resulting economic and political challenges will affect people in one form or another, Canada and worldwide. The ramifications of racial issues have permeated the consciousness and conversations of leaders, middle-level managers, and unions (including non-management employees) in a slow simmering manner. This might be due partly to the ascendency of the diversity, equity, and inclusiveness school of thought in human resources management and the associated rise of environmental, social, and governance principles in management prior to the arrival of the pandemic, partly to the destabilized economy and disrupted workplace, and partly to the increasingly louder voices from Indigenous and racialized communities outside the workplace and the political stewardship of the federal government over Indigenous, racialized, and gender agendas discussed earlier in this chapter. Such a combination of pressure on leadership and management is likely to impact on organizational planning for the future. Literature on board governance, leadership, and management have been populated with social justice issues in recent years and so are the themes and contents found in conferences and webinars. Obviously, social justice issues are competing with issues related to global conflicts, political upheavals, economic changes, and other social and technological issues. As the focus of this book is on racism and anti-racism, we will take a deeper look at the concept of racism and how the current workplace structures and processes and policies and programs impact on racialized and Indigenous peoples, without losing sight of the forces that are shaping the world outside the workplace and what the government, employers, and unions can do better.

CHAPTER 2

Shining a Light on Racism

This chapter examines the concept of racism and highlights its major features. Since people have difficult viewpoints on this concept, the chapter does not intend to reach a consensus among readers on how racism is defined; rather, it highlights the shared key features of these definitions, including the one working definition of racism that is proposed for this book.

RACISM IS MULTIFACETED AND MULTI-PURPOSED

People look at racism from different angles. Depending on their backgrounds and world-views, experiences, and personal preferences, they focus on different aspects of racism. Hence, it is difficult to reach a consensus on how racism is defined. Definitions serve particular purposes for different individuals, and they are meaningful only to each of them. This does not mean that one definition of racism is more correct than others. It merely reflects on what features of racism people wish to highlight for the purpose(s) of what they intend to present. Further complicating the matter is that it is not easy to draw a clear definitive boundary on the concept of "race" since it is an artificial construct for the benefit of describing a complex phenomenon.

In the real world, race also intersects with other human attributes (such as ethnicity and religion) that are hard to disentangle. If racism "purifies" itself solely on race, it detaches too much from reality, which renders the concept unrealistic and artificial and may not correspond well with the real world. As people with intersectional attributes (such as race, gender, class, and ability) may tell us, their experiences of racism based on their combined attributes are unique and are not comparable to others with different attributes. A racialized person from Africa may define "racism" in a different manner when compared with someone from the United States because their life experiences in two different continents and historical backgrounds are so different. Similarly, a racialized woman's experience on racial and gender issues does not align well with that of a disabled racialized woman.

And then there is the issue of language, which is a human tool for the purpose of communication. Within the confines of linguistic clarity or preciseness, it may still be possible to approximate the real world of matters specifically limited to race (as some lawyers or academics have maintained), while people on the street may not have that capability or inclination to do so. Many of us tend to lump ideas or behaviours together and subsume them under the term "racism" without distinguishing the fine specificities of multiple attributes (such as gender, class, and ability), the functionalities of racism (such as the hierarchy of power and value and their relationship with political ideologies) or the contexts in which racism is experienced (such as blatant racist remarks and subtle racial belittlement). The use of the concept of "racism" often comes with an intention. Some people use it with the intention of building an argument, highlighting other issues, and/or following up with additional human actions. In the legal domain, a definition of racism must connect with a body of constructs with the expressed objective of developing a legal framework or public policy. In the academic domain, a definition of racism has the objective of developing an explanatory framework or a social theory. In both academia and law, the definition of "racism" has implications on any combination of the following: theoretical constructs, regulations, law enforcement mechanisms, public education, human behaviours, social practices, institutional structures and processes, and, most important of all, the future of the world.

In the following sections, we will review some examples of the academic and legal perspectives on racism to get an understanding of the divergence of these definitions. One may note that academic theories focus on explaining why racism occurs and who benefits from it, and legal frameworks focus on what racism is and what adverse impacts are imposed on whom. Accordingly, academic definitions have the purpose of building a theoretical framework for describing and explaining the system of racial ideas and practices through time, while government definitions focus on the specific aspects of racial experience that the government plans to address in a formal legal manner or in an institutional programmatic manner. This divergence of purposes does not preclude these definitions from being cross-fertilized by each other to enhance their intellectual vigour or their pragmatic impacts.

Academic Perspectives on Racism

There have been many theories put forward by scholars in understanding racism through the ages. Franklin Frazier (1947, 265–71; 1972, 15–25) summarized the earlier ones in the nineteenth and early twentieth centuries. These "theories" appear more like opinions that served as justifications for slavery and racial injustice: racism was viewed as philosophically good for society (Hughes 1854), as a high quality of human achievement of a superior race (Whites) over an inferior race (Blacks) (Ward 1921), as a "consciousness of kind" that maintains racial exclusiveness (Giddings 1906), as a refusal of Blacks to assimilate with the Whites (Odum 1943), and a conflict of cultures, statuses, and interracial relations (R. Park 1950). These perspectives have a strong sense that racism is based on some hereditary attributes of Blacks and their lack of an assimilation mindset. In other words, biological and psychological factors have been used to understand racial differences and disparities.

However, as theoretical thinking evolved, some later theories on racism were more structural in nature and closely connected with how capitalism evolves and functions. This is a radical school of thought on racism. For example, Michael Reich (1978, 1981), a radical theorist, believed that racism is an ideological tool utilized by the ruling class to mystify the true of nature of capitalism. It enables White capitalists to get most of the wealth generated by the workers and splits the workers into two camps: White workers, who are getting ahead easier in their careers than the Blacks who they can blame for all the evils of the system. Meanwhile, Black workers get lower wages and have a harder time moving up in their careers. In creating an unequal and antagonistic relationship between Whites and Blacks, racism serves the interest of the capitalists (Prager 1972–73, 117–50).

Another radical theory on racism is the "industrial reserved army of labour," which argues that it is in the interest of capitalists to have a reserved pool of workers that can be called upon to work (with lower wages) when the economy expands and to be terminated when the economy shrinks. Migrant workers and immigrant workers are usually found in this sector. Nowadays, this army of labour could be a pool of surplus or seasonal workers like agricultural helpers, nannies, contract workers, part-timers, or people with precarious "on-and-off" employment history. As expected, there is resentment between the permanent full-time workers and those who are permanently "surplus." Once again, if this army of reserved labour is demarcated along race, ethnicity, or nationality lines, racism functions in splitting the working class into Whites and racialized people as well as native-born and foreign-born people, justifying low pay and poor working conditions and ensuring profit for the capitalists and more hard times for the racialized workers (Castles and Kosack 1973a; 1973b, 21).

As this radical school of thought evolved, the "Internal Colonial" theory, as advocated by Robert Blauner (1969, 393–408), emerged. It takes issue with the earlier-mentioned view that White capitalists are the beneficiaries of racism. This theory maintains that all Whites (not just capitalists) benefit from racism. It is in the interest of all Whites to subordinate racialized people just like the colonization process of forcing the colonized (that is, Third World countries) and destroys Indigenous values and ways of life. Therefore, racism is a principle of social domination by the superior Whites over the inferior racialized people in all aspects of their existence and not just the economic sphere. In ensuring the continuous subordination of racialized people, racism has its ideological and structural aspects, both help to stabilize the society and safeguard the privileges of the non-racialized people. The decolonization process is therefore not just about overthrowing capitalism but also uprooting the entire system of its White privileges and domination (Gonzalez Casanova 1965, 27–37; Blauner 1969, 393–408; Prager 1972–73, 117–50; Gonzalez 1974; Pinderhughes 2011, 253–56).

Critical race theory, pioneered by Derrick Bell (1980, 518–33) over forty years ago, views racism as a permanent social feature of which its adverse impact is diluted only when it is aligned with White interest (such as the emancipation of slavery in the United States). As a theory in racism, it blends identity politics, victimization, and political action together. Although it explains individual biases and prejudice, its main contribution is in articulating the functioning of institutional discrimination and oppression as a permanent structure with its historical and cumulative impacts on racialized communities. As the theory develops, it highlights the concept of white privilege, intersectionality, and power relations and views diversity as a diversion or even distraction of our attention on racial issues. It criticizes the contemporary diversity, equity, and inclusiveness school of thought as not demolishing the machinery of racial inequality. In sum, critical race theory uses race as the prism to analyze society and calls for a resistance stratgegy that aims to transform the socal structure of oppression. Richard Delglado and Jean Stefancic (2017) summarized the essence of critical race theory as a resistance stratgegy that aims to transform the socal structure of oppression (see also Butcher and Gonzalez 2020, 1–42; Cobb 2021, 1–21; Sawchuk 2021).

As the above summary shows, each wave of theoretical development changed the perspectives on racism in one way or another. The theoretical foci are different, and their explanatory frameworks vary. Overall, new perspectives attempted to make the understanding of racism more refined, comprehensive, and critical of the status quo. The concept of racism and terminology shifts as new perspectives emerged. One can increasingly hear the words "decolonization," "oppression," "white privilege," "exploitation," "Indigenization," "victimization," and "identity politics" in dialogues on racism among scholars and advocates in Indigenous and racialized people and communities. Even some government bodies and established institutions are beginning to adopt these new terms in their narratives, which may mean that they are permeating into the consciousness of the establishment.

Government Perspectives on Racism

Let us turn our attention to one federal government agency that has a mandate to enforce the federal *Human Rights Code* and one provincial government agency that has a mandate to develop policies and educational programs regarding a provincial human right code.

The Canadian Human Rights Commission does not have an official definition of "racism" that is readily available, but its officials talked about "racism" on different occasions. In marking the International Day for the Elimination of Racial Discrimination on 21 March 2021, Marie-Claude Landry, chief commissioner of the Canadian Human Rights Commission, issued a statement in support of the day, defining racism as "a system and a structure that is deeply embedded in the fabrics of our country." This system includes "white privilege," "racial biases," and "racial discrimination," which "contribute to injustice and inequality." It "continues to deny far too many Indigenous, Black and other racialized people a life free from discrimination, ... and in recent days, ... we have seen anti-Asian racism escalate to hate and violence" (Landry 2021). And, under the umbrella of racism, "xenophobia" was added (Landry 2020), as were the words "Islamophobia" and "antisemitism" (Malischewski 2023).

In response to the United Nation Committee on the Discrimination against Women's decision in favour of Jeremy Matson who had filed a petition alleging that the registration provisions of the *Indian Act* violated his rights and those of his children, the Canadian Human Rights Commission (2022) issued a statement urging the Government of Canada to "actively root out the enduring colonialism and systemic racism that are still woven into the fabric of far too many of the laws and policies that underpin our society."[1] Overall, it appears that the federal commission's use of the term "racism" covers at least race, Indigeneity, and religion. Meanwhile, the Ontario Human Rights Commission (n.d.b.), in one of its brochures to the public, stated that "racism is a social construct ... and is a broader experience and practice than racial discrimination." Accordingly, "racism is a belief that one group is superior to others." The brochure noted the overt and covert nature of racism: "Racism can be openly displayed in racial jokes, slurs or hate crimes. It can also be more deeply rooted in attitudes, values and stereotypical beliefs. ... [It has] become part of systems and institutions, and also associated with the dominant group's power and privilege." The commission further emphasized that "racial discrimination is the illegal expression of racism ... [and] racial harassment is a form of discrimination." This definition encompasses the cognitive, behaviourial, and structural elements of racism. The document further stated that racism impacts negatively on racialized communities, including Indigenous peoples. This definition is comprehensive and has enabled the commission to develop additional policies and programs and provides substance for the legal interpretation of Ontario's *Human Rights Code*.[2]

---

1 *Indian Act*, RSC 1985, c I-5.

2 *Human Rights Code*, RSO 1995, c H.19.

Convergence and Divergence

From these public statements, it seems clear that, while both the federal and Ontario human rights commissions were not as articulated as the radical theorists in explaining racism, they came to the similar conclusion that racism permeates human perception, attitude, and behaviours as well as social institutions and cultures. It is a prevalent deeply rooted societal issue. In addition, the commissions have also adopted some of the terminology utilized by radical theories such as white privilege, victimization, oppression, colonization, and intersectionality. As expected, the major divergence in the definitions is that the radical and critical theories placed the roots of racism in capitalism, capitalists, and everyone who is White, whereas the government commissions assigned responsibility to everyone who, and every institution that, treats people as if some are more superior than others based on their race, irrespective of their race. For political and pragmatic reasons, it appears that the government's definitions are more generic than the academic ones and do not assign "blame" to specific groups of the population.

WORKING DEFINITION OF RACISM

As noted earlier, academic definitions of racism are very much tied to their explanatory frameworks and their implied actions in ending racism. There are many other definitions such as those used by governments for public policy or legislative purposes. They boil down to the notion of an assumed hierarchy of people in human mindsets and social systems that are measured in terms of inferiority and superiority. With the earlier examination of how racism has been conceptualized by academics and government officials, this book proposes a working definition of racism that is applicable largely to the description (not explanation) of what is going on in the workplace and the larger society. It is intentionally broad in scope and generic in nature, and it shares some common grounds with the definitions that we have reviewed so far. This working definition could be applied alongside some of the explanatory frameworks discussed earlier in this chapter:

> Racism is a set of human perceptions, attitudes, actions and systems that treat people of different races, colour, ethnicity, nationality, ancestry, place of origin, citizenship, linguistic or religious backgrounds in a hierarchical, discriminatory, inequitable, and exclusive manner. At

both the individual and systemic levels, racism manifests itself overtly, but more often in a covert manner, with or without the knowledge or acknowledgement of individuals, organizations, or institutions.

This working definition consists of several integral components: (1) a combination of human psychology, behaviours, and social systems; (2) a range of personal and collective identities; (3) a hierarchical ranking of people with a demarcation in terms of separation, fairness, and acceptance; and (4) multiple levels of manifestation, subtlety, and subjectivity. This working definition describes *what* racism is, but it does not explain *why* it exists or *who* it harms or benefits like many academic definitions do. It serves us as a framework on *how* racism works at both the macroscopic-societal and microscopic-workplace levels.

At the broader societal level, when we find racial issues all over the multiple spheres of our lives, the working definition presents a framework for us to categorize the psychological and structural aspects of racism, the scope of impact at the individual or collective level, the manner in which racism impacts on them, and the level of awareness that individuals or organizations have when racial injustice is found. At the organizational or institutional level, the working definition serves the purpose of analyzing the mechanics of workplace racism without dwelling too much on the rationales behind it. It can become entangled with the political philosophies/ideologies or social theories of justice. This working definition will serve as a guide in sorting out all the human resources issues related to workplace racism. The working definition is pragmatic, with a focus on identifying the areas in the workplace that hide racism and how these areas operate.

CONCLUSION

Racism is a complex concept. It is complex because it has many facets and features and because the concept carries many meanings known only to people who use it. They also have their own individual objectives in using the concept and what they would like to communicate to other persons. Governments, with their political and pragmatic inclinations, have their own ways of using the concept of racism. They are interested in describing what racism is but fall short in explaining it. Meanwhile, academic perspectives reflect different schools of thought on racism, and they provide an assortment of explanations of why racism occurs and which stakeholder groups benefit from it. Their definitions are either supportive or critical of the status quo. Racism impacts on Indigenous peoples and racialized people adversely. The common usage of the term "racism" in the street is not limited to race. It also covers colour, ethnicity, nationality, ancestry, place of origin, citizenship, language, and religion. Ambiguities and confusions abound when people talk about racism. This book comes up with a working definition of racism to clarify what it is and sets the boundaries for the ways in which we wish to structure our discussion on the topic as it is relevant to the workplace.

CHAPTER 3

Racism Everywhere

This book is about racism in the workplace; however, in order to understand racism and how racism functions in a work environment, it is important to put the workplace in the context of Canada. When we realize that racism permeates almost all layers and corners of society, it is not surprising that it is also found at work. Workplace racism is therefore a microcosm of the larger society.

Using examples from the real world, this chapter argues that Indigenous peoples and racialized people experience different forms of racism—whether they are overt or covert—in all walks of life, from birth to death. These examples are not exhaustive of all racist practices or systems. They merely represent the tip of the racism iceberg, which is a massive phenomenon. Most of the examples of racism that will be exposed show how deep they are embedded in the institutions or ingrained in the culture. They also illustrate how racism can impact on individuals on a continuous basis from their birth and childhood, through their adulthood, until they reach the end of their lives. It impacts every aspect of a human being's life and their daily livelihood.

Racism is embedded extensively and deeply in a broad range of social institutions, and this is the social context of workplace racism in Canada. The experiences of racialized and Indigenous peoples affect them starting from their conception until the last days of their lives. There are not many chances to escape from them. It is the position of this book that workplace racism is a microcosm of the larger society and that it should not be viewed in isolation. Racist stereotypes, biases and attitudes, prejudice, harassment, and discrimination found in the work environment are an extension of the racism found outside the workplace. A good understanding of these experiences will enrich our comprehension and analysis of the racism noted in the workplace and gives us a better feel of how racialized and Indigenous people navigate their work lives in the workplace. It is important to connect the dots of racism in the lives of racialized and Indigenous peoples to understand more about why they think, feel, and behave in the ways in which they do. It is also important to note that many non-racialized and non-Indigenous peoples do not have the same or similar life chances of racialized and Indigenous peoples in or outside the workplace. One often hears the comment that racialized and Indigenous peoples carry "a chip on their shoulder" or that they look at the world through "a tinted glass." A closer reading of this chapter will enhance our understanding of how encompassing and overwhelming racial disparity is for them.

BIRTHS AND BABYHOOD

Indigenous Peoples

Indigenous and racialized peoples begin their lives with a huge disadvantage due to their race. It is not clear whether that is innate or environmental. It is increasingly apparent that social factors such as their poor living conditions, difficult domestic situations, poor parental health, unfair neglect in health services, or lack of resources have negative impacts on their babies and children.

Indigenous peoples start off their life journey at a disadvantage. They die early in their life. Statistics show that Indigenous infant mortality rate is double that of the Canadian population (Advisory Committee on Population Health 1999, xiv). Indigenous children also have a higher chance of being separated from their parents and experiencing domestic violence and maltreatment. It is a fact that Indigenous peoples aged fifteen and older (11 percent) are nearly ten times more likely than non-Indigenous peoples of the same age group (1.3 percent) to have been under the legal responsibility of the government during their childhood. This skewed representation might be partially due to child maltreatment, sexual or physical violence, or neglect. Child welfare services or the police are about three times more likely to be made aware of violence experienced by Indigenous children (16 percent) compared with violence experienced by non-Indigenous children (5.2 percent) (Perreault 2022). The Ontario Human Rights Commission examined the racial composition of children admitted to their care in Children's Aid Societies (CAS). The results show that, where data are available (in twenty-five out of twenty-seven CAS), 92.6 percent of them have a disproportionately higher number of Indigenous children. In fact, most of them are over-represented in their admission of Indigenous children, to the extent that the numbers of of Indigenous children are 2.6 times higher than that of the proportion of the Canadian child population.

Indigenous peoples are critical of the Ontario Human Rights Commission's data as they believe that the data have been undercounted mainly because Indigenous agencies have not been part of the commission's sample and that Metis children are often mistaken as White children. Indigenous children in foster care are disproportionately higher (seven-and-a-half times) than that of the Canadian child population. Indigenous children are also likely to be subject to Indigenous child welfare investigations. They make up a significant segment of the child welfare system. The causes of such a phenomenon are related to systemic racial discrimination, high poverty levels, intergenerational traumas, underfunding of the Indigenous CAS's operation on reserves, and long-term conflicts and tension between the child welfare system and Indigenous communities (Ontario Human Rights Commission 2018).

It is also a fact that 42 percent of Indigenous women are more likely than non-Indigenous women (27 percent) to have been physically or sexually abused by an adult during their childhood and have experienced harsh parenting by a parent or guardian. These childhood experiences seem to be connected with a lifetime of violent victimization (Heidinger 2022).

Racialized People

Racialized babies begin their lives (and even before their births) with disadvantages in their health. Preterm births among Black women (8.9 percent) are higher than those of White women (5.9 percent) in Canada. In Ontario and Quebec, African-born and Caribbean-born women have higher rates of preterm births than Canadian-born women. Other Canadian studies have identified additional adverse issues related to the babies of Black and Asian women, including higher stillbirth rates, lower birth weight, more inadequate gestational weight gain, and other birth problems when compared with White women.

The causes for these disparities are not clear, but research studies seem to suggest that they might be related to the disadvantaged socio-economic situations of Black and Asian women, their poor neighbourhoods, racial discrimination, lack of access to health care and insurance, psycho-social stress, and adverse health behaviours (McKinnon et al. 2016; Miao 2022).

The Ontario Human Rights Commission (2018) also did a study on the proportion of Black children admitted to the CAS in Ontario, and it noted that thirteen of the twenty-seven CAS showed disproportionately high admissions of Black children, to the extent that it is 2.2 times their proportion in the Canadian child population. Race data on the remaining CAS were not available, not collected, or missing because of data suppression. Looking at the same data set, more than half of the CAS (fifteen of the twenty-seven CAS or 55.6 percent) showed the under-representation of White children. The underlining factors of such over-representation include deep poverty and related risks, racial stereotyping and prejudice, and their associated assessment thresholds and different treatments. These factors compounded each other to increase the impacts of systemic biases.

POVERTY

Compared with Canadian-born White people, racialized and Indigenous babies tend to have a more difficult start in life as preterm babies, with higher infant mortality and lower birth weight as well as more chance of being separated from their parents, of having a more stressful environment, of being more likely to live in a violent environment, and of experiencing harsher parenting. They are more likely to be raised in a lower socio-economic environment.

Racial disparity in wealth among Canadians is obvious. Poverty is a central feature of a significant proportion of Indigenous peoples and racialized people. Statistical data on race and poverty in Canada highlight the disproportionate share of Indigenous peoples and racialized people living in poverty, and this suggests that they are more likely to experience miserable life chances than others.

More than one million Canadian children live in poverty today, and the consequences of their poverty are long lasting and pass from one generation to another. Since 2021, there are signs that indicate that more children now live in poverty than before (Racine and Premji 2024).

The brain development of children from poor backgrounds is slow, and this affects their physical and mental health well into their adulthood. Poverty means malnutrition, lack of clean water, poor hygiene, lengthy sicknesses, poor school performance, unlivable housing conditions, unaffordability in daily living expences, and shorter life expectancy (Children International, n.d.; Kapoor et al. 2022). Indigenous children and racialized children start their life journeys in a very disadvantaged position compared with the White population.

Earlier studies on the wage gaps of racialized and non-racialized people show that racialized families have three times the poverty rates of non-racialized families: the 2005 data show that "19.8% of racialized families lived in poverty, compared to 6.4% of non-racialized families" (Block and Galabuzi 2011). It is clear that, in Canada, poverty has been racialized, as indicated by the poorly paid jobs and poor health of the racialized sector. For racialized people, 9.5 percent of them were below the poverty line compared with 6.5 percent of non-racialized people in 2021. However, different racial groups experienced different degrees of poverty. The breakdown of poverty rates of racialized people in 2021 were "other visible minorities" (14.4 percent), Arabs (12.8 percent), Chinese (11.7 percent), Blacks (11.5 percent), Southeast Asians (9.1 percent), south Asians (7.0 percent), Latin Americans (6.8 percent), and Filipino (2.9 percent) (Statistics Canada 2023a; 2023l).

Other indicators of socio-economic disparity are family incomes and household incomes. The data show income discrepancies between races. Family incomes in the 2016 Census data show that racialized families tend to cluster at the bottom half of the income distribution range (60 percent) when compared with those of non-racialized individuals (47 percent) (Canadian Centre for Policy Alternatives 2019). Similar patterns were noted in a health study conducted by Statistics Canada using the 2001, 2006, and 2011 Canada Census Health and Environment Cohorts when household income data by race are categorized in five income quintiles. At the bottom, under two income quintiles on low income, Black males constituted 49.8 percent and Black females constituted 56.9 percent, whereas White males constituted 34.3 percent and White females constituted 39.4 percent. At the top two income quintiles on high income, the pattern was reversed: White males constituted 44.8 percent and White female constituted 40.4 percent—Black males constituted 40.3 percent and Black females 25 percent. These data suggest that Blacks are poorer than Whites and that Black women are even poorer. The study showed that low incomes have negative impacts on the health of Black people (Tjepkema et al. 2023).

When Canada was in the midst of the COVID-19 pandemic, 13.9 percent of Indigenous peoples aged sixteen and older were below the poverty line, which was close to double that of their non-Indigenous counterparts (7.4 percent). Among Indigenous peoples, 17.2 percent of First Nations living off reserve and 10.5 percent of Metis were below the poverty rate. The percentage for Inuit was too unreliable to be published by Statistics Canada 2023a, 2023b, 2023l).

Poverty is a structural phenomenon and has a racial component. We have a biased tendency to judge poor Indigenous and racialized children and adults as if they are personally at fault and are responsible for their poverty. In reality, they have done nothing wrong by just being born poor. And being poor is not a genetic attribute or criminal offence; rather, it is often a result of human prejudice, racial discrimination, and inequitable public or corporate policies and practices.

FOODS

Along with poverty, another aspect of life is secure access to nutricious foods on a continuous basis. The flip side of this is "food insecurity," which refers to the inadequate or unreliable access to healthy food due to financial constraints or poverty.

According to Statistics Canada (2023a, 2023l), food insecurity refers to living conditions that experience marginal, moderate, or severe food uncertainty. In terms of persons living in a household that experienced food insecurity in 2021, the proportion of people from the racialized (visible minority) population is 24.5 percent and from the non-racialized (non-visible minority) population is 16 percent. Within the racialized (visible minority) population, the breakdowns were as follows: Black (39.2 percent), Filipino (29.2 percent), Arab (27 percent), "other visible minority" (22.1 percent), Southeast Asian (22 percent), South Asian (21 percent), and Latin American (20 percent). For Indigenous people living off reserve, 30.9 percent experienced food insecurity in 2021. Once again, as an indicator of poverty, food insecurity has a racial component, and racial disparity is a key feature.

A recent study by FoodShare and PROOF (an interdisciplinary research program focusing on policy changes to reduce household food insecurity in Canada supported by the Canadian Institute of Health

Research) shows that race is the best predictor of food insecurity among Black Canadians, even after controlling for immigrant status, education, and homeownership (Sustain Ontario 2021). Food insecurity has been shown to be associated with low graduation rates, low self-esteem, low incomes, and poor neighbourhoods (M. Roberts 2020). With respect to the issue of low income, Valerie Tarasuk and Andy Mitchell (2020) noted that 60.4 percent of households in Canada that relied on social assistance experienced food insecurity. Most of these households are made up of racialized individuals in Toronto.

In 2024, rising prices impacted negatively on most Indigenous people as they have problems paying for their day-to-day expences. About four in ten Indigenous people living off reserve reported a rise in food prices, and six out of ten of them reported that they had problems buying healthy and nutritious food. Twenty-two percent of First Nations people, 23 percent of Metis, and 33 percent of Inuit living off reserve reported that the rising price of food caused them to not have enough food to last the week. Compared with 8 percent of the overall number of Canadian households, about one in five Indigenous people will depend on community organizations for food vouchers in the next six months (Statistics Canada 2025).

In addition to the adverse socio-economic consequences of food insecurity, Indigenous peoples and racialized people exhibit poor dietary patterns and diet quality. National representative nutrition surveys were used to examine dietary patterns and their association with socio-economic and socio-demographic factors and chronic conditions in the off-reserve Indigenous population in Canada (Health Canada and Statistics Canada 2004). The survey respondents identified their dietary patterns as measured by the Nutrient Rich Food Index. The overall results showed that most Indigenous peoples had unhealthy dietary patterns with a low diet quality (high fat and high sugar). Apparently, such patterns contribute to a higher incidence of obesity and chronic diseases, which is associated with the income level and smoking habits of adults and the physical inactivity of children among the off-reserve Indigenous population (Keshavarz et al. 2023).

In addition, being racialized also placed racialized people in a disadvantaged position. A systematic review of studies on the dietary patterns of racialized groups showed that Blacks are among the poorest consumers of fruit and vegetables and that Asian groups have high diet quality scores as a result of fish and low fat intakes compared to other groups (Bennett, Bardon, and Gibney 2022). The study also found that

Blacks and other racialized people in low-income neighbourhoods, such as the Jane-Finch area in Toronto, do not have access to much healthy food and that youth tend to buy unhealthy food in shopping malls and affordable fast food for lunch.

Rosie Mensah, a Ghanaian Canadian who grew up in this same neighbourhood in Toronto, coined this issue as "food apartheid," which describes "a community where residents have limited access to affordable, healthy food options." Now, a registered dietitian in Toronto, she has noted the prevalence of White European views on diets, the lack of racialized dietitians and perspectives on dietetics, and the minimal understanding of the complexity of racism, poor diets, and chronic diseases as the sources of the problem. Racial biases in dietetic education and access to finance and resources affect what racialized people eat, which, in turn, impacts on their health (Cukier 2021). Overall, racial disparity, poverty, food insecurity, unhealthy diets, and malnutrition are intertwined.

HOUSING

Adequate housing is a basic need for people. However, when compared with White people, Indigenous peoples and racialized people are more disadvantaged in satisfying this basic need. They live in housing with core housing needs. "Core housing needs" means that dwellings are unsuitable (that is, the size of the household exceeds the number of bedrooms required), inadequate (that is, major house repairs are needed), and unaffordable (that is, they are spending 30 percent or more of their income on the cost of shelter). Indigenous peoples and racialized people are also disproportionately found in rental housing stocks and overcrowded properties and suffer from homelessness, which are issues that are associated with all sorts of health and financial problems. Living in properties with core housing needs has a negative impact on the household's financial capacity to cover other essential expences including groceries, transportation, and clothing and the risk of infection and injuries on people living there, which, in turn, jeopardizes the development and education of children. In other words, poor housing is intertwined with many of the disadvantages that Indigenous and racialized peoples face in Canada. The following data on housing disparities suggests a structural racial divide in Canada that has ramifications on life chances and experiences.

In 2018, Indigenous households (63.9 percent) were less likely to own their dwelling than non-Indigenous households (68.7 percent). They were also likely to live in rental properties (36.1 percent), and 23.8 percent of those people living in rental properties lived in social and affordable housing, which is higher than the rate for non-Indigenous households (13 percent). In total, 35.3 percent of Inuit, 12 percent of First Nations people living off reserve, and 12.6 percent of Metis were experiencing core housing needs, as defined above. Overall, Indigenous peoples (13.5 percent) are more prone to experience core housing needs than non-Indigenous people (8.8 percent) (Hahmann and Masoud 2023; Statistics Canada 2023j).

Compared with non-Indigenous people, in 2021, Indigenous peoples were more likely to live in a crowded dwelling (17.1 percent for Indigenous peoples versus 9.4 percent for non-Indigenous people) and twice as likely to live in dwellings that need major repairs (16.4 percent for Indigenous peoples versus 5.7 percent for non-Indigenous people), and they were nearly three times more likely to report mildew in their dwellings and undrinkable water. Persistent underfunding of housing in Indigenous communities has been well documented (Hahmann and Masoud 2023; Statistics Canada 2023j).

Among these Indigenous peoples with core housing needs, a high percentage of them also reported financial difficulties: First Nations people living off reserve (52.3 percent), Inuit (69.1 percent), and Metis (65.7 percent). This is in contrast with the reported financial difficulty of non-Indigenous people with core housing needs (45.2 percent) (Statistics Canada 2023j). Financial hardship was higher among Indigenous renter households (41.6 percent), especially those living in social and affordable housing (55.8 percent), than among those who owned their properties (28 percent). Their life satisfaction and health levels also followed the above pattern but in reverse order (Hahmann and Masoud 2023; Statistics Canada 2023j). These data show that, even among those who have financial difficulties, Indigenous peoples are much worse off when it comes to housing and other aspects of their lives.

Indigenous peoples are over-represented in experiencing homelessness, financial instability, and poverty when compared with the rest of the population in Canada. Colonization and colonial practices such as the residential school system may explain such marginalization. A deprivation of using their native languages and practising their religions and a practice of forcing children to separate from their families and communities have had long-term negative impacts on Indigenous peoples.

In total, 54 percent of the women in Indigenous shelters have had a prior history of homelessness, whereas only 37 percent of women in non-Indigenous shelters reported the same. In addition, 44 percent of children living in Indigenous shelters had a prior history of homelessness, but only 28 percent of children in non-Indigenous shelters reported the same. The fact that more Indigenous women and children have a prior history of homelessness than their non-Indigenous counterparts may be due to the intergenerational effects of colonization and the residential school system, educational and employment barriers, and discrimination in the housing market (Statistics Canada 2022f). In other words, being Indigenous puts them in a position of long-term intergenerational misery with respect to housing, including homelessness.

During the COVID-19 pandemic, their overcrowded housing conditions and the lack of suitable and adequate housing (space-wise and health-wise) did not allow Indigenous peoples to isolate if they were not well. Their lack of access to clean water also prohibited them from proper handwashing. Supply chain issues, compounded by their isolation in dwellings throughout their communities, also made it difficult for people to get personal protective equipment to shield them against the COVID-19 virus. Their overcrowded housing conditions and a lack of mobility during the pandemic were restrictive for women living with abusers and were also conducive to domestic tension and violence and victimization (Statistics Canada 2022f).

Racialized people also have their own housing difficulties. In 2021, 11.3 percent of racialized people lived in a household with core housing needs. This percentage is higher than the "Canadian population" (7.7 percent). The breakdowns of racialized groups in core housing needs are: West Asian (19.5 percent), Korean (18.7 percent), Arab (14.9 percent), Black (13.2 percent), Chinese (12.9 percent), "racial group not included elsewhere" (12.4 percent), "multiple racialized groups" (10.3 percent), Southeast Asian (10.1 percent), Japanese (9.4 percent), South Asian (9.1 percent), and Filipino (5.1 percent).

As far as core housing needs are concerned, immigrants of racialized groups (11.4 percent) were more likely to have core housing needs than their non-immigrant counterparts (9.8 percent) (Statistics Canada 2023b). There were more racialized group members with core housing needs in urban areas, especially those with a higher proportion of racialized groups in Ontario such as Ottawa-Gatineau (14.3 percent), Toronto (14.2 percent), London (12.4 percent), Barrie (11.8 percent), Guelph (10.9 percent), and Catharine-Niagara (10.2 percent) (Statistics Canada 2023b). Such intersectionality of immigrant status, urban locations, and race adds a new dimension in racial disparity that should not be ignored.

In contrast, among racialized groups, Chinese (84.5 percent), Southeast Asian (71.9 percent), and South Asian (70.3 percent) populations had the highest proportion of home ownership in 2021. Meanwhile, Black (45.2 percent), Arab (48 percent), and Latin American (48.6 percent) populations had the lowest proportion of home ownership in the same year. The proportion of all Canadians who were homeowners was 71.9 percent in 2021 (Statistics Canada 2023b). Once again, the intersectionality of regional factors of where racialized people originated is an aspect that should be considered in racial disparity and housing.

EDUCATION

It has been well researched and documented that education has a large impact on the life chances of individuals. And there is a close relationship between having completed high school and post-secondary education and the improvement of an individual's employment and income level. This applies to Indigenous and racialized peoples as well as the rest of the population.

The lack of financial resources impacts adversely on Indigenous children's completion of high school or post-secondary education. Moreover, Indigenous parents who attended residential schools are usually associated with lower family income and children's lower educational attainment. The negative impact of colonization and residential schools on intergenerational schooling should be underscored (Statistics Canada 2023i). The lack of decent housing contributed negatively to the educational attainment of Indigenous people and racialized people. In 2016, First Nations off-reserve children living in unsuitable housing conditions (such as not enough bedrooms) were less likely to complete high school or any form of higher education (49.6 percent) than those living in suitable conditions (68.2 percent). The same pattern was found among Metis and Inuit children (Statistics Canada 2023i).

The 2016 data are available on the educational level of Indigenous women. The proportion of Indigenous women who attained a university certificate, diploma, or degree at the bachelor level or above was 13.6 percent, which is much lower than that of non-Indigenous women (31.7 percent). The educational attainment to this same level for Indigenous men was 7.9 percent and that for non-Indigenous people was 26.9 percent. The educational trend for women—Indigenous or non-Indigenous—is that more of them are getting post-secondary qualifications.

Data on professional education and race are scarce. However, a research study in Manitoba showed that White students are 3.8 times more likely to become registered dietitians than those from racialized backgrounds (Riediger et al. 2019, 44–46). Other studies have shown that 64–77.5 percent of students in the dietitian field in British Columbia are White. One study showed that 3 percent of university graduates in dietitian fields were Indigenous (when their population share is only 5.9 percent). A 2020 survey of recent graduates of dietetic programs across Canada showed that 79 percent are White, 12 percent are Chinese, 3 percent are South Asian, and 1.7 percent are Metis (Cukier 2021). These data have implications on the knowledge and cultural competence of graduates in this field, which, in turn, impacts on the nutrition awareness level of Indigenous and racialized peoples (College of Dietitians of British Columbia, n.d.).

Similarly, there is also limited enrollment of racialized people or Black, Indigenous, and People of Colour (BIPOC) in the therapy field, and BIPOC graduates have found themselves not equipped to work with their communities because they have been taught school curricula that are devoid of BIPOC's cultural milieux, perspectives, and skills (Gu 2020). Barriers in accessing post-secondary education or professional training have also been noted for Indigenous peoples specifically: a lack of academic preparation and guidance, not enough financial supports, intergenerational trauma (due to colonization), and the loss of family and cultural support systems (due to relocation) (Arriagada 2021). Overall, race data on students and teachers are not systematically collected and analyzed in the elementary and secondary school system in Canada (with the exception of the Toronto District School Board). At the post-secondary level, race data on students are almost non-existent (Grant and Balkissoon 2019, A10–11). Therefore, we do not have a clear understanding of which racial groups are at risk in school learning, school suspension, graduation, or children welfare (A10–11). And, needless to say, we do not have a readily available systematic comprehension of racial distribution and disparities of students and teachers in colleges and universities, the departments and programs they are in, how they perform, their graduation rates, their post-school employment status, and the scope and contents of the course curricula.

In examining the overall educational experience among Canadians, Statistics Canada's data show that, when attending school or classes, 16.9 percent of Whites reported that they have experienced discrimination, compared with 20.9 percent of non-Black racialized people, 26.9 percent of Indigenous people, and 29.4 percent of Blacks (Cotter 2022). It is telling that the percentage of Blacks (29.4 percent) reporting discrimination is almost doubled that of Whites (16.9 percent), and the percentage of Indigenous peoples experiencing discrimination (26.9 percent) is not far behind. As Black people have consistently pointed out, racism does not affect racialized people evenly. Anti-Black racism appears to be stronger than other forms of racism in the school system, which is illustrated in the following example:

> Black students talked about their personal racial experience in schools in Brampton, Ontario which included a prohibition of the use of the word "racism" by a teacher, a dismissal of slaves as badly treated as a myth, racial slurs in the hallway, belittling of Black students, teachers' assumption of Blacks having poor English skills due to their accents, disproportionately higher incidences of suspensions among Blacks, touching Black hair without permission, streaming Black students to applied courses, rather than academic courses, and micro-aggressions from teachers, along with other structural issues such as human resources practices, governance, administration and leadership. These racist incidents and structures found in schools under the Peel District School Board are documented in the report released by the Ontario Ministry of Education. (Raza 2022)

There have also been reports of widespread racial abuses and educational gaps in schools, including one study done by the Angus Reid Institute in partnership with the University of British Columbia in 2021, which surveyed 872 Canadian youth aged twelve to seventeen. Fifty-eight percent of these youths witnessed children insulted, bullied, or excluded based on their race or ethnicity at school. Fourteen percent reported that they had experienced it themselves. Racialized children are three times as likely, and Indigenous children are twice as likely, as their White counterparts to have confronted personal abuse themselves. The school curricula are not conducive for children to learn about racism in Canada, slavery, the internment of Japanese, the head tax imposed on Chinese immigrants, and the landing of South Asians from the *Komagata Maru* ship in Canada (Fletcher 2021).

Indigenous students also experience Indigenous-specific issues, often of a cultural and racial nature. Indigenous students from Rocky View Schools in Calgary, Alberta, reported a high tendency of chronic absenteeism (30 percent) during the 2017–18 school year. For on-reserve students, the chronic absenteeism rate was 80 percent. Reports of enrollment numbers of on-reserve students also showed a steady decline in the last five years. Rocky View Schools serve the Stoney-Nakoda First Nations communities of Bearspaw, Chiniki, Tsuu T'ina Nation, and Wesley. Barriers that contribute to such poor school attendance are related to cross-cultural anxiety and misunderstanding (as a result of the legacy of residential schools), the lack of a safe place in school for Indigenous students, the existence of White privilege and racism among educators, the embedment of racism in policy, curriculum, and classroom practices, knowledge gaps and pedagogy in the teacher education curriculum, and a lack of accountability for teachers to play a critical role in reconciliation (Fowler 2020).

While the above are merely a few examples of racism found in the school system, they illustrate how racial factors could be specific to individual racialized groups or generic to all of them. The examples also suggest that these experiences of racial discrimination could be prevalent in broader strata of the school system in various regions in Canada. The research findings also show that racism, a racist school environment and culture, low educational accomplishment, a lack of culturally appropriate school curriculum and educators, a lack of financial resources, and poor housing are all intertwined and hard to untangle; each factor reinforces the others in their adverse impacts.

RESEARCH AND KNOWLEDGE

While the educational system in Canada has exhibited various racial disparities in education attainment, Indigenous peoples and racialized people are also "screened out" in getting an equitable share of research money. The lack of well-funded research projects shuts them out from the opportunity of generating new knowledge or a fair share of the academic prestige in owning awards.

One example of racial disparity in the research arena is the Canadian Research Chairs program. This program awards funding that covers more than two thousand researchers at a time. It has been found to be biased and inequitable in its awards to researchers. In 2006, a settlement was reached between the federal government and eight female researchers requiring that the program set targets for awards to researchers who are Indigenous peoples, persons with disabilities, racialized people, and women. Between 2006 and 2019, universities seldom met or exceeded the equity targets. It is clear that, even in the field of academic research and knowledge generation, racialized people and Indigenous peoples have been largely denied annual funding, which currently amounts to between one hundred thousand dollars and two hundred thousand dollars in research money.

The Canadian Human Rights Commission, the Canadian Association of University Teachers, and the three major federal granting councils—the Social Sciences and Humanities Research Council, the National Sciences and Engineering Research Council, and the Canadian Institutes of Health Research—added higher targets for diversity representation in the program following the 2006 settlement. The targets for award representation in the ten years since 2019 are set against the representation rates in the general population. Thus, the targets are 4.9 percent for Indigenous peoples, 7.5 percent for persons with disabilities, 22 percent for racialized people, and 50.9 percent for women. The 2019 award program data show that 2.1 percent for Indigenous peoples, 1.6 percent for persons with disabilities, 15.9 percent for racialized people, and 33.5 percent for women. In both the 2006 and 2019 settlement arrangements, meeting targets for the award funding bodies remained optional, not mandatory. Future data will show how extensively racial bias in the program has been removed (Hannay 2019, A5).

There are numerous explanations for these half-hearted attempts to rectify the skewed situation of researchers and the associated distorted perspectives generated by research projects traditionally occupied by White male scholars. Numerous arguments have been put forward to explain the lack of progress. These include the institutional bias inertia in the academia, which is hard to dismantle; the lack of connection between Indigenous and racialized peoples (along with other marginalized groups) with research of a higher reputation and influence; and the relatively unknown profiles of Indigenous and racialized academics.

One of the adverse impacts of excluding Indigenous peoples and racialized people in the creation of new knowledge is the negation of their perspectives and their actual experiences. Such negations are manifested in knowledge gaps and knowledge distortion as a significant segment of the population has been excluded in research design and implementation. Hence, the research results have an inherent bias built into the knowledge that invalidates or distorts the validity of the findings.

The inaccessibility of Indigenous and racialized researchers to awards or publications means that their perspectives are not included in published research findings. As a result, knowledge and information are distorted and are not reflective of the real world. These gaps in education curricula and teaching materials do not enable a comprehensive education for future generations.

In the domain of health sciences, the lack of racial and ethnic data in the health sciences has been detrimental to the health and mortality of racialized people in Canada for many decades. Compared with other countries such as the United States and the United Kingdom, Canadian health professionals know little about racial differences on breast cancer between White and Black women or the development of leukemia among White and Black men. Similarly, inadequate health data on diabetes, suicide, and other health issues related to adults and children also jeopardize the progress in diagnosis and treatment among Indigenous peoples (Grant and Balkissoon 2019, A10–11).

How racism in health-care research for Indigenous peoples has harmful effects on them is also reflected in their exclusion in research and analysis. In the 1940s, the Canadian government observed the effects of malnutrition through the intentional denial of food and dental care to thirteen hundred Indigenous peoples (mainly children). People living on reserves who do not have postal service and those without permanent addresses are usually excluded from social surveys. Hence, their perspectives are ignored and are not taken into consideration in the design and development of health-care services. Meanwhile, there are also research projects run by universities that have collected data from Indigenous communities. Indigenous children and adults have been used as test subjects; some subjected to surgeries in "Indian hospitals." However, these universities do not share or return the objects of study, including biological samples. The deprivation of opportunities of preserving data sovereignty or telling their own stories by Indigenous peoples on their own behalf means that their voices are not heard, and non-Indigenous peoples are interpreting the research results through their own perspectives without a good grounding on Indigenous cultures, which might be distortive (Grant and Balkissoon 2019, A10–11).

HEALTH

So far, we have examined, in comparison with Whites, how Indigenous people and racialized people grow and live in social conditions that are full of racial disadvantages when they go through their babyhood, childhood, and adulthood. Wherever they turn, they are disproportionately submerged in poverty, food insecurity, inadequate and inferior housing, and poor education opportunities and attainment and excluded from research and knowledge generation, which deprives them of the contribution of their perspectives.

Racial disparity has been noted in the domains of food insecurity and poor housing. Poverty further perpetuates the less equal and more miserable housing conditions of Indigenous peoples and racialized people. We noted earlier that their health has been severely compromised by their poor diets and living conditions. In this section, we will provide more research findings in the health area to show that they have been found to be living in disproportionately unhealthy environments and are more inclined to poor health, as seen in the higher incidences of illness and injury than for non-Indigenous peoples.

Indigenous peoples (8.7 percent) were more likely than non-Indigenous peoples (3.1 percent) to report undrinkable water coming from faucets for more than one week and to have patches of mould and mildew that are larger than one square metre in their homes (13.2 percent versus 5.1 percent). Indigenous peoples also reported infestations of unwanted pests (First Nations people: 19.3 percent; Metis: 18.5 percent, and Inuit: 27.1 percent). A small segment of them reported on their ability of keeping a comfortable temperature in summer (20.1 percent) and winter (17.1 percent). In other words, most found their dwelling temperature was beyond their control (Statistics Canada 2023j).

Indigenous peoples who live with core housing needs (those properties that are unsuitable, inadequate, and unaffordable) reported a higher incidence of fair or poor general health (41.6 percent of those with core housing needs versus 20.8 percent of those without core housing needs), fair or poor mental health (32 percent versus 15.7 percent) and low ratings of life satisfaction (35.5 percent versus 15.9 percent) (Statistics Canada 2023j).

Between 2006 and 2011, Indigenous children and youth were consistently and significantly hospitalized more frequently irrespective of the causes (such as diseases of the digestive system, respiratory system, circulatory system, and mental and behavioural disorders) than non-Indigenous people. In 2011, the pattern of hospitalization disparity between the two identity groups stayed the same even when broken down by age. First Nations children living on reserve between the ages of zero and nine consistently had higher acute-care hospitalization rates in respiratory and digestive diseases and injuries than non-Indigenous people. Meanwhile, First Nations youth aged ten to nineteen living on reserve had consistently higher acute-care hospitalization rates in pregnancies, childbirth and puerperium, mental health, and injuries than those of non-Indigenous people (Carriere and Bougie 2023).

As for the health of racialized people, the 2016 Census data notes that Black people in Canada were disadvantaged for many social determinants of health, including education, income, employment, and housing. The Canadian Community Health Survey, along with other census and health administrative data provides a much comprehensive picture on mortality by ethnic origin. Health inequalities in diabetes and hypertension are noted between Black and White adults. In Ontario, for example, the Black population has a higher rate of having cardiometabolic risk factors such as obesity and smoking as well as lower physical activity, lower fruit and vegetable consumption, higher psychosocial stress, and higher alcohol consumption when compared with White Canadians (Gupta and Aitkin 2022; Tjepkema et al. 2023).

HEALTH-CARE SERVICES

There are many aspects of health-care services that Canadians need. If one examines whether Whites, Indigenous peoples, and racialized people have the same degree of services, it is easy to find examples of racial disparity. For example, Statistics Canada (2022f) notes that shelters for Indigenous peoples are less equipped with professional services than those for other people, and it includes data that demonstrated the following:

- In comparing the shelters for non-Indigenous people and those for Indigenous peoples, the latter offer fewer professional services such as mental health services (69 percent versus 60 percent) and individual counselling for adults (88 percent versus 77 percent).
- During the COVID-19 pandemic, 41 percent of Indigenous shelters reported difficulties in providing professional services, whereas only 29 percent of non-Indigenous shelters reported those difficulties. This may explain why Indigenous peoples in shelters may not get enough help with their mental health.

- When it comes to the issue of communicating with victims outside their facilities, 32 percent of Indigenous shelters reported difficulties in this area, but only 19 percent of non-Indigenous shelters reported difficulties.
- In the area of staff availability during the COVID-19 pandemic, 28 percent of Indigenous shelters reported challenges of staff shortage, whereas only 15 percent of non-Indigenous shelters reported such challenges.
- Compared with Indigenous peoples living off reserves, those living on reserves have less access to health-care services.

In the health-care area, Indigenous peoples seem to receive different treatment from their White counterparts. When Indigenous women reach out for assistance with physical and mental health, they feel that they are unheard, devaluated, ignored, and dismissed. They even avoid getting health-care services lest they are retraumatized again. Another report, titled *Plain Sight: Addressing Indigenous-Specific Racism and Discrimination in BC Health Care*, also notes prevalent stereotypes of Indigenous people as being less than capable, less worthy, non-complaint, and being more apt to be alcoholics, drug seekers, and bad patients (National Inquiry into Missing and Murdered Indigenous Women and Girls 2019a; BC Ministry of Health 2020, 74–75). Female Indigenous peoples are compounded by additional stereotypes of child apprehensions and are subject to misogynistic views and forced sterilization.

One example was the preventable death of Joyce Echaquan, an Atikamekw woman, in a hospital in Quebec that highlighted the abhorrent treatment of Indigenous people in a health-care environment. Before her death, Echaquan posted a livestream on her Facebook page of how the staff were making derogatory comments. It caused an international uproar and public anguish (Native Women's Association of Canada, n.d., 2). It might be an isolated case, but Indigenous peoples do not think so (Landry 2020).

Incidents of this racist nature are common, as Bernice Thorassie of the non-profit group Manitoba Keewatinowi Okimakanak (which means Northern Manitoba Chiefs in Cree) has witnessed. When Indigenous peoples find that they are not welcome in a health-care setting, they tend to miss their medical appointments, and this causes other people to stereotype them as forgetful or unreliable. There are other incidents in which Indigenous peoples are often not listened to even though they have an illness, an injury, or an infection. It was reported that an Indigenous man's complaint of a bone infection was ignored and misdiagnosed as a mental problem. But his condition deteriorated quickly to the point where his foot was almost amputated (Bains 2022). Another report of the death of a thirty-two-year-old Indigenous (Ojibways) man of the Onigaming First Nations, Joshua Kelly, who died because the White paramedic allegedly parked the ambulance on the side of the road outside of the reserve without entering Kelly's premises, after receiving a call that Kelly was problem breathing and non-responsive. The White paramedic stated that he was afraid of being attacked by Indigenous peoples since there was no police escort and the reserve was "red-flagged" on file, which usually relates to past violent incidents (Trinh 2022).

In the 1997 case *Canada (Canadian Human Rights Tribunal) v. Canada (Department of National Health and Welfare)*, the Canadian Human Rights Tribunal determined that racialized people have been discriminated against in the health-care profession as shown in their under-representation.[1] There are many negative impacts on racialized people when such a discriminatory environment exists in favour of Whites. When health care and medical training is poor in cross-racial and cross-cultural diagnoses, providers not familiar with Black, Brown, and Yellow skin may have difficulty in readily identifying clinical symptoms such as rashes, inflammation, bruising, or jaundice (Henley and Schott 1999, 129–30). This definitely has implications on the disparity in health care among people in different racial groups, including their prevalence, mortality, and levels of suffering due to mental and physical illness.

Sana Halwani (2004) has observed that the lack of services in minority languages constitutes a barrier to health-care services, among other things. For example, Arab and Tamil immigrants and refugees have found it difficult to get breast cancer screening or to get Arab interpreters in the past. This lack of linguistic competency in the health-care fields is further compounded by the lack of cultural understanding by health-care providers of how different racialized groups, due to their

---

1 *Canada (Canadian Human Rights Commission) v Canada (Department of National Health and Welfare)*, 2018 SCC 31.

immigrant cultures, perceive health risk and the prevention of diseases and communicate their distress and suffering. As a result, incorrect diagnoses may occur, which might further jeopardize racialized patients. One of the central medical principles is "informed consent." The inadequacies noted earlier in health-care services may also compromise this principle. Overall, Health Canada recognizes the heightened health risks of racialized people due to a lack of culturally sensitive services and delivery mechanisms. Such racial imbalance and skewedness on the part of health-care providers and services makes their adverse impacts on racialized people more obvious. In other words, in addition to poorer health, Indigenous and racialized peoples often do not receive the health services that they need to better themselves.

MEDIA

Racialized people are significantly under-represented in media outlets at every staff level. Only 4.8 percent of media board members and executives are racialized members. The Canadian Association of Journalists' 2022 Newsroom Diversity Survey noted that only 15 percent of Canadian newsrooms had racialized journalists in a top-three editorial position, although 25 percent of journalists in Canadian newsrooms were racialized. In comparison, the 2016 Census data shows that Indigenous and racialized people constituted 27 percent of the Canadian population. This concentration of Whites in the news selection and publication process and the dominance of White journalists often lead to news stories that largely reflect the perspectives of Whites and negate those of other voices (Cukier et al. 2011).

In one research study, in addition to documenting the general lack of representation of racialized people as journalists, racialized female journalists reported a hostile and precarious work environment, being disrespected for their work and expertise, and having limited decision-making power. These racialized women reported that they felt ghettoized in being assigned to work on "ethnic" topics and not allowed to branch out to other more mainstream topics; they also felt that their managers saw them as being less neutral than their male counterparts; and they also experienced harassment at work. Due to their precarious employment situation, they also felt that they were not able to speak authentically and "stand firm behind their ideas in their work." They felt that they had to put up with this working environment with poor pay and demanding conditions "indefinitely" (Cohen and Clarke 2024).

How news is reported is also racialized to the extent that readers and audiences do not get a real picture on what may have occurred. Such a pattern of news reporting tends to stereotype Indigenous or racialized peoples. There is a tenancy for journalists—mainstream or marginalized—to rely heavily on the narratives of the police services when it comes to crime incidents. Once again, these narratives have proven to be skewed to the disadvantage of racialized people, while the police are known for their biases and their negation of voices from Black, Indigenous, and people of colour (BIPOC) (Inclan 2022). There are also observed biases in how White journalists report crimes in the media: for Whites allegedly accused of committing crimes on racialized people, White journalists have a tendency to use mental illness and life stories of the accused in the story line before the court decisions have been made as if mental health issues can mask over racism or Islamophobia. The story line almost implies that "normal" White people would not commit crimes against racialized people. Meanwhile, news on racialized victims or racialized accused persons do not carry any life stories to "humanize" or "personalize" the individuals or mention mental illness as a likely cause of the crimes for the accused. White journalists have embedded perspectives on race that are often used for reinforcing their racial stereotypes and how they report the news (Khayambashi 2021).

Similar to the American portrayal of Blacks and other racialized groups, the Canadian coverage of crimes in Toronto news outlets often blames Black victims who have been wounded or shot by police officers as having been "known to police" even when they were not committing a crime when killed. The media's framing of the stories often involves gangs, drugs, and violence. It has been noted that media reports of sports often describe White players as intelligent and Black players as physically fit and innately talented. In general, the lack of racialized voices on news stories among journalists and editors is reflected in the White-skewed perspectives in the news. Crime news predominantly reflects the narratives of the police and the viewpoints of White journalists and not those of racialized people (*Media Smarts*, n.d.a, n.d.b).

Meanwhile, Black journalists are often accused of speaking publicly about their lived experience of racism under the guise of objectivity, which is often seen as a code of conduct and standard for journalists. However, they are used sometimes to work against BIPOC journalists as biased journalism, while the standards are eased for White journalists. The Association of Black Journalists views this as a double standard (Daly et al. 2023).

Mainstream media appears to be less in touch with racialized people, especially if they are concentrated in certain residential areas such as Scarborough, Ontario, where 73 percent of people are racialized. According to the University of North Carolina Centre for Innovation and Sustainability in Local Media's 2018 report, "news deserts" are usually found in lower income areas where many racialized people live but where there is not much media coverage. Anita Li's (2019) argument is that the mainstream media are disconnected with these people, and they are not reflected in their writing nor are their voices heard. There is hardly any media coverage on matters that mean a lot to racialized people, and, obviously, this is a disconnect that needs to be fixed. While there are "ethnic media" found in these racial "ghettoes," they are marginalized and less influential in impacting the political, economic, and social life of the country. Overall, these are some of the areas in media that exhibit a racial inclination to the detriment of Indigenous and racialized peoples.

PUBLIC SENTIMENTS AND COMMUNICATION

Public sentiments on race, ethnicity, immigrants, refugees, Indigenous peoples, religious groups, and various social identity categories have changed over time. Governments and research firms monitor them closely, and some survey results have sent alarm bells from time to time. In the earlier-mentioned social identity areas, in contrast with results found in European countries, extreme negative public opinions have not quite mushroomed yet, but xenophobia and negative racial/religious sentiments have been simmering, and, at times, some of these public opinions have manifested in disturbing comments or disruptive activities.

One way to find out the prevalence of public sentiments is found in our daily communication. Our ideas or feelings are expressed through our choice of words, tones, and manners of expression. These expressions could be conscious or unconscious and often creep in as colloquialisms. Racist stereotypes often emerge in words with double meanings such as the more polite word of "quiet" or "shy" (instead of "inscrutable") to describe Chinese people who do not speak what is on their minds or the more polite word of "money-conscious" (instead of "stingy") to describe Jews who are not hesitant to negotiate for a better deal.

Stand-up comedians often use some exaggerated forms of racial stereotypes to illustrate their images of specific ethnic or racial groups, and the laughter of the audience suggests that people are aware of these stereotypes and recognize their ridiculousness sometimes. Russell Peter, a Canadian comedian, tells his audiences about how he is afraid of saying the wrong things to people from the Middle East because he is afraid to die. His audience roars with laughter after he says this, which suggests that the audience has gotten the message from the comedian that people from the Middle East have a stereotypical image of being violent and that this has come from watching bombings or gun fighting in the Middle East in daily news. This example suggests that the way in which people communicate messages are often influenced by the media images of racialized people.

Daily communication may also take the form of micro-aggression in which Indigenous peoples and racialized people are verbally insulted, belittled, or degraded, consciously or unconsciously. Those who communicate in a manner that is interpreted as hostile and offensive may not be aware of the adverse impact that this type of communication has on their psychology or on the performance of racialized people. These kinds of racist aggressions, often based on biased assumptions of racialized people, are subtle, covert, and nebulous (Sue et al. 2007, 271–86). As one individual who has experienced such micro-aggressions on a daily basis described it, they are like "a thousand cuts," which implies that the injuries may be brief and small in scale, but they are cumulative on an ongoing basis.

Questions or comments from White people such as "where do you come from?" "you should go back where you come from," "your English is really good," and "you people are lucky" seem to have hidden meanings of illegitimacy of residence or belonging in Canada, unusual language skills, and incompetency. These hidden meanings are not hard to detect for racialized people as they confront these questions and comments many times to the point that they begin to doubt their residence in Canada. There are also statements like "I don't see colour when I interact with people" or "I treat everyone as human beings." These statements, on the surface, negate race or ethnicity, which may be interpreted as treating people as equals without being tainted by prejudice. In essence, they do not acknowledge the diversity of people, their uniqueness and heritage, and their legitimacy of being in Canada.

And then there are White people who prefer to prescribe a name or a collective term for some racialized persons. An Asian-looking person may be labelled as an "Oriental" and a Chinese person may be called a "Hong Kong Louise" or a "Kung-Fu guy." These racialized persons have their own names, but using these labels as substitutes for their real names seems more like fitting people to the racial stereotypes and as generic images that replace the actual persons in real time. When racialized people hear these terms, they feel degraded, and their humanness is reduced to an anonymous object, and they cease to be a unique person. Body language may also express micro-aggressiveness when White people avoid eye contact with racialized people when they are talking with them or not letting their bodies turning toward the racialized people. These body languages suggest that Black people are not perceived by Whites as being important and, therefore, deserving their full attention. Public sentiments toward Indigenous peoples were summarized in the 2019 National Inquiry into Missing and Murdered Indigenous Women and Girls, and they are noted for their racist, sexist, homophobic, and transphobic opinions.

Anti-Indigenous sentiments in the health-care sector were documented in an earlier chapter on "health-care services." One form of anti-Indigenous bias is racial profiling, which means any action taken for safety or security reasons that is based on "stereotypes about race, colour, ethnicity, ancestry, religion, or place of origin," rather than on reasonable suspicion, to single out a person for more scrutiny or different treatment (Ontario Human Rights Commission 2017).

The Ontario Human Rights Commission (2017) held a year-long listening exercise among Indigenous people as well as reviews of literature to learn more about how Indigenous peoples have been treated as suspicious "second-class citizens" in policing, health care, education, welfare, and commercial and social services. The study reported that they sensed that they were being "followed, watched, single out for scrutiny and/or treated as if they were a risk to others because of their ancestry or race." Public suspicion is often derived from the stereotyping of Indigenous peoples as intoxicated, drunk, dishonest, unreliable, unclean, having higher risks, and/or inclined to commit offences. Such stereotypes, often based on the culture and norms of White people or colonial biases passed down through generations, result in Indigenous peoples being closely monitored on the roads, followed in retail spaces, questioned in service environments or school settings, and treated in a rude manner (Ontario Human Rights Commission 2017, 2025).

HATE MESSAGES AND INCIDENTS

There are hateful messages and actions reported in Canada every year, and, in some areas, they are more frequent and intense than in others. Hamilton has been labelled as the Hate Crime Capital of Canada. The Hamilton Police Service reported an increase of hate incidents and hate-related criminal offences in 2022. Of the 174 incidents reported, most of them were related to racial bias (ninety-one), religion (forty-nine), sexual orientation (twenty-three), and gender identity (ten). Actual incidents may be more frequent than the police statistics, as most individuals did not report their incidents to the police. In 2022, Black people bore the brunt of the offences, followed by South Asians, East Asians, and Southeast Asians. For hate incidents related to religion, Jewish people were the dominant, followed by Muslims. It appears that graffiti messages are the dominant modes of expression (Carreno Rosas 2023).

In this section, three types of hate sentiments are highlighted to show the extent of the hatred that exists in Canada: anti-Semitism, Islamophobia, and anti-Asian hate.

Anti-Semitism

Anti-Semitic sentiments among Canadians seem to have been persistent, with their high and low points, throughout Canadian history. They have been manifested in hate messages in social media, print media, and graffiti as well as in hate crimes such as harassment, assaults, bomb threats, and vandalism. Online disinformation, hate, and abuse toward individuals and organizations are increasingly noted. The rise of the COVID-19 pandemic and political violence in the Middle East (such as the Israel-Hamas war of 2023) brought waves of corresponding anti-Semitism to Canada. As of May 2021, there had been 608 hate crimes in the country, mostly targeted at Jews, followed by Blacks and Muslims. B'nai Brith notes that, in 2021, there were 2,799 hate crimes and incidents combined and a 7.2 percent increase in hate incidents alone six years in a row in spite of the government's spending of one hundred million dollars through its Anti-Racism Strategy since 2019 (Government of Canada 2023d).

Islamophobia

Islamophobia (or Anti-Muslim hate) is a growing hate against Muslims, especially after the downing of the Twin Towers of the World Trade Center in the United States carried out by Al-Qaeda (a global network), aided by the Taliban, which is the current government in Afghanistan, on 11 September 2001. Islamophobia was declared by the United Nations to be a global phenomenon in 2021.

Muslims are viewed as "extremists," "terrorists," and "radicals," and such views are prevalent in Europe and America (European Academy on Religion and Society 2012). In Canada, some segments of the population have opinions that dwell on the perception that Islam is building its influence in Canada through immigration, that Islam is perceived to negate women's rights, and that its religious belief incites violence (Souissi 2021).

When compared with other religions (such as Buddhism, Judaism, Hinduism, Skihism, and Christianity), Islam elicits the highest negative sentiments among Canadians. An Angus Reid national survey of Canadians showed that two out of every five Canadians (39 percent) have unfavourable opinions of Islam, with the most prevalent negative views among one in two Quebecors (52 percent). Thirty percent of Quebecors and 16 percent of Canadians outside of Quebec hold very negative views on Islam and the religious practices of this faith. This survey also shows that Islamic symbols (such as a burka and a mosque) elicit highly negative sentiments among Canadians, especially from people in Quebec (Angus Reid Institute 2022).

While most hate incidents are not reported to the authorities officially, these incidents increased over 250 percent from 2012 to 2015. Most incidents were reported in Ontario and Quebec as many Muslims live in these two provinces. A study done by Forum Research in 2016 showed that 48 percent of Quebecers and 22 percent of Ontarians viewed Islam negatively. Data from Statistics Canada for the period from 2010 to 2019 reveal that Muslim women were the victims of reported hate crimes against Muslims. The most-cited violent attacks against Muslims include the Quebec City mosque shooting of six worshippers and the injuries of several others in January

2017 and the London, Ontario, killing of a family of four Muslims who were taking a stroll in the evening in June 2021 (Souissi 2021). Unfavourable views do not necessarily incite hate incidents or crimes. However, Statistics Canada's data in March 2023 show that reported hate incidents targeting Muslims increased by 71 percent from 2020 to 2021, which represents eight incidents per one hundred thousand Muslims in Canada. Anti-Muslim hate incidents tend to be committed on the streets, on the properties of Islamic worship, on hijab-wearing women, and in online platforms, which suggests that there is a correlation between negative public opinions and hate activities (Baig 2023).

Anti-Asian Hate

Lately, a significant segment of Canadians has become more reserved about the arrival of new immigrants. In April 2019, Ekos Politics reported that 40 percent of Canadians think that "too many" immigrants arriving in Canada are from "visible minority" groups (racialized people). Approximately 30 percent of New Democratic Party and Green party voters believe that there are enough racialized immigrants. Sixty-nine percent of those who identify as Conservative party voters also believe this. The extent that this "anti-racialized people" or "anti-immigrant" sentiment is conducive for the rise of hatred or White nationalism remains to be seen, but it is certainly an issue to be concerned about (Balkissoon 2019, A13).

Motivated by hatred and manifested in threats, slurs, stalking, assaults, and other actions, hate crimes are criminal offences against people and property. During the COVID-19 pandemic in 2020–23, Asian Canadians experienced a rush of anti-Asian hate messages in public places, with the racial assumption that the virus had come from China and that, because they were Chinese, they were presumably responsible for its spread. There was an element of racial hate as well as a sentiment of anti-immigration (Landry 2020). In Vancouver alone, anti-Asian hate incidents increased from twelve in 2012 to ninety-eight in 2020, representing a 717 percent increase. Since 2020, the number of incidents dropped from ninety-eight in 2020 to forty-four in 2022. The reasons for the decrease are not clear, but some have suggested that some Asian people have merely internalized the harassment and given up reporting to the police (Premji 2023).

The Toronto chapter of the Chinese Canadian National Council did a survey in 2021 and noted that there has been a 47 percent increase in self- and witnessed-reported incidents since 2020. Reported hate incidents also increased among South Asian people (318 percent) and Southeast Asian people (121 percent) in the same time period. As many women from these Asian regions are also followers of Islam, xenophobia and Islamophobia may play a role in these reported incidents. Their special cultural dresses have also singled them out for many expressions of hatred (Balintec 2022).

These anti-Asian incidents include verbal harassment, shunning, physical force/aggression/unwanted contact, workplace discrimination, vandalism, service denial, police abuse of power/police brutality, barring from the entrance or request to leave an establishment or transportation, the distribution of discriminatory literature, robbery/theft, the abuse of power by authorities, and other actions. While verbal harassment constitutes the most common conduct, violent attacks are a growing trend with people coughing in the faces of Asians or spitting on them. Without elaborating on the obvious, victims of anti-Asian hate have suffered mostly from mental distress and emotional harm, while a smaller segment of people have suffered physical harm, financial loss, loss of services and benefits, loss of employment, loss of housing, and other harms (Balintec 2022).

ENTERTAINMENT

Indigenous peoples and racialized people are under-represented on films and television shows (Mahtani 2001). Jennifer Yoon (2018) examined 780 Hollywood films from 1970 to 2018 and noted that "white actors are three times more likely to appear as characters in movies than their population size in the U.S. would predict." Racialized actors are "less visible on screen and they also speak much less frequently." The study also found that "two leading roles are 111 times more likely to go to White actors than to visible minority actors." Only forty-four (or 3.4 percent) of the thirteen hundred top-grossing films released between 2007 and 2019 featured an Asian actor in a leading role (Yuen et al. 2021). Similarly, racialized people represented 16.3 percent of speaking roles in Canadian television shows. While there have been more racialized people appearing on television shows recently, the impact of a single show like the Canadian series *Kim's Convenience* (which have mainly racialized actors) on representation statistics is significant (Parris 2019; Weaver 2021).

Canadians often watch American television shows and movies. In the past, White American actors usually played the roles of racialized people. This is changing gradually. In spite of this, racialized people are still portrayed as people inclined to commit crimes, have less education, and other "damaging stereotypes." It is a great concern for many racialized parents just for the sake of their children's self-esteem (Dow 2018). Children are influenced by what they see on screen. Makeda Green, Andrea Strauss, and Colleen Johnson (2021) did a study of children of different races and genders between the ages of nine and twelve in 2019 and 2020 who determined what their roles would likely be if they were cast in shows. The survey results show that 52 percent of all children selected a White boy as the "hero," followed by 19 percent who selected a Black boy and 12 percent who selected a Hispanic or Asian boy. White children are more likely to be viewed as smart (59 percent) compared to Black children (38 percent). Asian boys and girls are more likely than children of other races to be cast as the "smart kid" or the "nerd." Overall, it appears that children, irrespective of their race, have racial stereotypes already embedded in their brains by being exposed to entertainment media.

Video games are largely an American production, and the roles of racialized people in these games conform to their stereotypes. A content analysis of popular video game magazine and 149 video game covers shows that Blacks are "thugs" and are portrayed in muggings, shootings, and gang violence; Asians are portrayed in martial arts; and South Asians and racialized women are almost non-existent in video games. White male characters are usually the main characters, using military combat or technology (Burgess, Dill-Shackleford, and Burgess 2011).

It has been reported that racial slurs such the usage of the N-word are rampant among online gamers on the platform. The Anti-Defamation League (ADL) has reported that an estimate of twenty-five million US gamers aged ten to seventeen experience harassment on multiplayer platforms. The American Academy of Pediatrics maintains that racism has negative impacts on racialized children's mental and emotional health. It may explain the rise of the feeling of marginalization and suicide rates among Black youth in the United States. The ADL surveyed twenty-one hundred gamers in the United States, including those who play online multiplayer games, and it found that harassment based on race and ethnicity are high for Blacks (44 percent), Asians (40 percent), and Latinos (31 percent). The same study shows that 15 percent of those aged ten to seventeen were exposed to White supremacist ideologies in

2021. There seems to be a rising cultural trend of racist culture in online games. Some studies have linked the racist radicalization of killers in mass killings of Muslims (in Christchurch, New Zealand, in March 2019) and Blacks (in Buffalo, New York, in June 2022) with online games (Ramirez 2023).

Meanwhile, in the musical sector, Black Canadians and South Asian Canadians have carved out their own brands of rap and hip-hop music as well as Punjabi or Hindi lyrics (mixed with English) played with South Asian musical instruments (such as the sitar). In their own ways, they reflect the experiences of Blacks burdened with institutional racism and those of South Asians with the fusion of Canadian and South Asian cultures. Considering how limited their music is on the mainstream channels, it seems apparent that they have remained "ghettoized." In this sense, racism in the musical arena pushes racialized people to create their own music, which is creative, unique, and valuable; however, such ghettoization also reflects how difficult it is for them to break into the mainstream, which is more influential and far more financially and reputationally rewarding.

RECREATION

Due to colonialism, Indigenous peoples have a history of forced assimilation in residential schools, where Indigenous children were mandated to learn the colonizer's ways of recreation for children, such as learning activities usually practised by boy scouts or girl guides. In doing so, they negated their traditional life activities such as tanning hides or making snowshoes (Northwest Territories Recreation and Parks 2020). The residential school system has also attached a stigma to Indigenous ways of cultural play and limited them to more European cultures and a religious inclination.

There are stereotypes about racialized people that give the impression that racialized people do not like nature or wilderness, such as Black people cannot swim or do not play to play hockey or hike. It seems that the root cause for such stereotypes is segregation in the past where Indigenous peoples, Blacks, Jews, and Asians were not allowed at beaches, hockey rinks, swimming pools, parks, or theatres. This exclusion defined and delimited their worlds of recreation. Hence, recreational activities such as hiking, walking, having a picnic, and riding a bicycle in nature were not an integral part of their lives; hence, racialized parents diverted their children and grandchildren to other recreational activities and did not allow them to enjoy the traditionally prohibited venues of nature (Carratt 2022).

In the past, nature has been "White space" that was rarely seen by racialized people, and even Indigenous people, as a legitimate ground for their recreation. Outdoor activities and equipment were advertised using White models. It was not until 2018 when the Mountain Equipment Co-op started using racialized models in its advertisements. The image of nature is associated with White culture and White environmentalism. Racialized people are expected in urban centres. When they are found in natural parks, whether they are walking or just birdwatching, they are seen as oddities by White people (Morgan 2019; Scott 2020).

Meanwhile, there is actually a genuine fear of nature among racialized people, especially those who live in an urban environment. There are also barriers related to the integration of racialized immigrants with the host population, especially when these immigrants see themselves as being excluded from mainstream culture (or being "othered"). And then there is the issue of having a cottage vacation, which is a distinctive White cultural phenomenon as it requires additional financial support for cottage ownership over and above the basic cost of having "a roof over your head." The environmental movement remains dominated by a White privileged segment of the population, and any time spent in appreciating and living in nature remains foreign to racialized people.

Racialized people (Asian, African, and Caribbean people in particular) also have a fear of crime (such as mugging and racial attacks) in open outdoor space largely because they are more familiar with urban settings as well as a generalized anxiety of the unknown in the wilderness, where they feel isolated from the rest of the civilized world. To enjoy outdoor recreation activities like hiking, walking, biking, camping, canoeing, and fishing requires a sense of safety and security and not of anxiety and apprehension. Since outdoor camping and trips are not part of a racialized person's culture, having the proper racial composition among participants would ease the minds of parents before they enlist their children in these recreational activities as the parents are concerned about the degree of belonging and inclusiveness in outdoor activities (Scott and Tenneti, n.d.).

Overall, while racism is gradually being recognized as a social and cultural barrier for racialized people in engaging in recreational activities in nature, there is still a long way to go in removing these racial stereotypes. Therefore, racialized people have a restricted sense of recreation, especially in rural areas.

SPORTS

Sports can be viewed as an entertainment or a recreation. There are a lot of biases and reported racism to be unpacked in this field.

Statistics Canada (2024a) did a survey on the extent of perceived racism in sports and noted that 25 percent of Canadians felt that racism and discrimination in community sports was problematic in 2023 and that 18 percent of those who participated in a sport stated that they had actually experienced or witnessed unfair treatment, racism, or discrimination. Racialized people (26 percent) were more likely to experience racism than non-racialized people while playing a sport, especially for Blacks (34 percent), Filipinos (32 percent), and Koreans (32 percent). These victims or witnesses reported race and skin colour (64 percent), physical appearance (42 percent), and ethnicity or culture (38 percent) as the common features cited. Participants and athletes (64 percent), spectators (39 percent), and coaches and instructors (36 percent) were often responsible for acts of discrimination.

Insensitive jokes/comments (60 percent), name calling/insults/mocks (48 percent), being ignored by others and excluded from conversations/group activities (44 percent), talking behind the person's back (42 percent), threats or harassment (20 percent), and physical attacks/assaults (8 percent) have been cited as the types of discrimination. A significant portion (32 percent) of these incidents was never reported by the victim or witnesses. Only 23 percent of victims and witnesses reported at least one incident officially, and 35 percent informed other people about the incidents (such as teammates, friends, or social media (Statistics Canada 2024a).

In 2020, the Canadian Broadcasting Corporation hosted a panel discussion on racism in sport. Aaron Brown, representing Canada, won a bronze medal at the 2016 Olympic men's 4-x-100-metre relay described a continuous flow of micro-aggressions in the sports world, which has resulted in the build up of a lot of stress for racialized athletes. Aggressive comments like "you speak well for a Black person" or "all Black people steal—but not you" were psychologically distressful to him. In 2015, Khamica Bingham was the national 100-metre champion. A running magazine approached her to be featured on the cover after her victory. Later, she was told that her look did not "fit" the magazine's image of an athlete. Later, she found out that a White athlete was on the cover instead. She felt that being Black meant that she was "neglected in terms of beauty in the colour spectrum." Similarly, Chrisyabel Nettey, a long jumper who won gold at the 2015 Pan Am Games and at the 2018 Commonwealth Games, was also passed over for publicity by a few marketing companies. The latter picked up "a less successful white athlete instead" for the magazine feature (Dichter 2020).

In 2021, Ethan Bear, the Edmonton Oilers defenceman, was "racistly singled out and blamed" for the defeat of his team at the Stanley Cup playoffs. Christine O'Bonsawin, who teaches at the University of Victoria, commented on this social phenomenon: racialized athletes are seen as Canadian when they succeed in sports but are blamed as a racialized group that has failed Canada when they do not. Donavan Bailey, a Canadian track-and-field athlete, observed that racialized athletes commonly experience racism "on the field, in locker rooms, and from fans" (Rodriguez 2021b). This is one way to say that the sports world is saturated with racism.

Racism is not only experienced by star athletes; local youth athletes also experience it at the community level (Brown et al., n.d.). Najma Osman, a nineteen-year-old local athlete studying at Brandon University in Manitoba shared her experiences of racist treatment while she played basketball: "She ... had her hijab pulled off in public" and "has been called the N-word twice while playing sports." Her experience shows that "[racism] comes from everyone. You can even have your teammates be racist to you. You can have your own coach be racist to you. You can have other coaches be racist to you, the referee, parents." Andrew Jean-Baptiste from Winnipeg Valour Football Club reported an incident in which he and his teammates were yelled at with the N-word by spectators. Keagan Gaywish, a sixteen year old from Rolling River First Nation, reported an incident in which racist comments were shouted to him while he was playing hockey during a Westman High School Hockey League in the Town of Swan River in Manitoba (Petz 2021).

These are a sample of the experiences of a few athletes. While not exhaustive, they illustrate the persistent and prevalent nature of racial biases within sports organizations and of journalists who report on sports events, sports fans, and the general public.

Racism in sports in Canada has a longer history though. Garry Smith and Carl Grindstaff (1970, 19–30) describe the historical situation of Black athletes before the 1970s in a variety of sports in Canada (such as baseball, basketball, football, track and field, horse racing, bicycle racing, long jump, and boxing), and they note their accomplishments in sports but also the fact that they have experienced a range of racial discrimination as a result of the mainly American ways of training and organization in their sport organizations: the quota system, stacking, access to central positions, double standards of performance and injuries, compensation, and upward mobility in sport hierarchy. Some sports, such as tennis, swimming, golf, bowling, and hockey, are largely inaccessible to Black athletes. Without elaborating on the obvious, Black athletes in Canada also have to confront the racist remarks and conduct related to the non-sport domains in their lives.

Smith and Grindstaff also completed a quantitative study on Black players in the Canadian Football League (CFL) between 1955 and 1969 and noted that there was improvement in the number of Blacks from twelve players to fifty during this period. These numbers represent small percentages of the total number of players (49–65). In 1969, Black players represented 17 percent of CFL players. They did not have equal treatment with their White counterparts, and their opportunities were limited. In that period, there were numerous stereotypes for Black players—they were lazy, ignorant, apt to "fumble," more prone to get into difficulties, and more likely to "choke up" in a crisis.

SERVICES IN RETAIL, FINANCE, AND HOSPITALITY

Statistics Canada did a survey of Canadians and measured the extent of their experiences in discrimination in retail, financial institutions, and the hospitality industry. The findings show that there is a gradation of discrimination experiences by race: 28.2 percent of Whites experienced discrimination in a store, bank, or restaurant; 41.7 percent of Indigenous peoples reported discrimination; 45.2 percent of non-Black racialized people reported discrimination; and 51.4 percent of Black people reported discrimination (Cotter 2022). The relatively high incidence of reported discrimination in services provided in retail stores, banks, and restaurants may be illustrated further in the following studies.

Retail Stores

The Alberta Civil Liberty Research Centre at the University of Calgary documented patterns of consumer racial profiling, harassment, and discrimination in the retail industry. They include ignoring consumers, refusing service, providing slower service, uttering degrading racial terms, and/or showing physical actions such as detaining, interrogating, or arresting. Racial profiling works on the assumption that some racial or ethnic groups are more prone to shoplifting. Racialized people are more subject to stalking, questioning, searching, accusing, detaining, and/or removing them physically without just cause. As a result, profiled racialized people feel a loss of dignity and self-confidence and a loss of trust in retail establishments, and they often suffer from long-term psychological damage (Tuttle 2022). Similarly, one form of anti-Indigenous bias is racial profiling. Indigenous peoples are often suspected of shoplifting in retails stores, and they are often stalked and questioned. This suspicion is derived by the stereotyping of Indigenous peoples as dishonest, unreliable, prone to higher risk, and inclined to commit offences (Ontario Human Rights Commission 2017).

Another aspect of retail racism may be witnessed in how retail stores deal with White and racialized consumers with the return of their purchased goods. While Canadian studies are not readily available, Meirav Furth-Matzkin, an American professor of law at the University of California, Los Angles studied how four groups of people—Black men and women and White men and women, aged eighteen to twenty-five—were treated when they returned unused purchased items in their original packaging without a receipt. The median price of the returned goods ranged from five dollars to $350. The findings showed that Black men had the highest denial rate for their returns, followed by Black women. Both of these groups had the lowest chance of getting a refund. Meanwhile, "White consumers were 25% more likely to receive a concession by having their return accepted when it went against posted store policy" (Kestenbaum 2022). This study, along with others, is revealing as such racial biases and differential and inequitable treatment would not be known to individual customers without aggregating the data collectively.

Banks

People have unconscious bias about some segments of people based on their stereotypes without knowing them. Neha Chollangi (n.d.), a journalist in Osoyoos, British Columbia, reported a case where an Indigenous man—Maxwell Johnson—produced a Federal Indian Status Card as his identification card when he tried to open a bank chequing account for his twelve-year-old granddaughter. The bank's customer representative had many questions and was not prepared to accept that card as a valid identification. Things escalated, and the police service was called and ended up with the grandfather and his granddaughter being handcuffed and led away. Exactly what stereotypes the bank employee and the police officer had about Indigenous people in this particular case are not clear, but suspicion and distrust about Indigenous people grew in this banking process.

Chollangi also reported another case in which a Black man, who wanted to replace his debit card, was asked to produce several identification documents by the bank officer, and, when he had done so, even more questions were raised by the bank officer. It seemed that being Black had created distrust and that the Black man seemed to be "criminalized" and viewed as a security risk in spite of the documentation that he produced. He filed a complaint with the Canadian Human Rights Commission about his banking experience, which is still ongoing as of the time of writing. Numerous cases of alleged racism in banking practices (such as loan lending, money deposits, and accessing money from bank accounts) have been reported by the media.

Upselling bank products and services (such as "premium" credit cards, lines of credit, chequing accounts, overdraft protection, and balance protection insurance) to racialized people appear to be another form of racism. Bank employees seem to pitch racialized customers with inappropriate financial products more so than other customers. The Canadian Broadcasting Corporation's (CBC) Go Public program reported a concerning level of upselling to racialized people with supportive evidence from the Financial Customer Agency of Canada's own national review in 2018–19. This review covered the practices of the Bank of Montreal, the Canadian Imperial Bank of Commerce, the National Bank, the Royal Bank of Canada, Scotiabank, and the Toronto Dominion Bank. Such upselling seemed to make the assumption that Indigenous peoples and racialized people are prone to "default or overextend themselves." To Caroline Hossein, an associate professor of global development at the University of Toronto, such upselling is "systemic racism occurring in Canada's commercial banking system." Duff Conacher, the co-founder of Democracy Watch—a non-profit advocacy organization focusing on corporate and government accountability—maintains that Canada is decades behind the United States in requiring banks to monitor and track service lending and investment records by race and gender and to disclose data that shows discrimination (all quotations taken from E. Johnson 2022).

Restaurants

The hospitality industry includes travel and tourism, food and beverage, accommodation, recreation, and meetings and events. In terms of establishments, the hospitality industry covers hotel and restaurants, eateries, bars, casinos, cruises, entertainment venues, amusement parks, events and tours, and many other categories. In this section, we will highlight racism in a few settings, and they are by no means exhaustive and complete, but they nevertheless point out the various experiences of racialized people as customers.

Racial harassment and discrimination has a long history in Ontario. Although the Ontario 1944 *Racial Discrimination Act* and the 1954 *Fair Accommodations Act* were both in effect in 1954 and made racial discrimination illegal, three out of four restaurants in Dresden, Ontario, a small town just outside of Windsor, and three of the four barbers in the same town, did not serve Black people, according to the 28 September 1954 edition of the *Toronto Daily Star*.[2] Bromley Armstrong (a Black man) and Ruth Lor Malloy (an Asian woman) went to the Kay's Café in Dresden to see whether any staff there would serve them or not. They were not served (Levy 2021).

Fast forward to May 2014 when a number of Black youth went to Hong Shing—a Chinese restaurant—to celebrate the birthday of one of the youths (Emile Wickham). After ordering the dishes, they were

2 *Racial Discrimination Act*, SO 1944, c 51; *Fair Accommodations Act*, SO 1954, c 28.

asked by one of the restaurant staff to pay first before they could eat. They found out that they were the only customers who had to pay first. The Ontario Human Rights Tribunal found that they had been racially discriminated against, and the restaurant was ordered to pay ten thousand dollars to Emile Wickham. The tribunal ruled that the restaurant's staff member stereotyped Black people as untrustworthy, dubious, and possibly criminal (Boisvert 2018; Cecco 2018).

In April 2018, a video tape circulated in social media documenting the outburst of racist remarks and the threat of violence against a group of racialized men (at least one was from Afghanistan and Tajikistan) at a restaurant in Lethbridge, Alberta. A White woman was heard saying to these men: "Go back to your f**king country," "You're not Canadian," and "Speak English if you're going to speak. It's Canada." There were also counter-verbal exchanges from these men telling the woman to "shut the f*** up" and other unpleasant remarks. The police were called in, and the restaurant staff, after consultation with the police, asked the two groups to leave the restaurant, and both groups eventually left (Kornik and Heidenreich 2018).

In 2020–21, the legal case regarding the termination of the commercial lease of Elias Restaurant (8573132 Canada Incorporated), a restaurant serving Afro-Caribbean foods in North Toronto, by Keele Sheppard Plaza Incorporated was affirmed by the Ontario Court of Appeal, and it was determined that the termination was based on anti-Black racism. The restaurant was owned and operated by a Black man and his wife. The court noted that the concern of the Keele Sheppard Plaza was centred not on the family friendliness of the restaurant but, rather, on the kind of people they have as restaurant customers—families of Black and Caribbean backgrounds—who were different from those people who frequented the other stores in the plaza. This case suggests that having Black patrons in one's restaurant is like "catering while Black" (Morgan 2021).

Such examples of incidences in retail stores, banks, and restaurants are not exhaustive, but they highlight the multiple forms of racism as experienced by Indigenous peoples and racialized people. It appears that people have stereotypical images of these marginalized groups and that there is a lot of distrust and suspicion embedded in the culture. Depending on the historical period, some stereotypes are more negative than others, and some prejudice is more blatant. Nevertheless, the resulting conduct ends up racial harassment and discrimination. What we witness are those cases where the people get caught; most likely, most of the cases are submerged like an iceberg and never float to the surface and, hence, are never recognized.

TRANSPORTATION

A review of multiple published Canadian studies (completed between 2010 and 2020) and stakeholder roundtables on the experiences of Indigenous peoples, racialized people, and newcomers/immigrants who have used the public transit system in Canada shows that

> Indigenous peoples are targeted more than non-Indigenous peoples for fare inspection. The lack of adequate public transits between reserve and urban communities is often cited as having negative impacts on their access to educational, employment and medical/health-care opportunities and cultural activities. For Indigenous women, such inadequacy also made them difficult to escape domestic violence and subject them to more vulnerability if they hitchhike. The lack of accessible transportation also hinders Indigenous Elders to participate in social and cultural activities. (Linovski, Dorries, and Simpson 2021)

It has been well documented that racialized people experience all types of racism from passengers, operators, fare collectors, and transit police. Such discrimination includes racial slurs, harassment, and graffiti in transit washrooms. Racialized riders are often assumed to avoid paying fares and, therefore, are over-ticketed at more than seven times their share of the population. All these incidences tend to discourage racialized people from using public transit, but, unfortunately, public transit is the most cost-effective means of moving people around.

Newcomers and immigrants are usually transit dependent. Their complaints centre on the unaffordable fares, long travel time, and not going where people need to go. They also experience racial prejudice. For immigrants and newcomers who tend to reside in areas with lower rents, they must balance the lower cost of rents and longer commuter time, less frequent transit services, and longer walks to transit stops. For those who live in rural areas, they must give up employment opportunities, health and social services, and cultural activities due to the lack of transit services. All these difficulties are compounded by their low earnings.

Using examples from a number of American cities, Christof Spieler (2020) demonstrates that public transportation systems are often built around race, which means one system for Whites and another system for Blacks. This segregated system, with its racist overtones, may be manifested in various forms of governance structures and the schedules, fleets, route structures, and infrastructures of the transit system. Such a system might be seen to be too extreme as a "black and white" issue, but his position shows that systemic racial inequities do exist. An example of the legal challenges launched against the Los Angeles Metropolitan Transit Authority in 1996 illustrate how local rail or bus funding arrangements may have allegedly negative impacts on racialized people. A similar question was raised about former Mayor John Tory's Smart Track plan in Toronto and how it might indeed have created disparities for the Rexdale and Jane-Finch area (Jones 2015). The biased nature of public transit systems seems to be related to the geographical locations of where more low-income racialized people live and the availability of these transit systems, existing or planned.

Transportation has a lot to do with racial justice. It has the power to connect people and move them from one neighbourhood to another. Its accessibility and usage have immense implications for the welfare, education, employment, health, and housing of racialized people as well as for others. It may help to strengthen or weaken social justice in Canada. David Hulchanski and Maureen Fair (2011), of the University of Toronto and St. Christopher House, raise the issue of racial disparities due to the Toronto Transit Commission's (TTC) transit system with income distribution maps of census tracts in Toronto. One of the major findings shows that wealthier White neighbourhoods have access to three times more subway stations than the poorer racialized neighbourhoods that basically "force" the poorer people to own and use cars 10 percent more often than their richer counterparts. In addition, racial prejudice and the discrimination of TTC drivers seems to impact more on racialized women. Racism in public transit appears to have immense impacts on racialized people, and it can be systemic, cumulative, and intergenerational (Jones 2015).

This persistent issue of racial discrimination in public transit systems may be largely based on the lack of racialized voices at the planning stage, the historical evolution of neighbourhoods and the gap in transit networks, and the management of the transit system as it evolves.

Overall, the biased system may or may not be intentional, but it does pose an adversarial impact on racialized people.

VIOLENT CRIMES

The environments in which Indigenous peoples live are risky, unsafe, and insecure. Not only do they begin their lives with health issues, but they are also subject to unhealthy housing conditions, food insecurity, school systems that are not conducive to good performance, a lack of research funding, biased research findings, and poorer health and health-care services. Violence seems to be an integral part of their lives. They are murdered more often, and they are victims of sexual violence and other violent crimes more than the rest of the population.

Deep-rooted colonization policies and social and economic challenges are connected to criminal victimization. Between 2015 and 2020, the homicide rate of Indigenous victims was 8.64 per one hundred thousand Indigenous peoples, and this rate was 6.2 times higher than that of non-Indigenous peoples (1.39 per one hundred thousand). A significant number of these victims were First Nations. Of the 752 homicide victims for whom information on Indigenous identity was available, 25 percent (or 190) of them were Indigenous (Statistics Canada 2022d). During the same period of time, the murder rates of Indigenous women (4.7 percent) and non-Indigenous women (4.9 percent) by an intimate partner were more or less the same. However, the murder of Indigenous men (7.3 percent) was higher than that of non-Indigenous men (4.6 percent). It appears that the victimhood of children violence begets the victimhood of adult violence. In total, 27 percent of Indigenous people who experienced sexual violence in childhood were victims of violent crime in 2019, compared with 3.7 percent of Indigenous people who did not experience sexual violence in childhood (Perreault 2022).

Indigenous people between the ages of thirty-five and fifty-four (12.4 percent) were victims of violence three times more often than non-Indigenous people of the same age group (3.9 percent), during the last twelve months preceding the 2019 General Social Survey on Canadians' Safety (Victimization). One-third of Indigenous people experienced racial discrimination in the past five years before the same survey in 2019. And 14.9 percent of Indigenous people who experienced racial discrimination in the five years prior to 2019 were the victims of violent crime in 2019 compared with 5.1 percent of Indigenous people who had no experience of racial discrimination (Perreault 2022).

Based on self-reported information obtained from the 2019 General Social Survey on Canadians' Safety (Victimization), 40 percent of Indigenous people who are under the age of fifteen experience sexual or physical violence by an adult, while 26 percent of those aged fifteen to thirty-four and 54 percent of those aged fifty-five and older reported violence. During their childhood, sexual violence was more experienced by Indigenous women (26 percent) than by non-Indigenous women (9.2 percent) and by Indigenous men (5.8 percent) than by non-Indigenous men (2.8 percent) (Perreault 2022).

Intersectionality is also an important factor as Indigenous women are more likely to be the victims of sexual violence. In 2014, their rate of victimization due to sexual assault (115 incidents per one thousand people) is three times higher than their White counterparts (thirty-five incidents per one thousand people). Between 2011 and 2021, 21 percent (N = 233) of the victims of all gender-related homicides of women and girls were Indigenous, although they make up only 5 percent of females in Canada in 2021 (Perreault 2015; Sutton 2023). Seventy-one percent of Indigenous women perceived social disorder in their neighbourhood compared with non-Indigenous women (Perreault 2022). LGBTQIA+ Indigenous people, irrespective of their age, experienced more sexual or physical assaults, more intimate partner violence, and more non-intimate partner violence in the twelve months preceding the survey (Perreault 2022).

As defined in the 2018 Survey of Safety in Public and Private Spaces, violent victimization is "a physical assault (an attack, a threat of physical harm, or an incident with a weapon present) or a sexual assault (forced sexual activity or attempted forced sexual activity)." Fifty-six percent of Indigenous women have experienced physical assault, and 46 percent of them have experienced sexual assault in their lifetime. In contrast, 34 percent of non-Indigenous women have experienced physical assault and 33 percent of them have experienced sexual assault in their lifetime. Indigenous women (11 percent) were more likely than non-Indigenous women (2.3 percent) to have ever been under the legal responsibility of the government. Of these Indigenous women, 81 percent have experienced violent victimization (Heidinger 2022).

Meanwhile, the 247 homicide victims identified as racialized persons represented 32 percent of the total 762 victims for whom information on race was available. The homicide rate of racialized people was 2.51 per one hundred thousand racialized people, which is 38 percent higher than the rate of the rest of the population (1.81 per one hundred thousand people). Among the racialized homicide victims, 49 percent were Black, and 19 percent were South Asian (Statistics Canada 2022d). A study done on victimization by Statistics Canada earlier in 2014 showed that Canadian-born racialized people experienced violent victimization five times more than their immigrant counterparts (Simpson 2018). A study done by Statistics Canada earlier in 2004 showed a similar pattern, except that victimization for Canadian-born racialized people was three times more than their immigrant counterparts (Perreault 2004).

LAW ENFORCEMENT

Police Carding

The Government of Ontario appointed Chief Justice Michael Tulloch to conduct a review of street checks, which was reported in the *Report of the Independent Street Checks Review* in 2018. What he found was that police carding practices were common in Toronto. Police officers randomly ask individuals to provide identification even when they are not suspected of any offence and there are no suspicious activities. It is almost like police officers are collecting information on people on imaginary crimes. Carding impacts negatively on Black people, especially when they exercise their right not to cooperate. In 2011, four Black teenagers were punched, and one was arrested for not cooperating. In addition, one Black man who did not answer police officers' questions was handcuffed, punched, and left lying in the cold. While this is merely one incident of police carding, the report of Chief Justice Tulloch summarizes the prevalence of police carding (Tulloch 2018; *Globe and Mail* 2019, A10).

Police Stops and Checks

An independent report on racism completed by Victor Armory, Mariam Hassaoui, and Massimiliano Mulone shows that police officers practised systemic racism in Montreal. It reveals that Black people are four times more likely to be stopped than their white counterparts and that Indigenous peoples are 4.61 times, and Arabs are two times, more likely. Indigenous women are eleven times more likely than White women to be stopped by police officers. This report is based on an examination of data from tens of thousands of cases reported from 2014 to 2017. What is more surprising is that police stops actually increased 143 percent during these years, although the level of crime in the city remained constant. This report was commissioned by the city of Montreal. It is clear that racial profiling is practised and that it discriminates against racialized people disproportionately (Perreaux 2019, A3).

In Nova Scotia, reports of police stops and retail stalking are common. Black people are stopped and questioned by police officers because they are investigating a complaint about "suspicious people." Jermaine Parris, a Black man, complained about his banking fee in a local Royal Bank of Canada branch, and a bank employee called police on him saying that he had been "drinking and driving." Santina Rao, a young mother, was arrested by police and suffered a broken wrist, concussion, and other injuries in a store when she and her children were suspected of shoplifting and police officers were called by a store employee. These checking incidents, while they appear to be the tip of an iceberg, are confirmed by statistics showing the high chance of Black people to be street-stopped by police—six times more often than White people in the city of Halifax. Indeed, Dan Kinsella, the Halifax Police Chief, apologized for the practice of street checks (Mercer 2020, A10).

Police Misconduct

Allegations of police misconduct, racial harassment, and discrimination appear to be more common in several cities in Canada. News on the tensions between police services and racialized communities appear more frequently. The independent police watchdog in Ontario concluded in 2018 that nine sudden death cases of Indigenous persons in Thunder Bay were "tainted by systemic racism and neglect." And, in 2022, the Nishnawbe Aski Nation, which represents forty-nine First Nations in the Thunder Bay region, called for the disbandment of the Thunder Bay Police Service. The former police chief Sylvie Hauth announced her retirement in January 2023 weeks before she was to appear in a misconduct hearing for charges under the *Police Services Act* (Fiddler 2023, A4).[3]

Reporting to Police

Proportionately, Indigenous people (17 percent) were more likely to have little or no confidence in their local police service than their

---

3 *Police Services Act*, RSO 1990, c P.15.

Table 3.1: Experience of Discrimination When Dealing with the Police in Canada

	Whites (%)	Indigenous peoples (%)	Racialized people (Blacks) (%)	Racialized people (non-Blacks) (%)
When dealing with police	3.9	20.6	16.1	6.4

Note: Shaded data represent the highest percentage among the four racial groups.
Source: Cotter 2022.

non-Indigenous counterpart (9.2 percent) (Perreault 2022). Indigenous peoples showed great reluctance reporting to police when compared with non-Indigenous people. This may be related to colonization, systemic racism, racial profiling, and police violence. It is more common for victims from Indigenous communities to request that no further action be taken when they are involved in violent incidents compared with those in non-Indigenous communities. This may be related to the Indigenous distrust in law enforcement due to a long history of colonial policies and practices (Statistics Canada 2022f). Indigenous women (71 percent) were more likely to report not very much or no confidence in the police compared with non-Indigenous women (8.2 percent) (Heidinger 2022).

Overall, the patterns with people dealing with the police suggest that, when compared with Whites, Indigenous peoples and racialized people are more prone to report discrimination (see Table 3.1). Both Indigenous peoples and racialized people feel they are being harassed or discriminated by the police through carding, checking, and stops. They believe that the police abuse their power and that they are more likely to do them harm than to protect them. Therefore, they are reluctant to report incidents or issues to them since they do not feel the police are trustworthy.

COURT SYSTEM AND INCARCERATION

The Canadian criminal court system shows the over-representation of Blacks among those accused of homicide. The rate of Blacks accused of homicide was about six times higher than that of non-racialized people. Black males accused of homicide constitute 65 percent of all racialized males accused of homicide, and Black females accused of homicide make up 54 percent of all racialized females accused of homicide. In addition, Blacks are over-represented in being accused in criminal courts and face disproportionate outcomes. They represent only 3 percent of the population in Canada but account for 6 percent of all accused in 2015–16. Compared with their White counterparts during the period from 2005–6 to 2015–16, Black people who were accused were on average 24 percent less likely to be found guilty, 24 percent more likely to receive a custodial sentence, and 36 percent more likely to receive a long-term custodial sentence of two years or more (Government of Canada 2022d).

In 2020–21, Black adults represented 4 percent of the adult population in Canada. However, they were over-represented to various degrees in provincial admissions to correctional services (custody and community services) in Nova Scotia (3 percent of the population versus 11 percent of admissions to custody and 7 percent of admissions to community services), Ontario (5 percent versus 14 percent and 8 percent), Alberta (4 percent versus 5 percent and 4 percent), and British Columbia (1 percent versus 3 percent and 2 percent). For example, Black adults constituted 3 percent of the adult population in Nova Scotia, but they represented 11 percent of admissions to custody and 7 percent to community services in that province. Overall, compared with their representation in the larger population, Black people are over-represented among the federal offender population; they are more likely to be admitted to federal corrections for an offence that is punishable by a mandatory minimum penalty, and they are over-represented among those involved in use-of-force incidents in federal corrections (Government of Canada 2022d; Mercer 2020, A10).

Similarly, Indigenous peoples are over-represented in the criminal justice system in Canada. In 2014, 28 percent of Indigenous people (aged fifteen and over) reported being victimized in the previous years compared with 18 percent of non-Indigenous people. In 2016–17, Indigenous adults accounted for 4 percent of the Canadian adult population, but they constituted 27 percent of federal custody admissions, 27 percent of the federal in-custody population, and 30 percent of provincial/territorial custody admissions. Meanwhile, Indigenous youth accounted for 8 percent of the Canadian youth population, but they constituted 50 percent of the custody admissions. Indigenous proportions have been rising for over ten years. It appears that the root cause of the trending over-representations is related to colonization and its impacts on the Canadian criminal justice system as well as the trauma that was imposed on their well-being, compounded by their intergenerational poverty (Government of Canada 2023f).

Overall, the pattern showing people's experience dealing with the courts suggest that, when compared with Whites, Indigenous peoples and racialized people are more prone to report discrimination (see Table 3.2).

Table 3.2: Experience of Discrimination When Dealing with the Courts in Canada

	Whites (%)	Indigenous peoples (%)	Racialized people (Blacks) (%)	Racialized people (non-Blacks) (%)
When dealing with courts	1.7	3.9	No reliable data	2.3

Note: Shaded data represent the highest percentage among the four racial groups.
Source: Cotter 2022.

BORDER CROSSINGS

In 2017–18, there were more than 105 "founded" complaints of racism and rudeness against the employees of the Canadian Border Services Agency (CBSA), which makes up 12 percent of the 875 misconduct complaints for that period. "Founded" means that some aspects of investigations are found to be "valid." These were "allegations of racism, questioning of travellers' nationality, and name calling" by the CBSA's staff (Tutton 2018). In 2020, the CBSA conducted 215 "founded" investigations of its officers, which was up from 171 in 2019, despite a drastic reduction of recorded trips to and from Canada in that year—from ninety-four million trips in 2019 to a mere twenty-five million trips in 2020. Janet Dench, executive director of the Canadian Council for Refugees, maintains that "marginalized people, refugees and people without status in Canada, often racialized people, what we see is that CBSA has enormous power over the lives of these people. And in that circumstance, there is always the possibility of abuse of that power" (Tunney 2021b).

Human Rights Watch and Amnesty International alleged that thousands of asylum seekers were detained every year in abusive environments and that racialized people seem to be detained longer than others, often in provincial cells. The CBSA's reasons for detaining people are that the asylum seekers have criminal convictions, lack ties to the community, or pose a danger to the public or security of Canada. The CBSA is the only major law enforcement agency in Canada without independent civilian oversight (Canadian Press 2021). An external review of the CBSA at the Cornwall, Ontario, office by the Parriag Group took place in 2021, and the released report shows that there were incidents of harassment, discrimination, and violence. Specifics of these incidents were not available; however, this particular office in Cornwall provides border services for more than 1.5 million travellers, and one million of them are residents of the Mohawk communities of St. Regis, Quebec, and Akwesasne. Back in 2009, the proposed arming of border guards

Table 3.3: Experience of Discrimination When Crossing the Border into Canada

	Whites (%)	**Indigenous peoples (%)**	**Racialized people (Blacks) (%)**	**Racialized people (non-Blacks) (%)**
When crossing the border into Canada	2.0	4.6	No reliable data	12.2

Note: Shaded data represent the highest percentage among the four racial groups.
Source: Cotter 2022.

led to a six-week standoff around the post on Kawehno:ke (Cornwall Island) within Mohawk territory (Tunney 2021a).

The CBC reported that numerous racialized people have complained that they have been harassed and discriminated by employees who worked at the CBSA. These complaints have been reported by people who have racialized friends or relatives in their cars when going through a land border. The same racialized persons found that going across land borders were much easier when they have White passengers in their cars. According to these racialized complainants, about three out of four people believed that the difficulty crossing land borders seems to be related to race and ethnic or national origin. They usually felt upset, angry, scared, painful, humiliated, or ashamed about this kind of experience. The CBSA released a report saying that "1 in 4 officers witnessed colleagues discriminate against travellers" (J. Roberts 2022).

These patterns of incidents involving border crossings by Indigenous peoples and racialized people are summarized in Table 3.3, which shows that Indigenous peoples and racialized people (non-Blacks) are more prone to report discrimination when compared with Whites.

LONGEVITY AND MORTALITY

Indigenous Peoples

Numerous researchers have found that there are disproportionate rates of morbidity, mortality, and shortened life expectancy between Indigenous and non-Indigenous peoples. This may be due to a variety of factors including colonization, the lack of cultural relevance in programs, and systemically discriminatory practices (Carriere and Bougie 2023).

The 2006 data shows that Indigenous peoples' mortality rates are higher than those of non-Indigenous peoples and that they are especially more pronounced among the younger age groups. The mortality rate from all causes per one hundred-thousand-person years for Indigenous peoples was 581 (on reserve), 419 (off reserve), and 335 for non-Indigenous people. In 2011, the life expectancy of Indigenous men was 72.5 years and that of Indigenous women was 77.7 years. Thus, they are 8.9 and 9.6 years shorter than their non-Indigenous male and female counterparts. Moreover, they are more likely than non-Indigenous people to die prematurely. Between 1991 and 2006, Indigenous adults were two times more likely than their non-Indigenous counterparts to die from avoidable causes (Park 2021).

Deaths of Indigenous peoples are largely caused by heart disease, chronic liver disease and cirrhosis, unintentional injuries, and intentional injuries (suicide and assault). There are interlocking relationships between smoking, heart disease, and lung cancer and between a lack of exercise, poor diet, and type 2 diabetes. A combination of excessive alcohol consumption and smoking commonly found among Indigenous peoples more so than non-Indigenous people increased their risk of mouth and throat cancers (Park 2021).

Racialized People

Between 2001 and 2019, research findings showed that ischemic heart disease was the most common cause of death among Blacks and Whites. What followed were cerebrovascular disease, trachea, bronchus, and lung cancer for Black males; trachea, bronchus and lung cancer, and Alzheimer's disease and other dementias for White males; Alzheimer's disease and other dementias and breast cancer for Black females; and Alzheimer's disease and other dementias and trachea, bronchus, and lung cancer for White females. Black people's mortality risks of HIV/AIDS are higher than those for Whites. Black females' risks related to cancer-related deaths (stomach and *corpus uteri* cancers) are higher than their White female's counterparts, and so are Black males' risks of prostate cancer (Gupta and Aitkin 2022; Tjepkema et al. 2023).

Mortal inequalities between Blacks and Whites persisted or remained unchanged even when the social determinants of health (education, income, employment, and housing) were taken into consideration. A crucial factor of such experiences in discrimination was not factored into the analysis, and it is considered quite difficult to measure. This factor, however, seems to be related to risk factors such as smoking, binge drinking, and infrequent physical activity. The reasons for mortality disparities are not conclusive. They may be related to barriers in accessing proper treatments early in their diagnosis, the health-care system, immigration patterns, and hereditary features or other factors. Future studies may shed light on this issue (Gupta and Aitkin 2022; Tjepkema et al. 2023). Most recently, a study of the COVID-19 pandemic showed that the risk of dying from the virus was elevated for Black people when compared with White Canadians. This, too, requires further study (Gupta and Aitkin 2022; Tjepkema et al. 2023).

CONCLUSION

To understand the magnitude of racism in its reach in Canada, research studies and individual cases have been compiled and are presented in this chapter. The position of this book is that racism is found everywhere in Canada and that Indigenous peoples and racialized people experience racism from cradle to grave. While this chapter cannot be exhaustive in its presentation of racism in all social domains, it has covered racism in a wide range of people's lives: compared with White people, Indigenous peoples and racialized people are born with less chance of survival; they have more chances of being separated from their parents; they are poorer and are insecure in their food intake; they live in unhealthy, poor, and crowded housing units; they have a lower level of education; they are not included in well-funded research projects as researchers; they have mostly been neglected as research subjects; their livelihoods are less researched and, therefore, less understood, and there is less chance of them being included in public policy development; they are sicker and more unhealthy; they have less access to culturally appropriate health-care services; they are negatively portrayed in the media; they are talked down to more often, and they are less visibile in entertainment, more surrounded by negative public sentiments, and receive more hate messages; they are also less engaged in nature and other forms of recreation and sports; they are more mistreated in the retail, finance, and hospitality sectors and are more neglected in public transportation; they are more victimized in violent crimes, more scrutinized by the police, more mistreated in the court system and border services; and they die sooner.

In sum, Indigenous peoples and racialized people in Canada encounter many disadvantages and adversities throughout their lives, and most of these are related to race and other human rights grounds, according to a significant sample of research studies cited in this chapter. There are also a large number of research works on racial disparities between White people and racialized people and Indigenous peoples in many social domains in physical and mental health, health care, education, housing, food, transportation, media, entertainment, recreation, sports, communication, public opinions, retail, restaurants, financial services, and law enforcement. Overall, racism is encompassing and overwhelming, and it impacts deeply and extensively the livelihood of racialized and Indigenous peoples. Workplace racism and how they experience the workplace could be better understood in the context of the larger society.

PART TWO

WORKPLACE RACISM

Part 2 begins by reviewing the employment situation of racialized and Indigenous peoples, their workforce and occupational representation, employment incomes, and reports of discrimination in the workplace. It examines the prevalence of stereotypes and racial prejudice and their impact on them as well as their reactions.

This part devotes several chapters to examine how racism works at different stages of the individual's employment "life cycle" from recruitment (the entry of job candidates) to termination (the exit of employees from their organizations). It examines how barriers are erected at the entry points of hiring: recruitment and outreach methods, screening and selection processes, and hiring conditions. After they are hired, it looks at how employees move around the organization in bettering their careers, how their performance is evaluated, how succession is planned and managed, and how promotion and job movements are made. Furthermore, how employers retain their employees is discussed through an analysis of retention processes as well as corporate culture and practices with discriminatory and harassing impacts on racialized and Indigenous employees with an in-depth view on seniority, micro-aggression, and the conflict resolution mechanism.

Through a broad range of policies, programs, and practices related to these functions, Indigenous/racialized employees, in their intersectionality, encounter systemic racism fuelled further by racial stereotyping and prejudice. In the final analysis, workplace racism is made up of many structural blind spots and biased designs as well as individual subjectivity and discrete implementation. Most of them are unexposed, unrecognized, and unacknowledged.

CHAPTER 4

Racism in Employment

INTRODUCTION

As Chapter 3 illustrated, Canada is overwhelmed with evidence of racism from all walks of life. It would be difficult to imagine workplaces in Canada that are not embedding some form of racism that poses adverse impacts on Indigenous peoples or racialized people. It could also be construed that the adverse impact of racism could be discriminatory and harassing, individually or collectively.

As those who have been discriminated or harassed before and those who advocate for social justice have come to realize, finding evidence and proving racial discrimination and harassment can be a challenge. In the area of employment, individual employment data are confidential and private and usually not available to the public. Hence, workforce data on racial groups, such as Indigenous peoples and racialized people, in employment have to depend on Statistics Canada or its post-censual survey data, if large-scale Canada-wide data are needed. These workforce surveys are useful for cross-tabulations as well as studies on socio-economic, demographic, and geographic factors. Increasingly, as demonstrated in Chapter 3, many research studies have made use of these macro and micro data for the purposes of illustrating the racial biases that exist in a range of social arena in Canada.

However, there is also another set of data that proves to be relevant for our study of employment issues of Indigenous peoples and racialized people, and that is the employment equity data and board/executive parity data collected by both private and public sector employers under federal regulations (that is, the *Employment Equity Act* and the *Canada Business Corporations Act*) that have been mandated to improve their employment status.[1] These data provide both historical and structural data that allow some necessary cross-tabulations on Indigeneity and race by geography, gender, compensation, industrial sectors, occupations, and so on. Given these data are systematically collected and focused on multiple aspects of employment, they are useful to show how the employment situations of Indigenous peoples and racialized people are compared with non-Indigenous peoples and non-racialized people.

As these data are collected under regulations that aim at improving the status of Indigenous peoples and racialized people, along with others, the data have the tendency to show that the federally regulated employers have been being compliant with the legislation. Accordingly, if one takes a closer look at the historical data from these data sets, women's employment status has improved since 1987 (when the data were first collected), and their representation has been over and above the labour market availability. Similarly, data on racialized people has shown improvement lately in their representation. However, the data on Indigenous peoples and persons with disabilities remain under-represented, although Indigenous peoples have gained momentum in representation in spite of their overall under-representation when compared with the labour market availability. Overall, these data suggest that, despite the employment equity legislation that has been in effect since 1986, the progress in equitable employment has been slow and, at times, uneven and inconsistent for Indigenous peoples. As for racialized people, there has been progress in the past decade or so, and now they are generally over-represented and present in most occupational groups, as we will be examined later in this chapter.

To what extent these data reflect non-federally regulated employers is hard to say; however, one may cautiously suggest that equitable employment has not been on the priority list of many employers, and resources on human rights and employment equity have not been adequately allocated to improve the employment status of Indigenous peoples and racialized people. There are no special government policies and programs that mandate all private sector employers or territorial, provincial, and municipal employers on a massive scale, which has resulted in major

---

1 *Employment Equity Act*, SC 1995, c 44; *Canada Business Corporations Act*, RSC 1985, c C-44.

shifts in employment direction for these two groups of people. On a more local level, some progressive boards of education or city governments have programs that help to remove employment barriers for these groups to be hired and promoted, but the impact has been negligible. Due to all these contextual issues, the employment equity data that we are using to portray the current employment situation of Indigenous peoples and racialized people may not be as accurate as they should be for the purpose of generalizing the information across Canada. The data paint a narrowly defined segment of Indigenous and racialized employees in the federally regulated employment sector, and there are limitations to projecting their employment status in a broader context in Canada.

Having a preamble of this nature should not stop us from utilizing a variety of data sources to illustrate the extent to which Indigenous peoples and racialized people fare in employment, including the information pertaining to federally regulated employers.

EMPLOYMENT AND UNEMPLOYMENT

Indigenous Peoples

In general, there is a lack of race data on the labour force. In the United States, data on blacks, Hispanic, and Asian jobless rates are comparatively abundant; whereas in Canada, immigration data on the labour force are more prevalent than race and ethnic data (Grant and Balkissoon 2019, A10–11). To some extent, this lack of race data is reflective of the persistent resistance of government, business, and academic people to collect race data since race has been viewed as an irrelevant concept for academic and policy analysis as well as a politically sensitive concept. In the past century, race has been a taboo topic for public discussion, data collection, and public policy development.

In Canada, Indigenous peoples and racialized people cannot take employment for granted. The labour force and employment information discussed below show that being employed remains a struggle for Indigenous/racialized people.

Employment rates are the extent to which people are available to work in relation to the working age population (that is, those in the age group from fifteen to sixty-four). In general, the employment rate in Canada is approximately 60 percent. A high employment rate (say, 70 percent) is viewed as an indication of a healthy labour market, and a low employment rate (say, 50 percent) is viewed as problematic. Meanwhile, unemployment rates reveal the proportions of people in the labour force who do not have a job and are actively looking for a job. In Canada, Indigenous peoples have a lower employment rate and a higher unemployment rate in the labour market than their non-Indigenous counterparts, especially in occupations that require a higher educational level. The educational disparity between the two groups that was discussed in Chapter 3 may explain a part of this problem (Su and Jin 2023). Compared with non-Indigenous people (84.9 percent), the employment rate of Indigenous peoples (77.3 percent) age twenty-five to fifty-four, for all educational levels combined, were lower in 2022 (Statistics Canada 2023c, 2023d, 2023e).

There is still quite a disparity between Indigenous youth and non-Indigenous youth in their employment situation. In 2016, the employment rate for Indigenous youth was 39.3 percent, whereas for non-Indigenous youth it was 52.8 percent. Meanwhile, the unemployment rate of Indigenous youth was 23 percent and that of non-Indigenous youth was 15 percent (Statistics Canada 2021). These employment and unemployment rates illustrate that Indigenous communities have an unhealthy labour force in comparison with that of non-Indigenous people. The October 2023 data on youth employment (aged fifteen to twenty-four) shows that First Nations youth living off reserve who were employed was 16.4 percent and that of Metis was 13.2 percent. The youth unemployment rate in Canada for that month was 11.4 percent. Both figures appear to be an indication of a decline in Indigenous youth unemployment, which is reflective of the more robust economic situation in the post-COVID 19 era. In spite of this, the reality is that Indigenous youth have a higher unemployment rate than that of the total youth population (Statistics Canada 2023g).

Racialized People

In Canada, as of 1 December 2023, the employment rate of non-racialized people (fifteen years and over) is 60.3 percent, and their unemployment rate is 4.5 percent. The employment rate of racialized people is 65.8 percent, and their unemployment rate is 7.1 percent. There are variations of these employment rates among racialized people. The breakdown of the employment rates for different racialized people are as follows: South Asian (67.9 percent); Chinese (58.9 percent); Black

(67.0 percent); Filipino (73.8 percent); Arab (61.2 percent); Latin American (70.5 percent); Southeast Asian (66.6 percent); West Asian (62.6 percent); Korean (66.7 percent); Japanese (61.9 percent); racialized people not included elsewhere (63.2 percent); and multiple racialized people (61.7 percent) (Statistics Canada 2023f).

In 2006, racialized men and racialized women were more likely than non-racialized men to be unemployed (Block and Galabuzi 2011, 4). The 2016 Census data showed that racialized people's unemployment rate was 9.2 percent and that of non-racialized people was 7.2 percent in 2016. Breaking these data down by gender, racialized women's unemployment rate was 9.6 percent, and that of racialized men was 8.8 percent, while non-racialized men was 8.2 percent, and non-racialized women was 6.4 percent (Canadian Centre for Policy Alternatives 2019). Using the October 2023 data on youth unemployment (aged fifteen to twenty-four years), Statistics Canada (2023g) shows that racialized youth have higher unemployment than the average youth in Canada. Among other racialized youth, Black youth (17.7 percent) and Chinese youth (14.7 percent) were higher than the total youth population (11.4 percent) in Canada.

These data also suggest that the intersectionality of race, age, and gender does have an impact on unemployment and that, longitudinally, the labour market discrimination for racialized people has not improved that much between 2006 and 2016 (Block and Galabuzi 2011, 4).

WORKFORCE REPRESENTATION

In determining the extent to which Indigenous peoples and racialized people are equitably employed in organizations, the federal government generally uses three sets of data: employment data of federally regulated employers, labour market availability data, and attainment data.

Federally regulated employers are mainly found in banking and financial services, communications, transportation, and other sectors (including production industries, service industries, and public administration). The data cited here include a small sample of the nineteen thousand employers who employed 945,000 employees.

According to the federal government, the term "labour market availability" means the share of Indigenous peoples and racialized people, as well as other employment equity designated group members in the workforce, from which employers could hire based on data from Statistics Canada. These people are all available for work.

The "attainment rate" used to be called the "utilization rate." It means the extent to which employers employ Indigenous peoples, racialized people, and other employment equity designated group members (that is, women and persons with disabilities) in their organizations when compared with their representation in the "labour market availability" workforce. The rate is expressed in terms of the percentage of their employment based on their representation in the labour market availability. The term "availability" means that individuals are ready to be employed. If the rate exceeds the labour market availability, it means Indigenous peoples or racialized people are over-represented; if the rate is below that of the labour market availability, Indigenous peoples or racialized peoples are under-represented. This constitutes a measurement of the extent of equitable employment by employers. These rates could be further tabulated and analyzed by breaking them down into employment status, occupational groups, industrial sectors, and geographic locations.

In Canada, the labour market availability for Indigenous peoples in the 2016 Census was 4.0 percent and that of racialized people ("members of visible minorities") was 21.3 percent. In comparison, the representation of Indigenous peoples was 2.4 percent and that of racialized people was 27.4 percent of the federally regulated private sector employers with one hundred or more employees.

In 2021, these employers had 742,506 employees. Therefore, based on these data, the attainment rate of Indigenous peoples was 60 percent and that of racialized people was 128.6 percent in 2021 (Government of Canada 2022b). In other words, Indigenous peoples are under-represented, and racialized people are over-represented.

As noted for 2021, the number and representation of Indigenous peoples and racialized people in employment in federally regulated organizations continued its steady increase. The technical explanation is quite simple as it shows in the hiring, promotion, and termination data of Indigenous people. Their share of hires exceeded that of terminations, and this explains the increase in Indigenous employment in these organizations. However, their promotion share was lower, which suggests that they have difficulties in moving to positions with a higher status.

As for racialized people, their hires and promotions increased, and their termination rate was lower than that recorded for hires. This

Table 4.1: Representation of Indigenous Peoples and Racialized People and Their Attainment Rates in 2021

	Representation, 2021 (%)	Labour market availability, 2016** (%)	Attainment rate, 2021 (%)
Indigenous peoples*	2.4	4.0	60
Racialized people*	27.4	21.3	128.6

Notes: *Statistics Canada's terms used are "Aboriginal peoples" and "Members of Visible Minorities."
** These data are based on the 2016 Census data as the 2021 Census data were not available at the time of writing this book.
Source: Government of Canada 2022b, Table 1B: Designated Group Representation and Attainment Rates in 2020 and 2021 (by Percentage).

explains why their number and representation steadily increased during this period (Government of Canada 2022b).

The 1986 *Employment Equity Act* mandates federally regulated employers to improve the representation of Indigenous Peoples and racialized people. Since then, these employers have been working to improve their representation. The representation data of 2021 include the results of thirty-five years of employment equity work. And, yet, Indigenous Peoples remain largely under-represented, as noted in Table 4.1. There was a gradual increase in the representation of Indigenous Peoples since 1987, but it remains low and is currently "hovering" around 60 percent in their attainment (Government of Canada 2022b). The slow achievement in improving the representation of Indigenous Peoples is not anticipated, but it also means that there is still a lot of work to be done.

As for racialized people, there has been an upward trend in their representation since 1987, and they remain over-represented above 100 percent. In 2021, their representation was 128.5 percent (Government of Canada 2022b). In the context of the slow achievement of Indigenous Peoples' representation, the over-representation of racialized people after thirty-five years of employment equity work suggests that employment equity as a public policy still works in improving the status of racialized people. However, the data derived from federally regulated employers may not be typical of all employers in Canada as these data are skewed because these federally regulated employers have a legal obligation to increase the representation of employment equity designated groups, which include Indigenous Peoples and racialized people.

As for the representation of racialized people in the public sector, under the guidance of the Auditor General of Canada, during the period from 2018 to 2020, The Royal Canadian Mounted Police (RCMP) did not meet the external workforce availability representation rates, and the other five organizations were unsystematic in comparing the internal workforce data with the proper up-to-date external labour market availability data, and, consequently, these five organizations' representation rates of racialized employees are problematic. Similarly, the records of these six organizations show uneven representation in the fourteen occupational levels, especially those at the higher occupational levels (Auditor General of Canada 2023). In sum, the actual increase in the respresentation of racialized employees during this period remains unconvincing. However, it also means that the increase in representation to the extent that Indigenous Peoples would still be under-represented after thirty-five years is glacially slow.

OCCUPATIONAL REPRESENTATION

Representation and attainment rates can be broken down by occupational groups. The attainment rate is based on a division of data from representation by those from labour market availability. The lower the attainment rate, the less the talent of Indigenous Peoples has been utilized. Indigenous peoples are under-utilized in all fourteen occupational groups even after thirty-five years of federal government requirement for increased representation. They are mostly under-utilized in the "senior manager" occupational group (with an attainment rate of 40.7 percent). The reasons for their extensive and deep under-representation in a broad range of occupational groups even after such a lengthy period of federal requirement are a cause for concern and will be explored and discussed later in Chapter 5, Chapter 6, Chapter 7, and Chapter 8 (see Table 4.2).

Earlier in this century, racialized people were under-represented in the top levels. Using the 2006 Census data from federally regulated organizations in the communications sector, only 14.5 percent of these organizations include racialized employees, and only 5.1 percent of senior managers are racialized people. There is a range of concentration of racialized people in different sectors: leadership positions in the education sector comprise 20 percent racialized people. But racialized people constituted only 4 percent of the corporate sector (Human Resources and Skills Development Canada 2008; Diversity Institute in Management and Technology 2009). Such variation is still prevalent among federally regulated organizations. But, in considering the averages in

Table 4.2: Representation and Attainment Rates (Canadian Labour Market Availability) of Indigenous Peoples* in All Sectors by Occupational Groups in Canada, 2021

Employment equity occupational groups	Representation, 2021 (%)	Labour market availability, 2016** (%)	Attainment rate, 2021 (%)
Senior managers	1.3	3.2	40.7
Middle and other managers	1.3	2.7	52.6
Professionals	1.3	2.4	55.0
Semi-professionals and technicians	2.7	4.2	62.6
Supervisors	2.5	3.9	69.8
Supervisors: crafts and trades	3.6	4.3	94.6
Administrative and senior clerical personnel	2.0	3.5	63.1
Skilled sales and service personnel	2.0	3.7	56.2
Skilled crafts and trades workers	4.4	5.2	82.4
Clerical personnel	2.2	4.2	55.0
Intermediate sales and service personnel	2.8	4.5	60.4
Semi-skilled manual workers	3.4	4.8	75.3
Other sales and service personnel	3.9	5.8	65.4
Other manual workers	4.7	6.8	72.1
Total	2.4	4.0	60.0

Notes: *Statistics Canada's terms used are "Aboriginal peoples" and "Members of Visible Minorities," whereas the terms of "Indigenous Peoples" and "racialized people" are used in this book. ** These data are based on the 2016 Census data as the 2021 Census data were not available at the time of writing this book.
Source: Government of Canada 2022b, Table 2.14: Representation and Attainment Rate (Canadian Availability) of Aboriginal Peoples in All Sectors by Occupational Groups in 2020 and 2021 (by Percentage).

organizational variation, racialized people have made some improvement as time has progressed.

Unlike Indigenous Peoples, racialized people are over-represented in most occupational groups, and their corresponding high attainment rates show how well they do when compared with their labour market availability. Racialized people are over-represented in ten of the fourteen occupational groups. However, they are notably over-represented among administrative and senior clerical personnel (with an attainment rate of 191.9 percent). They are under-represented in four of the

Table 4.3: Representation and Attainment Rate (Canadian Labour Market Availability) of Racialized Peoples* in All Sectors by Occupational Groups in Canada, 2021

Employment equity occupational groups	Representation, 2021 (%)	Labour market availability, 2016** (%)	Attainment rate, 2021 (%)
Senior managers	14.4	11.5	125.5
Middle and other managers	30.6	17.6	173.9
Professionals	37.7	23.3	162.4
Semi-professionals and technicians	24.7	19.1	89.6
Supervisors	12.8	24.0	102.8
Supervisors: crafts and trades		11.1	115.1
Administrative and senior clerical personnel	31.4	16.4	191.9
Skilled sales and service personnel	37.1	27.7	134.0
Skilled crafts and trades workers	16.4	12.0	136.9
Clerical personnel	28.2	21.9	128.5
Intermediate sales and service personnel	29.5	25.4	116.1
Semi-skilled manual workers	18.5	22.4	82.6
Other sales and service personnel	18.1	26.5	68.2
Other manual workers	12.5	21.0	59.6
Total	27.4	21.3	128.6

Notes: *Statistics Canada's terms used are "Aboriginal peoples" and "Members of Visible Minorities," whereas the terms "Indigenous Peoples" and "Racialized people" are used in this book. ** These data are based on the 2016 Census data as the 2021 Census data were not available at the time of writing this book.

Source: Government of Canada 2022b, Table 2.16: Representation and Attainment Rate (Canadian Availability) of Members of Visible Minorities in All Sectors by Occupational Groups in 2020 and 2021 (by Percentage).

fourteen occupational groups: semi-professionals and technicians (89.6 percent), semi-skilled manual workers (82.6 percent), other sales and service personnel (68.2 percent), and other manual workers (59.6 percent) (see Table 4.3).

As noted, this dominant over-representation of racialized employees in a broad range of occupational groups, even in the high-status positions mentioned above, is not typical of Canadian workplaces. Studies

Table 4.4: Labour Force by Occupation in Canada, 2006

	Racialized		Non-racialized	
	Men (%)	**Women (%)**	**Men (%)**	**Women (%)**
All occupations	7.7	7.0	45.0	40.3
Management	8.2	4.6	55.1	32.1
Natural and applied sciences and related	15.8	4.8	62.4	17.1
Health	4.3	12.0	15.6	68.1
Business, finance, and administration	5.4	9.8	23.2	61.6
Social sciences, education, government services, and religion	4.2	7.3	27.7	60.8
Art, culture, recreation, and sport	5.2	5.2	39.6	49.9
Sales and service occupations	7.4	9.1	35.1	48.4
Trade, transport, and equipment operators and related	9.5	0.9	83.6	6.0
Occupations unique to primary industry	3.3	1.8	74.4	20.5
Occupations unique to processing, manufacturing, and utilities	14.0	11.2	52.7	22.1

Source: Statistics Canada, 2006 Census, Catalogue no. 97-564-XCB2006009; Block and Galabuzi 2011, 9.

on occupational representation based on the same fourteen employment equity occupational groups for non-federally regulated employers (such as those under the Federal Contractors Program) were not readily available. The Federal Contractors Program also has a government mandate to improve the representation of Indigenous Peoples and racialized people under the *Employment Equity Act*.

Sheila Block and Grace-Edward Galabuzi (2011, 9) have done a tabulation of racialized and non-racialized men and women in different occupations in Canada using the 2006 Census data. The occupational groupings are different from those used by federally regulated employers, and, therefore, they are not comparable. Furthermore, the Census data quoted by Block and Galabuzi do not include the labour market availability data for comparisons; hence, their data are not able to shed light on the representation and attainment rates of racialized people in various occupations. Nevertheless, Block and Galabuzi provide a profile of their distribution (not representation) compared to non-racialized people within each occupation as of 2006 (see Table 4.4).

As the labour market availability data are not available for comparison to determine the representation of racialized and non-racialized people, it is impossible to speculate how equitable racialized employees are in these occupations. In light of this deficiency, Block and Galabuzi (2011, 8–11) used the "all occupations" figures of 7.7 percent (for racialized men) and 7 percent (for racialized women) as a crude reference point for measuring racial distribution. Hence, the measurements utilized by Block and Galabuzi are not able to shed light on the issues related to representation. At most, these data provide a comparison of gender differences for each occupational group within the "racialized" and "non-racialized" groups.

HUMAN RESOURCES MANAGEMENT

There are many aspects in human resources management that have created representation issues for Indigenous and racialized people in the workplace. The key aspects are in the areas of hiring, promotion, and retention, among others. If Indigenous and racialized people are not recruited and hired on par with their representation in the population, if they are not promoted on par with their representation in the workplace, and/or if they are not retained and they decide to leave the organization and look for employment in other places, then these marginalized people will still be under-represented in the organization. In addition, there are situations when their retention rate is more or less the same as that of their hiring or promotion rates, and these situations would not resolve the issue of their under-representation or even lack of representation in some occupational groups at some levels of the organization. The following findings from studies in hiring, promotion, and retention may shed some light on the current situation.

Hiring

In a review of the federal hiring data covering the period from 2017 to 2021 conducted by the Government of Canada (2023e), it was noted that, overall, the hiring rate for racialized people was 19 percent and that of Indigenous Peoples was 2 percent. Clearly, with racialized people constituting 25 percent of the labour market and Indigenous Peoples constituting 5 percent (in the 2021 Census data), the federal hiring rates (with their percentage differentials compared to the labour market rates) were not enough to increase the overall representation of both racialized people and Indigenous Peoples in the federal workforce. Moreover, in the same five-year period, the departure (or termination) rates were 18 percent for racialized employees and 3 percent for Indigenous employees. With the departure of both groups almost on par with their new hires, their representation did not turn the dial too much in the end. Similarly, at the executive level, the hiring and departure rates for both groups were also quite similar, which basically signified that there had been very slow progress in raising representation at the executive level. During this five-year period, the federal government seems to have been going through the "revolving door" syndrome where the number of racialized people and Indigenous peoples hired was similar to the number of those who were terminated.

The findings of a longitudinal study on six Western countries—Canada, France, Germany, Great Britain, the Netherlands, and the United States—on hiring discrimination of African/Black, Asian, Latin American/Hispanic, and Middle Eastern and North African during a fifty-two-year period between 1967 and 2019 are not encouraging. The overall pattern is that hiring discrimination remains unchanged or slightly elevated. France is the only country that seems to have reduced the degree of hiring discrimination during this time period. Canada remained steady in its rate of hiring discrimination, and the Netherlands has increased. In general, hiring discrimination—especially, against those with Middle East and North Africa origins—has increased in the 2000s when compared with the 1990s (Quillian and Lee 2023).

Some studies in the past have suggested that, in Canada, there has been hiring discrimination against candidates with foreign names—job applicants with foreign names got a call back rate of 73.5 percent, whereas those with English names got a call back rate of 74.6 percent (Akintola 2011). Meanwhile, using data collected from Toronto and Montreal in 2007 and 2009, in which 12,910 resumes were sent out in response to 3,225 job postings, Rupa Banerjee, Jeffrey Reitz, and Phil Oreopoulos (2018) showed that hiring discrimination of Asian skilled applicants was substantially higher among smaller employers than in larger ones (with over five hundred employees). Larger employers are 20 percent less likely to call applicants with Asian names for an interview, and smaller ones are 40 percent less likely to call them for an interview. However, just based on perceptions and without empirical evidence on actual hiring data with racial comparisons, a survey by

KPMG on 1,001 Black Canadians that was released in 2023 revealed that nine out of ten Black Canadians observed that their employers had made progress on the diversity front in 2022, and 59 percent said that their employers had hired more Black candidates in the past twelve months (Douglas 2023a).

Promotion

Promotion appears to be an area with many complaints from racialized employees, especially when job applications were submitted for managerial or executive positions. While perceived promotion discrimination is not limited to just managerial or executive positions, racialized and Indigenous professionals often feel that their educational investment is not fairly translated into occupational mobility. When employees have applied numerous times for a promotion and failed, it is discouraging, and they do not see much future staying in the organization. Lack of promotion is often the main cause of employee disengagement and departure.

Public Sector

A number of promotion studies of public sector employees, cited by the Government of Canada (2022b), show that most of these studies were mainly a comparison of men and women in the workplace. There was a study done in British Columbia in 2015 that showed that racialized employees (11.7 percent) have a slightly lower chance than White employees (12 percent) of being promoted. Hence, the longitudinal studies of the Government of Canada published in 2022 intended to fill this vacuum. In the public sector, the Public Service Commission conducted an analysis of promotion data on all public servants hired on or after 1 April 1991 until 31 March 2018 (fifteen years). The results showed that Indigenous peoples have lower promotion rates (–7.5 percent) than their counterparts and that there was no appreciable difference between racialized people (0.6 percent) and their counterparts. For Indigenous peoples, the rate of promotion to the executive level was lower than that of non-Indigenous peoples. Overall, the promotion rate for racialized people to executive levels was lower than it was for non-racialized people (Government of Canada 2022b).

A second analysis was conducted on the promotion rates of new hires between 1 April 1 1991 and 31 March 2005 (fourteen years) and between 1 April 2005 and 31 March 2018 (thirteen years). The results show that an improvement was noted in the promotion rate of Indigenous peoples in the second period. However, there were no appreciable differences in the promotion rates between racialized people and their counterparts (Government of Canada, n.d.). For both Indigenous peoples (–8.2 percent [2005] versus –5.9 percent [2018]) and racialized people (–0.9 percent [2005] versus –1.6 percent [2018]), the noted improvements remained marginal and weak. This finding is consistent with that of the workforce report on the public service in British Columbia where racialized people's promotion rate (11.7 percent) is slightly below that of non-racialized people (12 percent). As for Indigenous peoples, their promotion rate (9.1 percent) was lower than that of their counterparts (12 percent) (BC Stats 2016; Government of Canada 2022b).

A third analysis was conducted on the share of applicants to the appointment process of Indigenous peoples and racialized people compared with their counterparts, and it compared these findings with their representation rates in the federal public service population and with the share of promotions over two fiscal years (2016–17 and 2017–18). The results showed that racialized people applied at a higher rate than their representation in the federal public service but that they, as applicants, had lower promotion rates than their representation (Government of Canada 2022b).

Private Sector

Unlike the public sector, which is mandated to collect promotion data under the *Employment Equity Act*, the private sector organizations seldom have internal promotion data unless they are under the Federal Contractor Program, the legislated Employment Equity Program, or have been studied by academics, which happens occasionally. As private sector employers' human resources data are considered proprietary and confidential, most of these data are derived from employee surveys that collect the perceptions of Indigenous and racialized employees regarding promotion. There have been occasional empirical studies, which we are citing here as examples, along with others that have studied how employees view the interplays of race and promotion.

Margaret Yap (2010) studied the promotion experiences of 22,338 employees who worked in a large Canadian company between 1996 and 2000. These employees were analyzed along race and gender lines, covering White men and women along with racialized minority men and women who all worked in a large Canadian company. The findings showed that White men have clear advantages over their counterparts both in terms of job levels and job families even after controlling for a broad range of variables (such as education, performance ratings, and so on). Overall, White employees (59.4 percent) received one or more promotions over racialized employees (55.7 percent) and male employees (57.2 percent) were also liklier than female employees (54.7 percent) to receive one or more promotions. The percentage differentials among them based on race and gender were statistically significant at the 1 percent level. After taking a more in-depth dive into the same data set, Margaret Yap and Alison Konrad (2009) observed that, for both White and racialized women, they were less likely to be promoted than White men at the lower end of the occupational hierarchy (which supports the "sticky floor" school of thought); for White women and racialized men and women at the middle occupational levels, they received fewer promotions (which lends support to the "mid-level bottleneck" school of thought); and racialized men remain promotionally disadvantaged at the high occupational levels (which supports the "glass ceiling" school of thought). Overall, race and gender have a decisive impact on promotions.

These findings were further reinforced by several studies on the broader public sector, such as the study by Frances Henry and colleagues (2017) regarding faculty members. This study was based on a four-year data set of a national sample of Canadian universities. The research results showed that racialized and Indigenous faculty members are poorly represented in the hiring, promotion, and tenure practices of those institutions. Another nationwide study on racialized and Indigenous Canadian academic research librarians by Mary Kandiuk (2014) also confirmed the lack of active outreach and recruitment, compounded by a lack of mentorships, organizational supports, and advancement opportunities as the source for their general low representation.

KPMG is a full-service audit, tax, and advisory firm, and it has over ten thousand employees across Canada. According to its study of one thousand Black Canadians between 19 December 2023 and 13 January 2024, almost three out of every four Black people (73 percent) perceived that their advancement in the workplace did not materialize due to their company's anticipation of a likely recession, cutbacks, or restructuring. Despite this, most felt that their prospects for advancement (such as project assignments, upskilling, and training opportunities) had improved over the previous year. Furthermore, 80 percent of Black persons viewed racialized people as being the first to lose their jobs last year. Overall, it was a mixed bag of feelings among Black people on various promotion issues during this uncertain time (KPMG 2024).

Retention

Statistics suggest that retention and race are highly interconnected: the retention rates of Indigenous peoples and racialized people are indeed lower than those of White employees. American and British literature on retention has shown that racialized employees have greater inclination to quit their current jobs, and, when compared with the retention rates of White employees, they are lower. A 2019 study of Coqual (an American think tank) noted that Black employees are likely to leave their companies 30 percent more often than their White counterparts. In Britain, Black professionals reported that they were 35 percent more likely to plan to stay for only two years or less than their White counterparts (Galea, O'Hara, and Bradshaw 2023). In some professions, such as academic professors in the United States, the retention of White assistant professors (61.3 percent) was higher than those of Asian (52.8 percent) or Black/Hispanic/Other (50.8 percent) minority faculty members (Abelson et al. 2018, 678–82). Similarly, Monique Payne-Pikus, John Hagan, and Robert Nelson's (2010, 553–84) study of the largest law firms in the United States confirmed that institutional racism was impacting the retention rates of racialized lawyers negatively.

Public Sector

In Canada, employee retention in the public sector is a topic that is seldom studied systematically. During the period of 2018–20, the Auditor General of Canada (2023) did an audit on six federal government departments and agencies—Canada Border Services Agency, Correctional Service Canada, Department of Justice Canada, Public Prosecution Service of Canada, Public Safety Canada, and the RCMP—and regretted to inform that the retention data were non-existent because all six government departments did not have a valid comparable reference of non-racialized people for their hiring and termination rates. However, examples of two additional government agencies are presented below, including the Indigenous and Northern Affairs Canada (INAC) and the Canada Energy Regulator.

INAC completed an internal study of its recruitment, development, and retention of Indigenous peoples and racialized people in 2015–16, which covered the period of 2010–15. The retention of employees may be measured in terms of the discrepancy between the departure (termination) rate of employees and their entry (hiring) rate. In this case, INAC had departure rates ranging from 9.08 percent to 13.30 percent during this five-year period. Throughout most of this period, their departure rates were higher than the entry rates, which means that INAC had low employee retention and their representation rates seldom improved. A number of factors have been attributed to such a discrepancy including restructuring, promotional and career developmental opportunities, employee well-being and satisfaction, work/life balance, and harassment and conflict resolution. The significance of these factors are to be determined. Despite this low retention, the representation of Indigenous peoples remains relatively high at 29.3 percent (in comparison with the workforce availability rate of 5.1 percent). The Indigenous representation rate of 29.3 percent was still below INAC's aspirational goal of having 50 percent Indigenous employees in its workforce (Government of Canada 2016). INAC's data may not be typical of all other federal departments. The results of the study on retention provide some insights on the retention of Indigenous and racialized employees.

The Canada Energy Regulator's (2022) *Employment Equity Report, 2021–2022* reported that the departure (termination) rate for Indigenous employees was 7.7 percent and that their hiring rate was 0 percent. Meanwhile, the departure (termination) rate for racialized employees was 7.7 percent, and their hiring rate was 2.7 percent. Departure and hiring rates for both groups are too small to have any meaningful calculation. The fact that racialized people are already under-represented means that any departures without new hires are bound to make them even more under-represented.

A review of the data on hires and separations within federal services between 2007–8 and 2014–15 shows that, for Indigenous peoples, their separation rate (5.1 percent) was higher than the hiring rate (3.8 percent) in 2015, which negatively impacted on their representation rate. During these eight years, their separation rate increased from 4.2 percent in 2008 to 5.1 percent in 2015, which shows a decrease in their retention. In contrast, the separation rate of racialized people was 9.9

percent, and their hiring rate was 16.1 percent in 2015, which positively impacted on their representation rate. During these eight years, their retention rate dropped as their separation rate increased from 6.8 percent in 2008 to 9.9 percent in 2015, which neutralized their gain in increased hires (Griffith 2016). This comparison of separation and hiring rates is an easy way to measure employee retention.

Private Sector

Catalyst and the Diversity Institute in Management and Technology (2007) at Toronto Metropolitan University (formerly known as Ryerson University) completed a study on seventeen thousand racialized executives, managers, and professionals in forty-three publicly traded and privately held companies and professional firms across Canada. Racialized employees were less satisfied with their careers than their White/Caucasian counterparts as they felt that their skills, education, and training were perceived as being under-utilized. Compared with their White/Caucasian counterparts, fewer racialized employees believed the talent identification and career development processes were fair. More racialized employees perceived an absence of role models, mentors, and networking opportunities; inequality in performance standards; fewer high-profile assignments; subtle forms of biases; and a less inclusive workplace.

As for the retention of racialized employees, their perspectives were revealed in a finding in which 79 percent of them and 83 percent of White/Caucasian employees intended to remain with their current employers. The discrepancy of these two groups diminished after additional regression analyses. This analysis result seems to be at odds with past research findings on retention: Lack of job satisfaction, career advancement and development opportunities, and utilization of employee skills, education and training usually ended up with lower employee retention.

A subset of the larger research project conducted by Catalyst and the Diversity Institute in Management and Technology (2007) was a study of 7,110 managers in nine Canadian companies in the information communications and technology sector. This more focused study noted that race played a key part in determining their organizational commitment to working in their current companies. Compared with their White/Caucasian counterparts (84 percent), racialized respondents (78 percent) were less inclined to stay with their organizations. And these racialized respondents were also less satisfied with their progress toward their overall career goals (65 percent versus 78 percent), income goals (51 percent versus 64 percent), goals for advancement (52 percent versus 67 percent), and the development of new skills (63 percent versus 72 percent) when compared with their White/Caucasian counterparts. Similar divergences were found in the opinions of these two groups based on race, with racialized respondents feeling more marginalized or negative in their relations with managers and colleagues, career advancement and development, and workplace inclusion (Cukier et al. 2007).

EMPLOYMENT INCOME

Employment income refers to income from salaries, wages, bonus pay, overtime pay, tips and/or commissions, and self-employment. For employers in Canada or individual provincial jurisdictions, the only available data have been provided by research studies by academic communities and think tanks. One of these studies is *Canada's Colour Coded Labour Market*, which was co-authored by Block and Galabuzi (2011), which examined the racial disparities in incomes from 2000 to 2005. Racialized people earned 81.4 cents for every dollar that non-racialized people earned, which is largely due to the fact that racialized people tend to work in jobs that are precarious, temporary, and poorly paid. These jobs may range "from call centres to security services to janitorial services." Racialized women earn 55.6 percent of what non-racialized men earn. Even among immigrants, non-racialized immigrant men and women earn more than racialized men and women, when controlling for education and age. Gender still plays a crucial role in the disparities between racialized and non-racialized people in earnings (Block and Galabuzi 2011, 3–4).

The study from the Canadian Centre for Policy Alternatives (2019) shows that income disparity between racialized people and non-racialized people remained more or less the same during the period from 2006 to 2016. Using the 2016 data, the income gaps of racialized and non-racialized people show the earnings of racialized women (fifty-nine cents per one dollar for non-racialized men), the earnings of racialized men (seventy-eight cents per one dollar for non-racialized men), the earnings of non-racialized women (sixty-seven cents per one dollar for non-racialized men), and the earnings of non-racialized men (one hundred cents per one dollar for non-racialized men. The data show that, although the gender factor is pertinent, the race factor is quite critical. And a comparison of incomes by race and gender data from 2006 and 2016 did not show much progress in closing these gaps (Canadian Centre for Policy Alternatives 2019). Similarly, a comparison of Black adults and youth and the Canadian averages for adults and youth in 2016 showed similar patterns of income disparities. Among racialized people, the 2016 Census data on Blacks in Canada show that they earned 75.6 cents for every dollar a non-racialized worker earned. As for the median annual employment income in 2016, Black adults (aged twenty-five to fifty-four) earned $35,008, while the Canadian average for adults was $42,374, and Black youths (aged fifteen to twenty-four) earned $7,517, while the Canadian average for youth was $9,938 (Spiteri 2023).

Salary Ranges in Full-Time Employment

In terms of cumulative salary ranges collected for employment equity purposes by federal regulated employers in 2021, non-Indigenous peoples have a slightly positive edge over Indigenous peoples on higher salaries overall. Similarly, non-racialized people have a slightly positive edge over racialized people on higher salaries overall (Government of Canada 2022e). Tables 4.5 and 4.6 illustrate the discrepancies in the distribution of Indigenous peoples and racialized people and their counterparts in salary ranges in 2021. Both of the tables suggest that non-Indigenous and non-racialized peoples have a slightly favourable edge over their counterparts in the distribution of salary ranges. Proportionately speaking, there are slightly fewer non-Indigenous and non-racialized peoples on the lower ends of salary ranges ($49,999 and under) and slightly more of them on the higher end of salary ranges (the $249,999 and under category).

Table 4.5: Discrepancies in the Distribution of Indigenous Peoples and Their Counterparts in Permanent Full-Time Employment by Salary Range as of 31 December 2021

Salary ranges	Cumulative distribution of Indigenous peoples* (%)	Cumulative distribution of non-Indigenous peoples* (%)
$49,999 and under	24.3	21.4
$149,999 and under	96.6	94.6
$249,999 and under	99.5	98.8

Note: *Statistics Canada's term used is "Aboriginal peoples."
Source: Government of Canada 2022e, Table 2B: Distribution of Aboriginal Peoples and Non-Aboriginal Peoples in Permanent Full-Time Employment by Salary Range as of December 31, 2021 (by Percentage).

Table 4.6: Discrepancies in the Distribution of Racialized People and Their Counterparts in Permanent Full-Time Employment by Salary Range as of 31 December 2021

Salary ranges	Cumulative distribution of racialized people* (%)	Cumulative distribution of non-racialized people* (%)
$49,999 and under	24.1	20.4
$149,999 and under	96.5	94.0
$249,999 and under	99.2	98.7

Note: * Statistics Canada's term used is "Members of Visible Minorities."
Source: Government of Canada 2022e, Table 2D: Distribution of Members of Visible Minorities and Non-Members of Non-Visible Minorities in Permanent Full-Time Employment by Salary Range as of December 31, 2021 (by Percentage).

Average Incomes

The data of Indigenous peoples ("Indigenous identity") fifteen years and over in private households in the Census data of 2021 (which based its income data on the year 2020) show that their average employment income was $42,240 and that of non-Indigenous peoples ("non-Indigenous identity") was $50,640. This is a $8,400 difference. The data show that Indigenous peoples are earning 83.42 percent of what non-Indigenous peoples earn. A breakdown on Indigenous peoples' average employment incomes shows some variations among them: First Nations ($39.960), Metis ($45,280), Inuit ($42,080), and multiple Indigenous responses ($40,240) (Statistics Canada 2022e).

According to the Census data of 2021 (which based its income data on the year 2020), the data of racialized people (or a visible minority group) show that their average employment income was $45,560 and that of non-racialized people (or "not a visible minority") was $52,550. This is a difference of $6,990. In other words, racialized people are earning 86.69 percent of what non-racialized people earn. A breakdown of racialized people's average employment incomes shows some variations among them: South Asian ($48,480), Chinese ($51,650), Black ($40,520), Filipino ($41,720), Arab ($43,320), Latin American ($43,280), Southeast Asian ($40,760), West Asian ($42,560), Japanese ($50,720), "visible minority, not included elsewhere" ($45,920), and "multiple visible minorities" ($45,520) (Statistics Canada 2022c).

In 2016, even among immigrants, whether they were racialized or non-racialized would impact their earnings. Racialized female immigrants earned fifty-two cents for every one dollar that non-racialized immigrant men earned, and racialized male immigrants earned seventy-one cents for every one dollar that non-racialized immigrant men earned.

Meanwhile, non-racialized female immigrants earned sixty-six cents for every one dollar that non-racialized men. Among younger immigrants (aged twenty-five to fifty-four), racialized immigrant women earned seventy-nine cents for every one dollar that non-racialized immigrant women earned (Canadian Centre for Policy Alternatives 2019).

In the private sector, the data on racial discrimination was less sector specific and readily available. Most studies focused on Canada as a whole without considering the private sector specifically. There is a disparity in average wages for different ethnic groups, and Black people experienced the largest earnings gap. The earnings gap for racialized people (aged twenty-five to sixty-four years) has been persistent and increased steadily over the past twenty-five years (Jackson 2001; Pendakur and Pendakur 2002). In 1991, racialized people earned 11 percent less than the average Canadian earned. Ten years later, they earned 14.5 percent less.

Due largely to their lower incomes and wider pay gaps, racialized people and immigrants, in particular, experience a higher incidence of financial difficulties. Coupled with the current economic uncertainty, Statistics Canada's data show that, in April 2024, almost all racialized people reported more difficulties meeting their financial needs in the past twelve months compared with non-racialized Canadians: West Asian (48 percent); South Asian (43 percent); Latin American (42 percent); Black (40 percent); Arab (38 percent); and Filipino (35 percent). In contrast, only 28 percent of non-racialized and non-Indigenous people reported financial difficulties in the same period. Chinese Canadians are the only group that has a lower percentage (22 percent) in reporting financial difficulty (Statistics Canada 2024e).

Pay Gaps: Hourly Wages, Bonus Pay, and Overtime Pay

Canada is the first country to report pay gap data on Indigenous peoples, racialized people, and other employment equity designated group members within federally regulated employers in 2021. Pay gaps show the differences in money earned between two groups of people. A pay gap is expressed in terms of the amount of earning of one group for every one dollar earned by another group. These gaps could be based on an hourly wage, bonus pay, of overtime pay. For the purpose of clarity in presentation, only data on "median pay gaps" are used to compare the pay of employees in the middle of the pay distribution for each group. First, we will present the three pay gaps of Indigenous employees compared with non-Indigenous employees. This will then be followed by a presentation of the three pay gaps of racialized employees compared with non-racialized employees:

- "hourly wage gaps" measure the difference in wages per hour among groups;
- "bonus pay gaps" show the mean and median gaps in annual amounts of bonus pay among employees or the proportions of employees who receive bonus pay in a given year;
- "overtime pay gaps" show the median gaps in overtime pay during the reporting year (Government of Canada 2022e, Tables 6A, 6B, 6C, 8A, 8B, 8C).

Using the "median" measurement of a hourly wage gap, each of the individual Indigenous employees made a median hourly wage of of $0.98 compared with one dollar earned by each of the median non-Indigenous employees. Four out of every ten employers (41.9 percent) paid the median Indigenous employees $0.99 or less for the one dollar paid to each of the median non-Indigenous employees. In other words, a significant proportion of Indigenous employees receive less than the median hourly wage of non-Indigenous employees (Government of Canada 2022e).

As for bonus pay gaps for median employers, the bonus pay of the median Indigenous employee was $0.93 for every one dollar paid to a non-Indigenous employee. Approximately, four out of every ten employers (44.2 percent) have no applicable bonus pay gap between Indigenous and non-Indigenous employees.

As for overtime pay gaps, the median employers paid overtime pay of $0.97 to each of the median Indigenous employees for every one dollar paid to the median non-Indigenous employee. Forty percent of employers have no applicable pay gap between Indigenous and non-Indigenous employees.

Once again, using the "median" measurement of hourly wage gap, each of the individual racialized employees made a median hourly wage of $0.95 compared with one dollar earned by each of the median non-racialized employees. Six out of ten employers (58.5) paid between $0.76 and $0.99 to racialized employees for one dollar paid to non-racialized employees. In other words, a significant proportion of racialized employees receive less than the median hourly wage of non-racialized employees.

As for bonus pay gaps for median employers, the bonus pay of the median racialized employee was $0.92 for every one dollar paid to a non-racialized employee. In total, 42.7 percent of employers paid each of their racialized employees a bonus of ninety-nine dollar or less, and 27 percent of employers had no pay gap between their racialized and non-racialized employees.

As for overtime pay gaps, the median employers paid overtime pay of $1.04 to each of the median racialized employees for every one dollar paid to a median non-racialized employee. In total, 22.5 percent of employers have no applicable pay gap between their racialized and non-racialized employees.

The overall picture of pay gaps is that, with the exception of higher overtime pay for racialized employees, most Indigenous and racialized employees receive lower pay for hourly wages, bonus pay, and overtime pay when compared with non-Indigenous and non-racialized employees.

A new report from the Brookfield Institute for Innovation and Entrepreneurship at Toronto Metropolitan University stressed that the employment and pay inequities for racialized people and immigrants had worsened between 2001 and 2016. Being racialized put people in a disadvantaged position in terms of wage disparities during the same period. Racialized people in this sector made an average of $3.89 per hour less than non-racialized people. Racialized immigrant women without a university degree who work in the same sector received $18.50 per hour less than White non-immigrant men with a university degree. This amounts to a difference of thirty-eight thousand dollars in annual income. The study shows that, in 2001, there was no pay gap between immigrant and non-immigrant tech workers; however, by 2016, a gap of $5.70 per hour had emerged (Canadian Press 2022).

REPORTED EMPLOYMENT DISCRIMINATION

Indigenous Peoples

According to Statistics Canada, there were more Indigenous people reporting discrimination in 2019 than in 2014: 44 percent of First Nations people, 29 percent of Inuit, and 24 percent of Metis have experienced discrimination (Cotter 2022). Deloitte interviewed a sample of Indigenous youth regarding their experience in schools and work. Dean Janvier, the director for Indigenous Prairies/British Columbia and

Government, Public Services, and Assurance Services at Deloitte, commented on how self-aware Indigenous youths are about racism and discrimination, not only of themselves but also of others who are less fortunate than they are. They talked about how other people do not believe in their competence, that they have to constantly prove themselves to others, that Indigenous people have problems even getting employment experience, and that they are way behind others in competing for jobs due to their lack of connections and networks (Douglas 2023b).

Benefits Canada did a survey of five hundred Indigenous Peoples who work in the information technology sector, and 59 percent of them said that they have experienced discrimination in their current organizations; 56 percent of them have hidden their Indigenous identity while working at their companies; 34 percent of them said they also have hidden their Indigeneity in their social media profiles; 62 percent of them have experienced bias when applying for a job; and 62 percent of them felt that they are unlikely to be promoted compared to other employees. Almost all of Indigenous employees surveyed (96 percent) believed that there are systemic biases against them, and two-thirds of them said that such biases are impacting them to a large or moderate extent. Once again, almost all of them (97 percent) said that they are not represented in the C-suite in the information technology sector, which includes 37 percent who said that it is to a large extent and 37 percent who said it is to a moderate extent (*Benefits Canada* 2024b).

Racialized People

Back in 2002, about one in four racialized employees reported racial harassment or discrimination in the workplace in Canada (Hiranandani 2012). Statistics Canada (2003) noted that 56 percent of its Ethnic Diversity Survey participants noted that discrimination or unfair treatment was mostly encountered in the workplace, especially at the job application and promotion stages.

Fast forward to 2020, and 45.6 percent of racialized people reported experiences of discrimination at work or when applying for a job or a promotion, five years before the COVID-19 pandemic, whereas 43.4 percent of non-racialized people reported discrimination during that time frame (Statistics Canada 2022a). According to the 2019 General Social Survey on Canadians' safety, 46 percent of Black people (over fifteen years of age) had experienced discrimination in the past five years, compared with 16 percent of non-Indigenous Peoples and non-racialized people. More Canadian-born Black people (65 percent) felt that they had been discriminated against than Black immigrants (36 percent) (Cotter 2022). The Conference Board of Canada (2023), in partnership with the Future Skills Centre, conducted a survey of over nine thousand working Canadians and found that Black Canadians, especially Black women, were more likely to report discrimination at work compared with White Canadians—close to 60 percent of Black men and just above 60 percent of Black women felt that they had been discriminated against in the workplace, whereas about 20 percent of White men and close to 30 percent of White women reported discrimination.

In a survey done by KPMG in 2022, 77 percent of unemployed Black Canadians found that getting jobs for them had not improved in the past year and a half, and approximately 40 percent of Black Canadians said that their chance of career advancement had not changed much over the same time frame (Aziz 2022). KPMG released a report in 2024 that stated that eight in ten Black Canadians (81 percent) said that they still faced discrimination in one form or another at work. This is a 10 percent increase in the statistics from the year before. However, more than half of the Black people surveyed reported that they faced less racism than in previous years, but 15 percent reported that they faced the same amount, and 13 percent reported that they faced more. In total, 78 percent felt that they had to work harder than non-Black people to be valued in the same way, with some variations among different occupational groups. Close to 80 percent of Blacks said that Black and other racialized people were among the first to lose their jobs the year before (Rana 2024).

In 2022, the Registered Nurses' Association of Ontario (2022) released a task force report on systemic racism experienced by Black nurses in the nursing profession. One of the research findings showed that 88.3 percent of Black nurses reported that they have experienced racism and/or discrimination, and 60.5 percent of Black nurses reported feeling uncomfortable or very uncomfortable in their academic and workplace settings because of their race, colour, or ethnicity. Furthermore, these Black nurses experienced systemic discrimination and felt that racial micro-aggressions affected their mental health moderately (32.7 percent) or strongly (30.2 percent).

Benefits Canada published the findings of a survey in 2024 conducted by the Coalition of Innovation Leaders against Racism that showed that half of Blacks, Indigenous, and People of Colour (BIPOC), especially those between the ages of thirty and forty-four years old in urban settings in Canada, found that they were uncomfortable or unwelcome in the workplace (*Benefits Canada* 2024a). This survey polled five hundred BIPOC employees and noted that 26 percent of them felt they were harshly judged, whereas only 9 percent of White managers felt that they were harshly judged. In total, 20 percent of BIPOC employees felt that their racial identity held back their career growth, whereas 10 percent of White managers had the same perception. As for professional development and/or special assignments, 23 percent of BIPOC employees felt that they were excluded due to their race, whereas only 10 percent of White managers had the same perception. Furthermore, 17 percent of BIPOC employees found it difficult to find mentors and/or sponsors to advance their careers compared to their non-racialized counterparts, and they were 10 percent more inclined to leave their company due to racial discrimination. In addition, 16 percent of BIPOC employees had encountered racial slurs at work, whereas only 12 percent of White managers had experienced similar treatment (*Benefits Canada* 2024a).

In the public sector, Correctional Service Canada reported that 55 percent of its racialized employees felt free to speak about racism in the workplace without worrying about reprisal, whereas 67 percent of non-racialized employees felt that way. For Black employees, the percentage dropped to 44 percent. The six federal government departments and agencies that were under audit by the Auditor General of Canada in the period from 2018 to 2020—Canada Border Services Agency, Correctional Service Canada, Department of Justice Canada, Public Prosecution Service of Canada, Public Safety Canada, and the RCMP—revealed that their racialized employees had reported discrimination at least 30 percent more often than non-racialized employees (Auditor General of Canada 2023).

The Re-Seasoning Coalition, a non-profit initiative aimed at facilitating higher representation of Black Canadians in the restaurant industry, in partnership with Technomic, a consulting firm specializing in food service industry research, completed a survey and noted that 69 percent of Black employees had experienced or witnessed racial prejudice, while the national average was 51 percent. Another finding from the same source was that 50 percent of Black employees have agreed that Black employees are more likely to experience or witness racial discrimination at work compared to 29 percent of employees of other races (*Baker Journal* 2022).

The 2019 General Social Survey on Canadian's Safety showed that 29 percent of Chinese, aged fifteen years and older, experienced discrimination or unfair treatment daily. Of those Chinese who reported discrimination, 27 percent of them said that they have experienced discrimination when at work or when applying for a job or promotion. A significant segment of Chinese who reported discrimination believed that they were discriminated on the basis of race or skin colour (22 percent), in relation to their ethnicity or culture (17 percent), and in relation to their language (11 percent) (Conroy 2023). These survey results were further confirmed by the 2021 Angus Reid Institute's survey of a total of 631 of Chinese, East Asians, or Southeast Asians. In total, 58 percent of respondents had experienced incidents of discrimination in the past twelve months. More than a quarter of them (28 percent) reported that experiences of discrimination occur "all the time" or "often" (Hernandez 2021).

The Environics Institute did a study in 2016 and found out that one-third of Muslims in Canada reported that they have been discriminated against in the preceding five years due to their ethnic origin, language, or religion. These discriminatory incidents were found mainly in the workplace or in public settings (Souissi 2021).

When it comes to workplace racism, they were also cognizant of the stereotyping and prejudice that was going on. They recognized that they might be reaching their job plateau sooner than other employees; they did find the workplace safe, and they realized they had to be on guard about not revealing their Indigenous identity. Meanwhile, racialized employees recognized their social isolation at work, their uneasiness in interactions with other people, and their feelings of being stereotyped, and they perceived more discrimination and felt that there was a lack of fairness in promotion (Siu 2021, 93–100). Racialized people's realization of racism has been consistently confirmed by various empirical studies (Deitch et al. 2003, 1299–1324; Banerjee 2008, 380–401; Irizarry 2012).

Catalyst conducted a survey with five thousand racialized and ethnic women, men, transgender, and non-binary employees in Canada, Australia, New Zealand, South Africa, the United Kingdom, and the United States. In Canada, 54 percent of those surveyed had experienced racism in their career, and 37 percent of them reported that they had experienced racism in their current jobs. In the Canadian context, racism included being passed over for a promotion, excluded from promotion opportunities, and wage gaps. Variations in experiences in racism are found among racialized women with different ethnicities, and intersectionality (race, gender, and class) played a distinct role in experiences as well (Reale-Chin 2023).

These findings were confirmed by the Black Canadian National Survey of York University. It showed that many Blacks (75 percent) and other racialized people (79 percent) viewed racism as a serious problem in the workplace, but only 12 percent of White people thought it was very serious. In hiring, promotion, and wages, 47 percent of Black people believed that they had been treated unfairly, while 24 percent of Asian/Southeast Asian people and 23 percent of Indigenous people reported similar unfairness. Among White people, only 15 percent thought so (Wilson 2023).

As shown above, there are numerous studies on the extent to which Indigenous peoples and racialized people experienced racism, some of which are outside the workplace, and some are in the workplace. This should not be a surprise to many people as Chapter 3 has illustrated with data and evidence that racism permeates almost all aspects of Canada and that Indigenous Peoples and racialized people experience or observe such racism every day.

CONCLUSION

In documenting the extent of racism in employment, we relied mainly on Statistics Canada's data and other studies on employment and unemployment. These data provide a big picture, and it shows that Indigenous peoples have higher unemployment rates than non-Indigenous peoples. Racialized people also have higher unemployment rates than non-racialized people, including both youth and adults. The intersectionality of race, age, and gender does play a role in these disparities.

Another level of analysis with respect to racism in employment concerns the total workforce and number of occupational groups in organizations. Here, most of our data concerning Indigenous and racialized people are from federally regulated organizations (using 2021 data and 2016 Census' labour market availability data). The bias here is that these organizations have a mandate to increase the representation of employment equity designated groups, and they include Indigenous and racialized people. The current situation is that, while Indigenous peoples are under-represented, racialized people are over-represented in most occupational groups. Using a much cruder method of determining the extent of "representation" of racialized people using their "distribution" data from various industrial sectors, Block and Gallabuzi (2011) concluded that racialized men and women are largely a "mixed bag" of over-representation and under-representation when compared with non-racialized men and women (using 2006 labour force data). Since the data sets used in these studies are different, they are not comparable. Further, they did not use representation data, and, therefore, their conclusions are likely to be questionable.

Another level of analysis of racism in employment concerns employment income. The data presented by the Canadian Centre for Policy Alternatives shows the impact of intersectionality of race and gender (using the 2016 Census data). Clearly, racial and gender disparities are apparent in the employment incomes of racialized men and women and their counterparts among non-racialized people. In terms of their average household employment incomes, Indigenous and racialized people earn less than non-Indigenous and non-racialized people. This pattern of disparities is also found among immigrants.

Yet another level of analysis concerns the salary ranges of full-time employees in federally regulated organizations (using 2021 data). Indigenous peoples are more clustered at the lower levels of salary ranges when compared with their non-Indigenous counterparts. A similarly skewed pattern is found for racialized people and non-racialized people.

Another level of analysis concerns the pay gaps of Indigenous peoples and racialized people in federally regulated organizations (using 2021 data). With the exception of higher overtime pay for racialized employees, most Indigenous and racialized employees receive lower pay in hourly wages, bonus pay, and overtime pay when compared with non-Indigenous and non-racialized employees.

With the exception of the over-representation of racialized employees in occupational groups in federally regulated organizations, all these measurements of employment disparities between Indigenous peoples and racialized people, on the one hand, and their counterparts, on the other hand, show that racism in the workplace is apparent. And, based on reports of racial discrimination collected from Indigenous peoples and racialized people, it is also apparent that they are aware of, and have experience with, racial discrimination in the workplace. Exactly what factors give rise to such extensive racism in the workplace, both subjective (perception) and objective (empirical), will be the topics of the next few chapters.

CHAPTER 5

Racism in the Air

INTRODUCTION

This chapter discusses the subtle forms of racism that are usually ingrained in individual thoughts (stereotypes) and emotions (prejudice). Like it or not, these thoughts and emotions often drive their behaviours. Negative stereotypes of, and feelings about, Indigenous peoples and racialized people constitute racism, and they are hidden, intangible, and discreet with no racist signs or concrete observable attributes until they manifest in human actions (like words, gestures, and any kind of actions). Here, we are talking about racism as something that is subtle, nebulous, invisible, and unprovable in the workplace, which defies logic and evidence. Some Indigenous peoples and racialized people describe this "something" as "everyday racism." It is like air that one cannot see, touch, hear, smell, taste, point at, or show to other persons, but it is there.

In this chapter, we will examine the perceptions and prejudice that centre on Indigenous peoples and racialized people. These cognitive and emotional attributes could be categorized under different terms (such as "dirty" and "untrustworthy"), and they are mostly hidden just below the surface of human interactions like our thoughts and feelings. Some of them may exhibit as racist acts in various shapes and forms in the workplace. Those that are more blatant or observable may be recognized more easily as spoken words or gestures of disrespect, micro-aggression, exclusion, belittlement, harassment, threats, bullying, violence, and discrimination. These negative stereotypes and prejudice could permeate throughout the work environment. In this chapter, we will examine only those manifested as daily human interactions in words and conduct and leave those that permeate, and are systemically embedded, in human resources policies, programs, practices, and cultures in the next few chapters.

STEREOTYPING

What Is Stereotyping?

In this book on racism in the workplace, stereotyping is defined as an act that simplifies the image of a person who, more often than not, does not correspond appropriately to the person it describes. It is often used to gloss over the differences among individuals and lump them into an oversimplified image of a group or groups of people.

Stereotyping may be a common human trait as we are not able to process too much information or too complicated a phenomenon. As a result, we categorize and rank people just as we categorize and rank things when they become too much (or to many) for us to handle in our brains. We ignore the variety of features of each individual and opt for common features. Worst still, we often defer to others to categorize and rank them for us as we are just too busy to give more thought to any one item in a single day. Unfortunately, some of the images that we have learned from other people or from the media are tainted with biases that tell more about the person(s) who says them or the media that broadcasts them. Once we have adopted those images, we repeat them in our brain, and, gradually, they constitute imprints that are hard to erase. When these images of people are consolidated in our thinking, they become our reference points whenever we must make a judgment on these groups of people in a hurry; hence, stereotypes become our yardstick of describing, measuring, and ranking people, correctly or incorrectly.

Where Do Stereotypes Come From?

Stereotypes of Indigenous peoples and racialized people in the workplace largely come from public opinions that we have learned from all sorts of media (such as social and printed media, advertisements, marketing messages, television shows, films, and broadcasting); the school system, including teachers, curricula, and learning materials;

family upbringing, including relatives, siblings, friends, and acquaintances; and our own interactions with these individuals. Scholars have long debated about which sources are more influential than others in impacting on stereotyping, but the verdict is not yet been determined. Let us assume then that stereotypes are multi-pollinated in their formation. For the purposes of this book, the ranking of influential power of these sources may not be of critical importance. These sources interplay with each other as people learn from multiple media channels and from each other. Individuals also formulate their thoughts as they interact with Indigenous peoples and racialized people and come to their own conclusions. After a while, these images are refined and transformed into stereotypes that are part of the collective consciousness, which we have in the back of our minds all the time.

Numerous research studies, media stories, and public opinions show that Indigenous peoples have been portrayed as incapable, unworthy, and rebellious; dishonest; unreliable; unclean; forgetful; dangerous and violent; risky; intoxicated; drunk; and inclined to commit offences. They are viewed as alcoholics, drug seekers, bad patients, and second-class citizens. These portraits of Indigenous peoples are all negative, and they elicit an image of them as undesirable persons who should not be hired, included in business deals, or even associated with.

Research studies, media stories, and public opinions show that racialized people (such as Black and Middle Eastern people) are portrayed as being related to gangs, thugs, violence, muggings, shootings, and drugs; they are more inclined to commit crimes, less educated, and have other negative stereotypes. Black people are specifically viewed as lazy, ignorant, and prone to get into difficulties. The image of Black female athletes is someone who is considered unfit to be included on sports magazine covers. Muslim people are viewed as extremists, terrorists, and radicals, and their religion is associated with misogyny, gun violence, and bombings. Asian people in video games are portrayed as smart nerds.

How Do Stereotypes Work?

Indigenous people must work very hard to overcome these negative images in order to survive in this country. Everywhere they go, they encounter barriers erected by people who have these negative images of them. And, similar to Indigenous peoples, racialized people are also burdened by negative images imposed on them. These public images are hidden below the surface and become some people's mental filter whenever they interact with racialized people on a daily basis. These mental filters constitue "unconscious bias," which is a common term used in the public and private sectors these days.

These negative images often become the stereotypes that are fixed in the minds of people, including those of Indigenous peoples and racialized people. The latter internalize them, and it becomes a part of their mental construct, which, in turn, affects their daily thoughts, feelings, and actions. The internalization of negative images for Indigenous peoples and racialized people is a long and cumulative process that begins during their childhood and consolidates during their adulthood. It is constantly reinforced not just by media coverage and public opinions but also by the words, gestures, and conduct of their school mates, participants in social gatherings, neighbours, and ordinary people on the street or in public transit, service providers, front-line workers, government bureaucrats, professionals, administrators, technicians, and manual/trades workers. Manifestations of these stereotypes, blatant or covert and in small or large doses, have various degrees of penetration into the minds of Indigenous peoples and racialized people. They are often described as mild or deep "cuts in a thousand pieces" on a daily basis.

What Are the Stereotypes in the Workplace?

A work environment does not exist in isolation. We bring this collective consciousness to the workplace without knowing exactly how and from where we learned it. The workplace has no firewalls around it when it comes to stereotyping. It borrows the negatives images of Indigenous peoples and racialized people and builds on them, making them more relevant and believable. New stereotypes may also be generated from within the workplace as we are surrounded by colleagues who have their own opinions based their own encounters with executives, managers, and coworkers/peers. We take our cues from them when interacting with individual employees.

In a work environment, the value of employees is contingent on what they can contribute to the organization, how they perform, how productive they are, what quality of work they can provide, how reliable they are, how they focus in getting results, and what reputation they yield for the organization. These are of high priority to the organization.

Indigenous Stereotypes

Negative stereotypes of Indigenous peoples at work are usually centred on these priority issues: that Indigenous employees are not punctual in their attendance at meetings or in their arrival at the workplace, they do not hand in their work on time as required, they do not complete their share of work in a team or on a cross-departmental work project, they are sloppy in their quality of work, they do not produce things quickly or get things done fast enough, they do not yield the results that are desired by their managers, and they do not raise the profile of the organization high enough.

A few of these stereotypes are related to time management. Unlike the Western way of viewing time as a linear progression of time from the past to the future, the Indigenous way of viewing time is non-linear and cyclical. There is flexibility built into time as it can be fluid and adjustable depending on the needs of the people and the community. This Indigenous world-view on time and its non-Indigenous interpretation appears to generate a number of time-related stereotypes that favour the Western value of time in attendance, submission of work, and productivity.

Other stereotypes seem to be related to teamwork and quality of work. As Indigenous peoples are often marginalized at work since they are not consulted or involved in decision making, they become gradually disengaged. As a result, the quality of their work performance declines over time, and so does their passion, sense of belonging, and loyalty. Once again, stereotypes about Indigenous contribution and performance may be an illustration of Indigenous disenfranchisement at work.

Racialized Stereotypes

In the workplace, negative stereotypes of racialized employees also cluster around several priority areas: competency, interpersonal skills, and leadership.

Black stereotypes dwell on their lack of competency and communication skills. Stereotypes of Black people's work emphasize their lack of a good work ethic and their intellectual capabilities (Kochman 1981). Outside of the workplace, the public has a stereotypical view of Black people as athletic and being good at sports (such as basketball).

It appears that this image of Black people carries over to the workplace as the flip side of this "sports" image is the idea that they may be strong physically but that they are weak intellectually and do not work hard enough. Hence, their competence is called into question. This is a common stereotype in the workplace, and it influences significantly their undesirability as professionals and technicians.

However, in workplaces where manual trade skills (such as construction) are required, the competence of Black people becomes an issue of work quality (as in measurement, soldering, or carpentry jointing). Stereotypes related to the Black people's quality of work are centred on sloppiness, hastiness, and the improper mixing of materials). These are just stereotypes, not factual evidence, which people communicate behind the backs of Black people, and they are difficult to prove.

Black people are also stereotyped as aggressive, confrontational, pushy, abrasive, and direct in their communication style (Mayovich 1972; Dixon and Rosenbaum 2004; Wingfield 2015). Not being tactful and diplomatic and overly blunt are considered to be qualities that are unfit for a work environment where having good interpersonal skills is important for workplace culture, morale, employee engagement, well-being, teamwork, liaison, management, and leadership. These negative stereotypes make it difficult for Black employees in employee retention, promotion to leadership positions, or any developmental opportunities. They also discourage co-workers from associating with Black people and raise alarm bells for putting them in supervisory or managerial positions or even working with them on a team. Having problematic communication style also raises the potential for doors to be shut in recruitment and hiring as having a new hire who has problems getting along with co-workers does not help to build a good work team or work environment.

Asian stereotypes tend to centre on their lack of people skills and management skills. Stereotypes of Asian people are that they are cold and non-dominant. They are also viewed as custodial, authoritarian, untrustworthy, inscrutable, and keeping to themselves. They are not good at taking charge (Berdahl and Min 2012; Askarinam 2016).

Asian people also have some positive stereotypes: they are competent in their technical and professional fields ("good in math" or "good in computers"), and they are meek, modest, hardworking, obedient, unassertive, cooperative, and humble (Kulik and Bainbridge 2006; P. Li 2008; Wong, Horn, and Chen 2013). These stereotypes appear to "ghettoize" Asian people in technical and professional occupations, without much chance to move into managerial positions. This has been the complaint of Asian workers for some time as promotions into these positions have been rare. Coinciding with the other stereotypes in the workplace mentioned above concerning a lack of management skills, it appears that these stereotypical images of Asian people may play a role in limiting their opportunities to move up the corporate ladder.

How Does Stereotyping Impact on Indigenous/Racialized Peoples?

Working relationships would be more harmonious if stereotyping did not occur in the workplace, but it does. How do employees know that stereotypes are alive and well in the workplace? One simply has to talk among Indigenous/racialized employees or among non-Indigenous/racialized employees; engage in employee resource groups or employee affinity groups, observing co-workers' gestures; listen to the words and tones used by management staff or non-management colleagues; participate in informal social gatherings after work hours or company retreats; and/or find out through the employee performance evaluation process from managers.

Stereotyping may enhance the building of a psychological filter when Indigenous/racialized peoples are recruited, promoted, trained/developed, or terminated. A psychological filter acts as a sorting mechanism in which the negative images of Indigenous/racialized peoples are utilized to make decisions on their hiring, selection, promotion, training, development, and other human resources management functions. Depending on how prevalent and deep-seated these Indigenous or racialized stereotypes are in the workplace, they might even act as a major obstacle in utilizing talents properly or strategically as these psychological filters may quickly exclude Indigenous/racialized people in hiring, promotion, training, or development. When Indigenous and racialized employees perceive stereotyping by management and experience persistent rejections in promotion opportunities, it deters them from applying for other promotions or blue-ribbon committee assignments and, worse still, may encourage them to leave the company.

Stereotypes marginalize Indigenous/racialized people and tend to place them in positions with less decision-making power. When we examine the stereotypical adjectives used to describe these workers, it is clear that most of them not only are negative but also exclude them from management and leadership positions. Even in working relationships, stereotypes of Black and Asian people tend to alienate them from the rest of the workforce. When we start labelling Asian people as being too "cold" or Black people as being too "abrasive," there is a greater chance that employees will start to stay away from them and not trust them. Stereotypes are not conducive to building cohesiveness and unity among employees, and they make the workplace divisive. This divisiveness often shuts off Asian and Black people from information from the non-racialized networks as well as from the Asian and Black networks. Overall, this fragments the organization further based on the race line.

In addition, negative stereotypes prescribe social boundaries for Indigenous/racialized people to behave. Stereotypes are sometimes called "prescriptive stereotypes." If Indigenous/racialized people deviate from these boundaries, they could be ostracized. Why? Stereotypes are expectations of people who have more power, status, and privilege than Indigenous/racialized people. These expectations are almost like a list of required conduct for marginalized groups and how they should conduct themselves at work. If Asian stereotypes are humble, cooperative, or unassertive, it would be a deviation if Asian workers become self-promoting, uncollaborative, and assertive. Those in authority positions would find the Asian person's conduct unacceptable, and they are likely to remind them to behave as the stereotypes prescribe. Thus, stereotypes are a social control mechanism that keeps Indigenous/racialized people in check—they should not be allowed to shine by performing or behaving well.

In sum, stereotyping is harmful to individual Indigenous and racialized employees and detrimental to the growth of the organization. Stereotypes and stereotyping are usually hidden behind the surface, but they have been reported on occasion. Indigenous peoples and racialized people are keenly aware that they exist, and they have complained about them. Although it is hard to pinpoint and prove, the impacts of stereotypes and stereotyping are usually manifested in their individual sense of uncertainty, disengagement, and a lack of belonging and a safe space; the general "segregation" of Indigenous and racialized people in non-management and non-leadership positions and a tendency to cluster these workers in low-level clerical and manual occupations; the lack of their integration in informal social networks within the workforce in the organization; the lack of, or slowness in, their promotional and developmental participation; the lack of their invitation to blue-ribbon or other higher profile assignments or committees; and the lack of their connection to the inner circle of leadership (Siu 2021).

How Do Indigenous and Racialized Employees React to These Stereotypes?

Negative stereotypes for Indigenous peoples and racialized people undermine their self-confidence and self-esteem, lower their performance and quality of work, and reduce their productivity and loyalty to their employers. There are Indigenous and racialized employees who possess these negative images and constantly wonder whether the words and actions of other people are reflections of their stereotypical views. The problem for them is that they are not 100 percent sure that the people surrounding them in the workplace are actually stereotyping them. Those suspicions and doubts swirl around in their heads in perpetual circles, and they are not able to stop them mainly because there is simply no solid proof or evidence that the deeds of others have sprung from these stereotypes. This psychological state creates a lot of stress and unnecessary tension for Indigenous peoples and racialized people inside and outside the workplace. On a daily, weekly, monthly, and yearly basis, they are constantly guessing, and the puzzle usually remains unresolvable. They are also in perpetual self-doubt about their work and are sensitive to whatever their bosses or colleagues say or do. They decipher and interpret their words and behaviours carefully and are constantly unsure of their actual meanings. This can become uncomfortable and stressful. The stress begins to damage their bodies and minds, just like inhaling polluted air and contaminated substances on a long-term basis.

There are some Indigenous/racialized people who fight against stereotyping. And the suspicion of being stereotyped creates stress and tension among employees and between themselves and the non-Indigenous/racialized employees around them. In the workplace, negative stereotyping puts everyone on guard as the workplace may gradually evolve into a battleground between Indigenous/racialized employees and non-Indigenous/racialized employees. It generates a distrustful relationship between them, and polarization may develop. There are groups of Indigenous peoples and racialized people who have rejected these stereotypes and are working hard to dispel them as misconceptions, falsehoods, lies, harmful labels, and racist biases. They combat them daily through counter-arguments and verbal hit-backs, and it can often deteriorate into physical fights, all of which are stressful and exhausting on both sides. Often, the issues on race remain unresolved on an individual basis, but they raise the temperature at the community level.

PREJUDICE

Stereotypes denote perception, and prejudice deals with emotions usually generated by perception. Therefore, these two features are closely related, and both, in turn, impact on the behaviours of people (Haddock, Zanna, and Esses 1994; Dovidio et al. 1996).

Shifting Prejudice against Indigenous Peoples

There are still non-Indigenous peoples who are prejudiced against Indigenous peoples because they are viewed as having been born inferior and their culture is not desirable. This old-fashioned view persists in certain pockets of the Canadian population (Brock and Morrison 2016). But, in this contemporary period, some non-Indigenous Canadians have made adjustments to their attitudes, but they are still mostly ambiguous toward Indigenous peoples. On the one hand, they see Indigenous history and culture as an integral part of Canada, and they are proud of them. On the other hand, they are dubious about their contribution as a nation in building Canada because they have received financial support from the federal government. They feel that Indigenous peoples are getting too many (read: unwarranted) benefits and still making a lot of illegitimate demands on the government (Durrheim and Dixon 2004). Negative feelings (such as anxiety, distrust, and anger) have grown between Indigenous peoples and non-Indigenous people (Werhun and Penner 2010). Citing from the survey from the Environics Institute for Survey Research (2016), *Aboriginal Peoples Television Network National News* (2016) reported that the attitudes of non-Indigenous Canadians seem to have improved somewhat in the mid-2010s: one-quarter of those surveyed showed appreciation for Indigenous peoples, and only one in ten had a less favourable view.

The Truth and Reconciliation Commission of Canada, which was launched during the regime of Prime Minister Stephen Harper and the commitment of the federal government to working with Indigenous organizations in implementing the recommendations in the commission's *Final Report* in 2019; the National Inquiry into Missing and Murdered Indigenous Women and Girls during the regime of Prime Minister Justin Trudeau; the media coverage of the discovery of dead bodies of children from Indian residential schools; and the organized efforts of Indigenous peoples in rallying community supports to look into these matters appears to have shifted public opinion on the plight of Indigenous peoples and their support in listening to Indigenous voices.

All of these initiatives have not automatically turned public attitudes to Indigenous communities completely away from racial prejudice, but they have enabled Indigenous peoples to amplify their concerns more openly and lessen or dilute the public negativity that has persisted for so many decades/centuries in the past.

Shifting Prejudice against Racialized People and Immigrants

Meanwhile, with respect to racialized people, Canadian attitudes toward people with European backgrounds are more favourable than they are toward racialized people (Angus Reid Institute 1991). However, a *CBC News* (2014) broadcast suggested that Canadian attitudes toward different ethnic groups (which include racialized people) seemed to have improved somewhat twenty years later. Even as more and more immigrants were coming to Canada during the 2010s (and most were racialized people), eight in ten Canadians believe that they are beneficial to the Canadian economy, according to the survey done in 2016 by the Environics Institute for Survey Research (2016), in partnership with the Canadian Race Relations Foundation. While the rest of the Western world appears to be going through a wave of xenophobia, Canadians have seemed to stand firm in their support for immigration. The small minority of Canadians in the survey who were concerned about the level of immigrants and refugees coming to Canada are usually concerned about the lack of Canadian capacity to support them, their potential for security threats, and their cultural misalignment with locally born Canadians (for example, immigrants not adopting "Canadian values") (Grant 2016, A10).

These concerns are still relatively rare in the early part of 2020s; however, as the housing affordability crisis runs deeper across Canada, especially in urban centres like Toronto and Vancouver, there is a growing concern that, perhaps, the immigration level was set too high in 2023 (reaching a government target of five hundred thousand per year), which resulted in "too many" people competing for housing and ended up with more homelessness (sleeping on the streets) or encampments (with temporary tents for shelters). Related to this housing affordability issue was the issue of which type of immigrants were arriving in Canada. Some Canadians commented that temporary workers and international students (who study in college diploma or certificate programs) may not be providing the high level of skills (when they graduate) that Canada wants to have. Some feel that Canada must have adequate infrastructure first before the federal government brings in immigrants.

At the time this book was written, public sentiments seemed to be turning sharply against immigrants and refugees coming to Canada. An Environic Institute for Survey Research's poll showed that most Canadians now believe that there are too many immigrants—57 percent of respondents reported that immigrants have failed to adopt Canadian values, and 35 percent reported that immigration is leading to more crime. With this backlash, the federal government has reduced the intake of immigrants by 20 percent, which represents a policy reversal. As a result, the Canadian population is expected to decline in the next two years (Hune-Brown 2025). This immigration policy reversal has not seemed to lessen the anxiety and antagonism toward immigrants. Now, for the first time in a quarter of a century, the Environic Institute for Survey Research's opinion poll in September 2024 shows that the majority of Canadians (58 percent) in a survey sample of 2,016 persons over the age of eighteen reported that they felt that there was "too much immigration." This percentage reflects a fourteen-percentage point increase since 2023, building on a seventeen-percentage point increase over the previous year of 2022–23. This "58 percent" is the highest proportion of Canadians who say that there has been too much immigration since 1998 (Neuman 2024).

The status of racialized people in Canada is related to international politics—when there are political conflicts between Canada and other countries, public sentiments shift negatively for those "other countries."

This has happened consistently in the past, as witnessed in the proliferation of degrading terms for Japanese (such as "Japs") and the rounding up of Japanese Canadians and sending them to internment camps during the Second World War when the relations between Japan and its Western allies (Canada included) deteriorated (Robinson 2017; Trafford 2018).

Hostility also grew between China and Canada when Meng Wanzhou, the chief financial officer of Huawei Technologies (a multinational technology corporation), was detained in 2018 and subsequently placed under house arrest until the charges against her were dismissed in 2022. During this period, prejudice against Chinese Canadians increased, and physical harassment and assaults further escalated as the COVID-19 pandemic persisted from 2020 to 2023. The Anti-Chinese Canadian racism appears to be a continuation of the nineteenth century's Canadian institutional racism against Asian people, in general, and the Chinese, in particular. Chinese Canadians were viewed as the bearers of the contagious COVID-19 virus. They were assaulted and felt threatened and intimidated (Evans and Li 2019; Angus Reid Institute and University of Alberta 2020; Chakraborty 2022).

Similarly, the Israel-Hamas War, which started in October 2023, led to the confrontation between Jewish Canadians and Palestinian Canadians, and the prejudice against both of these groups accelerated as the Canadian public began to take sides. Sentiments of anti-Semitism and Islamophobia became rampant. Both Muslims and Jews complained about incidents of verbal abuse, vandalism, hate messages, intimidation threats, and so on across Canada. Genocide messages against Jews were noted in rallies, and anti-Muslim slogans, such as "Kill All Muslims," were written on apartment hallways. The Toronto Police Service laid charges against some people who were arrested on the basis of hate crimes (related to the vandalism of the Indigo store in downtown Toronto) (Aziz 2023; Zimonjic 2023).

Prejudice in the Workplace

While blatant prejudice has been a regular feature in Canadian politics, to the demise of Indigenous peoples and racialized people, prejudice in the workplace does not manifest in such dramatic or violent manner. While workplace violence occasionally occurs, prejudice against Indigenous peoples and racialized people in the workplace is usually covert and discrete, just as the stereotypes about them lie under the veneer of collegial politeness.

Negative stereotypes of Indigenous peoples include the idea that they do not take seriously the Western values of work priorities, teamwork, collaboration, time management, punctuality, reliability, and trustworthiness, but the prejudice against them from these stereotypes may not be visible. In fact, occasionally, non-Indigenous employees in the workplace have been prepared to examine their biases in these stereotypes if indeed they are present, especially if policies on human rights, diversity, equity, and inclusiveness are official and prominently in place. Through my own focus groups and interviews when doing consulting work, Indigenous employees revealed that they have experienced unfair treatment at work through social isolation, ostracism, occupational "segregation," occupational immobility, the lack of managerial or collegial support, and, in general, lacking a sense of belonging to the organization in which they work.

Similarly, negative stereotypes of Black employees as abrasive/aggressive communicators and poor performers and those of Asian employees as not having many managerial or leadership skills and interpersonal skills may be the driving forces behind the prejudice against them, but this connection between stereotyping and prejudice is often built into the mindsets of people and is not openly demonstrable. In Canadian workplaces, collegial politeness remains a veneer masking individual racial prejudice. Through my own focus groups and interviews in organizations, racialized employees revealed their experiences of unfair treatment, just like the Indigenous counterparts. The major complaints from Black and Asian people were related to their lack of promotions and leadership developmental opportunities, their lack of supports from management and co-workers, and their lack of access to managerial development and the inner circle of corporate decision makers. These experiences confirmed for them that some forms of prejudice do exist in the workplace, although prejudice is not visible or even detectable, especially in office settings, unless it is exhibited in such behaviour.

Prejudice and Social Distancing

Due to the existence of negative stereotyping of Indigenous and racialized employees, White employees may develop social distancing as a way to avoid interacting with them. This is one way to develop an "in group" (Whites) and an "out group" (racialized people) in the workplace. The formation of "in groups" and "out groups" is divisive in an organization. Overtime, such distancing may create a milieu in which employees do not have a chance to get to know each other, which thus encourages a distrust between them. In the work environment, people tend to meet and talk in a formalized way as part of the normative workplace etiquette. In the context of workplace prejudice, unless they make an extra effort, employees would never develop more human and friendly interactions. In other words, a deeper level of humanity in working together is actually missing. On a daily basis, to interact deeper with other employees in a work environment is usually through informal gatherings like coffee breaks, lunch time, after work drinks, or doing things together (like shopping or going to watch movies) in non-work hours. Racialized employees do gather with each other informally, at work or outside work, but they seldom do so with the White people. This pattern of social gathering is also found among White employees who tend to mingle with other people of the same race.

Due to the relative absence of Indigenous employees in many workplaces (except in some trades or manual jobs), their informal social networks at work are rather limited. White employees and Indigenous/racialized employees are seldom intertwined in informal social get-togethers. This network pattern deepens the divide between them and makes it even more difficult for them to understand each other and allows prior stereotypical images and prejudice against Indigenous and racialized people to be diluted or dissipated. Over time, as expected, racial prejudice deepens and solidifies. The cleavage on racial lines among employees can become more entrenched unless their work leaders determine to change the workplace culture from one of stereotypes and prejudice to one of diversity and inclusiveness. Formal communication and collaboration for work purposes may also help to foster some degree of inclusion, but informal gatherings and interactions among employees that cross racial lines may be more effective in reaching a deeper humanity level at work and in reducing a culture of prejudice in the workplace.

To minimize the spread of social isolation and social distancing among Indigenous and racialized employees and other employees, the corporate culture has to change from the current culture to one of teamwork, collaboration, communication, learning, and networking.

In other words, the corporate culture must be inclusive and free of racial barriers. According to Adia Harvey Wingfield's (2023) research work, the new corporate culture that needs to be created is one of collaboration and an openness to a discussion on race at work. These two cultural features must be driven by the work leaders and a frank discussion on racial matters and working cooperatively to break down the racial barriers and silo working habits. These features would encourage dialogue, two-way communication, and an idea exchange and break down the isolation, ghettoization, and marginalization of employees, irrespective of their race and gender.

To break through this pattern of segregation in social networking at the same occupational level, Indigenous/racialized employees may have their own initiatives, which might include inviting White employees for coffee breaks, luncheons, and occasional drinks after work; the chance of having the invitations accepted by White people is usually low since they will often utilize one excuse or another. Meanwhile, White employees seldom invite Indigenous/racialized employees at the same occupational level for these social occasions. The notable pattern seems to be a White employee's decline of invitation from an Indigenous/racialized employee more frequently than a White employee's invitation of an Indigenous/racialized employee. Such a skewed pattern is reflective of the perceived gradation of racial status and the existence of prejudice in the workplace. Having active allies—non-racialized and non-Indigenous employees—champion, amplify, and sponsor racialized and Indigenous employees would break up the silos between racialized and Indigenous employees and other employees in their social networks and speed up the process of their formal and informal integration in the workplace (*Bloomberg* 2020).

Rationalization and Legitimization of Prejudice

While prejudice is often a discrete and subtle feeling that is well hidden below the surface, there are some prejudices that become overt but are rationalized and, often, glorified to the extent that they seem to be blatantly acceptable to employers. One type of "positive" prejudice is utilizing a business reason to consolidate prejudice and, subsequently, racial discrimination. One example is when some executives and managers are aware of the prevalence of racial prejudice in their workplaces but are not prepared to eradicate it either because they find it difficult to eradicate or because they see the few employees who are prejudiced against Indigenous or racialized employees as competent employees, and they depend on them to get good ratings in their own departments or feel that their customers would not want to be served by Indigenous and/or racialized people. For one or more of these reasons (and there may be others), these executives and managers do not change the status quo; rather, they prefer not to hire Indigenous or racialized persons to "disturb" the racial make-up of their departments. In this case, racial prejudice is rationalized and legitimized in business terms. As one may see, Indigenous and racialized persons may not be hired or promoted simply because they do not fit the business model that the executives or managers have created.

Another type of prejudice that is considered to be "positive" for Indigenous or racialized people is when executives or managers use racial stereotypes of special competancies and skills in professional or technical fields for hiring or promotion purposes. Non-Asian people may see Asian people as nerds who are good at computer work and other technical operations. They are good at numbers such as mathematics and finance. These are the "positive" stereotypes of Asian workers that was germinated in the racist past in Canadian history. In the past, Canada did not provide much chance for Chinese immigrants to earn a living except in working in laundry and restaurant businesses. Even nowadays, due to the fact that some of these people are not able to speak English as fluently as newcomers, they find themselves limited to fields of study where numbers, not English, is the dominant language of communication. This sets the stage for limiting their occupational skills and opportunities. Thus, the positive prejudice of White people in limiting Asian people's working areas to numerical and technical fields has the consequence of "ghettoizing" them to only those occupations, without much chance for them to work in non-technical and non-numerical fields (such as public policy, human resources, or communication fields) or management/leadership areas (such as strategic planning, change management, or public administration). It has been argued that such "positive" prejudice could easily hide the negative emotions that are directed toward Asians and subordinate them without much guilt (Werhun and Penner 2020).

In the final analysis, one may argue that there is no such thing as "positive" prejudice. All prejudices that limit the growth of Indigenous or racialized people in an organization are negative. The business reasons provided are merely masks over the negativism that comes with prejudice.

Prejudice and Workforce Representation

Racial prejudice is a feeling that is usually well hidden behind individual actions in the workplace, especially when prejudice is not politically correct to voice. When racial prejudice solidifies, it becomes a mindset that is intangible, invisible, or unidentifiable since it is a hidden well-guarded emotion. Like air, it has no shape or form, no smell, and no sound. But it is detectable only in behaviourial terms when one sees that Indigenous and racialized people, in various aspects of employment (such as hiring, promotion, training, and development), are excluded during social interactions when micro-aggressions, hurtful remarks, facial expressions, or hand gestures occur. The issue of representation of Indigenous/racialized persons will be discussed in greater detail later in this volume. But a few examples will be provided here to illustrate how racial prejudice, when translated into actions, will result in their discrimination in employment.

In the last century, it used to be quite common in Canada that Indigenous and racialized people were excluded from entrance to professional schools or associations; even after colleges and universities gradually opened their doors, Indigenous and racialized graduates still had problems getting professional, technical, or trade jobs after graduation. They were seldom hired for these positions. As a result, hardly any of them were represented at that level for a long time until the federal government enacted the employment equity legislation in 1986. Now, Indigenous and racialized people are hired more frequently in those positions, and we can see more of them represented in these fields.

But racial prejudice still makes it hard for them to be hired or promoted in management positions. This is witnessed in their under-representation in these positions. In addition, we see that only a few Indigenous or racialized people are appointed to senior executive positions and boards of directors. Hence, we can deduce that racial prejudice in the workplace is still alive and well at those levels (Siu 2021).

Each organization has its own patterns of representation of Indigenous and racialized employees. Racialized employees are under-represented in higher-salaried positions (such as professionals, managers, and executives). They are also very much unrepresented or under-represented on boards of directors. Indigenous employees are under-represented in many more positions with higher salaries than racialized employees in organizations. Similarly, Indigenous peoples are under-represented or even unrepresented on boards of directors (Siu 2021).

Racial prejudice has a lot to do with a lack of representation or under-representation. While the mechanisms of outreaching, screening, selecting, and hiring potential candidates for these positions will be thoroughly examined in the next few chapters, it should be noted here that these mechanisms are biased in many different ways. The gatekeepers of these positions are largely White, and the general mindset at the corporate decision-making level is that of unconscious bias.

"Unconscious biases" are incorrect assumptions, beliefs, and stereotypical views about certain segments of the population. These are usually embedded as mindsets that people are not aware of; as a result, their behaviours are derived from these mindsets unknowingly. These mindsets often designate White people and other racialized groups in a hierarchical manner and results in the preference of people with light skin tones over those with darker skin tones and European faces over African faces. People are also able to distinguish names that are likely to belong to Arab Muslims over those of other nationalities or other places (Project Implicit 2011).

These biases constitute the basis for decision makers at the organizational level in reaching out to communities for recruitment purposes, screening applications and resumes, selecting applicants, and hiring candidates. Because these biases are unconscious, corporate decision makers (managers or executives) are not even aware that they have prejudice in carrying out these human resources functions. As a result, when these decisions are made on a daily basis, the patterns of representation in different positions are skewed in favour of non-Indigenous peoples and non-racialized people. If racial prejudice also permeates the development and implementation of hiring and promotion tools and the design of the human resources management system, it is more than likely that the end result will discriminate Indigenous peoples and racialized people on multiple levels and components. This, in sum, is how racism works.

HOW DO INDIGENOUS/RACIALIZED EMPLOYEES REACT TO ALL THESE STEREOTYPES AND PREJUDICE?

As noted in Chapter 3, racism significantly affects the life chances of Indigenous peoples and racialized people. All their experiences outside the workplace have made them realize that being Indigenous or racialized means a life with hardship, and, compared with non-Indigenous and non-racialized peoples, there are no safe places for them to grow and be actualized as human beings. In fact, they are living in a harmful and dangerous world.

With this reality as the background, it is not surprising that some Indigenous individuals do not want other co-workers, managers, or executives in the workplace to know that they are Indigenous, especially when it is not evident from their physical appearance. This is because being Indigenous is not safe everywhere. I have conducted numerous interviews and focus groups in large corporations in order to find out the work experience of Indigenous employees. It was not a surprise to find out that being exposed as Indigenous is not something that these employees want. Indigenous employees are fully aware that they would face additional difficulties if their identity is made known. Some of the additional difficulties that they might encounter could include negative stereotyping, prejudice, social distancing, labelling as incompetent and unreliable, and limited developmental opportunities and promotion (Joseph 2013). Thus, they declined to check "yes" to the box on Indigenous peoples in their self-identification workforce survey forms related to the employment equity. This might explain why the statistical data on Indigenous employees is low. They hide their Indigenous identity and are constantly vigilant about what they say regarding their family, cultural, and community backgrounds in the workplace. In other words, they feel insecure and do not have a sense of belonging. They also recognize that their career paths are likely to be different from those of White employees since they witness that there is a better chance for White employees to be developed or promoted than they would otherwise have. They might even "self-censor" in applying for positions at a higher level as they are cognizant of the prevailing racial prejudice and discrimination against Indigenous peoples in the workplace (Dwyer 2003).

Based on many years of conducting focus groups and interviews with racialized employees, I have noted that most of them feel that some stereotyping and prejudice exist, but they are not sure of the extent to which it is prevalent. The number of years that the employees have worked in the organization makes some difference in their observations. The longer the employees have worked in the organizations, the more observant they are of what is happening on the race front. They have reported social distancing behaviours; uncomfortable conversations; feelings of isolation and being an outsider; unfairness in job competitions, performance evaluations, and developmental opportunities; a lack of connection with, and supports from, their supervisors or managers; a lack of belonging to the unit/department teams; and dissatisfaction with their jobs. Some of them believed that they had been discriminated against in the past. These reports are quite consistent with studies both in Canada and the United States (Banerjee 2008; Giscomme and Jenner 2009; Irizarry 2012).

Would they do anything to rectify the situation at work? Most said that they would not do anything, largely because they preferred to keep their jobs without making any waves. As expected, they would look for other job opportunities instead of trying to overcome or fight against racial stereotypes and prejudice. As we will examine in the next few chapters, when human resources mechanisms (such as hiring and promotion criteria and processes) are designed in a biased manner and are prone to the subjectivity of management (such as stereotypes and prejudice), it is very difficult for Indigenous and racialized employees to overcome. One of the results is that racial discrimination remains largely under-challenged.

CONCLUSION

Both stereotypes and prejudice are covert phenomena as they are part of our psychology; unless we say or act out the biased perception or negative feelings in public, Indigenous peoples and racialized people, and any other people, would not know. Moreover, individuals would not know that they stereotype or are prejudiced against them most of the time, unless someone points that out. The reality is that Indigenous and racialized employees may suspect that they are being mistreated, harassed, socially distanced, isolated, undermined, ostracized, discriminated, and a whole bunch of actions imposed by others in the workplace that make life at work uncomfortable and make them feel excluded. The difficult part is that it is not easy to prove the existence of racial stereotypes and prejudice (especially when they are subtle); they are like air, which is not visible and can only be felt.

However, there is evidence from what people say or do that demonstrates that stereotypes and prejudice prevail in the workplace. There are remarks and actions that show signs of prejudice and stereotypes. They reflect rationalized prejudice and the lack of Indigenous and racialized employees in different parts of the organization. As we will discuss in the next three chapters, the mechanisms of human resources that aim to recruit, select, hire, evaluate performance, train, develop, promote, and prepare for succession are loaded with human biases, and they result in racial harassment and discrimination. Similarly, corporate culture is also fermented with toxicity, which basically drives racialized and Indigenous employees out of many workplaces.

CHAPTER 6

Racism at the Gate

INTRODUCTION

This chapter discusses workplace racism beginning with what internal human resources mechanisms employers have placed at the entry points of their organizations for recruiting, screening, selecting, and hiring candidates.

The term "human resources mechanisms" covers all human resources functions, including hiring, training, development, promotion, retention, engagement, compensation and benefits, change management, succession management, and many other functions. It is an umbrella term with broad meanings. Some people call these mechanisms "personnel management," "human capital management," or "talent management"—the labels, like fads, last for a few years and then fade away. The key features are bringing in new candidates; onboarding them; managing their contributions; increasing their engagement and productivity; training and developing them; ensuring their well-being, safety, and security; and helping them to attain the organizational goals.

This book maintains that racial biases built into these human resources mechanisms, knowingly or not knowingly, and their net impact is that they, or parts of them, discriminate Indigenous/racialized people in one way or another. These mechanisms are designed and developed often with good intentions and claimed to be universally fair, neutral, and equitable. However, when they are executed with a lot of discretionary power by managers or executives, they can easily disadvantage for Indigenous and racialized people.

Despite the veneered fairness, neutrality, and equity that human resources policies, strategies, programs, tools, and practices carry, this chapter describes how racism is embedded in outreach, recruitment, job postings, job applications, screening and selection processes (such as screening and interview questionnaires, interview panelists, selection criteria, scoring and ranking, and decision-making methods), hiring, and probation arrangements. This chapter amplifies the subtleness of racial biases and how perception (stereotypes and unconscious bias) and prejudices (emotional negativism) of the organizational gatekeepers have made it harder for Indigenous/racialized people to be employed in the first place.

Throughout this chapter, we will take a closer look at the human resources mechanisms that are responsible for recruiting, selecting, and hiring external potential candidates for employment. As these mechanisms are also responsible for doing the same functions for internal candidates, we will deal with them in our discussion. But, first, we must be familiarized with the employment situation of Indigenous and racialized people to understand why an in-depth analysis of the current human resources "gatekeepers"—recruitment and selection—is critical.

The question we must ask is: what human resources mechanisms are at work in a work environment that discriminates Indigenous Peoples and racialized people in Canada?

RECRUITMENT AND OUTREACH

Individuals who are looking for jobs have to find out where the jobs are. They could do this in a number of ways: talk with their friends, acquaintances, or anyone they meet in a social gathering or networking event (that is, word of mouth); they could check job postings or advertisements online, in community centres, employment agencies, job counselling centres, colleges and universities, and social or printed media; and they could reach out to search firms (or headhunters). Similarly, if an organization is looking for qualified candidates, they might talk with their colleagues and people in the same industry (that is, word of mouth); reach out to where they are: professional associations, trade councils, hiring halls, colleges, and universities; consider job postings and advertisements; and retain the services of external search firms.

Word-of-Mouth

The advantage of the word-of-mouth method for recruiting potential candidates for positions is that, from the perspective of the employers, it is not costly at all, but its effectiveness in getting the right candidates depends largely on the social networks of the employers through their executives, managers, and supervisors. From the perspective of Indigenous or racialized persons, it also depends on their own social networks and the extent of their knowledge and connections with those who have positions to fill or who could create positions to fit the candidates. In any case, social networking is critical almost to the point that it is a prerequisite or a precondition for success, and it is also the source of racial bias when this recruitment method is utilized.

It has been demonstrated that the social networks of traditional leaders or management employees are very likely limited to White, able-bodied, and non-Indigenous men (Leighton 2010). In these kinds of networks, trying to find a qualified Indigenous or racialized candidate to fill the vacant positions may be quite difficult. Similarly, it is equally difficult for the social networks of Indigenous or racialized people to be familiar with what is available or what will come up in the job market because these networks are not saturated with people in the know. Leslie Woo, chief executive officer of CivicAction, has reported that 70–85 percent of open positions are filled through social networking; however, Black people's networks are limited (Amardeil 2024). It is not that Black people do not have networks of their own; it is just that their networks are not composed of people who are influential in human resources decision-making in the working world.

Therefore, using a word-of-mouth method as the only means of recruiting Indigenous and racialized people is not a great opportunity to match these qualified candidates with the vacant positions. More importantly, it is a method that perpetuates racism in recruitment as those responsible for hiring decisions are making Indigenous and racialized persons' employment opportunities much more limited and providing more chances for non-Indigenous and non- racialized people to be employed. Historically, this method of recruitment has benefited the more privileged segments of the population, and the these individuals continue to have an edge over the Indigenous and racialized people as far as employment is concerned.

Job Posting/Advertising

Internal job posting and external job advertisements publicize the availability of employment opportunities to everyone who has access to the media. These methods are much more egalitarian than the word-of-mouth method. Depending on the types of jobs that need to be filled, organizations are more selective in placing their postings and advertisements. For transparency and accountability reasons, more organizations opt for placing job advertisements and job postings as it will enhance their corporate reputation.

The effectiveness of job postings and job advertisements depends on many factors. Most relevant to the employment of Indigenous or racialized people is the wording used in outlining the qualifications and experiences required. There is a tendency for postings and advertisements to present the "ideal" qualifications and "ideal" experiences of people for the positions and not simply the basic or minimal requirements. For Indigenous people, a focus on high academic achievements would discourage them from applying for most jobs at the professional level and above simply because, at the working age of employment (twenty-five to sixty-four years of age), Indigenous people's educational attainment is often lower than it is for non-Indigenous people. While the proportion of Indigenous persons with less than high school education is improving, the gap between them and non-Indigenous people remains high (Gordon and White 2014). According to Michael Mendelson (2006), among the fifteen-plus age group, there were still 48 percent of them who had not completed their high school diploma, compared with 31 percent in the total population in 2001. And, in the same year, Indigenous peoples (25 percent) have almost reached parity with the total population (28 percent) in terms of college education attainment. As more people realize that a focus on academic credentials is, in itself, a barrier to people applying for jobs, a few companies are dropping the educational requirement to increase the diverse labour pool. It would certainly open doors for Indigenous people in terms of employment.

The same does not apply to racialized people who tend to have higher educational attainment than the total population (Lyon and Guppy 2019). However, the problem with the job postings and advertisements for racialized people is the common requirement of Canadian work experience. In the past decades, this requirement has been very prevalent. Nowadays, its usage is much more restrained. The reason for the requirement is that, without the experience of working in Canada, employers are concerned that immigrants (most of them racialized people) would find it difficult to perform optimally as they may not know the industrial standards, the cultural norms of customer service, the local municipal regulations, the health-care service procedures, and so on. This "Canadian work experience" requirement has become a hot topic of conversation and discussion as racialized people, who happen to make up the majority of immigrants and newcomers, find themselves in a "Catch-22" situation. They do not have Canadian work experience when they arrive in Canada, but they have problems getting jobs because of this requirement. Without a job, they cannot get Canadian work experience. This situation spirals downwards with no way out. As a result, they are unemployed for a much longer time, and employers have problems hiring qualified candidates, although most immigrants who are qualified to do the jobs are unemployed or under-employed on the sideline. As for the Canadian economy, this job requirement creates a massive labour shortage on a national scale as it acts as a huge barrier in meeting the employers' needs and in fulfilling the goals of the federal government's immigration policy.

In light of the labour shortage (especially in the health-care sector) during and after the COVID-19 pandemic, the Government of Ontario recently announced that new legislation would be introduced to make it illegal to list a requirement for Canadian work experience in job postings so that internationally trained immigrants would not be discriminated against (Dujay 2023). This provincial ban will end the public debates around the need for Canadian work experience as a job requirement, especially in the professional and trade fields, ever since the publication of the government report on the access of foreign trained individuals to professions and trades in Ontario (Cumming, Lee, and Oreopoulos 1989). This report has been on the provincial government's shelf for over thirty years with not many of its recommendations implemented. Meanwhile, the Ontario Human Rights Commission (n.d.a.) is still concerned about the potential covert "requirement" by some employers "under the table," even though job postings are no longer allowed to mention Canadian work experience as a job requirement (Ontario Human Rights Commission, n.d.a.).

The issue of "Canadian work experience" has been picked up as a topic for public discussion in Owen Guo's (2023, B4) article published in the *Globe and Mail.* He is an immigrant from China and formerly worked as a reporter for the *New York Times* in Beijing. His position is that the use of "Canadian work experience" will be illegal once the new Ontario legislation is enacted but that Canadian employers may still use other ways to screen out internationally trained individuals if they wish to discriminate against them with or without the term "Canadian work experience" written as a requirement in their job postings or job advertisements. It remains to be seen whether the current conservative government under Premier Doug Ford provides any positive impacts on stopping the employment discrimination of immigrants under the new legislation.

Search Firms (Headhunters)

Some employers also use external search firms (which are commonly known as headhunters) to recruit qualified candidates. This is especially prevalent for positions in professional, executive, or management fields. However, some search firms are specialized in certain types of occupations such as informational technology, artificial intelligence, finance, and other highly specialized occupation; some are specialized in administrative and clerical fields; some are specialized in recruiting certain segments of the labour force such as retired public or private sector executives, women, Indigenous peoples, persons with disabilities, racialized people, and LGBTQIA+ people; and some specialize in identifying candidates with industry-specific expertise. Search firms develop their expertise based on the trends of the human resources marketEmployers specify what candidates they need, and these search firms will provide the search services.

The usefulness of retaining the services of search firms in finding the right candidates for employers is contingent on several factors. Chief among them is the availability of a qualified pool of Indigenous and racialized people. For candidates in higher salary occupations, search firms usually create databases of candidates based on the firms' own networks, word-of-mouth referrals, speakers or attendees at conferences, webinars, or public events, media (social, electronic, and printed), websites of institutions, associations, and not-for-profit organizations, authors of publications, board directors and governors of the broad public sector, and many other sources.

In lower salary occupations, the services of search firms may not be retained to find Indigenous and racialized people as the latter do not have much difficulty in finding jobs through websites and other employment agencies. However, in high salary occupations, the databases of Indigenous and racialized people from search firms may not be adequate or up to date. This is mainly because they are not in a position to secure jobs that could give them a higher profile (through invitations to speak in public events or name recognition through media coverage). They are usually "under the radar," so to speak.

Do search firms have the resources to go beyond the traditional sources of collecting names and background information of candidates and digging deep to find out a pool of qualified candidates in the communities of Indigenous and racialized people? This will depend on how committed employers are to hiring Indigenous and racialized people and how committed these firms are to providing quality services to their clients. The chance is that the stronger the commitment of the employers, the more resources the search firms would allocate to build up-to-date databases on Indigenous/racialized people. At this stage, it seems unlikely that employers are prepared to pay high retainer fees to recruit them, maybe with the exception of senior executives or high-level professionals in very specialized fields.

Reaching Out

If utilizing the services of search firms is not perceived to be a cost-effective method to recruit Indigenous and racialized people, another way is to conduct special outreach efforts to connect with them and encourage them to apply for jobs. This is usually done through participating in job fairs, liaisoning with student organizations at high schools, colleges, and universities, and creating partnerships with job counselling and employment agencies, immigrant organizations, professional associations, trade councils, business associations, Indigenous and ethnocultural organizations, and other groups with special purposes (such as sports or health).

These efforts are usually carried out by the human resources department of a larger organization through their internal recruiters or through their business development or public relations departments to sponsor Indigenous/racialized community events as a way to build up their corporate profile with the hope of increasing the chance of members applying for jobs at their organization. Smaller organizations, with no human resources departments, may only do a one-time-only "outreach blast" or "email blast" to reach out to the communities. One of its purposes is to raise the corporate profile and encourage people to apply for jobs.

These special outreach liaisons, campaigns, partnerships, or community project-based events are concerted efforts that are often initiated by companies or organizations, with consultation with the Indigenous and racialized communities. They illustrate the commitment of organizations to connect with the communities and increase the diversity of their employees. Unfortunately, too few employers use this method of recruiting Indigenous and racialized people. So far, only large and a few medium-sized companies have used this method to raise their profile and attract people to apply for jobs in their organizations. It may well be the case that these outreach efforts are long-term commitments, and they are not quick fixes to increase the number of Indigenous/racialized employees. Tangible results of diversity, equity, and inclusiveness may take time to come to fruition, and racism takes time to be eradicated. Just as racial inequality in the workplace is not a superficial phenomenon, one should expect that it requires a more systematic long-term response to resolve the issue. And many employers do not have this long view or the patience, and, thus, the end result is that the representation of Indigenous/racialized employees in different occupational strata will come in waves, increasing at one time and decreasing at another, usually as a result of sporadic quick fixes.

SCREENING AND SELECTION

Once individuals are motivated and have applied for the positions that have been posted, an employer enters the second stage of bringing these individuals in for the screening and selection process. The screening of applicants is usually done in the first round of application reviews, and then a few candidates are short-listed for a more in-depth selection process. Depending on how thoroughly the employer plans to investigate the candidates, they may go through more than one round of interviews or tests.

The Canadian Human Rights Commission (2007) published a small booklet entitled *A Guide to Screening and Selection in Employment*, which outlines what should or should not be done in this area. There are questions concerning the prohibited grounds of human rights and what employers need to be careful about in screening and selecting candidates. Questions on candidates' birthplaces, nationalities, citizenship, race, colour of eyes, religious holidays or affiliations, and so on should be avoided. However, as this chapter illustrates, in the screening and selection process, there are a number of areas in which Indigenous and racialized candidates may be more likely to be screened out compared to non-Indigenous/non-racialized candidates as the process progresses even if employers do not ask questions that the commission cautions them to avoid.

Screening

In smaller organizations, the manager does the screening based on the application forms and resumes since they do not have special staff members to do the screening. In larger organizations, the screening process is usually done by the human resources department and not by the manager to which the successful candidate reports. The screening should result in a shorter list of candidates for the manager or interview panelists to question during the second round, which will be a more comprehensive job interviewing process.

The screening process is usually formalized with a checklist of items to be completed or a list of questions to be posed to the candidates on the phone or through a virtual meeting. At the screening stage, human resources generalists or recruiters usually carry out the task. Unfortunately, even in larger organizations, they do not have much cross-cultural or diversity training, thus their level of sensitivity to cultural differences is not as high as it should be. Thus, some level of unconscious bias does influence their assessment of the candidates at this screening stage as they do not feel comfortable talking or interacting with Indigenous and racialized candidates and may come to a hasty, and often incorrect, assessment that the candidate is not as competent or motivated as the other candidates because of their name, their ways of communication, and their expression of emotion.

There are several areas in which Indigenous/racialized individuals have a higher probability of being discriminated against by employers through the staff members who do the screening: First, Indigenous names (such as Dakaasin, Wakwi, Geezis, and Mikom) and names of racialized people (such as Bhavini, Jiya, Mingze, and Yuxuan) spell and sound different from English names (John, Richard, Stephanie, and Mary) or French names (Claude, Gabriel, Celine, and Isabelle). Names of different ethnic groups or nationalities are different, and studies have shown that they can elicit different racial or ethnic stereotypical images and feelings (Conaway and Bethune 2015). Other studies have suggested that non-European names increase the chance of being screened out through human prejudice and discriminatory acts (Martiniello and Verhaeghe 2023). Jean-Philippe Beauregard of the University of Laval found that job applicants with Arab family names are up to two times less likely to be hired. Similarly, the federal government did an anonymized recruitment pilot project based on resumes from 2017 and found similar results (quoted in Souissi 2021). According to a study done by Sonia Kang (2017) from the Rotman School of Management at the University of Toronto, Asian and Black resumes with names on them such as Tyrone, Jada, Wei, and Ming get 30–50 percent fewer responses from employers than those equivalent resumes with names of non-racialized people, such as Emily, Hannah, Scott, and Logan. Furthermore, the study demonstrated that racialized people must whiten their resumes to make them look whiter and less racialized by avoiding mentioning that they have received scholarships for minorities. The idea of whitening their resumes is to avoid discrimination just based on their resumes so that they have a better chance of getting into the interview phase. Moreover, discrimination by applicants' names is so prevalent that even organizations with explicit diversity and inclusiveness statements are not immune to it. Discrimination by job applicants' names is very common irrespective of whether organizations claimed that they are fair, diverse, or equitable.

Second, the ways in which Indigenous and racialized people speak and interact on the phone may be viewed and interpreted by people of different backgrounds. Some Indigenous and racialized individuals are gentler in their tones, more hesitant in their expression, and use more pauses and silences. This might be due to their cultural or family upbringing, their unfamiliarity with talking on the phone or interfacing in virtual meetings, their lack of experience in phone or virtual interviews, or their lack of familiarity with the interview questions. Whatever the sources are, the impressions created for the interviewers are that Indigenous and racialized candidates are shy, unprepared, lacking in self-confidence or self-esteem, and/or have poor communication or presentation skills. These attributes are evaluated as negative and do not score well. If English or French is their second language, the accents and linguistic usage of words may further accentuate the skewed impression of the screeners. Once again, the cultural lens used by the screeners to make a judgment on the Indigenous and racialized candidates are skewed in favour of the North American cultural norms to have a phone or virtual conversation, and anyone who does not follow the norms is likely to be evaluated as mediocre or poor. This may have nothing to do with race, and the associated attributes of culture and languages may contribute to prejudice and discrimination.

Third, among other things, one of the main objectives of screening is to find out how motivated the candidate is in getting the job that they have applied for. To find this out, the screeners assess the overall self-presentation of the candidates that they interview and determine how motivated they are in talking, their tone of voice, the words they choose, and their gesturing, facial expressions, eye contact, and other small movements that demonstrate their energy and passion. That might be a lot to look for in a short encounter, but this is what the screeners are looking for. Indigenous and racialized people can be quite animated and excited in other social settings where they feel safe and relaxed, but they do not appear this way in a "job interview." Job interviews are considered to be a more serious event, one that might determine their life chances, careers, and future. Culturally, an interface with a potential employer not only makes them a little nervous, but it also minimizes their informal and entertaining abilities. Compared with Americans or even Canadians, Indigenous and racialized people are less dramatic in their conversation, less passionate in their expression, and less energetic in their interaction with people. This, very likely, would work to their disadvantage in the first stage of screening. Hence, their phone or online encounters may not be counted as excellent as they do not demonstrate their enthusiasm about the positions for which they are applying, which is the key attribute that the screeners are looking for. Once again, technically speaking, the screening process might not be considered to be racist, but its impact is more adverse for Indigenous/racialized candidates than the non-Indigenous/non-racialized ones, and they get screened out more often.

Screening Out International Credentials?

The Task Force on Access to Professions and Trades in Ontario examined the issue of examinations, internships, and retraining sessions at length for foreign-trained medical doctors. It noted that there are numerous hurdles that they must go through to get the limited spaces for the certification of qualified medical professionals. The task force concluded that some of these hurdles are unnecessary to the point of inequity (Cumming, Lee, and Oreopoulos 1989).

One of the sore points of racialized or non-racialized immigrants is the barrier for them to getting into the health professions. Immigrants have difficulties entering health professions in Canada because their foreign medical credentials are not recognized by Canadian professional bodies (Halwani 2004). This has been the complaints of many professionals and tradespeople among immigrants.

The lack of access to the medical profession obviously hinders the employment of many foreign-trained medical professionals, and the findings serve to illustrate how other training/retraining and internship/apprenticeship requirements have slowed down, if not limited, the certification of other foreign-trained tradespersons and professionals, which, in turn, has deterred them from being employed in the same fields that they had been trained for or gaining work experience in other countries.

De-emphasizing Academic Credentials?

However, another trend in human resources management is the removal of post-secondary degree requirements from job postings in numerous large corporations such as Accenture, Apply, Delta Airlines, Ernest and Young, General Motors, Google, Microsoft, and Penguin Random House. The Harvard Business School and the Burning Glass Institute noted that 41 percent of US-based job postings required at least a bachelor's degree in 2022, which is a decline from 46 percent in 2019. These companies are shifting toward a skills-based hiring model. And this raises another question: what basis do recruiters use to determine the candidate they should hire? For technology companies, the shift is toward an internal professional certification model and apprenticeships to determine the skills of external hires. Other organizations are opting for an evaluation of job applicants' actual skills on site or in skill-testing assignments for assessing their contributions as well as the networks of readily available talents known to recruiters through word of mouth (Collahan 2023).

So far, no systematic and comprehensive studies have been conducted to find out whether such new models would impact negatively on Indigenous and racialized people without formal academic degrees, certificates, or work experience. Given that Indigenous people have a lower educational attainment in formal schooling, a shift away from formal academic credentials would theoretically help them since this used to be a barrier to their employment. However, the use of an in-house certification program and apprenticeships through the utilization of word-of-mouth and networking recruitment tools does not sound promising for Indigenous peoples and racialized people as they are usually disadvantaged by in-house tools. Utilizing in-house tools to screen candidates usually benefit those who have insider connections in the organizations to which they apply. Given that Indigenous and racialized people's social networks are not as robust as those of non-Indigenous or non-racialized people, they generally render them less apt to get hired.

For racialized people, the shift to less formal academic requirements may not affect them too much, but their networks through word of mouth may still be inadequate. A few research studies on racialized networks of people in the work environment suggest that their networks are restricted to other racialized people, who are still fairly distant from the more influential networks of White people, who are better connected to those people who can offer job opportunities. Due to their uprootedness, language barriers, lack of social supports, and lack of integration with the mainstream, racialized people's networks are limited in scope and poor in influence (Reitz 2007; Reitz and Banerjee 2007; Raza, Beaujot, and Gebremariam 2013).

The reality is that, as Indigenous and racialized people, as well as immigrant or non-immigrant segments of their population, have begun to learn, in employment either at the entry point (that is, hiring) or the advancement point (that is, promotion), who you know is more important than what you know.

Selection Panels

Having a selection panel is not mandatory in the selection of candidates for many organizations. In fact, especially for those candidates applying for lower-level positions (such as clerical or semi-skilled or low manual labour), having one person acting as the sole interviewer is quite common. The formation of a selection panel made up of more than one person is usually reserved for professional, managerial, and executive positions. There are several advantages of having a panel of people select candidates and recommend them for possible hires, and they include having multiple perspectives on the candidates and their resumes, reducing the chance of dealing with the unchallenged personal biases of one person, having a better division of responsibilities among panelists in the selection process, and providing greater opportunities for including diverse group members based on Indigeneity, race, gender, and disability. Having a panel has its own disadvantages: it is more difficult to organize the schedule of meetings and interviews, and it takes longer to come to a consensus and make a decision.

As in many organizations, many people of diverse backgrounds (especially women and racialized groups) tend to cluster at the lower strata of occupations. In addition, Indigenous and racialized employees in higher-level positions (professionals and above) are very small in number. This certainly has limited the creation of a diverse selection panel so that it can make use of the above advantages. In reality, having a diverse panel is extremely difficult to create. As a result, Indigenous and racialized candidates who manage to pass through the screening process seldom have the luxury of being interviewed by a diverse panel. The homogenous White panels are more of a norm. With that as a norm, the tendency for Indigenous and racialized candidates to be discriminated against is relatively high except when the organization is highly committed to increasing diversity and ensuring that a high standard of human rights prevails throughout the hiring process by educating/training executives and managers to have appropriate equity knowledge and skills.

At this stage of human resources development in Canada, we have not reached this level of sophistication on equity matters. For example, the racial, cultural, and linguistic issues identified in an earlier discussion on screening where the ethnic names of candidates and the ways in which they express themselves in conversation and carry themselves in interviews still elicit unconscious biases on the part of the screeners. It is hard to presume that unconscious biases of this nature are immune to executives and managers.

Selection Criteria

The importance of having an appropriate set of selection criteria should not be under-estimated. In order to identify the best candidate for the position, it is important to know what and how to measure the necessary criteria. Ideally, these criteria are aligned with the components of the job description for the position and the business directions and priorities of the organization. Hence, one of the prerequisites for the selection panel or for the manager (who happens to be the only person doing the selection) is to develop these criteria as explicitly as possible and match them with appropriate measuring tools (as in interview or test questions, assignment topics, or on-the-job demonstrations of knowledge and skills needed for the position). While this is an important part of the selection process, a large number of workplaces do not have a systematic and comprehensive set of criteria, which are agreed upon by the selection panelists, prior to the actual selection process. There are also reported cases where the selection panelists have asked ad hoc questions without consulting with their colleagues or having them agreed upon ahead of time. These cases actually illustrate how unstructured and disarrayed the selection process is for many selections in the past.

Currently, the ideal selection is based on a series of criteria that have been translated into multiple structured questions that are clearly written down and agreed upon by the panelists. These questions are to be weighed in terms of high, medium, and low priorities. There also should be a consensus among the panelists on what the ideal answers would be. And the answers of the candidate are then recorded so that a comparison of their answers and the ideal answers is made.

It is important to point out that, as in any formalized design of selection criteria and interview questions that are developed to ensure alignment with the criteria, when the actual selection takes place, there is still a chance for the formal design to become distorted and biased. The source of this problem largely hinges on the language that is used. Formally defined concepts can be interpreted in a culturally biased manner, tainted with personal subjectivity ("blind spots"), stereotypes and prejudice, power imbalances in a group setting, and/or conventional business practices. Even though these selection criteria and formal interview questions are written down on paper, discretionary personal interpretations may take over in the selection decision. If "organizational commitment" is a selection criterion, and a formal interview question was developed to probe how firm the candidate's commitment is to the company, the answer from the candidate, no matter how committed they are, could be filtered by stereotypes of Indigenous peoples as excessively loyal to their community and Asians as excessively loyal to their family, so that the general conclusion of those non-Indigenous and non-racialized panelists could be that, although Indigenous and racialized people may claim that they are committed to the organization, their commitment limit is to the threshold of the family and the community and no more. This may be a simplistic way of illustrating the limitation of even having a formal set of selection criteria and the impact of stereotypes as a psychological filter.

It is hard to estimate the extent to which this ideal process of developing a set of selection criteria and related structured questions or tests has been adopted. General observations suggest that, with the exception of those who have applied for professional and management jobs, many people have reported that their job interviews were not conducted by a panel of people and that the questions seemed to be "ad hoc-ish." This is yet to be researched further.

Without a set of structured interview questions (hiring tests or assignments) that are consistent with a clear set of selection criteria, the selection of the best candidate may wind up without clear directions on how best to make a selection decision. In this undefined situation, Indigenous and racialized candidates are likely to be assessed in a more biased manner. There are several reasons why this may happen.

First, in an undefined situation with no clear selection criteria, each one of the panelists may come up with their own selection criteria and interview questions that go with them. With no agreed upon criteria, the panelist(s) with the most influential power and communication strength may end up with the most convincing criteria, which may carry to the decision point. Accordingly, what this person thinks about the quality of the candidates' answers to the interview questions may likely override other panelists' opinions. In an organization, those who have higher status and power usually are more influential in affecting others' opinions (Ridgeway 2019; Nimon-Peters 2022). Thus, the racial stereotypes and prejudice of those influential panelists may be at work when they communicate their thoughts and feelings to the rest of the panel.

Second, it is also likely that the future direct report (that is, the manager who oversees the position to which the candidates have applied) may have the final say of who should be selected as the best candidate. In this case, the manager's stereotypes and prejudice could be the psychological filters when selecting the best candidate. Other panelists may just defer to their preference and decision. Not having a clear set of selection criteria agreeable by all panelists upfront also means that there may be a sham decision-making process that is riddled with subjectivity and unchallenged by the discretionary power of the manager.

Third, when there are no clear selection criteria agreed upon upfront by all panelists, often one conventional criterion stands out and is the "fit" criterion. This criterion is extremely vague and ambiguous because it is not well defined, and its definition depends on each panelist's view at a different time. Furthermore, it could be used as the rationalization that tailors to fit an argument or a decision.

The term "fit" may mean that the candidate is culturally in harmony with the mainstream culture ("culture fit"). In this case, the cultural socialization of Indigenous or racialized people in their own communities or families may instill in them special world-views, values and norms, and they will affect how they relate to other people (including clients and other employees); the ways in which they manage their time, tasks, and quality of work; and their perspectives on authority, order, privacy, and respect. Immigrants, especially newcomers, may have to learn a new set of values and norms just to fit in well with their new surroundings, be it the workplace or their neighbourhoods when they moved to Canada. This would affect their degree of being fit.

Some racialized people, due to their religions, may find it hard to fit well into a Christian or secular culture. Their religious beliefs may prohibit them from drinking alcohol, and this might interfere with their willingness to go along with the drinking culture in mainstream culture, thus rendering them uneasy at corporate receptions and social gatherings. Some people may find Indigenous and racialized people socially awkward, too shy or passive, too outgoing, too direct and undiplomatic, too formal and not good at small talk, and so on. Another example may be found in how people express themselves in social settings. Asians tend to contextualize a message in communication, giving other people the impression that they are indirect, not straightforward, and making the message too subtle to decipher. Another example may be found among some racialized individuals who are inclined to spend time in developing a longer-term relationship with their clients instead of wrapping up the relationship quickly and finishing a quick deal (Mills 2005).

Another way of looking at the issue of fit is the alignment of organizational values and those of the candidate. Each organization has its own corporate culture ("corporate fit"). When one moves from one workplace to another, one should note the subtle differences between the two organizations in terms of transparency, collaboration, inclusiveness, authoritarianism, client-centredness, result orientation, human respect, creativity and innovation, and other cultural traits. This realization that organizational culture is indeed an intangible entity can only be felt and observed when there are large contrasts between one organization and another. Such contrasts can also be felt by Indigenous and racialized individuals when the organizational cultures exhibit different values from what they have. Similarly, employers may find it difficult to work with an employee who does not share the values of the organization.

This uncertainty of value fit is prevalent when new hires are recruited from outside, irrespective of their Indigeneity or race. However, Indigenous and racialized people face another hurdle because the people who are hiring them (that is, executives and managers) are also not familiar with Indigenous/racialized community cultures. These executives and managers are also not sure that they fit in well in the current organizational culture. Thus, in addition to the ethnic community's cultural fit, the uncertainty for these hiring decision makers is compounded by the issue of the corporate cultural fit. Since corporate executives and managers are at a higher salary occupational level, their work circles do not enable them to have much experience working with Indigenous/racialized people (Mattis 2010). Hence, at the selection stage, there is a high probability that executives and managers must look beyond the candidates' capabilities and focus more on their own intuition and comfort level. In other words, the question in their minds is: could I work with the Indigenous or racialized candidate in front of us? Hence, the issue of corporate fit is very relevant to them. If and when a candidate is considered to be fit, it usually means that the panelists are comfortable with them in the organization. This is less than likely to happen at this historical juncture, and Indigenous and racialized candidates may have a higher probability than White candidates to lose out in the job competition, especially when the job is of high status and salary level.

Selection Measurements: Weighting, Scoring, and Ranking

Selection weighting, scoring, and ranking are tools for measuring the candidates' potential performance, which employers use in interviewing, testing, and assignment demonstrations. After deciding on the selection criteria and the formal interview questions, the panelists may attach weights to each question—a higher weight for higher priority questions and a lower weight for questions of lower priority. These weights could be done in percentage points, and they all should add up to 100 percentage points. Once that is done, the panelists can design a scoring and ranking system for recording the scores of candidates' answers to the interview questions and the ranking system after tabulating these scores at the end of interviewing all candidates and comparing their total scores. This would be an ideal arrangement for selecting the best candidate.

The advantages of this system of weighting, scoring, and ranking are to establish an inventory of interview questions, to establish a priority for each question as indicated by its weight, to quantify the quality of the candidates' answers in numerical terms, to compare the total scores of each candidate, and to make a decision based on those scores and ranking.

If an employer does not have a set of clear objective selection criteria and their associated structured interview questions (or tests and assignments), there is no need to go through this phase of measurement because the measurement tools would only measure the subjective and often personal criteria of the executives or managers, which is yet to be made explicit and defined. In this case, measurement serves no purpose of determining the best candidate in an objective manner that is agreeable to the executives and managers in the panel. Furthermore, Indigenous and racialized candidates may have a higher probability of being discriminated against due largely to the fact that personal biases often permeate in a subjective evaluation of candidates' potential performance and the selection decision is often not subject to critical review. It is hard to ignore the subtle impact of stereotyping and prejudice (as psychological filters) in a decision-making process. Although any personal biases are not hard to prove, the resultant representation of Indigenous and racialized people at higher salaried positions throughout Canada (as shown in the federal government reports on employment equity data since 1986) demonstrates the persistent and prevalent profile of their under-representation.

When an employer has a set of clear objective selection criteria and its associated structured interview questions (or tests and assignments), it does not automatically eliminate the possibility of racial biases in the selection process. This is because all selection through interviews, tests, and assignments goes through a human evaluation process on weights, scores, and ranking. This process has its inherent biases, and the identification and removal of these biases depends on how the panelists are cognizant of the embedded unconscious bias and their commitment to establishing a discrimination-free recruitment, selection, and hiring process. The inherent built-in biases in measurement in a work environment include the following categories.

Weighting of the Questions/Answers

One may classify the interview into three major components of questions/answers: knowledge, skills, and work experiences. When each question/answer is weighted, it means that the higher the weight, the more critical that question/answer is in the overall scoring. If skills are the focus of selection, the questions/answers related to skills are heavier in weight than those based on the candidates' knowledge or experience. The chance is that those who have more work experience would be in a better position to score higher when more questions are categorized as skills based or when those questions/answers command higher scores. Similarly, when work experience is weighted higher than skills or knowledge, those candidates with a long history or broader scope of experience may gain higher scores. If knowledge is weighted higher than skills or experience, then those candidates with higher academic specialty may score higher. As Indigenous individuals have less academic training and few work experiences (due to longer duration of unemployment or under-employment), they might have problems getting higher scores overall. Meanwhile, racialized individuals (especially immigrants) may have less work experience; they might get lower scores when the interview questions are weighted heavier in skills and experience. It has been generally observed that skills and experience are generally rated higher by employers, and foreign work experience may not have the same level of acceptance by Canadian employers (in light of their historical emphasis on "Canadian experience" in hiring).

Scoring of Candidates' Answers

Scoring answers from candidates during interviews (or test answers and assignments) could be quite subjective unless there are model answers agreed upon by the selection panelists. In addition, how a candidate answers the questions is as important as what they say. If there are no model answers agreed upon upfront prior to the interview, then personal discretion in scoring the answers could be subject to further discussion among the panelists. Which scores will win out through this discussion among the panelists depends on the status of the panelists and how each one of them communicates and influences the post-interview discussion period. We have noted that, in the previous discussion on the screening process, how these two factors—the agreed upon model answers and the candidates' communication skills—could affect the decision.

The issue of how candidates answer a question is, once again, skewed not in favour of Indigenous and racialized candidates.

Communication is an acquired skill, and its proficiency depends on the educational and literacy level of the speakers and audience. Due largely to their relatively low literacy and educational attainment level, Indigenous candidates tend to have limited vocabulary and grammar, and they may have difficulty in speaking or understanding complex words or phrases (Williams, n.d.). This may put them in a more difficult situation when the complexity of an issue raised in interview questions may be hard to put into words and is not commonly used in daily living.

As for racialized candidates, their communication skills are largely determined by whether they are newcomers, long-term immigrants, or locally born individuals. Newcomers and immigrants may have some difficulty in communicating complex issues since English/French is their second language, but, more importantly, their usage of words/phrases and accents may be an impediment for higher scores. Moreover, as the Ontario Human Rights Commission (n.d.a.) has expressed its concerns that, in a very discrete and subtle manner, the selection panelists may give lower scores for immigrant candidates who do not have Canadian work experience, have only foreign work experience, are not familiar with how the Canadian system works and what the local industry landscape looks like, are not proficient in English, or do not have the necessary soft skills to work in Canadian culture.

In both cases, Indigenous and racialized candidates' communication styles may be discriminated against under the seemingly neutral and objective selection system. It is because stereotyping and prejudice may be at work under the surface of scoring, and, unfortunately, no amount of legislation or policies can eradicate this scenario.

Ranking of Scores and the Decision-Making Process

As the scoring of all candidates is done, and the total scores of each candidate are tabulated, at the end of the interview session, the panelists may then rank these candidates based on each of their total scores. The candidate with the highest total score among all others would be ranked as the top candidate, which is how ranking is expected to conclude.

In the real world of selecting the best candidate, it might not work this way. There are several likely scenarios in which the final decision is made in a workplace.

Before ranking actually takes place, the panelists review the scores of each candidate for each set of questions/answers at the end of all the interviews to ensure that the discrepancy of scores among the panelists is not huge. Among the panelists, if the scores for a specific question/answer of one candidate vary hugely, this may suggest that each panelist was looking for different things in the answer; the panelists were impressed differently in terms of how the candidate answered the question; one or two panelists liked the example the candidate cites; or some other additional reason. After comparing notes of the panelists around the table, one or two panelists may be prepared to change their original scores by either increasing or decreasing them, so that the scores of the panelists become more aligned with each other. This comparison of notes means that at least one panelist has a higher status and better communication skills than others, and they have won over the other panelists in changing their scores. This adjustment of scores is usually limited to the top two candidates. However, if the top candidate stood out and ranked the highest, the adjustment of their scores is not needed.

It is common to see this score adjustment process after the interviews. This adjustment of scores is to resolve the differences among panelists in how they understand the answers of the candidates. It is also one way to create a consensus among panelists. However, it has its own dynamics. The panelist with the highest status and who has good communication skills is one who usually can convince others to have scores come closer to their score. Often, in the discussion among panelists, some biases become more explicit, which exposes panelists' assumptions of what the candidates have done or what their backgrounds are or why some answers gave certain impressions of the candidates. Based on the author's observations in job interview settings, these biases may or may not be racial in nature, but Indigenous and racialized candidates' answers tend to generate higher probability of different viewpoints among panelists due to linguistic, cultural, and/or racial factors. This area may require further research.

On some occasions, the adjustment of candidates' individual scores is orchestrated by one panelist because there was one candidate who clearly wanted to be the one with top ranking by that panelist. To make that happened, that particular panelist has to work hard to convince other panelists to change their scores not only on one question/answer but also possibly on others. This usually happens only when the panelist who wanted to reassess the scores happens to be the manager or executive who was doing the hiring, and they would like that person to be selected as the top candidate without saying it out loud. Usually, the rest of the panelists go along with their request for score adjustment. However, there might be favouritism or even nepotism at work here, and one must be extra cautious about racial prejudice and discrimination if one candidate with a higher score is an Indigenous or racialized person.

In ranking candidates based on the interview scoring, it is the general practice that the one with the top score will be hired. At least, the adjustment of scores that happens sometimes ensures that the final score is on the record, and other candidates' scores are recorded as a formal document to be submitted to the human resources department for filing purposes. However, there are still a few steps to go through before a hiring letter is sent to the winning candidate: reference checks and background checks (including education and criminal checks, if required in the human resources procedure) before the job offer to the successful candidate.

The Issue of "Over-Qualification"

Over-qualification is increasingly viewed as an under-utilization of human talents. On a human level, it means lower incomes and lower life satisfaction for over-qualified workers. Statistics Canada has defined over-qualification as "a situation in which university degree holders (bachelor's degree or higher) hold jobs that require no more than a high school education" (Cornelissen and Tyrcotte 2020). A study was conducted by Statistics Canada on the persistent over-qualification among immigrants and non-immigrants using the 2006 and 2016 Censuses. In both years, the proportion of over-qualified workers among immigrants was nearly 10 percent and among non-immigrants was 4 percent. Among immigrants, in both years, 14 percent of immigrants who studied abroad, and 4 percent of them who studied in Canada, experienced over-qualification. Immigrants who graduated from Southern and Southeast Asia were more likely to be over-qualified. Only 5 percent of recent and older immigrants (aged forty and above) have a greater tendency to be over-qualified. In general, in the last few decades, an increase in over-qualification rates has emerged.

Over-qualified immigrants are more likely to work in sectors that have been hardest hit by the COVID-19 pandemic such as accommodation, food services, health care, and retail). Who are likely to be overqualified among immigrants? They are highly educated and usually are recent arrivals to Canada, graduated in a foreign location, have a proficiency in an official language and literacy, have pre-immigration work experience, and so on. A prolonged period of over-qualification may result in losing skills, negative impacts on career paths, and longer period of unemployment. There are also intersectionality issues here as 33.8 percent of immigrant women experienced over-qualification more than once compared with 25.3 percent of immigrant men. 11.6 percent of immigrant women are persistently over-qualified. In contrast, only 8.7 percent of immigrant men are.

Over-qualification may act as a conduit to additional problems for immigrants to be hired or sometimes to be promoted. It is often used by management as an excuse not to hire racialized people or immigrants. The *Sangha v. Mackenzie Valley Land and Water Board* exposed subjectivity in a hiring case in which the complainant argued that he was not hired because he was considered as over-qualified by the respondent (that is the employer).[1] Although this was a case in racial discrimination in hiring, it has implications on promotion too because the mechanism in most promotion cases is similar to those used in hiring (Siu 2017, 1, 24-38–24-40).

Usually, in making a decision in hiring, one of the key issues is whether the candidates are qualified for the position. This issue is addressed at an early stage of screening when the candidates' resumes are reviewed. Candidates who are under-qualified are likely to be screened out for obvious reasons—their educational level, skill competencies, and/or work experiences are not on par with the requirements of the position. However, when candidates are over-qualified, it is difficult to argue that they cannot do the job because their qualifications are over and above what is required. Some of these "over-qualified" candidates are screened in for further review or selection. The issue is why these over-qualified individuals get rejected is an interesting question. The complainant in *Sangha v. Mackenzie Valley Land and Water Board* argued that rejection was an indication of racial discrimination. In addition, due to the fact that racialized people tend to have higher educational attainment, their attainment level is often used as one of the rejection reasons in hiring and promotion compeittions. Hence, disproportionately, these higher educated racialized candidates are discriminated against.

In *Sangha v. Mackenzie Valley Land and Water Board*, through research data, the expert witness noted that several issues, when

---

1 *Sangha v Mackenzie Valley Land and Water Board*, 2006 CHRT 9.

compounded together, would constitute racial discrimination. They were: (1) immigrants are more educated than native-born Canadians; (2) racialized immigrants have difficulties in securing employment at higher status jobs requiring a high level of qualification and so are forced take lower-status jobs that require low qualifications; and (3) as a result, racialized immigrants, as a collective entity, are under-represented in high-status jobs and are over-represented in lower-status jobs. Many racialized immigrants have high academic credentials or years of relevant work experience from the countries they have come from, but they are not able to get hired in jobs that they have been educated or trained in or that they have relevant work experience in, and, therefore, they seek jobs that they call "survival jobs." These jobs do not require the academic credentials that they have or the work experiences that they have, and these jobs are usually lower paid and have lower status. They usually get these jobs only because they downplay their qualifications or even remove them from their applications or resumes.

In human resources management, there are no principles in accepting or rejecting candidates due to their over-qualification. Thus, from the perspective of leaders, the hiring of over-qualified racialized people may likely result in risks for the organization because it may be difficult to retain such employees for long since they may look for other jobs or they may find the jobs too boring and demotivating because the nature of the jobs utilizes only a fraction of their talents. This may be the reason that employers try to avoid hiring over-qualified candidates. However, as *Sangha v. Mackenzie Valley Land and Water Board* shows, the adverse impact of such decisions on "over-qualification" is much more severe for racialized people, which renders such decisions as racial discrimination.

HIRING CONDITIONS: EMPLOYMENT STATUS, STARTING SALARY, AND PROBATION PERIOD

The initial employment status of Indigenous and racialized employees is very much determined at the time they accept their job offers from the employers. The hiring letter that the organization sends to them outlines the hiring conditions, which usually includes the job offer, job title, employment status, starting salary, starting date (to be arranged with the human resources department), probation period (and its optional extension), and the date the candidate must sign and return the job offer letter if they decide to accept the job offer. The scope and contents of these job offer letters vary by organizations, but the above examples illustrate a few human resources arrangements that impact on the starting points of an employee when they first receive their job offer.

As discussed in Chapter 3, Indigenous and racialized people live in a world full of racial disparities in almost every aspect of their lives, starting with their births and ending with their deaths. They are discriminated against every day, and they have to learn how to cope with stereotyping and prejudice. Having a job is not the most assuring life chance that they have, especially when the economy is not doing well and jobs are hard to come by or hard to keep. It has been a common experience for them that they have to apply to many jobs before they land on one when compared with White people (Vaswani et al. 2023). Given that it is hard for them to land a job, job offers include conditions such as employment status, starting salary, and probation period, which, while not ideal, are almost treated as "givens" and not to be contested or negotiated with their employers. In addition, given the limited resources and networks that they have, they would not be in an advantageous position to know the market rate of their starting salaries for their employment status or the usual practice of probation periods or conditions. And, given the secrecy (under the name of confidentiality) surrounding human resources matters, they are also not privileged to know the employment status, starting salary, and probation period of other candidates with job offers or current employees in similar positions. Hence, they are not in a position to negotiate with their offering employers on these issues in an informed manner. Furthermore, they are also not prepared to lose these job offers since they may not have any other jobs waiting for them. It may well be the case that they simply do not have the psychological security to decline the job offers, although the hiring conditions offered may not be as attractive as they should be. In a world full of perceived prejudice and discrimination and because of their own personal circumstances, Indigenous and racialized individuals may accept the job offers as they are presented with "gratitude."

Let us examine three human resources matters commonly found in job offers and discuss the dynamics of how racism works.

Employment Status

The employment status of the employee denotes whether they will work full-time, part-time, or on contract (with start and end dates). Unless the information about the employment status is clearly stated on the job posting—"full time," "part time," or "contract"—the manager has the discretion to offer the candidate a position with any of the above employment statuses after interviewing the candidates. This is most common for positions that are of a lower status and lower salaries or are semi-skilled or unskilled (such as those in hospitality, construction, manufacturing, and retail industries). Essentially, the manager reserves the right to have an employee to work on a short-term (part-time) or long-term basis (full-time), with or without a definitive time period (contract). That right is based on the discretionary power of management. While systematic academic studies are seldom carried out or not readily available, it is generally observed that, through employees' reports of comparisons of their own salaries with others, Indigenous and racialized peoples, newcomers, and women tend to get more part-time or contract jobs when compared with their White counterparts. This is usually due to the discretion of the managers who wish to allow themselves more time to observe whether Indigenous and racialized employees will work out all right (Block and Galabuzi 2011; Cook 2013).

Starting Salary

Unless job postings are explicitly clear about the starting salary or the salary range of the position for which people are applying, the manager has the option of designating the amount of salary per hour or per week (with a definitive number of hours) in the job offers. Once again, this situation is mostly found in jobs that are of lower levels and pay lower salaries or are semi-skilled or unskilled (such as those in hospitality and retail industries). (Fuller and Vosko 2008; Block and Galabuzi 2011). With exchanges of notes among these employees during their off-work hours, they often find out that they are paid differently—some earn more, and some earn less. Indigenous and racialized employees often find themselves in a lower pay category. The manager's expressed reason for such a discrepancy is the extensiveness of the work experience of employees—those with more work experiences should get higher starting salaries. Sometimes, this reason does not stand up to the employee's own research as it is not hard for them to compare notes on the length of work experience in similar fields.

Probation Period

Probation period is optional, but many employers prefer to establish them for new employees, usually for a period of three or six months, depending on the work categories. However, employers also have the right to extend the probation period longer, provided that they specify this option in the job offer or the contract upfront prior to the employees coming on board. Once again, there is a tendency for managers to reserve the right to extend the probation period longer for Indigenous and racialized people. This would allow them to have a longer period of time to monitor their performance before making a decision to give permanency to their employment status. This discretionary power of management is reserved to accentuate further the traditional authority structure (Holdaway and Barron 1997; Harcourt and Wood 2006).

CONCLUSION

As Chapter 3 articulated in greater detail, the extensive, persistent, and deep disadvantages and discrimination that Indigenous and racialized people experience since they were born—entrenched poverty, poor housing, low educational attainment, poor health and health-care services, unfair encounters with the police and the court system, and many other factors—and until they die, are loaded with tons of social injustice. What they must confront at the gate of employment are further prejudice and discriminatory human resources mechanisms that prevent them from being employed. This may explain the high unemployment rates among them compared with their White counterparts. They certainly feel that they have been discriminated against, although most do not expect that the methods used systemically by employers such as word of mouth, job posting/advertising, external search firms, and a lack of special outreach could essentially screen them out easily without their awareness. In other words, the subtlety of the discrimination by the human resources mechanisms at the entry points of employment often appear neutral and bias free. Unless Indigenous and racialized people themselves have experiences using these mechanisms, they would have difficulty in recognizing how they work to discriminate (for example, in recruitment, selection, scoring, and ranking).

For those few Indigenous/racialized people who have not been screened out from higher salaried positions, the use of selection panelists, undefined selection criteria, and measurement tools can also put them in a disadvantaged position. These are seemingly neutral mechanisms that, on the surface, are not biased and are applicable for everyone. But they produce discriminatory impacts. Human resources mechanisms of this nature are conducted and operated by human beings with their own bias filters. When these selection methods and tools are used, not only do personal perceptions and feelings permeate through, but their own personal discretion can also be manifested subtly, thereby affecting the decision-making process of hiring.

Once again, these are subtle processes of which their discriminatory power remains strong. In the final analysis, Indigenous and racialized candidates could be dropped at the final hiring decision point without evidence of any racial traits. They are unable to see how the seemingly neutral human resources mechanisms and tools could be biased and discriminatory when they are carried out by people who claimed to be fair and unbiased, and, thus, the mechanisms and tools are seen by many as fair and reasonable. To recognize the negative impacts of the recruitment and selection process of this nature on Indigenous and racialized people, one only needs to review their representation profiles on a regular and systematic basis.

CHAPTER 7

Racism on the Staircases and in Hallways

INTRODUCTION

Despite the workplace prejudice and stereotyping and the gatekeeping recruitment and selection mechanisms that are built into the hiring system, with the unintended result of screening them out, some Indigenous peoples and racialized people still manage to become employed. Once they are employed, however, it does not mean that racial prejudice and discrimination disappear from the organization in which they are hired. They still must overcome a broad range of adverse obstacles that potentially render them unable to be occupationally mobile and reach their potential like other employees.

In this chapter, we will examine the embedded racial biases in various human resources mechanisms in their design and implementation stages. These mechanisms include performance evaluation, training and development, coaching and mentoring, promotion, and succession management. In examining these mechanisms, we will expose how they work in impacting racialized and Indigenous peoples in an adverse manner.

PERFORMANCE MANAGEMENT

The Model

Performance management is a human resources mechanism designed and implemented for the purpose of monitoring and evaluating employees' performance so that their performance can align with the organization's vision, goals, and missions. Through its tools, policies, and procedures, performance evaluation becomes a formal system with a structure and processes.

The performance evaluation model, in its ideal form, enhances the mutual expectations of management and employees and encourages employees to aspire, grow, and excel. This model develops a process between management and employees in preparing their own individualized plan with performance goals and timetables, measuring and evaluating their performance progress and deliverables, and overseeing their training and development activities. In regular and impromptu meetings throughout the year, management coaching and performance feedback for individual employees are provided. Some employers even add a reward and recognition strategy to incentivize employees.

Each organization has its own system. In general, this model consists of five components: creating an individualized performance evaluation plan; monitoring ongoing employee performance; developing additional employee skills; evaluating the processes and deliverables of employees; and rewarding employee performance. When this model is applied by employers, they are able to make adjustments based on corporate culture and business needs. In reality, employers tend to be selective on what they wish to focus on and what they are capable of implementing. Some are half-hearted, lukewarm, and sporadic in their adoption, and some do not adopt a model at all.

Lately, this performance management model has been under intense scrutiny and criticism. Essentially, it is a model that both managers and employees find ineffective, and both will often try to avoid it. Employees complain that performance goals may be set but that they are seldom used for measurement or evaluation. Performance evaluation meetings may be arranged, but they are constantly postponed or even cancelled. Managers seldom give feedback on employees' performance, or their feedback is not carried out frequently enough to be helpful to employees (Van Vulpen, n.d.). All these signs suggest that management is not serious about such a system and that employees find it faulty. Despite these shortcomings, this system seems to be maintained in a half-hearted manner in many organizations, year in and year out.

Seemingly Neutral but Inherently Biased

From the perspectives of Indigenous and racialized employees, this generic model of performance management could be biased, unfair, and unhelpful. One of the central features of a performance management system is the setting of evaluation criteria, measuring tools, and a scale for scoring. Evaluation criteria include the employee performance level as agreed upon between the manager and the employee. For example, one may use the volume of sales, the revenue generated through sales, or the conversion rate from webinar attendees to product users per month/quarter as performance evaluation criteria. These criteria are operationalized using tangible indicators and quantitative measuring units; others may include indicators with qualitative measurements. Once these indicators and measuring units are established, the performance of the employee is then scored, usually from one (lowest score) to five (highest score)—a high total score for all indicators means an excellent performance, and a low total score means a poor performance.

This system of measurement and scoring look systematic, but the results are likely to be interpreted subjectively by executives, managers, human resources professionals, or employees. It is not clear whether there are distinct demarcations between each of the numerical scores along the scale of one to five or whether there are clear differences between "excellent," "good," "average," "passed," or "poor" (or "needs improvement"). Does each one of these scale markers refer to a standardized scale with national or international consensus and what we often referred to as "gold standards" or a reference point (or benchmark) yet to be defined by each manager or human resources department? It is uncertain whether the scores on such a scale have any meaningful application, comparison with peers, or acceptability among managers or executives.

There are cultural factors at work in scoring too. People who come from different cultural backgrounds may interpret same behaviours or processes in different manners. Performance may be measured in terms of what results an employee achieves and/or how an employee achieves the results. If the measurement focuses on the "how" part (such as the process used by an employee to get a short-term hard sale pitch to a client and not a longer-term nurturing of a client relationship), the scoring and rating of their performance would be very different depending on how the management views the values of these two processes and how frequent they get the sales. If the measurement focuses on the "what" part, then the sales volume may be of higher priority. Often, the relationship between how employees get their results is what needs to be measured, and, in that case, the employee's performance is then evaluated on those two aspects.

In this realm of performance measurement, it is important to note that Indigenous/racialized employees have a different approach in selling products or services. Instead of having a hard sales pitch to convince customers to purchase within a short duration of time and closing the deal quickly, they prefer to take a more long-term view in establishing a stronger rapport with the customers and influencing them to purchase more products from the store on a much longer-term basis. Such an approach is different from the North American quick sales approach. Without this cultural understanding of Indigenous and racialized employees, managers may be more focused on the results-oriented approach in getting quicker sales and thus inclined to evaluate their performance in a less favourable light.

And then there are the racial stereotyping and prejudices at work in scoring too. As Chapters 3 and 4 have meticulously shown, the racial stereotypes of Indigenous peoples and racialized people, the negative images and feelings toward them in the workplace and in society may taint the perspectives of the managers who do the scoring of employment performance. Examples of employee performance evaluations taken from two large corporations in Canada were examined by this author, and they show that the percentage of Indigenous managers with scores at the high end of the scale was consistently lower than that for non-Indigenous managers. Meanwhile, the percentage of Indigenous managers with scores at the low end of the scale was consistently higher than that of their non-Indigenous counterparts. This suggests that Indigenous managers are viewed as poorer performers by their executive bosses (Siu 2021, 171).

Having poorer scores in performance of this nature is not a new finding; an earlier study of American managers—White and Black—showed a similar pattern where Black managers have lower scores in their performance evaluation. More importantly, these Black managers also reported less chance of being promoted, felt that they had reached their career plateau earlier, and, without elaborating on the obvious, were less satisfied with their careers (Greenhaus, Parasuraman, and Wormley 1990, 64–86).

Subjectivity

As noted earlier, there is certain degree of subjectivity in performance evaluation on the part of management not just on scoring but also on the performance areas on which management wishes to focus. In one of the human rights cases examined by the author (who acted as an expert witness) that took place in the 2010s, the complainant was a police officer, and the respondent was a municipal police services board. The case was about alleged discrimination based on a prohibited ground ("race") in a workplace promotion case. While diversity and inclusiveness were one of the officer's main portfolios during his police service career, his good performance in this area had been largely ignored by those on the promotion panel as evidence of his performance. While this was not a performance management issue, the negation of a core responsibility that scored high marks for the officer in his application for a promotion to a new position suggests that the evaluation of employee performance can be a very selective process, in which the good performance results of Indigenous or racialized employees are often ignored either on purpose or through neglect. Similarly, cases were cited from university employees in the United States where their diversity and inclusiveness performance was ignored in their evaluation (Aguirre 2000).

As reported by many employees who experienced "selective performance evaluation," the evaluation was based either on dealing with only the "poor" performance of the employee or the "poor" performance based on the recency of the performance history as opposed to evaluating it in a more holistic and longitudinal manner that would cover the number of work months as deemed adequate by both the management and the employee. In both situations, skewed performance evaluation is considered biased by employees. The subjectivity, discretionary power, and selection perception ("picking cherries" in a reverse manner) of the panelists are always present and could be used to distort the arguments in favour or not in favour of specific candidates not only in performance evaluation but also in the selection of candidates for promotion purposes.

Discretionary Power and Secrecy

And then there are issues surrounding how managers or executives do their scoring and ranking of their subordinates in their performance evaluations. Since performance evaluation is a confidential process known only to the employee and the manager during specific sessions or throughout the employment period, communications between these two parties are not fully recorded, and, in some cases, only highlights are recorded. In fact, in some of these sessions, documentation is minimal.

The scoring and rating are not necessarily plotted on a statistical "bell curve," which would be considered fair by many employees. The executives or managers who do these scorings and ratings could, in their own discretion, give all subordinates similar high, medium, or low scores and ratings without triggering any sharing among employees unless they wish to. The confidentiality of performance evaluations further ensures the secrecy of these performance scores and ratings.

One human rights case that occurred in Ottawa, which was examined by this author (as an expert witness), shows how the confidentiality and secrecy of the performance evaluation process works to undermine the integrity of the system. The case in point involved a manager who basically gave top scores and ratings to all subordinates who reported to him for reasons that go beyond the confines of this examination. The result was that these employees all believed that they would be the top candidate in any job competition for a promotion. While this was a case about alleged racial discrimination, and the complainant was a racialized employee, the evidence collected did not confirm that the employee was discriminated against on the basis of his race due to his "top" score and rating in his performance evaluation results. Rather, it was the lack of differentiation in the performance evaluation results for different employees that may explain why the hiring manager in this case had to utilize other reasons to justify why a decision was made not in favour of the racialized complainant. When a performance management system is compromised or broken, it creates an environment in which managers are forced to use their own discretionary power to make their decisions, which are most often based on irrelevant grounds.

Another problem with this model of performance management is that it looks neutral, consultative, collaborative, and, to some extent, employee oriented. It even gives us an impression of being "scientific." However, due to the fact that it is a "negotiated" process between the managers and the employee, the model still enables the manager to exercise their discretion and give particular employees who are favoured higher scores if the manager anticipates that they "should" be promoted in the future. The distinctions between scores in the performance scale are often not as clear-cut as they look (especially between "excellent" and "good"). Furthermore, how a performance is judged is also subject to managerial priority, which is not often agreed upon between the manager and the employee. Unless performance measurement is rigidly defined, most performance evaluation tools are simply subjective and not clearly explained to employees, and the "consensus" between the manager and the employee is simply half-baked. If the manager is White and the workplace culture is contaminated with racial stereotypes and prejudice, the chance is that Indigenous and racialized employees may get lower scores in their performance evaluation rating. The differentiation of scores does not need to be dramatically huge. All they need to provide are some shades of difference.

While performance evaluation scores may not be the sole measurement indicator for promotion purposes, the lower scores discussed earlier would come in "handy" when the rationale for not making a favourable decision for Indigenous/racialized employees is to be made. One of the most common "official reasons" for not promoting someone is to tell that employee that "it is a very competitive market." By implication, it means that "the candidates in the job competition are all competent, including you. However, there is at least one successful candidate who has an edge in the competition over you." This is the reason that is often given to every unsuccessful candidate in a job competition. If any proof is needed, the lower scores of the unsuccessful candidate could be utilized. Hypothetically, there would be no suspicion of any signs of racial discrimination, but Indigenous and racialized people have heard of these reasons before and have a lot of experience of this kind of pass over as the scoring scale is not rigidly defined, and there is wiggle room between the categories of scores.

A decade or two ago, managers, human resource professionals, and colleagues might have consoled the unsuccessful Indigenous/racialized employee when they were passed over in promotion by saying: "It takes years to gain enough work experience to compete for the position that you have just applied. Be a little more patient, you will have your turn." This consolation is not comforting anymore because Indigenous and racialized people have seen people more junior and with less experience actually get promoted more often than they do. The performance evaluation model looks professional, and the scores seem so reasonable. The new "official reason" of competitiveness has now replaced the previous one of "experience counts ... and be patient."

Coaching

Coaching could be viewed as a component in an individualized performance improvement plan. It requires the active engagement of managers, as a more experienced person, to provide more in-depth guidance for their employees. This guidance helps employees to learn to achieve specific performance goals by giving employees ongoing feedback, advice, and joint exploration to find answers and solutions to work-related problems.

Coaching does require an additional time commitment and more effort with respect to employees on the part of the managers. Ideally, the managers should allocate equivalent time for each of their employees. However, in the real world, managers are more likely to spend more time in fighting "fires" (dealing with crises at work) rather than coaching employees. Unless some managers are very conscientious about coaching as a way to improve the performance of employees, they are likely to spend minimal time coaching. This begs the question of who should get the manager's attention, commitment, and time for coaching.

As discussed in Chapter 5, the issue of social distancing and isolation is very real for Indigenous and racialized employees, especially when they are perceived as an "out-group" member. Managers may not share "in-group" information with them. "In-group" information is usually shared with people that managers have an affinity with in terms of culture, values, norms, lifestyle, work approaches, family background, language, religion, age, gender, ethnicity, and race. There is an element of trust among "in-group" members and an element of distrust between the "in-group" and "out-group" members. At the level of management and leadership, White men are over-represented, and, increasingly, White women are more proportionately represented. Since executives/managers are broadly informed and usually have more experience in working in the organization or the field, "in-group" information from the management side may include working relations with other departments, decision-making process at a higher level, priority business issues, liaison strategies with other stakeholder groups, and other work-related issues or even personal opinions on industries and politics. All non-management employees would benefit from these "in-group" information; however, given the dominant features of prejudice and stereotypes regarding Indigenous and racialized people in society, and the resultant social distancing that often takes place in the workplace, executives, managers, and supervisors are comfortable with interacting with White employees, and they are more inclined to coach them rather than Indigenous or racialized employees. The information shared between them is often useful for employee performance improvement as well as for their career planning or promotion opportunities. While this coaching situation in the workplace may not come from deliberate or conscious racial discrimination, as far as the adverse impact for Indigenous and racialized employees is concerned, they suffer just as much.

Training

One of the central components of the above performance evaluation model is the establishment of an individualized training and development plan. The idea behind this component is two-fold. First, with respect to "training"—the provision of a skill-upgrading mechanism for employees to improve their performance and "development"—if employees wish to branch out into other related positions or get a promotion to a higher-status position, they might work with their executives or managers to develop their competencies and connections that fit well with a new career direction that the employee wishes to entertain.

It has been established that training and development expences are largely spent on executives and managers (Akofi 2016). Second, it has been demonstrated that these two classes of employees are largely made up of White, non-Indigenous, and non-racialized males, especially at the executive level. There has been an increased influx of White females, followed by racialized employees, at the middle management level in some larger corporations in Canada. There has also been a slower influx of them at the executive level (Innovation, Science and Economic Development Canada 2021, 2024; Grewal 2024). These data suggest that some inroads in training and development areas have been made for White females and racialized people.

In spite of these limited movements, management has been more generous when training is provided for non-management employees so that their performance would be improved. Training provided at this level is usually related to on-the-job training, job shadowing, in-house or external courses or technical and administrative skills upgrades, and lunch-and-learn sessions. The key feature of training is that it does enhance some degree of employee growth for promotion purposes, just to keep their jobs, and to help them do their jobs better.

While the term "development" is often connected to "training," for many strata of occupational groups below that of executives and managers, development education is largely neglected. These strata are largely focused on training and not on development. Unless there is a fixed departmental budget item allocated to employee training on a per annual basis, the sourcing of funds for employees in this area would be at the discretion of the managers. This often poses a problem for the manager to get funds for training purposes. Here, if the manager does not see the immediate organizational needs for training, they are likely to procrastinate on processing employees' requests or seeking approval from higher-level managers. It is often a process that seems to apply to every employee, irrespective of whether the employees are Indigenous or racialized.

Apart from organizational urgency, favouritism appears to be a critical factor in determining the granting of money for employee training (Schaffer and Riordan 2013; Afful 2024). It is a common inclination that managers may put forward a strong case for their direct report's approval for funding if there are employees who are perceived to be more favourable for a future promotion. Without elaborating on the obvious, training is an investment in employees, and, unless management believes that the investment is worthy to make on particular employees on a longer-term basis, such an expenditure is optional.

In an organization in which Indigenous and racialized employees are under-represented at its higher echelon, investing on their training may not be urgent or even necessary unless there is an immediate organizational priority in terms of skills training and/or an urgency to promote some employees to new or higher-status positions that require professional development. For example, nowadays, since artificial intelligence (AI), such as generative AI or chatGPT, is at the top of manager's priority list of organizational needs (as it is perceived as increasing efficiency), it might be easy to secure funding for training employees irrespective of their Indigeneity or race. However, if the requests for training are not topical, the chance for funding approval is unlikely. Therefore, Indigenous and racialized employees may have to wait longer to get their training or not at all. Not all organizations work in this manner, but, given the prevalence of stereotyping and prejudice in the workplace culture or in the mindsets of those in management and leadership, it is more common that Indigenous and racialized people will complain about their lack of management support in training, which makes it harder for them to be effective performers, while seeing other non-Indigenous and non-racialized employees getting more than their fair share.

SUCCESSION MANAGEMENT

Nature of Succession Management

When the term "succession management" is used, it is usually used to refer to a system to identify, plan, and develop middle-level managers to become higher-level executives. The idea behind it is to ensure that, if and when a higher-level executive is absent due to sickness, accidents, retirement, or termination, the organization has a readily available pool of potential executives who can replace them and that these potential executives have the knowledge and skills to carrying on the executive work that is left behind. It is a long-term process because pipelines need to be established so that new qualified candidates from other positions can gradually move into the executive positions. Succession management provides many benefits to the organization since it smoothes the process of power transition at the executive level to avoid the disruption that usually come with such a transition; it also retains internal talents and reduces turnover rates of employees who find themselves under-utilized.

In addition to executive succession, the term is also applicable when managers identify potential managers among professionals, semi-professionals, and technicians and develop them. And it could also apply to the identification of potential supervisors among administrative or clerical staff members and their development as supervisors. Essentially, it boils down to identifying and grooming employees to be a part of management irrespective of their levels—executive, managerial, or supervisory.

At each one of these levels, the process of managing succession are slightly different. The executive level of succession commands a much more comprehensive process than is used at the managerial level, which, in turn, is more comprehensive than the process used at the supervisory level. There are many tools—training, development, coaching, mentoring, and sponsorship—available to groom potential candidates for any of these successions. These tools will be examined here to see how Indigenous/racialized employees are impacted by them and how racism, if relevant, is integrated in these processes.

Currently, succession management does not seem to be a perfect corporate system for selecting and developing candidates and enabling a continuous flow of top talents, especially at the leadership and management level. Leonard Karakowsky and Igor Kotlyar (2012) observed that, based on their survey, approximately half of their survey respondents viewed succession management as "highly ineffective" or "somewhat ineffective" in their organizations. There seems to be a series of inherent deficiencies in the tools (such as talent identification and selection, training, and development) that the system is using that have made it incapable of reaching its goals. This is especially the case when it comes to the inclusion of Indigenous and racialized people in succession, promotion, or job movement.

Implementation of Succession Management

How to identify potential candidates who would be ideal for future executives, managers, or supervisors is one of the central questions. In the past, most organizations depend largely on the results of candidate performance evaluations when they are at lower occupational levels. The idea behind using this method is that it is important to know how candidates fare in executing organizational policies and procedures and how they do in middle management jobs. Despite the subjective biases inherent in the evaluation process, the evaluation results reflect the opinions of those who oversee employees, and this would be one factor to be considered in looking at whether the results are objectively correct or not. But the most insightful view about performance evaluation is that the evaluation really does not evaluate the potentiality of leadership in each candidate as it mesures only the performance of the candidates and does not measure the vision, strategic thinking and execution, and stewardship of these candidates. Hence, this is the key weakness of using performance evaluation results to identify potential executives.

The new direction of succession management is that it focuses on leadership and not management per se. It sees leadership development as a key concept, develops an inventory of high-potential leadership candidates, nurtures what these candidates have, such as their competency and their character, and provides experiential experiences, not just classroom courses. Usually, potential candidates are identified and graded without much transparency as having high, medium, or low potential, and learning and developmental modules are created to fit these grades. Based on the general observation of a small sample of organizations, this is a process that not even the potential candidates on the list know about it. There are inherent problems with secrecy (that is, non-transparency) because employees do not know how succession management works, especially the identification phase, and they have no idea what the identification criteria are and who are doing the identification. Without elaborating on the obvious, Indigenous and racialized employees usually do not how this process works; they too are in the dark.

Results of Succession and Representation of Indigenous and Racialized Employees

Succession management is envisioned and implemented as described in the above model. However, many organizations recognize that they are quite ineffective in identifying the right person for an executive position that they wish to fill. Some organizations have found themselves very unprepared to even do the succession planning (Kleinsorge 2010; Lafley 2011; Sengupta 2012). In fact, one example of the ineffectiveness of the implementation of most corporate succession management systems is their negation of diverse group members, including Indigenous and racialized people, on their lists of potential executive candidates. This may not be obvious to those in the decision-making process of identifying and selecting candidates. This is what is commonly known as "unconscious bias," and those who have biases of this nature do not even know that they are biased.

However, the outcome of succession management is that, when the names of new executives are announced, most (if not all) of them are White men and, increasingly, White women (Innovation, Science and Economic Development Canada 2021, 2024). This is telling because the identification criteria and the resultant selection process produce almost all-White results. We judge whether a succession management system is racially biased by its results, not by its motivations. It is therefore obvious that racism is working in succession management because of the result that is the under-representation of racialized and Indigenous peoples.

Why Indigenous and Racialized Employees Are Under-Represented?

If a succession management system produces an all-White result (which means the successful candidates in succession are White people, men and women), it is critical to find out how this works. This will be elaborated in the following paragraphs, beginning, first, with how the succession identification process works at the executive level, followed by how it works in the managerial and supervisorial levels. First of all, being competent is important for employees to be considered as likely candidates in a succession pipeline, and competency is usually noted in a performance evaluation. As discussed earlier in the subsection on performance management, there are several problems with this model, and they have implications on Indigenous and racialized employees.

At the executive level, competency is not only measured in terms of performance indicators through the performance management process, but it is also measured in terms of the recommendations of the executives to whom managers report. These recommendations are likely to be grounded in the performance evaluation results as well as the perceptions of these executives on a daily basis. At one organization that this author reviewed, each executive put forward the names of managers whom they believed were of executive material and why they should be considered for the succession pipelines. These names were then shared among a small group of senior executives who had working experience with these managers.

Visibility, Participation, and Networking

One way to increase the chance of oneself being selected for the succession pipeline or for the list of potential candidates for succession is visibility. In other words, employees must find ways to make themselves visible to the decision makers by participating in corporate program works (such as the United Way Fundraising Program); an organizing body for departmental retreats (such as corporate event organizing committees); cross-departmental task forces (such as external consulting service policy); or invititational staff supports at corporate meetings (such as regular business meetings involving the chief executive officer). In this manner, executives have more opportunities to work with these management employees, get to know them, and recognize their names as a result. This kind of participation is essentially a form of networking, which proves to be useful in succession and promotion.

However, such participation requires only a small sample of employees. As a matter of convenience, executives (most likely, White men and women) often nominate or recommend certain employees with whom they are comfortable to be involved in these programs, committees, task forces, or meetings. Hence, there is a certain degree of favouritism at work here. Only those employees in the inner circle of executives stand a good chance of being nominated or recommended because they have been accepted as one of the executives' in-groups and they are comfortable working with them. For White executives, their inner circles are likely to be White men or women. Such inclusion gives White employees more advantages in being considered in a succession pipeline (Brewer 1999). Being involved in these groups should be treated as a privilege.

Indigenous and racialized employees are very seldom found inside the inner circles of executives, as the latter have problems identifying any of them as board directors. One of the most common questions posed by executives when asked to include Indigenous and racialized people on their list of potential candidates for board directors, chief executive officers, or executives is: where can we find them? (Butler 2012).

Developmental Opportunities

Development education or opportunities include a broad range of programs and initiatives. They include self-assessment, personality tests, 360-degree performance feedback, home work, personal journal (diary) keeping, e-learning sessions, executive/management/professional breakfasts/presentations, or conference, job shadowing, rotational mentoring opportunities, special task force or project participations, networking sessions, team project management, "stretch" assignments (with extended responsibilities for a short-term learning week or month), and longer-term secondments (by leaving current positions for an extended period within the company or in connection with the public sector). Maternity leaves, educational absence, and sick leaves are ideal scenarios in which secondments could be arranged for potential executives, managers, or supervisors. These developmental opportunities are hard to come by, and they are usually created to meet some organizational need or longer-term restructuring process yet to be publicly announced.

Development education and opportunities are different from training in that they enhance the career future of employment by preparing employees for promotions, building better connections with higher-status employees, and providing exposure for their names in the organization or other workplaces. Development education and opportunities are usually initiated by executives and managers. It seldom originates from the employees as the latter are not aware of the changing organizational structure or the changing skill requirements or business priorities in the organization.

At the management level, succession management relies more on performance evaluation than at the executive level. This means that a list of potential managers for the future is still based on the perceptions of existing managers on how they have performed in the past. Unlike succession at the executive level, there are usually no requests from executives to managers to compile a list of potential managers for internal discussion among managers and executives. The executives have the autonomy to evaluate candidates on a regular promotion process in which they select their own candidates.

Despite this seemingly fair process, some executives may still carry out some forms of succession in which opportunities for grooming the next generation of managers arise. Executives may work with a departing or retiring manager to identify one or two candidates in professional occupations for special training in management areas in which the potential candidates have to learn more to become a competent manager or special development arrangement such as secondment in which the candidates are temporarily assigned new responsibilities as "acting managers" to acquire more on-the-job management training for a short period such as a few days/weeks depending on the circumstances. Similarly, identifying and grooming potential supervisors follows the earlier-mentioned process, usually at the discretion of the current supervisors.

Currently, it is fair to say that executives, managers, and supervisors are the drivers of development education and opportunities, and the latter are usually discretely carried out and not publicly announced until they are well into the process. The beneficiaries are employees who have been identified, selected, and groomed for succession and promotion by executives or other management staff. The names of the beneficiaries are kept confidential, and, sometimes, the beneficiaries are not even told. The current lack of Indigenous and racialized employees represented at the level of leadership and management suggests that they are usually not the ones groomed for development education and opportunities. As the process of identification, selection, and grooming is largely discreet, personal favourtism of leaders and managers becomes the principle of operation in excluding Indigenous or racialized employees.

Cloning

Who are likely to get developmental opportunities and what mechanism is put in place to make this succession happen?

When an organization does not have a policy that requires the posting of developmental opportunities, executives may exercise their own discretionary power to determine who should assume these positions. They may appoint any candidates that they like. In this situation, they would likely select those people with whom they feel comfortable working—people who look, think, and act like them and people who share similar perspectives on business and work approaches, lifestyles and hobbies, and so on (Leighton 1993; R. Smith 2002) As Fiona Sheridan (2013, 269–88) has observed, "people who are doing the judging unconsciously prefer people they're comfortable with, people they know, people who look like them, people whose experience they recognize." Incidentally, the chance of being cloned as White chief executive officers and White executives in an organization is high when the members of the board of directors are mostly White men (Brown, Brown, and Anastasopoulos 2002, 4).

Cloning reduces conflict between the people with authority and those without authority, and it increases the comfort level of the people with authority. Ryan Smith (2002) maintains that there is a tendency for people in authority positions to "reproduce themselves through exclusionary and inclusionary processes." As most executives are White men, it is likely that they would select White candidates who are within their comfort zones. Right now, the critical mass of White men at the executive level could easily clone new candidates in their own images, and such candidates may stay unchallenged for a long time. Indigenous and racialized employees really do not have much of a chance as long as cloning is a common practice at that level. Even at the managerial level, cloning is still dominant. Some studies have shown that White men are twice as likely to be promoted as managers when these positions are overseen by White men (Elliott and Smith 2004, 377).

Succession, as a corporate initiative, aims at stability, certainty, and harmony. Accordingly, the transition from one person to another person for positions must be as smooth as possible, with no drama and no tension. Cloning is an effective way to achieve that aim. Cloning basically means identifying a person who can replace an executive, manager, or supervisor when the time comes without much conflict. These positions are decision-making positions, and a person whose appearance, background, world-view, perspective, lifestyle, and approach are similar to the one who would be replaced, it lessons a lot of concerns and discomforts among the existing decision makers because they definitely fit with the corporate culture and could easily continue the normal corporate ways of getting things done or taking the organization to the next level that is on par with its vision and strategic directions. For these reasons, the most comfortable choice for a new successor in a conventional mode of White decision makers is a White man or, lately, a White woman. A selection of Indigenous and racialized person for a successor may be conducive to suspicion and unease, and, therefore, they are much less likely to be a person who is cloned by a White person who is in an authority position.

Some may argue that competency is the key principle for any upward succession of employees. Selecting a White person without any substantial competency for succession just because of their race would be at odds with this principle of human resources management. Smith (2002, 526, 530–32) notes that, for racialized people, competency plays a much stronger role at the lower end of the authority hierarchy (that is, lower-status positions) than for positions at the higher end. This finding also aligns with the life chances of racialized people in job movements. For employees who are "waiting to be promoted" due to their work histories, credentials, knowledge, and skills, it has been generally observed that competency is already a given attribute of almost everyone at that stage of their careers. In other words, these employees would not be competing only on the grounds of knowledge, skills, or work experience; they are also competing on other grounds. There are factors beyond competency that are at work here, and they play a more dominant role in securing executive, managerial, or supervisory positions. These factors are Indigeneity, race, ethnicity, gender, education, communication style, work approach, and experiences. Cloning gives White people an edge in securing development opportunities (Siu 2021, 181).

If developmental assignments are mandated to be posted internally first before appointments are made, then employees may scrutinize the appointment process. For posted job competitions, executives need to prepare job descriptions and schedule job interviewing processes. There are likely more candidates who come forward and apply for the positions, and these candidates may include diverse group members. There might be more monitoring by applicants and other employees on the progress of the selection process. In this sense, the developmental assignments are subject to more scrutiny.

In some cases, more transparent developmental assignments do not deter executives from providing opportunities for employees with whom they feel comfortable working. These employees look like them and have similar racial and cultural backgrounds, perspectives, work approaches, and lifestyles. The cloning phenomenon—executives/managers choosing people who are similar to them in succession, promotion, or appointment—has been well documented. Justification for cloning can be done on an ad hoc basis or as an afterthought, but, increasingly, it is more likely to be introduced at the stage in which the selection criteria, measurement, and interview panels are being prepared and organized. This usually means that the selection criteria and measurements are designed so that they can be aligned with the candidates' qualifications and experience, and the expected outcomes are in favour of those candidates who are "clones." Furthermore, the interview panelists are selected and gathered to represent the mouthpiece of the executives who designed the whole process. All these steps take some concerted effort to prepare and arrange, but human rights cases in the past provide evidence that supports this scenario (Berke 2005; Siegelman and Donohue III 2024). If the above process proceeds as designed, Indigenous or racialized employees could easily be screened out and fail to get these developmental assignments.

While the above example on executive or management developmental assignments provides insights on how racism in the form of cloning works, it could easily be adopted in many other development opportunities, including networking sessions and committee work. It can also be found at the supervisory level when developmental opportunities arise.

At first glance, cloning appears to be a "conspiracy" to promote people who are similar to the executives, managers, and supervisors. However, concerted efforts in human resources practices of this nature are common, and they could easily be incorporated in a broad range of activities such as outreach, recruitment, interviews, selection, hiring, succession, and promotion. Not all cases of succession or promotion work in this way. There are organizations that are trying hard to be more equitable and fairer and find ways to prevent cloning (as it tends to favour White males); the extent to which these practices succeed is questionable unless the entire succession management system is made more transparent and those in human resources decision-making processes are more Indigenous and racialized.

Leadership, Managerial, and Supervisory Values and Attributes

In some large corporations, appointing executives requires a process of determining whether the identified candidates for these positions are aligned well with leadership values that have been clearly articulated earlier in the process. Such values could include integrity, accountability, and collaboration, and every executive must adhere to them. There are usually two ways in which the values of these potential executive candidates are measured: primarily, through their work records and, secondarily, through job interview sessions. In addition, executive attributes (such as innovativeness, inclusiveness, and strategic leadership) and managerial/supervisory attributes (such as employee motivation, time management, and problem-solving) in terms of performance may also be used as reference points for matching. These attributes may be found in job descriptions.

Employees with prior experience working with executives directly definitely have an edge over other employees in getting passed this stage because, either through prior committee work, task force meetings, and so on, executives get a better sense of the values and attributes that the employee holds. That is why they are identified as candidates who are potential executives. At the managerial and supervisory levels where there are usually no clearly expressed sets of managerial or supervisory values, the reference points for measurement must be written organizational values. In job interviews, through candidates' descriptions of how they work as a team, how they bring in new ideas, how they influence and motivate others, or how they resolve problems or deal with crises, their values and attributes shine through. And these values could be compared with the stated organizational values, and their attributes could be compared with those listed on the job descriptions.

If there are no organizational values written or announced, then there are no yardsticks for measurement. In that case, the job interview panelists either have to come up with a clearly defined value statement or a list of attributes prior to the selection, or they can depend on their own personal discretion of what values should be used for evaluating candidates. If there are no clear values or attributes agreed upon up front, then the job interview process will likely be skewed in favour of the values held by the influential individual panelists.

Overall, the alignment with the leadership values (for executives) or organizational values (for managers and supervisors) and the alignment of their attributes with those listed in the job descriptions are important criteria for succession (and its related developmental opportunities). If these values and attributes are not delineated and communicated among the succession decision makers or are non-existent, then the chance for succession will be largely determined by the discretion of the executives, managers, or supervisors. And if some employees have the prior opportunities to work with these bosses in various capacities, then they will have an additional edge over others to be included in the succession pipelines. The conventional cloning practice and favouritism tendency—which higher-status persons use often to include lower-status people in their inner circles—is likely to be adopted. And, in an echelon of executives where White men and women largely dominate, Indigenous and racialized employees may not get a fair share in the succession pipelines or job competitions.

At the managerial and supervisory level where succession is seldom carried out as comprehensively as it is adopted at the executive level, developmental opportunities such as secondments and stretch assignments or training opportunities such as in-house courses may still be provided. These opportunities would likely be provided by managers or supervisors to give potential candidates that they favour some advantage in later job competitions. The most likely discrete opportunities for these candidates are for them to acquire additional responsibilities normally found in management or supervision in the form of developmental assignments (such as accompanying managers or supervisors to attend meetings with their superiors or working on a briefing note for an external meeting) so that they pick up additional knowledge and skills that are useful for positions in management and supervision along with their normal daily routines. Whether Indigenous and racialized employees will get these discrete responsibilities depends on how comfortable the bosses are in providing discrete "grooming" actions for them. Once again, it boils down to the trust level that the bosses have with Indigenous and racialized employees, the extent to which they have racial stereotypes and prejudices against these groups in their mindsets, and the social distancing that they exhibit in their relationship with these two parties.

Mentorship and Sponsorship

In a workplace environment, mentoring usually refers to a relationship between a more senior and experienced person with higher status and a more junior and less experienced person with lower status. Such a relationship enables the more senior and experienced person to provide guidance and nurturing support with the objective of grooming the junior person to build a career that the junior person has in mind. In contrast with the coaching discussed above, mentoring is more comprehensive in its approach, and it focuses on the development of an employee on a more long-term basis (including values, character, motivation, soft and hard skills, work-related training and developmental nurturing, and network building) and not just on their short-term performance or occupational skills. While this one-way top-down mentoring relationship is not the only kind of mentoring model (and there are other more egalitarian and peer-based mentoring models), it remains a dominant one, even today.

As a method for grooming candidates to become executives, managers, or supervisors, mentoring is not only limited to succession management, it can also be found as a formal method in any individualized performance improvement plan or even as an informal method for employees to get advice on career planning or problem-solving. Mentoring may not be limited to people working at one organization. A mentor may guide an employee from another organization and vice versa when an employee potentially finds a mentor who works in another organization. While it is usually a hidden agenda in mentoring for the mentor to equip the mentee with the right kind of knowledge, skills, and connections for their promotion or at least for them to retain their job or do it better, it is not explicitly expressed. Meanwhile, the mentee may also be motivated to learn from their mentor's wisdom how best to get an edge in promotion competitions as well as actualizing their inner potential. Since the mentor has been in the organization for longer, they will be able to provide needed guidance and support on how best to navigate the process of promotion, such as how to build one's networks both within the organization and outside, to prepare one's resume, and to prepare for interviews or testing assignments. There are definitely distinct benefits for Indigenous and racialized employees to have mentors either inside or outside their workplaces. Mentors may be able to guide and support them as they learn the "ropes" of surviving and prospering in their organizations.

Similar to coaching, mentoring may be a part of an individualized performance improvement plan that develops from the performance management system. But it does not have to be. At this stage, one general observation suggests that mentoring is a less common way for executives or managers to commit to help employees not only improve their performance but also reveal their commitment to groom them. This is because mentoring has not been formally incorporated as an integral part of performance management or leadership development. "Formally" means a mandatory requirement or corporate encouragement for executives or managers to mentor their employees. Such an organizational requirement/encouragement has led to mentoring becoming more structured, coordinated, and developed to the extent that it has an accountability framework and a set of program objectives and procedure. In larger organizations, there might be a special staff member whose portfolio has the responsibility for managing a corporate mentoring program. Currently, only some larger corporations in Canada have such formal mentoring programs. Even when a formal mentoring program exists, it is usually a small program in which an executive or manager can mentor no more than two employees at one time; otherwise, mentoring may become a burden to them and interrupt their normal day-to-day work. This demonstrates the limitation of mentoring as an impactful way to benefit employees and, thereby, their organizations.

In an organization, there are usually more employees who would like to be mentored by seasoned and experienced executives and managers, and the latter are usually fewer in number than the junior members, so a formal mentioning program is therefore constrained by this relative lack of senior managers and leaders as mentors. This means that there is a great chance that the mentees under this formal program are the result of management or leadership favouritism. Mentees are usually hand-picked by managers or executives in this program. Unless there are clear objective selection criteria prescribed and approved by the organizational leaders that are fair, equitable, and free from discriminatory practice, and the selection process is monitored and regularly reviewed and evaluated, personal biases are likely to permeate this process. This is one of the areas in formal mentoring programs that give executives and managers a lot of discretionary power to select their own mentees. Some progressive organizations have included in their formal programs equitable features such as giving priority to equity-seeking group members such as Indigenous peoples, LGBTQIA+, persons with disabilities, racialized people, and women. However, other organizations have shied away from mentioning these equity-seeking groups to avoid a backlash from the traditionally privileged group (such as White people) or resistance from employees as a whole. Hence, managers and executives tiptoe gingerly around this issue when selecting employees for mentoring.

Empirical studies on the composition of mentees in formal or informal mentoring arrangements in organizations are not readily available, but what has happened in corporate affinity groups in large corporate organizations shows some telltale signs of leadership and management biases. This author has conducted numerous focus groups based on affinity employee groups, and the findings show that events organized by Indigenous and racialized affinity employee groups in large corporations seldom attract executives and managers to attend. The only exception is women-affinity employee groups. Executives and managers attend their functions much more readily than any other affinity groups. Such a skewed situation might have changed a little considering the outspokenness of Indigenous peoples and Black people on colonialism and anti-Black racism, and their open protests have ignited a lot more media coverage and public discussion.

When it comes to mentoring and how mentees are selected by mentors, this skewness in the selection process for events organized by women-affinity employee groups suggests that there is a comfort zone between managers and executives, on the one hand, and female employees, on the other. It might be the gradual ascendency of White women in the upper echelons of management and leadership that has fostered such a comfort level, and it might be the larger size of the female workforce in the workplace that has solidified the closeness of the relationship between women employees and management and leadership. The implication is that executives and managers who are in a position to be mentors in a formal mentoring program have a tendency to select White women to be mentees rather than Indigenous or racialized men and women in a formal mentoring program run by organizations. Admittedly, there is an undercurrent that discourages the mentoring of women by men since men are concerned that such mentoring may be interpreted as gender favouritism, which is a topic of social gossip in the workplace.

There are mentoring relationships in organizations without a formal program, and they are better known as informal mentoring arrangements. Informal mentoring has the same objectives as formal mentoring, and they could be uni-directional (that is, top down in this case when a senior person mentors a more junior one). The main difference is that employees must find their own mentors in the workplace, whereas executives and managers in a formal program have to find their own mentees. This reverse pattern in informal mentoring makes it more difficult for Indigenous and racialized employees to find mentors. Why? When an organization is not inclined to develop a formal mentoring program, it suggests that the priority of leadership is not in mentoring or the growth of employees. Executives or managers may not have any moral high ground or corporate reason to encourage mentoring. The idea is to let employees develop their own mentorships if they so desire.

It would be difficult to see any executive and manager standing out and volunteering to be a mentor in this corporate culture as there is no corporate recognition or reward for doing so. Thus, when employees approach executives or managers to establish a mentoring relationship on their own, the response from them will likely be disappointing to these employees. It is even more difficult for Indigenous and racialized employees to secure a mentorship from any executives and managers considering their social distancing prior to their requests.

As discussed earlier in this section, it takes extra time and effort on the part of the executives and managers to mentor employees over and above their regular duties. As noted earlier, the remote work mode used in the COVID-19 pandemic and the hybrid work model that followed have made it even more difficult for executives and managers to manage the new work model and to get to know employees well enough, let alone Indigenous and racialized employees (Pickup 2022). While the current post-pandemic work situation warrants additional guidance and support from leadership, this situation can also encourage more burn-out among employees if they accept the additional responsibility of mentoring.

Sponsorship is an additional commitment that executives, managers, or supervisors offer to a few of their employees (who are already in a mentorship with them). In addition to the guidance and advice provided in an ordinary mentoring relationship, they actively promote these few employees as promotable employees to their superiors. In other words, the sponsors are committed to promoting their chosen employees to a higher level in the organization and continue to play this role until these employees under their "wings" are actually promoted. This commitment can be made known to the chosen mentees in a discrete and confidential manner. However, this is usually an unwise move on the part of the sponsors because workplace gossip networks like to connect the dots between the sponsors and the results of their future promotions. This might make it conducive for employees to be suspicious of any formal job postings that are faking fairness or openness.

In general, sponsorship is not a transparent act, and the short list of potential candidates for high-level executive positions is kept secretive. This keeps many potential candidates or employees who wish to be promoted guessing all the time. They look for clues and signs of employees getting special favours from their higher ups. Potential candidates on the short list probably notice that they are being asked to attend more meetings with people at a higher level; they are offered more leadership opportunities or management education (through their attendance at professional conferences) or given special assignments with critical importance to the organization; or they are asked to take the lead in new projects. All of these possibilities are either training or developmental opportunities offered at the discretion of executives or managers.

Executives usually play the role of sponsors mainly because of their high-status positions, their proximity to the inner circle of decision makers, and their influential power within that circle as well as their connections with other levels of the organization. Middle-level managers and supervisors may not have the influential power that executives have to play that role. Often, managers must team up with one or more executives to exercise the role of a sponsor. In general, sponsors have to converse not only with other executives, and, perhaps, their chief executive officer, to promote their mentees, but they may also need to give their mentees the opportunities to meet them or even work on a task together so that they are familiar with the values, attributes, and performance of their mentees. Unless these sponsors have absolute confidence in the calibre of their mentees and are totally comfortable with their conduct and performance, they would not "stick their heads" out and promote these mentees. Such confidence and comfort in a workplace are seldom found between executives, managers, and supervisors, on the one hand, and Indigenous and racialized employees, on the other. To introduce new segments of employees beyond the "old boys' club"—especially among the executives or even middle-level managers—destabilizes the status quo. Mentors may find it hard to break the homogeneity of Whiteness at that level since it introduces uncertainty and undermines the privilege of those at the decision-making level. Bringing in Indigenous/racialized employees in a traditional privileged group may raise suspicions and mistrust as new people usually do not have much allegiance to traditional ways of running an organization, and they may be viewed as a challenge, especially if they do not have a proven track record (Pettigrew 1992, 163–82).

This does not mean that some degree of confidence and comfort cannot be found between leaders and Indigenous/racialized employees, but they are much more rare. The one exception is found in a workplace with prevalent principles of diversity, equity, and inclusiveness and a firm commitment and active advocacy within leadership. Under these conditions, mentorship and sponsorship of Indigenous/racialized people are actively encouraged and executed.

In the findings of past focus groups and interviews in organizations in Canada that this author has gathered, the experiences of Indigenous and racialized employees show that they have difficulties in securing mentorship, let alone sponsorship, within their organizations. A few of them have explored mentorships beyond their own organizations through some community-based organizations or other informal networks cultivated by them. Whether these mentoring opportunities meet their needs or not remains to be determined, but they have managed to get some mentoring support. The problem with informal mentoring arrangements in the workplace is that it is more onerous for Indigenous/racialized employees to make those arrangements by themselves without much support or encouragement from leadership. Their social isolation, social distancing, and embedded prejudice and stereotypes suggest that they are uncomfortable with each other, and this further deters the initiative of mentorships. These employees may be good at networking among their peers but not with those higher in status and those who hold the decision-making power on their chance of promotion.

This discussion on mentoring makes it obvious that, whether or not there is a formal mentoring program in the workplace, Indigenous and racialized employees have a harder time securing a mentoring relationship with a more senior and experienced executive or manager. The workplace culture and structure that they are in is not conducive for them to gain the privilege of being mentored. Is racism part of the problem of this skewed situation where Indigenous and racialized employees are disadvantaged in being mentored or sponsored? The answer, in one word, is "likely." One thing that Indigenous and racialized people experience a lot is the ambiguous nature of human behaviour in the workplace. They are not 100 percent sure why they have not been selected to be the mentees by potential mentors in a formal mentoring program or why they are not able to secure the acceptance of potential mentors when they approach them. These potential mentors have come up with numerous seemingly legitimate reasons why they could not be the mentors to these employees such as: they are too busy now; they already have enough mentees and they cannot handle more; they are too new to the organization; they have too many commitments coming up soon and are unlikely to do a good job in mentoring; and other reasons. All these reasons sound legitimate and reasonable. Yet another set of questions swirling in the heads of Indigenous and racialized people are: are these potential mentors racists who have ignored my requests; are they being racially discriminatory when they have been mentoring White employees before but not me; are they rejecting me as a potential mentee because I am an Indigenous or racialized person or because I have Brown, Yellow, or Black skin or because I speak the language with an accent; and so on? These are questions that have no clear or definitive answers, and there is no empirical proof one way or another.

From their perspectives, the only thing that is certain and clear is that Indigenous persons and racialized persons have seldom been selected or accepted as a mentee in the organization, formally or informally. It is also clear that no one in the organization is able to provide concrete evidence that they have been discriminated against. The bottom line is that racism exists when one does not find a proportionate number of mentees who are Indigenous or racialized in the organization. We are clear that racism occurs when its adverse impacts in the life chances and career growth of Indigenous and racialized employees are measurable, and its subjective realized impacts on their mental health and well-being are felt. On both fronts, the adverse impacts are clear to them: they are not being mentored, and they feel unappreciated by this lack of mentorship opportunities. As this kind of racism is so subtle, it cannot be easily proven or not proven. It is an ambiguous yet perpetual situation in which Indigenous and racialized people find themselves, maybe even on a daily basis, as some Indigenous and racialized employees have claimed.

PROMOTION AND JOB MOVEMENT

Indigenous and racialized employees have many experiences in the workplace that they are not happy about. One of their main areas of dissatisfaction is their lack of promotion or even lateral transfers. Often, they do not know exactly the reasons why they have been passed over in the past, but one thing seems to be clear based on their experiences and that is that White employees—men or women—tend to have the advantage when it comes to promotion. Both the federal and provincial human rights commissions and tribunals have documented many cases of racial discrimination in promotions. Often, managers' allocation of work to employees, their evaluations of employees' performance, and their interviews and decisions on promoting specific employees are subjective in nature despite their seeming objectivity in nature. As noted earlier in this chapter, their subjectivity is entangled with the selection of employees for special work assignments or committees, the design of instruments used to measure performance, and the selection criteria for promotions.

Stereotypes and Prejudice

In the health-care profession, the *Canada (Canadian Human Rights Tribunal) v. Canada (Department of National Health and Welfare)* case in 1997 showed that Health Canada had discriminated against racialized people in scientific and professional jobs by making it difficult for them to be promoted to senior management positions (Halwani 2004).[1]

There are numerous reasons why getting a promotion from a professional position to a managerial position is difficult for Indigenous/racialized employees. The following "reasons" for not promoting them appear to be an extension of racial prejudice and stereotypes.

Leaders may believe that Indigenous and racialized employees may have difficulty in motivating their team members to follow their lead because, for a long time in history and even now, White people have been the dominant leaders, and White employees are used to reporting to them. If and when Indigenous and racialized people become bosses, it creates a "cognitive dissonance" that psychologists have labelled a mental state in which it is confronting a new situation that is at odds with what people are used to. The promotion of an Indigenous or racialized person to a managerial position destabilizes the status quo of our conventional mindset, and some people may have difficulty in accepting it.

To avoid such a scenario, leaders may opt for a safer option and that means that promoting a White person is less risky than promoting an Indigenous or racialized person, especially when the employees who would report to them are White people. Such risk avoidance is based on race and is most likely made when most employees are White, and these White employees are assumed to be reluctant to be subordinate to an Indigenous or racialized boss. Can this be an example of racial discrimination? If the decision of the leaders considered the race factor, and there is evidence for that, especially if the Indigenous and

---

1 *Canada (Canadian Human Rights Commission) v Canada (Department of National Health and Welfare)*, 2018 SCC 31.

racialized candidates are qualified and proven to be competent, there is a strong likelihood that it could be interpreted as a case of racial discrimination.

In addition, leaders may have another belief that the cultural upbringing of Indigenous and racialized employees may not be suitable for leadership. What is it in their cultural upbringing that impacts on their leadership? The term "cultural" is a broad concept. Individual views on this may vary. How Indigenous people or racialized people are brought up in their families and communities may be influential, but it is not clear how their upbringing could impact on the quality of leadership to the extent that they should not be promoted to become a leader. There is prejudice toward Indigenous people and a belief that they are not reliable and trustworthy or that their traditional leadership vision of egalitarianism, community orientation, and partnership are at odds with the contemporary mainstream hierarchical relationship, business orientation, and individual achievement. Meanwhile, Black people are seen as having poor communication skills and being aggressive, and Asians are viewed as being indirect in communication and passive in their actions (Siu 2021, 68–69, 72–75). Some leaders believe that these attributes are grounded in how Black and Asian children have been brought up: Black children learn to stand up when being tramped on and fighting fire with fire, while Asian children learn to be considerate of the people around them and to be quiet, humble, and modest—as an old Japanese saying goes: "nails that stand up get hammered." However, in none of these cases does one's cultural upbringing influence the quality of one's organizational leadership.

And there are leaders who believe that racialized people, especially Asian people, are capable of working as professionals and technicians but not capable of leading and managing people. Where this belief comes from is not clear. It might be linked with their belief that racialized people are not management material and that they would not be good as leaders or managers because of their attributes (as discussed in the previous paragraph). The relatively higher educational credentials that Asian people have acquired in information technology, finance, business and commerce, medicine, engineering, law, and data science (and they often excel in these fields) have historically "ghettoized" them as professionals or technicians, who are unable to be promoted to leadership and management positions. The image of Asian people as professionals or technicians has become their stereotype.

Over-Qualification

The issue of subjectivity among leaders who are in a position to make decisions on promotion is seldom reviewed. The Canadian Human Rights Tribunal's decision in *Sangha v Mackenzie Valley Land and Water Board* showed that using "over-qualification" as a reason for not letting racialized candidates have a job could be treated as racial discrimination.[2]

How can the qualification of candidates being interpreted as excessive to the point of "over-qualification" render these candidates as un-hirable or un-promotable? It is understandable that an employer may reject candidates on the basis that the qualifications of candidates are not aligned with those required for certain positions or that their qualifications are under- or unqualified for the positions. "Over" is a term that describes an excessive quality that is not required. This is a subjective imputation of an undesirable feature onto the qualification that is actually required by the position advertised and beyond. Such a subjective imputation of an "undesirable" feature is likely to be personal and is unlikely to be unsubstantiated by evidence that the excessive feature is harmful to the organization. In monetary terms, the employer is actually not just getting a person who can do the job as advertised but is able to do it "over and above" the requirement. One may even argue that over-qualified candidates are indeed resourceful for the employer as they, as employees, may be able to make a better contribution to the organization because of their "excessive" qualifications and that these candidates are ready and available for further promotions. Furthermore, the employer actually gets an employee (who is "over-qualified") for the same salary payment as one who is just qualified, and it is a cost-effective way to accomplish human resources management.

A general observation suggests that the issue of "over-qualification" has often been used as an excuse not to hire racialized people who have a higher education level, often with university or college credentials from abroad or even in Canada in the past several decades. Now, with graduates increasingly earning higher credentials on the job market, employers are seeing more of them applying or seeking jobs or promotions, even with qualifications that used to be labelled as over-qualification. Due to this change in the labour market, employers are increasingly hiring and promoting candidates who have historically been labelled

---

2 *Sangha v Mackenzie Valley Land and Water Board*, 2006 CHRT 9.

as "over-qualified." They could be racialized immigrants, women, and youth. It remains to be seen whether over-qualification is still a discriminatory factor that is reserved for racialized people (irrespective of their gender and age) but not for White people or youth. Only more research studies will tell.

Internal Job Posting or Not?

Like hiring, promotion follows similar processes of recruitment and selection. When positions are vacant or expected to be vacant in the perceivable future, or when a new position is created, employers have the option of making an announcement or "advertising" the position through an internal posting to the current employees or secretly arranging for an employee to fill that position without much fanfare.

General observations suggest that, for higher-status positions such as executive positions, most organizations still follow the traditional approach where secrecy remains the hallmark of promotion. The lack of transparency regarding how to get a promotion to these high-status positions is built into the succession management. For middle-level positions, such a hallmark is still prevalent in many organizations, but there are signs that it is changing in the direction of more transparency. In other words, managerial positions are subject to the increasing requirements of internal job postings, external job postings, or both. For supervisory positions, internal job postings are very common. However, in smaller organizations, these positions may not be posted, and secret grooming does take place upon the discretion of the supervisors in preparation for a replacement. Sometimes, an external job posting is carried out simultaneously to increase the number of applicants.

It appears that, as one moves through the hierarchy of positions, the higher the status of the position, the greater the chance that they are less transparent in the announcement of vacancy and the lesser the chance that employees have a fair chance to compete for those positions. Not being in the inner circles of leadership and management, in addition to the social distancing and isolation that they experience, Indigenous and racialized employees are not privy to the social gossip or workplace rumours on forthcoming vacancies, which gives them even less chance to do some informal navigation toward influencing those in the decision-making position on promotions.

No Internal Job Posting

The internal secret grooming of potential candidates for promotion can be carried on under the official radar. Those who have been "assigned" to identify potential candidates communicate in secrecy on how best to groom them. Reducing the promotion process from the formal mode of job posting and notification of selection and interview process to that of "word of mouth" at the discretion of one or more selected individuals introduces unfairness and renders Indigenous or racialized employees disadvantaged, even as they position themselves for the positions. They do not have access to the information on the forthcoming business directions or strategies, the personnel retirements or relocations, the restructuring of the workplace, or other organizational changes. With this information gap, they are not able to find ways to highlight how they could contribute to the organization and make a good impression on the decision makers.

Meanwhile, the decision makers tend to identify candidates through their histories of working with them in terms of assignments, projects, committee works, or being under their supervision. At the lower level, work performance may have a larger influence on their decisions, but the decisions boil down to trust—whether or not they trust these candidates. The cloning process, which has been discussed earlier, enables the decision makers to include those candidates who are similar to them in one form or another—race, ethnicity, gender, class, and so on—and are familiar to them through working relationships. In addition to the cloning process, the importance of a trusting relationship is harder to ignore in a work environment in which racial prejudice and stereotyping are embedded in terms of both corporate culture and human mindset. Prejudice and stereotypes make it difficult to establish or build up a long-standing trusting relationship between Indigenous and racialized people and the corporate decision makers in human resources. Without trust, Indigenous and racialized employees would not likely be identified as candidates for a promotion.

When the vacant or soon-to-vacant position is not made known to current employees, and, subsequently, an employee has filled in the position, employees will clearly be surprised. And an announcement that an employee has been promoted is perceived to be unfair and illegitimate for many employees. If a White employee gets the position, Indigenous and racialized employees will feel that they have been racially discriminated. Such a feeling may or may not be justified, but, in this context, it is clear that the employer has committed a management error in keeping the promotion opportunity secretive and not posting the vacant position. Whether racial discrimination is the driving force is not relevant because, in the final analysis, Indigenous and racialized employees have been deprived of the opportunity to compete for that position, and none of them have been promoted (or received a job transfer). In a corporate environment where racial prejudice and discrimination is a norm, this deprivation of social mobility could be construed as racist behaviour.

Internal Job Posting

When the position is posted and a White employee has filled that position, those Indigenous and racialized employees who applied and were not selected for interviews, or those who applied and were selected for interviews but did not get the promotion they wanted, will be concerned. As discussed earlier in Chapter 6, between the job application and hiring stages, there are many components in the process that are subject to policy biases and management system deficiencies including unconscious biases that people (including those decision makers) are not aware of. These biases are often embedded in the application, screening, interviewing, scoring, ranking, and selection processes—some are more obvious than others. When these biases are compounded by racial stereotyping and prejudice, no matter how extensive and intense they are, Indigenous and racialized employees may be subject to racial discrimination.

SENIORITY SYSTEM

Seniority has always been an issue to which unions have not been prepared to yield, despite the fact that it has been shown to be an employment barrier for racialized and Indigenous people. However, it is an issue that is multifaceted, and it is worth reviewing the context of how unions have been allowing the seniority system to perpetuate racial inequality instead of eradicating it.

Louise Delude (1992) prepared a working paper entitled "Seniority and Employment Equity" for the Canadian Human Rights Commission back in the summer of 1992, analyzing the complexity of seniority and how it indicates the extensiveness and comprehensiveness of how the seniority system works to the disadvantages of racialized and Indigenous peoples. Seniority is a fundamental principle for unions, and it remains a sacred cow in collective bargaining. This principle assumes that persons with the longest period of time working in an organization should be most preferred in employment.

Even if the seniority clause is not explicitly inserted in the collective agreement, the common use of "past practice" in arbitral jurisprudence related to an employer's way of doing things could be considered as a precedence for justifying centain practice. For example, an employer's reliance on seniority in determining vacation time is not necessarily included in a specific collective agreement. There are many implicit issues related to seniority that might emerge in the workplace. Arbitrators are often asked to consider the principle of past practice before their decisions.

Seniority Types

Depending on the organizations, the seniority clause has been inserted in collective agreements in many different ways:

- There is "competitive" seniority in human resources functions, including hiring and promotion, job transfers, job assignments, shift preference, training and development, the selection of work hours or days off, overtime arrangement, compensation, vacation time, access to parking or company housing, leaves, retention, termination, lay-off, and recall. These are competitive because employees are competing with each other, usually for definitive opportunities or positions.
- There are also "benefit" seniority features in other human resources functions such as pension eligibility and entitlements, insurance plans, vacation durations, paid holidays, severance pays, sick leave and maternity leave, profit-sharing benefits and bonuses, supplementary unemployment benefits, automatic wage increases, long service wage adjustments, and rewards. These functions are non-competitive as these functions are attached to the positions of the employees. Theoretically, once employees are secured in their positions, the benefits come with the positions.

Seniority as a Gradation of Priority in Decisions

While no definitive studies have been done on the presence of these seniority provisions in collective agreements, it suffices to say that a substantial number of them are present. Seniority rights could be carried out in hiring and promotion in an absolute (or straight or sole criterion of seniority), modest (where seniority is placed higher in priority), or mild (seniority is only one of several criteria) manner, which specifies the gradation of how candidates are hired or promoted at the discretion of the hiring manager or the criteria utilized according to the collective agreement. These managers could use seniority (length of service) as the sole criterion for selection, or they could use multiple criteria such as knowledge, educational credentials, ability, cross-sectorial experience, or physical strength.

In collective bargaining, even though unionists are adamant in using seniority rights as a tool, among competitive seniority provisions in collective agreements, most seniority rights are exerted in a modest manner, which means that a mix of seniority and other factors (such as skills) are commonly used in promotions, lay-offs, and recalls. Absolute (or straight) seniority is seldom used in promotions, and about one-quarter of lay-offs and recalls are constrained by the use of modest seniority, which means that other equivalent factors may be used in place of absolute seniority. Absolute (or straight) seniority is most often found in occupations with low-level skills (such as in the food and clothing industries) or in organizations with a relatively large number of employees who have a level of technical skill (such as in utilities or transportation).

Part-Time Work

Unions have often made it difficult for new people to join their unions. Seniority provisions are seldom made in collective agreements for part-time employees; in addition, some of them even specify that part-time employees are to be laid off first in case of staff reduction. Some collective agreements put part-time employees under separate bargaining units. In the construction and entertainment industries, new candidates must pay high initiation fees to join unions in their trades. Some unions require apprenticeships to be lengthy in order to regulate "graduates" so as not to threaten existing members. Similarly, some unions maintain low membership volumes so that existing members get their work regularly and steadily. All these measures are meant to restrict membership especially when more immigrants and racialized and Indigenous people are knocking at union doors. High industrial demands in the construction industry may be dealt with through temporary work permits for non-members.

Promotions and Transfers

Under the seniority system, discrimination based on race has largely been under-documented except where it has been made clear that there are separate job classifications and separate job titles, even though White people and racialized people perform similar tasks. Such discriminatory practices have been noted in some industries such as the steel industry. Seniority systems excluding women from promotions or having their job classifications excluded from promotion lines have been noted. The extent to which these segregated promotion lines also applied to racialized people and Indigenous peoples is unclear. The idea was to prevent them from integration, such as not hiring or promoting them in certain occupations.

In Canada, there has been a tendency for racialized and Indigenous peoples to be hired in occupations that are below their capabilities. There have also been employment barriers to promotion. Seniority systems usually worked against them as they were not allowed to transfer from one department to another one unless they were prepared to lose all their seniority years that they had accumulated in one department and start all over again (that is, at an entry level) in another department. Racialized and Indigenous people have a much higher tendency to be hired in a seniority unit that has lower wages or shorter wage ranges, and, once they are in this lower-wage seniority unit, they have greater difficulty in moving to another seniority unit that has higher wages or a broader range of wage increases as they have to start at the entry level (bottom level) of the other seniority unit. Since there are many ways to set up seniority units, people in each unit are placed in job ghettoes with little chance of escaping. It is also easier for employers to discriminate against racialized or Indigenous people as their work is usually compartmentalized. Furthermore, seniority rights may also create more steps or require more time for marginalized groups in their wage increases, thus forcing them to take more time to reach the same wage level as the dominant groups.

Having bargaining units for different employee groups within an organization is an employment barrier for racialized and Indigenous peoples. Due to the fact that seniority rights for employees are not portable across bargaining units, this results in job ghettoization without advancement as not many employees are prepared to drop all their seniority rights when they move out of their current department. Along this line is the fragmentation of the organizational workforce into different occupational groups with their own bargaining units and seniority systems, which further limit the promotion of employees once they have been initially hired in one type of occupational group, which usually happens to have lower wages and a narrower wage spectrum like those occupied largely by racialized or Indigenous peoples. Unionists are seldom prepared to give exemptions to those who wish to cross these departmental boundaries.

A seemingly neutral requirement for access to jobs could have an adverse impact on racialized or Indigenous peoples. Educational credentials and aptitude tests, when used in selecting candidates, may exclude some racialized or Indigenous employees in promotions or job transfers. These selection criteria may exclude these employees in a disproportionate manner as most of them do not have these credentials and would not fare well in these tests. Such adverse impacts on marginalized groups could be interpreted as discriminatory when seniority rights are accompanied with educational credentials or aptitude tests in decisions related to promotions or job transfers. In cases of this nature, employers must show that such a practice (which has an adverse impact in a disproportionate manner) is justified legally. To be legally justifiable, (1) employers must prove that the "discrimination" (or the selection criteria for hiring or promotion) must be "bona fide occupational requirements" and (2) employers must also provide accommodations to racialized or Indigenous people or any other historically disadvantaged people, which would enable them to do the job up to the point of undue hardship for the employers. These two "tests" are to be applied to the seniority principle to determine the legality of seniority systems. The "seniority principle" is that an employee is entitled to special employment benefits and preferences based on the fact that the employee has worked longer for the same employer (Delude 1992, 69). Based on the observations of Delude (1992, 77), Canadian employers and unions have seldom mitigated the negative impacts of the seniority system on racialized or Indigenous peoples. Unions seldom put in serious efforts to negotiate "short of undue hardship" accommodation in collective bargaining, and employers seldom explicitly justify their degree of accommodating racialized or Indigenous employees to the extent of short of undue hardship such as accommodation expences, workplace morale, major intervention on a collective agreement, or disruption of facilities.

There are also seniority units that encompass a production unit, department, or geographic area. In general, these units are restrictive especially when skills are more specialized and are difficult to transfer across work units. If seniority units are categorized by skills, benefits, or lay-offs, it would make movements from one position to another one immensely complicated. Currently, unionized workplaces exhibit different patterns of mixed seniority rights in collective agreements for promotions and transfers within a department. However, the issue of seniority rights becomes more inflexible when employees move from one department to another, especially when different (or competing) bargaining units are involved.

Benefits under a Seniority System

Rewards based on the length of service could be discriminatory when two groups of employees are differentially rewarded when one group's wage spectrum could be lengthened by additional progression steps that are not found in another group. Another discriminatory practice is to reward one group of employees by covering their seniority rights during absence from work due to illness, while other groups of employees do not have their seniority rights covered when they are absent due to specific illness. This second practice is usually referred to as gender-based seniority units when women are denied pregnancy-related leaves. For racialized employees, instead of special illnesses, it could be special religions, festivities, or cultural events that demand special time-off from work, which are not covered by seniority rights.

Policy Biases

There are several notable policy biases that are found in some organizations, and these biases work against the advancement of Indigenous and racialized employees.

Getting Permission before Application

Some organizations have a human resources policy that requires employees to notify their executives, managers, or supervisors and get their permission first before they can apply for a promotion (or a job transfer) within their organization. The main reason for such a policy is to make it easier for leaders to manage so that departure of some employees will not come as a surprise. However, a manager's primary priority is to manage their team well and keep it productive. Hence, employees who can meet this standard are likely to be retained as long as possible in the team. Such a policy actually encourages employees to seek job opportunities for a "promotion" elsewhere in other organizations, lest their requests for an internal promotion got rejected.

In this sense, the policy discourages all employees to apply for an internal promotion; however, it has a more adverse effect on Indigenous/racialized employees because they know from their own experience that applying for a higher-status position in another organization is much more difficult than one internally because they are "unknown commodities" outside their current organization. Thus, this policy places Indigenous and racialized employees in a more awkward position in seeking promotional opportunities. In addition to the difficulty in competing for an external position, they learn from their experience that their performance evaluation findings are usually not at the top level, and, thus, they may not get a chance to compete for an internal promotion, especially if their bosses are not prepared to speak highly for them, even though they have given them permission to apply internally. Therefore, Indigenous/racialized employees are between a rock and a hard place when it comes to job movement if they wish to have upward occupational mobility. They are often stuck in their current positions for a much longer time than their White colleagues.

Eligibility for an Internal Job Application

Some organizations have a human resources policy that requires employees to be in their current positions for a duration of time (such as two years) before they can apply for a promotion (or a job transfer). The rationale behind this eligibility rule is that it is usual for any employee to take about one or two years before they reach theie optimal level in any position. For this reason, it would be premature to move, or be promoted, to another position until the employee has reached this optimal point. This rationale has some problematic assumptions including employee learning curves, management supports, and workplace morale, and it has the potential to drive existing employees to leave their current organizations if they wish to advance in their careers more quickly. More importantly for understanding racism at work, such a requirement has a detrimental impact on employees who are fast learners and good performers on their job movements in an organization.

It also jeopardizes the chance for Indigenous and racialized employees to develop in their career because, historically, they have been slow in moving to positions where their talents can be fully actualized either to be promoted or to get lateral job movement. As a result, they tend to be stagnated in their job movements and stay in their positions longer than White employees, often measured in years. Such job stagnation is further reinforced by their lack of exposure to, and support fro higher-level employees; a lack of coaching, mentoring, and sponsorship; social distancing and isolation at work; and a lack of name recognition in the organization. All these factors have made it difficult for them to have a break in their job mobility either inside or outside their organizations or even for them to have some form of job movement; they experience role constraints, which results in the erosion of their skills (Collins 1997; Bean, Leach, and Lowell 2004; Wilson and Roscigno 2020).

Minimal Performance Evaluation Scores Prior to Internal Job Application

Some organizations have a human resources policy that requires employees to submit their performance evaluation results with at least the top two scores (as in "excellent" or "outstanding") along with their job application for a promotion or job transfer. Usually, these scores are part of the score scale of performance evaluation assigned by their executives, managers, or supervisors. The rationale behind this requirement is that employees with lower scores than the top two scores should spend more time at their current positions to improve their performance before they attempt to get a promotion or a job transfer. In other words, an employee should reach the peak of performance in their current positions before getting a new job with different or more extensive/important responsibility.

Such a requirement certainly impacts negatively on all employees as it hinders their job mobility and leaves the control of their careers fully in the hands of their current bosses prior to their screening, interviewing, and selection. It drives existing employees to look for external positions in other organizations, thus creating an outflow of talent in the organization. However, the impact on Indigenous and racialized employees is even more adverse. As shown earlier in the discussion of the biases inherent in current performance evaluation models, the relatively lower scores of the performance of Indigenous and racialized employees (when compared with White employees) at a collective level means that the chance for them to believe that they have a chance for internal promotion or any job movement is diminished. The result is that they would not be allowed to apply for positions that involve a promotion or a job transfer for them. It seems obvious that the door for career growth is therefore closed if they wish to stay in the same organization. Once again, this policy has the potential to drive Indigenous and racialized employees out.

Management System Deficiencies

There are also human resources management system problems that work against Indigenous and racialized employees when they come to the issue of job movement, like promotion and job transfers.

Undefined Career Paths

Some organizations do not have clear career paths showing how employees could be promoted or transferred to other positions. This is a management issue that frustrates many employees as they do not know how they can move laterally or upwards in an organization and, consequently, may end up being stagnated in their current positions.

It is unclear why so many organizations do not have this organizational feature in their human resources management; however, the most likely scenario is that human resources development has been managed in an ad hoc and unplanned manner, and efforts have not been made to systematically delineate the types and levels of competency needed for each position. A few global companies have managed to make headway in developing a "flow chart" or diagram for career development in some major office categories so that employees may use them for their career moves and the organization can use them for broader human resources development on a more long-term basis.

The lack of clear career paths explicitly and formally communicated to employees means that all employees have to find out how advancement works in the organization. For those employees who are not socially isolated or distanced from their co-workers or bosses, they may talk among themselves and exchange their observations, learn from their senior employees who have been working in the organization for a longer time, or learn from their bosses through coaching or mentoring.

For Indigenous/racialized employees, they are unable to benefit from these means. They are too distanced from other people in the organization to find out how people can move up or sideways. Having a mentor or sponsor would greatly help them to be informed on how they can move from one position to another with greater ease. But, as noted earlier in our discussion on mentoring and sponsorship in this chapter, Indigenous and racialized employees do not get involved in mentorship or sponsorship that easily. They have problems finding mentors or sponsors in an informal manner or being selected as mentees or being sponsored in a formal arrangement. Therefore, in an organization where career paths are not clearly defined on the organizational websites or communication pages, Indigenous and racialized employees may have fewer channels to get their information on career progression. They could observe who have received promotions or job movement, and, in a less equitable workplace, employees who have benefited most are usually those White employees who have been coached, mentored, or just have proper social connections that have given them advantages in job movements. Hence, a lack of formalized and explicit communication of how career paths are forged will end up causing a lot of guess work and suspicions and is likely to lead to distrust and feeling marginalized for Indigenous and racialized employees. Could this be viewed as racism? When it is perceived that White employees have benefited more in job movements and promotions in the work environment or that, in statistical terms, White people are more disproportionately represented in promotions or job transfers in workforce surveys and analyses, the chance is that racism is prevalent. But this must be verified in individual workplaces (Joseph et al. 2012).

Lack of an Employee Competency Data Bank

An employee competency data bank is a data management system for collecting, sorting, storing, and analyzing types and levels of competencies of employees in an organization. The major competencies of employees are directly collected and updated from all employees, which leaders and managers can access in identifying potential employees for job transfers (including promotions) across departments and geographic regions. The data also enable leadership to identify the profiles of the workforce in an aggregate manner and empower additional analyses to establish human resources patterns and potentials and align the data with the organizational business directions and growing needs.

The data bank enables more effective and efficient human resources development, easier and faster mobilization of employees across positions, and the accurate identification of employees for new positions within the organization across functional or geographic areas. For those few organizations that have this kind of data bank, the benefits are obvious (Dietrich, Plachy, and Norton 2014). This management system benefits all employees in their pursuit of job movements, including promotions. The lack of it means less fluid employee mobility and less effective promotions or job transfers. Many organizations do not have an inventory of employee competencies, and, thus, the data bank idea never materializes.

Having a data bank on employee competencies provides a more level-playing field for employees for job movements, including promotions, because it is the inputs of each employee on their competencies that get captured in the data bank without being filtered by their executives, managers, or supervisors. Traditionally, when an employer intends to find employees with certain competencies, the employer must depend on the inputs of its leaders. Apart from the subjectivity that is associated with management opinions about the competencies of employees, the selection of the leader(s) that the employer has made for consultation or requests also further filters the chance of a specific employee(s) being identified. These biases arising from racial prejudice or stereotypes toward Indigenous and racialized employees could be eliminated or reduced if an enterprise-wide data bank is used for identifying employee competencies.

CONCLUSION

There are a number of human resources mechanisms at work that disadvantage Indigenous and racialized employee to the extent that they actually contribute to their discrimination. The mechanisms discussed in this chapter are performance management, succession management, cloning, mentorship and sponsorship, promotion, and job movements.

The current model of performance management has a lot of biases, although it looks seemingly neutral in appearance. There are elements of subjectivity that are often related to the discretionary power and non-transparency on the part of management and inherent biases in the design and implementation of coaching and training for employees.

Succession management at the executive, management, and supervisory levels has some inherent deficiencies, especially at the candidate identification and selection stages. The end results are usually having more non-Indigenous and non-racialized individuals participate in promotion, job movements, and succession management. The general lack of visibility and the participation of racialized and Indigenous peoples in corporate initiatives, networks, and developmental opportunities deprives them from connecting with those in succession decision making. Cloning, mentoring, and the alignment of leadership values and organizational values constitute a critical component in succession management.

There are also multiple barriers for Indigenous and racialized employees in promotions and job movements: stereotyping, prejudice, the use of "over-qualification" as a way of screening and selection, the absence of internal job posting, policy and procedural biases (as in eligibility criteria and the submission of performance evaluation scores), and management system deficiencies (as in undefined career paths and the absence of an employee competency bank). When all these factors are compounding on each other, an environment for the exclusion of Indigenous and racialized employees is created and perpetuated.

CHAPTER 8

Racism in the House

INTRODUCTION

Indigenous and racialized employees may witness many hurdles in human resources functions, including performance evaluation, promotion, and succession management, in their attempts to be upwardly mobile. As employees, they are likely to have an opportunity to experience how these human resources functions work in one way or another. In the last chapter, we discussed how coaching, training, development, networking, cloning, and mentoring are essential mechanisms in helping employees move up in the organizational hierarchy and how they also hinder Indigenous and racialized employees to actualize their potential and advance in the organization. In this chapter, we will examine the extent to which organizational cultures and practices and the harassing and discriminatory conducts found in an organization could further lead Indigenous and racialized employees toward the exit. Recognizing the biases built into many of the human resources functions and the human mindsets in Chapters 6, 7, and 8 may be merely the first step in understanding the nature of workplace racism. Analyzing the toxicity of organizational culture and how management and non-management employees carry out these functions as well as how they conduct themselves in their daily interactions and work would help us to understand more deeply why racialized and Indigenous employee are often driven out of their workplaces. This chapter is a deeper dive on the relationship between employee retention, on the one hand, and corporate culture and racial harassment and discrimination, on the other.

RETENTION

Retention is the act of individual employees sticking around in an organization and the organizational ability to keep its employees. This is a simple way of describing retention in the workplace. High retention rates reflect the well-being of an organization and its ability to eliminate dysfunctional and avoidable attrition (Government of Canada 2022a). It has been observed since the 1980s that more and more employees have been growing disloyal to their organizations are prepared to leave their organizations at any moment. It may be due to their feelings of being uninspired, bored, or dissatisfied with their compensation or promotion opportunities. Since 2008, voluntary turnover has been increasing. At the executive level, in 2012–13, the turnover rate for Canadian senior executives was 2.4 percent; for executives, it was 3.3 percent; and for management groups, it was 4.5 percent. There are numerous variables that are related to this trend: structural factors (including economic changes and geographic locations) and organizational factors (including compensation, performance, and growth opportunities) (Bernier 2013).

There has also been a shift in the way in which employees view their careers. More and more of them feel that, instead of having a long-time career with one single organization, they like to hop from job to job in a series of organizations. Workopolis did a study and reported in 2014 that the proportion of Canadians who stayed in the same job had decreased from 60 percent in 1990 to 30 percent in 2002. This spelled uncertainty and instability in the workplace for employers. The latter preferred to retain employees who are experienced, knowledgeable about their companies, contribute well, keep their institutional memories, and have broad business and personal networks.

A New Challenge after the COVID-19 Pandemic

In these times of political, economic, and social change, discussed at the beginning of this book, their disruptive impacts on work, labour markets, workforce, and employee retention have been felt much more strongly in the workplace than they were in the pre-pandemic period. Employee turnover is relatively high and is expected to be even higher in the near future as Canada comes out of the pandemic. The ascendency of Donald Trump as the president of the United States, and the discruptive policies and actions that accompanied his second administration, have further unsettled and destabilized the Canadian economy and labour markets. The current models of remote and hybrid work disrupt the traditional model and generate waves of managerial concerns regarding organizational and business development, corporate culture of togetherness and cohesiveness, and financial implications for real estate rental arrangements. Meanwhile, employees have a tendency to pay more attention to their own individual goals rather than the collective organizational and business goals. Individual goals such as finding a balance of well-being, family, and work are taking a high priority. Personal advancement and succession opportunities in the workplace may not be able to meet the aspirations of individual employees (Tupper and Ellis 2022). For this reason, employees are less engaged and are looking beyond their organizations when their individual goals are not met. This is one of the reasons why it has been difficult to restore the traditional work arrangement after the COVID-19 pandemic and why some employees are opting for a hybrid or fully remote work environment to address the issues concerning work/life balance, teamwork, finances, and transportation.

Impacts of Retention Issues

When an employee leaves an organization, they take with them years of work experience, social networks, client trust, knowledge, and skills that cannot be replaced easily or quickly. This loss of work-related advantages can only be replaced with another employee who needs to accumulate these advantages at a cost for the organization through recruitment, training, and development. Furthermore, during this transitional period, the operation and function of the organization will take a hit and can only be replenished with a new employee who is equipped with expertise and experience after years of work in the same capacity. When employee turnover is high, the loss to organizational productivity and workforce morale can be immense and may take years to recover.

The human aspects of retention are equally concerning. When an organization stresses the value of employees and their well-being, employee commitment and engagement increase (Allen and Myer 1990), their productivity and the quality of their performance rises, and the satisfaction level with their jobs and organization is elevated (Allen and Myer 1990; Riketta and van Dick 2005). The reverse becomes evident when these employees are excluded, disrespected, or marginalized; they become cynical, uncommitted, and disengaged. They lose interest in staying in the organization and often try their hardest to quit (Aquino, Tripp and Bies 2006; Hakanen and Schaufeli 2012; Rahman and Nas 2013). Considering the negative impacts that have made in recent years in organizational growth and human wellness as well as the fact that Canada has the fourth worst attrition rate (16 percent) for employees in the world, there is cause for alarm (*Catalyst* 2019). Retaining employees therefore commands an increasingly elevated significance for corporate management and leadership.

WHY EMPLOYEES QUIT THEIR JOBS?

Knowing why employees stay and work in an organization is as important as finding out why they leave the organization. Externally, job opportunities that are available and changes in the larger financial and economic institutions, population changes, and family and community development are crucial in employee retention.

Internally, one may look into the issues of job satisfaction and the internal work environment. "Job satisfaction" is usually derived from individual achievement, social recognition, responsibility, growth, and other means of motivation as well as the compatibility between individual work ethics and how things get done in an organization. "Work environment" includes corporate values and culture, corporate policies and programs, procedures and practices, other human resource functions, and management approaches or styles. Employee engagement, morale, and co-worker experience may likely be included in these factors. Any discrepancies between individual expectation and what the organization offers is likely to increase tensions and upset the equilibrium between employees and management.

For the purposes of this book, especially Part 2, our focus is on the internal organizational issues that have implications for employee retention. The question then is: what workplace factors are retaining Indigenous and racialized employees and what factors are not? As previous discussions have noted, most employees are prepared to leave their companies when opportunities arise for a better job, and employers are looking for the sources of this inclination and the likely turnovers. More and more research shows that corporate culture, work environment, leadership, and management are crucial in the understanding of retention (Eichler 2016).

ORGANIZATIONAL CULTURE

Every organization has a culture of its own. However, when a large organization is dissected and looked at more deeply, it might have multiple subcultures based on geographic regions, branches, work units, occupational groups, and, often, its leadership and management. In fact, one may even argue that there are subcultures at the board and executive levels that are different from various segments of employees. Furthermore, when an organization is getting larger, whether it is global, national, or even local with multiple work units, there is a great possibility that micro-cultures will develop even within one location. Subcultures have their own work approaches and standards as well as production and service values, and each could exist nicely without competing or being at odds with others. During and after the COVID-19 pandemic, the hybrid and remote workplace models established special autonomy for certain occupational groups based on skills, functions, and customers, and they evolved into newer ways of cultural co-existence. Corporate culture is no longer monolithic, as reports of global businesses have portrayed.

However, this does not mean that the core corporate cultural norms and standards have not survived. The term "culture" is an umbrella term that covers many facets of the organization, including its mandate, vision, norms, values, and symbols. It also includes systems, policies, procedures, strategies, and operations. To put it simply, a corporate culture describes how people behave and how things are done in an organization. This architecture of values, norms, policies, and procedures make the organization more cohesive and standardized within an organizational-wide framework, and it may be strong enough to make employees working within it more cohesive and unified despite some of the localized micro-cultures that may stress autonomy and reflect local contexts. But this depends largely on leadership commitment, oversight and enforcement, and the collaboration and engagement of employees. Overall, employees may feel inclusive and have a sense of belonging locally and not feeling lost and alienated in a large organization. In addition, the organization can be more flexible and adaptable in today's changing world (Mensik 2024c).

One of the myths about corporate culture is that it is a long inflexible tradition abided by many employees—perhaps even generations of them—which is beyond the control of anyone. It was in existence before new employees joined the organization and is still there when existing employees left. It seems that it has its own will and is running at its own pace. The reality is that corporate executives and managers have the power to effect deliberate changes on any aspect of corporate culture, ranging from creating a statement of values; establishing employees' codes of conduct; formulating human resources strategies, policies, and procedures; and developing operational logistics and systems. Together, all these changes play a role in shaping and perpetuating how people conduct themselves and how things get accomplished. It is also important to note that, similar to recruitment, compensation and benefits, and training and development, cultural development for the organization is an integral part of the human resources management. In some larger corporations in Canada, there are designated staff members who are responsible for shaping corporate culture for the organization.

A poisonous culture is one that instills many negative and disturbing feelings among the employees: the feeling of being unwelcome, fearful, disrespected, harassed, belittled, undermined, uncertain, suspicious, intimated, bullied, isolated, distrusted, excluded, controlled, anxious, depressed, angry, and many other bad feelings compounding on each other. In this kind of culture, employees wish that they do not have to work in the organization and feel sick even when they get closer to the workplace every day that they go to work. This is what a poisonous culture does to employees, and it is especially the case when employees are at the receiving end of such feelings, and this means, for the purpose of this book, Indigenous and racialized employees.

A command-and-control culture is a clear demarcation of the leaders' (executives and managers) power to demand compliance with their orders from the non-leaders (that is, employees) without consultation with, and obtaining consensus from, the employees. In essence, it is a top-down approach reinforced by rewards and punishments. Without elaborating on the obvious, leaders create this kind of culture in an organization with the expectation that they can make corporate decisions without obtaining input from the employees or enlist their support without questions. In a command-and-control culture, leaders hold all major decision-making power, leaving employees to do the "leg work" of putting their decisions into operation. In the real world, there is a gradation of this command and control with those closer to the core decision makers having some say on the directions, strategies, and policies of the organization, and, as one moves down the hierarchy of power, employees are less and less involved in the control of corporate directions, strategies, and policies and more and more involved in the daily implementation and getting things done.

Based on these observations, it is safe to say that, in Canada, larger organizations are more bureaucratic and have a greater tendency to stress the command-and-control aspect of work relationships. Smaller organizations are less likely to be like this, but this is not always true. Some small organizations can be highly "command and control" with strong leadership and not much decentralization in their decision making, while larger organizations show more signs of decentralization in decision-making power once policies, rules, and procedures are put in place. While organizations may be placed along a spectrum with respect to a command-and-control culture, there are various shades of decentralized decision-making features in different parts and aspects of the organization along this spectrum.

In a command-and-control culture, being more isolated and distant from the networks of colleagues/co-workers, the efforts and contributions of Indigenous and racialized employees are less recognized by those around them and often go unnoticed by their leaders. This is because there is a huge social distance and contact gap between the leaders and their employees. The words and actions of leaders are more important than the formal written policies and procedures. Thus, the command and control of the leaders supersedes the constraints of written formalities as the latter are just words on paper and are easily ignored at the whim of those leaders. This is often indicated by the general lack of monitoring, review, and enforcement of these policies and procedures by the leaders in the organization. Clearly, for Indigenous and racialized employees, these policies and procedures are there for show, and violations of them bear few consequences. For example, it is common to find that managers are not taking the performance evaluation system seriously. Performance evaluations of employees are often carried out in a half-hearted manner or not at all, and senior executives barely notice it. The formal policy and procedural system set up in the workplace is largely undermined as a lack of leadership accountability has quietly taken it over in a command-and-control culture. And the leaders do not make a commitment to fix the broken system.

Excluded from Privileged Communication

The bad feelings generated by a poisonous culture, as experienced by Indigenous and racialized employees, are related to their marginalized status. Due largely to their generally low-status positions, compounded by race, they are more often than not isolated from the social networks within the organization that provide them with pertinent, up-to-date, and accurate information on the pulse of those with corporate authority, and they are not in the "gossip" networks of influential colleagues (or co-workers) who have insider information on who is doing what or who is in a good or bad relationship with whom. For these reasons, they are more disadvantaged than other employees in terms of climbing up the career ladders in the organization, knowing the impending changes in restructuring or lay-offs, and understanding the likely impacts of the actions of those in the higher echelon of the organization. Therefore, an organization that has a secretive and often selective communication system would leave Indigenous and racialized employees in the dark most of the time.

By having a secretive, selective, and non-transparent communication system, executives and managers have intentionally designed a system that picks and chooses the employees to whom they wish to communicate specific messages. These communications are usually informal, verbal, and personal, and they create a special class of employees who are privileged to know the insider information in a timely manner and another class of employees who are "internal exiles," as Gisèle Asplund (1988, 8) has labelled them, who are shut off from critical news that might benefit them in receiving promotion or succession opportunities, information on new assignments and developments, new directions in the organization, pending staff changes, or even individual performance criteria. Since these communications are privileged, Indigenous and racialized employees are not in the "inner circle" of leadership, and, overtime, these employees feel left out and "abandoned" and really do not feel they belong to the organization. They do not see much future working in the organization and are constantly looking for a way out.

One of the unintended outcomes of privileged communication being limited to a certain segment of employees is the development of gossip and rumours. Gossip and rumours are the hallmarks of a distrustful environment. Indigenous and racialized employees are deprived of knowing about the reality of the organization as they must constantly try to find out what is going on in the organization by initiating discussions with their own networks (usually made up of a few Indigenous and racialized employees) or by questioning people who might know more, directly or indirectly. The nagging search for the "truth" in the workplace uses up a lot of their mental energy and may even be crowding out their time for working or doing what they are supposed to be doing. The uncertainties of the information they receive through the grapevine and their inability to confirm the validity of the information puts them at a higher level of anxiety (especially when news of staff downsizing and changes or business restructuring is buzzing around). Gossip and rumours beget more of the same. In this culture of manufactured unauthorized uncertainty, Indigenous and racialized employees are absorbed to a greater extent than other employees (as the information they have is incomplete and unverifiable since the leaders are not prepared to take charge to clear the air, and, hence, gossip and rumours persist) and make them feel more stressed.

Selective Rewards and Punishments

In addition, the command-and-control culture acknowledges the contributions of only selected employees and rewards them with bonuses or perks, training and development, special assignments, and positions on high-profile task forces or committees. Such selection is not based on objective criteria but is more related to the subjectivity of the leaders. This way of running a workplace certainly places Indigenous and racialized employees in a position where they are less likely to be rewarded and more likely to be ignored by the leaders because this culture rewards only those in the inner circle of the leaders and not those who are marginalized (and often viewed as "out groups" where Indigenous and racialized employees are clustered). Such exclusion does not induce them to have a sense of belonging to the organization, and they see no reason to be engaged or loyal. As shown in some earlier studies, Indigenous and racialized employees will spend more time and effort trying to quit their jobs or leave the organization, more so than White employees.

In this kind of culture, Indigenous and racialized employees are penalized even when they do not know it. It is often done behind their backs. The structure is set up in such a way that there is no open discussion or consultation among staff members along with their managers or leaders. The commands come from the top and cascade downward in the hierarchy, and the reports come from the bottom and cascade upward. The work orders are issued from the leaders and are transmitted one level down at a time; similarly, staff reports come from employees one level at a time as they move upward. In this manner, what is said from one level to another could be highly orchestrated and packaged to the advantage of those in levels above and below, and these messages are transmitted often one on one in private offices. With this communication format, secrecy and non-transparency is the core principle. In protecting themselves and deflecting the truth, some White supervisors and managers often use Indigenous and racialized employees as scapegoats in order to explain why the problems have occurred or why the supervisors or managers have failed to get things done on time or deliver products or services in poorer quality. Since these remarks are made behind closed doors, Indigenous and racialized employees are not in a position of knowing. Hence, they end up feeling and bearing the blame and are "stabbed behind their backs," so to speak. Often, such scapegoating ends up with higher-level leaders having negative perception of these marginalized employees, while the White supervisors and managers come out as winners. In this sense, Indigenous and racialized employees are penalized without having done anything wrong and must bear the consequences of possibly being laid off later when the organization is downsized or not getting a bonus for their performance.

Secrecy

A command-and-control culture embraces secrecy, and this secrecy instills fear and anxiety among employees. As noted earlier in this discussion, only leaders play a key role in establishing a corporate vision, mandate, strategic direction, and policies. A central component in their decision-making are the human resources in key positions and their allocation of the resources in hiring, development, promotion, and termination for those positions. Employees are not sure whether or when the status quo of human resources will be disturbed; hiring, promotions, and terminations could be announced or not announced depending on the leaders' preferences; vacant staff positions could be filled or not filled; changes in leadership may be announced without much lead time; changes in mergers and acquisitions; and restructuring and downsizing are seldom publicized. Employees in general, and

Indigenous and racialized employees in particular, are often in a state of anxiety because of the uncertainty in their future. This is especially the case when the economy is in a downturn.

Why are Indigenous and racialized employees more fearful and anxious when working in a command-and-control work environment? This is because they are not part of the in-group that has connections with the leaders. They are more isolated and marginalized, and the culture they work in is not conducive to policy compliance, fair play, collaboration, openness, sharing and supportive networks, a sense of belonging, and clarity in corporate communication and transparency. Whether Indigenous and racialized employees are retained or terminated in the workplace is determined more by the likes and dislikes of their supervisors, managers, or executives than by the quality of the employee's performance. Compared with White employees, Indigenous and racialized employees are further away from the inner circles of leaders, and their images are tainted by the stereotypes and prejudices discussed earlier in Chapter 5. There are simply too few people in the organization who are prepared to say a few good words about Indigenous and racialized people. For these reasons, their job positions are more precarious and more susceptible to termination. They cannot count on other employees or any of their leaders to protect or empathize with them. It is a culture in which they are required to be subservient and marginalized, and it is not a comfortable environment; thus, they look for a way out.

Put Up or Shut Up

One of the cultural traits of a command-and-control workplace is the leadership's attitude of treating an employee's complaints or criticisms as unwarranted or unfounded. Any negative comments by employees are usually viewed by the leaders in this kind of culture as challenges or potential "revolts" or "resistance." And these comments are often dismissed as not worthy of consideration or further consultation. Hence, the leaders' usual response is to request the critical employees to accept the situation as it is and just stop complaining to them. In sum, it is a "put-up-or-shut-up" culture. This cultural trait impacts negatively on every employee, irrespective of their race, but its adverse impacts are more severe for Indigenous and racialized employees because they see themselves as being more unfairly or unequitably treated in their employment and in the workplace. As discussed in previous chapters, Indigenous and racialized employees are under-represented in many aspects of employment in Canada; some have been discriminated in promotion competition with or without their knowledge; others have been relatively deprived in training and development opportunities and have not been treated fairly and equitably in their employment histories. At least, that is how they feel about the workplace. They have much to complain about and are critical about various aspects of the workplace. And if they have to "put up or shut up," it is clear that the organization is not an ideal environment to work in because they may or may not have a conflict resolution mechanism that works effectively.

In smaller organizations, due to their lack of resources, they will attempt to resolve an employee's complaints by asking the employees to discuss the complaints with their immediate superior instead of retaining the service of a consulting or legal firm to investigate the allegations or using an internal ombudsman office. If the complaint issues are related to race (such as racial tension at work or harassment or discrimination allegations), their immediate superior (that is, their bosses) usually do not have the knowledge and skills to investigate the issues, and, more importantly, they may not be impartial enough to investigate or make a judgment by themselves. It has been observed that leaders of some organizations are hesitant to retain an external expert to investigate the issue at hand, and they try to do the investigation internally by having their own staff members (usually human resources staff) do the investigation. Such an investigation, by its very nature, is inherently biased as these individuals have vested interests to protect. A third party—especially, experts or specialists with proper investigative skills—could make the investigation more impartial and, at least, be seen as being impartial.

A "put-up-or-shut-up" culture is toxic because it creates an environment in which employees feel stifled or suffocated as their voices are smothered. When racial issues (such as prejudice, stereotyping, harassment, belittling, bullying, and discrimination) are experienced by Indigenous and racialized employees—and there are no mechanisms for their voices to be heard and they are in no position to improve the current work situation—their stress, frustration, and anger remains or grows stronger. As noted later in this chapter, compared with other employees, Indigenous and racialized employees are more isolated at work, and their social networks are less developed. Hence, they have more difficulty in airing their concerns about the unfairness they experience. With not much of a chance to express their perceptions and feelings and even less of a chance to have the situation improved, it is not surprising to find a higher rate of departure for Indigenous and racialized employees.

Corporate Hypocrisy

As noted in the previous section, in getting things done according to what they want, leaders in a command-and-control work environment often intentionally ignore the policies and procedures that their organization has established and that may be written formally on paper. Similarly, they may also say or do things that are in contradiction with their corporate values. For example, on the one hand, the organization may have a diversity, equity, and inclusiveness policy, a human rights policy, and a policy of respect and collaboration, but, on the other hand, the leaders do not walk their talk, which means that their behaviours are contrary to these policies. As Indigenous and racialized employees have observed, there are plenty of incidences of intolerance toward Indigenous and racialized people, allegations of prejudice, disrespect, harassment, and discrimination, and instances where leaders tackle these incidents in a half-hearted way or not at all. There are also no mechanisms put in place for the organization to respond quickly to allegations of misconduct, racial slurs, and bullying. Thus, social justice policies are merely symbolism and are seldom translated into actions. They set an example and give permission for their employees to ignore or bypass the codes of conduct, corporate values, and policies. However, given that these policies exist formally, leaders may enforce these policies for individual employees on a case-by-case basis, fostering the atmosphere of corporate hypocrisy throughout the workplace.

Hypocrisy breeds distrust between leaders and Indigenous and racialized employees through time. Leaders are viewed as unauthentic, two-faced, untrustworthy, and having a lack of integrity. When social justice policies are not enforced by the leaders, and the conduct of co-workers does not align with these policies and there are no negative consequences for these co-workers, Indigenous and racialized employees develop a deep sense of betrayal and mistreatment. The social justice policies are then viewed by these employees as lip service. They feel that they are "second class" and neglected despite the existence of these social justice policies. It is an environment that discourages engagement, loyalty, and devotion. They become cynical and passive. In fact, there is a great chance that they and other employees will see hypocrisy as a corporate value (Asplund 1988, 45). Since they have been treated unjustly, and this may be compounded by their lack of additional training, developmental opportunities, mentoring, coaching, or promotions, they do not see much future for themselves in staying with the organization. Ultimately, they will spend more time looking for another job outside the organization than doing their work.

Social Avoidance and Distancing

When White employees and Indigenous and racialized employees are trying to avoid interacting with each other in the workplace, we may witness a culture that breeds hostility, polarity, and toxicity. Employees in such an environment pretend not to establish eye contact, not to know each other, not to acknowledge that each other exists, not to exchange greetings in the hallways, not to seek help from each other, not to provide encouraging words or positive supports in meetings, and not to team up with each other at work or invite each other to social activities including coffee breaks or luncheons.

Through time, the workplace appears to have two groups with little communication or social interactions across the race line. There are also pockets of employees who form cliques based on racial, ethnic, religious, cultural, and linguistic lines merely through social distancing and avoidance behaviour. When White employees become an "in-group" without allowing the Indigenous and racialized employees to join, these employees become an "out-group" without much chance of integrating with their White colleagues. The demarcation line between these two groups of employees in some organizations is clearly marked, and, in others, the line is not obviously drawn. There are gradations of "segregation" of this nature among organizations, and the extent and intensity of social avoidance will make a difference in employee morale (as in cohesiveness and togetherness) and the workplace climate (as in trust and alienation). And this morale and climate do not instill optimism for Indigenous and racialized employees about their future in the organization.

Social avoidance among employees and between employees and leaders are cultural problems, and both leaders and employees are responsible for its existence and perpetuation. This kind of toxicity does not make working in an organization comfortable or collaborative. Polarity usually does not make employees feel safe or secure. Related to such polarity along racial lines, networking among employees can be skewed because the mingling of races in employee networks does not come easily. In some organizations, due to the influence of the current popularity of establishing employee affiliation networks (or employee resources groups) in some larger corporations, there are networks of racialized employees, Indigenous employees, female employees, employees with disabilities, and so on. There are multiple purposes for these networks, and one of them is the provision of supports and conduits with leaders to those who join. They are created based on identities, and there is a tendency for them to be in separate silos. Such networks have their limitations as they foster homogenous networking development as opposed to networking with other affiliation networks. Hence, it has been noted that these networks are not effective in enabling Indigenous or racialized employees to expand beyond their own individual races, and, given their marginalized status, their networks in the workplace are not particularly influential in helping them to move closer to the higher echelons in the organization.

ORGANIZATIONAL PRACTICES AND WORKPLACE CONDUCT

"Organizational practices" is a broad umbrella term that covers the manner in which many policies and procedures are put into operation by human beings, whether they are management or non-management staff members in an organization. It also encompasses the interaction of these staff members when they work together in putting into action all things that are needed to be done in running a business or an organization. Accordingly, most of the policies and procedures that are discussed in Part 2 of this book, when put into action, could be viewed as organizational practices, including what is being discussed in this chapter. This means that organizational practices include all actions related to many human resources functions in the hiring, promotion, and termination areas as well as basically all aspects of human interaction in the workplace.

"Workplace conduct" denotes all human behaviours found in the workplace, including sites or venues related to work (such as conferences, company get-togethers, and vehicles related to work events). These behaviours could be initiated and perpetuated by executives, managers, and non-management employees (whether they are front-line or back-room staff or professionals sitting by their computers). The include the day-to-day conduct of people working in close proximity with racialized and Indigenous employees and they include silence, verbal or non-verbal language, body movements and gestures, and written/visual/audio expressions (including graphics, words, and sounds) communicated through any form of media. This conduct (which includes all human actions in implementing human resources functions mentioned in the previous paragraph) is put on display and sensed by people who witness this conduct and may illicit different interpretations and reactions from them, including racialized and Indigenous people.

Managerial Biases

Middle-level management (including supervision in this context) is an important layer of people to whom many employees report. These managers and supervisors are the army of employees who put the policies and strategies of executives into action, who upgrade and develop the skills of employees, and who create a conducive environment for growth and sustainability. For all these reasons, the messages that managers communicate through their actions are critical, and, with their authority, they can create or change the culture of where they work. Therefore, how they interact with their employees and run their businesses becomes crucial. What they do and how they behave influence all those who report to them: are they ethical in their actions; do they play favouritism among employees; are they fair in treating people; do they listen to employees; are they engaging their employees; are they driving their employees too hard; do they respect and care for their employees? These are some of the areas in which employees take their cues and learn from them (Mensik 2024a).

Treating some employees better than others poisons their work environment. Those employees who do not benefit from the privileges see this as being unfair. When managers and supervisors provide opportunities for only a few employees, such as special assignments, interfaces with higher-level executives, and joining blue-ribbon committees, corporate networking, skill training, or development, other employees may see these opportunities as grooming tools for future promotion or succession. Indigenous and racialized employees are sensitive to these managerial manoeuvres and even label them as racial privileges, favouritism, or discrimination, as noted by the Canadian Human Rights

Commission in a case brought before the Treasury Board of Canada Secretariat. Nine employees from the Canadian Human Rights Commission filed a policy grievance through their unions in 2020, alleging that "Black and racialized employees at the CHRC (Canadian Human Rights Commission) face systemic anti-Black racism, sexism and systemiSee c discrimination." Carole Bidal, an associate assistant deputy minister at the Treasury Board of Canada Secretariat, announced its official ruling related to this grievance after an investigation. The Association of Justice Counsel, the Public Service Alliance of Canada, and the Canadian Association of Professional Employees also filed grievances and received the same decision. The grievance centred on the organizational culture of hostility and a toxic work environment in which Blacks and racialized employees were deprived of training and developmental opportunities as well as formal and informal networks. Consequently, these marginalized employees found themselves stagnated in their career development while their White counterparts advanced. The senior management echelon remains mostly White (Standing Senate Committee on Human Rights 2023; Thurton 2023).

There are also occasions in which Indigenous and racialized employees noted that managers and supervisors hold double standards in measuring employees' performance quality and punctuality based on gender, Indigeneity, and race. Some managers and supervisors may, on occasion, value ideas or suggestions from White employees more than their racial counterparts. On other occasions, Indigenous and racialized employees see their managers and supervisors providing more coaching to their White counterparts or engaging them more actively in work. All the above examples suggest that, due to their positions in the authority structure, managers and supervisors set examples for their employees and create their own subcultures in their work units or departments. Their particular work styles and treatment of their employees are ingrained in the workplace, and, if they seem unfair and inequitable, it may drive some Indigenous and racialized employees to quit their jobs sooner than others.

Racial Discrimination

Extent of Perception

An experience of racial discrimination is an overarching factor in driving racialized and Indigenous employees out from their workplaces. Catalyst's survey of more than five thousand employees in six Western

Table 8.1: Experience of at Least One Form of Discrimination on Human Rights Grounds in the Last Five Years

	Whites (%)	Indigenous peoples (%)	Racialized people (Black people) (%)	Racialized people (non-Black people) (%)
No specific grounds	16.5	33.5	46.0	27.1
Race or skin colour	2.8	13.8	41.0	19.0
Ethnicity or culture	2.3	14.8	21.9	17.3
Physical appearance	5.1	14.3	8.5	6.4
Religion	2.1	5.1	8.0	5.0
Language	2.1	2.5	9.0	8.6

Note: Shaded percentages represent the highest figures among the four racial groups.
Source: Cotter 2022.

countries (including Canada) revealed that employment and professional inequalities (32 percent), including unequal pay, missed promotions, and uneven workloads based on race, have been reported. Moreover, racial stereotypes (such as a preconception with intelligence, cleanliness, language skills, and COVID-19) and demeaning comments related to their cultures and identities have also been mentioned (Amanat 2023).

The survey also revealed that 41 percent of leaders, 36 percent of co-workers, and 23 percent of customers engage in racist behaviours. Both men and women, irrespective of their race, are equally responsible for initiating racism: White people initiated about 80 percent of racist acts, and 20 percent are initiated by racialized individuals (Amanat 2023).

An overview of the experiences of White people, Indigenous peoples, and racialized people in the larger society shows that there are significant disparities among them. According to one Statistics Canada's study more racialized people (Black people), proportionately speaking, experience discrimination on multiple human rights grounds than Indigenous peoples and racialized people (non-Black people). In comparison, the experience of discrimination on different grounds by White people is relatively low. The 2019 General Social Survey on Canadians' Safety, which looked at White people (that is, non-Indigenous and non-racialized people), Indigenous peoples, racialized people, and people aged fifteen years and older and shows their experiences of different forms of discrimination in the last five years (see Table 8.1).

Table 8.1 highlights two particular patterns: (1) Black people reported the highest percentages of experience of discrimination in all grounds except "physical appearance," and (2) all people experienced their highest sense of discrimination on "no specific grounds," which may be interpreted as they are unsure of why they have been discriminated against or their perceived grounds of discrimination do not fit the typology of human rights codes. Once again, Black people (46 percent), non-Black racialized people (27.1 percent), and Indigenous peoples (33.5 percent) reported the highest percentages of discrimination on "grounds" that are unclear or may not be related to human rights grounds. This finding suggests that, for Indigenous peoples and racialized people, there is a lot of ambiguity in their perceptions of why others "discriminate" against them or even whether they are confident that "race" is an ingredient of others' actions toward them. Such ambiguity explains why they feel more stressful all the time in their interaction with others. Ambiguity creates unease among people. This finding on ambiguity plays an important role in the guesswork and stress of racialized people (especially Black people) and other people in a variety of racial issues, including the perception of harassment, discrimination, and micro-aggression, which will be discussed in the remaining part of this chapter.

Furthermore, the Canadian Social Survey from January to March 2024 showed that more than one in three people (36 percent) over the age of fifteen in Canada experienced some form of discrimination or unfair treatment in all walks of life in the last five years (Statistics Canada 2024d). These forms of discrimination may include personal discrimination (possibly related to personality or other attributes, which may not be related to race). For racialized people, Indigenous people, and other marginalized people, discrimination affects them disproportionately. Using data from 2021 to 2024, just over half of racialized people fifteen years and older (51 percent) reported discrimination or unfair treatment in the past five years. This is a little less than double the 27 percent reported by non-racialized people. Such findings often raise the question of whether racialized people experience less racial discrimination.

Among different groups of racialized people, there were no significant differences in the reported discrimination. Canadian-born racialized people reported more discrimination than those who are foreign born. The types of discrimination reported are mainly related to race or skin colour (66 percent) rather than ethnicity (49 percent), culture (49 percent), accent (28 percent), and language (27 percent). In total, 46 percent of Indigenous people living off reserve reported experiences of discrimination, and only 33 percent of non-Indigenous people did. The types of discrimination reported were Indigenous identity and physical appearance. Compared with non-Indigenous people with disabilities (12 percent), mental or physical, Indigenous people with disabilities (23 percent) were twice as likely to be discriminated against due to their disabilities.

In various contexts, the workplace was cited as the most commonly cited context by people in this survey (41 percent), whether the discrimination was related to working, job applications, or promotions. Following the workplace, stores, banks, and restaurants (33 percent) and public areas (29 percent) were cited as common areas. More Black people reported discrimination (48 percent) than other racialized people (39 percent) or non-racialized people (41 percent). Proportionately, more Black people also reported discrimination in housing (13 percent) when compared with other racialized people (6 percent) or non-racialized people (6 percent). People who reported discrimination also reported lower life satisfaction, poor mental health, lower levels of meaning and purpose, lower levels of confidence in multiple institutions (such as school, courts, police, media, and Canadian Parliament as well as a lower sense of belonging in their local community.

Another study examined the experience of racial discrimination in the workplace between 2020 and 2022 (which was a more longitudinal study than the one cited above), and it showed that 27.6 percent of racialized people reported "discrimination at work when appling for a job or promotion since the beginning of the COVID-19 pandemic," while 24.9 percent of those who were "not a visible minority" reported discrimination as stated above. The breakdown of racialized people who reported discrimination at work included Black people, who ranked highest (39.7 percent), followed by Arab people (32.3 percent), South Asian people (31.4 percent), Filipino people (31.1 percent), Southeast Asian people (27 percent), and Chinese people (15.4 percent). However, when asked whether they felt discriminated against due to their race or colour (while not limited to work, hiring, or promotion), 19.8 percent of racialized people reported discrimination during the same period, while only 1.9 percent of those people who were "not a visible minority" reported discrimination. The variations of different racialized groups also changed, with 27.5 percent of Chinese reporting racial discrimination (the highest number), and only 3.9 percent of Arab people reporting racial discrimination. This suggests that, in terms of experience in discrimination, workplace discrimination has its own unique patterns among racial groups (including White people), and reports of discrimination specifically associated with "race or colour" are quite minimal among those people who are "not a visible minority" group (Statistics Canada 2024b).

A separate study released by Catalyst showed between 33 and 50 percent of racialized professionals at work are highly "on guard" as they are constantly expecting and consciously preparing themselves for potential bias or discrimination. Forty percent of racialized women anticipate ethnic and racial bias, and 38 percent of them anticipate gender bias (38 percent). Such proportions are greater than they are for racialized men (38 percent and 14 percent). For these racialized professionals who are highly on guard, 22–42 percent have sleep problems, and 50–69 percent of them seriously intend to quit their jobs (Thorpe-Moscon, Pollack, and Olu-Lafe 2019).

Proving Discrimination

The above statistics strongly suggest that racial discrimination is perceived by a significant segment of racialized groups as a part of their employment experience, although there are variations among them. Not all people agree with the perception of racialized and Indigenous people on this matter. Some would even argue that the perception is too subjective and that it does not correspond to the reality.

The federal Human Rights Tribunal applies the standard of the "reasonable victim," which means that, when assessing allegations of discrimination, both subjective and objective elements are considered. The test utilizes the objective, reasonable person standard in combination with the more subjective consideration of a hypothetical victim of similar cultural background to that of the complainant. In other words, the response of the complainant to the alleged discrimination (including harassment) is to be assessed in light of how a reasonable victim of the same racialized background would respond in similar circumstances. There is a possibility that, in some situations, a complainant may perceive that their failure to get a promotion or a work assignment with greater responsibility or advanced opportunity is due to their race and not to their performance or record of attendance. Thus, the issue of incorrect perception or misinterpretation on harassment or discriminatory practices is central to the assessment (Siu 2017, section 1.2.2.7).

Although the federal and provincial tribunals on human rights assess both subjective and objective elements in allegations of racial harassment/discrimination, employers and employees may not use such an assessment when complaints of this nature emerge. Non-racialized or non-Indigenous employers and employees may have an inclination to view these complaints as incorrect because they do not have the same or similar experience of harassment and they tend to view them as the result of racialized and Indigenous employees having "a chip on their shoulders." Whereas racialized and Indigenous employees, due to their long history of experiencing racial biases and unfair treatment and their observations of the frequent advancement of non-racialized and non-Indigenous employees, they see themselves as being occupationally blocked in their advancement.

Since the statistics on promotions, qualifications, and experiences of successful candidates in promotion competitions and the actual reasons for promotions are unavailable in most cases, the subjective allegation of discrimination and unfair treatment by racialized and Indigenous people are largely unverifiable. Hence, the non-transparency of most human resources decisions (such as hiring, promotions, or successions) under the premise of "confidentiality," and the accumulation of stress, suspicion, and distrust through time, often drives racialized and Indigenous employees to quit their jobs as they do not see any future in their workplaces.

The subjective interpretation of decisions on hiring, promotions, successions, and other human resources matters by racialized and Indigenous employees could be minimized through concerted management efforts in making these decisions more transparent and building a more trustful work environment. Often, an organization with distinctively biased methods of recruitment, outreach, selection, hiring, promotions, job advertisements or postings, and biased policies and procedures in training and development, coaching and mentoring, performance evaluation, and exclusive interaction and relationship building are conducive to an undercurrent of employee discontent and allegations of discrimination. If there are no concerted efforts to minimize biases in these human resources functions and the ways in which they are put into operation, racialized and Indigenous employees will find such organizations uncomfortable and stressful to work in as they do not think that they belong there.

Lay-offs and Recalls under a Seniority System

Seniority rights create the phenomenon of "last in, first out," which illustrates that the employees who are last hired are also the first ones who are laid off due to their lack of seniority. They are also the first ones to be terminated, especially if they do not have much work experience there. For those seniority units that have fewer positions, the impact will be more negative as employees have less room to move around within their units. While few employers prevent seniority from impinging negatively on marginalized groups, in abiding with their principle of seniority rights, very few unionists actually take a concerted effort to provide exemptions from seniority to racialized or Indigenous peoples in lay-offs.

Even with the current federal *Employment Equity Act*, seniority in relations to lay-offs and recalls to employment after a lay-off cannot be deemed to be employment barriers, and employees cannot use seniority as a ground for a complaint under this legislation.[1] With this limitation, unions continue to exclude seniority in any negotiations related to racialized and Indigenous peoples and other employment equity designated groups.

The seniority system that is currently set up still maintains a relatively high degree of rigidity in lay-offs and recalls. Unions can demonstrate to their members how protective they are about their job security. Different units of seniority—enterprise wide, departmental, or work unit—along with different gradations of seniority—absolute (straight), modest, or mild—also complicate their impact on racialized and Indigenous employees and how best to eradicate the negativities or biases.

Racial Harassment

Nature of Racial Harassment

One of the central drivers of a racialized and Indigenous employee's exit from their organizations is their experience of being harassed in the workplace. Racial harassment is a manifestation of discrimination. It describes behaviours (including verbal comments and gestures) that are defined by an individual in the workplace or work-related environment as unwelcome, inappropriate, intimating, humiliating, or degrading. These behaviours are racial in nature, which includes explicit or suggestive materials and verbal abuse, unwanted racial overtones or assaults, and activities to which consent is impossible due to intoxication, manipulation, coercion or force, and discriminatory actions related to Indigeneity,

1 *Employment Equity Act*, SC 1995, c 44.

race, colour, ethnicity, nationality, ancestry, creed, and citizenship. This seems to be a broad definition of racial harassment. Such a broad definition illustrates the reality of harassment because it is extensive in scope and format, varied in the manner in which it is carried out, intensive in the severity and degree of the hurts or harms, and, in many cases, it overlaps with more than one prohibitive ground and has a racial dimension. It impacts negatively on an individual employee's well-being, dignity, performance and adversely on the work environment.

The federal government's Bill C-65, *An Act to Amend the Canada Labour Code (Harassment and Violence)*, came into force on 1 January 2021.[2] It was an act that amended the *Canada Labour Code*.[3] It refers to the Work Place Harassment and Violence Prevention Programs. It provides a framework for employers and employees in the federal regulated sector to deal with harassment including bullying and sexual harassment (Aiello 2018). The act captures an expanded scope of conduct under the domain of "harassment," and the scope is embodied in the Harassment and Violence in the Workplace—Negative Behaviours Matrix (National Defence 2023).

The matrix, while not exhaustive, gives examples of inappropriate behaviours that cover any negative behaviours based on prohibited grounds of discrimination stated in the *Canadian Human Rights Act*.[4] These behaviours cover six major type of behaviours: psychological aggression, physical aggression, abuse of authority, online behaviour, criminal behaviour, and discrimination. In Table 8.2, examples of these six types of behaviours are summarized.

Subtle Racism, Micro-Aggression, and Bullying as Harassment

In Canada, the federal Department of National Defence and the Canadian Air Force have reported that "subtle racism and micro-aggressions" are common. Daily interaction among employees at work often generate conflictual situations largely due to different working approaches, unclear responsibility instructions or boundaries, various personal communication styles, and a host of other factors. There are five hidden stages of conflict among employees, and the first few of them carry a

2 *Act to Amend the Canada Labour Code (Harassment and Violence)*, SC 2018, c 22.

3 RSC 1985, c L-2.

4 RSC 1985, c H-6.

Table 8.2: Harassment and Violence in the Workplace—Negative Behaviour Matrix

Psychological aggression	Physical aggression	Abuse of authority	Online behaviour	Criminal behaviour	Discrimination*
Making inappropriate facial gestures (e.g., rolling your eyes) or laughing at someone.	Engaging in behaviour that does not involve physical contact (e.g., banging on a table, throwing an object).	Withholding information from someone who needs it to perform their work.	Purposefully leaving someone out of group emails who should be included.	Damaging some-one's property	Denying someone a promotion despite their qualifications.
Ignoring or ostracizing someone (e.g., not inviting a team member to a team lunch).	Standing over someone or invading their personal space.	Asking subordinates to take on personal errands.	Carbon-copying (Cc'ing) others when pointing out some's mistakes.	Engaging in voyeurism.	Refusing some-one a reasonable accommodation.
Being disrespectful to someone (e.g., purposefully misusing their pronouns or mispronouncing their name).	Engaging in behaviour that involves physical contact (e.g., spitting at someone, pushing someone).	Engaging in favouritism or disfavouritism.	Posting defama-tory material about someone online.	Sharing intim-ate photos of someone without consent.	Denying someone training oppor-tunities or limiting their training opportunities.
Coercing someone to engage in a ceremony or event (e.g., initiation rite) that demeans, belittles, or causes them personal humiliation.	Threatening to hurt someone (e.g., "I would like to hit you right now").	Belittling someone's work.	Being hostile toward someone online through words or pictures.	Stalking some-one or making death threats to someone.	Denying someone a transfer.
Speaking to someone in a con-descending, degrading, or abusive manner (e.g., using racial slurs).	Threatening to damage someone's property.	Taking advantage of a position of authority to exploit, intimi-date, blackmail, threaten, or mistreat someone.	Sharing material about someone online without consent.	Physical (e.g., hitting) or sexual (e.g., unwanted sexual touching) assault.	Denying someone a posting.
Making inappropriate sexual or non-sexual comments (e.g., making fun of someone's gender identity or sexual orientation).	Making inappropriate sexual gestures (e.g., gyrating in a suggestive manner).	Misusing power or authority to interfere with or influence someone's career.	Making online threats to someone.	Hate crimes.	Providing some-one with an unfair performance evaluation.

Notes: *Discrimination is an action or a decision that treats a person (or a group) unfairly for reasons such as race or disability. There are thirteen reasons (referred to as grounds) that are protected under the *Canadian Human Rights Act*. The thirteen grounds are race, national or ethnic origin, colour, religion, age, sex, sexual orientation, gender identity or expression, marital status, family status, disability, genetic characteristics, and a conviction for which a pardon has been granted or a record suspended. The behaviours listed under discrimination are not meant to be exhaustive.

Source: National Defence 2023.

mix of ambivalence, of which the motives of employees can only be left to their own guesswork. The ambiguity of the "offenders" in terms of their "real" reasons for discrimination was also noted in a Canadian national study by Adam Cotter (2022) in 2019. These stages, if left unmanaged properly, could easily lead to explicit confrontation with high emotion even in a public space (Chism 2024).

Interactions between Indigenous and racialized employees with other employees often take on a new dimension with racial overtones or intersectional race/gender ingredients. These interactions are often labelled as micro-aggressions, which could be interpreted as a form of harassment. Micro-aggression is a manifestation of prejudice, and it can target women, persons with disabilities, Indigenous peoples, racialized people, and people with special sexual orientation, gender expression, or identity. For the purposes of this book, we focus on Indigenous peoples and racialized people.

Micro-aggression may be manifested in short verbal comments or conduct (actions) that convey indignities or derogatory slights based on the above-mentioned personal identities (race, gender, and so on). Usually, the slights target a person or a group that is already marginalized. Unlike full-scale aggression, an incident of micro-aggression usually does not involve physical confrontation or a lengthy speech. It usually occurs in everyday life. A subset of micro-aggressions is the micro-invalidation that communicate with or without the intention of negating, excluding, or nullifying the thoughts, feelings, or experiential realities of individuals who are the recipients of micro-invalidations. These micro-invalidations may be subtle and appear harmless, but they hurt the recipients (Velazquez et al. 2022).

Racial micro-aggressive behaviours may manifest in comments, jokes, gestures, or actions usually made by White employees to Indigenous/racialized employees in a seemingly harmless way. The issue is that the White offenders do not even know how their behaviours can hurt the Indigenous and racialized employees and why some of the recipients of these aggressions make a big fuss about them. The context in which micro-aggression takes place is important to take into consideration. Same micro-aggressions may cease to be interpreted as such because the context has changed. The same words may be viewed as a belittlement or sarcasm in one context and just a neutral observation in another (Government of Alberta, n.d.b.).

Micro-aggressiveness may be found in the workplace on a daily basis, and it may seem harmless, but it hurts Indigenous and racialized people. It reminds them that they are "other" (that is, an "out-group"), and their racial diversity is not respected or valued. Due to the fact that these micro-aggressions come in small doses, they could be viewed as harmless. However, when they occur day in and day out, the stress may add up and starts eating away the self-confidence and self-esteem of Indigenous and racialized people, and they find themselves out of place and not belonging to the organizations they work in. These aggressions also negatively affect their productivity and performance. When the victims of these aggressions complain to their managers, and the latter do not take any actions to address the issue, they feel that management is ignoring their concerns and that nothing has been resolved (Government of Alberta, n.d.c.).

Over time, micro-aggressions increase stress and harm Indigenous and racialized people's mental and physical health. In some extreme cases, Indigenous and racialized peoples become unable to focus on work and may be driven to take drugs and become addicted to some toxic substances and exhibit eating and sleeping disorders and depression. Organizationally, micro-aggressions create conflicts and tension at work, reduce productivity, and undermine work quality. Indigenous and racialized people often hear remarks such as the following, which could be interpreted as micro-aggressive:

- "You speak good English," which may be interpreted as the speaker saying that an immigrant like you can speak in a way that the speaker still understands. The remark highlights the fact that you are an immigrant, and the speaker does not expect you to speak English well just like other racialized immigrants. It is a comment that demarcates the difference between you and the speaker.
- "You are quite successful in your life," which may be interpreted as the speaker not expecting a person with a racial background to be successful in Canada.
- "Your parents must be very proud of you," which may be interpreted as your accomplishments are unusually high in spite of you being a racialized person or an immigrant.
- "You do not look Indigenous," which may be interpreted as you do not have the physical appearance of an Indigenous person since the speaker has a stereotypical image of what an Indigenous person should look like.

- "You look just like any other person," which may be interpreted as you are not different and that the speaker is denying that you are as much an Indigenous or racialized person as anyone else. The speaker does not expressively acknowledge your identity.
- "I don't see colour," which may be interpreted as the speaker is not acknowledging you as an Indigenous or racialized person whose skin colour is a core part of your identity. The speaker may signal or try to convince you that they are colour blind and not racially biased.
- "When I talk with you, I don't even know that I am talking with a Black person," which may be interpreted as the speaker not acknowledging that you are Black and trying to tell you that they are not prejudiced against you as a Black person and that they are not racist.
- "Where do you come from?" which may be interpreted as the speaker trying to spotlight you as a foreigner or immigrant and intending to make you feel like an outsider.
- "Why do you wear that?" which may be interpreted as the speaker seeing themselves as a knowledgeable person who knows your culture well. They may be making fun of your cultural practice and being disrespectful.
- "Don't be so sensitive," which may be interpreted as the speaker being annoyed that they cannot even have a normal conversation without bringing up issues that bother you.
- "Time has changed ... it is time to move on," which may be interpreted as what annoyed you is no longer relevant at this point in time, and the speaker is signalling to you that they are not prejudiced against you.
- "Your name sounds funny," which may be interpreted as your personal name is not "Canadian" enough and the speaker is signalling to you that you have a "foreign" name or that you are not Canadian born.
- "So, what are you?" which may be interpreted as the speaker wishing to find out what ethnicity or nationality you are, instead of focusing on who you are as a person.

Here are some examples of micro-aggressive conduct:

- Interrupting an Indigenous or a racialized person while they are talking at a meeting, which may be interpreted as the speaker seeing themself as more important than you are as a racialized person. The speaker signals that they have no patience with you or are not interested in your ideas.

- Rolling eyes when an Indigenous or a racialized person is speaking, which may be interpreted as saying that their messages are ridiculous, unworthy, or simply "here you go again.
- Ignoring the suggestions or ideas of an Indigenous or a racialized employee but praising or supporting same suggestions when they are brought up by a White employee, which may be interpreted as a devaluation of an Indigenous or a racialized employee and their ideas or simply not paying attention to them when they speak.
- Telling a racist joke followed by saying "I was just joking," which could be interpreted as a degradation of an Indigenous or a racialized person in general because jokes often perpetuate racial stereotypes. The person who said "I was just joking" after their joke wishes to neutralize the offensiveness of the joke and lessen them from taking responsibility for the offending nature of the joke.
- Scheduling a meeting during an Indigenous or a racialized cultural or religious holiday, which may be interpreted as the primacy of non-Indigenous and non-racialized matters over the interest or priorities of the Indigenous or racialized people or simply not knowing much about the significance of the holidays or the holidays at all.
- Ordering only Western foods for an event or not meeting the dietary preferences of Indigenous or racialized people, which may be interpreted as the primacy of Western foods over Indigenous or racialized persons' dietary preference and signalling that they are of lesser significance or that Indigenous or racialized persons may just have to adapt to Western foods.
- Giving instructions or showing an Indigenous or a racialized person a way of doing a project without being asked, which may be interpreted as telling them that they do not know what they are doing as they are not as knowledgeable or skillful as the person who is giving the instructions is.

Some non-Indigenous or non-racialized employees' verbal and non-verbal remarks may be considered as masked put-downs, condescending and disrespectful remarks, or even biting sarcasm by Indigenous or racialized employees. They create discomfort and psychological disturbance, leading them to question themselves: "Am I too sensitive?" or "Did I interpret the situation correctly?" It is common for Indigenous and racialized employees to feel uncertain, unclear, and ambivalent about the other employees who have made these remarks or gestures. Some of them may rationalize the whole situation and pretend that it is a one-off incident. As the ambivalence of conflict remains unresolved, it creates an on-hold pattern of silent resentment and suspicion on the part of Indigenous and racialized employees, which often motivates them to seek confirmation from other employees regarding the interpretations of these interactions. Often, the "proof" or "evidence" of alleged negative behaviours never gets confirmed by the other employees, and the internal ambivalence never gets resolved. At some point during the course of working together with the other employees, an overt confrontation or burst of anger or emotions may erupt, and a "nasty" outbreak of inter-employee hostility with racial overtones may ensue.

Some have labelled these behavioural patterns as subtle racism on the part of non-Indigenous or non-racialized employees toward their counterparts. But the most difficult and hurtful impacts of such brewing conflict or perceived conflict for Indigenous and racialized employees is the ambivalence and uncertainty. This constant state of an unresolved puzzle is almost like the psychology of parents who have a missing child. It is never known for sure that the child is alive and well or is in danger of being tortured or harmed. The unknowns are what is torturous, and the case or situation has no closure.

Incidents of "full abuse of authority" imposed on Indigenous employees through overt threats of reprisal and senior officials in the federal government were found to be tolerant of such conduct (Burke 2016). Indigenous employees are twice as likely to be harassed than non-Indigenous employees in the workplace. This seems to be related to the negative stereotypes (such as an inclination toward drinking and gambling or a lack of education) that Indigenous Peoples have inherited. These stereotypes impact on their credibility and a lack of a sense of belonging. Non-Indigenous people do not have a sense of awareness of Indigenous norms, practices, and culture and have different perceptions of Indigenous looks, hairstyles, or powwows (Leblanc and Coulthard 2015; Waruszynski, MacEachern, and Giroux-Lalond 2019).

Bullying is one form of a dominant group of people attempting to put the "lesser" group in their place when the dominant group perceive or feel the "lesser" group to be smarter, better, or more advantageous than they are. Dr. Rumeet Billan, chief executive officer of Viewpoint Leadership, operationalized the concept of "Tall Poppy Syndrome." It stands for a phenomenon at work in which women, as a marginalized group, are harmed in their mental health, job satisfaction, morale, and employee retention because the dominant group (that is, men) see themselves as threatened by the advantages that some women (such as those with a higher educational level, articulated communication style, command of knowledge and skills) have in the workplace. Some men have attempted to weed these women out by putting them in their traditional place. In her study, she noted that 87 percent of women felt that they were undermined, belittled, and under-acknowledged in their accomplishments.

The syndrome could easily be adopted in the understanding of White people bullying racialized and Indigenous employees verbally in office meetings when the latter exhibit some form of "superiority" such as education, knowledge, skills, or even articulation in communication. Black men and women are often harassed and discriminated in the workplace in this manner. When they talk and put forward their ideas in group meetings in ways that might seem to be in disagreement with some White people, the latter often make an effort to erode the "authority" of the ideas expounded by racialized or Indigenous employees (*Make It Our Business* 2021). This form of "confrontation" adds up to job dissatisfaction, high stress, poor mental health, poor morale, and reduced retention at work.

Unique Features of Harassment

Racial harassment, similar to sexual harassment, carries the inverse proportion rule that means that, if the racial harassment is an isolated incidence, or when milder forms of racial harassment are carried out in a repetitive frequency over a period of time or when they are associated with violent conduct, it may not be construed as a claim of discrimination (Siu 2017, section 1.2.2.7). For example, an Indigenous employee may complain about a wage deduction as being severe when they are late for work when other employees do not face the same kind or degree of punishment. Or a racialized employee may complain about some employees uttering derogatory comments on their race on numerous occasions. These complaints are viewed by these racialized employees as persistent racial harassment.

Harassment has a detrimental effect on its victims, whether they are Indigenous or racialized people or anyone who happens to be the target of harassment. It undermines their dignity as human beings. It humiliates, disrespects, or belittles. Racialized people tend to get racial slurs, jokes, or derogatory comments on their behaviours, cultures, religious beliefs, foods, clothing, and lifestyles. They might be viewed as incompetent or unqualified and unfit for the jobs that they are doing and, hence, receive some biting remarks uttered by the harassers (Hughes and Dodge 1997, 581–99). Similarly, there might also be stereotypical jokes, slurs, insults, innuendo, comments, visual drawing or graphical material, negative evaluations, or physical assaults targeting Indigenous people as well as verbalized misinformation on their Indigenous status or cultures that are disturbing to them.

When determining the nature of the alleged harassment and the responsibility of the complainant, the federal Human Rights Tribunal takes into consideration whether the complainant is guilty of committing other forms of harassment (such as sexual harassment) and the corporate culture of disrespect. The tribunal takes the position that individual employees who complain about racial harassment must not be the persons who have a record of harassing other people (Siu 2017, vol. 1, section 1.2.2.7).

There are indications that, historically, in workplaces dominated by a significant number of White people, there is a greater chance that Indigenous or racialized employees will experience a higher degree of racial harassment. This is very similar to findings where sexual harassment is common in non-traditional workplaces where women begin to appear more among employees. When the corporate culture is more male-centred or White-centred, harassment can be more prevalent probably due to the fact that White people and men feel more "invaded" and, thus, threatened by their racialized and gendered counterparts (Schultz 1990, 1832–33).

Similar to liability in tort, the Supreme Court of Canada held that the employer is responsible for taking effective remedial action to remove undesirable conditions such as that of harassment. Even if non-management employees (and not those of management) were the ones doing the harassment, an employer must be responsible to address and stop the harassment (Andiappan, Crestohl, and Singh 1989, 827–49). Equally important is the employer's responsibility in eliminating the acts of harassment (whoever the harassers are) and the conditions that give rise to harassment. This indicates that the court's position is that racial harassment should be viewed as an organizational practice (and not an individual practice) and that management is responsible for its growth or elimination.

Extent of Racial Harassment

Racial harassment in the workplace is more widespread than what many people think. Catalyst did a survey on more than five thousand employees, including men, women, transgender individuals, and non-binary individuals in Australia, Canada, New Zealand, South Africa, the United Kingdom, and the United States. The results showed that 66 percent of the participants had reported workplace racism in the past and, currently, 52 percent of them were experiencing racism in their work. Workplace harassment (such as racist jokes and slurs) was reported as the most common type of workplace racism (reported by 48 percent of the participants) (Amanat 2023).

In some specific workplaces, such as the federal Department of National Defence and the Canadian Air Force, the reported rate of harassment of Indigenous Peoples is double that of the reported harassment for non-Indigenous peoples. The research findings also showed that women and Indigenous peoples are consistently higher than men and non-Indigenous peoples in reporting workplace harassment (Government of Canada 2022a). This is an example that shows the marked differences in harassment experiences between Indigenous and non-Indigenous employees.

However, there are also those studies that did not suggest workplace racism. In fact, some even show that non-Indigenous people complained more about harassment than Indigenous Peoples. In one study by Statistics Canada (2024c), 43 percent of Indigenous women and 30 percent of Indigenous men reported workplace harassment. In comparison, 48 percent of non-Indigenous women and 31 percent of non-Indigenous men reported workplace harassment. Such a contrast with the previous study cited above suggests that it might be related to the methodology or terminology used in conducting the study. When the term "harassment" is used without being specific about the nature of the harassment (such as sexual, racial, Indigenous, or personal), the respondents are then free to interpret the term in the way they want when they are completing the survey questionnaires. Unless the term has been made more precise as "racial harassment" or "workplace racial harassment," there is a greater chance that the survey respondents will tend to include "personal harassment" in their answers. Hence, these survey results were unable to indicate the extent of specific racial harassment that the people experienced.

Daniel Reale-Chin (2023) reported a global study of more than five thousand racialized people regarding their experience of racism in

Canada, Australia, New Zealand, South Africa, the United Kingdom, and the United States. Among them, Canada had the least proportion of racialized people who reported racism (37 percent), whereas South Africa had the highest (67 percent). Among Canadian women, there are variations in this kind of experience: Middle Eastern and North African women (56 percent), Latina women (50 percent), Indigenous women (50 percent), Black women (44 percent), and Asian women (37 percent) reported racism. Asian trans and non-binary employees (50 percent) reported a high incidence of racism. "Racism" in this study covered racial discrimination in promotion and racial harassment, including "slurs, stereotypes and derisive comments." And 48 percent of respondents reported racial harassment.

Lack of Adequate Human Rights Knowledge

Racial harassment and discrimination are a reflection of leadership and organizational culture. Josh O'Kane (2017) noted that organizational culture is the culprit of the widespread acceptance of harassment and discrimination as a behaviour pattern when leaders implicitly allow it; however, not many senior executives acknowledge it. One of the central components in the spread of discrimination and harassment in an organization is a lack of education and training on human rights issues for management and non-management employees.

The lack of human rights knowledge among employees lies squarely on the shoulders of the leaders because there is a misconception among them that human rights are not an integral part of business or organizational growth because social justice, like the current environmental, social, and governance school of thought, is just a management fad that is peripheral to the bottom line. In other words, human rights have seldom been used as a measurement on a return on investment.

When executives, managers, supervisors, and non-management employees have not been educated and trained on the basic principles of human rights and the application of these principles in the work domain, they are not cognizant of the nature of racial harassment and discrimination and their legal implications, and, consequently, human rights have not been ingrained in the corporate culture, in the tool box of management, or in their daily behaviourial patterns.

Overall, to ensure that the workplace is free from the toxic culture of racial harassment and discrimination, leadership is responsible for the lack of human rights education and training for all levels of management and all employees. Racial harassment and discrimination prevail in the workplace because organizational leadership is not committed to having a harassment-free workplace. As early as 1981, Commissioner Thomas Cumming of the Ontario Human Rights Commission confirmed that it is the duty of the employer to take reasonable steps to eradicate racial harassment and discrimination, including taking reasonably necessary steps to eliminate racial name calling and establishing race relations training in the workplace (Andiappan, Cresthl, and Singh 1989, 827–49).

Lack of a Functional Complaint and Conflict Resolution Mechanism

In addition to the lack of human rights education and training for management and non-management employees as a source of growing human rights complaints in an organization, the lack of an effective mechanism to investigate human rights violations and enforcement of the *Human Rights Code* would explain why racial harassment and discrimination can become unstoppable. An effective complaint and conflict resolution mechanism should have clarity in its objectives, processes, responsibility centres, time frame, deliverables, and communication. To gain trust among racialized and Indigenous employees or any other employees and encourage them to use it, management must make clear the purposes of the complaint and conflict resolution mechanism (that is, what the mechanism aims to accomplish); the different steps of actions and how one leads to another (that is, a flow chart of actions); the departments or persons responsible for the different steps of action (that is, who is accountable for what actions); the duration of each steps of action and the start and end dates of these actions as well as the total number of days/weeks/months needed for the entire conflict resolution process; the expected results at each step of action and the final results at the end of the process; and the communication expected at each step of action and the final communication on the results of the investigation of the complaints.

However, the perfect complaint and conflict resolution mechanism is often not found in real life at the corporate level. First of all, most organizations, especially smaller businesses, do not have a formal mechanism for complaints regarding human rights issues in the workplace or any other issues. Formal mechanisms for complaining about harassment or discrimination or other forms of unfair treatment on human resources issues are usually limited to larger private sector corporations, government departments, broader public sector agencies, and a few larger non-profit sector organizations.

While there are no systematic studies done on the effectiveness of the complaint and investigation of human rights allegation mechanisms across organizations, general observations have suggested that there is a broad range of mechanisms, and most do not instill confidence on the impartiality of the investigation process or the commitment of management to align the organization closer to the *Human Rights Code*. Some of the major problems noted in the author's review of complaint and investigation mechanisms on human rights are:

- Employees do not know how quickly they should file a formal complaint after an incident of harassment or discrimination.
- It is not clear to whom or where employees should send their complaints.
- Employees are not clear about the types and format of presentation of information that they should include in the complaints.
- The organization has not made clear who will be reviewing the complaint and how many people will know about the complaint and its details.
- The responsibility centre of the mechanism dwells within the human resources department or is the responsibility of the person responsible for human resources in the organization.
- There is no explicit timeline for management to start the investigation process once an employee complains about human rights issues.
- The investigator is not an external third party, and they are an employee of the organization—a manager, an executive, and a human resources professional.
- The investigator does not have the credibility or reputation of being impartial or neutral enough to launch an investigation.
- The investigator does not have training in human rights investigation and is not familiar with the human rights legislation.
- The investigator reports to the manager of the complaining employee or the human resources department.
- The backgrounds of the investigator are not appropriate, including race, ethnicity, religion, place of origin, sex, and other

prohibitive grounds of discrimination. Does the complaint have a say in the selection of an investigator?
- It is not clear to the employees what options are available for the organization to resolve the human rights complaints.
- It is not clear whether there is an appeal process if and when the management decision is not satisfactory to the complaining employee.
- It is not clear to the employees the pros and cons of going through the organization's own complaint, investigation, and conflict resolution process to preclude them from filing a complaint to the provincial or federal human rights commissions or tribunals.

These queries, which are by no means exhaustive, illustrate the broad range of issues that are not clear to employees. As long as they are not answered clearly, the mechanism may be negated by employees or at least put into doubt. When the mechanism has not been designed properly or is carried out half-heartedly, it gives the complaining employees reason to suspect its effectiveness. When employees shy away from using the mechanism, it becomes a useless mechanism. As such, allegations may remain allegations, and the work environment may become toxic with unresolved tension, suspicion, and distrust brewing.

The background of the investigator and the patterns of complaint dismissal may play a role in whether the mechanism is viewed as being legitimate or not. A case in point is the racialized employees from the Canadian Human Rights Commission who voiced their concerns about the high dismissal rate for human rights complaints from racial or religious groups. Their allegation is that the commission often assigns White investigators to those complaints who do not have relevant expertise and experience in investigating racism. As a reference, male investigators were not assigned to investigate sexual harassment or discrimination from the public. Advice from current or former racialized employees was often ignored as if the objectivity of the advice was questioned (Thurton 2023).

Impacts of Racial Harassment and Discrimination

A study of 119 immigrants and racialized women (aged twenty-six and over) and youth (aged between eighteen and twenty-five years old) in the Greater Toronto Area in online focus groups in July and August 2022 showed that many racialized and immigrant employees quit their jobs because of harassment and discrimination, including aggression and exclusion. The experience seems to be compounded by their lack of knowledge about human rights and the reporting mechanisms as well as their fear of reporting workplace harassment (Minors et al., n.d., 13).

In addition, Catalyst conducted a survey of more than seven hundred racialized people to estimate how they fared in the working world in 2016. It found out that an "emotional tax" was being imposed on racialized people. It is "a combination of feeling different from peers at work because of gender, race or ethnicity, being on guard for experiences of bias, and the associated effects on health, well-being, and the ability to thrive at work. As the demand is higher than the supply of skilled labour, recruiting and retaining talent has become a major problem in the technology sector. The report explained how racialized people are in a perpetual state of being "on guard" due to the omnipresence of bias and discrimination in and outside the workplace. This constant stress factor made 50–69 percent of racialized professionals express a "high intent to quit their current job." An additional set of interviews with candidates showed that 77 percent of them shared stories of exclusion (Kirkwood 2019).

How does racial harassment and discrimination drive racialized and Indigenous people out from their workplaces? Harassment and discrimination impact on individual employees at a very deep and personal level. As noted, there are many forms of human behaviours that aim at making people (racialized and Indigenous people included) feel annoyed, threatened, isolated, belittled, disrespected, humiliated, degraded, and abused. They wound them psychologically and/or physically. Often, they take these harassments lying down without any expressive response; at other times, they respond with angry voices and utter strong words that state that the harassers' conduct is not welcome and not acceptable. Some harassment is more physical than psychological: the harassers invade the private space of the harassed and/or stalk or assault them.

Some harassers are in positions of power (such as their supervisors or managers), and racialized and Indigenous people feel exploited, intimidated, and taken advantage of. Some harassed persons feel that they are manipulated or even coerced to do certain things that they are uncomfortable doing. Some of these harassers say negative things behind their backs and damage their chance of advancement or even networking. These harassing activities—subtle or blatant—undermine the dignity of racialized and Indigenous employees and make them feel uncomfortable and used. All these experiences end up stressing them, waking them up in the middle of the night, making them feel distressed and unable to perform well in the workplace, unable to connect or relate to co-workers, and ostracized and outcast, with no sense of belonging to the organization.

In addition to harassment, which could be ongoing or sporadic, discrimination in the workplace can be more focused on regular human resources functions such as training and developmental opportunities, promotion and succession, performance evaluation, coaching, mentorship, sponsorship, and rewards/benefits and compensation. Some discriminatory practices can be found in specific events, seasonal gatherings, or initiatives commonly carried out in social realms such as networking events, celebrations, idea competitions, honourary mentions in speeches, and awards. According to racialized and Indigenous employees, the most hurtful ones are those human resources functions such as developmental assignments, promotions, and successions where they are not selected, either in the form of job competitions or appointments. Indigenous employees have reported that they do not feel supported by their senior officials, and they feel that they were not able to advance in their careers in the government (Government of Canada 2022a).

Racial harassment is often ambivalent even when the harassing acts are silent (as in quietly ignoring the presence of racialized and Indigenous employees) and when the discriminatory acts occur in human resources functions or workplace events/initiatives. Both acts often leave racialized and Indigenous guessing: "Have I been racially harassed/discriminated against?" Information on job competitions (such as hiring and promotion), successions, performance evaluations, and other information-sensitive human resource functions that are confidential have made these domains non-transparent, and racialized or Indigenous employees have no way to find out why they have not been chosen to be the successful candidates. Hence, the elements of guessing and suspicion can only spiral without a definitive answer. Over time, with numerous unsuccessful attempts to get a promotion or obtain a developmental assignment, racialized and Indigenous employees' distrust continues to deepen. With a combination of both daily encounters of events or actions from management and co-workers, stagnation in their own positions, and no sign of their talents being fully utilized, as well as critical one-time events like promotions and appointments, racialized and Indigenous employees end up in a constant state of frustration, guesswork, and uncertainty. Over time, such a psychological state can only lead to stress and more stress, which constantly corroded both their psychological and physical well-being and safety.

Without putting much effort into making their workplaces more fair, equitable, and inclusive, organizations do not have a progressive program in educating and training executives, managers, and non-management employees in knowing more about the principles of human rights, the prohibited grounds of discrimination, and proactive and reactive human rights skills. There are also few signs that these organizations will even attempt to integrate workplace respect, human rights, and anti-racism in every aspect of their human resources functions. Moreover, when the complaint and conflict resolution mechanism is not in place or is improperly designed or dysfunctionally carried out, racialized and Indigenous employees really do not see any sign of hope and future for them to actually feel like they belong in their workplaces, let alone that they are growing in them. They literally wither away cognitively, emotionally, socially, and workwise. Hence, when growth opportunities arise outside of their organizations, they have no hesitation but to exit.

CONCLUSION

Chapters 6 and 7 demonstrated that there are inherent biases built into the systems that are designed to recruit, select, and hire external candidates, the systems that are designed to measure employee performance—to coach, train, develop, and mentor employees for succession purposes—and to promote and enable job movements for employees. These biases are embedded in the policies and procedures in all these areas. When put into operation by the employees entrusted to do the jobs, further biases are built into the decision-making process at each stage of operation, which makes it more difficult for racialized and Indigenous people to be employed and harder for them to succeed because these racial stereotypes and prejudices are now compounding the negative impacts of racially biased human resources systems, which further stifle the life chances of racialized and Indigenous employees.

This chapter has further broadened our understanding of racism in the workplace by examining the factors affecting the retention of racialized and Indigenous people in the workplace. It has focused on toxic organizational culture and biased practices; workplace conduct with special emphasis on racial harassment and discrimination. The evidence suggests that the cultural and behavourial patterns of the workplace cause deep wounds in the psychology of racialized and Indigenous employees and basically push them out from the organizations that employ them. The available data also shows that racial harassment and discrimination impact them adversely in significant ways.

PART THREE

CHANGE AGENTS

This part analyzes and assesses the strengths and weaknesses of the past and current legislation, public policies, strategies, and tactics utilized by the three key stakeholder groups in combating racism—the federal, provincial, territorial, and municipal governments, employers, and labour unions. These legislation, public policies, strategies, and tactics are in the realms of human rights, employment equity, anti-racism, and diversity and inclusiveness.

It is clear that all three stakeholder groups have established an extensive array of policies, programs, and initiatives in areas that could have impacted on racism in the past. It is also true that the progress in eradicating racism and strengthening equity by these parties is still considered moderately effective but still inadequate overall. There might be areas in which they could improve further. Their approaches, strategies, and focuses may need to be revised or innovated.

Recommendations are put forward in this section, and they focus on some key directions, approaches, strategies, and executions.

In employment equity, the coverage of employers needs to expand to more employers, and the monitoring and enforcement model needs to be strengthened. In human rights, the onus of proof needs to shift to employers, and more resources should be allocated. In anti-racism, having a specific anti-racism policy and strategy in employment and an anti-racism public education strategy is crucial. Employers are recommended to establish a clear diversity, equity, and inclusion policy statement, a focus on doing comprehensive employment systems reviews, data cross-tabulations and analysis, and more human rights education and training and broader coaching, mentoring, and community outreach. Labour unions should abandon the seniority system and make job movements for employees more flexible, do more consultation and joint responsibilities with employers, and be more active in getting justice for individual employees.

When these recommendations are put into motion, stakeholder groups' anti-racism, human rights, and employment equity efforts will be much more effective than what we have now.

CHAPTER 9

Governments: Defenders of Public Good

INTRODUCTION

This chapter examines the roles of governments in eliminating racism. The federal government has a number of mostly legislative and policy instruments in its toolbox to fight against racism or at least attempt to arrest the pace of racism's damages. It examines the major government tools and evaluates the merits and demerits of anti-racism strategies and policies, human rights laws, and employment equity legislation (including the amended *Canada Business Corporations Act*).[1]

After observing the problems with these strategies, policies, and laws, a few recommendations are put forward to tackle racism in the workplace. In these anti-racism strategies/policies, a focus on employment, public education, school-workplace transition, industrial alliance, and standardization of race data collection are recommended. In human rights, the shifting of onus of proof, resources allocation, and public education are recommended. Employment equity needs to expand its impacts more widely, rebalance its quantitative and qualitative components, and strengthen its legal enforcement.

ANTI-RACISM POLICIES, STRATEGIES, AND ACTIONS

Federal Government

The Government of Canada's first anti-racism strategy (2019–22) was announced in 2019. The current strategy is entitled Changing Systems,

1 RSC 1985, c C-44.

Transforming Lives: Canada's Anti-Racism Strategy 2024–2028, and it has the objective of tackling "systemic racism and mak[ing] our communities more inclusive and prosperous" by removing barriers and building a Canada "where everyone reaches the full potential—with equality, equity and fairness." Key themes emerging from this strategy are the customization of approaches for different marginalized communities (not "one size fits all") and a priority of addressing the challenges related to the intersectionality of race and other attributes such as sex and sexual orientation. There are four priority areas in this strategy: promoting empowerment; racial equity in immigration, health, and housing; advancing reforms in justice and law enforcement; and using international engagement to inform racial advancement. To carry out these priorities, the strategy explores legislative and system changes to enrich accountability and inclusiveness; prioritize and support communities; and strengthen relationships with national and international partners (Government of Canada 2024a).

The Federal Anti-Racism Secretariat was established back in 2019 when the first anti-racism strategy was launched. It aims to lead all federal departments in anti-racism by identifying gaps, coordinating responsive and new initiatives, and monitoring their impacts on racialized and Indigenous communities. Since its establishment, the Secretariat has funded anti-racism projects; fostered policy input from communities; developed an anti-racism framework for federal departments and developed anti-racism policies, programs, and services; established task forces with women and Asian communities; collected more data and built anti-racism tools; partnered with international bodies; and invested in the Canadian Race Relations Foundation (Government of Canada 2024a).

Based on the work that has been done so far, it appears that the federal Secretariat is focusing largely on consulting racialized and Indigenous communities in developing initiatives or policies and enabling the federal government departments to do anti-racism work. This is beneficial to racialized and Indigenous communities in the different ways in which the federal government has jurisdiction. However, there have been many community consultations, government task forces, think-tank research reports, and academic publications that have provided substantial and comprehensive information and analyses on racism and its impacts on racialized and Indigenous people and on the country as a whole. Instead of doing more of this kind of information gathering, the federal government may wish to focus its resources on taking concrete anti-racism actions based on the recommendations of past reports and publications, whose findings are very similar. Current consultations could be carried out just to establish priorities on these past recommendations in the context of more up-to-date racial data in different industrial sectors and geographic locations. Politically and historically, commissions, task forces, and consultations have been used to buy time for governments to deal with the public's anger and serve merely as symbolic value on anti-racism or other "hot potato" issues. Limited government resources may be better used in yielding concrete benefits for racialized and Indigenous communities or other long-term investments in building a more equitable social structure(s).

Provincial Governments

Some provincial governments also have their own anti-racism strategies or policies. Ontario, for example, announced its *Anti-Racism Act* in 2017 and its anti-racism strategic plan in 2023, formally known as the Building a Stronger and More Inclusive Ontario: Ontario's Anti-Racism Strategic Plan.[2] Since 2017, the province has focused on a sectoral approach in building a database: nine regulated areas were required to submit their racial data collection in a standardized manner in 2020: child welfare (Children's Aid Societies), education (school boards), and justice (Legal Aid Ontario; Special Investigations Unit, Office of the Independent Police Review Director; Adult Correctional Services; Youth Justice Division; Use of Force Report). There were also funds allocated to support entrepreneurship and address issues related to hate and racism. Special attention was paid to dealing with Anti-Black racism and Indigenous-focused anti-racism (as in Black economic development and Indigenous reconciliation and relationship building) (Government of Ontario 2023).

Meanwhile, similar to Ontario, the Government of British Columbia, enacted the *Anti-Racism Data Act* in 2022 as a starting point in enriching racial data sets.[3] The act emphasizes the importance of evidence-based anti-racism work and calls for the collaboration and support from Indigenous and racialized communities in creating anti-racism policies and

2 *Anti-Racism Act*, RSO 2017, c 15.

3 *Anti-Racism Data Act*, SBC 2022, c 18.

programs. It aims to dismantle systemic racism, measure the government's efforts in addressing racism, advance healing from racism's harms, and hold the government accountable (Government of British Columbia, n.d.).

The Government of Quebec, with the help of several ministers, proposed a series of anti-racism initiatives that aim to address racism for racialized and Indigenous people, and they are formally known as Racism in Quebec: Zero Tolerance—Report of the Groupe d'action contre le racisms. Among its recommendations on policing, housing, education, and government, it has a special chapter on access to employment for racialized people, which pays attention to the recognition of international credentials and experiences, increases racialized people's employment in construction jobs and the public sector, and encourages their appointments to boards of directors of state-owned enterprises. It also provides recommendations on public education, cultural safety, policing, access to justice, and housing conditions for Indigenous people but seems to gloss over the importance of the employment discrimination of Indigenous people (Government of Quebec 2020).

Examples from these three provincial governments—Ontario, British Columbia, and Quebec—may not reflect on the anti-racism work in other provinces; however, they shed some light on where these three provinces are at. It appears that they are in the early stages of anti-racism work, which includes doing research and gathering racial data as well as some ad hoc initiatives in response to what communities and institutions wished to see accomplished. If Canadian history tells us anything about the last five decades, these initiatives really did not yield many long-term structural changes in racial inequality and better livelihoods for racialized and Indigenous people. It is hard to say with confidence that the life chances of racialized and Indigenous people in the workplace or other domains have been improved over these last five decades. Overall, racial disparities in employment and other aspects of existence have remained more or less the same or are getting worse. Funds should be allocated to upgrading the employment opportunities for selected segments of the Indigenous and racialized population so that their livelihoods can be improved with better employment income and benefits.

Municipal Governments

At the municipal level, there are also examples of anti-racism policies and plans. In 2017, the City of Toronto launched a five-year anti-Black racism plan with a special focus on children and youth, health and community services, job opportunities and income support, policing and the justice system, and community engagement and Black leadership. In 2024, the city conducted an evaluation of this five-year plan and started drafting its ten-year action plan to tackle anti-Black racism with a year-long research and community engagement process. It is expected that 2024's planning process will build on to the success of the last five-year plan with systemic hurdles and strengthen Black people's contribution in the city (City of Toronto, n.d.b., n.d.c.).

It is not clear whether the City of Winnipeg has an anti-racism policy or plan; however, the city passed the Newcomer Welcome and Inclusion Policy in 2019, which has an anti-racism component. The term "newcomer" refers to recent immigrants, refugees, refugee claimants or asylum seekers, and temporary residents. The policy objectives are to demonstrate anti-racism leadership city-wide, launch anti-racism and cross-cultural competency in public service, foster community safety and trust, and build understanding between newcomers and Indigenous peoples. In addition to a focus on racism, this policy aims to develop better equitable and accessible services and build a representative workforce (City of Winnipeg, n.d.).

These two examples from Toronto and Winnipeg may not be representative of what municipal governments are all doing, but they are engaging communities and planning to create localized initiatives in fighting racism. Winnipeg is seeing newcomers as their focus for anti-racism work, and Toronto is viewing Black people as their focus. Once again, it appears that both municipalities are using a "shot gun" approach and hoping that some of their initiatives have some positive impacts. However, employment (such as hiring, promotion, and retention), human resources mechanisms (such as training and development), and workplace culture is not explicitly stated and linked specifically to racialized communities. More importantly, the types of racial biases, their sources, and solutions have been glossed over, making it difficult for the government to develop systemic plans for the eradication of racism with long-lasting positive impacts for these target groups.

Territorial Governments

Canada has three territories: the Northwest Territories, the Yukon, and Nunavut. All have made some headway in human rights and diversity, equity, and inclusiveness. As for special anti-racism efforts, the Northwest Territories has broadened its reach in numerous domains covering the school and health systems, social services, justice, housing, and government employment. The Yukon is beginning to branch into education and health. Nunavut appears to be the least progressive in terms of concrete advancements in anti-racism.

Northwest Territories

In 2021, the Government of Northwest Territories (GNWT) responded with Motion 29–19(2): Systemic Racism, which called for a review of its policies and practices for racial and cultural bias, especially as they relate to education, health and social services, justice, housing, and government hiring. The GNWT summarized its anti-racism initiatives in six areas a few years before 2021, including an Indigenous Cultural Awareness and Sensitivity Training program ("Living Well Together"); the Ministerial Directive on "Inclusive Schooling," which is in line with the Northwest Territories *Human Rights Act*; a ten-year Culture and Heritage Strategic Framework; an action plan that applied to all GNWT departments; and a Cultural Safety and Anti-Racism Unit to tackle systemic racism. Employment initiatives are limited to the public sector following the Affirmative Action Policy, which was established in 1989 and gives preference to Indigenous people in recruiting, hiring, and retaining and builds a representative public service. In 2018, programs were created for getting more Indigenous people into entry-level and management positions, and, in 2021–22, the government increased anti-racism training for employees. In addition, the government has developed an Indigenous Recruitment and Retention Framework and Action Plan and a Strategic Diversity and Inclusion Framework and Implementation Plan (Government of Northwest Territories, n.d.).

Yukon

The Government of Yukon (2023) announced its commitment to anti-racism and inclusive governance in the health sector in 2023. Its new legislation aims at creating a new authority on the health system with Yukon First Nations partners to be announced in 2024. The First Nation Education Commission saw the need for reviewing systemic racism in education. They then delegated funds and directed the Yukon First Nation Education Directorate and Yukon Child and Youth Advocacy Office to conduct a review of the ten years between 2014 and 2024. The review focuses on the experiences of First Nations students and other racialized students. In 2023, the Department of Education was notified about the review. It took place in 2024 and is expected to be completed at the end of that year, and the report will go to the Yukon Legislative Assembly (Yukon Child and Youth Advocacy 2023; Hatherly 2024).

Nunavut

Nunavut does not have an anti-racism policy or strategy per se, but it has a human rights policy and a harassment-free workplace policy. Both are not specific to the topic of anti-racism in employment, although, in principle, both policies have race as a central component.

OBSERVATIONS

The above examples on provincial, territorial, and municipal policies and plans suggest that each jurisdiction is in a different stage of addressing racism. Most policies focus on doing research and consultation on the issues facing racialized and Indigenous communities. The current status is that, on the one hand, there is an emphasis on collecting racial data so as to make evidence-based government policies and programs more relevant and, on the other hand, there are not many efforts to make legislative or policy changes in eradicating racism on a larger scale. Funding anti-racism efforts at the community and institutional levels could pre-empt the harms of racism in a localized community or small-scale manner, but these efforts remain ad hoc, and their impact may be limited.

Obviously, getting a job is the number one priority for Indigenous and some racialized people, but keeping their jobs and getting promoted to better jobs in the long term have been vocalized as a high priority too, and, for many years and numerous government programs, the aspects of employment discussed in Chapters 6, 7, and 8 have been glossed over by government programs at all levels, with the modest exception of the Northwest Territories. It may well be the case that the federal government seems to be depending on the *Employment Equity Act* to solve these employment problems, but they have not been reduced or removed.[4] Provincial and municipal governments still have not addressed the equity component of employment.

---

4 *Employment Equity Act*, SC 1995, c 44.

Historically, various government levels have utilized this funding method to showcase their commitment on various social justice issues, such as the many past initiatives on multiculturalism, racial equity, diversity and inclusiveness, and anti-racism. Their impacts were largely symbolic (in presenting the government as a leader in anti-racism), but they were short-lived because, as soon as the funds had dried up or the events/initiatives were over, their profiles at the community or institutional level did not last, and they did not have a long-term impact on concrete structural/organizational change benefiting racialized and Indigenous communities. Results from government-funded research projects and training ventures (which were usually generated in time of community or other political crises) may have had some lasting value, but, unfortunately, information and research data were limited in application and ceased to be topical unless that they were translated into government policies/legislation or knowledge/skills advancement immediately, which they often were not. Hence, it has become a recurring ritual for these projects to wither away once the funding cycles were over and the topical political heat had dissipated.

RECOMMENDATIONS

While community and institutional consultations and evidence-based data are essential ingredients for creating an anti-racism policy framework and actionable strategy, what comes after these research efforts are all that matters. Here are a few recommendations for various government levels in pursuit of anti-racism.

A Specific Anti-Racism Policy and Strategy in Employment

The current anti-racism policies and strategies available in a few government jurisdictions in Canada are relatively generic. They are broad enough to cover as many domains (such as education, health, and justice) and as many racialized groups as possible. In other words, these policies and strategies could be customized as specific jurisdictions are prepared. This feature has some merit as it could adapt to many constituents, industrial sectors, social spheres, and demographic groups.

Currently, anti-racism policies are focused on addressing the issues on racism with Indigenous people and Black people in the health-care systems and education services. Anti-racism in employment has not been a focus, although some attention has been paid to government employment. This is not impactful enough for racialized and Indigenous people (and their intersectionality with gender, class, or disabilities). Like other segments of the population, employment is a key financial source for racialized and Indigenous peoples, whether they are employed in the public sector (governments), the broader public sector (municipalities, universities, colleges, and hospitals), the private sector (federally or non-federally regulated industries), or the non-profit sector. A negation on employment and the workplace in fighting against racism is a major cavity in government policy, strategy, and action. An example of this negation is the lack of government focus in developing an anti-racism policy or strategy and the related actions serving racialized or Indigenous people with disabilities in the hospitality sector. There is simply no focus currently in this intersectional group on specific industries, and there does not seem to be any sign of urgency to address the experience of racism among these people.

A Specific Anti-Racism Public Education Strategy

Racism in the workplace has not sprung out of a vacuum. It is a microcosm of a larger issue in society, as Chapter 3 illustrated using information and data from many aspects of people's lives from their birth to their mortality. Evidence shows that, no matter where you look, you can see racism in action. It is therefore not surprising to find that people in general have an opinion that racialized and Indigenous people are inferior overall. With a negative stereotype of this kind, racial prejudice and discrimination against them are common in every sphere of our society. People believe that it is alright to have a low opinion about racialized and Indigenous people and to look down on them. In the employment field, they may even think that they are not discriminating against them, although, in essence, they are doing that by giving them lower scores in interviews, by not selecting them for special work assignments, by not offering them certain positions, or by not including them in the pool of candidates for succession planning. Under the pretense of impartiality and objectivity, human resources mechanisms are designed and executed as being merit focused, but, in reality, as discussed earlier in Chapters 6, 7, and 8, these mechanisms are merely tools for racial discrimination.

Before joining the labour force, people through their childhood and school years learn a lot about race through personal observations and personal comments/actions on racialized and Indigenous people. Through the mass media (including social media), there are prevalent problematic images and messages about racialized and Indigenous people that have not been challenged vigorously by anti-racism public education. There is also continuous misinformation or disinformation propagated through media that have not been blocked or neutralized by the government, influential people, or social forces (such as legislation, the police, or educational institutions).

One thing is clear: public education on anti-racism is quite limited in this country. All levels of government have not made much effort or expended many resources to educate the general public on racialized and Indigenous communities. To counter the negative forces generated from racism—both structural and psychological—requires relentless public education efforts, including media messages, public speeches, local forums and workshops, educational resources and community events, and government marketing (including billboards, posters, electronic messages, legal information alerts, and so on).

In the past, some of these public education methods have been utilized, usually through government funding of public "anti-racism" academic and community events, public speeches of politicians, government officials' announcements of new government policies or programs, and interviews with politicians. These have usually been ad hoc and reactive ways to get messages out, and these messages have not specifically been about anti-racism; rather, they are related to diversity, equity, and inclusiveness; multiculturalism; immigration and immigrants; refugees; and international students. Most were welcoming announcements for newcomers that showed how open our country is to helping more people who are from other countries that have humanitarian crises, internal conflicts, wars, and economic/political tension. The purpose and content of these anti-racism messages have been rather muted, and the impact of anti-racism has been minimal and ineffective in raising the level of social justice awareness and understanding of the general public.

An Anti-Racism Transition from Schools to the Workplace

Provincial governments have jurisdiction over the school system (including colleges and universities), and territorial governments also have authority provided by the federal government to manage their school systems. In other words, they have the responsibility to develop strong anti-racism curricula and educational resources to instill in students the vision, mindset, and skills to fight racism in schools as well as enabling students to transition to the workplace with a healthy view on race in an impactful manner.

The provincial and territorial governments may need to take on the responsibility of reviewing the current curriculum and educational materials in the school system (elementary and secondary schools) and identifying the current prevalence and types of racism in schools, the scope and content of the educational materials, the number of hours students spend in studying anti-racism and related issues, the capability of teachers in this field, their teaching methods, and the mechanism of evaluating anti-racism education in schools.

In addition to the work of employers who have accountability in building an anti-racism culture in the workplace, the school system plays an important role in developing the mindset and skills of students in learning and working with racialized and Indigenous people, and educators must see themselves as preparing students to join the working world. Hence, with the assistance and partnership of employers, the school system needs to equip students with the capability to work with their colleagues and interface with customers and service users when they transition to the workplace. It is difficult for employers to educate and train newly hired employees who have no idea how to conduct themselves or perform tasks in a work environment where interracial and intercultural workplace knowledge and skills are needed.

In preparing students for the workplace environment, which is different from that of the school system, "co-operative" programs for students are an ideal model to equip them with the necessary work-related technical/professional skills as well as work-related interpersonal skills. Here, employers may instill in these students real-life skills in working with racialized and Indigenous peoples as well as other diverse groups. Thus, one may formalize anti-racism, diversity/inclusiveness, and human rights types of educational materials in various "co-operative" programs and enrich students' mindsets and skillsets.

Integrating Anti-Racism Efforts across the Industrial Sectors

Currently, anti-racism efforts come from different jurisdictions or parts of a jurisdiction, and these efforts are not coordinated—hence, anti-racism resources are scattered between different players and are not cost-effective. Instead of having each government develop its own anti-racism policy for its own jurisdiction (such as the City of Toronto's policy for its own employees), it makes more sense for each provincial, municipal, and territorial government to call for a unified industrial sectoral anti-racism strategy. Such a strategy means that the municipal (or provincial) government could play a leadership role in calling for a united front in developing a cross-industry-wide alliance to fight against racism. This could be done by consulting and working with boards of trade, associations of various industries, major companies in multiple sectors, labour unions or trade councils, employee associations, and so on. The objective is to create institutional and industrial sectorial partnerships on developing an anti-racism strategy that would address issues raised by racialized and Indigenous people and share racial issues among employers, together finding common ground workplace solutions and developing/sharing resource materials so as to avoid multiple "wheel inventions" and make this process cost-effective. The municipal (or provincial) government merely plays the role of a catalyst for such industrial partnerships.

Standardize Racial Data across Federal, Provincial, Territorial, and Municipal Sectors

The current situation of research on racialized and Indigenous people across Canada is a patchwork of racial data collection. This means that data on racialized and Indigenous groups and their subsets are collected under different data types both within each jurisdiction and across jurisdictions. Racial data are sometimes mistakenly collected and tabulated under "proxy" racial categories such as religion, creed, ethnicity, nationality, language, and place of origin. As all these terms have different meanings, data derived from these categories are very different and cannot be compared across data categories or across jurisdictions. Some jurisdictions have only gathered data for the major race categories such as Black, Asian, White, and Indigenous; others have gathered data on their subset categories. For example, under the Asian group, subset data on South Asian, Southeast Asian, East Asian, and West Asian are also collected. There are advantages and disadvantages on these two ways of collecting racial data.

Furthermore, comparing data from more than one jurisdiction may pose some challenges, especially when the data sets are too small to have any statistical meaning. The major advantage of standardizing the collection of data on racial categories is that the research findings based on these data are comparable, especially if Statistics Canada's data categories are utilized as a reference point, and they can also be compared through time (years in history).

Given that there are so many aspects of racialized and Indigenous people's life that are impacted by race, it makes sense for the federal government or the provincial/territorial governments to sit down together and come to a consensus on what basic racial data categories should be used to cover some agreeable social domains (such as education, health, health care, housing, employment, transportation, and politics). Once such standardization is established, it makes it easier for more provinces, municipalities, and territories to do research on racial and Indigenous people and enable researchers, policy people, and politicians to have a common understanding on a broader spectrum of their livelihoods. As the broader public sectors (that is, municipalities, universities, colleges, and hospitals) receive provincial and territorial funding, it is more likely that these sectors will be more inclined to provide the necessary or relevant data on racialized and Indigenous people to supplement policy and program formation of jurisdictions at a higher level. In this manner of data collection and analysis, our understanding of the inequitable and discriminatory experiences of racialized and Indigenous people would be further enriched. This has been part of the data-building process on women in Canada in the last few decades. Once the momentum in research data collection begins, if political will and resources are available for research, the accumulative collected racial/Indigenous data would constitute a good foundation for better public policy development. This can only be accomplished through the concerted efforts of different levels of government.

HUMAN RIGHTS

Federal Government

As a part of the *Constitution Act 1982*, the *Canadian Charter of Rights and Freedoms* defines the rights and freedoms for all persons in Canada, including Canadian citizens, permanent residents, and newcomers.[5]

---

5 *Canadian Charter of Rights and Freedoms*, Part 1 of the *Constitution Act, 1982*, being Schedule B to the *Canada Act 1982* (UK), 1982, c 11.

Broadly speaking, all laws in Canada are consistent with the rules set out in the Constitution; however, the rights and freedoms in the *Charter* are not absolute, and they can be limited to protect other rights and important Canadian values. Section 15(1) of the *Charter* (on equality rights) states that "[e]very individual is equal before and under the law and has the right to the equal protection and equal benefit of the law without discrimination and, in particular, without discrimination based on race, national or ethnic origin, colour, religion, sex, age, or mental or physical disability." While the *Charter* came into force in 1982, section 15 came into effect in 1985.

In 1977, the Parliament of Canada passed for the first time the *Canadian Human Rights Act*, and, later in 1982, it specified that the Canadian rights of all people in Canada are protected from discrimination based on race, ethnic or national origin, colour, religion, age, sex, sexual orientation, gender identify or expression, marital status, family status, genetic characteristics, disability, and conviction for an offence for which a pardon has been granted or in respect of which a record suspension has been ordered.[6] This law aligns with the *Canadian Charter of Rights and Freedoms*, but it applies only to federal regulated activities. Non-federally regulated activities are subsumed under the provincial or territorial laws on human rights (Canadian Teachers Federation, n.d.). All provinces and territories have their own human rights legislation (Chun and Gallagher-Louisy 2018).

Provincial Governments

Ontario passed its *Racial Discrimination Act* in 1944, and the Saskatchewan law on human rights was first passed as a bill of rights in 1947.[7] Other provinces and territories followed suit in one form or another until Ontario established a formal provincial *Human Rights Code* in 1961, and the other provinces and territories followed.[8] Quebec's path in enshrining a human rights law was different. Quebec enacted its own provincial *Charter of Human Rights and Freedoms* in 1975.[9] When the *Canadian Charter of Rights of Freedoms* was incorporated as a part of

---

6 *Canadian Human Rights Act*, RSC 1985, c H-6.

7 *Racial Discrimination Act*, SO 1944, c 51; *Act to Protect Certain Civil Rights*, SS 1947, c 35.

8 *Human Rights Code*, RSO 1962, c 93.

9 *Charter of Human Rights and Freedoms*, CQLR, c C-12.

the *Constitution Act 1982*, it ignited a political battle between Quebec and the federal government about whether Quebec had to abandon its provincial *Charter*. However, the Supreme Court of Canada has the legal authority to bind without the approval of any provinces, so the *Constitution Act*, along with its *Charter of Rights and Freedoms*, was enacted in 1982. As a result, all Quebec laws must respect both the Canadian *Charter* and the Quebec *Charter* to be considered constitutional (Foot 2020).

It is clear that all provinces in Canada have their own human rights legislation. Provincial human rights legislation, similar to that of the federal jurisdiction, specifies protected (or prohibited) grounds such as race and sex and protected areas such as employment, housing, services, and membership in associations. The list of protected grounds for provinces are different, but those grounds related to racialized and Indigenous people are race, colour, ethnic origin, place of origin, nationality, and religion, and they are consistently common in all provinces.

There are some unique features in each provincial law on human rights. For example, Nova Scotia's *Human Rights Act* introduces Aboriginal origin as a protected ground in addition to race, ethnicity, and nationality.[10] Saskatchewan's *Human Rights Code* has perceived race as a protected ground (that is, the inferred race by another person).[11] Ontario's legislation in human rights has citizenship listed as a protected ground. In Quebec, its own *Charter of Human Rights and Freedoms* also lists social condition (as in educational level, occupation, and income level) as a protected ground (Chun and Gallagher-Louisy 2018).

Territorial Governments

Nunavut has had a human rights law since 2004.[12] Similar to the *Canadian Human Rights Act*, the prohibited grounds include race, colour, ancestry, ethnic origin, citizenship, place of origin, creed, religion, as well as nine more. It applies to all employees working in the Government of Nunavut and public agencies. In addition, Nunavut has a Harassment Free Workplace Policy that "promotes an atmosphere

---

10 *Human Rights Act*, RSNS 1989, c 214.

11 *Saskatchewan Human Rights Code, 2018*, SS 2018, c S-24.2.

12 *Human Rights Act*, CSNu, c H-70.

of mutual respect, fairness and concern" (Government of Nunavut 2016). It covers workplace harassment, sexual harassment, and personal harassment.

The Yukon's *Human Rights Act* applies similar principles as those found in the federal law on human rights.[13] It has some overlapping protected areas (such as housing, goods and services, and employment) and more or less the same protected grounds (as in race and colour, national origin, religion, age, and sex).

In addition to the usual protected grounds and protected areas found in other human rights law, the Northwest Territories *Human Rights Act* has a unique statement which confirms existing Indigenous rights.[14] Article 2 states: "Nothing in this Act shall be construed so as to abrogate or derogate from the protection provide for exiting aboriginal or treaty rights of the aboriginal peoples of Canada by the recognition and affirmation of those rights in section 35 of the *Constitution Act, 1982*" (Chun and Gallagher-Louisy 2018).

Municipal Governments

Not all municipalities in Canada have specific municipal policies on human rights to further their social justice vision. It appears that municipal policies in human rights and related areas are more likely found in larger cities. Progressive cities, like the City of Toronto, created its own Human Rights and Anti-Harassment Policy. While the City of Toronto's policy on human rights and anti-harassment is consistent with Ontario's *Human Rights Code*, it elaborates on the core principles of the provincial code and its scope in services and facilities, occupation of accommodation, contracts, and employment. The policy covers not only the city's employees but also visitors, contractors, consultants, elected officials, and even the general public (such as residents and recipients of city services). The policy also includes the roles and responsibilities of the city manager, deputy city managers, division heads, directors, managers, supervisors, human resources staff, corporate policy division, human rights office, and employees. Supplementary to the policy directives, procedures and guidelines are also available for implementation

---

13 *Human Rights Act*, RSY 2002, c 116.
14 *Human Rights Act*, SNWT 2002, c 18.

in processing human rights complaints. It also has its own Hate Activity Policy and Workplace Violence Policy (City of Toronto, n.d.a.).

Similarly, the City of Vancouver has a series of policies consistent with the intent of British Columbia's *Human Rights Code*,[15] and they include the Respect in the Workplace Policy (with accompanied procedures of operation); the Human Rights and Harassment Free Workplace Policy; the Preventing Violence in the Workplace Policy; and the Occupational Health and Safety Policy (City of Vancouver, n.d.a.). The Human Rights and Harassment Free Workplace Policy resembles British Columbia's *Human Rights Code* with an explicit statement of the protected (or prohibited) grounds of discrimination, examples of harassment, roles and responsibilities of the City of Vancouver, the Equal Employment Opportunity Program, supervisory staff and managers, and employees, harassment complaint procedures, and retaliation. Meanwhile, the Respect in the Workplace Policy focuses on disrespectful behaviour, including a fair and equitable process, privacy and confidentiality, corrective action, and the joint involvement of management, unions, and staff in resolving issues (City of Vancouver 2011).

OBSERVATIONS

All human rights laws in Canada have a list of prohibited grounds on discrimination (harassment included). Included in the list are race, colour, ethnic origin, nationality, religion, sex, and so on. People can complain about their alleged harassment and discrimination to the human rights commissions or tribunals in their own jurisdictions, and the gathering of evidence and investigation follows, and decisions are made by human rights tribunal adjudicators. Some jurisdictions have mediation for the complainants and respondents to see whether they can come to a mutual agreement on a settlement.

There are several problems with the current model of using human rights legislation to eradicate racism in the workplace.

Reactive and Complaint-Based Approach

The major problem with human rights legislation is its reactive process in getting social justice. A person (that is, the complainant) must

15 *Human Rights Code*, RSBC 1996, c 210.

complain to the government body (whether it is a commission or a tribunal) regarding a perceived human rights legal violation. The perceived "victim" must take a stand, gather their courage to fight racial harassment or discrimination, complete all the necessary forms, and prepare to spend a long time seeing the case go through the investigation and adjudication process. The tribunal deals with the complaints on a case-by-case basis, which is very similar to how social workers deal with their individual cases. In other words, social justice is not attained through a proactive process, and the end benefits of an investigation and tribunal decision belong to the complainant or the respondent. In the case of employment, benefits apply only to the individual employee (who has launched the complaint) or to the individual employer (who has defended their employment activities).

On a societal basis, the legal precedents could be seen as an indication of tangible benefits because these precedents could broaden the legal tests and enrich the arguments of subsequent legal cases. These legal precedents have value for furthering social justice and could provide richer legal arguments for some future individual human rights cases. The bottom line is that the human rights approach is basically the last resort for individuals to get social justice for themselves, but the approach does not make organizations more just in their structures and processes. In the realm of employment, it does not make the workplace less discriminatory or more equitable. Moreover, for the amount of effort and time, and the magnitude of resources, that the complainant and respondent need to put into "proving" or "not proving" discrimination or harassment, the result seems to be limited to one employee (or job candidate) or to one employer, and not the entire organization, the entire group of racialized or Indigenous people, or the entire group of employees.

Onus of Proof

The onus of proof on the complainant is common among human rights administrations in Canada. The complainant must demonstrate with evidence that they have been discriminated against. In the realm of employment, the racialized or Indigenous complainant must collect information from their co-workers or information/data from documentary review and personal recollection of what transpired through their recruitment, job interviews, promotion, and other processes. They may have to analyze human resources policies, programs, and procedures to determine how biased they are. Through these methods, the complainant must identify any racial stereotypes; policies, structures, criteria, and procedures that have, directly or indirectly, disadvantaged them; and other factors. Being an external job candidate or internal employee, the complainant may not be able to access any of the data sets in human resources of their organization. Given that almost all human resources information of other candidates in the job competition or succession planning are confidential, and that they will not be able to gain access to the evaluations of the job candidates, their interview scores and the rationale of managerial decisions, the complainant is at a much more disadvantaged position to gain the proper information or have sufficient information or data to "prove" that discrimination has taken place. In other words, human rights legislation and its enforcement design is skewed in favour of those in a position to discriminate and not the victims of discrimination. Hence, fighting against Indigenous people.

Administrative Biases

There are variations of how each province or territory structures the administration of its human rights legislation. In some provinces, commissions and tribunals are created to demarcate roles and responsibilities. Commissions may do public policy development, research, consultation, and public education (or informational dissemination), and tribunals may do investigation and adjudication. There may be more refinement in the coordination and information sharing between the administration bodies in human rights and more improvement in attaining impartiality in case review and enforcement, but they are not guaranteed (Government of Nunavut, n.d.; Chun and Gallagher-Louisy 2018).

The division of labour in the administration of social justice may have an impact on the probability of securing social justice. The shifting of the historical role of the Ontario Human Rights Commission from investigating human rights allegations to its current role of public policy development and public education have been criticized by communities of racialized and Indigenous people as lessening the chance of getting social justice because the complainants are left to utilize their own (usually limited) resources to argue for themselves, even with the assistance from the Human Rights Legal Support Centre in Ontario.

The latter merely provides the "basics" for completing forms for complainants to fight their cases. Compared with the large pool of resources available for respondents (that is, employers) to respond to complainants' allegations, the complainants are definitely at a disadvantage.

In the absence of a human rights commission, which used to gather evidence and investigate cases of allegations of racism in the workplace, giving racialized or Indigenous people the financial resources to retain lawyers or consultants to help frame their legal position and substantiate the relevant evidence is one way to minimize the disadvantages due to a lack of support from the commission.

RECOMMENDATIONS

Shifting the Onus on Proof of Discrimination to Respondents

As discussed earlier, human right legislation in Canada is based on a model of having the complainant prove their allegation of being discriminated by the respondent. This model poses many challenges to the complainant because, in the context of a workplace, the alleged discriminator is the employer or the management staff members. Not only must they have knowledge of how the human resources system (such as hiring or promotion) works, but they also must have the documents, data, and persons (past and present employees; complainants and non-complainants) at their disposal. They also must have the authority to produce those documents and data as well as to contact persons as witnesses as required by the government.

This does not mean that the complainant does not have the legal right to put forward their evidence to show that the allegation of discrimination is true or to challenge the evidence provided by the respondents. The complainant may also provide a list of the types of information, data, and persons that the government requires the respondent to produce or provide, if they are relevant to the case.

Clearly, both the complainant and the respondents have the legal right to retain a lawyer or expert witnesses to help them boost their arguments, as is currently allowed. There might be scenarios in which the complainant or respondents may not be financially equipped to retain these professionals; in that case, the government should provide financial support to aid them.

This recommended change to the model of operation requires a change in the current human rights legislation (and regulations, if warranted) to demarcate the conditions, scope, and process of operations. Clearly, a delineation of the new roles and responsibilities of the complainant and the respondent is in order.

Allocating Resources for Human Rights Commissions to Investigate Organizations on the Prevalence and Severity of Racism in the Workplace

Government bodies responsible for the execution of human right legislation have always played a passive role in eradicating racial harassment and discrimination. This is because they work on an operational model of reaction to individual complaints. If nobody complains about racial discrimination and harassment in the workplace, the government has nothing to react to. Hence, the human rights statistics on complaints based on race would reflect that. It is more likely that these statistics provide an under-estimated version of racial discrimination.

When talking with racialized or Indigenous people about racism and their willingness to file a complaint to the human rights commission or tribunal when they have experienced racism, one would realize that it would take a lot of courage, willingness, determination, and energy for them to take on a legal battle. Finding oneself not successful in a job competition and not sure about the reasons for such failure is not a situation that one would like to be in. In addition, filing a formal complaint means declaring to the management that they and their decisions are being challenged. The implication is that the complainant has spent a long period of time working in the organization unhappily and that the next scenario for the complainant is that they may have no chance to advance in the organization. Or when management interprets the action of the employee as unwarranted, they might not be treated well, and it might lead to their termination. As a result, the complainant may feel that they are not appreciated by the management and that they do not have a sense of psychological safety or a sense of belonging at the organization. After considering these scenarios, they might not file a formal complaint to the human rights commission or tribunal. Thus, a low number in the commission's statistics does not mean that incidents of racial discrimination are minimal. The statistics merely reflect the frequency of people filing their complaints and not the number of people who have experienced racial discrimination but do not file a complaint.

Focusing on the complainant's action for investigating the respondent's actions on racial discrimination in employment is not a sure way to reduce or eradicate racism. It is therefore necessary for the human rights commission to take a more active and proactive role in monitoring, reviewing, and investigating the hidden causes of racism in the workplace when the commission has enough evidence from various sources that the organization in question is discriminatory in their human resources functions. These sources could be formal or informal reports from existing or exited employees; whistle-blowers who have passed information to the media; academic research findings from scholars; investigative journalism published by the media; federal government's collected employment equity data from employers who are a part of the employment equity program or the federal contractors' program; and any other evidence or data obtained from other sources.

One example of this kind of probing was the Ontario Human Rights Commission's public interest inquiry of the admission of Black and Indigenous children to Children's Aids Societies in 2016. Section 31 of the Ontario *Human Rights Code* gave the commission the power to collect data on their practices and how services were provided to Black and Indigenous children and families (Ontario Human Rights Commission 2018). Through this type of inquiry and data collection, the government will be in a better position to identify certain patterns of racism not only in services but also in other domains, including housing and employment. Clearly, research methodology of this nature could be adopted to gain a better understanding of how employers conduct their human resources practices and the employment experiences of racialized and Indigenous employees in hiring, promotion, training, development, performance evaluation, and so on.

For adopting this kind of methodology in investigating organizations on human resources issues may require changes in the current human rights legislation. This could be done at the federal, provincial, and territorial levels. It will make the human right legislation stronger and give it more "teeth." It is likely that racism in the workplace could be reduced at a faster rate rather than by following the current model of reacting only to complaints and placing the onus of proof of discrimination on the complainant. Municipal governments are under the jurisdiction of their provincial governments, and, thus, they do not have the power to change their human rights legislation. However, their municipal human rights policies may be revised to give them the authority to ensure that their contractors' human rights performance records are in top shape (such as records of human rights training for managers and employees and no violations in human rights).

Extensive Public Education on Human Rights

One of the "sticky" issues that hinders the reduction and eradication of racism in the workplace is the lack of an understanding and knowledge of human right legislation among people in general. It is not only in the workplace that management and non-management staff members do not know much about human rights or have no training on issues related to it; the general public is also not familiar with the basic principles, protected grounds, and protected areas of human rights or what constitutes harassment and discrimination. There is little encouragement from those in power that fair treatment and human dignity are essential ingredients in achieving social peace. Human rights are not extensively taught in the formal school curriculum or in extracurricular programs, and there is not much promotion in media (such as billboards and television commercials) by the government. There are occasional conferences, forums, and events on human rights issues funded by the government through colleges and universities and non-profit/community organizations. However, most attendees of these initiatives are the usual "converted" audience—namely, human rights advocates, academic scholars, community organizers, consultants, and students in diversity, equity, and inclusiveness.

Along with a traditional reliance on legal compliance with human rights laws and the enforcement of the law, the government must realize that public awareness and education in human rights can only enhance legal compliance. The more the government can convince the public about the value of human rights, the greater the chance that racial conflicts and tensions can be neutralized. The workplace is a microcosm of the larger society: employees are people who go to the workplace to work or, in the contemporary social milieu after the COVID-19 pandemic, who work off-site at home (virtually). The socialization of people's racial images and attitudes is a round-the-clock slow simmering of ideas and feelings that are made on and off the job. It would be easier for people to adopt human rights perspectives and sentiments when they can learn incrementally in an ongoing manner. Even if employers provide human rights education and training in human rights for employees, there is a limit on the positive effects of this workplace education and training, unless it is further reinforced when these employees leave their work with the government to provide continuous human rights public education in one way or another.

The current situation of human rights education and training is simply not enough or prevalent enough: most employers do not provide it at work, and there is not much exposure on human rights knowledge or skills through existing learning or public awareness mechanisms, such as in schools, media, public institutions, and so on. Human rights are not a common topic, and they do not seem to be high on people's radar on a daily basis. When the government invests more resources (human and financial) in public education and devotes more time and exposure in educating people on this topic, one may notice gradual progress in this field.

EMPLOYMENT EQUITY

Federal Government

Canadian Charter of Rights and Freedoms

In addition to human rights, the *Canadian Charter of Rights and Freedoms* also enables employment equity laws, programs, and activities to rectify the conditions that disadvantaged people face due to their protected grounds such as race, national or ethnic origin, colour, religion, sex, age, or mental or physical disability and to treat them affirmatively with respect, dignity, and consideration as others. Section 15(2) of the *Charter* states:

> Subsection (1) [of the Charter (Equality rights)] does not preclude any law, program or activity that has as its object the amelioration of conditions of disadvantaged individuals or groups including those that are disadvantaged because of race, national or ethnic origin, colour, religion, sex, age, or mental or physical disability.

Employment Equity Act

The federal employment equity legislation was enacted in 1986. It has jurisdiction on federal regulated industries. These sectors include financial, transportation, communication, and other federally regulated entities. Private sector contractors (irrespective of their provinces or territories) are also under the *Employment Equity Act* and so are the federal public administration employers, plus the Royal Canadian Mounted Police and the Canadian Armed Forces (Government of Canada 2023b).

The *Employment Equity Act* basically requires these employers to eliminate employment barriers in their employment systems against racialized people (members of visible minority groups), along with Indigenous peoples, persons with disabilities, and women. It also requires employers to institute positive policies and practices and accommodation measures so that the above four designated groups can achieve their representation in the Canadian workforce or its segments. Accordingly, to fulfill these requirements, employers must collect and analyze the workforce data of their employees, identify employment barriers in their employment systems, prepare and implement an employment equity plan with goals and timetables, communicate to, and consult and collaborate with, their employees, monitor and review their progress, and revise their plans. They must also submit reports to the government and provide evidence that they have made all reasonable efforts and reasonable progress toward implementing employment equity (Government of Canada 2024c).

Canada Business Corporations Act

In addition to the *Employment Equity Act*, the federal government's amendments to the *Canada Business Corporations Act* came into effect on 1 January 2020.[16] The amendments require the boards of directors and senior executives of federally regulated companies to include the four groups designated under the *Employment Equity Act*—racialized and Indigenous people, women, and persons with disabilities—to reflect their representation in the population (Canadian Board Diversity Council 2016; McNelly and Batcho-Lino 2016; Milstead 2019).

Companies are not required to increase the representation of these four designated groups, but they must disclose their numbers and proportions among board directors and executives. If companies do not comply in increasing diversity, they must explain. This "comply-or-explain" model is a characteristic of the amendments. In 2025, the federal government will review the diversity disclosure. If diversity is not increased at the leadership level (board directors and executives), the government may consider additional amendments to the legislation in the future (Prusinkiewicz 2019). This approach ("comply or explain") to increase the diversity representation of the four designated groups is different from that of the *Employment Equity Act* ("goals and

---

16 *Canada Business Corporations Act*, RSC 1985, c C-44.

timetables"), though their objective is the same—namely, to increase diversity representation (Government of Canada 2024b).

Provincial Governments

Employment Equity Laws: Quebec and Ontario

Quebec's *Charter of Human Rights and Freedoms* is a statutory bill of rights and human rights code. It guarantees human rights and rights to privacy. It established the Human Rights and Youth's Rights Commission, the Human Rights Tribunal of Quebec, and employment equity programs.

The Government of Quebec has the *Act Respecting Equal Access to Employment in Public Bodies*.[17] It designates "women," "handicapped persons," "aboriginal peoples," and "persons who are members of minorities because of their race or the colour of their skin" and "persons whose mother tongue is neither French nor English and who belong to a group other than the aboriginal peoples or the visible minorities group." This law applies to public bodies commonly known as the broader public sector, including those with most directors appointed by the government, municipalities, urban communities, metropolitan communities, public transit authorities, and other municipal bodies composed of mostly elected municipal officers on their boards, school boards, colleges and universities, and public institutions in health and social services.

These public bodies have an obligation to conduct a separate analysis of the workforce with breakdowns by designated group members, their occupations, skills and experience, and the relevant recruitment area of the public body. These data are required to be submitted to the government annually. A public body is required to establish an equal access employment program with the object of increasing the representation of each designated group and correct practices in the employment systems. As in the federal employment equity program, this program in Quebec is based on a review of the employment systems and has the goals of occupation and designated group members, equal opportunity measures, support measures, measures to consult and inform, and a timetable for implementation and goal achievement. The legislation also has clauses dictating the process of compliance and the roles of the human right commission and tribunal as well as a series

17 *Act Respecting Equal Access to Employment in Public Bodies*, CQLR, c A-2.01.

of regulations outlining detailed procedures and deliverables. Quebec also has legislated employment equity in public procurements.

Ontario used to have a provincial employment equity legislation modelled on the federal government's Act. The legislation outlines the principles of employment equity and the essence of the legislation, including the coverage of employers and employees; the four designated groups—Aboriginal peoples, persons with disabilities, visible minorities, and women; key program components including workforce data analysis, employment systems reviews, employment equity plan, communication and collaboration, revision and review of the plan; and compliance and enforcement. Ontario's *Employment Equity Act* was enacted in 1993 by the government under the New Democratic Party, but it was repealed by the Conservative government on 14 December 1995 almost as soon as the government came into power. Since then, there has been no tangible effort to resurrect a separate employment equity act in Ontario.

"Special Programs" under Human Rights Legislation: Saskatchewan, Ontario, British Columbia, New Brunswick

In most human rights laws in Canada, there is a clause that clearly allows for the establishment of "special programs" to proactively address discrimination issues for specific segments of the population who have been disadvantaged by the protected grounds of discrimination. For example, the Saskatchewan Human Rights Commission, the Ontario Human Rights Commission, and the New Brunswick Human Rights Commission have the legal power to enable employers to create special programs in the workplace to act like an employment equity program that actively monitors the representation of designated groups in the company's workforce, identifies employment barriers, and utilizes positive, supportive, and accommodating measures to create a harassment- and discrimination-free workplace for racialized and Indigenous people.

For example, in Saskatchewan, as authorized by section 55 of Saskatchewan's *Human Rights Code*, the commission can "approve programs designed to prevent, reduce, or eliminate disadvantages experienced by groups of individuals because of a prohibited ground of discrimination in line with Section 55 of the Code" (Saskatchewan Human Rights Commission 2024a, 2024b).

New Brunswick's *Human Rights Act* has a special programs provision of which section 14 allows the New Brunswick Human Rights

Commission to approve "programs ... designated to promote the welfare of any class of persons." These programs cover employment, housing, and services in both private and public sectors, and their creation does not need the pre-approval of the commission, but commission-pre-approved programs would benefit from commission expertise and oversight and be protected from human rights discrimination challenges under the Act. New Brunswick has found it useful to use special programs to advance the human rights agenda of diversity, equity, and inclusion to neutralize the limitation of a complaints-based (reactive) model of the human rights legislation in the context of increasingly widespread nature of global migrations.

In addition, in 1984, in consultation with the commission, the Government of New Brunswick established the Equal Employment Opportunity Program with the expressed goal of providing Aboriginal persons, persons with disabilities, and members of a visible minority group's equal access to employment, training, and advancement opportunities in government employment. The provincial government has not introduced similar programs of this nature for the private sector (New Brunswick Human Rights Commission 2020).

Employment Equity Policies and Programs: Manitoba, British Columbia, and Alberta

In other provinces where there is no separate provincial employment equity legislation, some of them, like Manitoba, have instituted an employment equity policy in the job competition process for government positions: "Only individuals that are members of the employment equity group identified in the job advertisement are eligible to apply for the position." Also, for these specially advertised positions, these employment equity group members may be given special equity preference in consideration if they declare their identities in their applications. Employment equity groups are the same four designated groups in the federal *Employment Equity Act*, which include racialized and Indigenous people (Government of Manitoba n.d.a, n.d.b.).

British Columbia faced immense backlash when the government attempted to introduce employment equity to the private sector. Instead, the provincial *Public Service Act* gives agencies the discretion to development employment equity programs.[18] Like some other provinces, British

18 *Public Service Act*, RSBC 1996, c 385.

Columbia encourages employers of all sectors to take concrete action to ensure employment equity by removing employment barriers for people so that they are treated fairly and are free from discrimination "because of their race, age, gender or disability." These provinces provide resources material for employers who plan to establish an employment equity program, such as the BC Office of the Human Rights Commissioner (n.d.).

Alberta does not have a separate employment equity policy, but the Alberta Human Rights Commission provides assistance services to employers to reach their employment equity goals, including "compliance audits" to employers to see whether they fulfill their obligations under the federal legislation on employment equity for the four designated groups: Indigenous people, persons with disabilities, racialized group members, and women. Additional resource materials and fact sheets are provided to employers too (Inform Alberta, n.d.). Also, Alberta has a policy statement on diversity and inclusion and is committed to a diverse and inclusive public service workforce to meet the diverse needs of Albertans (Government of Alberta, n.d.a.).

Territorial Governments

The Nunavut Agreement is an example of employment equity legislation that Nunavut has with its Inuit population. It is an agreement of the Nunavut Settlement Area as represented by the Tungavik Federation of Nunavut and Her Majesty the Queen in Right of Canada. Article 23 of the Agreement ("Inuit Employment within Government") declares its objective "to increase Inuit participation in government employment in the Nunavut Settlement Area to a representative level." To accomplish this objective, the government agrees to conduct an analysis of the labour force of the Nunavut Settlement Area and prepare an Inuit employment plan with goals and timetables for employing qualified Inuit in all levels and occupational groups and an analysis of the employment systems and to remove biases in the systems, to institute measures to increase the number of job applicants and other equity related measures, and to build in review, monitoring, and compliance mechanisms (Nunavut Tunngavik, n.d.).

The Northwest Territories does not have a separate employment equity legislation, but the Northwest Territories's *Human Rights Act* allows employers to implement employment equity and other special programs with the objective of removing employment barriers for them so that their representation in the workplace is reflective of their proportions in the community population (Northwest Territories Human Rights Commission 2018).

The Yukon does not have separate employment equity legislation, but it has an employment equity policy that applies to all government departments. The purpose is to ensure "fairness in access to employment opportunities and to developing a public a public service which is representative of the Yukon population." Similar to the federal government's legislation on employment equity, this policy aims to achieve equitable representation of the target group members, identify and remove employment barriers, implement special measures and support programs, and contribute to fair and equitable access to employment opportunities. Target groups for this policy are "women, aboriginal people and people with disabilities." Accordingly, gender, race and disability data are to be collected and analyzed for employment equity planning. However, it is unclear whether racialized people are considered for this kind of planning as they are not explicitly stated as one of the three target groups, but race data are to be gathered. According to this policy, the Public Service Commission is the lead agency for implementing an employment equity program in conjunction with other government departments (Government of Yukon 1994).

As noted above, the three territories in Canada have three distinctive ways to approach employment equity: Nunavut has a specific legal agreement on Inuit employment in the government sector; the Northwest Territories utilizes its "special programs" provision to assist employers should they decide to implement an employment equity program; and the Yukon has an employment equity policy and program within its own government.

Municipal Governments

The City of Toronto (n.d.c.) has its own Employment Equity Policy and its related Employment Accommodation Policy and Guidelines. Accordingly, the city's core commitment is to "fairness and full equity in employment and services in recognition of its obligations and responsibilities as an employer and of its leadership role in the community." The Employment Equity Policy sets equitable representation as an objective and develops a proactive equity plan, and it implements measurement and monitoring mechanisms. The city's employment equity program includes communication and consultation, policy review and development, employment systems review, the removal of barriers, accommodation and supportive measures, and positive measures (City of Toronto 2000).

The City of Montreal has the Equal Access to Employment program, which "ensures a fair hiring process for women, aboriginal peoples, visible or ethnic minorities (whose first language is neither English nor French) and people with disabilities." The focus is on hiring the above diverse group members, as laid out in the Master Plan for Employment Diversity, Equity and Inclusion (City of Montreal 2024). Its 2021–23 plan focused on recognizing and valuing diversity, developing an inclusive culture, and strengthening communication and consultation in a proactive manner so as to "build a public service that is representative of the population" (City of Montreal 2021).

While a study on all the municipalities in Canada is not readily available for reference, one cannot simply assume that every city has its own employment equity policy like that of Toronto or Montreal. In fact, many smaller municipalities depend on their provincial human rights codes or general principles in diversity, equity, and inclusion in drafting their own statements on anti-discrimination and the elimination of biases. Those statements constitute a commitment on their part to provide a framework for striving for a barrier-free and discrimination and harassment-free municipality for people to live, work, play, and worship.

OBSERVATIONS

Patchwork of Social Justice Approaches across Canada

As an approach in reducing and eradicating discrimination against racialized and Indigenous people, along with other disadvantaged groups, employment equity has had an uneven development in Canada. While the Government of Canada introduced the *Canadian Charter of Rights and Freedoms* in 1982, and initiated legislation in employment equity in 1986 with the enactment of the *Employment Equity Act*, few provinces, municipalities, or territories have followed its lead in having a law on employment equity for individual jurisdictions. Instead, more provinces and territories have taken the route of utilizing the "special programs" provision in their own human rights codes to move employment equity forward. Even then, this "special programs" route has been seldom used. Basically, this route is more of a voluntary pathway depending on whether the employers are from the public or private sector. Another route to move employment equity forward has been to develop employment equity policies and programs by some provincial, municipal, and territorial governments or to provide resources or professional assistance to their own government departments or private sector/non-profit sector employers to develop their own policy frameworks or implement their own programs with some employment equity features.

Overall, it is a patchwork of employment equity, human rights, and diversity and inclusiveness initiatives, with some being more structural in their approach and yielding systemic results, while others are sporadic projects and initiatives of undetermined results. In terms of social justice for racialized and Indigenous people, almost all provinces, municipalities, and territories use the human rights legislation of their own provincial or territorial jurisdictions, coupled with initiatives mainly of diversity and inclusiveness.

Human Rights and Employment Equity: Different Approaches

The most significant difference between a human rights approach and an employment approach in addressing the issue of biases, harassment, and discrimination in the workplace is that the human rights approach is complaints based and, therefore, reactive (not proactive). It is of limited value in changing the embedded biases and discriminatory actions of individuals or employment systems. Whereas the employment equity approach is proactive (not reactive) and systemic and is more likely to result in tangible organizational changes in human resource policies, strategies, and procedures. The latter can positively impact racialized and Indigenous people in the workplace. While the rulings from a human rights tribunal could involve some policy and procedural changes in how people are recruited, interviewed, selected, hired, trained, developed, performance evaluated, or promoted, or may even result in the establishment of a special program with employment equity features, the occurrence of such results is often sporadic and unreliable, and they will not necessarily have a long-term impact because they are limited by the nature of the original human rights complaints. Meanwhile, employment equity legislation has some "teeth" in ensuring the regularity of annual government monitoring and reviews and even periodic audits of the performance of employers and their organizations on a long-term basis.

As noted earlier, human rights legislation is based on a model of placing the onus of proof on the complainant (that is, the employee), while employment equity legislation is based on a model of onus of proof on the respondents (that is, the employer) in the case of employment. These are two distinctive models. There are definite disadvantages in making employees gather evidence to prove that their allegation of discrimination is correct. When employers must prove their lack of discriminatory organizational structures and processes, policies, and procedures, with the government, acting as a regular monitor, reviewer, and auditor on a year-in-and-year-out basis using ongoing information and data updates, it is harder for employers to defend themselves unless they are on a path of yearly improvement of their own workforce representation data (stock data) and hiring/promotion/termination data (flow data). The pattern of inequitable human resource functions and practices on a collective (not individual) basis throughout the organization may be made more obvious and convincing than it would be in an individual case of complaints.

While there are several advantages in promoting employment equity over human rights in getting rid of racial and Indigenous harassment and discrimination in the long run, it does not automatically mean that the way in which employment equity is carried out is perfect at this stage. It is far from impactful for rectifying the biased and discriminatory inclination of human resource practices for racialized and Indigenous employees for a variety of reasons.

Employment Equity: Limited Coverage of Employers and Employees, Businesses, Board Directors, and Executives

Employment Equity: Limited Coverage of Employers and Employees

The federal *Employment Equity Act* covers only a small proportion of employers and employees in Canada. There were about nineteen thousand employers and 945,000 employees in the federally regulated private sector in 2021. Of these employers, only 551 of them with one hundred or more employees had submitted their annual reports to the federal government. These employers have 742,506 employees who represent approximately 3.6 percent of the Canadian workforce

(Government of Canada 2023b). According to Trading Economics (2024), the number of employed persons in Canada in June 2024 was 20,516,400. "Employed persons" are individuals of a minimum required age to work for a certain period of time for a business. It is obvious that the impact of the *Employment Equity Act* on racialized and Indigenous people is rather limited even if all employers are doing a perfect job in implementing their employment equity programs or if the federal government has been doing an excellent job in enforcing the compliance of all employers. As discussed later in this chapter, both the implementation of employers' compliance requirements and the enforcement of the government's monitoring, review, and audit power and actual activities are underwhelming.

Corporate Board Directorship: Limited Businesses

The *Canada Business Corporations Act* covers over 235,000 companies. Half of them are large publicly held companies in Canada. The amendments (Bill C-25) that require the disclosure of diversity information on board directorship and senior management in companies covered approximately seven hundred publicly held companies (or distributing companies) in the over 235,000 companies in Canada incorporated under the Act (Canadian Board Diversity Council 2016; McNelly and Batcho-Lino 2016; Milstead 2019; Vuicic 2019). The diversity information disclosure requirements do not cover other types of companies such as privately held corporations and government business enterprises (Statistics Canada 2023h). The definition of "distributing companies" (venture issuers and non-venture issuers) is far from clear and has posed reporting problems for the federal government to analyze the collected data, along with the failure of companies to file requirements and incorrect reporting. In 2020, the federal government identified 669 of these companies, and, in 2021, only 536 were identified (Innovation, Science and Economic Development Canada 2021). Hence, the statistical data is far from perfect. For the purposes of this book, the number "700" is used for publicly held (or distributing) companies in our analysis. However, given the imperfection of the reported data from the federal government noted earlier and the yearly variations in the actual numbers of these corporations, this number should be used with caution, especially when comparing data sets and years.

As of December 2021, there were 1.21 million companies in Canada: 1.19 million (97.9 percent) were small companies, 22,700 (1.9 percent) were medium-sized companies, and 2,868 (0.2 percent) were large companies. Out of this large pool of companies, GlobalEconomy.com (2024) listed 3,534 publicly held companies in Canada in 2022. It must be noted that this is only one of several ways to estimate the number of publicly held companies in Canada. The seven hundred publicly held companies impacted by the new amendments of the *Canada Business Corporations Act* are 19.8 percent of the 3,534 public held companies. It is only one-fifth of the publicly held companies in Canada. Even when only medium-sized and large companies are included in the calculation, the seven hundred publicly held corporations constituted only 0.3 percent. If all companies (1.21 million) are included in the calculation, the seven hundred publicly held companies are only 0.05 percent of all companies in Canada. It is obvious that the impact of the amended Act is quite limited in changing the needle in employment equity.

Corporate Board Directorship: Limited Seats

In Canada, a publicly held company must have at least three board directors and a maximum of fifteen board directors. Within these limits, these companies usually have seven to ten (or 8.5 on average) board directors each. Using the 8.5 directors for an average publicly held company, one may estimate that seven hundred publicly held companies may have 5,950 board directors. The actual number of board directors or director seats of companies, whether they are small, medium, or large companies in Canada, is not readily available. However, if one make the assumption that each small company has only one director seat (1.19 million x 1), and 8.5 director seats for each medium-sized (22700 x 8.5) or large (2,868 x 8.5) company, the estimated total board director seats would be 1,407,328. When the estimated 5,950 board director seats of these seven hundred publicly held companies in the context of the 30,039 board director seats of the 3,534 public held companies in Canada, the impact of the Act is 19.8 percent of board director seats in this type of company in Canada, which is one out of every five seats. Placing the estimated seven hundred publicly listed companies that have an estimated 5,950 board director seats in all the board director seats of the medium-sized and large companies, it is estimated that the amended *Canada Business Corporations Act* covers only 2.7 percent of board director seats (217,328) in these types of companies, and only 0.4 percent of board director seats (1,407,328) in all small, medium-sized, and large companies in Canada. These statistics show that the Act is impactful only on a very small scale.

Corporate Executives: Limited Executive Positions

"Senior managers" (also referred to as executive officers) are defined as a chair or vice-chair on a board of directors, a corporation president, a chief executive officer or a chief financial officer, a vice-president of a principal business unit, and anyone who performs a policy-making function within a corporation (Innovation, Science and Economic Development Canada 2021). In 2020, there were an estimated total of 14,807 senior managers in three types of organizations in Canada—public held corporations, privately held corporations, and government business enterprises. And, among them, there were 1,119 (or 7.5 percent) senior managers working in publicly held companies (Statistics Canada 2023h). These statistics strongly suggest that the impact of the amended *Canada Business Corporations Act* on workplace equity remains marginal as there is more room to grow at the senior management level.

Employment Equity: Problems in the Federal Government's Monitoring/Enforcement and Employers' Implementation

Prescribed Sequence of Doing Employment Equity

There are three core components of employment equity implementation according to the federal *Employment Equity Act*: workforce data collection and analysis, employment systems review, and employment equity planning and implementation. They are to be carried out in stages, one after another. Ideally, an employer should gather and analyze the workforce data first (which yields quantitative data on "what" representation patterns of designated groups emerged), followed by an analysis of the employment systems (which yields qualitative information on "why" under-representation of designated groups exists), and, based on these quantitative data and qualitative information, the employer then develops and implements an employment equity plan with goals and timetables on removing employment system biases and rectifying the under-representation situation with measures. With the sequence of implementing these three core components, beginning with workforce data collection and analysis, it is clear that having workforce data is a prerequisite to carrying out an employment systems review and employment equity planning and implementation.

Workforce Data Driving Employment Equity

By law, employers are obliged to collect workforce data and submit the data to the federal government on an annual basis. Both the government and the employers analyze the data and identify the representation gaps in different occupational groups by measuring the extent to which they deviate from the availability data. How does the federal government know whether the employers are making progress in employment equity? It monitors the pattern and size of these gaps and provides insights on the status of designated groups in the workplace. These are the gap patterns and sizes that the federal government monitors. These gaps could be "randomly" scattered throughout a spectrum of occupational groups across the four designated groups, or they could be concentrated in a specific designated group across occupational groups. Some gaps may be larger than others. Through time, some gaps may shrink or increase over time. If the gaps are shrinking, there is less of a requirement to address the issue of representation unless the gaps are considered unusually large in the first place. Improvement of representation data is considered to be "reasonable progress" in employment equity in accordance with the legislation. Persistently large gaps or an increasing gap size are considered to be problematic, and employers must find answers to the pressing question: what are the barriers in the employment systems of these occupations for specific designated group(s) that exhibit persistent or growing gaps? When the gaps are small, the pressure to identify employment barriers diminishes. When there are no gaps in the occupational groups, the pressure from the federal officials for the employer to conduct an employment systems review ceases to exist. In fact, the annual workforce data submitted by employers to the government in June each year is quite critical in determining whether an organization requires a formal audit. In addition to workforce data, the federal government also requires employers to complete a questionnaire in which questions on key aspects of the employer's employment equity implementation are posed. However, the questionnaire does not require details, which means that the government is unable to monitor the employer's implementation work as closely as it monitors workforce data collection.

With this review process, it is clear that the federal government's monitoring and enforcement strategy is workforce data driven. The government's priority is to first know the pattern and size of the representation gaps prior to making a decision whether a formal audit of an employer's efforts on employment equity is needed or not.

Lower Priority in Employment Systems Review

The federal prescribed (and ideal) sequencing of doing employment equity through workforce data collection and analysis, employment systems review, and employment equity planning/ implementation is often not followed by employers. This is because the federal government's method of reviewing the employers' employment equity performance often places employment systems review at a lower priority. Federal government officials seldom seek detailed information on the employment systems review—how employers review employment policies and procedures and the practices they have identified as being biased. For this apparent lack of attention on this component by the federal government, employers often skip this component and go straight to employment equity planning. The implication of skipping this important step of finding the reasons why representation gaps exist in the first place is that employers do not focus on the sources of under-representation of designated groups in specific occupational groups. Therefore, when employers work on the goals and timetables of increasing the representation of designated group members, they essentially work in a vacuum. As a result, the goals and timetables of increasing representation rates of racialized and Indigenous peoples are likely to be "wishful thinking."

Without knowing what causes the representation gaps and where the sources of the problem are in the employment systems, employers are not able to remove the employment barriers and build more equitable features into their employment systems. Therefore, the goals and timetables prepared in their employment equity plans are unrealistic and have little bearing on workplace reality. In fact, even if some of these goals are reached within the timetables that the employers propose, it is simply because they are lucky. In the final analysis, federal government officials are interested in finding out what measures employers will put into place for the next few years and what representation data is expected at the end of the plan cycle. There is little interest in finding out the connection between the actual problems in each part of the employment systems and the proposed measures that the plan puts forwards. It is therefore common to find that, at the end of the short-term employment equity plan, the proposed measures have not been proven to be impactful in reducing representation gaps in specific occupations. The reason is rather simple: the employers have not identified the actual employer barriers for specific representation gaps. Hence, the measures proposed in the plan are simply not evidence based.

Slower Progress in Employment Equity

In line with this observation, it is not surprising to find that the progress of many employers in employment equity has been rather slow for Indigenous people, persons with disabilities, and women from 1986 to 2020. However, progress for racialized people was slow prior to 2007, but it has sped up since. The progress of employment equity in the first twenty years of employment equity was slow overall for all designated groups. As far as operational issues are concerned, this was largely due to employers' slow start and half-hearted efforts as well as the federal government's leniency in monitoring and enforcing the legislation on employment equity. As shown earlier, employers' employment equity goals and timetables are not evidence based due to a lack of proper employment systems reviews, and the impact of their employment equity plans cannot be measured until after the short-term planning cycle is completed (say, three years). By the time federal government officials and employers find out the dismal impacts of their non-evidence-based (read: unrealistic) goals and timetables, and their ineffecetive proposed measures to remove employment barriers, a few years have gone by with a lot of time, energy, and resources wasted.

Due to this unique feature of the federal government's checking of employers' performance in employment equity and its monitoring and enforcement strategy with a focus on workforce data, paying minor attention to the employment systems review, employers' behaviour in running the employment equity programs follows suit. With over twenty years of experience in assisting employers to conduct their employment equity programs and in helping them to fulfill their legal obligations, this author has observed that employment systems review is one of the most neglected components. As a result of this neglect, employers'

Table 9.1: Representation of Designated Groups and Their Availability Rates in the Workforce in Canada, 1987–2009

	1987 (%)	AR (%)	1996 (%)	AR (%)	2001 (%)	AR (%)	2006 (%)	AR (%)	2008 (%)	2009 (%)
Aboriginal peoples	0.7	2.1	1.2	2.1	1.9	2.6	2.4	3.1	2.5	2.6
Visible minorities	5.0	6.3	9.2	10.3	10.4	12.0	12.3	14.5	13.6	14.1

Note: AR = availability rates in the labour market based on census data for 1986, 1996, 2001, and 2006.
Source: Ng, Haq, and Tremblay 2015.

goals and timetables for both qualitative (non-numerical) measures and quantitative (numerical) goals and timetables do not have much of a foundation. Hence, their employment equity plans are usually "wishful thinking" and unlikely to move the representation of designated groups forward.

Let us look at some employment equity statistics in Canada between 1986 and 2020 and assess the findings. The progress of employment equity may be measured by the representation rates of the four designated groups as compared with their availability rates in the workforce. The narrower the gap between these two rates, the greater the progress when compared with previous years. As noted, there are some fluctuations in these rates. Based on Table 9.1, there was some progression in the representation rates of Indigenous peoples and racialized people between 1987 and 2009.

However, the progress for Indigenous peoples as the senior managers, middle managers, and professionals during the period from 1996 to 2009 was not encouraging. Meanwhile, the progress for racialized people as middle managers and professionals was good, but less so as senior managers. A more up-to-date report by the federal government shows that, historically, the representation rates of Indigenous peoples in the federally regulated private sector workforce have been increasing since 1987 (0.7 percent). The rate reached is just above 2 percent in 2020. Meanwhile, the labour market availability rates increased from 2 percent in 1987 to 4 percent in 2016, and the representation gaps of Indigenous peoples were incrementally larger through time (see Table 9.2). One reason cited by the federal government was that the turnover rates of Indigenous peoples were relatively high in most of the federally regulated industries, which explains the gentler decline

Table 9.2: Representation of Designated Groups in Management and Professional Occupation Groups in Canada, 1987–2009

	1987 (%)	1996 (%)	2001 (%)	2006 (%)	AR (%)	2008 (%)	2009 (%)
Aboriginal peoples							
Senior managers	n/a	0.3	0.5	0.7	2.4	0.7	0.8
Middle managers	n/a	0.8	0.8	1.0	1.9	1.1	1.1
Professionals	n/a	0.7	0.9	1.0	1.8	1.0	1.0
Visible minorities							
Senior managers	n/a	3.0	3.7	5.1	8.7	3.8	6.1
Middle managers	n/a	8.4	8.8	12.2	14.0	13.7	14.0
Professionals	n/a	15.2	16.5	21.0	16.5	23.8	24.6

Note: AR = availability rates in the labour market based on census data for 1986, 1996, 2001, and 2006.
Source: Ng, Haq, and Tremblay 2015.

in the growth of their representation rates, even though more Indigenous people have participated in the labour market during this period (Employment and Social Development Canada 2022).

As for racialized people (or visible minorities in Statistics Canada's terminology), their representation rates were lower than their labour market availability rates from 1987 (5 percent versus 6.3 percent) to 2006 (15.3 percent versus 14.9 percent), but their representation rates surpassed those of their labour market availability rates from 2007 (15.9 percent versus 15.3 percent) to 2020 (26 percent vs. 21.3 percent). In 2020, racialized people were above the 100 percent threshold of representation rates in nine of the fourteen occupational groups in 2020, including senior managers, middle managers, and professionals. They were under-represented only in semi-professionals and technicians, supervisors, semi-skilled manual workers, other sales and service personnel, and other manual workers (Employment and Social Development Canada 2022).

For a long time and even now, some employees have viewed the very act of putting effort and resources into employment equity as being unnecessary because employment equity was peripheral to the bottom line of doing business. For smaller employers, there were no immediate benefits in making the workforce diverse or putting more staff members on collecting workforce data, reviewing human resources policies and procedures, and developing an employment equity plan. Hence, it is not unusual to find clerical staff members doing what is required by law, and these staff members may not get adequate employment equity implementation training. As a result, the collected workforce data, the review work on employment systems, the planning process, and other consultation and communication work required to launch employment equity programs are often substandard and are done half-heartedly. Moreover, there are also employers who only find out that they must do employment equity under the law when they receive a letter from the federal government that they have to submit some paper work or that they have to produce a report that should have been done over a year ago. All these are signs that employment equity is off their radar or, at least, low on their priority list.

Employment Equity Work Is Not Evidence Based

In addition to making "reasonable progress," employers also must demonstrate that they are making "all reasonable efforts" to do employment equity. This means that employers are obliged to follow the legislation and regulations to implement employment equity in great detail in all the aspects of doing employment equity (such as collecting and analyzing workforce data, reviewing all aspects of human resource management, developing and implementing an employment equity plan, doing consultation and communication, collaborating with bargaining agents, informing employees, reporting to the government).

In more than twenty years of working with employers on employment equity, I have found that one of the least implemented areas is employment systems reviews. This seems to be the result of the federal government's monitoring and enforcement strategy paying extra attention to the representation numbers without paying much attention to how employers do their employment systems review or how they prepare their employment equity plans. The government has not made it a high priority to connect "all the dots" together, such as the linkages between the representation gaps with occupation- and geography-specific employment systems, the human resources practices carried out by different levels/departments of an organization, and the patterns of hiring, promotion, and termination in accordance with occupations and geographic locations. This lack of comprehensiveness in analyzing both the quantitative data (through workforce data) and qualitative information (through findings from reviewing employment systems) may explain why the true causes of the representation gaps have not been clearly identified and acted upon by both the employers and the federal government. Furthermore, the federal government, in their review/audit process, have seldom insisted on employers reviewing their employment systems even when occupations or geographic locations have no representation gaps. Overall, employment systems have seldom been reviewed thoroughly by the employers or the federal government since the year the legislation was enacted. This may explain why, in some organizations, some representation gaps in some occupations are persistent or these gaps keep on popping up even in occupations that do not have a history of gaps. These gaps seem to have come in "waves," as some employers describe the phenomenon.

As employer barriers have not been properly identified, solutions for inequity and discrimination have remained unidentified. The federal government also does not have specific methodological requirements and a process prescribed on employment systems reviews for employers. Since the government seldom reviews employers' efforts in this area prior to their preparation of the employment equity plan, which requires a connection between the workforce data and data gaps, the types and extent of barriers identified, the measures that could rectify the inequitable situations of Indigenous and racialized peoples, and the numerical and qualitative goals of the employment equitu plan, it is therefore more likely that employers are less diligent in pursuing a rigorous review, and the government appears to also be lenient in this regard. Very often, since the federal government usually does not demand to see the result of the employer's employment systems review, the government officials and employers have no evidence of the actual employment barriers that have created the representation gaps identified in the workforce data analysis stage. Thus, employers have come up with a list of generic measures—barrier removal and supportive, positive, accommodation—without grounding them in real review findings and have developed an employment equity plan around them, and the government appears to be accepting employers' goals and timetables without many questions. Hence, these blind spots and hasty half-baked measures have not yielded the concrete positive results that would lead employers closer to the establishment of an equitable workplace. Several years later, after the implementation of the employment equity plan with the guesswork of measures to remove unidentified barriers, when the expected impacts are not forthcoming, the full cycle of government review, and employers trying some newer generic measures to rectify the inequitable situation of representation, usually starts all over again. So, there is no reset, just more repetition of the old ways of doing employment equity without solid evidence that could only be identified with a comprehensive employment systems review.

Employment Equity: Negotiable Compliance Timelines, Reasonable Progress/Efforts

The federal government has invested heavily in helping employers to make employment equity better. They have developed software that helps employers compile and analyze workforce numbers, create templates for statistical tables, and training materials for employers to review employment systems and prepare an employment equity plan. Without doubt, the software for workforce analysis saves employers' money, time, and other resources. More importantly, the software standardizes the reporting mechanisms and vastly improves the quality of employers' work on workforce analysis. The government has been weak in providing a practical methodology with tools and templates for employers to do their employment systems reviews and to develop an employment equity plan. As a result, employers efforts are less than adequate in doing these two major components of employment equity. These are the two areas in which quality work is not reliably being done.

However, this should not stop employers from developing their own methodologies, tools, and templates. Large corporations have invested time, money, and effort in doing employment equity, but, as noted earlier, their investment tends to be unfocused and misplaced, sometimes due to a lack of proper employment systems reviews and, hence, their misplaced efforts in developing employment equity. Smaller corporations have less resources and cannot invest as much as larger corporations in doing their employment equity. They depend more on the federal government's software, tools, and templates. Where the federal government is weak in supporting employers in certain areas such as employment systems review and employment equity planning, these businesses have demonstrated a poorer quality in these areas. With such weaknesses, irrespective of their employee size, corporations in general are notoriously unable to move employment equity forward faster due to unfocused and misplaced efforts.

With this situation, the federal government's monitoring and enforcement practices are crucial in identifying what has been done incorrectly and, thus, is not in compliance with the legislation. It also has a mandate to check on how employment equity is implemented by employers. The federal government has tended to be lenient, even though employers' goals and timetables both in workforce representation and in the removal of employment barriers are conservative or often not met. The federal government is likely to be satisfied as long as employers have made an attempt and failed to achieve their goals and timetables with explanations such as the economic development, industrial sectoral changes, organizational restructuring, employee turnovers, lead time for management improvement or training, community outreach, and program upgrading. Essentially, the federal government wants to give employers the impression that it is willing to work with them and facilitate their work rather than "coercing" them to comply. Therefore, it is not uncommon to see the government extend deadlines and provide new deadlines on tasks to be accomplished as long as employers have made some progress; no matter how minimal they are, as long as reasonable explanations are provided. This begins to sound like the comply-or-explain model that the *Canada Corporations Act* adopted for diversity representation on corporate boards of directors and senior management.

This lack of employers' proper execution of employment equity and the federal government's lenient monitoring and enforcement strategy has deterred the progress of employment equity, which explains why the status of employment equity progress has slowed, considering that it has a long history since 1986 and, without question, has had a tremendous amount of human and financial resources invested in it. Some forty years later, with the exception of women and racialized people (who have been beneficiaries in an incremental way), not much progress has been made on Indigenous people and persons with disabilities.

Back in 1992, Lubomyr Chabursky (1992, 335–38), in his evaluation of the *Employment Equity Act*, recognized some of the problems inherent in the federal government's enforcement model and attempted to use it as "non-confrontational" as possible in getting employers to move employment equity further along in the workplace. Without elaborating on the obvious, the model has made it difficult for the federal government to fulfill the spirit and goals of the legislation in the context of the half-hearted efforts of employers. The

Senate Standing Committee on Human Rights released two reports in 2007 and 2010 on employment equity in the federal public service, and both noted that progress toward equity has been slow, especially for Indigenous people and persons with disabilities (Government of Canada 2015). For the federal government, employers, and those who work in the employment equity field, representation data of the four designated groups are uneven across occupational groups and years. Furthermore, the under-representation of designated groups is still widespread across organizations and, in some case, severe and deep in a few occupational groups (especially senior managers). In reviewing the progress of employment equity, Carol Agnoc (2014) found that it still has a long way to go some thirty years after the legislative enactment.

The report of the Employment Equity Act Review Task Force, chaired by Adelle Blackett, summarized the ideas and suggestions of stakeholder groups based on a series of roundtable meetings and hundreds of written submissions and correspondences. The research findings showed that, in spite of the paperwork and efforts put into employment equity in almost four decades, employment barriers for the designated groups and their under-representation in some occupations remained. Current employment equity work seems to have been reduced to number-crunching exercises, checklists, and forms rather than a focus on removing employment barriers and strengthening equitable inclusion in the workplace. In the opinion of the report, a supportive well-funded regulatory apparatus is needed to incentivize compliance. The task force ended its report with 187 recommendations to revamp and remake employment equity in Canada (Government of Canada 2023c).

After almost four decades of doing employment equity work, employers' records of progress in this area is not encouraging or something to be celebrated. This is not reflected in the federal government's record of enforcement. There were only four federally regulated employers who received a notice of assessment of a monetary penalty. Of these four, the last penalty was issued in 1991, and it was for three thousand dollars, apparently the last penalty ever issued. No federal contractor has been found to be in non-compliance since 2013. This strongly suggests that the federal enforcement mechanism is not firm or strong enough to push employers to be fully compliant. It also shows that the federal monitoring system with its reviews and audits was and still is broken. The task force chaired by Adelle Blackett reported that the Canadian Human Rights Commission's Employment Equity Division seems to lack the financial and human resources to do much of an audit of employers, and the Employment Equity Review Tribunal was barely utilized to exercise its mandate to determine the violation of employers (Government of Canada 2023c).

Canada Business Corporations Act: Ineffective Comply-or-Explain Model

Relying on businesses to regulate themselves in the area of diversity among board directors and senior management may ward off the private sector's critique of the government trying to put its fingers in the sector's pie. But this approach may be too optimistic for the government to think in this manner. The main goal of doing business is to make money, and this is the bottom line for the private sector. It is a harder sell for businesses to view a diverse board of directors or a diverse senior management team as beneficial to their pockets because the connection between a diverse leadership and profit is not explicitly clear; it will take much accumulated evidence and data to show such a connection, and the duration between the organizational preparation for diverse representation and higher innovation, productivity, and market reach may be too lengthy. There was a period in the 1970s and 1980s when the federal government experimented with business voluntarism in implementing employment equity in the workplace. Not much was accomplished by the private sector during this period. Finally, the federal government decided to develop a piece of legislation mandating that the private sector do employment equity with strict requirements in 1986. This has been criticized by the private sector as being too heavy handed as the *Employment Equity Act* requires the private sector to set goals and timetables to make the workplace more equitable (Siu 2021, 300–3).

The *Canada Business Corporations Act*, with its enactment in 2020 of the new amendments on diversity representation and disclosure, aims to increase equity on boards of directors and senior management (executive officers). To avoid the private sector's criticism of the federal government's approach on employment equity, it adopted a softer approach of "comply or explain" in achieving this aim. What this model says is that publicly held business corporations should comply with the legislation by increasing the representation of the four designated groups—Indigenous peoples, persons with disabilities, racialized people, and women—in their boards of directors and senior management teams. Their diversity representation should improve through time, and their statistics are required to be disclosed to the federal government and the public. If any company does not comply with this diversity representation requirement, they are obliged to explain why their diversity representation has not increased and why they have not put in effort to make this happen.

The comply-or-explain model allows corporate flexibility in making their decisions in light of their businesses, offers opportunities for shareholders and other stakeholders to discuss the value of the legislated compliance, and gives the appearance that the government is not forcing corporations to adopt its vision of governance and management, provided that corporations can come up with good reasons with the support of evidence. Unfortunately, unless the government demands solid proof that compliance has adverse impacts on the corporations or that the conditions are not ripe for a change in governance and/or that corporations have made a reasonable effort to outreach, recruit, and appoint new diverse candidates but still failed to change the representation profiles of their boards and senior management, the government may find it difficult to enforce the legislation (Olaerts and Abma 2012; MacNeil and Esser 2022). Corporate explanations were noted for their lack of evidence and lack of substantiation, and their reports to the government were not convincing and were of poor quality. In the final analysis, this model did not have "teeth" to force corporations to comply and proved to be ineffective in changing the dial of diversity representation (Talaulicar and Werder 2008; Shrives and Brennan 2015).

The European experience in female parity on boards and senior management is more telling. The European Institute for Gender Equality reviewed the progress made by the largest listed corporations, central banks, and financial institutions in each of the twenty-seven European Union state members between 2003 and 2021. France, Italy, and Germany had their greatest improvement in female parity on boards between 2010 and 2015 with their introduction of a legislative quota system (European Institute for Gender Equality 2022). In 2011, the baseline for these member states was around 13 percent for women on boards. Ten years later (that is, in 2021), the proportion of women on boards was 16.6 percent in member states without government intervention (such as Bulgaria, the Czech Republic, Croatia, Cyprus,

Hungary, Latvia, Lithusania, Malta, and Slovakia); 30.3 percent in member states with soft measures (such as Denmark, Estonia, Ireland, Luxembourg, Poland, Romania, Slovakia, Spain, and Sweden); and 36.4 percent in member states with a legislative quota system (Austria, Belgium, France, Germany, Greece, Italy, Portugal, and the Netherlands). This suggests that corporate voluntarism, at least in Europe, was less effective for attaining female parity on boards than soft measures or legislative quotas. However, the contrast of their accelerating roles of corporate voluntarism, soft measures, and legislative quotas are less apparent at the executive level during the 2012–22 period (European Institute for Gender Equality 2022). The quota system has been showed to be very effective in getting female parity on boards; the European Union will begin implementing a legal binding 40 percent quota for women on corporate boards by June 2026 (Institutional Shareholders Service 2024; Women on Boards 2024).

This model of "comply or explain" has been tried in Canada since 2010s without much success in changing the representation of women at the board level. The data available shows that half the corporate boards still do not have female representation, but a provincial securities commission's report in 2018 found very modest progress on female board representation at 648 companies in Canada—from 11 percent in 2015 to 15 percent in 2018 (McFarland 2019). No matter how one looks at these data, the movement to parity remains slow. The amendment made to the *Canada Business Corporations Act*, effective as of 1 January 2020, which further expands the legislative coverage from women only to an addition of three more designated groups—Indigenous people, racialized people, and persons with disabilities—may make it more difficult to have parity progress for all four groups as the competition among these groups for limited board seats and senior management positions becomes more intense (Siu 2021, 303–4).

Innovation, Science and Economic Development Canada (2024) provides comparative statistics of the changes of the four designated groups in boards of directors and senior management teams in 2022 and 2023. It noted that the diversity disclosure amendments of the *Canada Business Corporations Act* became effective on 1 January 2020. During the four years since 2020, the data show that there have been some marginal and "yo-yo" (uneven) improvements on the status of these four designated groups under the comply-or-explain model. The data collected by the federal government covering a four-year period

Table 9.3: Percentage of Seats Held by Designated Groups on Boards of Directors in All Distributing Corporations

Designated groups	Available workforce (%)	2020 (%)	2021 (%)	2022 (%)	2023 (%)
Women	52.7	17	20	19	22
Indigenous people	4	0.3	0.4	0.6	0.7
Visible minorities	15.3	4	7	6	5
People with disabilities	9	0.3	0.4	0.4	0.5

Source: Innovation, Science and Economic Development Canada 2021.

Table 9.4: Percentage of Positions in Senior Management Held by Designated Groups in Distributing Corporations

Designated groups	Available workforce (%)	2020 (%)	2021 (%)	2022 (%)	2023 (%)
Women	52.7	25	25	27	29
Indigenous people	4	0.2	0.4	0.4	0.5
Visible minorities	15.3	9	9	12	13
People with disabilities	9	0.6	0.7	1.2	0.5

Source: Innovation, Science and Economic Development Canada 2021.

Table 9.5: Estimation of Years Needed for Designated Groups' Full Representation on Boards of Directors in All Distributing Corporations*

Designated groups	Net % Gain during 2020 and 2023 (4 years)	Average Net % Gain Every Year between 2020 and 2023 (4 years)	Representation Gap as of 1 January 2024 (%)	Estimated Number of Years Needed for Full Representation as of 1 January 2024
Women	+5	+1.25	30.7	24.56 years
Indigenous people	+0.4	+0.1	3.3	33 years
Visible minorities	+1	+0.25	10	40 years
People with disabilities	+0.2	+0.05	8.5	170 years

Note: * The numbers in this table are built on the data from Table 9.3.
Source: Innovation, Science and Economic Development Canada 2021.

from 2020 to 2023 show that the progress to diversity representation has been slow, uneven, and marginal. More importantly, it also shows that all four designated groups are very far from reaching their

Table 9.6: Estimation of Years Needed for Designated Groups' Full Representation on Senior Management Level in All Distributing Corporations*

Designated groups	Net % Gain during 2020 and 2023 (4 years)	Average Net % Gain Every Year between 2020 and 2023 (4 years)	Representation Gap as of 1 January 2024 (%)	Estimated Number of Years Needed for Full Representation as of 1 January 2024
Women	+4	+1	23.7	23.7 years
Indigenous people	+0.3	+0.075	3.5	46.67 years
Visible minorities	+4	+1	2.3	2.3 years
People with disabilities	+0.1	+0.025	8.5	340 years

Note: *The numbers in this table are built on the data from Table 9.4.
Source: Innovation, Science and Economic Development Canada 2021.

representation in the available workforces of women (52.7 percent), Indigenous people (4 percent), visible minorities (racialized people) (15.3 percent), and people with disabilities (9 percent). The data of the available workforces of designated groups is based on the *2021–2022 Employment Equity in the Public Service of Canada* report (see Table 9.3, Table 9.4, and Table 9.5).

The uneven, marginal, and slow progress of designated groups on boards of directors makes their progress even harder to predict what will happen after 2023. But, on average, the minute net gain per year for all designated groups using the comply-or-explain model is clear. Under the model, it may take 24.56 years for women, thirty-three years for Indigenous people, forty years for visible minorities (racialized people), and 170 years for people with disabilities to gain full representation. If we assume twenty-five years to be one generation, this means it will take somewhere between one to seven generations to attain full representation on boards of directors depending on the designated group status. Similarly, the uneven, marginal, and slow progress of designated groups in senior management makes their progress even harder to predict what will happen after 2023. But, on average, the minute net gain per year for all designated groups using the "comply or explain" model is clear. Under the model, it may take 23.7 years for women, 46.67 years for Indigenous people, 2.3 years for visible minorities (racialized people), and 340 years for people with disabilities to gain full representation. If we assume twenty-five years to be one generation, this means it will take somewhere between one to fourteen generations to attain full representation in senior management depending on the designated group status. The only exception, as noted, is racialized people whose gain was steady (without the "yo-yo" effect), and their baseline in 2020 was considered to be high. With a net gain of one percentage point per year, the full representation rate of 15.3 percent is within reach by 2024 (see Table 9.6).

Overall, the comply-or-explain model expounded in the *Canada Business Corporations Act* is demonstratively ineffective in achieving the diversity representation goal in leadership positions.

RECOMMENDATIONS

Extend the Impact of Legislated Employment Equity to the Public and Private Sectors in the Provinces, Territories, and Municipalities

The federal government's employment equity legislation is limited to federal civil servants, federal regulated corporations, and federal contractors. Quebec has an employment equity law for the broader provincial public sector but not for the private sector. As noted in the observations section of this chapter, the existing legislation covers only a small group of corporations and employees. Apart from these two pieces of law, the country has a patchwork on employment equity-related activities at the provincial, municipal, and territorial level utilizing the "special programs" clause in the provincial human rights acts and limited employment equity policies or programs. Overall, employment equity impact is quite limited in Canada. Similarly, the latest amendments made to the *Canada Business Corporations Act* on diversity representation covering the same designated groups as the federal *Employment Equity Act*—racialized and Indigenous people, persons with disabilities, and women—are also quite limited in their impact as they only cover leadership positions (that is boards of directors and senior management) as well as the fact that they cover only a small fraction of publicly held corporations and leadership positions.

In order to broaden the benefits of employment equity for racialized and Indigenous people as well as women and people with disabilities, making employment equity a legal tool across the provinces, territories, and municipalities would be the first crucial step. Currently, only large corporations and government departments and, to some extent, the broader public sector organizations such as hospitals and school boards have instituted employment equity policies and programs; smaller organizations do not have employment equity policies or programs. For this reason, racialized and Indigenous people are not benefiting from employment equity. In addition to extending the legal framework of employment equity to the provinces, municipalities, and territories, including smaller organizations and corporations with fewer than one hundred employees would be another way to broaden the benefits. The current employer size of one hundred employees and over severely limits the scope of benefits of employment equity. When the federal employment equity legal framework was first introduced in 1986, there was intense resistance to include smaller organizations for fear of backlash from employers and politicians. Whether the political climate is now ripe for such reforms remains to be seen, but the impact of employment equity on racialized and Indigenous people should be expanded.

Refocus the Government's Monitoring Practices on Both the Quantitative and Qualitative Aspects of Employment Equity

In the last few decades, when the federal government has been monitoring the progress of employment equity among employers, it has been workforce data driven (quantitative components) and gave less priority to the employment systems review (qualitative component) and employment equity planning (both quantitative and qualitative) components. Even less priority was placed on communication, consultation, and collaboration (qualitative components) in doing employment equity. In order to ensure that employment equity is done properly in an integrated manner in accordance with the legislation and regulations, more attention is needed on how workforce data are connected with the qualitative components and how the qualitative process of employment systems review and employment equity planning are carried out in a more human relationship-centred process. This would make employment equity work more integrated, holistic, and aligned with the legislation and regulations, both in spirit and substance.

Discard the Comply-or-Explain Model and the Negotiable Goals-and-Timetables Model and Focus on a Stronger Enforcement Model for Equitable Employment

The comply-or-explain model has been adopted as a way for the *Canada Business Corporations Act* to induce or gently "push" corporations to start the process toward higher representation from the four employment equity-designated groups to be appointed to boards of directors and senior management. Similarly, the federal *Employment Equity Act* utilizes two "tests"—"reasonable progress" (section 11) and "all reasonable efforts" (section 12)—stated in the legislation to measure the performance of employers in employment equity and requires the employment equity plan's goals and timetables for both the quantitative and qualitative components to edge toward more equitable employment.

As the workforce data (after forty years of enactment since 1986) and data on leadership positions (after four years of enactment since 2020) show, both models are not working as expected. This is partially due to the fact that there is an "escape clause" in these two models that allows corporations to explain away, if needed, why they are not able to have equitable appointments (in leadership positions) or equitable employment (in other positions). It is clear that the goals and timetables model could be inflexible and enforceable, if needed. However, that was not the intent when the *Employment Equity Act* was prepared under Judge Rosalie Abella back in the 1980s.

As observed, the slow progress of employment equity in the workplace seems to be related to the inability of employers to discern the actual causes of the representation gaps through a proper employment systems review and to incorporate the solutions (measures) for these actual causes in their employment equity plans in the form of goals and timetables (both for the measures and representation data). In other words, employment systems reviews must be properly done and should be evidence based as per the legislation, regulations, and guidelines put forward by the federal government.

Along this line of thinking, the federal government's enforcement may need to be more focused on ensuring that employers are actually doing what they are legally required to do before and after they prepare their employment equity plans: identify the employment barriers; develop property measures (positive, accommodation, supportive or barrier-removal measures); focus on the processes to properly inform, communicate, consult, and collaborate; implement the plan with adequate resources and efforts; and regularly review and revise the goals and timetables for both quantitative and qualitative processes. Currently, the weakness of the government's enforcement, as observed, does not reflect the comprehensiveness of the qualitative components of employment equity and is too fixated on checking boxes to denote employers' "reasonable efforts" and checking the workforce representation goals and timetables to denote employers' projected "reasonable progress."

It is important to see through the "cosmetic" non-evidence information gathering and the reasons that employers often use to explain away their lack of progress on equitable employment and the lack of reasonable effort in carrying out the tasks that make employment equity successful.

The federal government's enforcement process needs to have clearer and firmer review and compliance auditing criteria, extensive and comprehensive practice, adequate enforcement funding, a systematic and 360-degree evaluation process, stricter and timely due dates, and a heavier penalty regime.

The legislation has a clear set of review and compliance auditing criteria; what is needed is the further articulation of indicators that could be subsumed under each criterion. To further elaborate on the extensiveness and comprehensiveness of reviews and audits, one may identify the scope and contents of documents and the positions of people needed for reviews and conversations. Adequate enforcement funding necessitates more human and financial resources as well as time allocation. The evaluation of documents, data, and people performance may need to be more systematic and thorough, especially when the organizations under review or being audited are spread far apart geographically and are functionally specialized in different ways. Violations and continuing violations could lengthen the timetables for employment equity. There may be multiple due dates for undertakings, and they could be made more restrictive, especially when the direction in which the trends of employment are going is unclear and progress has slowed down. Hence, stricter due dates and heavier penalties may speed up the process of compliance.

The current models of compliance—comply-or-explain and negotiable goals and timetables—are there to give employers some flexibility and, at the same time, to present the government as a reasonable enforcer. The pay-off is that these models do not advance the employment status of racialized and Indigenous people and other designated groups too much. If one considers all the resources, efforts, and investments that have been made in employment equity in the last few decades, the impacts are dismal. It may be time to consider a stronger enforcement model like what the European Union is doing, and this may mean a rethink of the current legislation and regulations.

CONCLUSION

The most prevalent government tool to deal with racism in Canada is human rights legislation. It is found in the federal, provincial, and territorial levels of jurisdiction. However, it is not as impactful as it should be. The complaint-based reactive model of this legislation, coupled with its onus of proof on discrimination on complaints, undermines its effectiveness.

Meanwhile, legislated employment equity legislation is found at the federal level and at the provincial level in Quebec, but their coverage of employers and employees is rather limited. Furthermore, Canada's newly amended *Canada Business Corporations Act*, which addresses the issue of diversity representation disclosure at the leadership level (that is, board of directors and senior management), covers only publicly held distributing corporations but no other corporations. Although these laws are modelled on a proactive process of systematically reducing or eliminating racism and actively building a more viable sustainable environment in the workplace, they are still not as impactful as they should be because these legislative tools do not have a strong and effective monitoring and enforcement system. Hence, equitable employment and appointments are still only progressing glacially.

In Canada, we have a patchwork of anti-racism efforts, and most are rather localized, while some are still at a research and community consultative stage. A few have focused on anti-Black or anti-Indigenous racism. These efforts are not focusing on employment; rather, they are focusing on other aspects of racialized and Indigenous people's livelihoods such as housing, health-care services, and so on. Given that racism is generalized and often has a local flavour, such efforts are not meaningless. Unfortunately, some coordination across industries, municipalities, and territories may be needed to make these efforts more impactful and with more institutional supports.

Since weaknesses in these government tools at various levels have been identified, this chapter presents several recommendations that could expand their coverage to people and institutions and increase their impact.

In the anti-racism area, we need a specific policy and strategy in employment, a specific anti-racism public education strategy, and an anti-racism transition from schools to the workplace, integrating anti-racism efforts across industrial sectors and standardizing racial data across municipalities, provinces, and territories.

In the area of human rights, we need to shift the onus of proof on discrimination to respondents (employers), allocate resources for human rights to investigate organizations on the prevalence and severity of racism in the workplace, and extend public education on human rights.

In the area of employment equity, we need to extend the impact of legislated employment equity to the public and private sectors in the provinces, municipalities, and territories; refocus the government's monitoring practices on both the quantitative and qualitative aspects of employment equity; discard the comply-or-explain model and the negotiable goals-and-timetables model; and focus on a stronger enforcement model for equitable employment.

These recommendations, if adopted, will require a stronger political will, more changes in public policy development, legislation, and resources allocation, and support from institutions and communities.

CHAPTER 10

Employers: Money Guys

INTRODUCTION

With the rise of diversity, equity, and inclusion (DEI) management in Canada in the 1990s, employers have gradually gravitated to this management perspective in pre-empting and resolving racism. For those employers who are impacted by the federal *Employment Equity Act*, their human resources policies, programs, mechanisms, and activities are increasingly adopting a DEI favour.[1] Thus, we see that more companies have developed DEI policies and built diversity feeder pools; instituted program changes as in education and training, community outreach and marketing, coaching, mentoring, sponsorship, and employee engagement; and put into place diversity leadership councils, DEI committees, employee resources groups, and board reforms. The magnitude of these activities is very much a function of the company's size and resources and the extent to which these companies are driven by a DEI value system.

It has been observed that a DEI management system is often a hallmark of larger corporations that have designated professionals working in a distinct unit in human resources in organizations. In medium-sized companies, the person in charge of human resources is also in charge of DEI, no matter how small scale the DEI program is. In smaller companies, DEI as a distinct mandate is almost non-existent formally. Nevertheless, DEI has been a theme in human resources for more than

1 *Employment Equity Act*, SC 1995, c 44.

two decades in Canada, and some corporate activities (such as lunch and learns or employee appreciation events) have a DEI flavour. While DEI activities are progressive, there are more things that employers can do. In this chapter, some recommendations are put forward for their consideration.

This chapter outlines some of the major policies and/or programs (or initiatives) that the private sector has put into place to address social justice issues related to racialized and Indigenous peoples in the workplace. There is also an "Observation" section after this outline that provides a critique of some of the key activities launched by corporations. Similarly, common programs and initiatives conducted by companies are also presented to illustrate their scope and shortcomings as ways in which to address racism.

This chapter also recommends a series of actions for employers to collaborate with employees (and unions). These actions include collecting and analyzing racial data in the workforce; joint labour and management reviewing employment policies, programs, and practices; removing unconscious biases among leaders, managers, and employees through regular training; developing a strategy for anti-racism and proactive actions; increasing anti-racism and human rights competency among managers and leaders; establishing diversity and equity progress as a performance evaluation of leaders and managers; allocating appropriate resources for diversity and equity work; strengthening leadership engagement with employee resources groups; and regular management reporting of diversity and equity progress. It is anticipated that when the private sector puts into action these recommendations, it will be in a position to reduce or eliminate racism in the workplace.

POLICIES

Larger- and medium-sized Canadian companies and organizations have a mix of social justice policies made up of elements from the DEI school of thought, employment equity, and human rights. A few offsprings from these schools of thought (such as accommodation and workplace respect) that are important enough for some organizations have also been developed. Observations suggest that smaller organizations usually have very few formal policy statements but that they may have a few sentences included in their employee handbooks or corporate releases that could be counted as brief official policy statements. Policy statements in themselves are not an accurate measurement of corporate commitment of social justice for employees, but they are symbols of progressiveness in the management philosophy of corporations. Even if they do not generate tangible achievements in social justice for employees or, in the context of our discussion, for racialized and Indigenous people, these statements nevertheless elevate the corporate reputation of these organizations.

Diversity, Equity, and Inclusiveness

Since DEI has become more prominent in Canada since the 1990s and remains a strong component in management among corporate leadership, it is important to highlight it first. DEI is a school of management thought that emphasizes the value of human differences and how these differences benefit everyone in a work environment as well as the growth of an organization. Its emergence was the context of a global labour movement and high demands for labour in many countries (Urbancova, Cermakova, and Vostrovska 2016). The idea is to maximize the supply of labour irrespective of their differences. DEI are a set of values that emphasize the contribution of a variety of people with differences in their personalities, birth features (race, sex, ability, and so on); social attributes (marital status, religion, education, and so on); organizational attributes (occupation, seniority, department affiliation, and so on); fairness and equality in treatment; and a sense of belonging and acceptance by the organization and its people (Gardenswartz and Rowe 1998, 25).

The DEI school of management emphasizes diversity in the workplace and holds that high work efficiency is fundamental to organizational growth and competitive edge. Why? Employees from diverse backgrounds are unique human resources. They are culturally sensitive, efficient in marketing, and full of innovativeness and creativity. Furthermore, the diversity of employees enables better group performance, problem solving, and decision making and creative thinking, especially in workplaces that focus on cognitive skills. For global businesses, diversity furthers intercultural negotiation and entrepreneurial activities. DEI is more of a process than a goal. The idea is to integrate the values of DEI in all aspects of human resources management so that organizational strategies, policies, programs, procedures, and activities are carried out to elevate employees to a higher performance and grow the organization with a competitive edge. However, a diversified workforce also brings in more risks such as misunderstandings and tension, low morale, weaker communication flows, and group incohesiveness (Urbancova, Cermakova, and Vostrovska 2016).

To minimize these pitfalls and to maximize the value of diversity, more contemporary DEI management places emphasis on two other aspects of diversity management, which are equity and inclusion. These two terms have special meaning, and they must be carried out in their fullness in order to reap the expressed advantages of DEI. The term "equity" is seldom elaborated clearly in the language of DEI professionals. It is often defined as fairness or equality in treatment. But the term "equity" in DEI is best defined as "employment equity" and is used in section 2 of the federal *Employment Equity Act*, where its purpose is

> to achieve equality in the workplace so that no person shall be denied employment opportunities or benefits for reasons unrelated to ability and, in the fulfillment of that goal, to correct the conditions of disadvantage in employment experienced by women, Aboriginal peoples, persons with disabilities and members of visible minorities by giving effect to the principle that employment equity means more than treating persons in the same way but also requires special measures and the accommodation of differences.

While the Act targets the four employment equity designated groups, the meaning of the term "equity" in DEI is not restricted to these four groups but can be extended to include any other groups (such as gays and lesbians, single or young persons, low income persons, and so on). Furthermore, it is important to highlight that "equity" is a process with the aim of reaching "equality," which means, in the context of an organization, it is a process that includes changes in corporate values, cultures, strategies, policies, programs, procedures, and practices—essentially, any changes that might help to accelerate employees closer to a state of equality.

"Inclusion" is a process that enables an organization to benefit most from diversifying its workforce, including making all employees feel safe and motivated to be productive, collaborative, and supportive in working as a team. "Inclusion" is sometimes viewed as an integral feature in an organization's culture. This type of culture has all sorts of welcoming signs for new employees and makes them feel comfortable and at ease; existing staff members get to know new employees and provide opportunities for all of them to be familiar with each other; all employees are encouraged to feel a sense of belonging to the organization; the organization provides ongoing supports, coaching, and helpfulness to employees; and the environment makes it easy for all employees to develop and maintain a relationship with other colleagues both within and across work units/departments even in different geographic areas. Overall, employees in an inclusive workplace experience psychological safety, feel secure, and see themselves growing in the organization.

In many ways, DEI is a rejection of the American "affirmative action" and the Canadian "employment equity" models of addressing social justice issues related to people and, in this context, those related to racialized people and Indigenous people. DEI believes that the differences in people should be treated with respect, and, therefore, their contributions to the organization should be valued and harnessed. In this context, differences based on race are not to be hierarchized and nor are the social injustices that result from racial differences. While racial discrimination should be rectified, racialized and Indigenous peoples should not be singled out for special treatment as if they deserve priority hiring or promotion or any other human resources conditions that could be made advantageous to them so that they can gain special privileges in employment. The central argument of this DEI management school of thought is that merit should still be the guiding principle, not race or any human rights grounds or diversity features. Such a way of thinking is at odds with affirmative action or employment equity, which believes that, in order to reach equality, management must provide special measures in the form of accommodation, support, positive measures, and even collective actions to provide advantages to racialized/Indigenous people in all human resources practices.

In addition, unlike the complaint-based model of social justice, the human rights school of thought emphasizes the need to initiate complaints from racialized/Indigenous people so as to trigger the process of investigation, remedy, and/or settlement. The affirmative action and employment equity model insists that management must be proactive in creating and maintaining an organization structure and culture that emphasizes the provision of eliminating discriminatory practices and biased attitudes throughout the organization.

Currently, contemporary DEI is a modified version of the old "diversity management" school of thought in which the attributes of equity and inclusion (described earlier) are now incorporated in DEI management. This means that the DEI practices that contemporary corporations are adopting are those that have elements related to workforce representation of marginalized groups, including racialized and Indigenous people, equitable human resources policies, programs, procedures, and practices, and inclusive treatment in a very broad sense. Since human rights are a part of the corporate remedy for social injustice in some organizations, a few elements of these elements are incorporated in their human resources management practices.

Sample of Policy Statements

Thus, in larger corporations, it is common to see a few of the following policies that cover DEI, employment equity, human rights, and other social justice issues formalized.

DEI Policy

This policy statement usually outlines the underlining principles of DEI, followed by examples of organizations that translate the policy into programs or initiatives. This statement may also highlight a few committees or task forces that have been created to lead or support certain aspects of these programs or initiatives, including senior management councils on diversity, employee affinity groups (or resources groups), and data/policy committees (Ernst and Young, n.d.).

Employment Equity Policy

This policy is usually required or recommended if the organization is under federal regulations. As a formal policy, it basically summarizes all the key ingredients of the employment equity legislation, including the four designated groups covered by the Act; the purpose and program components (such as workforce data collection and analysis, employment systems review, and the employment equity plan with representation goals and timetables); communication and informational sharing, consultation, and collaboration; and any other management and employee obligations (City of Toronto 2024).

Anti-Workplace Violence Policy

This policy emphasizes the importance of a harmless and non-threatening work environment that does not jeopardize the physical and mental safety of employees. It usually gives examples of violent acts and words and prescribes a process in which employees can report violence at work. It also demarcates the roles of different players in the organization both in monitoring, reporting, investigations, and resolutions. It often incorporates the legal requirements of the health and safety legislation of the jurisdiction (Michener Institute of Education at University Health Network 2010).

Human Rights Policy

This policy is largely based on the human rights legislation of the jurisdiction in which the organization is located. It highlights the monitoring, reporting, investigation, and resolutions of human rights violations. It also describes the roles and responsibilities of management and employees in relation to a human rights commitment and obligations (Bank of Nova Scotia, n.d.).

Anti-Discrimination and Anti-Harassment Policy

This policy is usually an offspring of the current human rights legislation in which the organization is located. It focuses on the meanings of harassment and discrimination and often provides examples of these behaviours and the impacts they impose on employees. It elaborates the prohibited grounds (such as race, sex, marital status, and so on) and the people under the protection of the legislation. The policy highlights the roles of management and employees and the employment areas in which the legislation covered. This policy is often an offspring of the human rights policy (BC Hydro, n.d.).

Accommodation Policy

This policy also adheres to human rights legislation as well as the federal employment equity legislation (if relevant to the organization). It discusses the prohibited grounds and the concept of "undue hardship" in accommodation for employers. It gives examples of what accommodation measures look like and the roles and responsibilities of management and employees. It describes the process of accommodation from employee requests to resolutions (City of Montreal, n.d.).

Social Responsibility Policy

This type of policy may cover a broad range of responsibilities related to social justice, environmental justice, climate change, health and safety, community well-being, and Indigenous relations. Most of these policies are along the lines of environmental, social, and governance (Telus, n.d.).

Code of Conduct

Although the term "code" is used to describe how management and employees should conduct themselves in the workplace, it is actually a policy statement on human behaviour at work. Among many human behaviours such as conflict of interest, confidentiality, and privacy issues, this code covers discrimination, harassment, violence, and security. The messages are a confirmation of the other policy statements on social justice issues in organizations (PriceWaterhouseCooper 2023).

Publications like *Canada's Best Diversity Employers, Canada's Top Employers for Young People* (2024), or *Canada's Top 100 Employers* (2024) often identify organizations with social justice policies and programs. The Canadian Centre for Diversity and Inclusion (2024) often reports "Success Stories" of larger corporations and outlines their diversity policies and programs across industries.

Observations

As noted earlier, policy statements on social justice issues (such as DEI, anti-discrimination, and anti-harassment) are hallmarks of larger corporations, and they put on public displays through their own organizational websites and showcase them in annual competitions with their peers to gain recognition and build their reputation. However, for smaller organizations, their policy statements on social justice are often succinct without much elaboration. In fact, they are often glossed over in their public releases or annual reports lest these social justice messages crowd out, obscure, or distract their core business or functions.

In the development of policy statements, while there are some observable discrepancies between larger and smaller organizations in the ways in which they support social justice issues (in policy elaboration, frequency of publicity, and centrality of DEI in their businesses), policy statements are not a true indicator of how DEI, employment equity, human rights, and anti-racism are embedded in their human resources practices or organizational culture. In fact, there is an undercurrent of mild resentment among racialized and Indigenous employees toward the corporate use of these policy statements as a facade of progressiveness that masks over social injustice found in the workplace. The word "hypocrisy" is often used to describe executives and managers who do not "walk the talk." We must take a look at the programs and initiatives that organizations have developed and implemented in putting these policies into action.

STRATEGIES, PROGRAMS, AND INITIATIVES

In translating their policies on social justice, employers have used a broad range of measures and adjustments to improve the situation of racialized and Indigenous people in their workplaces. Usually, this is the result of organizational self-reflection and program reviews and a determination to find new ways to deal with complaints from racialized and Indigenous people and to make the organization fairer in treatment, more equitable in human resources processes, and more inclusive in culture. *Canada's Best Diversity Employers* (2024) reports the accomplishments of many Canadian organizations, ranging from public, broader public, private, and non-profit sectors. Some of these accomplishments at the strategy and program levels encompass numerous new ventures, adjustments, and directions that correspond to their corporate policy changes.

Development of New Strategies and Programs

In order to translate their policies on human rights, employment equity, diversity and inclusion, anti-discrimination and anti-harassment, and workplace respect, organizations often find themselves in need of new strategies and new actions. These strategies could be new pathways in reconciliation and decolonization, new approaches in addressing issues related to racism, or new action plans to engage employees or newcomers. Along with these new strategies are new recruitment, selection, and hiring methods, new internships or summer student programs, new mental health programs or initiatives, new mentorship and coaching programs, new training and development programs for employees of specific backgrounds, new accountability measures, new employee champions programs, and new anti-racism education programs. These programs mentioned below give us a few examples of what had been developed and implemented in organizations, and these examples are not meant to be exhaustive or complete.

Noting that its previous ways of attracting and retaining racialized and Indigenous people as well as other diverse groups were not as effective as expected, the Bank of Canada was determined to develop a new strategy to make the organization more equitable and inclusive. In

2022, a new diversity and inclusion strategy was announced that incorporated the reconciliation and inclusion of Indigenous people as well as accessibility. Furthermore, acknowledging native land and establishing protocols for events and speaking occasions as well as enabling employees to have dialogue with Indigenous people and other diverse groups became emerging necessities for employee engagement and learning about diversity. Hence, the establishment of the Indigenous Engagement Guidelines was timely. Scholarship, summer employment, and mentorship programs for racialized and Indigenous students were also developed to increase their numbers in the Bank of Canada.

Blake, Cassels & Graydon also developed new programs to recruit more racialized and Indigenous people in their company. Coffee breaks offer virtual networking sessions to create pipelines of new candidates from these communities. The Black@Blakes internal network was created to support and advance Black lawyers, and Black@Blakes internship for Black law students was created in 2020. To facilitate the development of relevant initiatives and programs, the firm launched a survey from its internal teams to collect data on how best to improve its mentoring, training, and other DEI programs.

Home Depot Canada launched their new development program for Black people, Indigenous peoples, and people of colour and identified opportunities for these employees at networking opportunities to increase their visibility to peers as well as arranging sponsorships for them to move into leadership positions with active support from the executives. In 2023, IGM Financial developed the Indigenous Strategy in consultation with Indigenous people. And Thomson Reuters, working in partnership with McKinsey, created the Diverse Talent Academies, which were open to all racialized/Indigenous people. The program has three tracks: executive leadership, management accelerator, and leadership essentials. It utilizes virtual workshops, fireside chats, sponsors, and peer support groups to train racialized/Indigenous people to be leaders.

Adjustment and Enrichment

Instead of creating brand new strategies, programs, or initiatives, some employers have made adjustments to their existing plans or programs so that they can meet the needs of racialized and Indigenous employees as well as their organizational directions and goals. For examples, some employers have made adjustments to their hours of work to make them more flexible, allocated additional funds for health and wellness programs, enriched their health-care plans and mentorship or internship programs, revamped their promotion processes, made special adjustments to their communication formats, diversified their job interview panels, and recalibrated their training programs. Some employers have completed reviews of their DEI training for their management staff and non-management staff and made adjustments to their generic off-the-shelf DEI training, making these training sessions more customized and specific, with clarity in their DEI goals tying them to their corporate values and goals, aligning them with with special organizational events/milestones, and adding measurements to their training (Chang 2025).

These examples are not exhaustive, but they are highlights of what were accomplished by some employers when they tailored their DEI initiatives and programs more. Enbridge employs over seven thousand employees throughout Canada, does an annual review of their compensation, performance evaluation management, leadership development, and succession planning across ethnicity and gender, and determines how fair they are in the impact on employees' career development. Adjustments are made to ensure equitable and discrimination-free programs.

Loblaw Companies updated its commitments for truth and reconciliation by building allyship, championing the employment of Indigenous peoples, and strengthening the economic development of Indigenous communities. The company sponsored the Canadian Council for Aboriginal Business' Indigenous Women in Leadership Award.

IGM Financial, in ensuring DEI performance accountability, evaluates the DEI performance of its leaders who have more than three direct reports. Their performance includes targets for under-represented employees and is tied to their compensation.

Acceleration of Progress

Some employers have upgraded their goals and timetables by hiring and promoting racialized and Indigenous people by removing some employment barriers. After a few years working in the area of DEI and human rights, organizations usually recognize that this kind of social justice work requires a lot of supports. Otherwise, the progress may slow down as there are not enough professionals with expertise in these fields. Hence, the upgrading of facilitators in selection and hiring is important. These employers are usually subsumed under the federal regulated industries as they have to prepare goals and timetables for the representation of employment equity designated groups. But there are other private sector employers who also have goals and timetables in their employment equity programs. Here are a few examples of how organizations can aim to accelerate progress in social justice in this way.

Through an employee listening initiative in 2020, Enbridge created two special programs with a focus on meeting the intersectional needs of women and Black/Indigenous women's participation in leadership, and the programs reached at least 4 percent of target participants. Actions have been created to ensure that 20 percent of leadership representation is composed of racial and ethnic employees by 2025. The company also launched pay equity analysis annually. The Diversity Targets campaign reviewed internal workforce data and set targets annually for representation. It also reviewed their inclusion initiatives, examined their impacts, and recommended future efforts. IGM Financials has determined to improve its pipeline for more diverse employees by setting the hiring goal of 50 percent of its 2022 summer internships to be made up of Indigenous Peoples, racialized people, and other diverse groups. The target of 50 percent was exceeded in 2023 when 77 percent of interns identified themselves as racialized people and half as women.

McMaster University employs over three hundred facilitators to help executives, managers, and department heads work on search committees so that more racialized and Indigenous people are hired more often. McMaster University has also collaborated with Indigenous groups, the Indigenous Education Council, and McMaster Indigenous Research Institute to formulate the Indigenous Strategic Directions to move reconciliation forward in research, education, student experience, and leadership and governance. Loblaw Companies has instituted measurable goals for racialized employees for their boards of directors, executives, and managers. The company has now exceeded its 2024 goal of 30 percent in middle management positions and its 2024 goal of 25 percent in executive roles for racialized employees (Loblaw Companies Limited, n.d.). Similarly, Thomson Reuter Canada established representation goals and timetables: 30 percent of its senior leaders will be racial and ethnic employees. In 2022, racial and ethnic representation reached 18 percent. Using "stay interviews" as a method to retain diverse talent seems to have been effective. All executives of Women's College Hospital have an equity goal in their talent action plan and participate in the Government of Canada's 50-30 challenge. This

50-30 challenge means that the representation goals for women is 50 percent and for other marginalized groups such as Indigenous peoples and racialized people is 30 percent. It is an equity challenge that more and more companies are taking up (Women College Hospital 2023).

Anti-Racism Actions

There are organizations that have a focus on the issues of racialized and Indigenous peoples in addition to other diverse groups, multiple prohibited grounds related to human rights, and other social justice issues. A focus on anti-racism may mean that the organization is setting a higher priority on racism and is determined to find new solutions. Accordingly, some organizations may develop a plan identifying racial issues or specializing on Black people or Indigenous peoples rather than Asian people or immigrants in general. Some organizations emphasize providing adequate anti-racism education or training sessions for both management and non-management staff, and some may dive deeper into anti-racism issues (such as micro-aggressions or workplace safe spaces) and come up with innovative solutions. Here are a few examples of anti-racism actions organized by organizations.

Since 2021, Loblaw Companies has targeted 160,000 employees to complete two DEI courses—Building a Culture of Inclusion and Being an Ally—and this goal has been reached and exceeded by forty thousand employees at the end of 2024. Blake, Cassels & Graydon's Black lawyers developed anti-racism training and contributed to the annual Black History Month client events. Canadian National Railway Company provides DEI leadership training for senior executives, middle managers, and supervisors to help them become better equipped with DEI tools. Women's College Hospital has established an Anti-Black Racism Task Force to oversee and advise on strategies to advance anti-Black racism priorities. This task force is expected to tackle the themes identified by employees and implement recommendations from the *Black Community Consultation Report*. The hospital also developed an equity roadmap to address anti-racism and other equity and inclusion issues. Legal counsel specializing in systemic racism also reviewed the human resources policies and recommended further anti-racism actions. There was an anti-Black commitment in 2020 with the goal of dismantling anti-Black racism by 2023. In addition, the hospital's Centre for Wise Practices in Indigenous Health Gathering Place provides stakeholders (such as faculty, staff, and community members) to access traditional medicines, exercise Indigenous ceremonial practice rights, and engage with Elders, Knowledge Keepers, Traditional Practitioners, and Educators (Women College Hospital 2023).

In Canada, there has been a renewed focus on employee retention, especially that of racialized employees, with the help of some professional and advocacy organizations. Under the BlackNorth Initiative, which was established by Wes Hall in 2020, and Black Professionals in Tech Network, which was founded by Lekan Olawoye, business organizations are finding ways to retain Black employees, especially those with the potential to become corporate leaders. Dahabo Ahmed-Omer, the executive director of the BlackNorth Initiative, said that "there is no point bringing Black people into a space that is not ready to accept them. Retention means you are giving employees opportunities to grow." Air Canada, the Business Development Bank of Canada, Enbridge, Healthcare of Ontario Pension Plan, and Maple Leaf Sports and Entertainment are a few examples of corporate Canada taking steps to improve the retention rate of Black employees with some successful results (Galea, O'Hara, and Bradshaw 2023).

Observations

Programs and initiatives introduced by employers with the objectives of eradicating racism and promoting DEI and human rights are commonly found in larger corporations and some medium-sized firms. It is harder to find this kind of program among smaller employers due to a lack of resources and expertise.

Weak in Employment Systems Reviews

The strategies, plans, programs, and initiatives reported earlier in this section are all useful DEI programs and initiatives, and most improve the quality of the workplace. The key unresolved issue is the extent to which they actually remove barriers so as to increase the chance for racialized and Indigenous employees to be less discriminated and treated more equitably. The potential serious problem of new or adjusted programs is their unclear impact on removing employment barriers or discriminatory conditions and on accelerating the rectification of biased conditions or strengthening an equitable and inclusive work environment. Often, this boils down to a lack of creditable information and data gathered through evidence-based methodology conducted by internal professionals or external experts.

The following steps need to be investigated prior to the development of new strategies, policies, or plans or new or adjusted programs or initiatives.

- Did management expose and review the root causes of the under-representation of racialized and Indigenous people in specific occupations such as senior management, professionals, or skilled manual workers?
- Did management retain the services of external consultants (an arms-length party) to check unconscious biases of management, inequitable policies and programs, and toxic culture?
- Did management retain legal experts to investigate human rights complaints or the dubious conduct of employees on racial issues?

Unfocused or cosmetic solutions tend to yield negative or neutral results, and they are not obvious until a few years after their implementation. Lost time and wasted efforts usually deepen the unjust conditions in the workplace and delay the process of rectification or eradication of racism. While organizations that are under federal regulations are required to do a comprehensive review of the employment system (such as hiring and promotion policies and procedures), a sizable number of organizations skip this step prior to their employment equity planning. Hence, a lot of non-evidence factors are at play, which render poor non-systematic planning.

Lack of Comprehensive Data Collection and Analysis

Data collection and analysis in DEI is an exercise commonly put into practice in larger corporations. It is also quite popular for leadership to tap the pulse of employees in job satisfaction, management practice, employee engagement and growth, morale, training and development, and occupational health and safety. However, one item that has not received the attention of management is the collection and use of employee data. These data are based on self-identification surveys, which are often adopted in federally regulated industries. These data, primarily collected for the purposes of employment equity programs, could be used to link other human resources functions (such as performance evaluation or training opportunities) to show how racialized and Indigenous people fare. Such uses are still consistent with the purpose of employment equity as their objective is to make human resources functions and processes less biased and fairer in the long run.

Lack of Human Rights and Anti-Racism Education and Training

The majority of organizations nowadays focus on DEI education and training and not on human rights or specific anti-racism training. In the past few years, larger organizations tend to organize training sessions for executives in eliminating unconscious biases. These training sessions are supposedly rolled out incrementally from the executive level to the management level; however, either due to changes in priority settings, funding, or logistic and workload issues, mving such training down to managers or supervisors may pose a challenge in operation. Hence, in some organizations, these training sessions have not been arranged beyond the executive level.

There is not much of a momentum of human rights training for both management and non-management employees. Most social justice training has been related to DEI, and, more distinctively, training focuses largely on perception, attitudes, and unconscious biases that cut across gender, race, religion, sexual expression and identity, transgender issues, disability, and, to a minor extent, ageism. These are all very relevant topics for training, and they raise the consciousness of managers and executives. As observed, these training sessions are seldom extended to non-management staff, leaving them largely deprived of progressive perspectives in these fields. As for human rights training, it has been largely neglected because this field is considered not fashionable and "old school," and DEI is considered more popular.

Related to human rights training, anti-racism training is also largely absent in organizations. Racism has been considered to be a sensitive subject because the term itself, like sexism, seems to be loaded with negative emotion and accusations of White privilege. In the 1960s, race relation training, cross-cultural training, or ethno-cultural training appeared to be more neutral without a presumption of White dominance. Anti-racism training is currently associated with decolonization and reconciliation of Indigenous people, Black Lives Matter, anti-oppression, and other seemingly radical and critical race theoretical thoughts. It is considered to be difficult to do the training or to be trained and is seldom picked as a training project in organizations.

Lack of Anti-Racism Strategy

Closely connected with anti-racism training is the development of a strategy for anti-racism. The federal government and a few other jurisdictions have carried the banner of anti-racism. This was outlined and discussed earlier under Chapter 9. However, at the corporate level, such anti-racism programs seldom surface. Culturally and politically, it is difficult for corporate management to acknowledge that racism exists in the organization. Racism is not just a perception or an attitude, but it is also embedded in human resources policies, programs, and initiatives and, more importantly, in values and culture.

Lack of Coaching, Mentoring, and Sponsorship

Two human resources initiatives that have been demonstrated to be very useful for racialized and Indigenous people are coaching and mentoring. They are beneficial because, as discussed earlier in Chapters 7 and 8, racialized and Indigenous employees are relatively isolated and are usually not in the inner circles of influential employees or decision makers in the organization. Coaching and mentoring by their managers may be helpful for them to improve their performance, to know how the system works in the organization, and to connect better to the inner circles. Coaching and mentoring by peers are also quite helpful to them for the same reasons. Unfortunately, these two initiatives have not been adopted extensively by management. As a result, these initiatives have not been concretized into more permanent and formal programs with proper guidelines and training for all stakeholders.

In larger organizations, there are some degrees of coaching and mentoring of potential candidates for succession planning or promotion, and this has been very limited to a few employees who may or may not be members of racialized or Indigenous people. In fact, sponsorship as an initiative to proactively arrange corporate appointments or influence decision makers to promote specific employees has been actively promoted as a way to speed up the advancement of these employees, whether they are racialized or Indigenous employees. In the past, these special employees tend to be White men and, increasingly, White women. There have been occasional racialized or Indigenous employees among these special employees, but they are few and far between.

Lack of Community Outreach

In order to increase the pipelines of racialized and Indigenous people to fill in positions that traditionally have not been occupied by them or positions in which they are under-represented in spite of various recruitment or hiring methods, organizations continue to use the usual recruitment methods such as word of mouth, job advertising agencies, headhunting firms, professional association websites, job or trade fairs, trade councils, and hiring halls. The problem of utilizing only these methods is that they are often not frequented by racialized or Indigenous peoples, and, thus, they miss these opportunities to learn about the these available jobs. Obviously, they should utilize these sources for information on job opportunities. More importantly, organizations need to outreach to their communities, but not much has been done about that.

There is also a need to enrich the feeder pools for those positions that are under-represented by racialized and Indigenous peoples. The feeder pools for positions for executives are managers, and those for managers are professionals, and those for professionals may or may not be semi-professionals (such as a para-legal), but other tuition supports for furthering education of semi-professionals may be in order. If these feeder pools are dried up, organizations may need to reach out to the communities of racialized and Indigenous people to increase the feeder pools, but this does not seem to have been widely adopted.

Lack of Performance Evaluation

One of the human resources areas that needs to be revamped is the performance evaluation system as it is an area that affects the life chances of racialized and Indigenous people. Racialized and Indigenous employees often complain that there are biases in management's evaluation of their performance as indicated by their lower performance scores. It has been observed that the performance of these employees tends to be poorly evaluated by the corporate performance evaluation system when compared with White employees. It is also clear that getting lower scores and more negative comments will affect their promotion chances and has implications on succession planning. Unfortunately, this is a neglected area.

Furthermore, the evaluation of executives' performance in the DEI, human rights, employment equity, and anti-racism areas has been largely neglected. In order to put a higher priority of social justice for racialized and Indigenous people and get better results, executives' performance in these areas should also be monitored and evaluated so that they are held more accountable and, at the same time, compensated. In fact, middle-level managers and supervisors also seldom get evaluation on their performance in these areas and are treated as if these areas are merely add-ons without proper evaluation criteria and tools. Hence, management evaluation is an area that needs to be improved. Currently, not much thought has been given to upgrade the performance evaluation system for everyone at work.

STRUCTURES

Several special bodies have been created to advance policy changes and program implementation. They are usually found in larger corporations.

Diversity Leadership Councils

To lead the organizational efforts to build a discriminatory-free, equitable, and inclusive workplace, employers usually establish a special body made up of chief executive officers (CEO) and a number of senior executives or even selected members from the board of directors. This body embodies significant status and command respect. This body is often called a Diversity Leadership Council or Inclusion Council, and it develops strategies and plans to advance the organizational agenda, and reports are submitted for discussion at the council level regularly. Two examples of Diversity Leadership Councils are explored here. The Royal Bank of Canada (RBC) established the Global Diversity Leadership Council in 2001, and it has been chaired by the president and CEO ever since. Led by a vice president, the Global Diversity and Inclusion Centre of Excellence formulates strategies to ensure RBC is making progress on its DEI goals and commitments and depends on all RBC business units and functions and other teams to help advance DEI (Royal Bank of Canada 2024). Loblaw Companies has the Inclusion Council, which is made up of twenty leaders. It oversees the progress of DEI activities and reports regularly to its Board of Directors and Management Board. Each council member is responsible for their own committee and Employee Resource Group.

DEI Committees and Advisory Groups

Meanwhile, committees are set up to translate the strategies and policies of the organization into actions and prepare DEI plans accordingly. In addition, advisory groups are created to provide advice to the DEI committees, which, in turn, are mandated to follow the directions from the leadership council and cascade activities through managers and supervisors in advancing the DEI agenda. Advisory groups can be composed of community representatives, area experts or faculty members, and/or employees or other stakeholder groups (such as students in colleges and universities). Two examples of diversity committees and advisory groups include the following. The University of Calgary has struck a Presidential Task Force on DEI and Accessibility to conduct consultation with a range of the university's internal bodies and external communities, research, and review data and has put forward a strategy and implementation plan to carry out its work on DEI. This task force also helped in drafting an Indigenous Strategic Plan in 2017 to implement recommendations from the Truth and Reconciliation Commission's report with advice and consultation with the Indigenous communities. Corus Entertainment has a DEI team with focus on diversity and authentic representation. It analyzes data and conducts in-depth sessions with the company's business areas, determines objectives, and creates dashboards for the business area with measurement.

Employee Resource Groups

Employee resource groups (ERGs) are groups of employees with specific identities based on race, Indigeneity, gender, ability, sexual orientation, or other diversity identities. These groups may have different objectives in different organizations: networking, education/training, professional development, peer support, coaching, mentoring, or resources sharing. These groups are endorsed by senior executives, and, in limited duration, they have interfacing with these executives. A few examples of ERGs include the following. Enbridge has nine ERGs with over forty chapters in the company. Each ERG is overseen by an executive and provides advancement opportunities, leadership development, peer support, and networking events. These nine ERGs include Ethnically Diverse Resource Group, Indigenous Employee Resource Group, and Caregivers, Allies, Resources Education Support. Embrace Your Roots in Loblaw Companies is an employee resource group made up of employees from multicultural and Indigenous backgrounds. It celebrates employees from different cultures. Women's College Hospital has an African, Black, and Caribbean employee group. The Children's Aid Society of Toronto has also established Black, Muslim, and East Asian employee groups.

Observations

These structures are created to carry out activities related to removing employment barriers, supporting racialized and Indigenous people to advance their status, and making the workplace discrimination free and more equitable and inclusive. Without diversity leadership councils, committees, and advisory groups, DEI, human rights, and employment equity would not be advancing in such a coordinated and timely manner. The ERGs provide needed help and supports for racialized and Indigenous people. However, observations and experiences suggest that they might not reach their potential in interacting with higher-level executives or managers. This is because executives and managers do not attend the functions of these groups very often and, thus, are not keeping their finger on the pulse of racialized and Indigenous employees enough so that they can offer concrete help.

If ERGs are conduits for the members in the diversity leadership councils or DEI committees/advisory groups to learning how best to develop strategies, policies, plans, programs, and initiatives to meet the needs of racialized and Indigenous employees, this might explain why policies, strategies, and programs do not have enough funds or other resources to advance the DEI agenda. Moreover, for programs and initiatives to work properly, regular reviews and consultation with participants need to be conducted so that emerging needs can be identified on time and new ideas can be generated. Instead of completing a formal survey, an informal conversation or consultation with members of the ERGs may be sufficient. Given that employers often use surveys as a means to find out the pulse of employees, employees often experienced "survey fatigue." Thus, connections or liaisons with ERGs may yield a better response rate.

RECOMMENDATIONS

Application of Employment Systems Reviews

While the term "employment systems reviews" is familiar to organizations that are regulated by the federal *Employment Equity Act*, it has not been consistently and comprehensively carried out by these organizations, as discussed earlier in this book in Chapter 9. Organizations not under the coverage of this legislation may not be aware of the value of such reviews and may not be in a hurry to apply these reviews. "Employment systems review" is an examination of every policy, program, procedure, guideline, and rule created and implemented in human resources management as well as the value and culture of an organization. The examination includes all of them when put into practice, formally and informally, written or undocumented, individual cases as well as collectively. The purpose of such an examination is to identify employment biases (including barriers) for racialized and Indigenous people as well as other groups in a systematic manner and to analyze how these biases impact on these groups adversely both in the long and short run. The review also includes an examination of the reasonable accommodation of the particular needs of these diverse groups so that they can be fully represented and can participate in the organization.

This examination must be systematic, covering all human resources functions for each occupation in each geographic location, especially when under-representation has been noted. In other words, both occupationally specific human resources policies and practices and organizational-wide human resources policies and practices are to be examined. Examples of human resource functions include recruitment, selection in hiring and promotion, training and development, coaching and mentoring, performance evaluation, retention and termination, employee engagement and social inclusion, accommodation of special needs, and workplace and occupational specific and geographic/local values and cultures. Employment systems reviews, while focusing on human resource systems, also examine the perception, attitudes, and values of executives, managers, and supervisors. How they apply policies, procedures, and practices, including consistency and fairness and extent and process, are all critical areas that need to be examined.

The application of the human resources policies and practices becomes critical when an organization is going through expansion, downsizing, moving to a new business direction, restructuring, merging with another company, or acquiring a new company. All these new business ventures and organizational changes usually affect the application of human resources policies and practices, and management needs to be vigilant about how to regularly monitor the changes through the lens of an employment systems review. There is a set of methodological processes that could be put into place for an organization to carry out an employment systems review. Ideally, an impartial person or company with expertise in this kind of review should be retained to do the review as there are many vested interests surrounding human resource policies and practices, especially when they have been there for years. An external specialist may help to identify issues related to employment systems without much emotional attachment to them. Once the biases are identified, it is up to management to decide what to do with the review findings.

Essentially, the review methodology includes creating an inventory of all the policies, programs, procedures, guidelines, and rules related to human resources functions (such as hiring, promotion, and so on) as well as any occupational specific human resource policies and practices; reviewing previous corporate surveys of employees related to their opinions on job satisfaction and so on; collecting documents related to these matters; reviewing these documents with the core review question on how the policies and practices affect racialized and Indigenous people adversely; reviewing corporate documents on business directions and human resources functions; developing a list of employees covering management and non-management staff members from multiple occupational groups, geographic locations, and demographic backgrounds; grouping them into different focus groups or interviewing them and finding out what the policies and practices are as they experienced them in their current or previous positions and how they have been affected by them; interviewing employees who have left the organization and reviewing their exit interview results (if any); interviewing representatives from multiple bargaining units; interviewing employees who work in the areas of human rights, employment equity, DEI, and other social justice issues; and categorizing employment biases (and barriers) and summarizing review findings.

There are usually a lot of preparation works to be done prior to the actual employment systems review. Preparation includes seeking the commitment and endorsement of the CEO and the executive team, seeking collaboration from the human resources department and all major business departments as employees from their departments will likely be involved in focus group discussions and interviews. If circumstances allow, one should create a joint labour and management committee to review employment policies, programs and practice, and so on so that a dialogue could be forged between these two groups on some commonly identified employment issues. Overall, this review is basically a research project aimed at finding out the sources of why racialized and Indigenous people are not represented or under-represented in some occupations and geographic areas. With the results of the research in hand, it is easier to focus on the sources of the problems and develop options to tackle them.

The failure of organizations to do employment systems reviews deprived their benefits for racialized and Indigenous groups. It is therefore critical to highlight the importance that these reviews will do for making the workplace fairer and equitable for every employee and discrimination free for racialized and Indigenous people. Without an employment systems review, it would be very difficult to pinpoint in a specific manner that certain features in human resources management and the employment systems it created are indeed biased, pose barriers, and discriminate racialized and Indigenous people as individuals or as a group. With the review findings, it is also difficult to prepare an action plan that would remove the identified employment barriers and establish a framework of programs and initiatives that would make the workplace equitable and discrimination free.

Data Cross-Tabulation and Analysis

Organizations regulated by the federal *Employment Equity Act* are required to collect demographic data on their workforces, including racialized and Indigenous peoples. These data are used to link with their occupational positions, salary status, part-time and full-time status, along with other specifics so as to provide evidence whether there are biases in employment when compared with the Census data. This is a limited way to demonstrate whether there is employment equity in the occupational groups.

However, there is an added value in linking the data on their demographic backgrounds with data in human resources functions. For example, race and Indigeneity data could be connected with employees' participation in training or developmental opportunities. In analyzing the linked data, it is easier to identify the extent to which racialized and Indigenous employees participated in training sessions/ programs or participated in developmental programs. Another way is to link the race and Indigeneity data with the scoring system usually found in performance evaluation systems. In this manner, one may evidence whether racialized and Indigenous employees are clustering in higher or lower evaluation scores. And if these data could be disaggregated by departments, occupational groups, salary levels, part-time/full-time status, or geography, they would also shed light on whether racialized and Indigenous employees are highly or lowly scored when compared with each other or among races.

Similarly, demographic data could be collected on programs on onboarding, mentorship, and succession and on corporate task forces, conference attendance, corporate awards, career counselling, human rights complaints, benefits (such as tuition reimbursement programs or wellness programs), disciplinary actions, and many other human resources initiatives. Once data sets are linked, patterns of usage or participation by racialized or Indigenous employees could be identified and analyzed.

A Strategy on Anti-Racism

Policies on human rights, employment equity, and DEI often implicitly include their ways in which to address racism issues and describe what needs to be done to fight against racism, but they are not considered to be anti-racism strategies. As discussed earlier in Chapter 9, there are some examples of anti-racism strategies across jurisdictions, starting with the federal government. Organizations that plan to develop a strategy to fight against racism may follow the lead of the federal government (Canadian Human Rights Commission 2023).

Having a strategy on anti-racism puts racism in the organization's focus. This may be why corporations seldom have a strategy in this field as it implicitly acknowledges that racism is a corporate problem. There are only a few organizations that have explicit strategies on anti-racism, and they are mainly in the broader public sector. Broader public sector organizations (such as hospitals, colleges, and universities) are more willing to develop an anti-racism strategy because they are providing services for the public with public money—hence, their mindset is focused on serving the public and public good. Private sector organizations are less than eager to wave banners on social justice, environmental degradation, climate change, and other social issues. Nowadays, with the environmental, social, and governance movement in the corporate sector, the focus on social issues may be elevated, and CEOs may be paying more attention and willing to extend themselves in this direction.

A strategy on anti-racism basically announces to the public that the organization is committed to tackling racism in the workplace. This strategy may include several major components:

- executive commitment to anti-racism;
- organizational and systems reviews on racism;
- anti-racism in human resources management;
- anti-racism values, norms, and culture;
- communication, education, training, and engagement on anti-racism messages;
- anti-racism action plan;
- implementation; and
- monitoring and evaluation.

A strategy may focus on workplace racism beginning with a review (such as taking the corporate pulse in a survey, town hall meetings, focus groups, or roundtables)—the idea is to listen and learn from the people who work there as well as to take a critical look at the corporate policies and programs in the human resources areas as well as the culture of the organization. One may share the review findings with leaders and get them onboard. Meanwhile, the review should continue by talking with more employees and other stakeholder groups, including customers and contractors. An action plan should be prepared with goals and timetables on hiring and promoting racialized and Indigenous peoples. Benchmarks can be set, and progress toward them can be monitored. Finally, implementation of the strategy itself must be monitored and evaluated, and any necessary adjustments to the action plan should be made periodically once it is determined if it works or not (White 2022).

Human Rights Education and Training

Increasing human rights education and training among leaders, managers, and employees is of a high priority if racism is to be eradicated in an organization. The prohibited grounds of discrimination (such as race, colour, place origin, ethnic origin, citizenship, ancestry, age, sex, disability, family status, marital status. sexual orientation, gender identity, gender expression, receipt of public assistance, and records of offences) and the protected social areas (such as housing, employment, services, contracts, membership in unions, and trade or professional associations) where discrimination is prohibited are the basic foundations for human rights to ensure that everybody is entitled to equality, dignity, and respect. However, many people in the workplace are still not clear about these entitlements and are not familiar with the basic concepts such as discrimination, harassment, bona fide occupational requirements, and accommodation.

Employees who do not know the basic features found in human rights legislation will likely encounter some missteps when interacting with co-workers and potentially violate the law. For management employees, they not only need to know the basic legal framework of human rights, but they also must create a culture to prevent human right infringements, meet the accommodation needs of employees, and institute a process for reporting allegations of discrimination and harassment and a process of investigating and resolving issues related to them.

In other words, all these management and non-management staff members must know the human rights of employees so as to ensure that the workplace is respectful. While employees need basic education on human rights legislation, leaders and management staff members need more than a basic education; they need training in human rights competency with the skills to manage in accordance with the principles of human rights.

Coaching and Mentoring

When coaching and mentoring become an integral part of the corporate culture, the organization can be transformed into a caring, collaborative, supportive, motivating, and productive workplace. Coaching is usually a working relationship between management and non-management staff that enables the less experienced or knowledgeable members to gain a better understanding of what needs to be done and how best to accomplish it. It works best when the two parties are genuine and sharing, and it entails a motivating energy for developing a better way of doing tasks or interacting with people. It has the potential to raise the level of job satisfaction, engagement, commitment, and productivity of the persons being coached. Collectively, it fosters a culture of learning and development, a more confident workforce, and a greater sense of organizational pride and commitment.

Mentoring often involves coaching and supporting. It provides an environment for at least two persons—the mentor and the mentee—to learn from each other and for the more experienced mentor to pass along their wisdom and knowledge, which enables the mentee to upgrade them. Mentorship is more holistic than coaching as it involves the whole person and their future and does not just focus on the job and tasks as coaching does. A mentor can help mentees change their positions or advance in their careers. Mentorship could be formal or informal. A formal mentorship program in the workplace can help racialized and Indigenous people reach their potential in a much more systematic way, and it allows for an optimal way to overcome employment barriers. Coaching and mentoring are important tools to enable racialized and Indigenous people to understand how the systems in the organization work ("learning the ropes"), especially for new employees or employees with immigrant backgrounds; to learn how best to perform and how best to work in a work team; to get insights on what management does and how they appraise employees and their work; to get to know more about the business direction of the organization; and to upgrade oneself and prepare to advance to a new position or career.

While coaching and mentoring are practised in organizations to some degree, only a very few have a formal arrangement (as in mentoring programs) or requirements (as in professional development or performance evaluation). Overall, it has been observed that they are not embedded in corporate culture. Those who are fortunate to find their own coaches or mentors informally and are able to benefit from such an arrangement are not usually racialized or Indigenous people. Many of the latter have testified that they seldom have coaches or mentors who help them navigate the employment process in their organizations. By this statement, they mean that they do not know how to get training and developmental opportunities, how to get a fair performance evaluation from their bosses, how to become involved and participate in higher profile committee or task force activities, or how to be successful in promotion attempts. When coaching and mentorship are elevated to a formal arrangement, and racialized and Indigenous people get a fair share of these arrangements, the workplace can become a more equitable and fairer place to work.

Community Outreach

Even though many corporations have under-representation of racialized or Indigenous people in their overall workforce, their specific occupational groups, or their workforces in certain geographic regions, they seldom use community outreach as a recruitment tool in changing the composition of their workforces. Community outreach may mean many things to people, but here it means the action of corporations in reaching out to communities of racialized and Indigenous people for their specialized knowledge, skills, and experiences. It definitely does not mean "casting the net wide and hope you can catch a few you want." It means at least three things: corporations may need to do some research and identify (1) where people with target competencies are readily available; (2) where people are being educated, trained, or in the pipeline with these targeted competencies; and (3) where people are prepared to join the pool of positions in the organizations where they will be trained with these targeted competencies.

For example, after doing some market research, it has been noted that Indigenous people tend to cluster in colleges for their education, and racialized people have heavier clusters in university education. Therefore, corporations and agencies may be wise to publicize their professional job opportunities among racialized university students and their semi-professional or technical job opportunities among Indigenous college students. Corporations and agencies may do research to find out where racialized and Indigenous people with legal, financial, nursing, social work, or construction work skills are located and whether these people have their own race-based or Indigeneity-based associations so that they can prepare an outreach strategy to work with them. There are also recruitment agencies that specialize in potential employees from racialized or Indigenous backgrounds. Finally, corporations or agencies may create internship programs for potential interns of racialized or Indigenous backgrounds who wish to learn or be educated in target skills within their own organizations. In this manner, such internship programs can attract potential interns through community organizations or recruitment agencies. When corporations and agencies use this target approach in reaching out, the results can enrich the diversification of candidates ready to work in the targeted job positions or increase the pool of feeders through these pipelines.

Performance Evaluation

There are two aspects of the performance evaluation system in organizations that must be revamped. One is to make it fairer for racialized and Indigenous employees, the other is to hold management staff members more accountable through their performance evaluation system. As discussed in the earlier section on corporate programs in this chapter, although performance evaluation is carried out in most organizations, there is a relatively high degree of subjectivity in the way in which employees' performance is evaluated. For racialized and Indigenous employees, the prejudice and stereotyping of management, the lack of coaching and clear communication on both sides (management and non-management staff), the lack of frequency in giving employees feedback, the lack of clear criteria and indicators for measuring performance, and the scoring and ranking system are conducive to a lack of fairness. Based on these observations, improvements must be made to better the quality of performance evaluation. And if the basic framework is not sound (as illustrated by the growing critiques from human resources professionals toward the current performance evaluation system), another system must be developed with a greater emphasis on coaching and mentoring to equip employees with the right knowledge and skills. A revamped performance evaluation system can benefit the training and developmental component for employees rather than the evaluation component of the current system.

As for using the performance evaluation system to hold leadership and management accountable for their commitment and performance on DEI, human rights, employment equity, and anti-racism, the inclusion of social justice would work as one key performance evaluation criterion. Furthermore, with this new performance evaluation criterion, leaders and managers' compensation would now be tied to their performance in promoting social justice in the workplace, which would be a good start. This means that if management staff's overall performance in promoting social justice at work is neglected, their performance scores would be lowered and their compensation would also be reduced. In this manner, it is expected that social justice performance would command higher priority and attention in the organization. Such a performance evaluation system is increasingly used in the public sector and larger private sector corporations.

CONCLUSION

In Canada, larger organizations have a greater tendency to develop some form of social justice policy for the workplace, including DEI, employment equity, human rights, and anti-racism. On paper, these policies are progressive; however, some racialized and Indigenous employees see them as being hypocritical because leaders do not "walk the talk."

Smaller and medium-sized organizations may not be that sophisticated to create their own social justice policies for their organizations. In translating some of these social justice policies, larger organizations have developed and implemented numerous programs and initiatives that aim to be beneficial to the workplace and the people who work there. Some have designed programs that intend to remove employment barriers, support racialized and Indigenous people, provide outreach to their communities, increase their representation, make them feel included and give them a sense of belonging, and accommodate their special needs.

The central issue is whether organizations have done a lot of research on finding the sources of the inequitable issues in the workplace prior to their development of programs and initiatives that claim to be effective solutions. Current findings from more than two decades of work from employment equity and human rights suggest that a significant share of "solutions" on removing employment barriers and on elevating the representation and inclusion of racialized and Indigenous people tend to be cosmetic and have been ineffective even after putting them into practice for years. This is because these "solutions" were not evidence based in their design and were half-hearted in their implementation.

The key structures created as the result of launching DEI management in the last few decades are diversity leadership councils, DEI committees and advisory groups, and employee resources groups. All three are of critical importance in leading, managing, and supporting DEI efforts. To make these structures more effective, the pulse of employees must continue to be monitored, their needs must be identified, and adequate funding needs to be delivered. In other words, the effectiveness of these structures must be regularly checked and financially supported.

The pitfalls of what employers have been doing to make the workplace less discriminatory and more equitable are related to their lack of effectiveness. Results take a much longer time to surface; hence, finding more effective measures, programs, or initiatives has been delayed. Unless employers invest more time, resources, and efforts to remove biases and build fairness in the employment system in a targeted and focused manner, progress toward greater representation and advancement for racialized and Indigenous peoples is destined to be slow. The federal government has played a role in developing untargeted and unfocused ways forward, and the private sector under federal regulations has been more lenient in monitoring and enforcing employment equity legislation, especially the mandatory requirements for a comprehensive and regular employment systems review. While larger corporations have done their share in implementing some programs or initiatives in the social justice areas, smaller and medium-sized corporations have a long way to go. Here, as suggested in Chapter 9, it is these types of employers that the federal, provincial, territorial, and municipal governments must start mandating so that they can play a more critical role in advancing the equitable status of racialized and Indigenous people.

CHAPTER 11

Labour Unions: Negotiators and Advocates

INTRODUCTION

Employees are the receiving end of what management offers to them in an employment relationship. However, for those working in a unionized organization or a workforce segment that has a bargaining agent representing them, they may be able to negotiate some changes in the working relationship or environment. In a non-unionized workplace, the situation is much different as they are not represented by anyone—a union or an association. In other words, they are on their own.

While employers have a major say in who can be hired, promoted, transferred, retained, paid, trained, developed, and treated, there are instances in which unions have traditionally been involved in negotiating the life chances of racialized and Indigenous peoples, along with other marginalized groups, in the workplace. For example, unions control the hiring and training of employees in the construction industries. They control the types and qualifications of people gaining access to work through hiring halls, and they play a role in "segregating" racialized and Indigenous peoples along with other marginalized groups.

Union practice therefore is pivotal as it impacts on people adversely in particular segments of the job market. The domination of racialized and Indigenous peoples by White people has been documented well in history books, and it is also reflected in the dominance of White people in the labour movement and within the organizational structure of labour unions in Canada (Nangwaya 2011). Hence, White people's control of racialized and Indigenous people in the occupational world is not unusual and is consistent with the pattern of White people in other social domains.

This chapter recommends a series of practical actions and programs that unions may implement in eradicating racism in the workplace. Unions are encouraged to negotiate human rights and equity measures in collective agreements; organize proactive education programs; develop support networks of racialized employee groups; encourage mentoring and coaching activities or programs; foster allyship development and learning circles; and establish working committees made up of human resources people and racialized and Indigenous employees to identify and remove employment barriers.

UNIONIZED WORKPLACE

Unions play a critical role in advocating labour rights and human rights on behalf of their members. They have a mandate to negotiate for stronger protections in collective agreements and push for stronger legislation in social justice. It is clear that, under the federal and provincial legislation on labour relations and human rights, employers and unions are not allowed to discriminate racialized people and others with prohibited grounds of discrimination in any collective agreements.

In Canada, we have multiple layers of unions: consolidated unions that speak on behalf of labour unions, largely on political matters (such as Canadian Labour Congress (CLC), large national unions covering public sector unions (such as Canadian Union of Public Employees (CUPE), and large national unions covering multiple private sector unions (such as Unifor). These large unions set policy frameworks on social justice issues as well as launching campaigns in promoting and protecting Indigenous and racialized people and their human and worker rights.

Canadian Labour Congress

The CLC was founded in 1956. It has over fifty affiliates (including the Canadian Federation of Nurses Unions, the Canadian Union of Postal Workers, the International Association of Fire Fighters, the National Association of Teachers, the Public Service Alliance of Canada). The CLC plays a leading role in political actions in calling the federal government to protect and defend Canadian workers' rights and livelihoods and in solidarity with other social justice movements. As far as racial discrimination issues are concerned, the CLC has recently focused on eradicating colonialism, systemic racism, violence, Islamophobia, and transphobia, which negatively impacts on Indigenous communities and racialized and intersectional communities. Although the CLC (2021) focuses on broader Canada-wide issues (rather than local workplace issues), it plays a leadership role in setting the socio-political framework on race, racism, and Indigeneity, leaving local anti-racism work to the more local unions to tackle.

Unifor

Established in 2013, Unifor amalgamated the Canadian Auto Workers Union and the Communications, Energy and Paperworkers Union of Canada. The name "Unifor" is made up of united ("unis") and strong ("fort"). It is a union for everyone. It is the largest private sector union in Canada, covering twenty-nine sectors with 696 locals and 2,883 bargaining units. It has 320,000 members from a broad range of industrial sectors. Many of Unifor's policies are related to diversity and human rights: accessibility, gender equality, gender-based violence, human rights, LGBTQIA+ issues, racial justice, and harassment (Unifor 2024a). These policies have established frameworks for its member unions in defining their own social justice policies. Unifor also sets an example for its members on workplace justice, focusing on Indigenous people, racialized people, women, LGBTQIA+, and persons with disabilities. It has the Local Union Equity Fund to encourage the fight for equity in the local union's work and launched campaigns on issues related to Indigenous communities ("Stop Violence against Indigenous Woman and Girls"). Like the CLC, Unifor also has a larger social mandate that goes beyond the workplace. It set up the Unifor Social Justice Fund to support national and international non-government sector and community groups in their fight for human rights, equity, and insecurity (Unifor 2024b).

Canadian Union of Public Employees

An excellent example may be found in CUPE, which has 740,000 members (as of December 2023) and more than twenty-one hundred union locals. Its Constitution was developed at the founding convention in 1963. It includes an Equality Statement that condemns discriminatory speech or conduct that is racist, sexist, transphobic, or homophobic and states that harassment is a form of discrimination that abuses, devalues, or humiliates. It insists that CUPE's policies and practices must reflect the union's commitment to equality. CUPE has its Code of Conduct to which its members must comply. The code is consistent with CUPE's National Constitution, the Equality Statement, and applicable human rights legislation. Internally, it has a set of procedures for handling complaints.

CUPE emphasizes the importance of raising awareness of Indigenous communities and their history and cultures. In aligning with the recommendations of the Truth and Reconciliation Commission of Canada, CUPE (2019) pays special attention to implementing Call for Action 57, which focuses on educating public servants:

> We call upon federal, provincial, territorial, and municipal governments to provide education to public servants on the history of Aboriginal peoples, including the history of legacy of residential schools, the United Nations Declaration on the Rights of Indigenous Peoples, Treaties and Aboriginals rights, Indigenous law, and Aboriginal-Crown relations. This will require skills-based training in intercultural competency, conflict resolution, human rights and anti-racism.

With this focus, CUPE urges its locals to support this call to action and work with employers to offer training and education to its members and provide solid support for Indigenous rights and justice issues as a priority.

CUPE also has several councils and committees to advocate social justice. It has the National Indigenous Council, the National Racial Justice Committee, the National Women and Gender Rights Committee, the National Persons with Disabilities Committee, and the National Pink Triangle Committee. These bodies of active union members all promote fairness and justice for their identified groups in the development of policies and programs as well as negotiating with employers in this area in their collective bargaining.

As an example, CUPE's National Indigenous Council developed a mechanism to protect Indigenous employees' rights, to develop CUPE policies in anti-racism, and to support employment equity. Its focus is on truth and reconciliation bargaining (as manifested in the development of *Truth and Reconciliation: CUPE Taking Action through Collective Bargaining*, a guidebook to help CUPE locals strengthen their reconciliation work) (Canadian Union of Public Employees 2022). Many of the issues discussed in the guidebook are employment issues that are pertinent to Indigenous peoples such as occupational representation, hiring, in-service training, work hours, wages, pension plans, and the inclusion of Elders at grievances and other meetings. The *Walking the Talk: A Practical Guide to Reconciliation for CUPE Locals* document enables union members to work on issues and set up a protocol for reconciling with the Indigenous communities (including land acknowledgement and the inclusion of Elders, Chiefs, and other representatives) (Canadian Union of Public Employees 2019).

Back in 1999, CUPE's National Convention adopted the CUPE Policy Statement on Workplace Racism, and, in 2021, its National Convention adopted a CUPE-wide Anti-Racism Strategy. Its key strategic direction is to break down barriers and build a more inclusive union. The ten strategic goals focus on governance; representation (especially in union leadership), anti-racism education, and training, lived experiences of Black, Indigenous, and racialized employees; anti-racism organizing and community outreach; bargaining for better jobs; the enforcement of collective agreements' anti-racism activities; data collection on racialized members for further union actions; political actions to fight systemic racism; and coalition work with allies and other social movements.

Despite what the larger umbrella unions have provided as a framework for furthering workers' human rights for racialized and Indigenous employees, it does not necessarily mean that each of the member unions or their locals are diligently following the footsteps of their national or provincial unions on this front. What seems to be noticeable is that, as far as formal adherence to human rights legislation is concerned, the provincial and their local unions are at least formally acknowledging the centrality of human rights. For example, under the Federation of Labour in British Columbia, the United Steelworkers Local 1-1937's has a collective agreement with the Veterans Memorial Housing Society, which is active from 22 February 2024 to 21 February 2027, in which Article XX on Harassment and Discrimination clearly states: "The Parties to this Collective Agreement agree that the employee have the right to a working environment that is free from harassment and discrimination. The employer shall provide a working environment that is free from harassment and discrimination." This is an example of the extent to which a collective agreement can explicitly adhere to the principles of a harassment- and discrimination-free workplace. The local unions must do more to ensure that these principles are translated into actions.

Human Rights

Ideally, every collective agreement should include the protections mandated by human rights legislation. If that is the case, the grievance procedure in the collective agreement provides an additional option for employees to get human rights enforced over and above the legislative procedures. Human rights issues arising from the workplace in some organizations have been dealt with through the grievance and arbitration mechanism available in the collective agreement. Such procedures benefit both the employers and employees as they both can resolve racial allegations that are at stake right in their workplaces. Examples of such provisions are found in the agreements negotiated by the CUPE and the Canadian Auto Workers Union. Collective agreements like these contain clauses that enable the unions to defend and promote the human rights of all employees, especially those of racialized and Indigenous people and others who are subjected to discrimination and harassment.

What is more important is the extent to which specific work arrangements and human resources functions are detailed in the rest of the collective agreement, such as those itemized in different articles of the agreement (examples include work hours, wages, pay days, vacation with pay, call time, health and welfare, seniority, leave of absence, safety equipment, permanent closures, severance pay, disciplinary records, adjustment of grievances, arbitration, strikes and lockouts), and ensuring that they are aligned well with the principles and provisions of the human rights legislation, health and safety, and employment equity (BC Labour Relations Board 2024).

However, explicit details on the the equitable and fair components of human resources functions and work arrangements are usually not specified in the collective agreements. The knowledge and competency of union negotiators becomes crucial in the wording of the agreements. The expertise and comprehensiveness that the local unions invested in critically examining the collective agreements prior to the signing of the document become the crux of the matter. Are union officials, stewards, and members well educated and trained in scrutinizing the agreements? Do they place a high priority in fighting and securing social justice for all segments of their memberships, including racialized and Indigenous employees? Do these collective agreements have a built-in framework to ensure that employers invest more in their employees' education and training and build in more safeguards for pre-empting racial inequities in the workplace?

Historically, unions have called upon the union officials and members' legal knowledge and analytic skills on how best to identify discriminatory clauses in their collective agreements and scrutinize them in light of past court decisions. There could be discrepancies between one group of workers versus other groups on the provision or denial of benefits; benefit payments; employment eligibility (such as age); employment requirements (such as education levels and work experience); selection tests; interview practices; remedial actions (such as special measures for racialized people); work rules and schedules, and so on. Unions have been called upon to negotiate with the employers to give marginalized groups such as racialized and Indigenous peoples a break lest they are loaded down by the historical accumulation of systemic discrimination, giving them an opportunity to prove to themselves that they are able to work in new jobs or giving them a chance, as a collective group, to build a critical mass in positions that have been voided of their presence. This book is unable to examine every single provision in the existing collective agreements to come to a conclusion, but general observations on the complaints and grievances of unionized employees (especially among Black and Indigenous employees in the public sector) reflect a growing discontent on racial equality fronts.

This is why it is important that unionized workers do not lose the right to file complaints to human rights tribunals (or through human rights commissions) despite their collective agreements. The availability of two options for unionized workers is the concurrent jurisdiction model. Back in 2022, there was a short period when the concurrent jurisdiction model of workers' rights concerning human rights complaints at the Human Rights Tribunal of Ontario (HRTO) or relying on their collective agreements was under review by the Government of Ontario, the Ontario Federation of Labour, and the Coalition of Black Trade Unionists. The above unions maintained a firm stand on such workers' rights as they saw the value of concurrent jurisdiction, but the Government of Ontario intended to review the model. The model had been in place for more than two decades. Finally, later that year, the

HRTO confirmed that the model would continue after the review. This decision reasserted the right of unionized workers to file their human rights complaints either through the collective agreements or the HRTO (Ontario Federation of Labour 2024).

Education and Training in Human Rights

In raising the awareness and understanding of human right issues, unions take on the responsibility of establishing an organizational framework aligning with human rights principles, and they see one of their mandates as advocating human rights in the workplace, including eradicating racism. They usually provide education and training for their stewards and members, especially those who have a role to play in collective bargaining. However, unions have also negotiated with their employers to have more human rights training for every employee and additional training for employees with special responsibility in preventing and resolving workplace tension that is related to human rights issues. Such negotiations have held the unions accountable to their members and, if successful, hold the employers accountable too.

Larger unions like CUPE have the resources to provide a wide range of courses on human rights for their members. CUPE has numerous courses on this front: anti-harassment and bystander training (which focuses on enabling learners to identify disrespectful behaviour and to acquire the skills to intervene before, during, and after a harassment or violent situation); challenging racism (which helps learners to identify what racism looks like and how to challenge it); the duty to accommodate (which enables learners to explore case law and prohibited grounds under human rights legislation, to learn to make the case for accommodating employees and developing accommodation measures, and to break down stereotypes and stigma of accommodation); the introduction to allyship (which enables learners to be allies with different marginalized employees and learn more about white supremacy, privileges, and strategies for collective action); essentials for inclusive unions (which examines the concept of unconscious biases, comfort zone, and inclusiveness); safer spaces for Two-Spirit, trans, and non-binary workers (which examines safer workplaces for Two-Spirit, trans and Non-binary employees); sexual violence and harassment at work (which helps learners to recognize sexual harassment and sexual violence, know human rights, roles, and responsibilities, and learn how to deal with and prevent violence and harassment); creating accommodation-friendly workplaces (which emphasizes the legal framework of accommodation and works with employers on this issue); disability and ableism in the workplace (which explore ableism, accessibility, and visible and invisible disabilities); solidarity with Indigenous workers (which explores colonialism and reconciliation); women breaking barriers (which explores the oppression of women, barriers and challenges, and personal leadership) (CUPE, n.d.).

OBSERVATIONS

It is a well-established observation that labour unions have been active in fighting for workers' rights and human rights, and the efforts they have put forward in educating and training workers on anti-racism and human rights are noticeable. However, it is also common to learn from racialized and Indigenous members that there is still a lot of work to be done in educating union executives and members on this front. Racism is a complicated social phenomenon, and, in workplaces, it assumes many features that are not easily noticeable from those found on the street—racist comments and actions are more subtle and more polite; admittedly, there are some blatant and raw interactions that are hard to ignore.

There are also union executives who are less familiar about how racism has developed in white-collar work domains, especially in the advance of micro-aggressions and challenges to White privileges and colonialism. More importantly, with respect to the racial biases embedded in human resources mechanisms, which are the topics of Chapters 6, 7, and 8 in this book, it is much harder to understand the actual extent of the embedded racism and how it is also ingrained in corporate culture and management style. These are harder to "prove" as being discriminatory mainly because some of these phenomena are not quantifiable and the Canadian research data are not easily available. The situation concerning the lack of substantial data on racism is very similar to the situation of gender research studies in the 1960s and 1970s when modern-day feminists had problems "proving" their cases of gender discrimination due to a lack of empirical evidence.

This lack of racism awareness and empirical data on race often gave the impression to racialized and Indigenous union members that their submitted human rights allegations (complaints/grievances) or their views on the racial bias inherent in the union structures and processes have not been whole-heartedly supported by their labour unions. These two deficiencies—a lack of racism awareness and empirical data—are two areas that labour unions need to address among their executives and members. It is a call for more human rights and racism education and training and more research on the status of Indigenous and racialized people and their experiences in the workplace.

Another issue that labour unions have seemed to negate intentionally is seniority. Empirical studies have shown consistently and persistently that they impact on racialized and Indigenous peoples adversely in employment. Our discussion in Chapters 7 and 8 suggests that labour unions' rigidity and semi-rigidity in keeping a seniority system in place for a broad range of positions and their traditional insistence on its supremacy in job movements (transfers), promotions, terminations (lay-offs), recalls, and other employment-related issues have kept racialized and Indigenous people "perpetually" in unfair employment conditions. So far, labour unions have not been prepared to yield on this ground. Ideally, labour unions should find other ways to secure their negotiations and bargaining powers and protect workers and "liberate" racialized and Indigenous workers from this mode of operation. Failing this, labour unions need to find ways to make seniority systems less rigid.

RECOMMENDATIONS

Labour unions may consider various ways to make the workplace more discrimination free through management-union partnerships. To do that, both management and unions must be cognizant of the multiple factors that impact on the workplace, including the general composition of the workforce in terms of race, age, gender, and other prohibited grounds in human rights, the trends of the industry, the types of educational and skill levels of the workforce, the technological level of the company, the wage structure, and others factors that both management and unions are knowledgeable about. Thus, in order to arrive at a solution, both parties must work together as they both have a common understanding of what factors need to be addressed.

Joint Consultation with Employees

In managing human resources, one lesson that has been learned through time is the importance of engaging employees and soliciting their opinions and suggestions on how best to work with them so as to increase the quality of their performance and productivity as well as workplace morale. Therefore, in the interest of all unionized employees, especially racialized and Indigenous peoples and other marginalized groups, unions need to consult with employees as a priority item to be included in the collective agreements. For the purposes of this book, such consultations should be related to human rights, employment equity, anti-racism, and diversity and inclusion.

In working with management, unions may incorporate a consultation process in the collective agreements or a standalone consultation process apart from any collective agreement. In other words, this option should not be part of the collective bargaining process; rather, it should be a separate process with the objective of joining hands with management in consulting employees so that both the unions and management understand the perspectives of employees together without tying consultation to a collective bargaining process. Using either approach, consultation with employees is accomplished. In the context of the tradition of unions' inclination or habit of negotiation in the long history of collective bargaining, unionists have problems collaborating with management without actually negotiating at all. Hence, such collaboration in consulting with employees would be a radical change from the union's past style of bargaining. Given that union-management collaboration is very different from bargaining, unions often resent this kind of cooperation between two parties that have been antagonistic to each other for a long time.

To ensure success one way or another, several factors should be considered when employee consultation is the goal: be specific on how a "consultation" is defined and maintain a common understanding between management and unions: which groups of employees are to be consulted and how anonymity is to be kept; which bargaining agents are to be consulted (especially in larger organizations); what issues are to be consulted; how confidentiality of information is to be kept; how transparent is the consultation; and how communication with employees/bargaining units is to be arranged. If a piece of law is related to employee consultation, the roles of the union and management must be defined clearly in legislation. These are the questions that must be resolved between the two parties.

However, without working with management, unions may also consult with employees to find out the concerns of the employees on issues that are not directly related to social justice. For example, compensation and benefits may be one of the fields that has social justice implications. In preparing for a collective bargaining process, unions may review employee data on wage and benefits and note that racialized or Indigenous employees are paid differently and that their benefits may also have inherent biases. A consultation with employees prior to collective bargaining would help unions negotiate more effectively.

Joint Responsibilities in Employment Equity

For federally regulated industries, the federal *Employment Equity Act* specifies that unions and management have a joint responsibility to work on employment equity in the workplace.[1] There are three major components to employment equity according to the legislation: workforce data collection and analysis; employment systems review; and employment equity planning and implementation. It is recommended that unions to do more in educating employees on the value of employment equity as related to racialized and Indigenous peoples along with other designated groups (women and persons of disabilities) and in communicating and encouraging employees to self-identify in workforce surveys.

In addition, it is recommended that unions do more to engage employees to participate in interviews, focus groups, surveys, and town hall meetings and share their opinions and feedback on their work experience with their employers. There is evidence that some employers complete their employment systems reviews in a half-hearted manner; hence, their review findings are not informative or insightful. Some employers often skip their reviews altogether, as required after their workforce data collection and analysis. The federal government (that is, the Canadian Human Rights Commission) may not even be aware of some employers' lack of employment systems reviews as they do not audit federally regulated employers when their workforce data findings show that they are well represented in most occupational groups in

1 *Employment Equity Act*, SC 1995, c 44.

the organizations. Unions must monitor and ensure that employment equity reviews be regularly carried out to identify employment barriers for racialized and Indigenous employees.

Since an employment equity plan prevails over all relevant collective agreements, if and when inconsistencies are detected, it is in the interest of the union to be involved in the development of any provisions in the employment equity plan that might affect the collective agreement rights. Unions, if not every employee, should ensure that the goals and timetables for hiring and promotion of employment equity designated groups are reasonable on a yearly basis. Furthermore, unions and the employees must also monitor the extent to which employers are removing employment barriers and implementing the employment equity plan with sufficient effort. The federal Employment Equity Tribunal has the power to revise an employment equity plan that prevails over a collective agreement whenever inconsistencies are identified. The revised version of the plan has implications for employees who are covered by a collective agreement. In relation to employment equity, the tribunal has the power to order an amendment to the collective agreement whenever the orders are not strong enough to ensure compliance with the *Employment Equity Act*. Given the power of the tribunal, it makes sense for unions to be engaged in the employment equity planning process.

Unions must remember that the joint responsibilities of unions and management in employment equity are distinct from the collective bargaining process and that the legislated employment equity standards cannot be traded off for other concessions in collective bargaining. One of the key strategies for employees and unions is to establish a management-union partnership on key items related to human rights. It is a joint responsibility between the two parties on agreeable items within the legal confines of labour relations and human rights legislation.

The benefits of such a partnership is that, when the two parties work together for the well-being of their employees, whether they are racialized, Indigenous or not, items such as training and development, occupational health and safety, workplace violence and respect, employee and management conduct, employee engagement and inclusion, harassment and discrimination, diversity representation, compensation and benefits, accommodation, and many others could be elevated to a level where employers and employees' interests are balanced to achieve better labour relations, human rights, diversity and inclusion, employment equity, anti-racism, and other social justice goals.

Take accommodation as an example, both employers and unions have the duty to accommodate employees short of undue hardship. Some racialized employees need to have their religious observances, and, in some workplaces, work rules in the collective agreements (such as a requirement for employees to work on Saturday) may jeopardize religious observance for some racialized employees. In issues related to accommodation, unions cannot be a bystander with the assumption that the employers have the sole responsibility to accommodate. Meanwhile, employers may find it helpful when unions are involved in accommodation especially when accommodation is arranged on a collective level to enhance the performance of an entire racialized group or Indigenous group. Partnerships can be carried out in good faith, trust, and transparency by both the unions and employers. Collective bargaining is not the only means to establish a partnership, and collective agreements are not the only instruments through which collaboration can be developed.

There are values in partnership building, and it can be carried out in various formats:

- formally incorporating the joint responsibilities for selected items in the collective agreements;
- meeting of the two parties on how best to meet their obligations, including setting a structure (such as a committee or task force), agreeing on the goals, mission, time frame, and composition of the structure to tackle the issues; and
- sharing information on pertinent issues of mutual interests when they are related to racialized and Indigenous people or other marginalized groups in the workplace.

If and when a structure (such as a committee) is created to collaborate on human rights issues or complaints between management and unions ,and if the structure and process of human rights issues or complaints are clearly communicated to employees and both parties agree to ensure that its mandate is carried out with proper resources, the structure may focus on its proactive mechanism in making the workplace discrimination free and build up a respectful climate of human rights and simultaneously develop its reactive mechanism in response to human rights grievances. Leaving the option open for employees or unions to file claims to human rights tribunals, such an in-house human rights structure and process would be beneficial for the employees.

Historically, management and unions have been considered to be antagonistic to each other as they have opposing interests. This basic tendency has not changed too much, and the management-union relationship in some industries is quite negative. It has not been the general or common practice for management and unions to consult with each other, and it would pose legal questions in the process of collective bargaining if consultation was made compulsory or the word "negotiation" was replaced with "consultation." A legally binding arrangement may prove to be legally challenging for enforcement purposes. For social justice issues, formal management-union consultation may prove to be beneficial.

In a non-unionized workplace, an internal human rights mechanism to address human rights claims or complaints would be beneficial to employees and employers. Through this mechanism, employers may monitor the status of human rights as experienced by employees, especially racialized or Indigenous employees. In addition, employees may get their complaints resolved internally sooner if there is management expertise in human rights and a streamlined process that is acceptable to both employees and management instead of waiting for the human rights agency to respond. To ensure that the internal human rights mechanism works, employee representatives or their association representatives are well represented in the governance and operation of this mechanism. Employee input is crucial to the success of any internal human rights mechanism because employees who have experiences with this kind of mechanism have found that they often do not yield much positive changes because the mechanism is largely designed and controlled by management without much input from the employees.

Strengthen Union's Roles in Human Rights Education and Training

Union members have expressed a demand for unions to strengthen human rights education and training for all employees, especially those representing the unions. This kind of education and training could be conducted by the union alone if resources are available. However, it is also feasible and, in fact, desirable for both the employer and the union to jointly be responsible for human rights education and training. One way to introduce this approach is to put it in writing in a collective agreement. It is in the interest of both employers and unions (and employees) to have human rights education and training: human rights education and training enables employees to know the rights of their co-workers and their own rights; it is also important for employers because having this kind of knowledge enables employees to know the human rights law and increase the chance for them to obey the law and show respect to each other. If this line of thinking is correct, the workplace should be more respectful.

In this context, there is a difference between "education" and "training." Human rights education offers a process for employees to learn the basic principles of human rights, prohibited grounds of discrimination, social areas in which human rights are legally observed, the roles and responsibilities of employers and employees, the legal rights of people at work, the basic concepts of human rights and their meanings: discrimination, harassment, accommodation, and undue hardship. Education is the process of enabling everyone at the workplace to know the general framework of the human rights law.

However, human rights training is a step further for people who have basic knowledge of the legal framework and have an obligation at the workplace to practise human rights. Human rights training is built on the knowledge gained through the educational process mentioned earlier. Who are the people who need human rights training? Human resources professionals including human rights specialists, DEI specialists, executives, managers and supervisors of different divisions, departments, work units or agencies, and union representatives all provide supports to employees when they want to find a solution to their concerns, allegations, and alleged discrimination or harassment. They need to have the skills to help employees navigate when they allegedly confront "biases," "discrimination," or "harassment," no matter what form they take. In the context of unions helping employees, training includes skills development in learning how to help employees to identify human rights issues, how they properly document human rights incidents (such as racial slurs or being passed over in job competitions), how to collect evidence to "prove" their cases, what processes that they have to take in the grievance process, what the time frame of the grievance process is, what witnesses are needed, and how to write up a formal grievance.

Playing a More Active Role in Getting Justice for Individual Union Members

Union members have expressed a call for unions to negotiate harder for their members, especially putting in place mechanisms to identify employment barriers for racialized or Indigenous people in addition to other marginalized groups. Furthermore, unions must eradicate discriminatory practices found in a broad range of human resources functions, including hiring and promotion policies, procedures, and practices; training and developmental opportunities; performance evaluation system, coaching, and mentoring; succession planning; termination (lay-off) and recall; and compensation and benefits.

Based on consultations with union members, union negotiators should negotiate with employers on what employees consider to be positive and supportive measures and include them in collective agreements. "Positive measures" (such as skills upgrading programs or credential acceleration programs) are programs or initiatives that help racialized and Indigenous employees to gain fair treatment and equitable status in human resources functions on an interim basis until such time as they become competitive on par with other employees. "Supportive measures" (such as peer support programs or coaching) are those programs or initiatives that facilitate racialized and Indigenous employees to gain and maintain momentum in advancing their careers or in securing their jobs.

These two types of measures are quite important for racialized and Indigenous people because, without them, the workplace is not equitable enough for them to compete for jobs or get fairer treatment. Clearly, in a unionized environment, through the collective bargaining process, unions can push further for a discrimination-free workplace.

At the individual level, unions could also work through a grievance and arbitration process to get justice for union members. However, the success of unions in fighting for employees' human rights depends on the legal knowledge of human rights of union representatives as well as that of employees. Not knowing too much about the case law often puts the union and the employees in a disadvantaged position in the grievance process. As discussed in the previous subsection on human rights education and training, a more sophisticated and comprehensive understanding of human rights legislation and case law can strengthen the arguments of the union and employees and better their chance of success. There are also benefits for employers too as the grievance and arbitration process allows unions and them to work out a solution without involving the government as a third party—a solution that fits better for their workplace.

However, to get justice for individual union members or for a collective group such as racialized and Indigenous people, such "localization" of human rights grievances for individual workplaces needs at least two preconditions so that social justice could be awarded for these two marginalized group members. Both the union representatives who handle the human rights case(s) and the arbitrators who are responsible for the case(s) must be familiar with the intricacies of human rights cases so that human rights are not delegated to be secondary in priority. Here, employees as citizens may have to play an active role in pushing the government to instill stronger human rights training for public sector arbitrators and lawyers dealing with collective agreements. Such training must be mandated for arbitrators and associated lawyers, and they must be certified to adjudicate collective agreements with human rights components according to the standardized tools and procedures aligned with those used in the human rights tribunals.

Even though employees and unions could grieve about discrimination cases, they could also file a claim under the human rights legislation. In case the employees and unions do take these two options, it makes sense for the grievance and arbitration processes to proceed first, followed by the claim-filing process to the human right tribunal, if the employees and unions elect to do so. It is possible that the arbitration process may be partially faulty or that the arbitrator has not examined the case thoroughly, and so letting the case go through the tribunal process may ensure that justice is reached. Meanwhile, the employers and unions may jointly collaborate in developing internal procedures related human rights grievances. However, the resulting procedures may not be viewed by employees as fair or legitimate and that there are no standards on internal procedures in the organizations. In the final analysis, employees must have the option of filing a human rights claim with the human rights tribunal or using internal workplace human rights procedures.

Be Innovative in Seniority Issues

Seniority Exemptions

While seniority is a sacred cow in collective bargaining, unionists seemed to be finding new ways to remove or neutralize its negative impacts by creating different seniority categories so as to circumvent the rigidity of the seniority system. The idea behind these categories is to make it more flexible to get around the classic "absolute" (or straight) seniority that it imposes on the workplace reality. These seniority types are useful only when they are incorporated in collective agreements. The first two are to protect union officials and younger employees, while the third one is to help racialized and Indigenous peoples.

- "Super-seniority" is assigned to higher positions on the seniority lists for all union officials. The aim is to ensure they do not get laid off. This type of seniority does not help to rectify the disadvantaged position of racialized and Indigenous people as they seldom reach the status of union officials in the past.
- "Reverse seniority" is applicable when young (and junior) employees are assigned more seniority so that they do not get laid off due to their short length of service in the company. Such assignment is created so that more young (and junior) persons can replace retired employees.
- "Retroactive seniority" is given to people who do not have the duration of service in the company, but they are given this type of seniority with the objective of compensating them as a result of their past discrimination at work. The seniority is given to them on the date that they were supposed to get the positions if they were not discriminated against. Theoretically, this type of seniority does make it more equitable for racialized and Indigenous people if this occurs; however, empirical evidence is not readily available to confirm this.

In protecting effectively racialized and Indigenous peoples in the workplace, the key measure is to make a statement in the collective agreements that seniority rules are not to be applied to them. For example, a statement could be explicitly made that in all cases where hiring, promotion, job transfer, termination and recall from lay-off, racialized and Indigenous peoples are to be considered provided that they have the skills to work, irrespective of their seniority. Only when this policy is clearly stated in the agreement can one get an affirmative result that overcomes the discrimination that is embedded in the workplace.

Another way to enable racialized and Indigenous employees to compete more equitably with other employees is to credit them with seniority years that resemble the average of the seniority within the job classification, provided that they have the competency needed for the position that they are competing for in the promotion and job transfer of which they are under-represented, along with lay-off or recall when they are in question. When such a clause is inserted in the collective agreements, it might make the job competitions more equitable under the seniority systems.

An additional measure to enable Indigenous employees to address the shortcomings of the seniority system is to accommodate their traditional cultural needs such as rice harvesting, trapping, and hunting by allowing them to take longer leaves of absence and still maintain their seniority during these leaves. To do that, the system needs to incorporate such arrangements in the collective agreements, or one may incorporate a different clause in the collective agreements for Indigenous people to waive the seniority requirement for the positions for which they wish to compete, thus giving them access to positions that are beyond their seniority years.

To increase the chance for racialized and Indigenous employees in seniority systems in which they are in disadvantaged position is for the employers to adopt a policy to promote employees internally, especially when racialized and Indigenous employees are "ghettoized" in jobs at the lower levels. Such a policy would "force" employers to promote these disadvantaged employees before hiring from outside. The policy would also enable these disadvantaged employees to compete with other employees even though their current seniority level normally does not allow for this. It is important to note that such a policy would only work in an enterprise-wide seniority system; guaranteed wages would be unchanged for the positions irrespective of who wins the competitions and under which seniority systems they come from; and training programs would be developed for racialized and Indigenous employees once they are successful in their job competitions. Internal training programs that would help to "bridge" racialized and Indigenous employees who do not have the technical skills or experience are essential for their transition or promotions.

Moreover, there is an occupational hierarchy based on seniority that requires employees to move from a lower position to a higher position, one step at a time through a series of positions in a prescribed line of promotion. This hierarchy must be removed so that racialized and Indigenous employees or any other employee can apply irrespective of their seniority rights using their enterprise-wide seniority as opposed to their work unit-based occupational seniority. Once this seniority system is dismantled, racialized and Indigenous employees would be freer to get promotions. In addition, in terms of promotions and job transfers, in order to allow racialized and Indigenous employees to have an equitable chance to succeed, unions must ensure that collective agreements are inclusive of a more flexible seniority system. This is especially the case for racialized employees with a higher educational level who have historically been marginalized and under-utilized in their competency and not able to secure positions due to their lack of seniority in the organization. While management has a tendency to favour a narrower version of seniority such as departmental or work-unit seniority for promotions and even horizontal transfers because employees with a longer work history in the department or work unit are more familiar with the special localized work culture and locational specific knowledge and skills, unions may wish to secure broader seniority units (such as enterprise-wide seniority) and a more flexible version of modest or mild seniority systems (such as a mix of knowledge, skills, and other selection factors and not just absolute or straight seniority) so that more of their members can be eligible and competitive for advancement.

Elimination of the Last-in-First-out Rule

Historically, similar to women, Indigenous and racialized peoples are discriminated against. They are usually the last group of people to get hired, and, due to the constraints of the historical seniority clause, they have the least senirority—hence, they are the first to get terminated. For these unique historical reasons (due to seniority requirement), they are discriminated against. They are the "last in, first out" in employment.

Unions should also push to eliminate the "last-in-first-out" (LIFO) rule in seniority systems, which is discriminatory unless seniority is adjusted for racialized and Indigenous employees as if they had not been discriminated. This is harder than it seems since not only is it difficult to trace back when they first applied the positions in which they were discriminated in the same company, but it is also difficult to assume that they have the competency to do the jobs for which they first applied. One solution is to assume that their seniority is equal to the average seniority of non-racialized and non-Indigenous employees of the same age. Although this is an approximation, it tends to resemble the seniority of non-marginalized employees. In this manner, when racialized or Indigenous employees are to be promoted to another position, even under an enterprise-wide seniority system, they should be immediately formally credited with the seniority years equal to the average seniority within the classification of the position to which the employee has been promoted, thus avoiding the fate of the LIFO rule, which is discriminatory in nature.

Another way to make the employment system fairer and equitable for younger marginalized employees under the seniority system is to ensure that the proportion of lay-offs of younger racialized or Indigenous employees is similar to that of older employees before and after the lay-offs. In this manner, younger marginalized employees would not be disproportionately penalized due to their younger age and usually lower seniority years even though the crediting method mentioned above is in effect. Unions may also try other ways to alleviate the pain of lay-offs and, at the same time, ensure fairness to racialized and Indigenous employees, which might include the elimination of overtime work and hiring freeze; converting some permanent full-time positions to part-time positions; the elimination of temporary work; the lowering of the retirement age; the use of vacation times ahead of their schedule; the sharing of work among employees; and the requiring of employees on pay-roll to fill subcontract positions or outright banning of subcontracting positions.

Unions have a tendency to treat individual seniority as if it relates to the duration of employment in specific work units or departments. Thus, when individuals move from one unit/department to another one, their seniority must be recalibrated again. This often works to the disadvantage of racialized or Indigenous peoples, especially when their seniority is usually shorter than that of White people because, historically, they were not hired equitably or promoted in a broad spectrum of industries. This also means that their seniority is so limited that they hesitate to apply for jobs either in terms of horizontal transfers or vertical promotions lest their seniority be jeopardized with this job mobility. Therefore, in order to break away from this problem in seniority, unions may consider in times of lay-offs:

- using an enterprise-wide or plant-wide seniority model, with bumping allowed for some related occupational groups;
- selecting employees with fewer than ten years of company services may be bumped within their departments and those with more than ten years of services may utilize their bumping rights within their company;
- specifying a department unit for temporary lay-offs and an enterprise-wide unit for permanent lay-offs due to technological or some business restructuring changes;

- calculating seniority based on different seniority units such as using enterprise-wide seniority to determine departmental seniority only when employees with a specified long duration of services in the company and those with shorter duration of company services would not be counted in the departmental seniority; and
- utilizing portable seniority among bargaining units with the same employer or group of employers in the same industry (a system of how portability would work could be developed and agreed upon upfront prior to lay-offs).

These are examples of options available to make seniority rights more flexible, and they could be used to ensure that racialized or Indigenous employees are not jeopardized in a rigid seniority system that essentially puts them at a disadvantaged position when lay-offs occur.

Accommodation

Accommodation is one of the ways in which unions (and employers) can address the discriminatory implications of seniority rights in a unionized environment. It is commonly understood that both unions and employers have a duty to accommodate up to the point of undue hardship. Accommodation measures, if implemented, constitute a substantial departure from the terms and conditions of employment as defined in the collective agreement, which may be interpreted as undue hardship in the business operation of the employers. Similarly, high expences for accommodation or the disruption of the operation of the unions may also be considered as undue hardship for employers. However, a prevailing attitude among employees that is at odds with a human rights code and its spirit could not be construed as posing undue hardship on the employers. Employers therefore cannot use racial prejudice or opposition among employees as a reason for not accommodating.

Meanwhile, unions also need to accommodate racialized, Indigenous, and other employees up to the point of undue hardship. But their "undue hardship" is different from that for employers. Unions have to consider how the accommodation measures impact on other employees and not just on the individual complainant. The question for the unions should be: would the accommodation measures discriminate or interfere with the rights of other employees? Therefore, the duty to reasonable accommodation short of undue hardship remains unresolved if the accommodation measures mean that the seniority rights of other union members have to be waived or modified. And would this be an "undue hardship" for the unions?

It is clear that the federal employment equity legislation deems seniority not to be an employment barrier, but it is unclear whether seniority is viewed as discriminatory or not in the context of human rights legislation, federal or province wise. In areas in which the law is unclear, unions and employers may need to develop policies for clarification (Lace 1995, 15–20). In addition, unions and employers cannot set up work rules that are discriminatory and incorporate them into the collective agreement. All provisions in the collective agreement are drawn up by the two parties. Therefore, unions must take responsibility to ensure that reasonable accommodation is provided for employees, and if unions are not cooperating with an employer's accommodation for an employee, they are, in essence, participating in the discriminatory act, either in policy making or in practice. Hence, unions must contribute to not discriminating employees by working with the employers to accommodate short of undue hardship. Unions cannot stand aside and do nothing even under these circumstances, though they do not have the initial responsibility of accommodation.

Support Networks for Racialized and Indigenous Peoples

In larger organizations nowadays, with the blessing of employers, employees have an opportunity to form their own "employee resource groups" (or "affinity groups"). The aims of these groups vary: fuller employee engagement, better professional development, more opportunities for career advancement, more frequent interfacing with management, and richer networking and relationship building. Some place higher priority on one or two of these aims, and some have a mix of all of them. These employee resource groups are organized under the banner of diversity, equity, and inclusiveness, and they tend to be organized around their identities. These identities could include gender, race, ability, age, sex, sexual orientation, sexual identity and expression, and Indigeneity.

Each one of these identity groups has their own common themes in their work experience that results in particular issues related to them alone and some common issues that are shared with other identity groups. For example, many Indigenous employees are keenly concerned about the negative impacts of colonialism and are struggling to regain their dignity after their traumatic experiences in residential schools. They have been marginalized and isolated at work and do not have much confidence to take initiatives or express their viewpoints in meetings or teamwork. Meanwhile, many racialized employees are deeply concerned about the lack of recognition for their contributions to the organizations and are constantly undermined and undervalued by their co-workers and management. Under these circumstances, unions may play a more active role in giving them support in encouraging them to be more engaged and participatory at work, in helping them to get the professional development opportunities that they need, in securing coaching and mentoring experience with management, in advancing them in their career paths, in interfacing with management, and in networking with other employees as well as building relationships with management. Unions can do all the above by providing support to employee resource groups in their collective agreements on specific matters pertinent to racialized and Indigenous people:

- in working with management, racialized and Indigenous employees can identify employment barriers and discriminatory practices that are embedded in human resources policies, programs, and practices;
- developing resources materials on the nature of racism and how racialized and Indigenous employees can support each other, the importance of allyship, and the availability of coaching and mentoring;
- enabling unions and employers to work together and organize events to promote awareness among employees on the plights of racialized and Indigenous employees and how best to raise awareness and cooperation among employees;
- negotiating with employers to prepare career paths of different occupations (or occupational groups) in the organization so that racialized and Indigenous employees can find their paths to advancement as well as other employees; and
- securing a fair share of opportunities for professional development and relationship building with management for racialized and Indigenous employees so that they are not left out.

These are a few suggestions that employee resource groups may wish to incorporate for their organizations. When unions are able to support these groups' mandates, they can strengthen their networks and, in turn, consolidate the supports of these racialized and Indigenous employees.

Allyship Development and Learning Circles

One of the most noticeable work experiences that racialized and Indigenous employees have is isolation and marginalization. As a result, they do not have a sense of belonging to the "work team," and, for some, their productivity and quality of performance declines. In a unionized work environment, wherever there are racialized and Indigenous employees as well as other non-racialized and non-Indigenous employees, unions could actively encourage allyship formation among the latter employees and build a more caring, supportive, and inclusive workplace. There are several activities or programs that unions could implement to facilitate the growth of allyship:

- establish an allyship program that identifies non-racialized and non-Indigenous employees who are willing to be allies with racialized and Indigenous employees in building a discrimination-free and inclusive workplace;
- develop a learning program for allies with adequate resource materials and trainers in support of racialized and Indigenous employees and campaign for their rights and fair treatment;
- work with racialized and Indigenous employees to develop and implement networking opportunities with allies; and
- develop coaching and mentoring opportunities for racialized and Indigenous employees utilizing the expertise of their allies.

CONCLUSION

Labour unions play an important role for employees in the workplace, especially in a unionized environment. They can advocate workers' and human rights for employees and negotiate with employers on behalf of employees in collective bargaining. There are several levels of unions—national, provincial, and local unions in Canada. National and provincial union organizations are more focused on political actions, policy directions, and power consolidations of multiple unions in a broad range of public and private sectors. The CLC, Unifor, and CUPE have been cited as examples. All of them have their emphasis on social justice, including human rights, equity, diversity, and inclusiveness with special reference to racialized and Indigenous peoples, along with other marginalized groups. Local unions can focus on negotiating better terms for their members in their collective agreements.

Unionists have been working hard on consolidating their human rights work in collective agreements, fighting for individual members' human rights, promoting education and training in human rights for their members, and advocating for more consultations with employees. Unfortunately, seniority rights are a central principle for labour unions. The seniority systems that unions have set up contain many complicated issues, are highly rigid in their application, and have placed a lot of restraints on human resources, including promotions and job transfers, lay-offs and recall, and employee benefits. For racialized and Indigenous employees, seniority systems have slowed down or even hindered the struggle for equality for racialized and Indigenous peoples. Until seniority rights cease to be the foundational principle of union work, this book recommends several measures for unions to adopt in order to speed up the process of social justice in employment: unions must establish a partnership with employers on social justice issues (as in joint responsibility in implementing employment equity); unions' roles in human rights education and training must be strengthened; unions must play a more active role in getting justice for individual members; and unions must be innovative in modifying seniority systems, including creating exceptions, removing the LIFO rule, instituting accommodations, supporting networks for racialized and Indigenous employees, and developing allyship and learning circles.

PART FOUR

NEW CHALLENGES, NEW DIRECTIONS

Part 4 summarizes the evidence and arguments puts forward in this book and places them in an organizational and global context. Internally, organizations have their own constraining and distorting forces when individuals fight against racism—namely, employee resistance against the diversity, equity, and inclusiveness (DEI). Vested interest from different departments may also pose barriers for organizations to remove embedded racist biases in the system. Getting external assistance is one way to remove racism. As an anti-racism action, boycotts are discussed in detail.

Externally, organizations are surrounded by many political, social, and technological forces, chief among them are geopolitical conflict; growing authoritarianism, illiberalism, and populism; hate crimes, hate speech, and violence; rising challenges to DEI and the anti-wokeism movement; and the transformative nature of artificial intelligence with all its biases. Racism is expanding its reach and intensity with the support of these forces. Due to the macroscopic nature of these forces, it is recommended that all three parties—governments, employers, and labour unions—collaborate closely in combating racism, and, more importantly, in times of crises, that there is an urgency to fight racism. The key words in fighting racism are collectivity and urgency.

CHAPTER 12

Fighting Racism from Within

This chapter summarizes and reviews the key messages of the book so far. It shows how racism is ingrained in human minds and employment systems. To reshape the workplace, governments, employers, unions, (and employees) must focus on different approaches and implementation issues in addressing racism and achieving fairness and equity for racialized and Indigenous peoples.

This is despite the legislation, policies, and programs instituted by various government levels in fighting workplace racism and pushing for a better work environment; employers' compliance with the law and their establishment of human resources management systems aiming to make the workplace discrimination free and more equitable; and labour unions also fighting for worker rights and human rights and putting additional efforts into diversity, equity, and inclusiveness (DEI). Progress made by these three parties has been promising at times. Overall, considering the resources and efforts that they have made in addressing racism and building a fairer work environment, this progress has still been sporadic in nature and glacial in pace.

So far, several recommendations have been put forward in this book to address the shortcomings and blind spots noted in the work of governments, employers, and unions. Each of them has been mostly working on its own to wrestle with the enormous century-old system of racism that has been too ingrained to remove. In this chapter, we are taking a fresher look at racism and anti-racism again and identifying some salient and emerging features. This time, we will be more holistic and critical in seeing whether we have been running on a "treadmill" of anti-racism, and we will examine:

- the workplace power structure as a restraining force;
- the DEI ideology as a distorting force;
- the resistance to DEI and anything that is anti-racism; and
- the rise of artificial intelligence (AI).

WORKPLACE RACISM AND ITS COUNTER FORCES

The empirical data cited in this book clearly show that racism is an integral part of the experiences of racialized and Indigenous peoples in Canada. They have more of a chance of being discriminated against in the workplace and, indeed, throughout their life cycles. Prior to being hired and during their tenure in the workplace, they face employment barriers with discriminatory features inherent in human resources policies, mechanisms, and tools of their organizations. While national statistics show that they are cognizant of racial discrimination in segments of the population, employee satisfaction survey results of individual companies usually show that racialized and Indigenous employees are less convinced about racial discrimination than what is found in Canadian national polls. This difference in survey findings on the perception of racialized and Indigenous peoples on discrimination is noticeable, especially in light of the meticulous analysis of the stereotypes and prejudice in the workplace as well as the biased nature of human resources mechanisms established in the workplace.

Racialized and Indigenous employees' relative weak verbalized awareness of racism at work suggests two forces that are at work here: the power structure of the workplace and the corporate DEI ideology. It is feasible that racial biases are inherent in the human resources mechanisms but that its discriminatory features are very subtle and not easily recognizable.

Let these forces be made clearer in the following sections.

Workplace Power Structures as a Restraining Forces

Most workplaces are hierarchical with a power structure. Smaller organizations are flatter in their structure, and their levels of authority are limited. They also have organizational policies, procedures, programs, and practices. Along with their organizational cultures, they take on the roles of maintaining employees' behaviour in alignment with their organizational vision, norms, and rules. In the public sector, deputy ministers and high-level bureaucrats usually follow the instructions of the elected politicians in power in shaping the government policies and programs. In the private sector and non-profit sector, boards of directors or governors usually provide strategic policy directions to their workforces, and their executives and managers carry out those directions, while non-management staff members implement them. Corporate policies, procedures, programs, and practices are enforced sets of rewards and punishments, and employees' activities are monitored, measured, and reviewed regularly. In a work environment with a power structure, racism may be analyzed on two levels: individual and organizational.

Individual Level

At the level of individual employees, based on the discussion in Part 2 of this book, it is clear that racism, in the form of negative attitudes and stereotyping as well as biased organizational policies and programs, structures, and processes, is an integral part of an organization. Not all organizations manifest racism in the same way, and the intensity and severity of racism also varies. Employees must manage racism as they observe or experience it in a way that does not jeopardize their relationship with their managers and co-workers.

Working in a structure of authority requires racialized and Indigenous employees to reflect and analyze each interaction with the people around them and to comply with organizational policies and procedures with caution. They may interpret some of their daily encounters and what and how they are treated as signs of racism. The interpretations of how people speak/talk and how people act in a workplace resemble a "mind game" because there are no rigid rules on behaviour as long as they are viewed as respectful, non-violent, legal, and legitimate.

In an organization in which values, visions, and norms are said to be in line with the principles of DEI, it makes the interpretation of social interaction at work not as easy as it may seem. This is because (1) terms such as DEI are not uniformly understood by people in the same manner and (2) the organizational DEI culture does not progress evenly. This means that all executives, managers, and employees have different expectations of how people should behave at work, which becomes quite tricky when "racism" is under scrutiny in an organization with

DEI as its ideology. There might not be a consensus of what "racism" is all about.

There are many instances on a daily basis in which some racialized and Indigenous persons feel that they have been discriminated or harassed against or that the policies and programs that they have to abide by are biased and could be defined as racially biased. In spite of this, they are not prepared to stick their heads out and "cry racism" whenever they are uncertain that there are racist elements in their encounters or even racial tones. They are not able to confront or strike a conversation with their supervisors, managers, or executives about this issue, especially when the conflict resolution mechanism is not in place to deal with "racial" issues. The power dynamic in the work hierarchy requires racialized and Indigenous employees to be very careful of what they say about anything related to "race." Race is a sensitive topic. Negative ramifications (such as social ostracism, isolation, revenge, and so on) may surface when management or co-workers react to allegations of racism.

Any explicit uttering of the word "racism" is a serious matter because allegations of this nature require not only courage but also an immense need for evidence. There are instances of ambiguity in daily encounters that leave racialized and Indigenous employees to puzzle over their "racial" components. No one in the organization is prepared to help them to interpret their daily work experiences and confirm that they have or have not been discriminated against.

The persons who have alleged discrimination must bear the responsibility of proving that the allegations are on firm ground. Without evidence, the allegers may lose all creditability. Meanwhile, such ambiguities, when accumulated day in and day out, increase the stress level of racialized and Indigenous employees. They are not easily resolvable, even when they exchange notes among themselves, talk with their spouses, relatives, or friends, or talk with experts in DEI or human rights. Both the confirmation of their suspicions and the reduction of their stress lie in the collection of relevant data and credible testimonies, and this may take time and effort. It is not something that can be accomplished in a matter of days, weeks, or even months. Hence, anxiety, paranoia, suspicion, irritation, and anger continue to simmer inside their psyche, and, if they persist, it definitely impacts on their work performance and quality of life both in their workplaces and at home.

For many employees, the workplace is a place where they spend seven or more hours a day, five days a week. Some spend more, even on the weekends, and some spend fewer hours if they are on contract or are working part-time. Apart from sleeping hours and hours spent at home or for leisure, people spend a significant portion of their lives at work.

These working hours have implications for these employees. First, employment is their source of income, which brings food to their tables and pays for other expences for their livelihoods. Second, the workplace is also a place where employees work with each other, usually in small circles of co-workers day in and day out. Thus, when racialized and Indigenous sense or observe that something that is considered to be racist has happened to them or other employees in the workplace, they may react to the incidents immediately, but, most likely, they digest what has just happened and ask the following questions: what has actually taken place; was it a racist act; who were the "offenders"; who were the victims; were there witnesses around? But when the incidents happen to specific employees, they will have two key questions subject to reflection many times over in their heads: (1) should these incidents be reported to the management and (2) should they confront the "offenders"?

The fact that the livelihood of employees depends on the work offered by the employer and their working relationship with other employees means that they must be cautious about an allegation of "racism" related to the "offenders." The workplace has its power dynamics. There are multiple networks among employees, networks between managers and employees, and networks among managers and executives. These networks of people generate their opinions over a sensitive matter like race and racism in an unpredictable manner. Once it becomes "public" and reverberates in the hallways and on the floors of the workplace, management and individual employees must be extra careful in how they handle the allegation as an item of gossip.

Since an allegation of "racism" has its implications on employee's morale, engagement, performance, and productivity, it is important for employees to think twice before taking the next step in tackling the issue at hand. Thus, workplace racism, even as an allegation, has a magnitude of individual ramifications and organizational consequences. It upsets employees and destabilizes the work environment.

Anti-racism efforts of an organization are often determined by the magnitude and intensity of the employees' complaints or outcries and the external pressures from industrial peers, law enforcers, government policies/legislation, and community protests. At the individual level, the power structure of an organization exerts tremendous restraining forces on individual employees to keep their mouths shut. Employee resources groups and labour unions may play a role in exposing racial biases or racist conduct to the higher level of the authority structure, and it is up to that level to determine whether some changes are needed or not. As for individual experiences, the power structure tends to diminish the voices of racialized and Indigenous peoples; unless the organization has a formal conflict resolution mechanism in place, often individual complaints are limited to small circles of colleagues (co-workers) at most and most of the time, these complaints are bottled up. Hence, anti-racism efforts from the organization are limited. If the organization has a DEI policy or program, the best that it can do is to continue its usual DEI activities, which, in the minds of racialized and Indigenous employees, really do not have much impact on eradicating workplace racism.

Organizational Level

At the organizational level, workplace racism, as embedded in corporate strategies, policies, programs, procedures, structures, and processes (discussed in Part 2 of this book), represents the results of group thinking and the group interests of its top executives. Organizational leadership and its departmental interests may perpetuate the embedded workplace racism. These racial biases undermine the long-term goals of social justice as represented in the DEI management approach. This is because strategies, policies, programs, procedures, structures, and processes are developed with the interest of achieving other organizational goals (such as making profits or building a customer base) in addition to the corporate DEI management. Each department or work unit has a vested interest in facilitating that achievement of their own interest.

For example, to increase business profits in the private sector organization, a production unit is interested in getting workers who can produce high quality products with proper skills, and the sales department is interested in assembling a team of salespersons who can identify the sources of potential customers and have the communication skills to get the products sold fast. For these reasons, community outreach and the recruitment of human resources becomes a priority item for the organization. Given that the human resources department has limited staff members, recruiting racialized and Indigenous peoples with different skill sets for different departments (such as production and sales) would need a lot of effort from the human resources department. Sometimes, it is a strain on the staff members of the human resources department to acquire different talents as they may come from different sources.

Streamlining these efforts necessitates skewing the recruitment process in a certain direction that might jeopardize the chance of recruiting racialized or Indigenous peoples. As a result, there are "winners and losers" in departments that need racialized or Indigenous peoples. A case in point is that when organizations need candidates with a broader range of skills for different departments, they focus largely on university (not college or hiring halls) recruitment, making them "successful" in getting professionals (such as salespersons and marketers) and "unsuccessful" in finding qualified tradespersons and technicians (such as welders and appliance producers). This streamlining of recruitment efforts for racialized and Indigenous peoples has implications on diversifying the workforce because a higher proportion of Indigenous peoples in post-secondary education are found at colleges or hiring halls, not at universities. Recruitment methods that focus on universities may negate the chance of recruiting more Indigenous peoples from colleges.

Not using college recruitment means less chance of hiring Indigenous peoples to do technical production in the organization. The recruitment bias (recruitment streamlining) is an employment barrier for Indigenous peoples and is a part of the larger systemic racism across organizations in Canada. It boils down to not recruiting from pools of qualified Indigenous tradespersons or Indigenous potential trades graduates from colleges. It may start off as a money-saving decision in cutting corners in recruitment and outreach. It might reflect a blind spot in DEI group mentality due largely to a lack of accurate information of where Indigenous peoples with technical and trades skills are. It might also be related to the organizational inertia in hiring university (not college) graduates for the organization's co-operative program, and those managing these co-operative programs have yielded good results in the past and might see no reason to change their traditional targets on universities or include colleges for a change.

In reviewing organizational policies, strategies, programs, procedures, structures, and processes, it is not difficult to find examples of this nature. Past policy or program successes beget institutional inertia in making any new changes; hence, blind spots become racial biases and are gradually built into the human resources mechanisms in recruitment methods, job posting tools, selection procedures, training and development protocols, background checking processes, and so on. Often, it takes more than employee complaints about these biases or self-reflection on the part of human resources department to identify the source(s) of biases. Each of these biases often reflects the interests of the stakeholder groups (such as departments) and why they see the biases as a business necessity to the point that the biases remain where they are so that the stakeholder groups can achieve larger corporate goals (such as profits or market share). Under these circumstances, the final decision of keeping these racial biases or finding alternatives must be escalated upwards to the top executives or even the board directors.

Racism at the organizational level is harder to tackle since it is ingrained in corporate culture, policies, programs, structures, and processes. It often represents blind spots and the interest of stakeholder groups' interest within the organization. Due to the fact that racism is ingrained, it takes longer to discover and identify it, but it is often hard to prove unless empirical evidence (data) is collected and made available, and it is harder to eradicate this racism as the decision must be escalated to the top executives or board directors if it is major.

If the organization has DEI as its corporate vision or management approach, anti-racism efforts could be subsumed under the DEI umbrella. However, in the eyes of racialized and Indigenous employees, the DEI umbrella seldom deals with extensive or deep racism issues (such as systemic biases in promotion or succession policies or procedures or extensive racial harassment). If the organization does not have a DEI approach, racism issues are often "swept under the rug" and considered not to exist, and, hopefully, the "whistle blower" just gets fed up and exits the organization, and that would be the end of the racism story.

Corporate DEI Ideology as a Distorting Force

Racism in the workplace is a multifaceted phenomenon. Workplace racism often varies by the public, broader public, private, and not-for-profit sectors, and, within the private sector, there are also great variations of the industries that organizations are in, such as construction, manufacturing, entertainment, hospitality, financial, and agriculture. Each one of these sectors and industries has its own histories and cultures and this, in turn, influences how racialized and Indigenous peoples are treated. There are different ways to classify sectors, and one common way is to categorize the four government levels: federal, provincial, territorial, and municipal as the public sector. Some are also subsumed as crown corporations and public service agencies in the same sector. The broader public sector consists of colleges, universities, and hospitals and other publicly appointed or arms-length agencies. As the governments are the custodians of taxpayers' money and considered as leaders for the public good, and the broader public sector is spending taxpayers' money, they are conscientious of the mass media's scrutiny, and are more careful than the private sector on how they present themselves to the public, how they communicate messages, and how they set themselves as models for other sectors to emulate. Currently, in Canada, these sectors see that having DEI as their corporate vision is a wise move as it is considered to be fair and progressive. The extent to which these two sectors are committing themselves to these practices is subject to debate.

However, this does not mean that private sector organizations and established non-profit organizations are negligent on these fronts. In fact, they are just as keen as the public and broader public sectors to build up their good reputations as well as gaining support from the communities that they serve or do business with under the DEI banner. All of the above employers see themselves as being accountable to their stakeholders—their employees, customers, contractors, service users, and the larger public. They are prepared to meet the standard of the current human resources management, of which DEI is one of the core pillars, and treat their employees accordingly. Once again, the extent to which they are committed to all these standards are to be verified. However, there are sceptics in the business sector who do not see much value in adopting DEI to improve company performance. They see the public perception of corporate hypocrisy, the loss of creativity, and the corporate risks in changing the cultural landscape as pitfalls of DEI (Foss and Klein 2023).

Meanwhile, smaller businesses and not-so-established non-profit organizations (both unionized and non-unionized) do try to emulate larger corporations or the governments in their human resources management's school of thought to the extent possible, but, due to their lack of resources, they are not able to do too much concrete DEI work in their organizations. Overall, they are able to use DEI as a general reference and cite DEI in their communications pieces, but it is unclear the extent to which they can follow the spirit or substance of the

DEI school of management. Currently, human resources management emphasizes the importance of DEI and pays tribute to this school of thought, which has been in vogue for over the last thirty years. In general, the Canadian public and broader public sectors have adopted the vision of DEI and have been using DEI as a core principle in organizing their human resources activities. However, this is easier said than done. Racialized and Indigenous peoples do not find DEI effective in eradicating racism, although they welcome its management philosophy. DEI is not considered to be an effective management tool because it often glosses over racism as a "diversity" issue rather than an "equity" issue or an "inclusiveness" issue.

Our working definition of "racism," cited in Chapter 2, states that "racism is a set of human perceptions, attitudes, actions and systems which treat people of different races, colour, ethnicity, nationality, ancestry, place of origin, citizenship, linguistic or religious backgrounds in a hierarchical, discriminatory, inequitable, and exclusive manner. At both the individual and systemic levels, racism manifests itself overtly, but more often in a covert manner, with or without the knowledge or acknowledgement of individuals, organizations, or institutions." When this definition is deconstructed, it has (1) a combination of human psychology, behaviour, and social systems; (2) a range of personal and collective identities; (3) a hierarchical ranking of people with the demarcation of separation, fairness, and acceptance; and (4) multiple levels of manifestation, subtlety, and subjectivity. The current DEI management school does not deal with this kind of complexity in workplace racism. Therefore, racialized and Indigenous peoples have been disappointed by the current DEI.

At the individual level, having this school of management as a corporate practice, however, does make employees more cognizant of what they say and do in interacting with each other. Daily conversations between managers and employees and among employees become more collegial most of the time, and blatant prejudice and stereotyping become much less frequent or more subtle. At the policy and procedure levels, as noted in Chapters 6, 7, and 8, they are still racially biased and are embedded in human resources operations. As discussed earlier in Chapters 9 and 10, these biases, which are mostly systemic, have not been removed because they are not officially identified as biases or because organizations are only half-heartedly doing DEI work. In addition, the government has been lenient in reviewing organizational practices and in enforcing the employment equity legislation. It has made no visibly concerted efforts to rein in the non-compliant activities of organizations. As it stands, most biased human resources functions are still very much in practice, and they are conducive in discriminating racialized and Indigenous peoples.

Racism in these organizations is coated with the DEI ideology as if the organizations are progressing perfectly under this ideology. When racialized and Indigenous employees experience discrimination in their quests for an equitable share of training, development, and promotion—opportunities that are on par with their non-racialized and non-Indigenous counterparts—their perceived "discrimination" experiences are often explained away by management: "There are many qualified candidates in the job competitions, and this does not mean that you are not qualified. Unfortunately, there is only one position vacant for so many qualified candidates" or "It is a matter of time until your promotion will come" or "You may need to market your knowledge and skills better because jobs are very competitive in this company." While racialized and Indigenous peoples, as a collective entity, are statistically shown to be disproportionately under-represented in certain occupations (such as management) or in opportunities for advancement, their experiences of being discriminated, both individual and collective, are seldom recognized or acknowledged. Thus, with the corporate banner of DEI above their heads, some racialized and Indigenous peoples view their organizations as just as hypocritical because, on the one hand, management talks about DEI and how they are being fair to everyone, and, on the other hand, they experience discrimination often one job competition after another. According to these employees, management is not walking the talk, and DEI is just an empty shell.

Another way to look at workplace racism is that racial prejudice and discrimination remains the current theme of organizational life, and the organizational DEI ideology and programs are only skin deep in their impact. DEI ideology is appealing to many people as it treats employees as individual entities and not as identity groups in a collective sense (such as gender, age, race, ethnicity, and immigrant status). While DEI preaches diversity as an embodiment of identity groups or social groups, this school of thought sees employees as a pool of individuals; while in a pool, each has their own unique merits and contributions to the organization. They are not superior or inferior to each other, just different. When these diverse individuals work with each other, the cross-fertilization of their individual perspectives and experiences actually make the team better for the organization as a whole. This school of thought has a certain attraction to management and employees as it puts each individual employee on an equal footing. Unlike the schools of employment equity and human rights that focus on group identity and give specific groups special "protection" in terms of employment opportunities—women, Indigenous peoples, persons with disabilities, racialized people, and other identity groups under the prohibited grounds of discrimination because of their past historical marginalized status, disadvantages, or discrimination—DEI has gained broad acceptance in many sectors.

DEI is a rejection of the perspectives that are inherent in the employment equity or human rights legislation. And, due to the fact that DEI focuses on the positive aspects of individual contributions to an organization, it is in direct contrast with the schools of employment equity and human rights that focus on the negative aspects of discrimination and employment barriers. As such, DEI "sells" well to Canadian corporations and individuals. It is more popularly accepted than the application of employment equity and human rights.

Within a DEI framework, racism is considered to be a form of employment barrier. It could be a negative attitude and stereotype, and it could be a negative behaviour or adverse strategy, policy, procedure, program. The ways in which it is carried out in operation or put into practice may negatively impact racialized and Indigenous people. More importantly, racism may be embedded as a part of the organizational culture as an expressed social interaction, vision, value, and norm. Given that racism can be hidden behind the beliefs and feelings of managers or co-workers, integrated in numerous human resources mechanisms, or ingrained in the organizational ways of getting things done in the organization, to single out or call out one or two features as the manifestation of racism would be challenging. It takes additional knowledge and skills to identify racism in some seemingly neutral activities; hence, it is not easy for individual employees to complain about racism in the workplace since expertise expertise in the analysis of racism is rare, and there are different gradations of knowledge among people in this field in the workplace.

In a workplace with DEI as an organizational ideology, there are many factors that could contribute to racism, but these factors could easily be interpreted as many manifestations of non-inclusiveness—a form of marginalization—but not really racism or even racial in nature. In human resources matters, due to confidentiality, privacy, and non-transparency, it is extra hard to show that racism is at work simply because available documents to shed light on job competitions and the qualifications of job candidates are not readily available for release. Consequently, the reasons for the failure of some racialized and Indigenous employees in securing a promotion are not easy to determine. Within the DEI framework of human resources management, racial factors are hard to isolate and determine as employment barriers are often generic and are applicable to other employment equity designated groups, not just racialized or Indigenous peoples. Within this DEI framework, specific impediments for racialized and Indigenous peoples to have fairer treatment and discrimination-free employment practices are harder to single out and overcome, especially when the biased organizational structure, management practices, and toxic culture are all integrated together seamlessly and there are no clear signs that management is dismantling them as they have difficulties in understanding holistically how each human resource item is related "universally" with others.

Resistance to Social Justice Measures in the Workplace

Resisters, Threats, and Reactions

A DEI management philosophy and its programs have not been happily received by some employees in the workplace. From a socio-psychological perspective, they are resisting DEI because of three specific threats over their status, merits, and moral stands (Shuman, Knowles, and Goldenberg 2023). Some people felt threatened because they believe that their status is being usurped by marginalized people as DEI programs appear to favour their race or gender or any other designated identities by these programs now or in the future. As the people who feel threatened are not proclaimed as being part of the DEI programs, they fear that they will lose out. Some of them may even be concerned about their next generation as they are not able to change their race, gender, and so on. They see job opportunities as "zero-sum": when these DEI-designated beneficiaries get a share of the employment pie, other people like them may lose out. Some people felt threatened because they believe that they are where they are now (that is higher-status positions) because of their individual merits (competency, diligence, and so on) and that the DEI programs appear to be redistributing these positions to certain marginalized groups not because of their qualifications (such as knowledge, skills, competencies) but purely on their identities such as gender or race. This perception is based on an assumption that these marginalized people are not really qualified for the positions and that they are only succeeding in getting hired or promoted because of the DEI programs. Some people see equality and fairness in employment as a moral high ground, and they see themselves possessing these moral principles. They believe that they are employed in high-status positions because their moral principles are in action. However, DEI programs seem to suggest that they are not legitimate in being employed in those positions and that their own moral images are being questioned by the DEI programs. The DEI programs seem to enable groups such as racialized or Indigenous people to claim these moral rights and share the employment system and the unequal status of racialized and Indigenous peoples.

Although these three psychological threats are distinctly categorized, in reality, one or more of these threats could be felt in mixed forms, and people may not know exactly the nature of their fears, except that they are feeling a generalized form of anxiety. Under these perceived threats, employees usually exhibit several forms of resistance to DEI: some of them may deny the assumption of a biased employment system. Some defend the status quo and do not see racialized or Indigenous peoples as being discriminated against. Some distance themselves from DEI and take no responsibility for social prejudice as they do not believe that they are prejudiced against racialized and Indigenous peoples and do not discriminate against them. They also do not see themselves being benefited by social inequality and living or working in an environment of privileges (Shuman, Knowles, and Goldenberg 2023).

Building on Eric Shuman, Eric Knowles, and Amit Goldenberg's 2023) study discussed above, Lauren Park and Lin Grensing-Pophal (2023) further explored the psychology of people who have pushbacked to DEI. These people perceived a loss of control or autonomy when DEI symbolized the launching of a new set of criteria for personal success in the workplace that does not depend solely on merit or hard work; an emphasis on some individual differences (read: skin colour) being higher than others; and a new group of people (read: White people) who become disadvantaged through no fault of their own.

Gartner Incorporated, a global management consulting firm that conducts regular surveys of employers and employees to identify their pulse on DEI and other issues, appears to be more interested in how these psychological emotions (fears, in this case) have manifested explicitly in the visible behaviours of employees. Their survey concludes that there are three types of DEI resisters in the workplace that are identified by the way in which they behave—they deny, disengage, and derail DEI efforts (Rai and Dutkiewicz 2022). Essentially, employees who deny do not see DEI as a problem. They do not recognize or acknowledge race, gender, and other identities that may result in their discrimination or under-representation in the workforce or certain occupations. For example, remarks like "we have no racism here" or "I am colourblind in my relationship with people."

Employees who disengage do not see DEI as their problem. They do not support DEI as a concept or as a program. They tend to shy away from any discussions, events, training sessions, or actions related to DEI, and they are afraid to say anything that may displease others and distance themselves from racialized groups. They take no personal responsibility for the problems or solutions related to DEI. Remarks made by people who have disengaged include: "I did not say anything about the incident, as I did not see it as my problem" and "Racism is not my problem. I did not cause it and I do not know how to solve it." Employees who derail DEI view it as a low priority item among all other problems. They dismiss the concerns of racialized people and see no reasons to spend efforts on DEI. There is a tendency that sidetracking racism is one way to protect the dominant group and belittle the marginalized group. The following remarks show signs of the derailment of DEI: "We should focus on competencies and merits, not on race or gender" and "Black lives matter, so are other lives."

Resisters to social justice measures in the workplace are a part of the larger anti-wokeism movement outside the workplace in contemporary Western society. This topic will be discussed in greater detail in the next chapter. Suffice it here to say that employers in Canada appear to be cognizant of growing anti-employment equity and anti-DEI sentiments and have been cautiously introducing the DEI management approach in the workplace due to concerns over employee backlash. The private sector's resistance to the employment equity legislation passed by the federal and Ontario government in the 1980s and 1990s was largely based on their resistance to government "encroachment" on business management and contempt of the government's attempt to regulate their human resources management. All these resistances to social justice measures in the workplace suggests that anti-racism was being viewed as a part of the social justice continuum that posed challenges to the traditional culture at work.

Canada

Historically, even if we go back to the 1950s when the concept of having an equal opportunity program was first introduced in Ontario, there was resistance from people who questioned the need for such a program when no "unequal opportunity" (read "discrimination") existed, or so the people who opposed the program claimed. In the 1960s, human rights legislation was passed in Canada, and Ontario and the rest of the Canadian provinces followed one after another. It, too, was resisted and opposed by people who saw legislation against discrimination in employment, housing, services, and associations for numerous groups with prohibited grounds as "overkill."

Soon, in the 1980s, the federal government introduced employment equity legislation that was enacted in 1986. Resistance to this piece of legislation was noticeable across Canada. The Government of Ontario attempted to prepare a similar piece of legislation in the 1990s and was massively opposed, led by the media including editorials by the national *Globe and Mail*. In the end, the new Conservative government came into power in 1995 and repealed the newly passed employment equity legislation under the New Democratic Party a few months earlier in 1996. Since then, no provincial and territorial governments have ever developed any legislation on employment equity across Canada.

But the idea of DEI rose in popularity, first among the larger private sector organizations, followed by various provincial and municipal governments and the non-profit sector. The federal government, due to its employment equity legislation (which has persisted since 1986), was shy of openly endorsing DEI for fear of undermining its own legislation, but its federal government departments have developed and conducted DEI programs in one form or another that paralleled with their employment equity programs.

Employees in Canada are less resistant to DEI than to the federal *Employment Equity Act*, which was enacted in 1986.[1] Nevertheless, there were a lot of misunderstandings with the legislation and its purposes and principles in the early 1980s. It is noticeable that the federal

---

1 *Employment Equity Act*, SC 1995, c 44.

government's key pre-employment equity preparation prior to the launching of employment equity legislation and during the early stage of implementation was the education of employers and the training of human resource professionals. The idea behind this strategy was to ensure that the legislation was properly carried out. The government also spent less money on doing public education as if consultation with the stakeholders (such as businesses, unions, employment equity designated groups, community organizations, and so on) was more than enough. As a result, many working employees did not, and still do not, understand the concept of employment equity. The government left it to the employers to educate their employees, but that was seldom carried out with earnest.

Rosemary McGowan and Eddy Ng (2016) did a study of employees in a mid-sized organization in Canada and noted that they did not know too much about employment equity and that they saw the employment equity programs as problematic mainly because they thought individual merit should be the foundation of any proper hiring and promotion, not race, gender, disabilities, and Indigeneity. Worst still, these employees saw racialized and Indigenous employees, as well as women and persons with disabilities, as being not quite qualified enough to get the positions that they got through hiring or promotion; consequently, they were being marginalized at work. Needless to say, there were tensions not only among employees but also between management and employees as to the implementation of employment equity initiatives. DEI (which was later imported from the United States) is more acceptable as DEI programs do not single out designated groups for "special treatment," and "merit" remains a central feature in employment. And corporations usually used DEI as a "marketing" tool to ease in employment equity initiatives where it was able to lower the tension somewhat in the workplace.

One research project showed that some immigrants were not happy with DEI management. It showed that African immigrants noticed some gaps in DEI policies and were not integrating well in the workplace. The challenges that these African immigrants faced included racial discrimination and the cultural competency of management. They were disappointed with DEI, and they were looking for ways to make DEI better. Although DEI talks about inclusion, the African immigrants did not feel inclusive in their organization. In fact, they felt that the DEI policies were too rigid and exclusionary and that management had communicated these policies to them poorly. The African immigrants felt that the DEI initiatives were not well customized for them and that accessibility and accommodation were not provided to them well (Dimingu 2024).

United States and the World

In spite of its broadened base of endorsement and implementation by organizations in the public, broader public, private, and non-profit sectors, the resistance to DEI from a small segment of employees persisted in the United States. Coca-Cola, Home Depot, and Google have reported incidents of some employees not participating in DEI training initiatives, expressing concerns about lost opportunities, and filing lawsuits on alleged reverse discrimination (Park and Grensing-Pophal 2023). These resistances ranged from passive disengagement to active pushbacks against corporate policy changes and program implementation. There have been extensive studies on resistance to DEI changes at the attitudinal, cognitive, and behavioural levels (Gundemir et al. 2024).

Emily Strother, senior principal at the Gartner Human Resources Practice, reported that a Gartner survey of 3,516 employees in September 2021 showed that 42 percent voiced their resentment toward DEI and viewed their organization's DEI efforts as divisive. The survey showed that 44 percent agreed that a growing number of their co-workers felt alienated by the DEI efforts of their organizations (Gartner 2022). Another study of American employees by the Conference Board of the United States (2024b) showed that 17 percent of these employees saw that DEI has a detrimental effect on workplace productivity, and 52 percent of these employees saw that measuring DEI targets has a neutral or negative impact on their work experience because they perceived DEI targets as quotas and could disadvantage some groups unfairly.

The American Productivity and Quality Centre published its survey of 312 DEI leaders from global organizations in 2022 and noted that employee resistance to DEI could be one of the factors why organizations announced their commitment to DEI but, in practice, were not implementing enough DEI initiatives: only 26 percent of them have DEI measures, and 25 percent tied DEI goal achievement to executives' compensation. The lack of DEI prevalence may be due to management's lack of clear communication on the reasons for DEI implementation to employees and their lack of attentiveness to employees' concerns. (American Productivity and Quality Centre 2022; Park and Grensing-Pophal

2023). There are also studies that show that employers who have DEI policies and programs in the workplace may be responsible for some of the dissatisfaction and resentment of employees toward DEI because employers have not clearly communicated the purposes of DEI and executed the DEI programs effectively (Geiger et al. 2023).

HOW TO ADDRESS WORKPLACE RACISM IN AN INNOVATIVE MANNER?

Individual Employees' Complaints

Either from the individual or organizational perspective, racism in the workplace is ambiguous and often subtle to the point that it is not noticeable, but it is there, and it is not easy to prove. Some of these racial issues are seemingly neutral or harmless, and, when highlighted by racialized and Indigenous people, one may even be accused of "having a chip on the shoulder" or "just being too sensitive." In fact, many people—racialized or Indigenous or not—have problems even identifying the manifestation of racism. Such subtlety and ambiguity make even the mentioning of racism difficult. In each organization, there is usually a handful of employees who do know or understand what workplace racism is about, how racism harms, who is being harmed, and the extent to which racism impacts on racialized and Indigenous employees. Observations and consultations with employees in several large corporations in Canada suggest that the majority of employees (and management included) do not have a deep comprehension of racism. And this makes any efforts to counteract the spread of workplace racism very trying.

The difficulty in fighting racism in the workplace boils down to several factors: a hierarchy of power dynamics, work as a major financial source for workers, a low level of racism literacy (awareness, knowledge, understanding, and empathy) among management and fellow employees. However, if employees could enlist the support of management and unions (if unionized), the latter two parties could adopt the strategies and measures mentioned in Parts 2 and 3 of this book, and they could slowly reduce and remove employment biases and dismantle obstacles at both the attitudinal and organizational levels. On these fronts, it is not so much a lack of anti-racism ideas or options but, rather, a lack of will on the part of management and unions to deal with racism. Moreover, as discussed in Parts 2 and 3, there are many ways in which the governments can tackle the issue, including legislation, policies, strategies, and programs, but, once again, the lack of will on their part has slowed down any progress on anti-racism.

These special features of workplace racism suggest that individual employees do not have much power to counter racism by themselves as it is a collective force. Once an allegation of racism is made known to management and/or to the employee(s) who is viewed as the "offender," the allegation may be filed as a complaint directly to the management (either through a corporately prescribed mechanism of conflict resolution or a union's grievance process), and management may likely "close their ranks" and unite as a collective force to protect the good name of management, or the "offender" may be likely to galvanize to create a circle of supporters among their co-workers to support them. Both parties are likely to treat the complaint (or allegation) as political and not just an "impartial" workplace conflict to resolve. If the complainant takes the route of filing a complaint to a human rights commission (provincial or federal), the process is likely to be paper driven (with lots of paperwork), and the process is likely to be drawn out and lengthy process.

In these scenarios, the "complainant" (employee) is likely to be viewed by management as a "troublemaker." Such labelling or stigmatization is likely to reduce the "complainant's" chance for further advancement in the organization in the long run or, worse still, marginalize or ostracize them at work, whether or not they "won" or "lost" the case. It is better for the "complainant" to start looking for a new job outside the organization, which is the fate of many corporate whistle-blowers in Canada. Even then, not many employers are prepared to offer a job to a "troublemaker" who has complained about racism. The stigmatization process continues even when the case is over. In the end, allegers of racism continue to be punished by people who have worked in the same workplace because they are seen as less trustworthy or difficult to work with. Not all racialized or Indigenous allegers follow this fate in a mechanical manner and to the same degree of hardship. It depends largely on how the process of allegation, investigation, review, mediation, and settlement has unfolded in human rights cases of this nature. Usually, the process that these cases take put the allegers or complainants on a lengthy journey of stress and depression.

Therefore, it is critical to keep in mind that racism is best dealt with in a proactive manner and not to react after racism has hit. Here are a few ways to take a proactive stand on fighting racism. First, create employee resource groups if they do not exist in the workplace. These groups aim to establish a forum for employees to talk among themselves on the issues that are important to them as a group and how to address them. It might take some time to accomplish this mission. But, once this is done, these groups can be utilized as a forum to start a conversation with the human resources department and senior managers and executives, relay concerns, and make suggestions for improvement. This will also take time, but at least a communication channel is established between those in authority (management) and those who are not (employees). This could also be a platform for employees to exchange ideas with labour unions (if unionized) and urge them to work on racial issues that are pertinent to racialized and Indigenous peoples in a proactive and reactive manner.

Second, since the lack of racism literacy is a large part of the problem, it is critical to create a work environment in which the literacy level of the entire workforce and management is elevated through time. Education is a lengthy process even at the best of time. Encourage management and unions to collaborate with the employee resources groups to conduct "lunch and learn" sessions, webinars, corporate speaker series, and human resources development events and to create a dialogue and idea exchange process so that more people at work understand racism and/or acquire some skills in how best to interact and work together as a team. The idea behind these educational sessions is to create a better working environment and better reception for support in case "racial" issues arise.

Third, employee resources groups need to explore outreaching to, and partnering with, external professional associations and trade councils and community and non-profit organizations to establish joint events in raising awareness of racism and additional functions that could better the relationship between external organizations with private or public sector organizations. Employers, unions, and non-profit groups need the opportunity to collaborate with each other so as to develop trust among themselves in tackling issues related to racism. Too many "silo" activities, even in racial matters, may be counter-productive as stakeholder groups may view other groups as competing with them.

Fourth, a lack of information and data in racism research has often been cited as an impediment to making progress in racial matters. A large investment in research on women and gender issues in the past few decades in Canada is largely responsible for yielding more insights and solutions to those issues that promote the status of women. Similarly, at this stage, when race data and information is largely inadequate, governments, employers, unions, employee resources groups, academic institutions, consulting firms, and DEI-advocacy organizations may take a lead in funding or partnering with each other to do research projects that shed light on racism and practical solutions in addressing pertinent issues in the employment fields (such as unemployment or under-employment, performance management, or succession planning).

Organizational Responses to Employees' Resistance to Social Justice Measures

Meanwhile, at an organizational level, when there are pushbacks against DEI, employment equity, or anti-racism from a segment of employees in the workplace, it is important to find out why. Gartner (2023) did a survey with DEI leaders to identify the causes of resistance in 2022, and the survey findings show that 51 percent cited that corporate leaders fail to take ownership for driving DEI results; 33 percent mentioned that they limited power to effectively drive decisions that shape DEI results; 31 percent noted ineffective coordination of DEI efforts across disparate operating units or functions; 29 percent indicated their limited staff dedicated to DEI to make meaningful progress; and 23 percent noted that they must navigate and plan for employees who resist DEI efforts.

In sum, the lack of executive leadership commitment, limited authority of DEI leaders, ineffective coordination, limited staff members to implement DEI, and a lack of know-how and planning to deal with DEI resisters. These circumstances do not help DEI become effective, and they render DEI leaders incapable of handling the workplace dynamic effectively. The dynamic is the relationship between two groups of employees: racialized and Indigenous groups (marginalized group) and non-racialized and non-Indigenous groups (dominant group). When this dynamic is conflictual and distrustful along race lines, it likely results in high tension and low morale and productivity. If management is unable to pre-empt it from happening or unable to resolve the racial issues, the workplace will likely be toxic and lead to higher turnover rate.

For all of these reasons, leaders need a long-term strategy to change the racial dynamic from negative to positive and "turn the ship" around. Like wrestling with the impact of racial incidents after they have occurred, individuals find it much harder to deal with than before the incidents have occurred. Similarly, collective racial tension is much harder to resolve once it is embedded in the corporate culture and allowed to simmer.

As each organization that is grappling with racial tension has its own history, culture, structures, processes, and resources, it would be difficult to go into specifics. Suffice it here to outline three key components in developing a long-term strategy to deal with racism in the workplace.

First, start with a strong commitment from the top and work with cooperation from the bottom. Since it is enterprise-wide research to find the factors that give rise to racial tension, leadership commitment is crucial, and this commitment has to be communicated clearly to all employees, including management. This commitment includes a clear mandate, a workable structure and process to do the research, a sufficient allocation of resources, a clear set of deliverables, and a viable time frame.

Second, retain a reputable, impartial, and experienced third party to conduct a research project on workplace racism. A researcher or team of researchers that is retained from outside with no vested interest in protecting the status quo and is well known for their neutrality, thoroughness, and insights in doing the project is needed. The project must have terms of reference that are agreeable by both the employer and the employees (and labour unions, if applicable). The resultant research report (with recommendations) should be reviewed by all parties involved.

Third, work on strategic and operational plans. Upon the completion of the research project report and the approval of the recommendations by the review parties, strategic and operational plans are to be developed for implementation with committed resources and a realistic timetable.

While these three components are critical in eliminating biases, racism, and other forms of workplace injustice, they still do not guarantee the end of racism. The reason is simple: those in power (that is, leadership and management) are not willing to abandon the traditional ways of doing things and may not be ready to acknowledge that their organization has been discriminatory. Many organizations still have structures that enable chief executive officers (CEOs) to have a major influence in governance (that is, who should be on the boards of directors/governors) and have a major say in operations (that is, who should be on the executive and management teams). With this kind of structural arrangements, CEOs who are not committed to DEI or social justice are unlikely to invest human and financial resources in DEI, human rights, anti-racism, and employment equity. In fact, as we will discuss in the next chapter, the collective efforts in these fields in the workplace are shrinking, and the frameworks that promote these fields are under pressure to reverse their trends with the approval of CEOs and executive/management teams.

Responses from External Organizations and the Public

While a smaller organization has a flatter reporting relationship, a larger one usually has its power gravitating toward the CEOs and executive/management teams. The government, employer, and labour unions are three parties that wield the lion's share of power, which can determine the life chances of racialized and Indigenous employees. This book has devoted many pages on these parties and how they impact on the work experience of employees. These three parties play key roles in the employment histories of employees in various stages and aspects of their employment. Racism, which is largely embedded in human resources mechanisms and how they are carried out in practice, determines the kind and degree of racism that racialized and Indigenous peoples experience. In this chapter, we take a closer look at racism and see how these employees can manage—individually and collectively—in a racially biased work environment. What the governments, employers, and labour unions can do in eradicating racism have been elaborated in Chapters 9, 10, and 11. The discussion here is limited to the actions that individual employees can take by themselves and collectively and how they can harness or leverage what external organizations can do in eradicating racism. External organizations cover a spectrum of vested interests such as community organizations, racial/ethnic or Indigenous organizations, consumer groups, professional associations, trade councils, social justice advocacy groups, neighbourhood associations, the mainstream/social media, and the public.

If racism is a systemic issue, racialized and Indigenous employees or any segments of the employees of an organization may first seek solutions with employers or labour unions (if unionized). If this fails to elicit any effective solutions and the concerned employees are running out of patience, they may have to look beyond the organization that employs them. Non-profit organizations such as social justice advocacy groups, racial/ethnic organizations, professional/business organizations, and neighbourhood groups may lend sympathetic ears to individual racism cases, but, given their general mandate, they are more prepared to put in efforts on issues or cases related to systemic racism, which have widespread impacts on racialized or Indigenous groups as a whole. As most of these non-profit organizations are limited in resources, they do need employees to have more thoughts on how best to approach these organizations and to convince them to take up the challenge of resolving racism issues. Once one or more organizations are prepared to collaborate with the employees, more ideas on how to resolve the racism issues may emerge.

If and when racialized and Indigenous employees are able to connect with some external groups, and if these groups are sympathetic to their causes, they may form an alliance to fight against racism in a variety of ways that go beyond the conflict resolution mechanism normally found in a workplace such as the filing of grievances, negotiations, and internal human rights investigation and remediation.

Once racism-related discontent moves beyond the originating organization, the fight against racism usually goes beyond the control of the racialized or Indigenous employees who made the complaint in the first place. The external organizations that formed the alliance will likely take over the complaint and take on the major role in the anti-racism fight. The alliance may utilize social or political activism tools, including boycotts, legal challenges, petitions, and other civil disobedience activities that aim at exerting pressure on the employer or parties that lend support to the organization.

Working with external groups on racism issues requires an effective strategy. Having mainstream and social media and public involvement will add momentum to the employees' efforts at anti-racism. Media coverage of racism issues will put the organization on notice that there is perceived racism and discontent brewing in the organization and that any prolonged negative publicity may damage the organization's reputation (especially if it claims to be progressive and to practice DEI). Broader and prolonged publicity of workplace racism is likely to discourage other racialized and Indigenous people to apply for jobs there, to jeopardize the growth of the business or reduce/cut off organizational sponsorship or endorsement, and to distract the core activities of the organization. If the concerned organization is in the public or broader public sector, media coverage of anti-racism activities may further embarrass the politicians in power and put extra pressure on those bureaucrats who are running it because, currently, nearly all public sector organizations subscribe to the DEI management philosophy and must also abide by the human rights legislation or, at the federal level, the employment equity legislation. For those on the boards of directors/ governors of the concerned organization, they too must be cognizant of the reputation of the companies they represent.

The key point here is that when external organizations are committed to taking on systemic racism that originates in an organization, racism as a workplace issue could become a larger social issue worthy of attention by those organizations that are connected with the organization from which workplace racism is alleged to take place. Workplace racism is now a political issue with more people involved in it and no longer just one employee or a few employees of racial or Indigenous backgrounds.

Boycotts as an Effective Social Change Tool

Boycotts are one of the many protest tools that have been used by people in a non-violent manner to raise public awareness on racism as well as to "punish" organizations and institutions that perpetuate and support it. Boycotts have been used extensively in anti-racism struggles well beyond the workplace. Social justice groups and movements, such as Black Lives Matters and the Boycotts, Divestment and Sanctions (BDS) movement, have used this method to draw attention to their anti-racism stands.

In response to the death of George Floyd in 2020, boycotts of stores that did not support the Black Lives Matter movement were planned (Marcos 2020). The current BDS movement is boycotting people, companies, institutions, organizations, and countries that support the Israeli government and its anti-Palestinian activities (BDS, n.d.).

There are studies that show that the success of boycotts in reaching their goals is not guaranteed and that only a small minority of them are successful (Hawkins 2010; Maira, 2018; Lawson 2024). Successful boycotts for moral, political, environmental, and social reasons, not necessarily of an anti-racism nature, are well documented. Consistent and prolonged media coverage of boycotts and growing and extended support of the public appear to be crucial for the success of boycotts.

For example, the boycott of the sugar industry founded on slavery reduced the sales of sugar by one-third to one-half in England in 1791. And there was the boycott against South African products and companies by South African exiles and their supporters in opposition to the apartheid (racial segregation, discrimination, and racial violence), which started in 1959 and finally ended in 1994 with the collapse of apartheid. In 1955, the refusal of Rosa Parks to move to the back of the bus, where bus seats were designated for Blacks, led to a widespread boycott of the bus services in the United States (the Montgomery Bus Boycotts). In the United Kingdom, there was also a boycott of the Bristol Omnibus Company for its refusal to hire Black employees in 1963. These boycotts were the catalyst for the first *Race Relations Act* in 1965, which prohibited racial discrimination in public places and made racial hatred illegal (Asare 2023; Ethical Consumer Research Association 2025).

There have been many consciousness-raising and successful boycotts since then. Successful boycotts of Nike's products due to labour exploitation were reported throughout the 1990s, and the boycotts resurfaced again in the 2010s on the same issues; the boycotts of Mitsubishi for its environmental violation in Mexico in the 2000s; the boycott of Nestle's baby milk in 2003; the successful boycotts of PricewaterhouseCoopers's business in Burma in 2003, Aon Corporation (insurance) in Burma in 2005; and Austrian Airlines, Eastravel, and FromersGuides's discontinuation of promoting tourism to Burma in 2005. In 2008, over one thousand universities in the United States, the United Kingdom, and Canada joined the garment boycott against Russell Athletic, the owner of Fruit of the Loom, and pressured the company to shut down its Honduran factories. In 2011, an international coalition of health and environmental groups' boycotted Johnson and Johnson and pressured the company to stop the use of formaldehyde preservatives in its baby products.

There were also bitter but successful boycotts of Mini Babybel's cheese in France in 2012, the long running boycotts of Nestle's baby milk formula from 1974 to 2014, the boycott of a Sodastream factory in an occupied Israel settlement on Palestinian land, which has a long history of racial discrimination against Palestinians in 2015, the boycott of five Israeli banks by the United Methodist Church and the PGGM, the largest Dutch pension fund, in 2016. They announced the withdrawal of investments from these banks from 2014 to 2016, the boycott of Seaworld's captive orca-breeding programs and its orca shows in 2016, the boycotts of Cartier's gemstones mined in Myanmar in 2017, the boycott of the Body Shop's and L'Oreal's products with animal testing in 2018, the boycott of several airlines, car rental companies, Chubb Insurance, and First National Banks of Omaha, which offered discounts and incentives to members of the National Rifle Association in 2018, the boycott of over seventy large companies with financial ties to the Trump administration from 2018 to 2020, the boycott of Merline Entertainment brands due to its treatment of captive animals in 2018, the boycotts of Burberry's fur in 2018, the boycotts of HSBC due to its investment in the Israeli weapons manufacturer Elbit Systems in 2018, the boycott of hotels in Brunei due to anti-gay bills in 2019, the boycott of Constellation Brands's brewing business, which impacted negatively on the water supply of the region in 2020, the boycott of Dogs4Us's puppy farms in the United Kingdom in 2020, the boycott of L'Oreal regarding its hypocrisy on diversity matters in the United Kingdom in 2020, the boycott of Kirin Group for its relationship with the Myanmar Economic Holdings Public Company in 2021, the boycott of Fortnum & Mason due to its force-feeding practice of geese and ducks in 2021, the boycott of two television channels in the United Kingdom for their breaches of impartiality in 2021, the boycott of Canada Goose's fur products, the boycott of Ben & Jerry for its ice cream products in the Israeli settlements on Palestinian land in 2021, the boycott of Swatch regarding its gemstones from Burma in 2021, the boycott of AXA's involvement with the Hunting Office in the United Kingdom in 2022, the boycott of the first international LGBTQIA+ conference, which was organized by the UK government as the government announced its ban of conversion therapy in the United Kingdom in 2022, the boycott of Air France for its practice of shipping monkeys for experimentation in 2022, the boycott of Pillsbury for its violation of Palestinian rights in 2020, the boycott of House of Fraser for its sale of fur in 2022, the boycott of G4S for its violations of Palestinian prisoners' rights, the boycott of Klook for its wildlife cruelty in the tourism industry in 2023, the boycott of Puma for its sponsorship of the Israeli Football Association in 2023, the boycott of Twitter/X for its harmful and inaccurate content in 2024, the boycott of brands operating in Russia and Russian exports, the boycott of Baillie Gifford's (Scotland-based investment firm) investments in illegal Israel settlements in 2024, the boycott of Pret (coffee chain) for its investment in Israel in 2024, and the boycott of Barclays for its investments in arms companies supplying Israel with weapons and military technology in 2024 (Ethical Consumer Research Association 2025).

This brief chronological history of boycotts on different fronts (such as human rights, animal rights, and labour rights) in Europe and the United States strongly illustrates that boycotts have been effective. Their success is also based on raising public awareness and connecting with elected politicians and other social change tools.

Erica Chenoweth (2013), a political scientist at Harvard University, examined hundreds of campaigns in the twentieth century (1900–2006) and concluded that non-violent campaigns are twice as likely to achieve their goals as violent ones. In spite of this success rate, Chenoweth noted that 47 percent of non-violent resistance still failed even when the magnitude of public support was large, as shown in the failed attempt of four hundred thousand people (2 percent of the East Germany population) in the peaceful protest against the communist party in the 1950s.

In her research, she showed that, with the participation of around 3.5 percent of the population, some serious political change during the last century could happen, and success is almost guaranteed. Examples may be found in the peaceful protest of the People Movement in Manila, Philippines, in 1986 that toppled the Marcos regime in four days and the bloodless Rose Revoluiton of the people of Georgia who held flowers in their hands, stormed the parliament building, and outsed Eduard Shevardnadze in 2003 (Robson 2019; Wambach 2025).

This "3.5 percent" is a magical number.

In a country like Canada, when its population reached 40 million in 2025, 3.5 percent of them mean 1.4 million people must participate in an anti-racism boycott or a non-violent protest of this nature to reach its goal. It is not an easy target to reach, but it is feasible with the proper alignment of stars (Robson 2019; Asare 2023). The current patriotic Canadian boycotts of American products and services triggered by the Trump administration's tariffs and threats of annexation in 2025 may yield some successful results. It may also be a lesson on boycotts for anti-racism should a company exhibit an unacceptable racism record.

CONCLUSION

In examining the issue of workplace racism more deeply, it is clear that racism seriously impacts the life chances of individual employees as well as racialized or Indigenous peoples as a collective entity.

Employers have many tools at their disposal to end racism in the work environment or at least minimize the effectiveness of their policies, programs, structures and processes—conduct and practices that create a toxic discriminatory environment or build a more respectful and discrimination-free work environment. We also know that different levels of government and labour unions can also do more to hold employers accountable to their employees. But, nowadays, most workplaces remain problematic in terms of racist attitudes and stereotyping, biased policies and programs, and inequitable structures and processes as well as toxic corporate cultures. Racism that starts small in a small work unit may germinate and grow to an unresolvable phenomenon that spills over to the larger society.

The theme of this chapter is obvious: racism is embedded in many aspects of the workplace, and the power structure of most workplaces does not allow racialized or Indigenous peoples to thrive without fighting with their employer. Perceived social injustice is best pre-empted before it solidifies into antagonism or alienation, and it should be resolved as quickly as possible. Otherwise, not only will the negative impacts of racism be spread further and deeper, but it might spread to the societal domain beyond the workplace. Racism destabilizes and polarizes the public. Once it gets to that stage, the resources for containing and neutralizing it could be costly.

And, as some historical studies have suggested, there is a chance that, close to half of the time, protests of this nature may succeed. If anti-racism protests fail, the unresolved issue of racism will likely emerge again in a matter of time.

CHAPTER 13

Fighting Racism from Without

INTRODUCTION

Throughout this book, there is a focus on racism and its manifestations in the workplace. The theme is that racism is a structural phenomenon as it is embedded largely in policies, programs, and corporate culture, and it is perpetuated through our perceptions and attitudes. Accordingly, the roles of government, employers, and labour unions are important in eradicating racism mainly because they have the power and resources to change the status quo. It is not clear whether they have the will to make that happen.

Building on the research studies cited and the arguments presented in this book, we have come to a point where we should be reflecting on how racism and fighting racism in the workplace demands a good grip on the complexity of the power dynamics in a work environment and on how much leverage an individual has and can have. It is not easy to end racism if racialized and Indigenous employees do not have much power or resources to leverage. Employers and their managerial representatives who are working along with union officials in the workplace can only accomplish their goals of building a discrimination-free work environment if they have the will to do so. At a certain point, racialized and Indigenous peoples, at both the individual and collective level, must go beyond the confines of the workplace and seek external support and draw in more power as alluded in the last chapter when external forces are to be considered.

The research findings and analytical discussion in this book has so far led us to a realization that there is also the bigger picture and a series of external forces with which racialized and Indigenous peoples have to reckon. In this historical juncture, there are a number of changes that must be taken into consideration in understanding the nature of racism and fighting against it in the workplace. These changes are macroscopic in nature involving global politics, political ideologies, social trends, cultural shifts, and technological transformation. We need to have a good understanding of the shifting landscape of the world and a recognition of the tsunami of racism that is washing on shore from abroad and the hidden evil germinating from within our society. Currently, we are living in a world with:

- widening geopolitical conflicts;
- the growth of authoritarianism, illiberalism, and populism;
- the ascendency of hate crime, hate speech, and violence;
- rising challenges to diversity, equity, and inclusiveness (DEI); and
- the spread of artificial intelligence (AI) and biases.

All these political, social, and technological changes have immense implications for racialized and Indigenous peoples and the prevalence of racism and how best to fight against it in the workplace. The key social agents—the governments, employers, and labour unions—must take note of these shifting realities and build a work environment where most people are active and interact with each other while they are at work. The prevalence of these large changes outside of the workplace, and the politicians, employers, and labour unions that are not able to arrest the pace of conflict and deterioration, shows that the larger social environment (in which these workplaces are located) is actually edging toward the tipping point of collapse.

In this chapter, we are going to examine the extent of how the five major social trends mentioned earlier are spreading and the inability of the key stakeholder groups to fix them quickly and effectively. The implications of the situation are alarming as these large social trends are giving permission to the public and to working people to victimize racialized and Indigenous peoples further, and, worse still, they are allowing racism to become more deeply ingrained in the social fabric, making it more difficult to eradicate it and further embedding racism in its various manifestations in future generations.

WIDENING GEOPOLITICAL CONFLICT

Encircling the Communists

Immediately after the Second World War, the Western allies (mainly the United States, the United Kingdom, France, and the other Western powers), anxious over the expansion of communism in Europe and Asia, focused on building stronger economic and military defence "walls" barricading the Soviet Union and the People's Republic of China. This meant that, according to the Western allies' strategy of containment, their neighbouring countries (such as Germany and Japan), even though they were defeated fascist countries, could not be allowed to be economically and militarily weak. They had to be rebuilt to be stronger under certain agreed upon conditions after their surrender in 1945. Hence, the North Atlantic Treaty Organization (NATO), which comprises thirty countries forming an alliance, was born in Europe and North America, and the North Pacific Rim countries of South Korea, Japan, Taiwan, and a string of Southeast Asian countries formed a geopolitical alliance in defence of the Western allies' security and freedom.

This defence design of encircling communist countries (Soviet Union/Russia and China) with strengthened economies and countries friendly to the political system of democracy (the "free world") included the active engagement of the American allies in securing further diplomacy, business, economic, and military cooperation among poorer developing countries (that is, the "Third World"). Under this system, the world enjoyed over seventy years of relative peace and prosperity and improvements in the standard of living for some countries. However, during these decades of a strong economic and military America, there were still wars and cross-country conflicts that were quite persistent, which brought misery to many people around the world. Yet these conflicts did not escalate on a global scale like the world wars, but they did break up some countries. There was the Korean War of 1950–53, the Algerian War of 1954–62, and a series of wars in the Middle East (such as the Israel's War of Independence, the Suez Crisis, the Lebanon War, and the second Lebanon War), and military conflicts in Asia, Europe, South America, and Africa. More recently, the Russia-Ukraine War, which started in 2022, and the Israel-Hamas War, which started in 2023, are still ongoing at the time of writing, although attempts have been made to contain the war's destruction and bring peace.

Unravelling Lines of Defence

During these years of sporadic conflicts and underlining hostility between nations or within the confines of a country (that is, internal civil wars), it is getting clearer that the world order that was constructed after the Second World War under American leadership has been unravelling and that shifts to a new world order are yet to be defined. The two geo-defence lines of alliances (Europe and Asia) constructed after the Second World War are still fulfilling their mandates in securing a Western style of democracy, freedom, and security. However, these alliances are facing increased challenges from Russia (the former Soviet Union) and China, and countries along the geo-defence lines are reducing their commitment and are shifting their alignments.

Both Russia and China are reclaiming their territories that were lost some time ago. The war currently taking place in Ukraine after Russia's invasion three years ago and the constant threat that China is posing in the South China Sea and the Taiwan Strait are examples of political and military aggression. Mostly importantly, Russia is teaming up with other countries: with China on the economic front to ease the pressure on the Russian economy under Western sanctions and with North Korea on the military front to combat the depletion of Russian military resources. Meanwhile, China is teaming up with numerous countries along the Belt and Road Initiative throughout Central Asia and Europe and acting as an economic partner with over twenty countries in African and South/Latin America.

The Belt and Road Initiative was established to counteract the financial and economic might of America's economic reach. The economic alliance made between Brazil, Russia, India, China, and South Africa (BRICS) has been formed to act as a competitor to the economic alliance of the United States, Europe, Canada, and Australia on the world stage. The membership of BRICS now includes additional countries such as Egypt, Ethiopia, Indonesia, Iran, and the United Arab Empirates.

Rise of China

After many decades of military defeats at the hands of European powers in the nineteenth century, and decades of civil wars and poverty, China gradually emerged in late twentieth century as a manufacturing centre for many global products. In this century, it has become a rising industrial nation. While the manufacturing industry is only one aspect of measuring economic strength of a country, America has lost its shine in this industry. The United States used to manufacture half of the world's output immediately after the Second World War, and now it manufactures about one-sixth of the output. Clearly, the American might of manufacturing has weakened in the last eighty years. China has now taken the lead and is responsible for 35 percent of global manufacturing. By 2030, the United Nations expects that it will rise to 45 percent. The United States is now using tariffs to pull in more investments and jobs from other countries. Time will tell whether they will work or not, although many economists have their doubts.

China and the United States are the two largest competing economic powers in the world, and it is this competition for world dominance that has created trade tension and economic uncertainties all over the world. The United States is actively decoupling China as it views the country as an existential threat. In response, China is opening up its economy by eliminating all tariffs on goods from the least developed countries. China's trade surplus worldwide is one trillion US dollars. Compared with the US share of global exports (8.5 percent), China's share was 14 percent in 2023. China is now diversifying its markets and avoiding US tariffs through its Belt and Road Initiative's infrastructure investment funding with 150 countries. In addition to using tariffs as a weapon, the United States is also "weaponizing" its dollars by freezing the dollar assets of sovereign countries and applying US laws and sanctions related to its dollar's reserve status for other countries. It is not clear whether the BRICS countries could replace the American dollar with other financial tools (Narine 2025). The global fight over economic dominance between the United States and China (and other American adversaries) may trigger a military showdown.

Tension in the Middle East

Meanwhile, with a long history of enduring fights, the Middle East and North Africa has emerged as an epic centre of political turmoil. It is a geographic region made up of many countries, including Egypt, Iran, Iraq, Israel, Jordon, Kuwait, Lebanon, Libya, Oman, Palestine, Qatar, Saudi Arabia, Syria, and the United Arab Emirates. The creation of Israel and the split of Palestine into separate Jewish and Arab states by the United Nations is a historical source of ongoing conflicts there.

The recent Israel-Hamas war started in 2024 and does not seem to be ending, although ceasefires were declared several times. At the time of writing, the two sides were still unsettled on their co-existence. Given the unresolved issues of territories, the emboldened aggression of Israel, and the negation of humanitarian supports in the region, the historical anguish and resulting unrest do not seem to be subsiding anytime soon.

Adversaries

Raphael Cohen (2024), the director of the Strategy and Doctrine Program at the Rand Corporation's Project Air Force, observed that geopolitics has made the world tense and unstable. The world order has largely been created, developed, and guarded by the United States since the Second World War. In the last few years, with wars raging in Ukraine and the Middle East and the simmering tension in the South China Sea region, NATO and the United States have been busy "putting out fires," and, at the same time, the political and military ties among China, Russia, Iran, and North Korea are consolidating. These four countries have supported each other in terms of troop deployment, the supply of weapons, economic assistance, treaty signing, and various forms of assistance.

The United States has simultaneously found itself involved in more than two wars (Russia/Ukraine and Israel/Palestine), which is depleting its resources. This is in contrast with American government's traditional preference of engaging in no more than two wars at the same time. The United States has found itself in an untenable situation with this current military scenario, especially when China's military resources and power have increased formidably. With the alliance of China, Russia, Iran, and North Korea focusing their fight against the United States, the world is facing a more insecure order, and the United States must find ways to deal with the emerging "axis of adversaries."

US Ambitions

With the arrival of President Donald Trump's second term, the political signals being sent out from the White House appear to be one of US disengagement from international organizations (such as the United Nations) and from other countries (and treaties and agreements), including NATO. The administration is prepared to "negotiate" a peace talk on Ukraine between Russia and the United States without the involvement of the Ukrainians or any NATO members and to control Gaza and remove the Palestinians from the area without consultation with the Palestinians at the time of writing. This indicates that the United States is abandoning its historical allies and friends and preparing to appease Russia, although Russia invaded Ukraine two times in the past ten years without any provocation from the Ukrainians. In the case of Gaza, the United States is preparing to negate the rights of Palestinians and acquire Gaza under the ownership of the United States. In both cases, the United States is bypassing a multilateral process of negotiation and finding solutions to reach enduring peace with specific countries and not multiple stakeholder countries nearby.

In international trade, while both Mexico and Canada are historical free-trade allies of the United States, the United States is denouncing the United States-Mexico-Canada Agreement, which was signed in 2020, and is preparing to impose on its trading partners 25 percent tariffs on all imported goods (and 10 percent on oil and gas from Canada), along with another 25 percent tariffs on steel and aluminum imported from Canada, and other foreign importers worldwide irrespective of their allyship and friendship with the United States. In other words, the United States is acting as a bully and not negotiating with its partners.

The expansionist ambition of the United States is beginning to look like those of its adversaries (Russia and China) in their plans to gain more territory of geopolitical and economic importance. For Russia, it is the Ukraine and the Arctic, and, for China, it is Taiwan, the South China Sea, and the Arctic as well. The United States has expressed its ambition to annex Canada, Greenland, and Panama through economic or military force and acquire Ukraine's natural resources (I. Kapoor 2025). Ambitions of this nature resemble the carving of "spheres of influence" in different parts of the world by the European colonial powers in the nineteenth century. Such an expression of ambitions can unsettle many countries as it does not abide by international law, treaties, or agreements, and these ambitions often bring cross-country suspicion and tension.

Implications

Historically, racial prejudice in Canada has grown when there have been external conflicts and threats. In the Second World War, when

Japan joined Germany in its fight against the Allies, Canadian antagonism and distrust toward the Japanese Canadians increased. Japanese Canadians were labelled by the Canadian government as "the enemy from within," and their properties were confiscated, and they were then rounded up and put in internment camps. The coordinated 9/11 attacks on the Twin Towers of the World Trade Centre in New York City and the Pentagon in Arlington, Virginia, in the United States on 11 September 2001 were executed by Al-Qaeda, an Islamic extremist group. Close to three thousand people died in what was the single largest loss of life from a foreign attack on the US home front. Since then, Muslims have been cast as terrorists, and Islamophobia has taken hold in many Western countries, including Canada. Religious and traditional symbols and clothing elicit fear among Canadians. With the war raging on between Israel and Palestine since 2023, both anti-Semitism and anti-Palestine hate activities have erupted. During the COVID-19 period from 2019 to 2022, the virus was rumoured to have originated in China and been deliberately spread all over the world through the Chinese government's actions, mismanagement, and disinformation. Chinese people in Canada were seen as conspiring with China to infect Canadians (according to conspiracy theories). More Chinese Canadians were verbally abused, spat upon, and physically assaulted on the street. Waves of anti-Asian hatred prevailed across Canada. These racist activities illustrate that global conflicts—wars, terrorism, or the pandemic crisis—and their interpretations or conspiracy rumours can intensify the traumas of racialized people.

Which issues the government stands on is also important. Any gestures seen as endorsements of political positions give permission to people to respect or hate racialized or Indigenous peoples or other marginalized people. The government's treatment of Japanese Canadians permitted people to suspect and distance themselves from them. Silence on the part of the authorities, be it in the political, corporate, or religious arena, may be interpreted as the "quiet endorsement" of racialized, ethnic, or religious biases. The inaction on the part of the authorities regarding public hate toward Chinese Canadians seemed to give permission people to disrespect and harass that particular racialized group. Public condemnation of group activities, if not clearly communicated, may also be interpreted as public blaming. An example of this type of blaming can be found in the current finger pointing at South Asians who have been shouldering the blaming for housing unaffordability and asylum application backlogs in Canada and the negative experiences that Muslims and Jews have to bear in police-community relations and border crossings, along with hate activities imposed on worshippers, religious buildings, and schools (Su 2025). In spite of the changing geopolitical turmoil and the Russian invasion of Ukraine, anti-Russian sentiments are rising in Canada both in the media and on the street, in addition to the sanctions that have been imposed on Russia.

Geopolitical tensions have intensified through shifting military reinforcement and encounters in Europe, Asia, and the Middle East, which have increased attention on built-in historical and structural issues, most of which are unresolved given the hardening of the positions of the current political players. One would expect that the racist activities that have surfaced sporadically will continue until negative international relations subside. The racism that is generated through these escalated tense international conflicts often permeates to the work environment, and it is expected that some racist remarks or violence will erupt. Emotion generated by external international events in the larger society needs to be diffused by governments and civic leaders, and the hatred or bigotry that is expressed must be sanctioned and condemned; otherwise, such government negation or leniency may be interpreted by people as demonstrating that the authorities are giving permission to people to translate the prejudice and stereotyping into actions. For the same reason, politicians, corporate executives, and leaders of other social domains (such as education, religion, sports, entertainment, and so on) need to join hands in standing up and calling out against racism before the general public begins to accept bigotry as the "new normal" and the governments falling into patterns of authoritarianism, illiberalism, populism, hate crimes and violence, and anti-wokeism.

More importantly, when governments, corporate leadership, and civic/community leadership are not taking actions to pre-empt the racial ramifications of geo-conflicts with the progress made so far on DEI or the human rights fronts, "catch up" jobs that reverse the likelihood of an influx of new types of prejudice and stereotypes from forces outside the workplace will become difficult. One can easily learn lessons from the Israel-Hamas war in Gaza, which erupted so quickly, and the rising hostility and violence between the Jews and the Palestinians in Canada that developed in a matter of a few weeks in 2023–24. Corporate executives and managers, as well as human resources professionals, were not prepared for the dynamics of ethnic, religious, and racial tensions to change so quickly. Similarly, the rising Islamophobia that simmered and erupted after the 9/11 attacks in September 2001 and how fast such fear and anxiety toward Muslims and their communities spread across Canada and how persistently the phobia has lasted for over a decade should encourage government, corporate management, and civic/community leadership to rethink how best to neutralize, reduce, and eliminate racism in the workplace and beyond, lest it descends unexpectedly and without warning. The reality is that what happens outside the workplace is likely to impact employees and the workplace. Workplace racism and geopolitics are intertwined.

GROWING AUTHORITARIANISM, ILLIBERALISM, AND POPULISM

Marlies Glasius (2018) defines "authoritarianism" as repeated actions that negate the accountability of those in power to people by making decisions in secret, disseminating disinformation, and blocking people's voices. This pattern of power exercises is often associated with "illiberalism" of which its actions infringe on individual autonomy, human dignity, and human rights. Authoritarianism is therefore a threat to democracy.

One must be aware that authoritarianism may be created through democratic elections. It could be a full-blown regime covering vast territories, or it could manifest on a smaller scale like limiting its practices to only small parts of the government apparatus or its local branches. Democracy is "a free competition for a free vote" (Schumpeter 1943, 260, 271), which is founded on tenants like "respect for freedom of expression, access to information and freedom of association" (Dahl 1971, 3). In contrast, authoritarianism could be viewed as a defective democracy that has no free elections and no respect for these freedoms.

Meanwhile, "populism" could be an offspring of authoritarianism as it focuses on the direct relationship between a populist leader and the people, often bypassing the intermediate government bureaucracy or agencies. Often, the leadership assumes that it has a mandate to exercise unilateral power without being hindered by traditional institutional, or even legal, restraints.

Authoritarianism, illiberalism, and populism are three political environments that are conducive to the spread of racism mainly because they set an example for people to propagate racist messages and encourage racist assaults or other activities. The authorities in power under these systems often launch their own inequitable and unfair human resources mechanisms and institute laws, policies, and programs that pose adverse impacts on people and those who advocate the rights and fair treatments of racialized and Indigenous peoples and other marginalized groups.

Authoritarian Practices

Authoritarian practices involve "a pattern of actions, embedded in an organized context, sabotaging accountability to people ('the forum') over whom a political actor exerts control, or their representatives, by disabling their access to information and/or disabling their voice" (Glasius 2018, 527). Examples of authoritarian practices include denying access to information by those in authority positions; deliberately misinforming and providing inaccurate information to the public; discouraging critical information; blocking queries from the public, parliamentarians, journalists, human rights advocates, activists, internal critics, and whistle-blowers; and eliminating opportunities for passing judgment on those in authority (through elections, sermons, songs, journalism, and non-governmental organizations), interfering with critics of specific actions or decision, and censorship (Glasius 2018).

The Hungarian 2010 Media Law is a good example of information control.[1] The law was established by an oversight body run by the government. The legislation consists of two laws: (1) The 2010 Act 104 on the Freedom of the Presss and the Fundamental Rules on Media Content (which regulates media content and the rights and obligations of the media); and (2) The 2010 Act 185 on Media Services and Mass Media (which deals with media services and products, the establishment of Media Council, and administrative procedures for media law enforcement). The body has the authority to prohibitively level high fines on radio and television outlets. The government body is overseen by a party-controlled body with broad powers and biased tendering procedures (Human Rights Watch 2024). In India, the Modi government canceled permits for non-government organizations to receive foreign funding licences and cracked down on the foreign press by not renewing the work permits for correspondents from Australia

1 Article 19, 2011, reprinted in *Hungarian Media Laws Q & A, Country Report*, www.article19.org/data/files/medialibrary/2714/11-09-01-REPORT-hungary.pdf.

and France. The Indian police also raided the New Delhi office of a portal and the homes of journalists in 2023 in an effort to disable critical voices (Kumar 2024). These practices were authoritarian in nature, although the regimes have seldom been labelled as authoritarian, but their practices may be endemic to their mode of governance.

Illiberal Practices

Illiberal practice is "a pattern of actions, embedded in an organized context, infringing on the autonomy and dignity of the person" (Glasius 2018, 530). This pattern of practices includes interference with legal equality, legal recourse, or recognition before the law; infringement of freedom of expression, fair trial rights, religion, and the right to privacy; and violations of physical integrity rights. In sum, illiberal practices are human rights violations, and they harm human autonomy and dignity. Illiberal practices suppress the voices of those who pose a threat to those in power (Glasius 2018).

A failure to hold free and fair elections and a failure to separate powers who sabotage accountability are both considered to be authoritarian. Through a pattern of presidential decrees or thwarted or corrupted judicial oversight to bypass parliament is a form of authoritarian practice because it blocks the dialogue of accountability. These could also be illiberal practices because they infringe on individual autonomy and dignity.

Examples of a mix of authoritarian and illiberal practices with a populist appeal may be found in the Russian government's repression of homosexuality and Filipino President Rodrigo Duterte's killing of drug users (Human Rights Watch 2023, 2025). The Trump administration's deportation of Venezuelan "gangsters" from the United States to El Salvador in March 2025 misused the *Alien Enemies Act* of 1798 without the approval of Congress is a good example of an authoritarian act. The same Act was used to put 120,000 Japanese Americans in jail without trial during the Second World War (Santos 2025).

Populist Practices

Populism focuses on two segments of society: the people and the elites. Contemporary populism stresses the importance of a direct connection between the leader and the people, relies extensively on the authority of the audience, and attempts to diminish the power of the intermediary actors (political parties, mainstream media, institutional rules, and bureaucracy). It is worth noting the social context from which populism arises. It is likely to impact on the content and style of public discourse. In Canada and the United States, populism seldom changed regimes, but it enabled a large segment of people to be democratized in a common language (Urbinati 2019).

Nowadays, populism tends to rise in emerging democracies or fully democratic countries, while it does suspend free elections, it might take the form somewhere between constitutional government and dictatorship. And there is a tendency for dualism to be created between the elite and the people—the "honest many" and the "corrupt few," and the "we good" and "they bad" dichotomy or partisanship. Polarization may often emerge acutely near election time (Urbinati 2019). According to Kurt Weyland (2001, 14), populism is "best defined as a political strategy through which a personality leader seeks or exercises government power based on direct, unmediated, uninstitutionalized support from large numbers of mostly unorganized followers." There is usually an anti-establishment rhetoric among populists.

Wealthy candidates such as Silvio Berlusconi in Italy and Ross Perot and Donald Trump in the United States are part of the wealthy elite. However, they appeal to the many populists who are looking for someone who has "made it" and are competent. Populism likes to acquire power through elections as plebiscites. When a populist candidate is in power, there is a tendency for that leader to believe that they have been mandated by the population to act unilaterally without institutional consultation or support. Populist electoral victories are often interpreted as "taking the country back," and populist leaders directly communicate to the people, bypassing the intermediary organizations, such as parties or the media, and show that they do not need to abide by institutional rules (Urbinati 2019).

These observations are based on numerous research findings that reflect quite accurately the general behaviour of Donald Trump as the "saviour" of the American people, especially in his second term. Some of his executive orders are either unconstitutional or do not follow the established institutional protocols or traditional norms. He presides as if he can act alone without any restraints from the people (even his loyalists) around him, the law, or the Constitution. He can punish his critics or enemies, and he can terminate the employment of employees in the federal government if they have done something that he does not like. These leaders intend to have unlimited power and stay in power as long as possible by changing the Constitution and disbanding the Parliament or Congress of the country. According to Nadia Urbinate (2019), former President Hugo Chavez of Venezuela, former Prime Minister Silvio Berlusconi of Italy, and President Trump of the United States have all exhibited these behavioural patterns during their regimes.

In the contemporary American style of populism that is currently unfolding within Trump's second term of presidency, there is a strong focus on drumming up political messages that Trump wants people to hear, whether or not the messages are true, especially the people who support him. These messages could be misinformation or disinformation. In an age of populism, they are abundance. For populists, there are values in actively promoting disinformation to confuse people and inform people with falsehoods. This is because they could easily destabilize the status quo, make the public increasingly confused about the validity of the elites' communication, and become unable to anchor oneself with other people and the world. When people cannot tell the differences between "truths" and "falsehoods," they are more susceptible to the messages of populists who speak with great confidence and keep repeating the messages as if they are true (Kost 2025).

A Few Examples

Historically, it is not uncommon to find that democratic countries beget authoritarian governments. One may find that dictators have been elected by people through the ballot box. Russia, Turkey, Hungary, Poland, India, Philippines, Venezuela, Peru, and Ecuador—once in power, these political leaders roll back democracy. David Frum (2017) maintains that the pre-conditions for an autocracy are here for "'democratic backsliding' .... down a path toward illiberalism" in the United States (Glasius 2018; Parker and Towler 2019).

Meanwhile, a recent review of studies on global political trust from 1958 to 2019 showed that, at least since 1990, trust in parliament and government has declined by an average of 8.4 and 7.3 percentage points respectively in democratic countries in the world. In both Hungary and the United States, political distrust has been a powerful predictor in the elections for Viktor Orban in Hungary in 2010 and for Donald Trump in the United States in 2016. A significant number of Republican voters for Trump were distrustful of the federal government when compared with Democratic voters. This public disenchantment with authority is a strong factor that has given rise to authoritarianism, illiberalism, and populism. There are other contributing factors such as a polarization of political trust between the two segments of the population, economic distress, negative attitudes toward immigration and refugee claimants, and cultural wars of wokeism (Valgarosson et al. 2025).

The United States witnessed authoritarianism during the period after the Civil War, a twelve-year period from 1865 to 1877, when there was unresolved racial tension between White people and Black people in the southern part of the country. The civil and political rights of Black people were undermined, and the growing violence of the Ku Klux Klan devastated Black southerners. The removal of civil liberties and the imposition of punitive actions against opposing critics at that time were signs of authoritarianism among those in power. Blacks remained segregated and disenfranchised, their housing and education situation worsened, and White supremacy remained the ideology and practice well into the twentieth century. While racism manifested changes through time, authoritarianism seemed to be related to the social anxiety that was generated against racialized people, and Black people were perceived by White people as social threats. Throughout the period between the last quarter of the nineteenth century and much of the twentieth century, there were efforts by civil society and the government to instill human rights and the fair treatment of all people. However, the undercurrent in the United States is still authoritarianism, which is associated with conformity to the White race and culture. Any deviation from this conformity is considered to be a threat (Parker and Towler 2019).

Hence, the drive to build an affirmative action legal framework since the civil rights movement and a DEI culture in the last thirty or more years has been an uphill struggle both in the workplace and in the non-work environment (such as education institutions). There have been numerous court challenges in the United States regarding the affirmative action program at the post-secondary education level. The latest one was pursued by Edward Blum and other conservative activists. Blum founded the Students for Fair Admissions, which brought the cases of Harvard University and the University of Southern Carolina to the US Supreme Court. He challenged race-conscious admission policies and laws on voting rights that had reached the Supreme Court in the past. The Supreme Court's rulings on affirmative action on college admissions of these two universities signalled the rise of political conservatism. Blum is on Do No Harm, a conservative activist group, board of directors. This organization had challenged DEI programs in the health-care industry, including a case against Pfizer. The latter was challenged as Do No Harm alleged the company's fellowship program had discriminated against White and Asian-American applicants in the past (Liptak 2023).

The presidency of Donald Trump in his first term in the United States in 2016 signalled the growing momentum of authoritarianism. Along with other political leaders who have claimed to be a "strong man," Trump portrayed himself as the saviour of the country who could and would "Make America Great Again." There have been many indicators, through his words and deeds, that, in his second term as president in 2025, he would lead like an authoritarian by undermining democratic norms (such as the freedom of speech) and institutions (such as the freedom of press) and bring the country closer to authoritarianism (some have even used the term "fascism") by dismantling the separation of judicial, legislative, and executive powers and muster more power onto himself so he could preside without the approval of the Congress and the Senate and ignore the judicial system.

Trump has the hallmarks of an authoritarian who is racially biased, tolerant toward violence, and prepared to curtail civil liberties and ignore democratic rules. In his campaign speeches, he constantly repeated that Latinos are illegal migrants, criminals, murderers, and rapists. He also was silence on the violence of insurgents who stormed the US capital building in Washington, DC on 6 January 2021 in his defence. Immediately after his inauguration on 20 January 2025, he issued numerous executive orders to deport migrants to their home countries and smashed all DEI policies, programs, and initiatives of the federal government and their infrastructures, funding, and human resources. At the same time, the government was preparing a strategic plan and the groundwork for ending DEI in the private and non-profit sectors (Parker and Towler 2019).

Racism and Xenophobia

Populism is viewed differently by people in different parts of the world. In the United States, the term is viewed as being extremely right-wing or left-wing, whereas, in Canada, it is associated with fascism, extremism, and Trump. In Europe (France and Italy), populism represents demagoguery and nationalism/patriotism (Wagner and Brigevich 2024). Despite these variations, one central theme of populism is the people versus the elite, with a high inclination toward xenophobia and racism (Clark 2024). Populism, as a form of authoritarianism, has often led to the formation of political parties or party politics. What attracts people to join the momentum of populism is its ability to make politics seem personal. People identify with the cause as it has personal meanings, and the political right is inclined to connect politics with personal experiences and cultures as witnessed in the anti-woke cultural wars in the United States, which will be discussed later in this chapter (Zack 2023).

Right-wing racist, nationalist, anti-immigrant, and Islamophobic movements and political parties are on the rise in Europe. Examples may be found in the ascendency of the Golden Dawn in Greece, the National Front in France, the Alternative fur Deutschland and the Patriotic Europeans against the Islamisation of the Occident (PEGIDA) in Germany, the Party for Freedom in the Netherlands, the Swedish Democrats in Sweden, the English Defence League in the United Kingdom, and One Nation in Australia. And, now, the Republican Party in the United States has joined the list of populist movements and parties (Vieten 2016).

In Canada, far-right groups such as the Ku Klux Klan, the Nazis, and other fascists in the 1920s and 1930s surfaced and were active, as was the Heritage Front in the 1980s and 1990s. Nowadays, in the aftermath of the 9/11 terrorist attacks of the Twin Towers and the Pentagon, there has been widespread anxiety over the Islamic religion. PEGIDA Canada and La Meute and other far-right organizations began their White supremacist, anti-Semitism, and anti-government populist communication messages and recruited thousands of followers. Their key platforms of propaganda are digital, and their contents are largely provoking and engaging and of dubious quality and accuracy. There are those who spread hate messages and those who instigate physical violence (Leman-Langlois, Campana, and Tanner 2024).

History suggests that, at the time of economic crisis, scapegoating of certain segments of the population is common. The creation of an "out group" or several "out groups" is receptive to people who are prepared to find fault with others as an explanation for widespread economic turmoil. In the 1930s, Jews, communists, gays and lesbians, and elites were scapegoated in fascist Germany. In late 1970s and early 1980s, the "New Right" movement gained ascendency under Prime Minister Margaret Thatcher in the United Kingdom and President Ronald Reagan in the United States with its nationalist and xenophobic rhetoric focusing on opposing the elites and foreigners (as reflected in the drive for Brexit in United Kingdom). The rise of Jörg Haider in Austria, Marine Le Pen in France, and Republicans in Germany and the United States normalizes the far-right politics, policy, and White supremacy in the West. Nowadays, most new populist movements are on the far-right spectrum, with "we" the pure people and "them" the corrupt elite, and the projected enemy is the Muslim and the Jew. An analysis of the rhetoric of the Finns Party in Finland shows that the current DEI management policies and programs that assigned special privileges for minorities is odds with the populist movement. The latter's interpretation is that "true" Finns are being discriminated by the elites and the minorities in their own country in the name of DEI (Vieten 2016).

Implications

The ascendency of right-wing parties and social movements has added momentum to the spread of authoritarianism, illiberalism, and populism all over the world. It is a political phenomenon that has escalated in its momentum in the last decade. As noted, the hallmarks of authoritarianism are blockages to correct information, the spread of disinformation and misinformation, and the reduced opportunity to express opinions or ask critical questions. Populism favours the rise of dictators and neutralizes the effectiveness of intermediary institutions (or the "deep state"), thus enabling the further acquisition of power in the hands of the dictators. The latter can just make laws and policies as they see fit.

These structural and process changes in a democratic society could easily amplify the messages of the government or those of authoritarian, illiberal, and populist movements that are usually in different shades of nationalistic, fascist, and racist themes. These political, usually anti-human rights and denial of freedoms messages have either gradually seeped through or forcefully entered the mainstream media and public discourses. When these messages are intentionally propagated through the government, they present a theme that is more right of centre: anti-race centred, anti-gender centred, and anti-DEI. The theme can be more modest or more extreme depending on the nature of the social movements or the official ideology of the populist/authoritarian government.

In a more extreme form, the communication messages could be more fascist and similar to Germany's Hitler regime where people were categorized in a hierarchy of superiority and inferiority, "in" groups and "out" groups, or "us" or "them" groups. Since this regime was modelled on a "strong man" mandate and is a winning model, the communication messages are usually commanding and authoritative, and people tend to be attracted to this "halo effect" and adopt its messages to some degree. As the messages on race, gender, human rights, and DEI have shifted in the larger society to correspond to those of the new regime, more managerial staff and employees in the workplace may also adopt the tone of the new messages, and the treatment of racialized and Indigenous people may also align with the new messages. Soon, the managerial style in the workplace may also shift from a collaborative team approach (as in a DEI mode) to a custodial "command-and-control" approach (which aligns with the "rule by fear" of the new regime). All these cascading communication messages and shifts in values and managerial styles in the workplace could be slow or fast in motion depending on how the authoritarian/populist regime enforces the new policies and laws.

HATE CRIME, HATE SPEECH, AND VIOLENCE

While there are conceptual ambiguities surrounding the term "hate crime," it still has its value in public policy development and in community alliance formation (Ignaski 2008). Hate crimes are also known as bias-motivated crimes. These crimes are perpetuated against racialized and Indigenous peoples along with other marginalized groups (such as Muslims, women, trans-gendered people, gays and lesbians, and people with disabilities) based on prejudice and hatred. They instill fear or cause harm among members of these groups based on their personal identities. The fear is often instilled through speeches, written words, and graphic/symbols of hate in addition to other forms of victimization such as micro-aggressions, intimidation, harassment, or discrimination, and the harms to the victims include assault, murder, arson, and/or vandalism. Victims of hate crimes usually feel unsafe and anxious and have no peace of mind on a daily basis (Farrell and

Lockwood 2023). Making segments of the population afraid of other people or their surroundings, and feeling stigmatized and traumatized, is one effective way to control marginalized people.

Hate speech is motivated by hatred, and it portrays segments of the population as vermin, excrement, or animals and advocates genocide and incites violence and terrorism. Hate speech, both online and offline, is a threat to racialized and Indigenous peoples, plus other marginalized groups (Woolf 2024). When hate speech poses a challenge to government regulation, such a challenge remains unresolved as it seemingly impinges on the freedom of speech.

Currently, the effectiveness for the existing legal means to muzzle hate speech remains unclear and is judged on a case-by-case basis. The federal government has proposed having the Canadian Human Rights Commission address the issue as a human rights complaint, but it did ignite some opposition. And the current *Online Streaming Act*, due to its coverage of online platforms, does invite smaller online platforms (such as Gab) to become havens for hate as they are not regulated by the federal legislation on online streaming.[2] Until such time in which a specific federal legislation that could eliminate hate speech is available for effective enforcement, digital hate speech remains unchecked (Patel 2023).

Canada

In Canada, hate crimes that target Jews, Muslims, and Black people have increased in a staggered manner between 2009 and 2017. The crime rate rose 47 percent to 2,073 in 2017. Both violent and non-violent crimes have increased and so have hate-related property crimes (such as graffiti and vandalism) and the incitement of hatred, threats, assaults, and harassment. Vandalized property damages have amplified the visibility of hatred in the public eye, thus deepening the traumas of harms experienced by victims and their communities. During the COVID-19 pandemic, reports of anti-Asian hatred increased as people hurled insults, threw garbage, and spat at Asian Canadians. In public transit, people changed seats so as to avoid sitting close to them. Anti-Asian harassment and assaults were commonly noted (Lederman 2023).

Increased anti-Muslim incidents in the country have been linked to the far-right populist movement, and mosque shootings have set the

2 *Online Streaming Act*, SC 2023, c 8.

tone of hurt throughout Muslim communities. The highest rates have been in Ontario and Quebec. Statistics Canada claimed that these statistics, while heightened, are likely "under-counts" of the real extent of hate crimes in Canada (Grant 2018). Police-reported hate crimes increased by more than 30 percent in 2023 when compared with those in the year before. Even then, there is a tendency that hate crimes have been under-reported largely due to the lack of a clear definition of what constitutes a "hate crime" and that people are not trained in identifying them and in knowing the legal standard or government guidelines for law enforcement and prosecution (Woolf 2024).

In addition, there is growing online extremism that connects racism and violence. In the first three months of 2018, 2.5 million of hateful messages were found on Facebook, and, between April and June, YouTube users flagged more than 6.6 million hateful videos (Tenove, Tworek, and McKelvey 2018). Some of these online ideological messages have led to anti-Semitic or anti-Muslim violent incidents. As a result of the Israel-Hamas war, police have noted an increase of online hate, graffiti, and assaults in many major cities across Canada. B'nai Brith Canada reported approximately twenty-eight hundred anti-Semitic incidents in 2022, with 75 percent of them occurring online. Social media (such as TikTok, Instagram, and Snapchat) is now the largest anti-Semitic medium (Smith and Proudfoot 2023).

Anti-South Asian hate showed an increased severity. In 2014–15, South Asians in Canada were scapegoated for numerous social problems (such as housing unaffordability and shortage and asylum application backlogs in the government system). In 2017, there were violent killings at a mosque in Quebec City. In 2020, a South Asian cab driver was stabbed to death in Winnipeg. In 2021, a Pakistani Canadian Muslim family was run down by a truck, and a judge described the incident as white nationalist terrorism due to Islamophobic hate and the online radicalization of racism. Some scholars have noted that these far-right messages have increasingly adopted and propagated the Great Replacement Theory to increase hatred toward racialized migrants as if the latter intended to replace the White people as the dominant population and take over the historically rightful place of the White people in Canada. In 2024, the federal government's announcement of drastic cuts to the number of people admitted into Canada once again sent a clear signal that immigrants, temporary migrants, and international students are to be blamed for housing unaffordability, inadequate health-care services, and the lack of infrastructure supports (Kukreja 2024).

The public took a hint from the government's negative attitudes and actions toward immigrants and international students as permission to disrespect, even to the point of "dehumanizing" South Asians. Many South Asian international students also reported anti-Indian accusations online saying, so to speak, that they were taking jobs away from local Canadians and damaging the future of Canada. Reported hate crimes against South Asians and Muslims appear to be increasing. One in six people reported that race-based hate crimes were against South Asians in 2023, but it was only one in ten in 2022. There was also a large increase in reported hate crimes against Muslims. Most of these hate crimes were limited to threats or graffiti, but 12 percent of them were physical assaults. In 2023, 44.5 percent of hate crimes with South Asian and Black people facing higher rates of hate threats and assaults (Brunner and Coustere 2024; Su 2025).

In 2023, the Royal Canadian Mounted Police reported the arrest of a young man, alleging his role in the making of videos for a US-based neo-Nazi group promoting hate and terrorist activities. This, along with other cases related to White supremacy and terrorism (such as Atomwaffen, also known as National Socialist Order), represents increased cases that connect racial hate with terrorism. This group also provides firearm-training camps for people attacking racial, ethnic, and religious groups (Hayes 2023). More than half (55 percent) of the hate crime perpetrators were White people in 2020. Unlike the organized Ku Klux Klan of the old days (with White members), contemporary hate crimes are committed by ordinary people meeting online, sharing white supremacy ideas, and planning for offline hate activities. Nowadays, these "ordinary people" may not be White; they are more heterogeneous and diverse in their social backgrounds (Schafer 2002).

Hate crimes are often carried out in retaliation against terrorist attacks. Hate crimes related to race, ethnicity, or immigrant/migrant status occurr when offenders feel threatened by the victim's groups and assert their dominance in the social hierarchy. Some hate events may not be properly categorized as hate crimes, but they nevertheless cause harm to the victims. In the current context of polarized speeches or overt behaviour as well as extreme ideology, driven by prejudice and hatred, some ordinary individuals, who are not related to any hate groups, seem to get "social" permission and feel "entitled" to express hatred and anger (through assaults or micro-aggressions) toward migrants, immigrants, asylum seekers, native-born racialized, or Indigenous peoples when the offenders believe that their space or activities have been intruded upon or disturbed (Farrell and Lockwood 2023).

United States

During the COVID-19 pandemic in 2019–22, there was an increase of hate crimes and victimization—notably, among Asian communities and among Muslim and Jewish communities during the violent war activities in the Middle East. Hate messages are increasingly noted online through social media, especially in those media being lenient or inclined to right-wing messages. In the United States, that would be X (formerly known as Twitter), Rumble, Truth Social, Parler, Gab, Gettr and even YouTube. X has a huge participant base with more than $4.5 billion in December 2024. And since Elon Musk's takeover of X in 2022, he has restored about sixty thousand accounts formerly suspended. These accounts included those of white nationalists, neo-Nazi, and conspiracy theorists. The threats of harm messages are also broadening with a mix of anti-democracy ideologies and racism spilling over to the government, the public health and education sector, and the private sector (Farrell and Lockwood 2023).

In the United States, law enforcement agencies classified several thousand hate crime cases; most were motivated by racial bias. In 2020, police in the United States reported 8,052 criminal incidents motived by bias that were considered to be hate crimes, and Federal Bureau of Investigation witnessed the largest increase in hate crimes based on race, ethnicity, or ancestry (mainly, Black individuals) since 2001. Hate crimes against Asian Americans increased by 76 percent between 2019 and 2020. In spite of the statistics on growing hate crimes and speech, under-reporting of hate crimes is considered common by law enforcement agencies due to inadequate police training in this field. The police reports of hate crimes are a fraction of the reports of victimization by non-governmental organizations such as Anti-Defamation League and the Southern Poverty Law Centre and self-reporting through the National Crime Victimization Survey (the Bureau of Justice in the United States) (Dovidio et al. 2010; Farrell and Lockwood 2023).

Implications

Hatred of certain segments of the population is proliferating and is spreading across a broad spectrum of society. Hate is no longer limited to the fringe of societies in many Western countries and is permeating into the mainstream. What we have witnessed in the United States is the expanding targets of hate on racialized and Indigenous people, feminists, LGBTQIA+, religious communities, migrants, refugees, and immigrants (Dovidio et al. 2010).

The ascendency of hate crimes and hate speech (especially online) has created a culture of blaming racialized and Indigenous people for social and political problems. Although these crimes and speeches have mostly occurred in a non-workplace environment, the very fact that they are commonly found in neighbourhoods and every walk of life means that prejudice, scapegoating, and hatred toward certain segments of the population are increasingly mainstream. Hate crimes and hate speech have become more of a social norm than a social deviance. The frequent occurrence of hate crimes and hate speeches in the larger society gives permission to employees at work to behave with hatred, especially when these activities of hatred have increased outside the workplace, and the current legal framework is not effective in curtailing these activities.

Empirical evidence on the impact of the authority-endorsed legalized bigotry and the government leniency toward public bigotry has begun to emerge. In Western societies such as the United States and United Kindom where anti-DEI sentiments are endorsed or even legalized and fair treatment at work is not considered to be a human resources requirement, where authorities give a green signal to bigotry, blatant prejudice, and overt discrimination, and where past support and protections for disadvantaged groups (such as racialized and Indigenous peoples) have been withdrawn and harassment, bullying, intimidation, intolerance and micro-aggressions are increasingly experienced and reported by employees. A recent Cypher's survey of four thousand adults in the United Kingdom, cited by Tony Case (2025b) of *Worklife Daily*, revealed that more than three-quarters of the Black respondents reported that they had been recently discriminated against and that sexual harassment is reported to be on the rise, especially among the LGBTQIA+ employees. When the government's number of arrests is unable to keep pace with the number of hate crimes and hate speech, and the people who have offended go unchecked and unpunished, people who are attracted to their speeches and have endorsed hate crimes against racialized and Indigenous peoples are emboldened to do more of these crimes.

More importantly, the messages of hatred that degraded racialized and Indigenous people and stripped them of their human dignity and painted them as less than human beings were intentionally created to influence people, and they are gradually settling in the psyche of more people. Repetitions of language of hatred and news of unchecked or unresolved hate crimes have demonstrated to some people that the government is not serious in stopping or ending them. Workplace racism, whether it is manifested as some modest racial jokes or comments, simple but continuous micro-aggressive conduct, passive-aggressive resistance to cooperate, or outright verbal abuse or physical assaults, can be the offspring of masked racial hatred. Some words or gestures that are belittling, jabbing, or intimidating may be a reflection of the negative perceptions and attitudes toward them. Clearly, in times of emerging unchecked hate speech and hate crimes in the larger communities, corporate and civic leadership must take extra measures to ensure that workplace culture and morale are not contaminated with any shades of racial hatred, and proactive works are needed to pre-empt employees from being influenced by bigotry.

RISING CHALLENGES TO DEI

US Supreme Court and Legal Challenges

As a school of management thoughts, DEI began its ascendency in the United States, Canada, and the rest of the Western countries in the later part of the twentieth century. Its popularity among major corporations went relatively unchallenged for over thirty years. Lately, DEI suffered some setbacks, especially when affirmative action programs in the education sector in the United States were challenged numerous times. There was a marked increase in federal lawsuits targeting DEI programs, which was compiled by New York University's School of Law's Meltzer Centre: eleven filed in 2021, fifteen in 2022, and forty in 2023. Some of these lawsuits could be called reverse discrimination lawsuits, and some involved diversity training. These lawsuits were launched well before Trump declared the death of DEI in 2025 (Mensik 2024b).

Although there have been challenges to social justice policies and legislations in the past few decades, the latest wave of challenges appeared to be triggered by the US Supreme Court's decision on affirmative action. In June 2023, the Supreme Court ruled that Harvard University and the University of North Carolina's race-conscious admissions were unconstitutional, violating the Equal Protection Clause of the Fourteenth Amendment. Speaking for the majority, Chief Justice John Roberts wrote that both universities' programs "lack sufficiently focused and measurable objectives warranting the use of race, unavoidably employ race in a negative manner, involve racial stereotyping, and lack meaningful end points." The chief justice maintained that applicants must be assessed as individuals "not on the basis of race" but, rather, on their own individual experiences (quoted in Liptak 2023).

This ruling by the US Supreme Court has tipped the balance of ideology in favour to the right for at least a generation. Affirmative action, which was once entrenched and symbolized the equitable society that democracy cherished, is now losing a lot of its old political clout that was gained through the civil rights movement of the 1960s. Even in the last days of its strength, affirmative action in university education was able to tilt the scale; of Black students, only 1.5 percent of the admitted class of 2026 at Harvard University were poised to join the elite. The end of affirmative action meant further erosion of the chance for Black and other racialized people to access higher education in the United States. The re-election of Donald Trump in 2024 is likely to have further cemented the decline of social justice and human rights in the United States for more generations to come (Thompson 2023).

Another side effect of this 2023 ruling is that the US Supreme Court also seems to have laid the groundwork in setting legal limits on workforce diversity. It is expected that employers would examine their DEI policy after this ruling and may hesitate to consider race in hiring, which will further restrict the pipeline of highly qualified minority candidates (Wiessner 2023). The chilling effect of the declared end of affirmative action for the university sector is reflective of the decline in the private sector's public mentioning of their environmental, social, and governance (ESG) initiatives. ESG reporting aims to enhance corporate accountability and transparency, meets investors' demands and engages stakeholders, manages risks and sustainability, and increases corporate competitiveness. In the United States, there are standardized reporting requirements (such as Global Reporting Initiative). According to Axios, a media company in the United States, the number of companies reporting ESG initiatives was down 64 percent in the fourth quarter of 2021 from its peak. Factset found that ESG that was mentioned in the transcripts of management calls declined in four of the past five quarters. Companies were not comfortable in showing their ESG initiatives because they perceived ESG to have a negative connotation in a woke culture (Shufelt 2023).

Ever since the US Supreme Court overturned affirmative action in 2023, corporate DEI programs and initiatives on multiculturalism face uncertainty in the United States. Even the subsidiaries of many companies located in Canada have the dilemma of deciding whether to follow the policies of their headquarters or to adhere to the Canadian norms and legal framework. Some corporations in the United States do not have a clear plan or goal for their DEI programs. Companies, such as Ford Motors, John Deere, Bud Light, Miller Lite, Adidas, Lowe's, Harley Davidson, and Molson Coors are now facing a public that is increasingly associating the DEI brand with "woke" culture. These companies want to stay away from cultural conflict and their commitments made in the aftermath of the death of George Floyd. They see that DEI has become a polarizing force, and they do not want their brands to be built around that concept. Some right-wing investors (such as Robby Starbuck) are boycotting companies that support "woke" initiatives and/or ceasing to invest in them (McCoy 2024).

Furthermore, some companies have found that the global political and economic future is uncertain and risky. Consumer spending is slowing down. They have started to divest money from their DEI initiatives. Consulting and marketing firms that depend on DEI or multicultural marketing have found their revenues shrinking. There are also increased legal risks in conducting DEI programs that address issues related to employment discrimination, target hiring/promotion, and DEI training. Cutbacks on DEI initiatives include the reduction in funding on education and training of executives and managers on unconscious bias and cultural awareness, undoing the metrics for measuring executive performance in DEI, shifting financial resources from DEI programs, and laying off DEI staff members. The gains that were made in the last ten years on the DEI front in both the United States and Canada are gradually being diminished, at least in terms of public appearance and narrative, though not necessarily of substance and operation (Hall and Soliman 2024, B4). And DEI and ESG are increasingly viewed as intertwined management concepts and seen as evils by anti-wokeism activists.

The Conference Board of the United States (2024a) published its survey report entitled "DEI under Pressure" in 2024 showing that DEI in the United States is under tremendous political, legal, and social pressure, although the business case for DEI remains relevant. Due to growing concerns from shareholders, activists, lawmakers, and government agencies, 63 percent of executives see that DEI is under pressure and acknowledge that the 2023 US Supreme Court's decision on affirmative action has had a negative impact on their DEI programs. Sixty-nine percent of these companies expect persistent external scrutiny of their DEI efforts.

To avoid political or legal risks related to DEI as a result of the US Supreme Court's 2023 verdict, 53 percent of these companies have modified their DEI terminology to mitigate their risks and downplay the DEI program's conventional target groups, and 20 percent more are expected to do the same. Despite this adverse environment, fewer than 10 percent of these companies are cutting back on their DEI resources in the next three years. They are using broader concepts like "engagement," "inclusiveness," and "belonging" (to replace "diversity"). Instead of using the term "diversity recruitment" in the past, companies are now using "broadening talent pool," which is less prone to legal challenges and not as likely to be perceived to be "woke." A small percentage of the surveyed companies will scale back their external communication on DEI in the next few years (Conference Board of the United States 2024a).

Anti-Woke Movement

Being "woke" means being concerned about social justice issues such as racism or sexism. Increasingly, the term is associated with progressive advocates who stay alert to social or racial injustice and discrimination. The phrase "stay woke" was coined by Huddie "Leadbelly" Ledbetter who ended a song advising Black people to "stay woke ... Keep your eyes open" when travelling through Alabama in 1938. It means staying alert to societal issues and asking people to be vigilant and advocate for needed social change. "Stay woke" tends to be associates with the civil rights movement. Academically, woke is translated nowadays into the curricula of DEI studies, feminism and gender studies, postcolonial theory, queer theory, disability, and fat studies.

According to anti-woke activists, the meaning of "woke" changed drastically from positive and inspiring to negative and pejorative. It is now twisted by anti-woke activists to mean that using group identity, rather than individual merits, as a means to allocate or redistribute resources and opportunities is unfair and unequal and undermines the principles of individual merits and individual rights. It emphasizes ideological conformity and suppresses individual dissent. It sees people basically in two groups: the oppressors and the oppressed. One example cited by anti-woke activists is the people in the Black Lives Matter movement who see themselves as being politically awake on collective racial justice but negate individual merits (Paulson 2024). In other words, anti-woke activists want society to go back to old-fashioned "individualism" when individuals were responsible for their own fate through their hard work and accomplishment, and their advancement should not depend on their collective identities such as race or sex.

Canada

The concept of "woke" keeps on changing its meanings through time and culture. Some anti-woke people (as in the Stop Woke movement in Canada) see wokeism as a school of thought that opposes free speech, reason, open inquiry, and individual autonomy. In the name of social justice, anti-woke activists view DEI as leveraging identity politics and victimhood and fostering social fractures and authoritarianism. DEI in the workplace makes people feel that they are being judged by their identities rather than their merits and competencies. In Canada, anti-woke culture sentiments tend to associate DEI with opposition to privately funded medical care and support for medical assistance in dying, abortion, gender self-identification, native land acknowledgement, and immigration growth. These sentiments reflect the nostalgia of classic liberalism and traditional family values. Anti-woke activists believe that the historical niceties and compassionate nature of Canadians have eased these woke ideologies to infiltrate the political, social, and business elites and permeate many institutional visions and policies to the extent that they go along with wokeism. In the end, wokeism has eroded the traditional world order of classic liberalism, democracy, and freedom and built its ideologies as the foundation of the social framework without much pushback from Canadians. Anti-work activists believe that woke ideology is connected to "society's current ills," and they advocate for "merit, equality, and fairness" or "dignity, equality, and solidarity" to replace "diversity, equity, and inclusion" (DEI) (Copeland 2024).

The anti-woke movement in Canada is at its early stage of development. Eric Kaufmann (2023, 2024) reported to the Macdonald-Laurier Institute's website that media coverage of "cultural wars" between cultural socialism (which prioritizes protection for minority groups) and cultural liberalism and conservatism (which prioritizes free speech, objective truth, due process, and national heritage) has exploded in the West since 2015. John Rustad, leader of the BC Conservative Party, has been vocal about the demise of a "woke ideology." According to Professor Francis Dupuis-Deri of Universite du Quebec in Montreal, the concept of "woke" appeared to capture many different kinds of discontents under a large tent and seemed to reflect the concerns of a segment of right-wing movements in Canada, the United States, and France. The current anti-woke movement seems to be a re-surfacing of the previous anti-political correctness movement that emerged at the end of the twentieth century. This new movement has a new focus on race, gender, and sexuality with its theme on the "white men as poor victims of sexism or reverse racism" (Olaniyan 2024).

Anti-woke movement is also a reaction to both the domestic conflicts in Canada and those external wars that have broken out on the world stage in the past years. Internally, in response to numerous police-community conflicts and the killing of George Floyd in the United States, waves of anti-racism activities organized by the Black Lives Matter movement were organized, along with the advocacy movement of transgender identities and the mobilization of Indigenous people represented by Idle No More, the Indigenous-led railway blockade, and the anguish over residential school children graves. And then there is the mobilization of Palestinians over the wars in Gaza between Israel and Hamas in the Middle East. The political tension and military activities there have stirred up anti-Semitism and anti-Palestinian animosity (Olaniyan 2024).

Based on a national survey conducted by Maru Voice Canada in 2023, among many of its findings, there is an alignment of Canadian opinion with those in the United States and United Kingdom, which is two to one against the cultural socialist position (which is considered "wokeism"):

- "by a 78 to 22 margin, Canadians agree that 'political correctness has gone too far'";
- "by a 70 to 30 margin, Canadian oppose the idea that Canadian is a racist country";
- "by a 2 to 1 margin, people said we talk too much about race";
- "those who have taken diversity training are significantly more woke than those who have not"; and
- "results indicate that diversity training, as currently practiced, needs to be reformed or abolished in organizations as it heightens employee anxiety and advances contentious beliefs" (Kaufmann 2023, 2024).

These findings suggest that there is a large segment of Canadians who do not subscribe to DEI ideas, programs, or approaches that focus on race, racial matters, or racism. The overall implication is that DEI is too woke and is not in line with public opinion. This may lead to an organizational rethink of using DEI as a corporate vision for the workplace. The DEI banner does carry a political risk these days, especially when the anti-woke movement specifically mentions DEI as being too "woke" (which is an insulting word these days).

In recent years, more and more Canadian corporations are retreating from their own DEI policies and programs. The brewing company Molson Coors in Montreal has abandoned its DEI mission and has taken a "broader view" in welcoming employees. It announced that it will end its DEI training programs, and diversity "representation goals" will no longer be required in 2025. The company will no longer require its suppliers to meet diversity goals. The Ford Motor Company chief executive officer (CEO) Jim Farley also announced that the company has stopped involving itself in external cultural surveys on diversity matters (Bongiorno 2024; Wilson-Smith 2024).

United States

The growing momentum of anti-DEI sentiments in the United States seems to be a part of the anti-woke movement. Some anti-woke activists are against progressive policies on race, gender, and queers. Moms for Liberty, founded in 2021, managed to get one-third of its candidates on their school boards. "Woke" teachers have lost their jobs over their activities with anti-racism and LGBTQIA+ (in Colorado), gender-neutrality (in Florida), and gender non-binary teaching material (in Georgia). Florida and Arkansas also banned African American studies and psychology; and Florida also required pupils to be taught about the benefits of slavery. Since 2021, forty-four states have introduced bills or taken additional steps to restrict the teaching of critical race theory, and eighteen states have imposed bans on the theory (*The Economist* 2023).

Florida governor Ron DeSantis positioned himself as a warrior against wokeness: "We fight the woke in the legislature. We fight the wok in the schools. We fight the woke in the corporations. We will never, ever surrender to the woke mob. Florida is where woke goes to die." Wokeness in 2021 appeared to denote engagement in civil rights and social justice. But anti-woke culture became an ideology for the right to brand its bigotry as a resistance movement. He saw himself as the leader of the anti-woke movement and introduced the *Stop Woke Act*, which pre-empts any attempt of the school system or businesses to teach anything that would cause anyone to "feel guilt, anguish or any form of psychological distress" due to their race, colour, sex, or national origin. The proposed act was challenged in the federal court, leading to its enforcement being blocked against businesses (Paulson 2024). Other warriors in this movement include Tucker Carlson of Fox News (who labelled Black Lives Matter and Brown M&Ms as woke warriors), Steve Bannon, Vivek Ramaswamy, Toby Neugebauer, Elon Musk, and Piers Morgan. They see themselves as defending the United States from DEI, Black history, trans rights, homosexuality, and feminism (Harriot 2022).

In the United States, DEI has been politicized and become a partisan issue. Large corporations used to praise and promote DEI, but corporation such as Meta, McDonald's, Walmart, Boeing, Ford, Target, and a host of other corporations are retreating from this school of thought now. Walmart, for example, is scaling back its DEI racial equity training programs and its evaluation of supplier diversity, and so is Target on its removal of hiring and promotion goals for women and racialized people. Companies are now facing more backlash from political and legal institutions, and there is a threat that, as more and more companies are retreating from their DEI commitments, more companies may follow suit. Companies focusing on incorporating DEI into their vision may be seen as being "woke" in spite of their business justification (L. Johnson 2024). Anti-DEI activists, like Robby Starbuck, have been attacking DEI, and Starbuck claimed that the end of Walmart's DEI programs was the result of such attacks. The company cancelled its racial equity centre and diversity training programs (Kabelka and Sost 2025).

With the re-election of Donald Trump in 2024, the anti-woke movement gained a lot of validation and became much more vocal and energized. As a settlement with Edward Blum, an anti-woke activist, the Fearless Fund agreed to close its grant program for Black women entrepreneurs as the program allegedly violated the *Civil Rights Act* of 1866 as it discriminates based on race. Stephen Miller, a new cabinet member, has already filed lawsuits against Meta and Amazon, alleging that their DEI programs were discriminatory against White people. More companies are expected to go through lawsuits under the second administration of Donald Trump, but they plan to minimize the risks. It appears that corporations are rethinking how to avoid political, social, and financial risks when using DEI as a corporate vision or business strategy. They do not wish to have their profits reduced, brand name shattered, consumer market diminished, employee morale reduced, and higher turnover rate. However, according to a survey of the Conference Board of the United States, most companies (around 80 percent) are still keeping their DEI values and programs over the next few years. As a term, "DEI" may be changed to fairness, belonging, respect, or engagement, but organizations are keeping their commitment to these high corporate values (Kabelka and Sost 2025).

In fact, the anti-woke movement is now being institutionalized by the Trump administration. On the first day of his second term as president of the United States, he announced in his inaugural address of shutting down DEI in the federal government and de-funding all DEI programs. According to Kenji Yoshino, a New York University lawyer, Trump's orders are "a way of striking fear into organizations' hearts" (Chemtob 2025). Trump further announced a new US policy that "there are only two genders: male and female." He accused the previous government of "trying to socially engineer race and gender into every aspect of public and private life." With the re-election of Trump, the essence of the anti-woke movement has now been institutionalized in law, policies, and programs beginning on 20 January 2025.

In furthering his anti-woke annihilation of DEI policies, programs, and practices, Trump started out by revoking former President Joe Biden's executive orders and executive memoranda related to DEI because they are "harmful" and "divisive and dangerous." They included Executive Order 13985 on Advancing Racial Equity and Support for Underserved Communities through the Federal Government, Executive Order 4035 on Diversity, Equity, Inclusion, and Accessibility in the Federal Workforce, and Executive Order 14069 on Advancing Economy, Transparency, and Effectiveness in Federal Contracting by Promoting Pay Equity and Transparency. In addition, Trump directed federal agencies to terminate their DEI offices, positions, plans, programs, initiatives, grants, and contracts and all their DEI performance requirements for federal employees, contractors, and grantees. Furthermore, Trump requires the identification of federal contractors who provided DEI training to federal agencies and all grantees who received federal funding for DEI or environmental justice programs since 20 January 2021. In place of DEI, Trump mandates monthly oversight meetings to monitor areas needing presidential or legislative action to advance "equal dignity and respect" for White males and other groups that have not been given DEI preference in the past (Olson and Shaw 2025a, 2025b).

On the next day after the Inauguration, Trump signed another executive order titled Ending Illegal Discrimination and Restoring Merit-Based Opportunity by revoking several executive orders including Executive Order 11246, which was the foundational executive order from 1965 that imposed affirmative action obligations on federal government contractors and subcontractors, thus ending the affirmative action requirements for federal contractors that had been enforced for the last sixty years. The executive order also revoked Executive Order 12898 on Environmental Justice, Executive Order 13583 on Federal Workforce Diversity Initiative, Executive Order 13672 on LGBT Workplace Protections, and Presidential Memo (2016) on National Security Diversity Goals. It also requires federal agencies to eliminate DEI practices through specific actions such as removing DEI principles from the federal acquisition, financial assistance, contracting, and grant-making processes. Trump ordered federal employees to report on colleagues who continue DEI activities and dismissed officials who oppose his orders and are not "reliable, loyal, trustworthy."

More importantly, the executive order directs all federal agencies to take action against "DEI discrimination" throughout the private industry, casting DEI as a discriminatory human resources mechanism. Essentially, the Trump administration supports the "equality of opportunity for all" principle in federal civil rights protections and designated

DEI policies as a violation of civil rights laws. Within 120 days of the inauguration, the executive order directed the attorney general to develop a strategic enforcement plan for ending DEI discrimination, which identifies sectors of concern within each government agency's jurisdiction, the "most egregious" DEI practitioners in each sector of concern, outlines specific deterrence steps for DEI programs deemed discriminatory, and includes potential litigation strategies and regulatory actions. Each federal agency must identify up to nine potential investigation targets focusing on larger employers including corporations, non-profit organizations, state/local bars, medical associations, and universities (Olson and Shaw 2025a, 2025b).

The general thrust of these executive orders (and other related administrative and legislative tools) is to remove all existing remnants of DEI policies, programs, and practices from the federal government, government contractors, and private sector companies and non-profit organizations, large or small, and to include only inclusion policies, programs, and practices that treat everyone equally (including White males and other marginalized groups often ignored by traditional DEI efforts in the past) within a short time frame during Trump's second term (Smith 2025a). Citing Trump's executive orders, Google responded immediately by eliminating its diversity goals. Some of these executive orders are being questioned on their legality, and the enforcement of DEI orders related to the private sector, including federal contractors, was paused and blocked by a federal district judge for a number of legal reasons (Smith 2025c).

To broaden his anti-DEI policy reach, Trump signed another executive order on 29 January 2025 to revoke federal funding for Kindergarten to Grade 12 schools that teach "radical gender ideology and critical race theory." This would affect tens of thousands of school districts nationwide; however, the federal government does not have jurisdiction over school curriculum at the state level (Chemtob 2025). A month after Trump's inauguration, the Education Department and schools had two weeks to terminate their race-based programs (US Department of Education 2025). Trump also immediately fired two Democratic commissioners at the US Equal Opportunity Commission (EEOC) and removed some EEOC guidance on its website that had been issued during the Biden administration. The guidance may be considered as illegal DEI-motivated race and sex discrimination (Smith 2025b). To further legitimize and publicize his designated DEI as discriminatory and illegal, Trump claimed that the Federal Aviation Administration's DEI policies were the cause of the fatal plane crash that occurred in Washington, DC, on 30 January 2025 without any evidence. Such allegations implied that the pilot and/or co-pilot were incompetent because they were hired under a DEI policy. The DEI policy had existed for years under Trump's first administration (Basu 2025). Trump also assigned DEI as one of the causes for the inability of the Federal Reserve chair, Jerome Powell, to stop inflation, which seemed to allege that the chair or staff members were "DEI hires" (Gavin 2025). The Trump administration also threatened universities and other institutions that have DEI policies and programs and has been prepared to block federal funding to them if their DEI policies and programs continue. Accordingly, in light of this threat, the University of California announced that it would be dropping its diversity statements in its hiring process.

In spite of this demolition of DEI policies and programs in the United States, there are still some organizations that value the business case for DEI and are continuing to integrate DEI principles in their business (Case 2025c). JPMorgan CEO Jamie Dimon has maintained that his organization's DEI programs will stay despite the challenges from conservative activist shareholders, and so are 98 percent of the shareholders of Costco who rejected Costco's anti-woke proposal and voted to keep the current DEI policies (Guynn and Schulz 2025).

United Kingdom

In the last thirty years, the world has witnessed the ascendency of a powerful return of authoritarian values and views in democratic countries. These values have gradually but persistently occupied a more dominant role in shaping public policy, be it related to immigration, judicial powers, media freedom, and, as Bart Cammaerts (2022) has argued, the re-normalization of racist and fascist ideas and, simultaneously, the abnormalization of people or organizations that fight against racism and sexism through an anti-woke culture war. In the United Kingdom, anti-woke activists are members of parliament such as John Hayes, James Sunderland, David Maddox, Kemi Badenoch, and Garth Bacon, and broadcasters such as Andrew Neil (who formed *Great Britain News*, which specializes in attacking wokeism), newspaper columnists such as Dan Wootton, Doug Murray, and Oliver

Harvey. These members of parliament speak with authority when they are anti-woke. Kemi Badenoch, the minister of equality, was against the decolonization agenda in a debate on Black History Month: "I want to be absolutely clear that the Government stand unequivocally against critical race theory. ... We do not want teachers to teach their white pupils about white privilege and inherited racial guilt" (Badenoch 2020).

Anti-woke activists appear to see themselves as victims of DEI, which focuses on addressing the historical inequity in a wide range of social reality. According to these activists, any progress made by racialized and Indigenous peoples means the further victimization of White people, further "white distress," and "white suffering." Anti-woke activists have described wokeism as "religious, totalitarian fanaticism," "extremist, authoritarian, intolerant, ideological," "destructive, totalitarian, divisive, negative and anti-democratic." Such adjectives for DEI, anti-racism, and anti-sexism activities positioned themselves as politically deviant and extremist and going against the sovereign will of the public and a threat to the country. In the United Kingdom, there is a tendency to cast social justice activists as an irrational and vindictive "mob." Hence, the term "woke" is associated as "mob" and increasingly seen as derogatory. A survey of over thirty-six hundred persons in the United Kingdom conducted by Bobby Duffy and Gideon Skinner (2023) showed that the term "being woke" has been increasingly heard a lot by 51 percent of the surveyed people in 2023. Back in 2020, the percentage was only 33 percent. The term "woke" is increasingly viewed as an insulting term by 42 percent of the public, up from 24 percent in 2020. While the percentages vary across different age groups, the trend is that being "woke" is viewed increasingly as pejorative over the last few years. The Conservative Party and media have played a key role in defining public opinions on "woke." There has been an explosive usage of the term "anti-woke" in the media. In 2022, the number of mentions was 882 in UK newspaper articles, up from ten in 2019.

The survey findings also showed that 15 percent of people see themselves as "anti-woke," especially those who are age fifty-five plus (24 percent) and male (21 percent). A much larger share of people who voted Conservative (34 percent) than those who voted for Labour (3 percent) see themselves as "anti-woke" and so were men aged sixty and over (31 percent). One interesting observation based on this survey is that more people across gender, age, and political voting lines now view politicians as inventing or exaggerating culture wars as a political tactic (62 percent) in 2023, which is up from 44 percent three years earlier in 2020. In 2023, 56 percent of the public believed that politicians are trying to use cultural wars to distract people from other important issues and divide the society further. The survey findings also showed that, in 2023, for the first time in recent history, the majority of people (52 percent) believe that culture wars are a serious problem for the United Kingdom compared with 42 percent in 2020. Overall, the public still feel the media have a negative impact on making cultural wars a real-world problem (Duffy and Skinner 2023).

To command attention from people, anti-woke activists advocate free speech to defend anti-woke messages on racism and hate speech. Andrew Neil claimed that *Great Britain News* (which some people have labelled as the British version of Fox News in the United States) has the mandate to expose the threat of cancel culture to free speech and democracy (quoted in Landler 2021). Andrew Neil also stated that "cancel culture is insidious, it stands against everything we have stood for since the Enlightenment onwards and that is why it is serious" (quoted in Ritter 2021). James Sunderland and David Maddox, two famous anti-woke activists defend free speech to the extent that people should have "the right to offend people and debate from different perspectives are at the heart of freedom of speech" (Cammaerts 2022).

Anti-woke movement, through right wing media, has been attempting to discredit anti-racism activities such as the BlackLivesMovement with the support from a populist Conservative government that does not put much effort into ending systemic racism in the United Kingdom. The conservatives have waged a long campaign against political correctness, cancel culture, and wokeism. This campaign gave rise to Boris Johnson's brand of populism. The UK government set up the Commission on Race and Ethnic Disparities in 2021, chaired by Tony Sewell in response to the BlackLivesMovement's protests. The report that followed appeared to maintain the government's anti-woke stand by questioning systemic racism, white privilege, and decolonizing; downplaying racism and racist incidents; criticizing DEI programs (such as unconscious bias training) and quotas; belittling anti-racism as destroying statues; dismissing identity politics. It appears that the anti-woke movement was further supported by the commission's report with the blessing of the government (Pilkington 2022).

Implications

As a human resources management school of thought, DEI emerged to counteract the blunt edge of affirmative action (in the United States) and employment equity (in Canada) that maintains that racialized and Indigenous peoples, along with women and persons with disabilities, should be equitably treated. While DEI has been focused on valuing the contribution of everyone in the workplace, unfortunately, it has increasingly been associated with favouring hiring and promoting only racialized people even though they are perceived as not having the necessary merits or competency to do the job. This incorrect perception of the DEI approach and the negative stereotyping and prejudice against racialized people appears to be the founding factor of an anti-woke movement that has become politicized and institutionalized through government policies and practices, at least in the United States and the United Kingdom.

With the rise of right-wing parties, DEI has been construed and labelled as an "unfair" and "inequitable" anti-merit method of hiring and promoting people, especially racialized people. Wokeism is built on that perception and label. The US Supreme Court case of making affirmative action illegal in the university sector, and the killing of DEI in President Trump's executive orders have pressured more and more organizations to retreat or abandon DEI policies, programs, and practices.

The waves of DEI retreat have already arrived in Canada, and companies are increasingly re-evaluating the future of DEI in the workplace, and human resources professionals are uncertain about the next stage of the development of DEI and, as matter of fact, employment equity and human rights. It is difficult to predict whether the anti-woke movement is gaining traction or not in Canada as that movement is one of the contextual factors of Trump's executive order on anti-DEI.

Anti-wokeism is one of the central features of right-wing movements and governments (as shown in earlier discussion on authoritarianism, populism, and illiberalism). The recent political climate in Europe and the United States demonstrates the fast ascendency of far-right parties (as in France and Germany), which, in turn, has induced a larger segment of the population to become very concerned about immigration and economic issues to the point that they see immigrants and asylum seekers as taking over their jobs, countries, and cultures and changing their rightful place and the control of their future. Their world-views are increasingly against the conspiracy theory known as the Great Replacement Theory (with a strong fear of White people being replaced by racialized people and a strong xenophobia and urge to reclaim White supremacy).

While Canada has not quite reached the same level of phobia and paranoia about foreigners as that of the United States, there are sentiments of anti-immigrants and anti-racialized and Indigenous peoples targeting Asian people (especially South Asian international students and Chinese people related to COVID-19 and political interference), Black people (related to Black Lives Matter and anti-Black racism curriculum), and Indigenous peoples (related to residential schools and mass graves). Conspiracy theories abound on all these peoples. The momentum is building. In Canada, the People's Party of Canada (headed by Maxime Bernier) is advocating a "common sense" approach that is similar to Donald Trump's "common sense" and Pierre Poilievre's "Common Sense Conservatives" (Conservative Party of Canada). Incidentally, the former Ontario premier Michael Harris's "Common Sense Revolution" won the provincial election in 1996 and executed a series of anti-woke measures, including the immediate repeal of the Ontario *Employment Equity Act* and the restructuring of the government bureaucracy and defunding progressive programs.

It is expected that, once these conservative political parties gain momentum in their political campaigns or if and when they become governments, like what the People's Party of Canada said about its political platform, they are likely to end official multiculturalism; demolish "racist and sexist" DEI ideology, policies, and programs; prohibit DEI education and training; stop funding DEI groups; support DEI victims; deport illegal immigrants; promote free speech and academic freedom; preserve Canadian values and culture; and reject climate change policies and programs.

Hence, if history has any lessons to be learned, anti-wokeism will follow in the footsteps of Trump in dismantling DEI and other measures that promote social justice. It may not be limited to the government, but it is likely to spread to the broader public and private sectors and the nonprofit sector. Shopify in Canada has rolled back their DEI programs and removed the web pages of their DEI programs ("Build Native," "Build Black," "Social Impact and Empowered"). Shopify's staff that are responsible for the management/administration of DEI programs no longer work there. Hundreds of technology leaders in Canada have signed an open letter condemning Shopify for their political move (Galea 2025).

The political environment, which is largely beyond the mandate of corporations or community organizations, has a large impact on workplace racism. Legislation and government policies can change and, like what is happening in the United States in 2025, they could also drastically affect the employment and occupational status of racialized and Indigenous peoples in the workplace, and, worse still, they can impact on their livelihoods beyond the workplace.

Hence, to enable the private and non-profit sectors to have more autonomy and independence in managing their workplaces, organizational anti-racism in the forms of political influence, lobbying, and government liaisons must be a long-term strategy to embed social justice (very much like the environmental, social, and governance) as the management standard so that DEI or anti-racism remains a pillar in business and community growth.

The workplace in the United States during the post-election period (after the inauguration day on 20 January 2025) witnessed intense political tension among employees, often with daily heated political debates according to a Resume Now's survey report of over one thousand American employees. More than half of the employees avoided co-workers who had opposing political views. Such an atmosphere would damage teamwork and productivity. Ninety percent of surveyed employees perceived political leanings of executives and believed that these biases would impact the career opportunities and promotion of employees, thus raising doubts about equity in the workplace.

This kind of workplace polarization, at least in employees' conversations, could be manageable if the organization had workplace policies in place to regulate political discussion. Polarization could escalate when employees are allowed to have non-verbal communications such as wearing Black Lives Matter T-shirts or Make America Great Again hats in their workplaces (Case 2025a). Organizations need to prepare guidelines for productive discussion on race, racism, and racial matters and guiderails against verbal abuse or violence on racial issues. In Canada, provincial occupational health and safety legislation may have provisions and workplace committees to safeguard the safety of employees. If organizations have workplace respect policies and programs and code of conducts, it will help if they are enforced. Otherwise, political polarization along racial matters, triggered by anti-woke activities in the workplace, could affect their workplace safety, which could easily deteriorate. Under that scenario, an anti-racism strategy and program for each workplace may be in order.

But these short-term anti-racism measures may not be able to arrest the prevalence of anti-wokeism across many countries, to which Canada may not be immune. As noted in the spreading of the demolition of all things woke-ish in the United States and the United Kingdom, the private sector and non-profit sector may need some strategies to block off or neutralize any attempts from above or below to the coming harms to racialized and Indigenous peoples and other marginalized groups in the workplace and beyond. When anti-wokeism becomes a government policy as soon as authoritarian, illiberal, and populist parties come into power and form a government, it may be too late to stop the anti-wokeism tide.

ARTIFICIAL INTELLIGENCE AND BIAS

In addition to the widening geopolitical conflicts; the ascendency of authoritarianism, illiberalism, and populism; the intensification of hate crimes, hate speech, and violence; and the rising challenges to DEI that have been discussed in the previous sections of this chapter, there is another macroscopic force that is increasingly dominant in impacting the growth of racism, and that is artificial intelligence (AI) biases. AI is a learning system that uses inputted data to accomplish goals in a fast-paced manner. The system, when trained, is able to digest data, identify patterns, make predictions, and formulate recommendations. It aims to simulate what a human being can do with increased accuracy, reliability, time savings, cost-reduction, and computing power, which are at least the projected potentials of AI.

People working in the AI field see AI as a technological advance that has the potential to revolutionize the ways we do things in many fields. Clearly, both the private and public sectors are moving ahead in investing more resources in AI as a management tool. In the early stages of AI progress, the business sector, especially human resources professionals, believed that, given that its command of information is broad, its nature is data and algorithm driven, and its operation is arm-length from stakeholders' interest, there was a greater tendency for AI to make objective and impartial decisions without much human bias. In other words, compared with the current human decisions that might be skewed in so many directions due to self-interest and non-rational considerations, AI should be objective, fairer, impartial, and equitable.

While the scope of AI adoption in management is broad, this section focuses on how it impacts on human resources management, in general, and on racialized and Indigenous peoples, in particular. In examining these issues, the potential racism that is inherent in AI and the recommended anti-racism in the workplace that should take place will be highlighted.

AI and Human Resources Management

AI has evolved over a number of decades, and it has now become more and more prominent in Canada. The COVID-19 pandemic, with its disruptive impact on the organization of work, patterns of people interaction, and a complete lockdown on the workplace where employees used to work together in a location, sped up the process of disruption through an acceleration of technological changes at work. While changes have taken place in the traditional human resources functions (such as onboarding, coaching, and training) and business functions (such as planning, staff meetings, sales, customer services), most were moved to an online platform. With the exception of most face-to-face services, including merchandise production and transportation, most people were forced to adapt quickly to the new work order (Minbaeva 2021).

AI is essentially a data-driven machine. Unfortunately, human resources management is not the vanguard or passionate friend of data analysis. In fact, not many human resources departments use data as a way to drive forward their mission. This may be one of the reasons why human resources management is seldom on par with other departments in the organization in terms of engagement in the CEO's inner circle. Only in the last ten years has there been a slight push to collect more data on human resources to drive management. The application of AI provides an opportunity for human resources departments to gain an inroad to CEO's inner circle. In the past, workforce data collection and analysis enjoyed a boost by requiring employment equity or affirmative action legislation. But this limited use of data may not bring human resources management to a new level in which additional data are needed to enable AI and machine learning to broaden their application to research, develop, and evaluate policies, programs, procedures, and other processes as they connect to human resources (not just individual employees).

Right now, it appears that AI has been helping human resources management do its administrative, operational, and clerical tasks faster and cheaper (such as preparing job descriptions, job posting, sourcing, screening, job offering letters, scheduling, interview questions, briefing notes, and meeting agenda) and to improve recruitment, learning, and performance management processes. AI, with its automation processes, can reduce human efforts and time for delivering results, decrease costs for hiring, and simplify operational steps. It can provide job applicants with different job advertisements and help employees determine their training areas/courses, help management screen resumes, evaluate video interviews, recommend who should be promoted, and decide who should be terminated.

AI also has the capability to personalize compensation and benefits packages for employees and help human resources administrators manage these personalized packages. Employee career counselling and development, mentoring, and responses to employees' inquiries can also be personalized en masse. Once employees have been hired, AI can assist employers to monitor employees' pace of work, track their movement through wearable technology, assess facial expression, voice, and other movements, scrutinize employees' emails, keystrokes, or cursor activities, and analyze customer feedback on employees' performance. Obviously, some of AI's capabilities are viewed as contentious and may be unethical or even illegal. In spite of these advantages, AI has not quite enabled human resources management to become more strategic, to build management models, to integrate into corporate decision-making processes, to increase productivity and engagement, to optimize organizational performance, to improve workplace morale, and to grow the organization, but the opportunity to do so is there (Nawaz et al. 2024).

AI's Bias and Discriminatory Potential

As is commonly known to social scientists, human learning and accomplishments in every domain are infused with social and cultural context and social relationships. When AI systems are created to learn from human beings through the information and data we have gathered and analyzed, they inherit all the human findings through the ages, but they also learn all the biases and mistakes made by human beings. At the end of the day, AI systems are composed of all "the good and the bad" that human civilization possesses. Beyond the social justice areas, examples of misinformation or disinformation are rampant. There are much medical misinformation embedded in the Internet, and it is accessed by many people. A survey conducted by the Canadian Medical Association reported by Kelly Grant (2025) in the *Globe and Mail* showed that 62 percent of those surveyed in 2024 found out that the information they obtained from the Internet was false or misleading occasionally, often or all the time. Such misinformation may lead to life and death issues or delays in seeking property medical treatment.

At this stage of AI evolution, AI systems have a long way to go both in terms of strategic capability and administrative details, but they also need to have ethics and values and address systemic discrimination. AI learns from multiple large datasets, and, unfortunately, as noted, these datasets have inherent biases or misinformation, and AI is unable to resolve these problems easily. In the earlier days of AI development, Dany Rastelli (2018) saw the value of "bringing HR and AI together" with the assumption that AI could not discriminate on the basis of race, gender, disability, and sexual orientation. This was too quick of a conclusion. However, a few years later, 34 percent of global CEOs are still concerned about the increase of the "bias toward specific groups of customers or employees" through the use of generative AI in the next twelve months (PriceWaterhouseCooper 2024). This is a legitimate concern. Whatever biases we have, they are part of the AI systems, and AI experts are trying to disentangle these biases from the systems that could be of great help to us.

AI has an algorithmic bias problem that results in the perpetuation of societal bias (Zajko 2021). An example of the potential biases in generative AI is its ability to create images based on algorithms. The resultant images reflect the datasets found in its training. Hence, the images of Indigenous peoples from generative AI are people wearing traditional headdresses, those of Black people are reflective of Blacks doing low-level menial jobs; those of Chinese people are working in laundry, computer, or information technology fields; and those of South Asian people are gig workers in food delivery occupations. An instruction to AI to show CEOs or high-level executives usually end up with images of White men. As AI-generated images are all based on the datasets that the Internet has, these images have many incorrect assumptions about age, gender, class, and race (Schual et al. 2022). These stereotypes are formulated on the images that AI learned from the past datasets fed for AI to learn. Currently, these narrow views are limited by AI's memory of images. With these memories and images, AI systems may have difficulty placing higher priority on giving professional positions to Black people, let alone CEO positions. It has been noted that AI systems reflect existing biases and under-representation from the large datasets that they learned from. One example is Microsoft's Tay Twitter chatbot, which reposted racist tweets. Such incidents of repeated racist biases are damaging to organizational reputations, and it might also disturb racialized employees and other groups who have felt unsupported or alienated. Some AI systems turn men into astronauts and sexualize women. These might reinforce stereotypes and create a biased work environment (Blanchette 2024; Larkin 2024).

It is expected that AI systems will gradually improve their accuracy when their training is diversified by increasing the volume of diversified images fed into the system. It is noted that increasing a thousand additional images to a model of more than two billion would reduce the above stereotyped results significantly. Most images of racialized people are reflections of people from Western cultures, and their images are based on US-centric training sets for AI (Stokel-Walker 2024). Melissa Heikkilä (2023) illustrates how three popular AI image-generating models—DALL-E2 and two versions of Stable Diffusion—have amplified stereotypes of people of different races, ethnicities, genders, and professions. Depending on how researchers pose their instructions to the AIs, different stereotypes are clustered around specific wordings of the instruction (such as identities, countries, cultures, adjectives, and so on). One critical problem with the current AI systems is that they are not able to identify the reasons why they have come to their own conclusions.

In spite of these shortcomings, over three thousand employees in the United States seem to have hope in the potential value of AI in the human resources areas. Over 80 percent of them believe algorithms could give more accurate performance reviews than their managers. Another study from Gartner showed that over 60 percent of US employees believe that AI is less biased than human beings in making decisions on compensation. However, those involved in performance reviews management recognize that whether AI can do well in reviews depends largely on some foundational issues such as data quality related to employee behaviours and management communication in a work environment under stress and cultural issues rather than the narrow project goals and outcomes.

The issue of bias on race and gender as well as the verdict on AI's benefits is still unclear (Mensik 2025).

Examples of AI's Discrimination

According to the Society for Human Resource Management's (SHRM) survey in 2022, nearly a quarter of organizations surveyed reported that AI or automation support human resources-related activities (such as recruitment and hiring) are used by employers mainly to save time and increase efficiency. There is a difference between using AI for administrative/operational work and using AI for hiring decisions. We cannot afford to make wrong hiring decisions because the risks are high and these risks are related to the fact that, at this stage of development, AI still has serious misinformation and bias. AI can either amplify the biases that it learns from its data sources, or it can manufacture its own based on its algorithms. These are the two major sources of AI bias. For example, in job competition, if the datasets are based largely on White people, men, older age groups, workplaces, educational institutions, hiring decisions, and so on for the positions, the chance is that the selection of candidates will be based on biases related to patterns of employment decisions in the past. If past hiring decisions were skewed in favour of White males who graduated from certain institutions in certain urban centres, their skills, education, and work experiences would then be used as references for candidates' resumes to match.

A recent survey by the Society for Human Resource Management (SHRM) on the confidence level of human resources professionals suggested that approximately half of them have confidence in the hiring recommendations of AI despite evidence of biases exhibited by Amazon a few years ago (Larkin 2024). The hiring biases of Amazon were based on the quality of AI's training data and its AI-driven hiring tools that received their training on the past ten years of Amazon's hires of men in the technology fields. The tools showed that they continued that gender bias by downgrading information on resumes with the word "women's" or graduates from two all-women's colleges and gave higher priority to "male" words such as "executed" or "captured" in describing their work actions. Subsequently, upon learning of the gender bias, Amazon now limits those AI tools to their rudimentary administrative tasks as opposed to more sophisticated hiring tasks (Dastin 2018). Along with other studies and observations, this example on Amazon does illustrate the risks of using AI in making talent management decisions, not just in hiring but also other human resources functions. This does not mean that, as AI develops, it will not resolve this issue on AI bias and its discriminatory potential, but, at this stage, it requires caution.

AI tools may be designed to favour candidates with better and more prestigious educational institutions that only richer people can attend. Thus, the algorithms now have wealth markers that might pick up candidates with specific prestigious extracurricular activities or internships, family connections, postal codes, school names, or language (terms) used in the resumes. These are unintended consequences and criteria used for hiring decisions, and they do not have much relevance to a candidate's actual abilities or qualifications (Dhiman 2025). In light of this kind of finding, human resources professionals and hiring managers have to be very careful in setting the priority on how well the AI tools used are trained to align with organizational values, strategic directions, and operational needs in screening and reviewing resumes for hiring or promotion.

There are reports of AI systemic bias against racialized people and women, and the *Artificial Intelligence and Data Act* (*AIDA*) was developed to address these issues, among others. It has not been enacted or enforced yet at the time of writing this book. While AI may not use race or gender directly for formulating its recommendations, it may use their proxies (such as incomes or neigbhourhoods) as ways to determine their creditworthiness, availability of health-care service delivery, or safety precautions (Government of Canada 2025). The *AIDA*'s strength is its narrow focus on the freedom from discrimination using the current Canadian human rights model. This narrowness is also its main weakness because it does not deal with the bias that is related to human rights (such as surveillance, policing profiling, militaristic suppression, torture, human dignity, and censorship), which is the kind of human rights that Human Rights Watch and Amnesty International are concerned with (Scassa 2024).

The US Employment Opportunity Commission (EEOC), concerned about potential discrimination, held a public session entitled "Navigating Employment Discrimination in AI and Automated System: A New Civil Rights Frontier." Its intention is to explore the roles that AI plays in employment decisions and how the EEOC could regulate its use. The American Civil Liberties Union in New York City noted that AI can lead to more discriminatory results than human-driven processes. Learning Collider, a research lab in New York City, compared AI-driven versus human-driven hiring and found that AI-driven tools selected 50 percent fewer Black applicants than humans did. Very likely, data on criminal legal proceedings, evictions, and credit history of Black applicants might be tinting the AI-driven screening and hiring processes, and the AI algorithms might be lowering the overall ranking of Black applicants (Gonzales 2023).

There are other examples of bias that is not related to employment such as face recognition where the training algorithm is on White people (hence, producing poorer quality of face recognition for racialized and Indigenous people). In the United States, with respect to loan approval screening where the training algorithm is largely based on male business owners, the screening results show that female business owners have problems getting loans (Zettelmeyer and Suh 2019). Moreover, racism is embedded in the American health-care system. In 2019, researchers found an algorithm that was used to predict patients who need extra medical care. It was found that White patients needed more than Black patients. Black patients incurred lower health-care costs. AI bias in the Correctional Offender Management Profiling for Alternative Sanctions system predicted twice as many false positives for recidivism for Black offenders (45 percent) than White offenders (23 percent) (Datatron, n.d.). These examples in the non-employment fields also reinforce the notion that, at this stage, AI still has an undetermined extent of inherent bias built into its system. If not cautious, human decisions that emerge from AI findings or recommendations may carry immense risks.

Sarah Kaplan and Carmina Ravanera (2022) synthesized research works on the linkages between AI and equity issues and noted that AI has the potential to both amplify and mitigate bias. Overall, the research findings show that, due to the fact that AI uses methods in statistical prediction, it can avoid human cognitive biases in equity issues through programming; however, AI could reinforce biases through the use of biased data sets and reproduce the bias all over again in its own manner. Facial recognition software has problems in racial identification, and this has negative implications for policing and other surveillance work. Some AI and automation in specific occupations may impact adversely for racialized and Indigenous people or women. Racial and gender inequality and inequity may result from embedded bias or omissions in AI's datasets. In addition, there is a misalignment of AI and algorithms with social values (such as fairness), a lack of transparency from the AI developers or practitioners, a lack accountability due to lack of legal or policy oversight or obligations, and a lack of multiple diverse perspectives in the design and developmental of AI. In sum, with these shortcomings, AI has a long way to go in eliminating all biases in the technology.

How Best to Address AI's Racial Bias?

As AI develops, there will be many opportunities for incorporating more human resources functions in AI. As noted earlier, some of the administrative functions of human resources management (such as writing job descriptions and interviewing questions) have already constituted a part of AI. It is being applied in screening resumes and job applications, assessing interview videos, and other early stages of candidate selection processes. Increasing, human resources professionals are testing AI's ability in deciding who should be on the short lists of hires and promotions, how employees' performance is evaluated, how their training and development needs are assessed, how their compensations and benefits are personalized, and so on. As AI is getting in the "sensitive" areas in human resources management, more efforts are needed to figure out how to reduce or remove bias in the system, lest its potential biases become riskier.

Data Quality

Bias and discriminatory potential are a function of the data that AI has been trained on. If the data are collected through teams of people who come from diverse backgrounds such as gender, race, ethnicity, geography, education, income, lifestyles, perspectives, cultures, and so on, the chance is that their data sets will be more representative, and AI will be more "intelligent" if it is trained using those diverse data sets. This is one of the areas in which human beings could be used to identify and remove them prior to feeding in the training programs for AI (Kaplan and Ravanera 2022). The involvement of social scientists in multiple disciplines (such as psychology and AI specialists, anthropology, sociology, political science) in the data training stage, along with data scientists, would help tremendously (Stackhouse 2020). Having said this, there are still assumptions made on the non-biased inclination of people from different backgrounds or social scientists from multiple disciplines. From our observations and experiences, we know that even racialized or Indigenous peoples have their own biases on race and ethnicity, women have their biases on gender, and social scientists are biased in many different ways. One cannot speak with confidence that they are not biased. The issue remains whether there will be a point when human beings are self-reflective enough to uproot their own biases in their AI training datasets and be transparent about them and whether it is indeed feasible for human beings to contain their biases and for AI to recognize and remove their inherent biases.

Data sources have been cited as one of the key areas seeking solutions for these issues. To advance the quality of AI systems and tackle the issue of data bias, AI experts know that increasing the volume of the data set is one way to resolve the bias issue. Currently, it is not clear how best to increase the volume of data because there are limitations in the availability of datasets. Most of the digital text on the Internet has been utilized. New methods of sorting through the domains of human knowledge seem to work in empirical areas such as science and mathematics, but they are of limited use in the humanities and the arts. Unless innovative ways are designed and tested, it is an issue that cannot be resolved yet. As we are reaching the plateau of progress, removing biases from AI will be increasingly difficult. Furthermore, running data centres for AI uses a tremendous number of resources (especially water), and, therefore, it is capital intensive. Therefore, the issue of cost-effectiveness is one of the major considerations in enlarging the volume of data (Metz and Mickle 2024).

Organizational leaders and professionals must take on the responsibility to remove all biases, as AI can only express these biases in a variety of formats after their training. Right now, it is up to human beings to do the sanitization and to be vigilant in weeding out racist and discriminatory contents. At this stage, some would argue that it is not clear whether one can depend on AI to do the eradication of biases itself.

Management and Accountability

Ideally, AI leaders, developers, and users must include DEI principles—fairness, transparency, data representativeness, impartiality, human oversight—in AI training so as to pre-empt the occurrence of blind spots. Furthermore, it makes sense to build in a clear accountability framework and practice with the power to verify AI outputs and to enable explicability (ability to explain and justify results) and bias correction mechanisms. Accountability encompasses numerous critical issues in AI: governance, technical, ethical, and regulatory (Basiouny 2025). In addition, they include integrating an accountability framework and practices in AI development, along with establishing an effective strategy involving diverse teams working in a safe and inclusive environment with constant skill upgrading and strong transferable skills, regular review and auditing, and establishing partnerships with multiple stakeholder groups for an all-encompassing ecosystem (Blanchette 2024).

PriceWaterhouseCooper (2024) has utilized a similar framework as above and built a foundation for responsible AI systems that aligns with the organizational values and AI ethics that people can trust. With that foundational principle, an organization needs to develop a road map that provides concrete implementation framework and processes with a clear AI strategy and accountable deployment specifics—most importantly, in the areas of decontaminate datasets for training AI. The AI developers must be committed to verifiable data with constant monitoring and mitigation of discriminatory biases (especially in the area of DEI, employment equity, and human rights). The mitigation of biases involves the identification of vulnerabilities and potential for misuse (as violations of personal privacy and confidentiality). AI strategy has to build on trust. Its alignment with the European Union's *General Data Protection Regulation* is a good start and an aspirational goal. PriceWaterhouseCooper's framework has a governance model, it aligns AI with public policy and regulatory trends, ensures legal compliance, adheres to industrial standards, manages risks, regularly improves model performance, and improves metrics for monitoring purposes.

The trust factor is critical in AI management. A PriceWaterhouse-Cooper's 2017 survey of CEOs showed that 76 percent said potential biases and lack of transparency were impediments for AI adoption. And 73 percent said that having governance and rules to control AIs are needed. Anand Rao and Euan Cameron (2018), both from PriceWaterhouseCooper, reiterated that AI systems must be transparent, their decisions must be explainable, and their results must be repeatable. AI must have data integrity, and its unintentional biases must be removed. Moreover, AI developers, analysts, and management must work hand in hand to ensure that the AI data and analytics must be aligned with industrial standards and government regulations; institute a transparency model; focus on sustainability, robustness, and reliability; measure bias and fairness; ensure system cybersecurity and data privacy;

and pre-empt physical harm. PriceWaterhouseCooper's AI management model is responsible, and it enables AI to be accountable in pre-empting, reducing, and eliminating bias.

Similar management ideas to deal with AI bias are also proposed at the Kellogg School of Management, Northwestern University, and the US Equal Employment Opportunity Commission (Zettelmeyer and Suh 2019; Gonzales 2023). A strong AI management framework is vital for the pre-empting, reducing, and removing all biases that are detrimental to racialized and Indigenous peoples, women, and any other marginalized groups.

Legal Frameworks

In addition to a viable AI management framework, governments must step in, not just provide guidelines but also regulate AI and hold all parties that are involved in the development and implementation of AI responsible. In this historical juncture, the Canadian government has proposed *AIDA*, which is a part of Bill C-27, the 2022 *Digital Charter Implementation Act*, which some experts maintain hs stifled AI adoption and failed to provide clarity to make AI systems better.[3] Lately, Joe Castaldo (2025) reported that, in both Canada and the United States, momentum to move forward legislative change has slowed a bit, although with the Trump's presidency, there may be some changes in this momentum with a special focus on "ideological bias" (O'Brien and Parvini 2025).

Nevertheless, the federal government's *AIDA* approach and its Sovereign AI Compute Strategy may not be able to stop the decline of Canada's AI ranking on the world stage (based on Stanford University's AI vibrancy ranking) from third in 2017 to fourteenth in 2023 because they have not addressed AI's risks and safety issues. Geoffrey Hinton, a Canadian who won the 2024 Nobel Prize in physics for his AI work in Canada, firmly believes that these risks and safety issues might pose existential threats to humankind. Clearly, mitigating AI bias and harms and boosting economic productivity and growth should guide the assessment of government AI policy, legislation, and strategy (quoted in Khurana 2024). AI, with all its data decoding and predictive power, is promising in its abilities to resolve world problems and may

3 *Digital Charter Implementation Act*, 2022, Bill C-27.

have convinced some experts to believe that it can identify the pattern of geopolitical changes and even to end global poverty. However, AI's achievement on this front may be negligible, and some may even expect to see a rise of further global inequality and erosion of human rights. In fact, AI may bring in more world problems and deepen our economic and security issues, information confusion, and the spread of falsehoods and geopolitical conflict. Rachel Adams (2024a, 2024b), the CEO of the Global Centre on AI Governance and author of *The New Empire of AI: The Future of Global Inequality*, argued that, so far, AI seems to moving in a direction where the countries with the fastest AI development will also see economic growth and those that show little progress in AI development and adoption will face further economic stagnation or decline. While the concern about cybersecurity risk topped the global CEOs' concerns about generative AI (64 percent), according to a PriceWaterhouseCooper's (2024) survey, the spread of misinformation ranked second (52 percent) on their list of concerns. This suggests that there is a significant number of CEOs who believe that misinformation is likely to increase with the rise of generative AI.

In the human resources areas, with the arrival and experimentation of AI, there are two specific risks to manage in the race and Indigeneity areas: wrongful dismissal claims (arising from the substantial changes in some employees' responsibilities that may be construed as constructive dismissal) and employment discrimination (arising from AI decisions allegedly related to prohibited grounds as they apply to individual employees). *AIDA* requires employers to assess whether their AI systems are high-impact systems; if so, they must establish mitigation measures, publish a plain-language description of the system, expect risks of material harm, and notify the designated minister. When the automated decision systems are utilized, employers must provide, in plain language, an account of those systems to make predictions, recommendations, or decisions about individuals that could have a significant impact on them and provide these individuals with an explanation of the organization's decision-making process upon request.

Furthermore, the federal government launched the Voluntary Code of Conduct on the Responsible Development and Management of Advanced Generative AI Systems in September 2023. This is voluntary, and its effectiveness is contingent on how many businesses are receptive to support the code and how companies enforce the code. And, in March 2024, Ontario's Bill 149 on *Working for Workers Four*

Act received royal assent, and one special amendment (Part III.1) will come into force on proclamation, which requires a statement disclosing the use of AI to screen, assess, or select applicants for employment in publicly advertised job postings, subject to exceptions (Levy and Verlint 2025). It appears that both the federal and provincial governments are beginning to think of ways to tackle legal issues emerging from the adoption and experimentation of AI in human resources areas. So far, the steps taken by governments are preliminary attempts. The value of these attempts is in their calls for transparency and some degree of managerial responsibility.

In order to resolve the issue of bias as it relates to the potential for racism and discrimination, along with misinformation and disinformation, which are prevalent in social media and the AI environment, governments appear to be leaving them to AI designers, developers, and practitioners to resolve with no inclination to make AI safer and more responsible. This is a large and significant gap in AI regulations. It makes more sense for the sake of human rights, diversity, equity, and inclusiveness to incorporate the management models proposed by AI experts and academics discussed earlier in this section (such as PriceWaterhouse-Cooper) as much as possible in a legislative framework. As of now, it may be difficult to resolve these issues, but more public education, more responsible regulations, more research funds, and more continuous dialogues among experts and marginalized communities may yield new solutions on these issues. Not resolving these issues will not pre-empt adverse impacts at the individual, institutional, and societal levels.

MORE THOUGHTS

Each of the five selected social, political, and technological trends—widening geopolitical conflict; growing authoritarianism, illiberalism and populism; ascendency of hate crime, hate speech and violence; rising challenges to DEI; and the rise of AI—has its own implications on racism, anti-racism, and racialized and Indigenous peoples.

When it comes to geopolitical conflicts, Canadian history shows that, whenever there are political and economic conflicts, some racialized and ethnic groups in Canada are likely be the victims of racism as their international status changes. The prevalence of hate speeches and crimes and related violence shows similar patterns. The political parties and their platforms involved with authoritarianism, illiberalism, and populism may also jeopardize some ethnic and racialized people and Indigenous peoples. Policies and programs (such as DEI and employment equity), which attempt to reduce or eliminate racism, are also under attack, thus giving permission to people that devalue the values of these policies and programs. AI, which is thought to be impartial in human resources matters, is noted for its biases with no solutions in sight.

These five macroscopic forces, which originated outside of the workplace, are taking us in new directions in the realm of racism and anti-racism. Any strategies and measures designed for eradicating racism at work must take these forces into consideration. Some of these forces could be managed; others are beyond the capability of individual organizations to deal with.

Compared with the private sector and labour unions, only the government has influence over them, but, even then, international collaboration is needed.

Governments can forge peace in political conflict zones; find diplomatic ways to neutralize or contain authoritarian, illiberal, and populist regimes; put legal restraints on hate speeches, hate crimes, and the violence they generate; protect racialized and Indigenous peoples from further dismantling DEI, employment equity, human rights, and other measures and laws; and regulate the use and misuse of AI to further equality.

This does not allow the private sector or labour unions to be bystanders on the side. They should be doubling down on proactively building a work environment without racial prejudice and stereotypes and one with all the safeguards in fairness, equity, and respect. These historical and political forces give permission to disrespect and hurt disadvantaged groups of people and have the potential for victimizing them further. AI has the potential to save the world from further degradation, but it may not in the context of what is going on in the world. Individual businesses and organizations as well as labour unions could band together collectively and push for a more equitable social agenda and a discrimination-free and harassment-free employment system for racialized and Indigenous peoples. There are plenty of examples in which corporations, large and small, have collectively withdrawn their businesses and services from regimes that are corrupt and dictatorial or have withdrawn their support and collectively voiced their values in protest against their governments when their values do not align. The key word here is "collectively."

CHAPTER 14

Final Thoughts

This book is written in times of global crises in health and health care, economic uncertainty, and political turmoil. Canada has gone through a series of pandemic disruptions that have exposed numerous economic, health-care, housing, educational, and social disparities, and all of them have social justice ramifications. They have also triggered a rethinking process of racial disparity in the workplace as discontent is galvanized in anti-racism community protests from below and government policy changes on racial matters from above. There has been relative silence in the middle (the institutional workplaces) on racial disparities.

Racism is a complex term with multiple meanings and little consensus. Academic definitions are for research and practical perspectives for public policy development and community politics. A working definition is offered for a discussion on workplace racism. Our discussion on racism starts with an overview of the experiences of racialized and Indigenous peoples. Racism is found everywhere and permeates every aspect of their lives (food, health, housing, sports, border crossing, and so on) from birth to death. It is overwhelming and inescapable. The workplace is merely a microcosm of the larger society. Racism surfaces at the entry points of recruitment and hiring, through their attempts to move up in their careers (promotion and job movements), and their journeys to move out (termination) of the organizations they have worked in. As they see, feel, and experience them, workplaces are mostly saturated with racial stereotypes, prejudices, micro-aggressions, harassments, and discriminations.

Human resources mechanisms (job selection criteria and processes, performance evaluation, and so on) look impartial and fair on the surface, but, deep down, they are biased through their designs and executions. Racism is subtle so that not many racialized and Indigenous peoples notice how embedded it is. They can sense it only after several attempts to navigate within their workplaces when the experiences of discrimination begin to seep in. In organizations that proclaimed diversity, equity, and inclusiveness in their corporate vision, values, and mission, such a veneer makes it even harder to decipher the workplace reality.

Various levels of government have developed legal frameworks, strategies, policies, and programs to make racism disappear, but there are all sorts of problems in their frameworks and law enforcement. Employers also have their own strategies, policies, and programs to deal with inequity, harassment, and discriminatory practices, but racism is seldom specifically targeted for removal. Their measures on raising awareness and training fall short of having any enduring impact on racism eradication. Labour unions' work on racism is advocacy and negotiation with employers, but their insistence on having a seniority system in place does not help. Overall, racism remains a permanent feature in the workplace despite the efforts of these three change agents. There are few signs that racism is in retreat. For this reason, this book put forwards numerous recommendations on addressing racism, especially in those areas in human resources mechanisms, perceptions and attitudes, and corporate cultures where they have failed to make a dent in racism.

However, this may not be enough as we take a closer look at racism in the context of the dynamics in the workplace as well as the larger society on the world stage. There are a number of internal constraining forces that make individual employees fighting racism and the removal of systemic biases in corporate policies and programs difficult. In addition, there are several external forces on the political, social, and technological fronts—geopolitical conflicts, extremist regimes, hate crimes/speech, anti-woke movement and measures, and artificial intelligence—which have broadened and intensified racism in the workplace and made anti-racism more complicated and harder to fight.

As a result, a few anti-racism themes have emerged that could be viewed as effective. It appears that a solo fight against racism by oneself is seldom effective in the workplace; fighting workplace racism must move outward to the public arena, and help from external organizations may increase the chance of success. Moreover, the three key change agents—governments, employers, and labour unions—need to work collectively to address workplace racism, workplace violence, hate speech/crimes, public displays of racism, state racism, and artificial intelligence's inherent biases. These macroscopic forces that have been gathering momentum through time may be getting insurmountable for one party to wrestle. Stronger determination, resources, collaboration, and legislation are needed to combat racism at the macro-level so that the micro-level racism at work can be resolved.

There is also a need for us to recognize the urgency of fighting against racism in times of crises like we have now on a world scale. Racism that comes with a change in political regimes from a democratic one to one that is authoritarianism, illiberalism, or populism is much harder to wrestle down. Fighting racism on a large global scale is a zero-sum power exercise. There may still be hope that artificial intelligence may save us from further human misery related to racial bias, but, so far, its progress is not promising.

An immediate focus on having positive political, legislative, and cultural change with collective efforts from the change agents may be more impactful.

Bibliography

ABELLA, JUDGE ROSALIE SILBERMAN. 1984. *Report of the Commission on Equality in Employment*. Ottawa: Human Resources and Skills Development Canada.

ABELLA, JUDGE ROSALIE SILBERMAN. 1985. *Research Studies of the Commission on Equality in Employment*. Ottawa: Royal Commission on Equality in Employment.

ABELSON, JONATHAN S., NATALIE Z. WONG, MATTHEW SYMER, GREGORY ECKENRODE, ANTHONY WATKINS & HEATHER L. YEO. 2018. "Racial and Ethnic Disparities in Promotion and Retention of Academic Surgeons." *American Journal of Surgery* 216(4): 678–82. Online: https://doi.org/10.1016/j.amjsurg.2018.07.020.

Aboriginal Peoples Television Network National News. 2016. "Negative Attitudes toward Indigenous Peoples Highest in the Prairies Provinces, National Poll." 8 June. Online: https://aptnnews.ca/2016/06/08/negative-attitudes-toward-indigenous-peoples-higest-in -prairie-provinces-national-poll-2.

ADAMS, RACHEL. 2024a. "AI Is Bad News for the Global South: The Coming Wave of Technology Is Set to Worsen Global Inequality." *Foreign Policy*, 17 December.

ADAMS, RACHEL. 2024b. *The New Empire of AI: The Future of Global Inequality*. New York: Wiley. Online: www.wiley.com/en-us/The+New+Empire+of+AI%3A+The+Future+of+Global+Inequality-p-9781509553112.

ADVISORY COMMITTEE ON POPULATION HEALTH. 1999. *Toward a Healthy Future: Second Report on the Health of Canadians*. Ottawa: Minister of Public Works and Government Services Canada.

AFFUL, CHRISTIAN ACKON TAWIAH. 2024. "Underlying Factors That Perpetuate Race-Based Discrimination in the Workplace in Washington State." PhD diss., Department of Philosophy Management, Walden University. Online: www.proquest.com/openview/63c382853b8c08a-497135526de5cfd2f/1?cbl=18750&diss=y&pq-origsite=gscholar.

AGNOC, CAROL. 2014. *Employment Equity in Canada: The Legacy of the Abella Report*. Toronto: University of Toronto Press.

AGUIRRE, ADALBERTO, JR. 2000. *Women and Minority Faculty in the Academic Workplace Recruitment, Retention, and Academic Culture*. San Francisco: Jossey-Bass.

AIELLO, RACHEL. 2018. "House Passes Bill Aimed at Tackling Harassment in Federal Workplaces." *CTV News*, 7 May. https://www.ctvnews.ca/politics/article/house-passes-bill-aimed-at-tackling-harassment-in-federal-workplaces/.

AKINTOLA, ABAYOMI R. 2011. "Hiring Discrimination in Racially Diverse Labour Market: A Cross Country Study." MA diss., Karlstad Business School, Handelsh ogskolan vid Karlstads Universitet. Online: https://doi.org/10.1111/ijtd.12082.

AKOFI, SOLOMON. 2016. "Evaluating the Effects of Executive Learning and Development on Organizational Performance: Implications of Senior Manager and Executive Capabilities." *International Journal of Training and Development* 20(3): 177–99. Online: https://doi.org/10.1111/ijtd.12082.

ALLEN, MARY. 2018. "Police-Reported Crime Statistics in Canada, 2017." *Statistics Canada* (23 July). Online: www150.statcan.gc.ca/n1/pub/85-002-x/2018001/article/54974-eng.htm.

ALLEN, NATALIE J. & JOHN P. MYER. 1990. "The Measurement and Antecedents of Affective, Continuance and Normative Commitment to the Organization." *Journal of Occupational Psychology* 63(1): 1–18. Online: https://doi.org/10.1111/j.2044-8325.1990.tb00506.x.

AMANAT, HAYATULLAH. 2023. "Two-Thirds of Workers from Marginalized Backgrounds Face Racism at their Jobs: Survey." *CTV News* (16 October). Online: www.ctvnews.ca/business/two-thirds-of-workers-from-marginalized-backgrounds-face-racism-at-their-jobs-survey-1.6604260.

AMARDEIL, TANIA. 2024. "Advancing Black Canadians in the Workplace." *Innovating Canada, Mediaplanet Content Hub*. Online: www.innovatingcanada.ca/diversity-and-inclusion/advancing-black-canadians-in-the-workplace/.

AMERICAN PRODUCTIVITY AND QUALITY CENTRE. 2022. "Workforce Diversity, Equity, and Inclusion: Survey Report" (27 September). Online: www.apqc.org/resource-library/resource-listing/workforce-diversity-equity-and-inclusion-survey-report.

ANDIAPPAN, PALANIAPPAN, MARK CRESTOHL & JANG SINGH. 1989. "Racial Discrimination in Employment in Canada." *Relations Industrielles /Industrial Relations* 44(4): 827–49. Online: https://doi.org /10.7202/050536ar.

ANGUS REID INSTITUTE. 1991. *Multiculturalism and Canadians: Attitudinal Study 1991: National Survey Report*. Ottawa: Multiculturalism and Citizenship Canada.

ANGUS REID INSTITUTE. 2022. "Islamophobia in Canada: Four mindsets indicate negativity is nationwide, most intense in Quebec." Online: https:// angusreid.org/islamophobia-canada-quebec/.

ANGUS REID INSTITUTE & UNIVERSITY OF ALBERTA. 2020. "Blame, Bullying and Disrespect: Chinese Canadians Reveal Their Experiences with Racism during COVID-19." 22 June. Online: http://angusreid.org /racism-chinese-canadians-covid19/.

AQUINO, KAL, THOMAS M. TRIPP & ROBERT J. BIES. 2006. "Getting Even or Moving On? Power, Procedural Justice, and Types of Offence as Predictors of Revenge, Forgiveness, Reconciliation, and Avoidance in Organizations." *Journal of Applied Psychology* 91(3): 653–68. Online: https:// doi.org/10.1037/0021-9010.91.3.653.

ARRIAGADA, PAULA. 2021. "The Achievements, Experiences, and Labour market Outcomes of First nations, Metis and Inuit Women with Bachelor's Degrees or Higher. *Insights on Canadian Society*. Statistics Canada." 20 October. Online: www150.statcan.gc.ca/n1/pub/75-006-x /2021001/article/00009-eng.htm.

ASARE, JANICE GASSAM. 2023. "Do Boycotts Actually Work? Examining the Use of Boycotts to Drive Social Change." *Forbes*, 22 December. Online: www. forbes.com/sites/janicegassam/2023/12/22/do-boycotts-actually-work -examining-the-use-of-boycotts-to-drive-social-change/.

ASKARINAM, LEAH. 2016. "Asian Americans Feel Held Back at Work by Stereotypes." *The Atlantic*, 26 January. Online: www.theatlantic.com/politics /archive/01/asianamericans-feel-held-back-at-work-by-stereotypes/458874/.

ASPLUND, G. 1988. *Women Managers: Changing Organizational Cultures*. Toronto: John Wiley and Sons.

AUDITOR GENERAL OF CANADA. 2023. "Inclusion in the Workplace for Racialized Employees." Online: www.oag-bvg.gc.ca/internet/English /parl_oag_202310_05_e_44338.html.

AZIZ, SABA. 2022. "Black Canadians Seeing Progress in the Corporate Sector bnut Want More Senior Roles." *Global News*, 19 February. Online: https:// globalnews.ca/news/8633231/black-employees-corporate-canada-poll/.

AZIZ, SABA. 2023. "Antisemitism, Islamophobia Rising in Canada Amid Israel-Hamas Conflict," *Global News*, 19 October. Online: https://globalnews.ca /news/10035853/israel-hamas-conflict-islamophobia-antisemitism-canada/.

AZPIRI, JON & BEN DOOLEY. 2017. "Thousands Protest against Anti-Islam, Anti-Immigration Rally at Vancouver City Hall." *Global News*, 19 August. Online: https://globalnews.ca/news/3682727/vancouver-anti-islam-anti-immigration-rally-and-counter-protest-planned-for-saturday/.

BADENOCH, KEMI. 2020. "Closing Statement to the House of Commons on Black History Month in the United Kingdom." *American Rhetoric*, 20 October. Online: www.americanrhetoric.com/speeches/kemibadenoch-blackhistorymonth.htm.

BAIG, FAKIHA. 2023. "Islamophobia Is Widespread in Canada, Early Findings of Senate Committee Show." *Global News*, 19 April. Online: https://globalnews.ca/news/9636076/islamophobia-canada-senate-committee/.

BAINS, CAMILLE. 2022, "No Single Fix for Anti-Indigenous Racism in Canada's Health –Care System: Doctor." *CTV News: Health/News*, 30 September. Online: www.ctvnews.ca/health/no-single-fix-for-anti-indigenous-racism-in-canada-s-health-care-system-doctor-1.6090855.

Baker Journal. 2022. "Group Aims to Increase Black Representation in Restaurant." 28 September. Online: www.bakersjournal.com/group-aims-to-increase-black-representation-in-restaurant-industry/.

BALINTEC, VANESSA. 2022. "2 Years into the Pandemic, Anti-Asian Hate is still on the Rise in Canada, Report Shows." *CBC News – Toronto*, 3 April. Online: www.cbc.ca/news/canada/toronto/2-years-into-the-pandemic-anti-asian-hate-is-still-on-the-rise-in-canada-report-shows-1.6404034.

BALKISSOON, DENISE. 2019. "The Inescapable Scent of Canada's Ripening Hatred." *Globe and Mail*, 19 April.

BANERJEE, RUPA. 2008. "An Examination of Factors Affecting Perspectives of Workplace Discrimination." *Journal of Labour Research* 29: 380–401. Online: https://doi.org/10.1007/s12122-008-9047-0.

BANERJEE, RUPA, JEFFREY G. REITZ & PHIL OREOPOULOS. 2018. "Do Large Employers Treat Racial Minorities More Fairly? An Analysis of Canadian Field Experiment Data." *Canadian Public Policy* 44(1): 1–12. Online: https://doi.org/10.3138/cpp.2017-033.

BANK OF NOVA SCOTIA. N.d. "Global Human Rights Statement." Accessed 23 October 2024. Online: www.scotiabank.com/ca/en/about/responsibility-impact/human-rights.html#:~:text=Scotiabank%20is%20committed%20to%20providing,discrimination%2C%20harassment%2C%20and%20violence.

BASCARRAMURTY, DAKSHANA, CARLY WEEKS & ERIC ANDREW-GEE. 2020. "New Data show that Immigrants and Low-Income Earners are more Susceptible to COVID-19." *Globe and Mail*, 23 May. Online: www.theglobeandmail.com/canada/article-how-covid-19-is-exposing-canadas-socioeconomic-inequalities/.

BASIOUNY, ANGIE. 2025. "Why Accountability Matters in AI Development and Governance." *Knowledge at Wharton*, 7 February.

BASU, ZACHARY. 2025. "Trump's Blame Game Returns after Deadly Plane Crash." *Axios*, 31 January. Online: www.axios.com/2025/01/31/trump-blame-game-plane-crash.

BC HYDRO. N.d. "Statement of Respect, Inclusion and Diversity." Accessed 22 March 2025. Online: www.bchydro.com/toolbar/about/who_we_are/corporate_citizenship.html.

BC LABOUR RELATIONS BOARD. 2024. "Federation of Labour in British Columbia, Collective Agreement." Online: www.lrb.bc.ca/media/22510/download?inline.

BC MINISTRY OF HEALTH. 2020. "In Plain Sight: Addressing Indigenous-Specific Racism and Discrimination in B.C. Health Care." Online: https://engage.gov.bc.ca/app/uploads/sites/613/2020/11/In-Plain-Sight-Summary-Report.pdf.

BC OFFICE OF THE HUMAN RIGHTS COMMISSIONER. N.d. "Employment Equity Toolkit." Accessed 31 August 2024. Online: https://bchumanrights.ca/resources/employment-equity-toolkit/.

BC STATS. 2016. "Workforce Profile Report: BC Public Service. British Columbia." April. Online: www2.gov.bc.ca/assets/gov/data/statistics/government/worforce_profile_report_2015_bcps.pdf.

BDS (BOYCOTT, DIVESTMENT, SANCTIONS). N.d. "FAQs." Accessed 11 January 2025. Online: https://bdsmovement.net/faqs#collapse16239.

BEAN, FRANK D., MARK LEACH & B. LINDSAY LOWELL. 2004. "Immigrant Job Quality and Mobility in the United States." *Work and Occupation* 31(4): 407–23. Online: https://doi.org/10.1177/0730888404268902.

BELL, JR., DERRICK A. 1980. "Brown v. Board of Education and the Interest Convergence Dilemma." *Harvard Law Review* 93(3): 518–33. Online: https://doi.org/10.2307/1340546.

BENEFITS CANADA. 2024a. "Half of Canadian BIPOC Employees Felt Uncomfortable or Unwelcome at Work: Survey." 1 February. Online: www.benefitscanada.com/news/bencan/half-of-canadian-bipoc-employees-feel-uncomfortable-or-unwelcome-at-work-survey/.

BENEFITS CANADA. 2024b. "Majority of Indigenous IT Workers have Experienced Workplace Discrimination: Survey." 11 January. Online: www.benefitscanada.com/news/bencan/majority-of-indigenous-it-workers-have-experienced-workplace-discrimination-survey/.

BENNETT, GRACE, LAURA A. BARDON & EILEEN R. GIBNEY. 2022. "A Comparison of Dietary Patterns and Factors Influencing Food Choice among Ethnic Groups Living in One Locality: A Systematic Review." *Nutrients* 14(5): 1–21. Online: https://doi.org/10.3390/nu14050941.

BERDAHL, JENNIFER & JI-A. MIN. 2012. "Prescriptive Stereotypes and Workplace Consequences for East Asians in North America." *Cultural Diversity and Ethnic Minority Psychology* 18(2): 141–52. Online: https://doi.org/10.1037/a0027692. Medline: 22506817.

BERKE, DAVID. 2005. *Succession Planning Management: A Guide to Organizational Systems and Practices*. Greensboro, NC: Centre for Creative Leadership. Online: https://books.google.ca/books?hl=en&lr=&id=hOs2DwAAQBAJ&oi=fnd&pg=PR7&dq=cloning+as+a+succession+management+tool&ots=ZVN80wqNA8&sig=2jKYG9uHiaomUMiPao7lSH5awW0#v=onepage&q&f=false.

BERNIER, LIZ. 2013. "Rising Turnover Cause for Concern." *Canadian HR Reporter*. 18 November.

BLACK LIVES MATTER CANADA. 2023. "Fighting for Justice & Liberation for Black Communities and Individuals from Coast to Coast to Coast." Online: www.blacklivesmatter.ca/.

BLANCHETTE, SIMON. 2024. "Beyond Bias: Equity, Diversity and Inclusion Must Drive AI Implementation in the Workplace." *The Conversation*. 17 November.

BLAUNER, ROBERT. 1969. "Internal Colonialism and Ghetto Revolt." *Social Problems* 16(4): 393–408.

BLOCK, SHEILA & GRACE-EDWARD GALABUZI. 2011. Canada's Colour Coded Labour Market: The Gap for Racialized Workers. Ottawa: Canadian Centre for Policy Alternatives.

BLOOMBERG. 2020. "Race and Ethnicity in the Workplace: The Road to Active Allyship." 7 December. Online: www.bloomberg.com/company/stories/race-ethnicity-in-the-workplace-the-road-to-active-allyship/.

BOISVERT, NICK. 2018. "Toronto Restaurant Ordered to Pay Black Man $10,000 after Asking him to Prepay for Meal." *CBC News*, 30 April. Online: www.cbc.ca/news/canada/toronto/hong-shing-tribunal-decision-1.4642009.

BONGIORNO, JOE. 2024. "Molson Coors Ends Diversity, Equity and Inclusion Policies, Moves to 'Broader View'." *CityNews*, 6 September. Online: https://ottawa.citynews.ca/2024/09/06/molson-coors-ends-diversity-equity-and-inclusion-policies-moves-to-broader-view/.

BREWER, MARILYNN B. 1999 (Fall). "The Psychology of Prejudice: Ingroup Love and Outgroup Hate." *Journal of Social Issues* 55(3): 429–44. Online: https://doi.org/10.1111/0022-4537.00126.

BROCK, MELANIE & TODD G. MORRISON. 2016. "Exploring the Roots of Prejudice toward Aboriginal Peoples in Canada." *Canadian Journal of Native Studies* 36(2): 13–42.

BROSSEAU, LAURENCE. 2020. Recognition of the Foreign Qualifications of Immigrants. Ottawa: Library of Parliament, Parliament of Canada.

Online: https://lop.parl.ca/sites/PublicWebsite/default/en_CA /ResearchPublications/202086E.

BROWN, CRAIG C., NIKOL VEISMAN, DALIMA CHHIBBER, JESSICA PRAZNIK, DARIA JORQUERA PALMER, ALLEN MANKEWICH, LEISHA STRACHAN, SARAH TEETZEL, LORI WILKINSON NIKOL VEISMAN, DALIMA CHHIBBER, JESSICA PRAZNIK, DARIA JORQUERA PALMER, ALLEN MANKEWICH, LEISHA STRACHAN, SARAH TEETZEL & LORI WILKINSON. N.d. *Exp*eriences of Racism and Anti-Racism in Sport in Winnipeg: Final Report. Winnipeg: University of Manitoba and Immigration Partnership Winnipeg.

BROWN, DAVID A.H., DEBRA L. BROWN & VANESSA ANASTASOPOULOS. 2002. Women on Boards: Not Just the Right Thing ... But the "Bright" Thing. Ottawa: Conference Board of Canada.

BRUNNER, LISA RUTH & CAPUCINE COUSTERE. 2024. "Migration Experts Scruitinize Justin Trudeau's Explanation for Immigration Cuts." *The Conversation*, 24 November.

BURGESS, MELINDA, KAREN E DILL-SHACKLEFORD & STEPHEN R. BURGESS. 2011. "Playing with Prejudice: The Prevalence and Consequences of Racial Stereotypes in Video Games." *Media Psychology* 14 (3): 289–311.

BURKE, A. 2016. "Indigenous Military Members Under 'Systemic' Racism, Report Claims." *CBC News*, 13 December. Online: www.cbc.ca/news /canada/ottawa/canada-military-indigenous-racism-report-1.3891862

BUTCHER, JONATHAN & MIKE GONZALEZ. 2020. "Critical Race Theory, the New Intolerance, and Its Grip on America." *Backgrounder* 3567: 1–42.

BUTLER, SELETHA R. 2012. "All on Board! Strategies for Constructing Diverse Boards of Directors." *Virginia Law and Business Review* 7(1): 730–43. Online: https://doi.org/10.1177/09579265221095407.

CAMMAERTS, BART. 2022. "The Abnormalisation of Social Justice: The 'Anti-Woke Culture War' Discourse in the UK." *Discourse and Society* 33(6): 1–14. Online: https://eprints.lse.ac.uk/114596/1/095792652210 95407.pdf.

CANADA ENERGY REGULATOR. 2022. Employment Equity Report, 2021–2022. Ottawa: Government of Canada. Online: www.cer-rec.gc.ca/en/about /publications-reports/employment-equity-reports/2021-2022/employment-equity-report-2021–2022.pdf.

CANADA'S BEST DIVERSITY EMPLOYERS. 2024. *Canada Stop 100*. Online: www.canadastop100.com/diversity/.

Canada's Top 100 Employers: 2022 Winners. 2021. *Globe and Mail*, 12 November. Online: https://issuu.com/ct100./docs/ct2022-magazine-issuu.

CANADIAN BOARD DIVERSITY COUNCIL. 2016. "2016 Annual Report Card. Toronto." Online: http://boarddiversity.ca/sites/default/files /CBDC-Annual-Report-Card-2016.pdf.

CANADIAN CENTRE FOR DIVERSITY AND INCLUSION. 2024. "Success Stories." Online: www.ccdi.ca/success-stories/.

CANADIAN CENTRE FOR POLICY ALTERNATIVES. 2019. "By the Numbers: Race, Gender, and the Canadian Laboir Market." Online: https://monitormag.ca/shorthand/by-the-numbers-race-gender-and-the-canadian-labour-market-200221160640/index.html.

CANADIAN FEDERATION OF INDEPENDENT BUSINESS. 2020. "Your Business and COVID-19 Survey – Part Three." Online: www.cfib-fcei.ca/sites/default/files/2020-03/COVID-19-survey-results-March-31.pdf.

CANADIAN HUMAN RIGHTS COMMISSION. 2007. A Guide to Screening and Selection in Employment. Ottawa: Minister of Public Works and Government Services.

CANADIAN HUMAN RIGHTS COMMISSION. 2022. *More Must Be Done to Dismantle the Lasting Effects of Colonialism*. Ottawa: Canadian Human Rights Commission. Online: www.chrc-ccdp.gc.ca/en/resources/more-must-be-done-dismantle-the-lasting-effects-colonialism.

CANADIAN HUMAN RIGHTS COMMISSION. 2023. "Anti-Racism and Organizational Change: A Guide for Employers." 23 October. Online: www.chrc-ccdp.gc.ca/en/resources/publications/anti-racism-organizational-change-a-guide-employers.

CANADIAN PRESS. 2021. "Canada Locks up Black Immigrants, Asylum Seekers Longer Than Other Detainees: Report." *CBC News*, 17 June. Online: www.cbc.ca/news/canada/asylum-seekers-detention-canada-1.6069327.

CANADIAN PRESS. 2022. "Tech Sector Employment, Pay Gaps Persist for Women, BIPOC Community: Survey." *Benefits Canada*, 5 December. Online: www.benefitscanada.com/news/bencan/tech-sector-employment-pay-gaps-persist-for-women-bipoc-community-report/.

CANADIAN TEACHERS FEDERATION. N.d. "Speak Truth to Power Canada. A Short History of Human Rights." Accessed 17 August 2024. Online: https://sttpcanada.ctf-fce.ca/human-rights/history/#:~:text=Canadian%20provinces%20and%20territories%20created,Other%20provinces%20and%20territories%20followed.

CANADIAN UNION OF PUBLIC EMPLOYEES. 2019. "Walking the Talk: A Practical Guide to Reconciliation for CUPE Locals." Online: https://cupe.ca/walking-talk-practical-guide-reconciliation-cupe-locals.

CANADIAN UNION OF PUBLIC EMPLOYEES. 2022. "Truth and Reconciliation: CUPE Taking Action through Collective Bargaining." CUPE National Human Rights Branch. Online: https://cupe.ca/orders/truth-and-reconciliation-cupe-taking-action-through-collective-bargaining.

CANADIAN WOMEN'S CHAMBER OF COMMERCE & DREAM LEGACY FOUNDATION. 2020. Falling through the Cracks: Immediate Needs of Canada's Underrepresented Founders. Toronto: Canadian Women's Chamber of

Commerce. Online: https://canwcc.ca/wp-content/uploads/2020/05/Falling-through-the-Cracks_CanWCC_May2020.pdf.

CANADIAN WOMEN'S FOUNDATION. 2021. "The Facts about the #MeToo Movement and Its Impact in Canada." 22 November. Online: https://canadianwomen.org/the-facts/the-metoo-movement-in-canada/.

CARRATT, EBANY. 2022. "How the History of Segregation Impacts Recreation." *Canadian Parks, Protected and Conservative Areas Leadership Collective*, 23 March. Online: www.cppcl.ca/how-the-history-of-segregation-impacts-recreation/.

CARRENO ROSAS, AURA. 2023. "Hamilton Sees 61% Increase in Hate Incidents in Hamilton in 2022: Police Report." *CBC News*, 25 April. Online: www.cbc.ca/news/canada/hamilton/hamilton-hate-incidents-2022-1.6821072.

CARRIERE, GISELE & EVELYNE BOUGIE. 2023. "Changes to Acute-Care Hospitalizations among Indigenous Children and Youth: Results from the 2006 and 2011 Canadian Census Health and Environment Cohorts." *Statistics Canada*, Health Reports, 18 January. Online: www150.statcan.gc.ca/n1/pub/82-003-x/2023001/article/00002-eng.htm.

CASE, TONY. 2025a. "America's Political Tensions Threaten to Turn the Workplace Upside Down." *WorkLife Daily Briefing*, 25 February. Online: www.worklife.news/culture/americas-political-tensions-threaten-to-turn-the-workplace-upside-down/.

CASE, TONY. 2025b. "'Bigotry is Suddenly Acceptable Again': Anti-DEI Push meets with Spike in Workplace Discrimination." *WorkLife Daily Briefing*, 20 February. Online: www.worklife.news/culture/bigotry-is-suddenly-acceptable-again-anti-dei-push-meets-with-spike-in-workplace-discrimination/.

CASE, TONY. 2025c. "'I don't think it's over': Former Head of DEI on Corporate Diversity's Uncertain Future," *WorkLife Daily Briefing*, 26 February. Online: www.worklife.news/culture/bigotry-is-suddenly-acceptable-again-anti-dei-push-meets-with-spike-in-workplace-discrimination/.

CASTALDO, JOE. 2025. "Momentum to Pass Regulatory Legislation for AI has Slowed Considerably in Canada and the U.S." Momentum to pass regulatory legislation for AI has slowed considerably in Canada and the U.S." *Globe and Mail*, 20 January. Online: www.theglobeandmail.com/business/article-momentum-to-pass-regulatory-legislation-for-ai-has-slowed-considerably/.

CASTLES, STEPHEN & GODULA KOSACK. 1973a. "The Function of Labour Immigration in Western European Capitalism." *Selected Studies in International Migration and Immigrant Incorporation* 1: n.p.

CASTLES, STEPHEN & GODULA KOSACK. 1973b. Immigrant Workers and Class Structure in Western Europe. London: Oxford University Press.

CATALYST & DIVERSITY INSTITUTE IN MANAGEMENT AND TECHNOLOGY. 2007. Career Advancement in Corporate Canada: A Focus on Visible Minorities. Toronto: Catalyst Publication. Online: www.torontomu.ca/diversity/media/Full%20Report.pdf.

Catalyst. 2019. "Empowering Workplaces Combat Emotional Tax for People of Colour in Canada (Report)." 24 July. Online: www.catalyst.org/research/emotional-tax-canada/.

CBC NEWS. 2014. "CBC News Poll on Discrimination." November. Online: www.documentcloud.org/documents/1362391-cbc-discrimination-poll-november-2014.html.

CECCO, LEYLAND. 2018. "Dining While Black: Toronto Restaurant Fined after Charging Customers Upfront." *The Guardian*, 1 May. Online: www.theguardian.com/world/2018/may/01/toronto-restaurant-emile-wickham-race-discrimination.

CHABURSKY, LUBOMYR. 1992. "The Employment Equity Act: The Examination of its Development and Direction." *Canadian Law Review* 24(2): 305–61. Online: www.canlii.org/en/commentary/doc/1992CanLIIDocs35#!fragment//BQCwhgziBcwMYgK4Ds-DWszIQewE4BUBTADwBdoByCgSgBpltTCIBFRQ3AT0otokL-C4EbDtyp8BQkAGU8pAELcASgFEAMioBqAQQByAYRW1SYAE-bRS2ONWpA.

CHAKRABORTY, CHANDRIMA. 2022. "Contagious Minorities: Chinese Canadians During the Covid-19 Pandemic." *Journal of Canadian Studies* 56(3): 393–409. Online: https://doi.org/10.3138/jcs-2022-0017.

CHANG, EDWARD H. 2025. "Rethinking DEI Training? These Changes Can Bring Better Results." Working Knowledge, 23 January. Online: www.library.hbs.edu/working-knowledge/rethinking-dei-training-these-changes-can-bring-results.

CHEMTOB, DANIELLE. 2025. "Jamie Dimon Defends DEI Efforts amid Trump's Crackdowns." *Forbes Daily*, 24 January. Online: https://www.forbes.com/sites/daniellechemtob/2025/01/24/forbes-daily-jamie-dimon-defends-dei-efforts-amid-trumps-crackdown/.

CHENOWETH, ERICA. 2013. "Fear and Loathing." *TedBoulder Talk*. Online: https://tedxboulder.com/speakers/erica-chenoweth.

CHEUNG, ADRIAN, SARAH BRIDGE & SHANIFA NASSER. 2017. "Toronto – Anti-Islamophobia Motion Brings Out Hundreds of Protest and Anti-Protest." *CBC News*, 4 March. Online: www.cbc.ca/news/canada/toronto/m103-protests-toronto-1.4010235.

CHILDREN INTERNATIONAL. N.d. "The Poverty Problem: Facts and Issues." Accessed 18 July 2023. Online: www.children.org/global-poverty/global-poverty-facts?rs_id=451&utm_campaign=rkd-fy23grant&utm_medium=cpc+grant&utm_source=google&gad=1&gclid=Cj0K-

CQjw8NilBhDOARIsAHzpbLD7QC06069N7Ahge_5JVjV2gCRLjnYf-3d6WWZMzdMOqCSUcKnX_cZMaAqotEALw_wcB.

CHISM, MARLENE. 2024. "Uncovering 5 Hidden Stages of Conflict." *SmartBrief*, 6 May. Online: www.smartbrief.com/original/uncovering-5-hidden-stages-of-conflict?utm_term=DB12F525-A96A-49B9-B241-4AF940FC0B18&l-rh=e93a66d4cf1f844922e5bd6f95ad503b952bdceb89c03109991e-3d039ef4b33e&utm_campaign=77F8DA5B-9982-431B-9E20-444163A3CF79&utm_content=9EF254DD-8846-43CD-8110-E65FE7D-B27CD&utm_source=brief.

CHOLLANGI, NEHA. N.d. "Unconscious Bias at the Bank." *KOHO Financial*. Accessed 5 September 2023. Online: www.koho.ca/learn/unconscious-bias-at-the-bank/.

CHUN, JIWON & CATHY CALLAGHER-LOUISY. 2018. "Overview of Human Rights Codes by Province and Territory in Canada." *Canadian Centre for Diversity and Inclusion*, January. Online: https://ccdi.ca/media/1414/20171102-publications-overview-of-hr-codes-by-province-final-en.pdf.

CITY OF MONTREAL. N.d. "Charter of Rights and Responsibilities." Accessed 3 October 2024. Online: https://montreal.ca/en/topics/montreal-charter-rights-and-responsibilities.

CITY OF MONTREAL. 2021. "Master Plan for Employment Diversity, Equity and Inclusion." 9 June. Online: https://montreal.ca/en/articles/master-plan-employment-diversity-equity-and-inclusion-14942.

CITY OF MONTREAL. 2024. "Diversity, Equity and Inclusion in Employment." 7 March. Online: https://montreal.ca/en/articles/diversity-equity-and-inclusion-employment-2994.

CITY OF TORONTO. N.d.a. "City of Toronto Human Rights and Anti-Harassment Policy." Accessed 25 August 2024. Online: www.toronto.ca/legdocs/mmis/2008/ex/bgrd/backgroundfile-13239.pdf.

CITY OF TORONTO. N.d.b. "Confronting Anti-Black Racism." Accessed 18 August 2024. Online: www.toronto.ca/community-people/get-involved/community/confronting-anti-black-racism/.

CITY OF TORONTO. N.d.c. "Toronto Action Plan to Confront Anti-Black Racism." Accessed 18 August 2024. Online: www.toronto.ca/legdocs/mmis/2017/ex/bgrd/backgroundfile-109127.pdf.

CITY OF TORONTO. 2000. "Employment Equity Policy." 4 July. Online: www.toronto.ca/city-government/accountability-operations-customer-service/city-administration/corporate-policies/people-equity-policies/employment-equity-policy/#:~:text=Policy%20Statement,leadership%20role%20in%20the%20community.

CITY OF TORONTO. 2024. "Employment Equity Policy." Online: www.toronto.ca/city-government/accountability-operations-customer-service

/city-administration/corporate-policies/people-equity-policies/employment-equity-policy/.

CITY OF VANCOUVER. N.d. "Respect in the Workplace." Accessed 26 August 2024. Online: https://vancouver.ca/your-government/respect-in-the-workplace.aspx.

CITY OF VANCOUVER. 2011. "Administrative Report, Supports Item No. 3, City Services and Budgets (CS&B) Committee Agenda." 3 March. Online: https://council.vancouver.ca/20110303/documents/csbu3-CodeofConductHumanRightsandHarassmentPolicyandRespectfulWorkplacePolicy.pdf.

CITY OF WINNIPEG. N.d. "Appendix B – Newcomer Welcome and Inclusion Policy." Accessed 18 August 2024. Online: https://clkapps.winnipeg.ca/DMIS/ViewPdf.asp?SectionId=556654.

CLARK, BRENT, JR. 2024. "They Are Not Like Us Citizens: Reconsidering the Racism and Populism Relationship." PhD diss., Department of Sociology, University of California, Irvine.

CLC (CANADIAN LABOUR CONGRESS). 2021. "What We Care About." Online: https://canadianlabour.ca/what-we-care-about/.

CLC (CANADIAN LABOUR CONGRESS). 2022. "Asian Heritage Month: Canada Must do More to Eliminate Anti-Asian Racism." 30 April. Online: https://canadianlabour.ca/asian-heritage-month-canada-must-do-more-to-eliminate-anti-asian-racism/.

COBB, JELANI. 2021. "The Man behind Critical Race Theory." *The New Yorker*, 13 September. Online: www.newyorker.com/magazine/2021/09/20/the-man-behind-critical-race-theory.

CLOUBROUGH, JILL. 2018. "Manitoba: More Survivors Coming Forward to Report Assaults after #MeToo Movement." *CBC News*, 9 March. Online: www.cbc.ca/news/canada/manitoba/winnipeg-police-sexual-assault-reports-up-metoo-1.4568787.

COHEN, NICOLE & SHANNON CLARKE. 2024. "Reporting on Precarious Ground: Women in Digital Journalism." *Canadian Journal of Communication*. Online: www.gendereconomy.org/reporting-on-precarious-ground-women-in-digital-journalism/.

COHEN, RAPHAEL S. 2024. "China and North Korea Throws U.S. War Plans Out of the Window: The Intervention of Asian Powers in Europe Nullify Decades of U.S. Strategic Planning." Foreign Policy, 2 December. Online: https://foreignpolicy.com/2024/12/02/us-military-defense-strategy-china-russia-north-korea-war-geopolitics/.

COLLAHAN, CLOEY. 2023. "If Hiring Candidates with No Degrees, What Should Recruiters Look For?" *Worklife Newsletter*, 17 February. Online: www.worklife.news/talent/degree-free-hiring/?utm_campaign=worklifedis&utm_source=worklifedaily&utm_medium=email&utm

_content=121423&utm_medium=email&utm_campaign=Worklife%20 Briefing%2012142023&utm_content=Worklife%20Briefing%20 12142023+CID_8831c8f60556a3e9db391a9912d28852&utm _source=wldis&utm_term=If%20hiring%20candidates%20with%20 no%20degrees%20what%20should%20recruiters%20look%20for.

COLLEGE OF DIETITIANS OF BRITISH COLUMBIA. N.d. "Indigenous Racism and Colonialism in Dietetics in BC and Canada." Accessed 29 July 2023. Online: https://collegeofdietitiansofbc.org/wp-content /uploads/2022/02/3_5_220223_Indigenous-specific-racism-and -colonialism-in-dietetics-FINAL.pdf.

COLLINS, SHARON M. 1997. "Black Mobility in White Corporations: Up the Corporate Ladder but Out on a Limb." *Social Problems* 44(1): 55–67. Online: https://academic.oup.com/socpro/article-abstract/44/1/55 /1646504?login=false or https://doi.org/10.2307/3096873.

CONAWAY, WENDY & SONJA BETHUNE. 2015. "Implicit Bias and First Name Stereotypes: What Are the Implications for Online Instruction?" *Online Learning* 10(3): 162–78.

CONFERENCE BOARD OF CANADA. 2023. Leveling the Playing Field for Black Canadians: A Call to Action for Leaders. Ottawa: Conference Board of Canada. Online: https://fsc-ccf.ca/wp-content/uploads/2023/11/levelling-the-playing-field_2023.pdf.

CONFERENCE BOARD OF THE UNITED STATES. 2021. "CEOs and Other Business Executives Discuss Addressing Health Inequality." 4 March. Online: www.conference-board.org/press/CEOs-discuss-health-inequality.

CONFERENCE BOARD OF THE UNITED STATES. 2024a. "DEI under Pressure: Report." 28 October. Online: www.conference-board.org/publications /DEI-under-pressure.

CONFERENCE BOARD OF THE UNITED STATES. 2024b. "Press Release: Despite DEI Backlash, Nearly 60% of US Workers Support DEI Policies." 30 October. Online: www.conference-board.org/press/dei-backlash.

CONROY, SHANA. 2023. "Experiences of Discrimination in Daily Life among Chinese people in Canada, and their Perceptions of and Experiences with the Police and the Justice System." *Statistics Canada*, 28 August. Online: www150.statcan.gc.ca/n1/pub/85-002-x/2023001/article/00005-eng.htm.

COOK, CHARLENE. 2013. "Poverty and Employment Precarity in Southern Ontario." EPSO Policy Options Working Paper no. 15: How to Increase Equity and Reduce Discrimination. February. Online: https://pepso.ca /documents/pepso-wp-15-equity-discrimination-2014-05.pdf.

COPELAND, PETER. 2024. "Canada Is Poised for a Counter Cultural Movement of Its Own: Peter Copeland in the Hub." *Macdonald-Laurier Institute*. 21 October. Online: https://macdonaldlaurier.ca

/canada-is-poised-for-a-counter-cultural-movement-of-its-own-peter-copeland-in-the-hub/.

CORNELISSEN, LOUIS & MARTIN TYRCOTTE. 2020. "Persistent Overqualification Among Immigrants and Non-Immigrants." *Statistics Canada.* 2 September. Online: www150.statcan.gc.ca/n1/pub/75-006-x/2020001/article/00004-eng.htm.

COTTER, ADAM. 2022. "Experiences of Discrimination among the Black and Indigenous Populations in Canada." *Statistics Canada.* 16 February. Online: www150.statcan.gc.ca/n1/pub/85-002-x/2022001/article/00002-eng.htm.

COUSINS, BEN. 2023. "Deadline Extended for Repayment of COVID Business Loans." *BNN Bloomberg*, 15 September. Online: www.bnnbloomberg.ca/ottawa-extends-deadline-for-interest-free-ceba-repayment-1.1972023.

CTV NEWS. 2020 "What's Essentials? List of Services and Workplaces Allowed to Be Open Gets Smaller." 24 March. Online: https://toronto.ctvnews.ca/what-s-essential-list-of-services-and-workplaces-allowed-to-be-open-gets-smaller-1.4865668.

CUKIER, ABIGAIL. 2021. "Canada's Dietitians Are Lacking in Diversity – But Things Are Changing." *Best Health.* 28 October. Online: www.besthealthmag.ca/article/dietetics-canada/.

CUKIER, WENDY, MARGARET YAP, MARK ROBERT HOLMES & SARA RODRIGUES. 2007. "Gender and Visible Minority Status: Career Advancement in the Canadian Information and Communications Technology Sector." Online: www.torontomu.ca/diversity/research/abstracts/5.pdf.

CUKIER, WENDY, JOHN MILLER, KRITEN ASPEVIG & DALE CARL. 2011. "Diversity in Leadership and Media: A Multi-Perspective Analysis of the Greater Toronto Area, 2010." *Proceedings for the 11th International Conference on Diversity in Organizations, Communities and Nations, South Africa*, 20–22 June. Online: www.international.gc.ca/world-monde/ism-racisme.aspx?lang=eng.

CUMMING, PETER A., ENID L.D. LEE & DIMITRIOS G. OREOPOULOS. 1989. *Access! Task Force on Access to Professions and Trades in Ontario.* Toronto: Ontario Ministry of Citizenship, Queen's Printer for Ontario. Online: https://km4s.ca/wp-content/uploads/Access-Task-Force-on-Access-to-Professions-and-Trades-in-Ontario-1989.pdf.

CUPE (CANADIAN UNION OF PUBLIC EMPLOYEES). N.d. *Workshop Catalogue.* Accessed 24 November 2024. Online: https://cupe.ca/mrm-union-education/workshops.

CUPE (CANADIAN UNION OF PUBLIC EMPLOYEES). 2019. "Walking the Talk: A Practical Guide to Reconciliation die CUPE Locals." 24 September. Online: https://cupe.ca/walking-talk-practical-guide-reconciliation-cupe-locals.

DAHL, ROBERT. 1971. *Polyarchy: Participation and Opposition*. New Haven, CT: Yale University Press.

DALY, BRIAN, DEXTER BROWN, JULIE SOBOWALE & NADIA STEWART. 2023. "Amplifying Voices, Protecting Lives: Addressing Systemic Racism in Media." *Government of Canada*. 26 January. Online: www.international.gc.ca/world-monde/ism-racisme.aspx?lang=eng.

DASTIN, JEFFREY. 2018. "Insight: Amazon Scraps Secret AI Recruiting Tools that Showed Bias against Women'" *Reuters*, 9 October. Online: www.reuters.com/article/world/insight-amazon-scraps-secret-ai-recruiting-tool-that-showed-bias-against-women-idUSKCN1MK0AG/.

DATATRON. N.d. "Real-Life Examples of Discriminating Artificial Intelligence." *Datatron Blog*. Accessed 27 December 2024. Online: https://datatron.com/real-life-examples-of-discriminating-artificial-intelligence/.

DEITCH, ELIZABETH, ADAM BARSKY, REBECCA M. BUTZ, SUZANNE CHAN & ARTHUR P. BRIEF. 2003. "Subtle yet Significant: The Existence and Impact of Everyday Racial Discrimination in the Workplace." *Human Relations* 56(11): 1299–1324. Online: https://doi.org/10.1177/00187267035611002.

DELGLADO, RICHARD & JEAN STEFANCIC. 2017. *Critical Race Theory: An Introduction* – Critical America. 3rd ed. Vol. 30. New York: New York University Press.

DELUDE, LOUISE. 1992. *Seniority and Employment Equity*. Ottawa: Canadian Human Rights Commission.

DHIMAN, SHIVANI. 2025. "Bias in AI Resume Screening: What Every HR Leader Needs to Know." *People Box*, 18 January. Online: www.peoplebox.ai/blog/ai-resume-screening-bias-hr-guide/.

DICHTER, MYLES. 2020. "Canadian Athletes detail Experiences with Racism in Sports." *CBC Sports*, 2 July. Online: www.cbc.ca/sports/olympics/summer/trackandfield/track-and-field-panel-story-1.5615142.

DIETRICH, BRENDA L., EMILY C. PLACHY & MAUREEN F. NORTON. 2014. "Analytics Across the Enterprise: How IBM Realizes Business Value from Big Data and Analytics." *International Business Machines Press*. Online: https://books.google.ca/books?hl=en&lr=&id=lGOVAwAAQBAJ&oi=fnd&pg=PR13&dq=IBM+-+employee+competency+data+bank&ots=cNmLMDV39J&sig=G3OzI6TWtUMuGzusvf44FUOD1BU#v=onepage&q&f=false.

DIMINGU, HENRY. 2024. "Workplace Integration: A Phenomenological Study of Immigrants' Experiences in Northern Canadian Organizations." PhD diss., School of Business and Management, California Southern University, 24 September. Online: www.proquest.com/openview/760c0705b341e7d31c882a9bf9833aa9/1?pq-origsite=gscholar&cbl=18750&diss=y.

DIVERSITY INSTITUTE IN MANAGEMENT AND TECHNOLOGY. 2009. "DiverseCity Counts: A Snapshot of Diversity in the Greater Toronto Area." Online: www.ryerson.ca/diversity/news/CourtsReport_CONFIDENTIAL.pdf.

DIXON, JEFFREY & MICHAEL ROSENBAUM. 2004. "Nice to Know You? Test Contact, Cultural, and Group Threat Theories of Anti-Black and Anti-Hispanic Stereotypes." *Social Science Quarterly* 85(2): 257–80. Online: https://doi.org/10.1111/j.0038-4941.2004.08502003.x.

DOOLITTLE, ROBYN. 2018. "Unfounded Rates Start to Fall in Cities across Canada." *Globe and Mail*, 2 August. Online: www.theglobeandmail.com/canada/article-unfounded-rates-start-to-fall-in-cities-across-canada/.

DOUGLAS, EMILY. 2023a. "Canadian Companies Commit to Anti-Racism, but Employees Worry About Recession Cuts." *Human Resources Director*, 30 January. Online: www.hcamag.com/ca/specialization/diversity-inclusion/canadian-companies-commit-to-anti-racism-but-employees-worry-about-recession-cuts/434443.

DOUGLAS, EMILY. 2023b. "People Still Ask Me If I'm a Diversity Hire: Indigenous Youth Still Face Racial Bias at Work." *Human Resources Director*, 21 June. Online: www.hcamag.com/ca/specialization/diversity-inclusion/people-still-ask-me-if-im-a-diversity-hire-indigenous-youth-face-racial-bias-at-work/450066.

DOVIDIO, JOHN, JOHN C. BRIGHAM, BLAIR T. JOHNSON & SAMUEL L. GAERTNER. 1996. "Stereotyping, Prejudice, and Discrimination: Another Look." In *Stereotypes and Stereotyping*, edited by Neil Macrae, Charles Stangor and Miles Howstone, 276–319. New York: Guilford Press.

DOVIDIO, JOHN F., MILES HEWSTONE, PETER GLICK, VICTORIA ESSESS, REFAELA M. DANCYGIER & DONALD GREEN, ED. 2010. "Hate Crime." In *The Sage Handbook of Prejudice, Stereotyping and Discrimination*. London: Sage Publications. Online: https://doi.org/10.4135/9781446200919.n18.

DOW, DAWN M. 2018. "The Never-Ending Task of Shielding Black Kids from Negative Stereotypes." *The Atlantic*, 9 April. Online: www.theatlantic.com/family/archive/2018/04/black-parents-media-stereotypes/557408/.

DUFFY, BOBBY & GIDEON SKINNER. 2023. "Woke vs Anti-Woke Culture War Division and Politics." *Ipsos and the Policy Institute, King's College London*, October. Online: https://kclpure.kcl.ac.uk/portal/files/243269329/woke-vs-anti-woke-culture-war-divisions-and-politics.pdf.

DUJAY, JOHN. 2023. "Province to Ban Canadian Experience Requirement in Job Listings." *Canadian Human Rights Reporter*, 9 November. Online: www.hrreporter.com/focus-areas/employment-law/province-to-ban-canadian-experience-requirement-in-job-listings/381261?hsmemberId={{contact.

hs_object_id}}&utm_source=GA&e=aW5mb3dvcnRoQHJvZ2Vycy5jb20&utm_medium=20231109&utm_campaign=CHRRW-Breaking-20231109&utm_content=F292ADEF-94C5-4E9A-A09E-D4255369EB79&tu=F292ADEF-94C5-4E9A-A09E-D4255369EB79.

DURRHEIM, K. & J. DIXON. 2004. "Attitudes in the Fibre of Everyday Life: The Discourse of Racial Evaluaiton and the Lived Experience of Desegregation." *American Psychologist* 59(7): 626–36. Online: https://doi.org/10.1037/0003-066X.59.7.626.

DWYER, ROCKY. 2003. "Career Progression Factors of Aboriginal Executives in the Canadian Federal Public Service." *Journal of Management Development* 22(10): 881–89. Online: https://doi.org/10.1108/02621710310505476.

THE ECONOMIST. 2023. "Anti-Woke Activists Are Winning the Culture Wars in America." 9 December. Online: www.economist.com/united-states/2023/12/09/anti-woke-activists-are-losing-many-of-their-school-board-battles.

EICHLER, LEAH. 2016. "Two-Thirds of Employees Are Ready to Jump." *Globe and Mail*, 1 October.

ELLIOTT, JAMES R. & RYAN A. SMITH. 2004. "Race, Gender, and Workplace Power." *American Sociological Review* 69(3): 365–86. Online: https://doi.org/10.1177/000312240406900303.

EMPLOYMENT AND SOCIAL DEVELOPMENT CANADA. 2022. "Employment Equity Act: Annual Report 2021." 13 July. Online: www.canada.ca/en/employment-social-development/corporate/portfolio/labour/programs/employment-equity/reports/2021-annual.html#h3.10.

ENVIRONICS INSTITUTE FOR SURVEY RESEARCH. 2016. Canadian Public Opinions on Aboriginal Peoples: Final Report. Toronto. Same Institute.

ERNST AND YOUNG. N.d. "Global Executive Diversity, Equity and Inclusiveness Statement." Accessed 3 October 2024. Online: www.ey.com/content/dam/ey-unified-site/ey-com/en-gl/about-us/diversity-and-inclusiveness/documents/ey-gl-ge-dei-statement-08-2024.pdf.

ETHICAL CONSUMER RESEARCH ASSOCIATION. 2025. "History of Successful Boycotts." *The Ethical Consumer*, 19 December. Online: www.ethicalconsumer.org/ethicalcampaigns/boycotts/history-successful-boycotts.

EUROPEAN ACADEMY ON RELIGION AND SOCIETY. 2012. "Islamophobia: Becoming a Global Epidemic." *News*, 7 July. Online: https://european-academyofreligionandsociety.com/news/islamophobia-becoming-a-global-epidemic/?gclid=EAIaIQobChMI1OqU1dvDgAMV8g-tBh2T3wBJEAAYASAAEgKqzPD_BwE.

EUROPEAN INSTITUTE FOR GENDER EQUALITY. 2022. "Statistical Brief: Gender Balance in Business and Finance 2021." Online: https://eige.europa.eu/sites/default/files/documents/20220905_pdf_mh0922067enn_002.pdf.

EVANS, PAUL & XIAOJUN LI. 2019. "Introduction: The Meng Factor in Canadian Views on China." *University of British Columbia*, 13 March. Online: https://sppga.ubc.ca/wp-content/uploads/sites/5/2019/03/Introduction-to-Public-Opinion-Survey-13March2019.pdf.

FARRELL, AMY & SARAH LOCKWOOD. 2023. "Addressing Hate Crime in the 21st Century: Trends, Threats, and Opportunities for Intervention." *Annual Review of Criminology* 6: 107–30. Online: https://doi.org/10.1146/annurev-criminol-030920-091908.

FIDDLER, WILLOW. 2023. "Thunder Bay Police Force Appoints New Chief." *Globe and Mail*, 22 March.

FILLION, STEPHANIE. 2021. "Justin Trudeau Adds New Faces in Top Roles for Gender Equal Cabinet." *Forbes*, 26 October. Online: www.forbes.com/sites/stephaniefillion/2021/10/26/justin-trudeau-adds-new-faces-in-top-roles-for-gender-equal-cabinet/?sh=23139cf16d59.

FLOWERS, VINCENT S. & CHARLES L. HUGHES. 1973. "Why Employees Stay." *Harvard Business Review*, July. Online: https://hbr.org/1973/07/why-employees-stay.

FLETCHER, THANDI. 2021. "Half of Canadian Kids Witness Ethnic, Racial Bullying at School: Study." *UBC News*, 19 October. Online: https://news.ubc.ca/2021/10/19/half-of-canadian-kids-witness-ethnic-racial-bullying-at-school-study/.

FONTAINE, TIM. 2016. "Canada Officially Adopts UN Declaration on Right of Indigenous Peoples." *CBC News*, 2 August. Online: www.cbc.ca/news/indigenous/canada-adopting-implementing-un-rights-declaration-1.3575272#:~:text=Link-,There%20were%20cheers%20in%20the%20United%20Nations%20as%20Canada%20officially,adopted%20by%20the%20General%20Assembly.

FOOT, RICHARD. 2020. "Canadian Charter of Rights and Freedoms." *The Canadian Encycolpedia*, 2 March. Online: www.thecanadianencyclopedia.ca/en/article/canadian-charter-of-rights-and-freedoms.

FOSS, NICOLAI J. & PETER G. KLEIN. 2023. "Why Do Companies Go Woke?" *Academy of Management* 37(4): 1–45. Online: https://doi.org/10.5465/amp.2021.0201.

FOWLER, TERESA ANNE. 2020. "Racism Contributes to Poor Attendance of Indigenous Students in Alberta Schools: New Study." *The Conversation*, 29 September. Online: https://theconversation.com/racism-contributes-to-poor-attendance-of-indigenous-students-in-alberta-schools-new-study-141922.

FRAZIER, FRANKLIN E. 1947. "Sociological Theory and Race Relations." *American Sociological Review* 12(3): 265–71.

FRAZIER, FRANKLIN E. 1972. "Sociological Theory and Race Relations." In *Intergroup Relations: Sociological Perspectives*, edited by Pierre van den Berghe, 15–25. New York: Basic Books.

FRUM, DAVID. 2017. "How to Build an Autocracy." *The Atlantic*, March. Online: www.theatlantic.com/magazine/archive/2017/03/how-to-build-an-autocracy/513872/.

FULLER. SYLVIA & LEAH F. VOSKO. 2008. "Temporary Employment and Social Inequality in Canada: Exploring Intersections of Gender, Race and Immigration Status." *Social Indicators Research* 88(1): 31–50.

GALEA, IRENE. 2025. "Hundreds of Tech Leaders Condemn Shopify Diversity Rollbacks, Defend DEI in Open Letter." *Globe and Mail*, 25 February. Online: www.theglobeandmail.com/business/article-hundreds-of-tech-leaders-condemn-shopify-diversity-cutbacks-in-open/.

GALEA, IRENE, CLARE O'HARA & JAMES BRADSHAW. 2023. "Companies Seek Strategies to Retain New Hires as They Work toward Goals on Work Force Diversity." *Globe and Mail*, 14 August. Online: www.theglobeandmail.com/business/article-workforce-diversity-hiring-strategies/.

GARDENSWARTZ, LEE & ANITA ROWE. 1998. Managing Diversity: A Complete Desk Reference and Planning Guide. Rev. ed. New York: McGraw-Hill.

GARTNER. 2022. "How HR Can Address DEI Pushback: Q&A with Emily Strother." 16 June. Online: www.gartner.com/en/newsroom/press-releases/06-15-2022-how-hr-can-address-dei-pushback.

GARTNER. 2023. "Gartner HR Survey Identifies Top Five Challenges Facing DEI Leaders." *Gartner*, 25 January. Online: www.gartner.com/en/newsroom/press-releases/1-24-2023-gartner-hr-survey-identifies-top-five-challenges-facing-dei-leaders.

GAVIN, WILLIAM. 2025. "Trump Claims Fed Chair Jerome Powell Was Too Busy with DEI and Climate Change to Tackle Inflation." *Quartz*, 30 January. Online: https://qz.com/donald-trump-jerome-powell-fed-inflation-criticism-dei-1851751084.

GEIGER, LAUREN, CARRIE P. MASTLEY, MELANIE THOMAS & EDDIE RANGEL. 2023 "Academic Libraries and DEI Initiatives: A Quantitative Study of Employee Satisfaction." *Journal of Academic Librarianship* 49(1): n.p. Online: https://doi.org/10.1016/j.acalib.2022.102627.

GIDDINGS, FRANKLIN H. 1906. "Race Improvement through Civilization." *Independent* 61: 383–84.

GISCOMME, KATHERINE & LAURA JENNER. 2009. "Career Advancement in Corporate Canada: A Focus on Visible Minorities – Diversity and

Inclusive Practices." *Catalyst*. Online: www.rbc.com/diversity/docs/diversity_and_inclusion_practices.pdf.

GLASIUS, MARLIES. 2018. "What Authoritarianism Is … and Is Not: A Practice Perspective." *International Affairs* 94(3): 513–33. Online: https://doi.org/10.1093/ia/iiy060.

GLOBALDATA. 2023. "Canada's Economic Growth to Stay Below 1% in 2024, Forecasts *GlobalData*." *Business Fundamentals*, 10 October. Online: www.globaldata.com/media/business-fundamentals/canadas-economic-growth-to-stay-below-1-in-2024-forecasts-globaldata/#:~:-text=Canada's%20economic%20growth%20to%20stay%20below%201%25%20in%202024%2C%20forecasts%20GlobalData.

GLOBALECONOMY.com. 2024. "Canada: Listed Companies." Online: www.theglobaleconomy.com/Canada/Listed_companies/#:~:text=Number%20of%20companies%20listed%20on%20the%20stock%20exchange&text=The%20latest%20value%20from%202022,to%202022%20is%202396%20companies.

GLOBE AND MAIL. 2019. "It's Time to End Carding Once and for All." 4 January. Online: www.theglobeandmail.com/opinion/editorials/article-globe-editorial-its-time-to-end-police-carding-once-and-for-all/.

GONZALES, MATT. 2023. "EEOC Solicits Recommendations to Curb AI-Driven Discrimination." *Society for Human Resource Management*. 1 February. Online: https://doi.org/10.1007/BF02800542.

GONZALEZ CASANOVA, PABLO. 1965. "Internal Colonialism and National Development." *Studies in Comparative International Development* 1(4): 27–37.

GONZALEZ, GILBERT. 1974. "A Critique of the Internal Colony Model." *Latin American Perspectives* 1(1): 154–61. Online: https://doi.org/10.1177/0094582X7400100110.

GORDON CATHERINE E. & Jerry P. White. 2014. "Indigenous Educational Attainment in Canada." *International Indigenous Policy Journal* 5(3): n.p. Online: https://doi.org/10.18584/iipj.2014.5.3.6.

GOVERNMENT OF ALBERTA. N.d.a. "Diversity and Inclusion Policy." Accessed 31 August 2024. Online: www.alberta.ca/diversity-inclusion-policy.

GOVERNMENT OF ALBERTA. N.d.b. "Examples of Microaggression in the Workplace." Accessed 30 November 2023. Online: https://alis.alberta.ca/succeed-at-work/manage-challenges/examples-of-microaggression-in-the-workplace/#:~:text=Microaggression%20can%20be%20so%20common,doesn't%20really%20look%20black.

GOVERNMENT OF ALBERTA. N.d.c. "Microaggression in the Workplace." Accessed 30 November 2023. Online: https://alis.alberta.ca/succeed-at-work/manage-challenges/microaggression-in-the-workplace/.

GOVERNMENT OF BRITISH COLUMBIA. N.d. "Meet the Anti-Racism Data Committee." Accessed 18 August 2024. Online: https://antiracism.gov.bc.ca/data-act/meet-the-committee-members/.

GOVERNMENT OF CANADA. N.d. "About the Federal Anti-Racism Secretariat." Accessed 12 November 2023. Online: www.canada.ca/en/canadian-heritage/campaigns/federal-anti-racism-secretariat/about.html.

GOVERNMENT OF CANADA. 2015. "Employment Equity Act: Annual Report, 2014." Online: www.esdc.gc.ca/en/reports/labour_standards/employment_equity_2014.page#h2.2-h.3.1.

GOVERNMENT OF CANADA. 2016. "Evaluation of Recruitment, Development, and Retention Activities at Indigenous and Northern Affairs Canada: Final Report." Project no. 1570-7/14096. January. Online: www.rcaanc-cirnac.gc.ca/eng/1532020262694/1542209736701#chp6.

GOVERNMENT OF CANADA. 2021. "Building a Foundation for Change: Canada's Anti-Racism Strategy 2019–2022." 23 June. Online: www.canada.ca/en/canadian-heritage/campaigns/anti-racism-engagement/anti-racism-strategy.html.

GOVERNMENT OF CANADA. 2022a. "Canadian Air Force Retention Strategy." 6 October. Online: www.canada.ca/en/department-national-defence/corporate/reports-publications/caf-retention-strategy/annex-a-underrepresented-populations-in-the-retention-strategy.html.

GOVERNMENT OF CANADA. 2022b. "Employment Equity Promotion Rate Study." *Public Service Commission*, 28 November. Online: www.canada.ca/en/public-service-commission/services/publications/employment-equity-promotion-rate-study.html.

GOVERNMENT OF CANADA. 2022c. "Inequalities of Mental Health of Adults Before and During the COVID-19 Pandemic: Summary." 31 October. Online: https://health-infobase.canada.ca/covid-19/mental-health-inequalities/summary.html.

GOVERNMENT OF CANADA. 2022d. "Overrepresentation of Black People in the Canadian Criminal Justice System." 15 December. Online: www.justice.gc.ca/eng/rp-pr/jr/obpccjs-spnsjpc/index.html.

GOVERNMENT OF CANADA. 2022e. "Overview of the 2022 Annual Employment Equity Act Report." Online: www.canada.ca/en/employment-social-development/corporate/portfolio/labour/programs/employment-equity/reports/2022-annual.html#tbl-1b.

GOVERNMENT OF CANADA. 2022f. "Social Inequalities in COVID-19 Deaths in Canada." 26 August. Online: https://health-infobase.canada.ca/covid-19/inequalities-deaths/.

GOVERNMENT OF CANADA. 2022g. "Truth and Reconciliation Commission of Canada." 29 September. Online: www.rcaanc-cirnac.gc.ca/eng/1450124405592/1529106060525.

GOVERNMENT OF CANADA. 2023a. "Canada's Anti-Racism Strategy." 24 March. Online: www.cbanada.ca/en/canadian-heritage/campaigns/anti-racism-engagement.html.

GOVERNMENT OF CANADA. 2023b. "Employment Equity Act: Annual Report 2022." 21 August. Online: www.canada.ca/en/employment-social-development/corporate/portfolio/labour/programs/employment-equity/reports/2022-annual.html.

GOVERNMENT OF CANADA. 2023c. "Executive Summary: A Transformative Framework to Achieve and Sustain Employment Equity." 11 December. Online: www.canada.ca/en/employment-social-development/corporate/portfolio/labour/programs/employment-equity/reports/act-review-task-force-summary.html.

GOVERNMENT OF CANADA. 2023d. "Factsheet – Antisemitism in Canada." 2 February. Online: www.canada.ca/en/canadian-heritage/corporate/transparency/open-government/standing-committee/ahmed-hussen-pch-contract-cmac/antisemitism-canada.html.

GOVERNMENT OF CANADA. 2023e. "Representation and Hiring Targets." September. Online: www.canada.ca/en/department-finance/corporate/transparency/transition-binders/2023/representation-hiring-targets.html. .

GOVERNMENT OF CANADA. 2023f. "State of the Criminal Justice System Dashboard: Understanding the Overrepresentation of Indigenous People in the Criminal Justice System." *Department of Justice*, 13 April. Online: www.justice.gc.ca/socjs-esjp/en/ind-aut/uo-cs.

GOVERNMENT OF CANADA. 2024a. "Changing Systems, Transforming Lives: Canada's Anti-Racism Strategy 2024–2028." 13 August. Online: www.canada.ca/en/canadian-heritage/services/combatting-racism-discrimination/canada-anti-racism-strategy.html.

GOVERNMENT OF CANADA. 2024b. "Diversity of Boards of Directors and Senior Management." 10 May. Online: https://ised-isde.canada.ca/site/corporations-canada/en/business-corporations/diversity-boards-directors-and-senior-management.

GOVERNMENT OF CANADA. 2024c. "Employment Equity Act S.C. 1995, c. 44." Online: https://laws-lois.justice.gc.ca/eng/acts/e-5.401/page-1.html.

GOVERNMENT OF CANADA. 2025. "The Artificial Intelligence and Data Act – A Companion Document." 31 January. Online: https://ised-isde.canada.ca/site/innovation-better-canada/en/artificial-intelligence-and-data-act-aida-companion-document.

GOVERNMENT OF MANITOBA. N.d.a. "Manitoba Government Job Opportunities." Accessed 31 August 2024. Online: www.gov.mb.ca/govjobs/info/eequity.html.

GOVERNMENT OF MANITOBA. N.d.b. "Manitoba Government Job Opportunities." Accessed 31 August 2024. Online: www.gov.mb.ca/govjobs/about/definitions.html#Employee_categories.

GOVERNMENT OF NORTHWEST TERRITORIES. N.d. "Government of the Northwest Territories Response to the Motion 29-19(2): Systemic Racism." Accessed 18 August 2024. Online: www.ntlegislativeassembly.ca/sites/default/files/legacy/td_442-192.pdf.

GOVERNMENT OF NUNAVUT. N.d. "What Is the Nunavut Human Rights Act? English Guide." Accessed 21 August 2024. Online: https://nhrt.ca/wp-content/uploads/2020/02/EN_GUIDE_what_is_the_human_rights_act.pdf.

GOVERNMENT OF NUNAVUT. 2016. "Harassment Free Workplace Policy." 7 January. Online: www.gov.nu.ca/sites/default/files/documents/2021-11/harassment_free_workplace_policy_4.pdf.

GOVERNMENT OF ONTARIO. 2023. "Annual Progress Report2023: Ontario's Anti-Racism Strategic Plan." 20 September. Online: www.ontario.ca/page/annual-progress-report-2023-ontarios-anti-racism-strategic-plan.

GOVERNMENT OF QUEBEC. 2020. "Racism in Quebec: Zero Tolerance." December. Online: https://cdn-contenu.quebec.ca/cdn-contenu/politiques_orientations/Groupe_action_racisme/RA_GroupeActionContreRacisme_AN.pdf?1607993548.

GOVERNMENT OF YUKON. 1994. "Employment Equity, Policy 3.55, Human Resource Policies." In *General Administration Manual*. Vol. 3. 27 October. Online: https://yukon.ca/sites/yukon.ca/files/psc/psc-hr-policy-employment-equity.pdf.

GOVERNMENT OF YUKON. 2023. "Yukon First Nations and Health System Partners to Guide Development of Health Wellness Yukon and Putting People First." 23 October. Online: https://yukon.ca/en/news/yukon-first-nations-and-health-system-partners-guide-development-health-and-wellness-yukon-and-putting-people-first.

GRANT, KELLY. 2025. "One-Third of Canadians Turn to Their Internet for Health Information Due to Lack of Access to a Doctor." *Globe and Mail*, 21 January. Online: www.theglobeandmail.com/canada/article-one-third-of-canadians-turn-to-the-internet-for-health-information-due/.

GRANT, TAVIA. 2016. "Canadians Still See Newcomers in Positive Light, Study Finds." *Globe and Mail*, 25 October. Online: www.theglobeandmail.com/news/national/canadians-still-see-immigration-in-positive-light-study-finds/article32508784/.

GRANT, TAVIA. 2018. "Statscan Reports Sharp Rise in Hate Crimes." *Globe and Mail*, 30 November. Online: www.theglobeandmail.com/canada/article-hate-crimes-in-canada-rose-by-47-per-cent-last-year-statscan/.

GRANT, TAVIA & DENISE BALKIAAOON. 2019. "How Canada's Racial Data Gaps Can Be Hazardous to Your Health, and More." *Globe and Mail*, 7 February. Online: www.theglobeandmail.com/canada

/article-how-canadas-racial-data-gaps-can-be-hazardous-to-your-health-and/.

GREEN, DENISE O'NEIL. 2021. "United against Anti-Muslim Racism and Islamophobia: A Call to Action in the Aftermath of Hate-Motivated Attack on Muslim Family." *TorontoMet Today*, 8 June. Online: www.torontomu.ca/news-events/news/2021/06/united-against-anti-muslim-racism-and-islamophobia/.

GREEN, MAKEDA MAYS, ANDREA STRAUSS & COLLEEN RUSSO JOHNSON. 2021. "How Would Kida Cast Themselves?." *Kidscreen*, 15 June. Online: https://kidscreen.com/2021/06/15/how-would-kids-cast-themselves/https://kidscreen.com/2021/06/15/how-would-kids-cast-themselves/.

GREENHAUS, J., S. PARASURAMAN & W. WORMLEY. 1990. "Effects of Race on Organnizational Experiences, Job Performance Evaluations, and Career Outcomes." *Academy of Management Journal* 33(1): 64–86.

GREWAL, RAMANDEEP K. 2024. "Board Diversity in Canada: Progress and Plateaus." *Knowledge Hub, Stikeman Elliott*. Online: https://stikeman.com/en-ca/kh/canadian-securities-law/board-diversity-in-canada-progress-and-plateaus.

GRIFFITH, ANDREW. 2016. "Employment Equity: What the Latest Government Report Tells Us." *Policy Options*, 31 May. Online: https://policyoptions.irpp.org/2016/05/employment-equity-latest-government-report-tells-us/.

GU, JUDY ZIYI. 2020. "Why Are There So Few BIPOC Therapists in Canada?" *Best Health*, 7 October. Online: www.besthealthmag.ca/article/bipoc-therapists-in-canada/.

GUNDEMIR, SEVAL, ROUBEN KANITZ, FLOOR RINK, INGA J. HOEVER & MICHAEL L. SLEPIAN. 2024. "Beneath the Surface: Resistance to Diversity, Equity, and Inclusion (DEI) Initiatives in Organizations." *Current Opinion in Psychology* 60 (December): 1–6. Online: https://doi.org/10.1016/j.copsyc.2024.101922.

GUO, OWEN. 2023. "'Canadian Experience' Requirements Are Not Just Discriminatory – They Harm the Economy." *Globe and Mail*, 19 November.

GUPTA S. & N. AITKEN. 2022. "COVID-19 Mortality among Racialized Populations in Canada and Its Association with Income." *StatCan Covid-19: Data Insights for a Better Canada*, Catalogue no. 45-28-0001, 30 August. Online: www150.statcan.gc.ca/n1/pub/45-28-0001/2022001/article/00010-eng.htm.

GUYNN, JESSICA & BAILEY SCHULZ. 2025. "Costco Won't Join DEI Backlash. Why Shareholders Rejected Anti-'Woke' Proposal." *USA Today*, 24 January. Online: www.usatoday.com/story/money/2025/01/23/costco-dei-shareholder-proposal-rejected/77907655007/.

HADDOCK, G., M.P. ZANNA & V.M. ESSES. 1994. "The (Limited) Role of Trait-Laden Stereotypes in Predicting Attitudes toward Native Peoples." *British Journal of Social Psychology* 33(1): 83–106. Online: https://doi.org/10.1111/j.2044-8309.1994.tb01012.x.

HAHMANN, TARA & MOHAN B. KUMAR. 2022. "Unmet Health Care Needs during the Pandemic and Resulting Impacts among First Nations People Living Off Reserve, Metis and Inuit." *Statistics Canada*, 30 August. Online: www150.statcan.gc.ca/n1/pub/45-28-0001/2022001/article/00008-eng.htm.

HAHMANN, TARA & HUDA MASOUD. 2023. "Housing Experiences and Measures of Health and Well-Being Among First Nations People Living Off Reserve, Metis and Inuit: Findings from the 2018 Canadian Housing Survey." *Statistics Canada*, 4 April. Online: www150.statcan.gc.ca/n1/pub/41-20-0002/412000022023001-eng.htm.

HAKANEN, JARI J. & WILMAR B. SCHAUFELI. 2012. "Do Burnout and Work Engagement Predict Depressive Symptoms and Life Satisfaction? A Three-Wave Seven-Year Prospective Study." *Journal of Affective Disorders* 141: 415–24. https://doi.org/10.1016/j.jad.2012.02.043.

HALL, WES. 2022. No Bootstraps When You're Barefoot. Toronto: Random House Canada.

HALL, WES & WALIED SOLIMAN. 2024. "Canada Must Stand Firm on DEI as U.S. Retreats." *Globe and Mail*, 26 December. Online: www.theglobeandmail.com/business/commentary/article-canada-must-stand-firm-on-dei-as-us-corporations-retreat/.

HALWANI, SANA. 2004. "Racial Inequality in Access to Health Care Services." Race Policy Dialogues Paper, Ontario Human Rights Commission. December. Online: www.ohrc.on.ca/en/race-policy-dialogue-papers/racial-inequality-access-health-care-services.

HANNAY, CHRIS, 2019. "Canada Research Chairs to Increase Equity Targets." *Globe and Mail*, 1 August.

HARCOURT, MARK & GEOFFREY WOOD. 2006. "A Critique of Probationary Employment Periods." *New Zealand Journal of Employment Relations* 31:2: 17–29. Online: https://search.informit.org/doi/abs/10.3316/informit.129790998807652.

HARRIOT, MICHAEL. 2022. "War on Wokeness: the Year the Right Rallied around a Made-Up Menace." *The Guardian*, 21 December. Online: www.theguardian.com/us-news/2022/dec/20/anti-woke-race-america-history.

HASHAM, ALYSHAH. 2017. "Crime: A Year after Ghomeshi Verdict, Sexual Violence Experts See 'Significant Advances'." *Toronto Star*, 26 March. Online: www.thestar.com/news/crime/a-year-after-ghomeshi-verdict-sexual-violence-experts-see-significant-advances/article_e9a93a8c-d02e-5f05-a951-c66a6128a005.html.

HATHERLY, DANA. 2024. "Systemic Racism in Yukon's Education System under Review." 30 March. Online: www.yukon-news.com/news/systemic-racism-in-yukons-education-system-under-review-7335752.

HAWKINS, RICHARD A. 2010. "Boycotts, Buycotts and Consumer Activism in a Global Context: An Overview." *Management & Organizational History* 5(2): 123–43. Online: https://doi.org/10.1177/1744935910361644.

HAYES, MOLLY. 2023. "Ottawa Man Faces Simultaneous Hate, Terrorism Charges in First for Canada." *Globe and Mail*, 6 July.

HEALTH CANADA AND STATISTICS CANADA. 2004. "Canadian Community Health Survey, Cycle 2.2, Nutrition Focus – Food and Nutrition Surveilance." https://www.canada.ca/en/health-canada/services/food-nutrition/food-nutrition-surveillance/health-nutrition-surveys/canadian-community-health-survey-cchs/canadian-community-health-survey-cycle-2-2-nutrition-focus-food-nutrition-surveillance-health-canada.html.

HEIDINGER, LOANNA. 2022. "Violent Victimization and Perception of Safety: Experiences of First Nations, Metis and Inuit Women in Canada." *Statistics Canada*, 26 April. Online: www150.statcan.gc.ca/n1/pub/85-002-x/2022001/article/00004-eng.htm.

HEIKKILÄ, MELISSA. 2023. "These New Tools Let You See for Yourself How Biased AI Image Models Are." *MIT Technology Review*, 22 March. Online: www.technologyreview.com/2023/03/22/1070167/these-news-tool-let-you-see-for-yourself-how-biased-ai-image-models-are/.

HENLEY, A. & J. SCHOTT. 1999. Culture, Religion and Patient Care in a Multi-Ethnic Society: A Handbook for Professionals. London: Age Concern England.

HENRY, FRANCES, ENAKSHI DUA, AUDREY KOBAYASHI, CARL JANES, PETER LI, HOWARD RAMOS & MALINDA S. Smith. 2017. "Race, Racialization and Indigeneity in Canadian Universities." *Race Ethnicity and Education* 20(3): 300–14. https://doi.org/10.1080/13613324.2016.1260226.

HERNANDEZ, JON. 2021. "More Than Half of Asian Canadians Experienced Discrimination in Past Year: Survey." *CBC News – British Columbia*, 8 June. Online: www.cbc.ca/news/canada/british-columbia/anti-asian-discrimination-angus-reid-poll-1.6056740.

HIRANANDAN, VANMALA. 2012. "Diversity Management in the Canadian Workplace: Toward an Antiracism Approach." *Open Access*. Online: https://doi.org/10.1155/2012/385806.

HOLDAWAY, SIMON & ANNE-MARIE BARRON. 1997. "On Probation: Responding to Racial Prejudice and Discrimination." In *Resigners: The Experience of Black and Asian Police Officers*, edited by Brenda Yeoh Saw Ai, Fabio Perocco, Rita Segato, Carlos Vargas, Ajmal Hussain, Olga Jubany, and Saskia Sassen, 95–109. London: Palgrave MacMillan. Online: https://doi.org/10.1007/978-1-349-14345-0_7.

HUGHES, DIANE & MARK DODGE. 1997. "African American Women in the Workplace: Relationships between Job Conditions, Racial Bias at Work, and Perceived Job Quality." *American Journal of Community Psychology* 15(5): 581–99.

HUGHES, HENRY. 1854. *Treatise on Sociology: Theoretical and Practical.* New York: Negro Universities Press.

HULCHANSKI, DAVID & MAUREEN FAIR. 2011. The Three Cities within Toronto: Income Polarization among Toronto's Neighbourhoods, *1970–2005*. Toronto: Neighbourhod Change Research Group, Cities Centre, University of Toronto.

HUMAN RESOURCES AND SKILLS DEVELOPMENT CANADA. 2008. "Employment Equity Act: Annual Report." Online: www.hrsdc.gc.ca/eng/labour/equality/employment_equity/tools/annual_reports/2008/docs/2008report.pdf.

HUMAN RIGHTS WATCH. 2023. "Russia: Supreme Court Bans 'LGBT Movement' as 'Extremist'." 30 November. Online: www.hrw.org/news/2024/02/13/hungary-media-curbs-harm-rule-law.

HUMAN RIGHTS WATCH. 2024. "Hungary: Media Curbs Harms Rule of Law." 13 February. Online: www.hrw.org/news/2024/02/13/hungary-media-curbs-harm-rule-law.

HUMAN RIGHTS WATCH. 2025. "Philippines' 'War on Drugs'." Online: www.hrw.org/tag/philippines-war-drugs.

HUNE-BROWN, NICHOLAS. 2025. "What Do Changes to Immigration Mean in a City of Immigrants?." *The Local*, 14 January. Online: https://thelocal.to/immigration-toronto-editors-letter/.

IGNASKI, PAUL. 2008. "Hate Crime" and the City. Bristol, UK: Policy Press. Online: https://books.google.ca/books?hl=en&lr=&id=4Cn-BfqsKNbcC&oi=fnd&pg=PR7&dq=Hate+crime&ots=keL0TdEX-IC&sig=obSob5u_ER05uROV2BZk-fvvtzE#v=onepage&q=Hate%20crime&f=false.

INCLAN, ISABEL. 2022. "Canadian Journalism and Its Struggle with Race, Racism, and Diversity." *New Canadian Media*, 14 April. Online: https://newcanadianmedia.ca/canadian-journalism-and-its-struggle-with-race-racism-diversity/?doing_wp_cron=1691078259.8307969570159912109375.

INFORM ALBERTA. N.d. "Employment Equity". Accessed 31 August 2024. Online: https://informalberta.ca/public/service/serviceProfileStyled.do?serviceQueryId=1085257.

INNOVATION, SCIENCE AND ECONOMIC DEVELOPMENT CANADA. 2021. "Diversity of Boards of Directors and Senior Management of Federal Distributing Corporations: 2021 Annual Report." Online: https://ised-isde.

canada.ca/site/corporations-canada/sites/default/files/attachments/2022/diversity-report-2021-e.pdf.

INNOVATION, SCIENCE AND ECONOMIC DEVELOPMENT CANADA. 2024. "Diversity of Boards of Directors and Senior Management of Federal Distributing Corporations –2023 Annual Report." 10 May. Online: https://ised-isde.canada.ca/site/corporations-canada/en/data-services/diversity-boards-directors-and-senior-management-federal-distributing-corporations-2023-annual.

INSTITUTIONAL SHAREHOLDERS SERVICE. 2024. "EU Female Directors Quotas Are Coming: Is Europe Ready?." *ISS Insights*. Online: https://insights.issgovernance.com/posts/eu-female-director-quotas-are-coming-is-europe-ready/.

IRIZARRY, AMBER H. 2012. "Understanding Diversity: Top Executives' Perceptions of Racial and Ethnic Diversity in Public Relations." MA thesis, Georgia State University, Atlanta. Online: http://scholarworks.gsu.edu/cgi/viewcontent.cgi?article=1092&context=communication_theses.

JACKSON, A. 2001. Poverty and Racism. Ottawa: Canadian Council on Social Development.

JOHNSON, ERICA. 2022. "Business Go Public - RBC Agent Pushes Unnecessary Chequing Account on Customer, Comments on His Accent." *CBC News*, 28 June. Online: www.cbc.ca/news/business/banks-racial-discrimination-report-1.6473715.

JOHNSON, LAUREN. 2024. "Backlash Is Real, Warns Scotiabank's VP of Global Inclusion." *Human Resources Director*, 3 December. Online: www.hcamag.com/ca/specialization/diversity-inclusion/dei-backlash-is-real-warns-scotiabanks-vp-of-global-inclusion/516459.

JONES, SCARLETT. 2015. "Where Are We Going? Public Transit and Racial Equity in Toronto." *PP+G Review*, 8 January. Online: https://ppgreview.ca/2015/01/08/where-are-we-going-public-transit-and-racial-equity-in-toronto/.

JOSEPH, BOB. 2013. "8 Basic Barriers to Aboriginal Employment." Online: www.ictinc.ca/8-basic-barriers-to-aboriginal-employment.

JOSEPH, DAMIEN, WAI FONG BOH, SOON ANG & SANDRA A. SLAUGHTER. 2012. "The Career Paths Less (or More) Travelled: A Sequence Analysis of IT Career Histories, Mobility Patterns, and Career Success." *MIS Quarterly* 36(2): 427–52. Online: https://doi.org/10.2307/41703462.

KABELKA, LAURA & ANNIKA SOST. 2025. "Anti-Woke: With Trump Returning, US Firms Back Off on DEI." *In Focus: Deutsche Welle*, 15 January. Online: https://corporate.dw.com/en/about-dw/s-30688.

KANDIUK, MARY. 2014. "Promoting Racial and Ethnic Diversity among Canadian Academic Librarians." *College and Research Librarians* 75(4): 492–556. https://doi.org/10.5860/crl.75.4.492.

KANG, SONIA. 2017. "Discrimination in Hiring." *Insights Hub (Rotman).* Online: www-2.rotman.utoronto.ca/insightshub/talent-management-inclusion/discrimination-in-hiring.

KAPLAN, SARAH & CARMINA RAVANERA. 2022. "An Equity Lens on Artificial Intelligence." *Social Sciences and Humanities Research Council*, 7 April. Online: www.sshrc-crsh.gc.ca/society-societe/community-communite/ifca-iac/evidence_briefs-donnees_probantes/skills_work_digital_economy-competences_travail_economie_numerique/kaplan_ravanera-eng.aspx.

KAPOOR, GARIMA TALWAR, MOHY TABBARA, SHERRI HANLEY & SASHA MCNICOLL. 2022. How to Reduce the Depth of Single Adult Poverty in Canada. Toronto: Maytree and Community Food Centres Canada.

KAPOOR, ILAN. 2025. "Trump's Tariff and Land Grab Threats Signal U.S. Expansionist Ambitions." *The Conversation*, 14 February. Online: https://theconversation.com/trumps-tariff-and-land-grab-threats-signal-u-s-expansionist-ambitions-249924.

KARAKOWSKY, L. & I. KOTLYAR. 2012. "Do 'High Potential' Leadership Programs Really Work?" *Globe and Mail*, 2 January. Online: www.theglobeandmail.com/report-on-business/careers/management/do-high-potential-leadership-programs-really-work/article4248330/.

KAUFMANN, ERIC. 2023. "The Politics of Culture Wars in Contemporary Canada?" *Macdonald Laurier Institute*, 15 February. Online: https://macdonaldlaurier.ca/politics-of-culture-wars-canada/.

KAUFMANN, ERIC. 2024. "Canadians Aren't Actually 'Woke'." *The Hub*, 15 February. Online: https://thehub.ca/2024/02/15/eric-kaufmann-canadians-are-not-actually-woke/.

KEMEI, JANET, MIA TULLI, ADEDOYIN OLANLESI-ALIU, MODUPE TUNDE-BYASS & BUKOLA SALAMI. 2023. "Impact of the COVID-19 Pandemic on Black Communities in Canada." *International Journal of Environmental Researchnd Public Health* 20(2): n.p. https://doi.org/10.3390/ijerph20021580.

KESHAVARZ, PARDIS, GINNY LANE, PUNAM PAHWA, JESSICA LIEFFERS, MOITABA SHAFIEE, KELLY FINKAS, MARISA DESMARAIS & HASSAN VATANPARSAST. 2023. "Dietary Patterns of Off-Reserve Indigenous Peoples in Canada and their Association with Chronic Conditions." *Nutrients* 15(6): n.p. Online: https://doi.org/10.3390/nu15061485.

KESTENBAUM, RICHARD. 2022. "On Sale for the Holidays: Racism in Retail Stores." *Forbes*, 15 November. Online: www.forbes.com/sites/richardkestenbaum/2022/11/15/on-sale-for-the-holidays-racism-in-retail-stores/?sh=6d4a2a803904.

KHAYAMBASHI, SHILA. 2021. "Implicit Bias within Canadian Media Often Means Porviding Excuses for White Accused." *The Conversation*, 6 July. Online: https://theconversation.com/implicit-bias-within-canadian-media-often-means-providing-excuses-for-white-accused-162887.

KHURANA, RYAN. 2024. "Canada Has a Nobel Prize for AI. But Our Red Tape Will Strangle Us." *Globe and Mail*, 26 December.

KIRKWOOD, ISABELLE. 2019. "'Emotional Tax' for People of Colour Is Contributing to Canada's Retention Problem." *Betakit*, 26 July. Online: https://betakit.com/emotional-tax-for-people-of-colour-is-contributing-to-canadas-retention-problem/.

KLEINSORGE, R. 2010. "Expanding the Role of Succession Planning." *T+D (American Society for Training and Development)* (April): 66–69.

KOCHMAN, T. 1981. *Black and White Styles in Conflict*. Chicago: University of Chicago Press.

KORNIK, SLAV & PHIL HEIDENREICH. 2018. "B.C. Woman Fired from Car Dealership after Racist Tirade Caught on Camera at Lethbridge Restaurant." *Global News*, 9 May. Online: https://globalnews.ca/news/4197330/lethbridge-restaurant-racist-facebook-video/.

KOST, DANIELLE. 2025. "Meta Faces the Limits of Policing Misinformation." *Working Knowledge, Harvard Business School*, 13 January. Online: www.library.hbs.edu/working-knowledge/meta-faces-the-limits-of-policing-misinformation.

KPMG. 2024. "Employers Are Making Headway in Eradicating Anti-Black Racism." 5 February. Online: https://kpmg.com/ca/en/home/media/press-releases/2024/02/canadian-employers-make-progress-on-anti-black-racism.html.

KUKREJA, REENA. 2024. "Anti-Immigrant Politics Is Fueling Hate toward South Asian People in Canada." *Queen's University Arts and Science News*, 7 November. Online: www.queensu.ca/artsci/news/anti-immigrant-politics-is-fueling-hate-toward-south-asian-people-in-canada.

KULIK CAROL & HUGH BAINBRIDGE. 2006. "Psychological Perspectives on Workplace Diversity." In *Handbook of Workplace Diversity*, edited by Alison Konrad, Pushkala Prasad & Judith Pringle, 25–52. London: Sage Publications.

KUMAR, RAKSHA. 2024. "Inside Modi's Crackdown on the Foreign Press in India." *Reuters Institute for the Study of Journalism*, 13 November. Online: https://reutersinstitute.politics.ox.ac.uk/news/inside-modis-crackdown-foreign-press-india.

LACE, CATHY. 1995. "Impact on Collective Agreements and Collective Bargaining." In *Union/Management Issues in Employment Equity: Fulfilling Joint Responsibilities and Developing Effective Coordinating Committees*, edited by Canadian Institute, 1–38, 6 June.

LAFLEY, A.G. 2011. "The Art and Science of Finding the Right CEO." *Harvard Business Review*, October.

LANDLER, MARK. 2021. "Britain's New Entry in Conversative Media Is Off to a Splashy, but Shaky, Start." *New York Times*, 18 June. Online: www.nytimes.com/2021/06/18/world/europe/britain-media-gbnews-neil.html.

LANDRY, MARIE-CLAUDE. 2020. *The Time to Address Indigenous Racism Is Long Past Due*. Ottawa: Canadian Human Rights Commission. Online: www.chrc-ccdp.gc.ca/en/resources/the-time-address-anti-indigenous-racism-long-past-due.

LANDRY, MARIE-CLAUDE. 2021. *Statement – It's Time to Step Up to End Racism*. Ottawa: Canadian Human Rights Commission. Online: www.chrc-ccdp.gc.ca/en/resources/statement-its-time-step-end-racism-0.

LARKIN, ZOE. 2024. "AI Bias – What Is It and How to Avoid It?." *Levity*, 30 September. Online: https://levity.ai/blog/ai-bias-how-to-avoid#:~:-text=For%20example%2C%20a%20facial%20recognition,equal%20opportunity%20and%20perpetuates%20oppression.

LAWSON, ANDREA. 2024. "Could a Loblaw Boycott Really Work? Probably Not, Experts Say." *Brighter World, McMaster University*, 1 May. Online: https://brighterworld.mcmaster.ca/articles/could-a-loblaw-boycott-really-work-bradley-ruffle-francois-neville/.

LEBLANC, DANIEL. 2015. "'Cultural Shift"' Required to Address Sexual Harassment in Canadian Forces." *Globe and* Mail, 30 April. Online: www.theglobeandmail.com/news/politics/report-says-canadian-armed-forces-marred-by-sexualized-culture/.

LEBLANC, M. & J. COULTHARD. 2015. "The Canadian Forces Workplace Harassment Survey: Findings from Designated Group Members. Director General Military Personnel Research and Analysis Scientific Letter, DRDC-RDDC-2015-L179." June. Online: www150.statcan.gc.ca/n1/pub/85-603-x/85-603-x2019002-eng.htm.

LEDERMAN, MARSHA. 2023. "B.C.'s Report on Pandemic Hatred is Titled from Hate to Hope. It is Hard to See the Hope." *Globe and Mail*, 8 March. Online: www.theglobeandmail.com/opinion/article-bcs-report-on-hate-during-the-pandemic-is-called-from-hate-to-hope-its/.

LEIGHTON, DAVID S.R. 1993. "How Can Women Access Boards?" *Women in Management* 4 (2): 1–7.

LEIGHTON, DAVID S.R. 2010. "Making Boards Work." In Women on Corporate Boards of Director: International Challenges and Opportunities, edited by Ronald J. Burke and Mary C. Mattis, 253–61. Dordrecht: Kluwer Academic.

LEMAN-LANGLOIS, STEPHANE, AURELIE CAMPANA & SAMUEL TANNER. 2024. "How the Far Right Is Evolving and Growing in Canada." *The*

Conversation, 14 November. Online: https://theconversation.com/how-the-far-right-is-evolving-and-growing-in-canada-242004.

LENARDUZZI, JAKE. 2023. "Business Confidence Continues to Fall." Canadian Economics, 19 October. Online: www.conferenceboard.ca/insights/business-confidence-continues-to-fall/?utm_source=cboc_blast&utm_medium=email&utm_campaign=marketo_economics&utm_content=eqt_oe_oct1923&mkt_tok=MDk0LUVHRi02MzkAAAGO7KlU6W9AF-0cr8BqmUa-IUZso5MeU8dxnoxCh01GGEy6h3YErvhdD9nAnSeWp-DIC1wyGKFMPzTh0ELjKj3WWHKUq3N0Yg_sAwVzLmdaP46C2D.

LEVY, GENELLE. 2021. "How Activists Fought Racist Restaurateurs in Southwestern Ontario." *TVO Today*. Online: www.tvo.org/article/how-activists-fought-racist-restaurateurs-in-southwestern-ontario.

LEVY, RHONDA B. & MONTY VERLINT. 2025. "Regulation of AI in the Canadian Workplace: Technological Advances from AI bring Legal Risks for Employers." *Canadian Human Rights Reporter*, 6 January. Online: www.hrreporter.com/focus-areas/employment-law/regulation-of-ai-in-the-canadian-workplace/390503#:~:text=Prohibited%20grounds%20of%20discrimination%20include,performance%20management%2C%20and%20pay%20equity.

LI, ANITA. 2019. "Canadian Media Lacks Nuance, Depth n Racial Issues." *Policy Options*, 10 September. Online: https://policyoptions.irpp.org/fr/magazines/september-2019/canadian-media-lacks-nuance-depth-on-racial-issues/.

LI, BERNARD, SHIVANI SOODS & CHRIS JOHNSTON. 2022. "Impact of Covid-19 on Small Businesses in Canada, Four Quarter of 2021." *Statistics Canada*, 6 January. Online: www150.statcan.gc.ca/n1/pub/45-28-0001/2021001/article/00043-eng.htm.

LI, PETER. 2008. "The Market Value and Social Value of Race." In Daily Struggles: The Deepening Racialization and Feminization of Poverty in Canada, edited by Maria Wallis and Siu-ming Kwok, 21–33. Toronto: Canadian Scholar Press.

LINOVSKI, ORLY, HEATHER DORRIES & SHERYL-ANN SIMPSON. 2021. "Public Transit and Equity-Deserving Groups: Understanding Lived Experiences." December. Online: https://tspace.library.utoronto.ca/bitstream/1807/110044/1/Public%20Transit%20and%20Equity_Final%20Report.pdf.

LIPTAK, ADAM. 2023. "U.S. Supreme Court Rejects Affirmative Action at Universities." *Globe and Mail*, 30 June. Online: www.theglobeandmail.com/world/article-us-supreme-court-strikes-down-university-race-conscious-admissions/.

LOBLAW COMPANIES LIMITED. N.d. "Diversity, Equity and Inclusion." Accessed 5 October 2024. Online: www.loblaw.ca/en/dei/.

LYON, KATHERINE & NEIL GUPPY. 2019. "Canada: A Review of Research on the Race, ethnicity and Inequality in Education from 1980 to 2017." In The Palgrave Handbook of Race and Ethnic Inequalities in Education, edited by Peter A.J. Stevens and Gary Dworkin, 253–300. London: Palgrave Macmillan. Online: https://doi.org/10.1007/978-3-319-94724-2_7.

MACNAB, AIDAN. 2022. "These Two Events Highlight Importance of Having Women in Leadership Positions, Said Nadia Effendi." *Canadian Lawyer*, 16 August. Online: www.canadianlawyermag.com/resources/practice-management/these-two-events-highlight-importance-of-having-women-in-leadership-positions-says-nadia-effendi/369062.

MACNEIL, IAIN & IRENE-MARIÉ ESSER. 2022. "The Emergence of 'Comply or Explain' as a Global Model for Corporate Governance Codes." *European Business Law Review* 33(1): 1–56.

MAHTANI, MINELLE. 2001. "Representing Minorities: Canadian Media and Minority Identities." *Canadian Ethnic Studies* 33(3): 99–133.

MAKE IT OUR BUSINESS. 2021. "Black Women in the Workplace and Tall Poppy Syndrome." *Western Centre for Research and Education on Violence Against Women and Children*, 3 March. Online: www.makeitourbusiness.ca/blog/2021/black_women_in_the_workforce_and_tall_poppy_syndrome.html.

MAIRA, SUNAINA. 2018. Boycott! The Academy and Justice for Palestine. Oakland, CA: University of California Press.

MALISCHEWSKI, CHARLOTTE-ANNE. 2023. *Eliminating Racism Is Our Collective Responsibility*. Ottawa: Canadian Human Rights Commission. Online: www.chrc-ccdp.gc.ca/resources/newsroom/eliminating-racism-our-collective-responsibility.

MARCOS, CORAL MURPHY. 2020. "'Boycott for Black Lives': People Plan to Stop Spending in Companies that Don't Support BLM." *USA Today*, 18 June. Online: www.usatoday.com/story/money/2020/06/18/boycotts-people-plan-stop-spending-stores-dont-support-blm/3208170001/#:~:text=Boycotts:%20People%20plan%20to%20stop,that%20don't%20support%20BLM.

MARTINIELLO, BILLIE & PIETER-PAUL VERHAEGHE. 2023. "Different Names, Different Discrimination? How Perception of Names can Explain Rental Discrimination." *Frontiers in Sociology* 8: n.p.

MATTIS, MARY C. 2010. "Women Corporate Directors in the United States." In Women on Corporate Boards and Directors: International Challenges and Opportunities, edited by Ronald J. Burke & Mary C. Mattis, 43–56. Dordreht: Kluwer Academic.

MAYER, STEVE & ANDREW WILLIS. 2022. Unprecedented: Canada's Top CDEOs on Leadership during Covid-19. Vancouver: Signal – Penguin Random House.

MAYOVICH, MINAKO KUROKAWA. 1972. "Stereotypes and Racial Images: White, Black, and Yellow." *International Journal of Social Psychiatry* 18(4): 239–53. Online: http://doi.org/10.1177/002076407201800402.

MCCOY, KIMEKO. 2024. "'We Can't Cry About the Milk That's Spilled': As DE&I Fallout Continues, Multicultural Agencies Grapple with Changes." *Worklife Daily Briefing*, 6 November. Online: www.worklife.news/dei/we-cant-cry-about-the-milk-thats-spilled-as-dei-fallout-continues-multicultural-agencies-grapple-with-changes/.

MCFARLAND, J. 2019. "TD Study Calls for Regulators to Stay the Course on Gender Disclosure Policies." *Globe and Mail*, 27 March.

MCGOWAN, ROSEMARY A. & EDDY S. NG. 2016. "Employment Equity in Canada: Making Sense of Employee Discourses of Misunderstanding, Resistance and Support." *Canadian Public Administration* 19(2): 310–29. Online: https://doi.org/10.1111/capa.12171.

MCKINNON, BRITT, SEUNGMI YANG, MICHAEL S. KRAMER, TRACEY BUSHNIK, AMANDA J. SHEPPARD & JAY S. KAUFMAN. 2016. "Comparison of Black-White Disparities in Preterm Birth between Canada and the United States." *Canadian Medical Association Journal* 188(1): E19–E26. Online: https://doi.org/10.1503/cmaj.150464.

MCLAUGHLIN, KATY. 2022. "COVID-19: Briefing Note #100, April 13, 2022." Executive Briefing: COVID-19: Implications for Business. *McKinsey & Company*, 13 April. Online: www.mckinsey.com/capabilities/risk-and-resilience/our-insights/covid-19-implications-for-business.

MCNELLY, ALLISON & STEFANIE BATCHO-LINO. 2016. "Gender Disparity: Quotas May Be Only Way." *Globe and Mail*, 17 November. Online: www.theglobeandmail.com/report-on-business/quotas-may-be-only-way-to-counter-lack-of-women-on-canadian-boards/article32878679/.

MEDIA SMARTS. N.d.a. "Racial and Cultural Diversity in Entertainment Media." Accessed 31 August 2023. Online: https://mediasmarts.ca/digital-media-literacy/media-issues/diversity-media/visible-minorities/racial-cultural-diversity-entertainment-media.

MEDIA SMARTS. N.d.b. "Race and Cultural Diversity in News Media." Accessed 3 August 2023. Online: https://mediasmarts.ca/digital-media-literacy/media-issues/diversity-media/racial-cultural-diversit y-news-media.

MENDELSON, MICHAEL. 2006. Aboriginal Peoples and Postsecondary Education in Canada. Ottawa: Caledon Institute of Social Policy.

MENSIK, HAILEY. 2024a. "How Manager Complicity is Driving Toxic Workplaces." *Worklife*, 1 May. Online: www.worklife.news/leadership/toxic-workplaces-manager-complicity-leaders/?utm_campaign=worklifedis&utm_source=worklifedaily&utm_medium=email&utm_content=50124&utm_medium=email&utm_campaign=Worklife%20Briefing%205012024&utm_content=Worklife%20Briefing%205012024+CID_689844dc7d6c34f6ebbc525ed454da3d&utm_source=wldis&utm_term=How%20manager%20complicity%20is%20driving%20toxic%20workplaces.

MENSIK, HAILEY. 2024b. "Why Anti-DEI Lawsuits Are Piling Up This Year." *WorkLife*, 20 August. Online: www.worklife.news/dei/why-anti-dei-lawsuits-are-piling-up-this-year.

MENSIK, HAILEY. 2024c. "WTF Are Microcultures? (and Why They Are Important in Workplaces Today)." *Worklife*, 14 February. Online: www.worklife.news/culture/wtf-are-microcultures-workplace-hybrid-work-rto/?utm_campaign=worklifedis&utm_source=worklifedaily&utm_medium=email&utm_content=50624&utm_medium=email&utm_campaign=Worklife%20Briefing%205062024&utm_content=Worklife%20Briefing%205062024+CID_4a9a148e2f961acde1dac8df-0fc46a2e&utm_source=wldis&utm_term=ICYMI%20WTF%20are%20microcultures%20and%20why%20they%20are%20important%20in%20workplaces%20today.

MENSIK, HAILEY. 2025. "Can AI Make Performance Reviews Less Biased?" *WorkLife*, 20 January. Online: www.worklife.news/technology/can-ai-make-performance-reviews-less-biased/.

MERCER, GREG. 2020. "Nova Scotia Still Faces a Disturbing Racism Problem." *Globe and Mail*, 25 January. Online: www.theglobeandmail.com/canada/article-nova-scotia-still-faces-a-disturbing-problem-with-racism/.

METZ, CADE & TRIPP MICKLE. 2024. "Experts Are Divided on Whether the Tech Industry Is Already on the Cusp of an AI Slowdown." *Globe and Mail*, 27 December.

MIAO, QUN. 2022. "Racial Variations of Adverse Perinatal Outcomes: A Population-Based Retrospective Cohort Study in Ontario, Canada." *PLoS One* 17(6): e0269158.

MICHENER INSTITUTE OF EDUCATION AT UNIVERSITY HEALTH NETWORK. 2010. "Michener Anti-Violence Policy." 14 January. Online: https://michener.ca/discover-michener/policies/workplace-anti-violence-policy/.

MILLS, D. QUINN. 2005. "Asian and American Leadership Styles: How Are They Unique?" *HBS Working Knowledge*, 27 June. Online: www.library.hbs.edu/working-knowledge/asian-and-american-leadership-styles-how-are-they-unique.

MILSTEAD, DAVID. 2019. "Board Appointments of Women Hit Five-Year Low." *Globe and Mail*, 27 February. Online: www.theglobeandmail.com/business/article-board-appointments-of-women-drop-to-lowest-number-in-five-years/.

MINBAEVA, DANA. 2021. "Disrupted HR?" *Human Resources Management Review* 31(4): n.p. Online: https://doi.org/10.1016/j.hrmr.2020.100818.

MINORS, JHOANNA GONZALES, UDUAK MACKENZIE, ASHELY LANDER & ABIGAIL ISAAC, SEASONOVA GROUP INC. N.d. *Addressing Barriers to Employment for Immigrant and Racialized Women and Youth: What We Heard Report*. Ottawa: Women and Gender Equality Canada.

MO, GUANGUING, WENDY CUKIER, AKALYA ATPUTHARAJAH, MIKE ITANO BOASE & HENRIQUE HON. 2020. "Differential Impacts during COVID-19 in Canada: A Look at Diverse Individuals and Their Businesses." *Can Public Policy* 46(S3): 261–71.

MOORE, RYAN. 2019. "Hundreds Blocked Small Far-Right Crowd from Spreading Hateful Message in Toronto." *Canada's National Observer*, 24 March. Online: www.nationalobserver.com/2019/03/24/news/hundreds-blocked-small-far-right-crowd-spreading-hateful-message-toronto.

MORGAN, ANTHONY. 2021. "Anti-Black Racism in Canada's Food Sector." *The Monitor*, 1 September. Online: https://monitormag.ca/articles/anti-black-racism-in-canadas-food-sector/.

MORGAN, D.M. 2019. "Being a Shark: Reflections on Blackness in Canadian Wilderness." In *Black Writers Matter*, edited by W. French, n.p. Regina: University of Regina Press.

MURPHY, JESSICA. 2015."Trudeau Gives Canada First Cabinet with Equal Number of Men and Women." *The Guardian*, 4 November. Online: www.theguardian.com/world/2015/nov/04/canada-cabinet-gender-diversity-justin-trudeau.

NANGWAYA, AJAMU. 2011. "Race, Resistance and Co-operation in the Canadian Labour Market: Effecting an Equity Like Race Matters." PhD diss., Department of Adult Education and Counselling Psychology, Ontario Institute for Studies in Education, University of Toronto. Online: https://central.bac-lac.gc.ca/.item?id=NR78313&op=pdf&app=Library&is_thesis=1&oclc_number=1019464842.

NARINE, SHAUN. 2025. "While the U.S. Threatens Tariffs and Builds Walls Around Its Economy, China Opens Up." *The Conversation*, 23 February. Online: https://theconversation.com/while-the-u-s-threatens-tariffs-and-builds-walls-around-its-economy-china-opens-up-245012.

NATIONAL COUNCIL OF CANADIAN MUSLIMS. 2021. "NCCM Recommendations - National Summit on Islamophobia." 19 July. Online: www.nccm.ca/wp-content/uploads/2021/06/Policy-Recommendations_NCCM.pdf.

NATIONAL DEFENCE. 2023. "Harassment and Violence in the Workplace – Negative Behaviours Matrix." 16 May. Online: www.canada.ca/en/department-national-defence/services/benefits-military/conflict-misconduct/new-workplace-harassment-and-violence-prevention-regulations-for-defence-team-public-servants-bill-c65/negative-behaviours-continuum.html.

NATIONAL INQUIRY INTO MISSING AND MURDERED INDIGENOUS WOMEN AND GIRLS. N.d. "Timeline of Key Milestones." Accessed 10 September 2023. Online: www.mmiwg-ffada.ca/timeline/.

NATIONAL INQUIRY INTO MISSING AND MURDERED INDIGENOUS WOMEN AND GIRLS. 2019a. "Reclaiming Power and Place: The Final Report on the National Inquiry Into Missing and Murdered Indigenous Women and Girls." Online: www.mmiwg-ffada.ca/final-report/.

NATIONAL INQUIRY INTO MISSING AND MURDERED INDIGENOUS WOMEN AND GIRLS. 2019b. "Supplementary Report: A Legal Analysis of Genocide." Online: www.mmiwg-ffada.ca/wp-content/uploads/2019/06/Supplementary-Report_Genocide.pdf.

NATIVE WOMEN'S ASSOCIATION OF CANADA. N.d. "Anti-Indigenous Systemic Racism in Canadian Health Care Systems: Policy Brief." Accessed 11 November 2023. Online: https://nwac.ca/assets-knowledge-centre/FNIHB_Systemic_Racism_in_Healthcare.pdf.

NATIVE WOMEN'S ASSOCIATION OF CANADA. 2023. "United Nations Declaration on the Rights of Indigenous Peoples (UNDRIP) Act and Implementation." Online: https://nwac.ca/policy/united-nations-declaration-on-the-rights-of-indigenous-peoples-undrip-act-implementation.

NAWAZ, NISHAD, HEMALATHA ARUNACHALAM, BARANI KUMARIPATHI & VIJAYAKUMAR GAJENDERAN. 2024. "The Adoption of Artificial Intelligence in Human Resources Management Practices." *International Journal of Information Management Data Insights* 4(1): n.p. Online: www.sciencedirect.com/science/article/pii/S266709682300054X?via%3Dihub.

NEUMAN, KEITH. 2024. "Canadian Public Opinion About Immigration and Refugees – Fall 2024." *Environics Institute, Focus Canada*, 17 October. Online: www.environicsinstitute.org/projects/project-details/canadian-public-opinion-about-immigration-and-refugees---fall-2024.

NEW BRUNSWICK HUMAN RIGHTS COMMISSION. 2020. "Special Programs and the Meaning of Equality and Discrimination." October. Online: https://vivreaunb.ca/content/dam/gnb/Departments/hrc-cdp/PDF/SpecialPrograms-Guidelines.pdf.

NG, EDDIE S., RANA HAQ & DIANE-GABRIELLE TREMBLAY. 2015. "A Review of Two Decades of Employment Equity in Canada: Progress and Propositions." In *International Handbook on Diversity Management at Work: Country Perspectives on Diversity and Equal Treatment*, edited by Alain Klarsfeld, Lize A.E. Booysen, Eddy Ng, Ian Roper, Ahu Tatli, 46–67.

Cheltenham, UK: Edward Elgar. Online: www.researchgate.net/publication/295912390_A_review_of_two_decades_of_employment_equity_in_Canada_Progress_and_propositions.

NIMON-PETERS, AMANDA. 2022. "The Science of Who Speak in Team Meetings." *Psychology Today*, 28 July. Online: www.psychologytoday.com/ca/blog/the-leadership-brief/202207/the-science-of-who-speaks-in-team-meetings.

NORTHWEST TERRITORIES HUMAN RIGHTS COMMISSION. 2018. "Human Rights and Employment." October. Online: https://nwthumanrights.ca/wp-content/uploads/2015/08/Employment-Guide-WEB.pdf.

NORTHWEST TERRITORIES RECREATION AND PARKS. 2020. "Racism in Recreation and Parks." 15 June. Online: www.nwtrpa.org/post/racism-in-recreation-and-parks.

NUNAVUT TUNNGAVIK. N.d. "Nunavut Agreement Article 23." Accessed 31 August 2024. Online: https://nlca.tunngavik.com/?page_id=2301.

O'BRIEN, MATT & SARAH PARVINI. 2025. "Trump Signs Executive Order on Developing Artificial Intelligence 'Free from Ideological Bias'." *Globe and Mail*, 24 January. Online: www.theglobeandmail.com/world/article-trump-signs-executive-order-on-developing-artificial-intelligence-free/.

ODUM, HOWARD W. 1943. *Race and Rumors of Race*. Chapel Hill: University of North Carolina Press.

O'KANE, JOSH. 2017. "Canadian Executives say Sexual Harassment isn't an Issue at their Companies Report." *Globe and Mail*, 18 December. Online: www.theglobeandmail.com/report-on-business/canadian-executives-say-sexual-harassment-isn't-an-issue-at-their-company-report/article37359943.

OLAERTS, MIEKE & RIENTS ABMA. 2012. "Is the Comply or Explain Principle a Suitable Mechanism for Corporate Governance throughout the EU?: The Dutch Experience." *European Company Law* 9(6): 286–99.

OLANIYAN, OLAMIDE. 2024. "Stepping into the Big, Weird 'Anti-Woke' Tent." *The Tyee*, 24 June. Online: https://thetyee.ca/News/2024/06/24/Stepping-Inside-Anti-Woke-Tent/.

OLSON, CAMILLE A. & SEYFARTH SHAW. 2025a. "Navigating President Trump's Executive Actions on DEI." *Society of Human Resources Management*, 29 January.

OLSON, CAMILLE A. & SEYFARTH SHAW. 2025b. "Navigating the Two Executive Orders: Merit-Based Practices and Belonging in the Evolving Policy Landscape. *Society of Human Resources Management*, 29 January. Online: www.shrm.org/events-education/education/webinars/navigating-two-dei-executive-orders-merit-based-practices.

ONTARIO FEDERATION OF LABOUR. 2024. "Human Rights Tribunal Confirms Concurrent Jurisdiction in Ontario." Online: https://ofl.ca/hrto-confirms-concurrent-jurisdiction/.

ONTARIO HUMAN RIGHTS COMMISSION. N.d.a. "Policy on Removing the 'Canadian Experience' Barrier." Online: www3.ohrc.on.ca/en/policy-removing-canadian-experienc-barrier.

ONTARIO HUMAN RIGHTS COMMISSION. N.d.b. "Racial Discrimination." Online: www3.ohrc.on.ca/en/racial-discrimination-brochure.

ONTARIO HUMAN RIGHTS COMMISSION. 2017. "Under Suspicion: Research and Consultation Report on Racial Profiling in Ontario." Online: https://www3.ohrc.on.ca/sites/default/files/Under%20suspicion_research%20and%20consultation%20report%20on%20racial%20profiling%20in%20Ontario_2017.pdf.

ONTARIO HUMAN RIGHTS COMMISSION. 2018. "Interrupted Childhoods: Over-Representation of Indigenous and Black Children in Ontario Child Welfare." Online: www.ohrc.on.ca/en/interrupted-childhoods.

ONTARIO HUMAN RIGHTS COMMISSION. 2025. "Fact Sheet: Recognizing Anti-Indigenous Discrimination and Harassment in Retail Settings." Online: www3.ohrc.on.ca/en/fact-sheet-recognizing-anti-indigenous-discrimination-and-harassment-retail-settings.

ONWUACHI-WILLIG. 2018. "What About #Us Too?: The Invisibility of Race in the #MeToo Movement." *Yale Law Journal* 128: 2018–19. Online: www.yalelawjournal.org/forum/what-about-ustoo.

PARK, JUNGWEE. 2021. "Mortality among First Nations People, 2006 to 2016." *Statistics Canada*, 20 October. Online: www150.statcan.gc.ca/n1/pub/82-003-x/2021010/article/00001-eng.htm.

PARK, LAUREN & LIN GRENSING-POPHAL. 2023. "Why DEI Backlash Exists and What to Do about It." *SAP: Best Practice Guide*, 30 August. Online: www.sap.com/resources/why-dei-backlash-exists#:~:text=In%20a%20similar%20vein%2C%20another,to%20feel%20disadvantaged%20or%20marginalized.

PARK, ROBERT EZRA. 1950. Race and Culture. Glencoe, MN: Free Press.

PARKER, CHRISTOPHER SEBASTIAN & CHRISTOPHER C. TOWLET. 2019. "Race and Authoritarianism in American Politics." *Annual Review of Political Science* 22: 503–19. https://doi.org/10.1146/annurev-polisci-050317-064519.

PARRIS, AMANDA. 2019. "There's Never Been a Show About a Black Female Canadian Lawyer – until Now." *CBC News*, 5 March. Online: www.cbc.ca/arts/there-s-never-been-a-show-about-a-black-female-canadian-lawyer-until-now-1.5043520.

PATEL, RAISA. 2023. "Online Safety Bill Limited." *Toronto Star*, 5 July.

PAULSON, KEN. 2024. “The Woke Movement and Backlash.” *Free Speech Centre, Middle Tennessee State University*, 3 July. Online: https://firstamendment.mtsu.edu/article/the-woke-movement-and-backlash/.

PAYNE-PIKUS, MONIQUE R., JOHN HAGAN & ROBERT L. NELSON. 2010. “Experiencing Discrimination: Race and Retention in America’s Largest Law Firms.” *Law & Society Review* 44(3–4): 553–84.

PENDAKUR, K. & R. PENDAKUR. 2002. “Colour My World: Have Earnings Gaps for Canadian-Born Ethnic Minorities Changed over Time?” *Canadian Public Policy* 28(4): 489–511. Online: https://doi.org/10.2307/3552281.

PERREAULT, SAMUEL. 2004. “Visible Minority and Victimization.” *Canadian Centre for Justices Statistics, Statistics Canada*. Online: www.publicsafety.gc.ca/lbrr/archives/cnmcs-plcng/cn000033859531-eng.pdf.

PERREAULT, SAMUEL. 2015. “Criminal Victimization in Canada, 2014. Juristat.” *Statistics Canada*, 30 November. Online: www150.statcan.gc.ca/n1/pub/85-002-x/2015001/article/14241-eng.htm#a2.

PERREAULT, SAMUEL. 2022. “Victimization of First Nations People, Metis and Inuit in Canada.” *Statistics Canada*, 19 July. Online: www150.statcan.gc.ca/n1/pub/85-002-x/2022001/article/00012-eng.htm.

PERREAUX, LES. 2019. “Report Finds Systemic Discrimination in Montreal Police Force’s Practices.” *Globe and Mail*, 8 October.

PETTIGREW, A. 1992. “On Studying Managerial Elites.” *Strategic Management Journal* 13(S2): 163–82. Online: https://doi.org/10.1002/smj.4250130911.

PETZ, SARAH. 2021. “Manitoba Athletes Talk Frankly about Racism in Sport in New V ideo at Combatting Discrimination.” *CBC News*, 7 December. Online: www.cbc.ca/news/canada/manitoba/racism-in-sport-video-1.6276636.

PICKUP, OLIVER. 2022. “Remote and Hybrid Working Highlights the Widening Gulf between Work-Life Conditions of Senior and Junior Employees.” *Worklife*, 15 February. Online: www.worklife.news/talent/remote-and-hybrid-working-highlights-the-widening-gulf-between-work-life-conditions-of-senior-and-junior-employees/?utm_campaign=worklifedis&utm_source=worklifedaily&utm_medium=email&utm_content=122823&utm_medium=email&utm_campaign=Worklife%20Briefing%2012282023&utm_content=Worklife%20Briefing%2012282023+CID_868eb3ed7836d263cb361d7ebc9f400b&utm_source=wldis&utm_term=Remote%20and%20hybrid%20working%20highlights%20the%20widening%20gulf%20between%20work-life%20conditions%20of%20senior%20and%20junior%20employees.

PILKINGTON, ANDREW. 2022. “Perspective Chapter: Black Lives Matter and the Anti-Woke Campaign in the UK.” In *Effective Elimination of Structural Racism*, edited by Erick Guerrero, 131–48. London: IntechOpen. Online: https://books.google.ca/books?hl=en&lr=&id=n9ZyEAAAQBAJ&oi=fnd&pg=PA131&dq=anti-woke+movement+in+UK&ots=X6MD32hgXL&sig=3gFHzPp7Xx5kC27NkyImjCVJPqM#v=onepage&q=anti-woke%20movement%20in%20UK&f=false.

PINDERHUGHES, CHARLES. 2011. "Toward a New Theory of Internal Colonialism." *Socialism and Democracy* 25: 235–56.

PORTER, JOHN. 1965. The Vertical Mosaic: An Analysis of Social Class and Power in Canada. Toronto: University of Toronto Press.

PRAGER, JEFFREY. 1972–73. "White Racial Privilege and Social Change: An Examination of Theories of Racism." *Berkeley Journal of Sociology* 17: 117–50.

PREMJI, ZAHRA. 2023. "3 Years into the Covid-19 Pandemic, Anti-Asian Hare Still Prevalent in Metro Vancouver: Advocates." *CBC News – British Columbia*, 26 January. Online: www.cbc.ca/news/canada/british-columbia/anti-asian-hate-in-metro-vancouver-2023-1.6725671.

PRICEWATERHOUSECOOPER. 2023. "Code of Conduct: Living Our Purpose and Values." September. Online: www.pwc.com/ca/en/about-us/assets/pwc-code-of-conduct-en.pdf.

PRICEWATERHOUSECOOPER. 2024. "From Principles to Practice: Responsible AI in Action." *Strategy+Business*, 20 February. Online: www.strategy-business.com/article/From-principles-to-practice-Responsible-AI-in-action?utm_source=itw&utm_medium=NL20240312&utm_campaign=resp.

PROJECT IMPLICIT. 2011. "Implicit Association Test (IAT)." *University of Virginia, Project Implicit.* Online: https://implicit.harvard.edu/implicit/user/demo.canada/ca.static/selectatest.html.

PRUSINKIEWICZ, KATHERINE. 2019. "New CBCA Diversity Disclosure Requirements Confirmed." *Norton Rose Fulbright*, July. Online: www.nortonrosefulbright.com/en-ca/knowledge/publications/806cb42e/new-cbca-diversity-disclosure-requirements-confirmed.

PUGLIESE, KARYN. 2020. "Indigenous Women Leaders are Having a #MeToo Moment." *Canada's National Observer*, 23 December. Online: www.nationalobserver.com/2020/12/23/opinion/indigenous-women-leaders-metoo-harassment.

QUILLIAN, LINCOLN & JOHN J. LEE. 2023. "Trends in Racial and Ethnic Discrimination in Hiring in Six Western Countries." *Proceedings of the National Academy of Sciences* 120(6): n.p.

RACINE, NICOLE & SHAINUR PREMJI. 2024. "Child Poverty Is on the Rise in Canada, Putting over 1 Million Kids at Risks of Life-long Negative Effects." *The Conversation*, 29 January. Online: https://theconversation.com/child-poverty-is-on-the-rise-in-canada-putting-over-1-million-kids-at-risk-of-life-long-negative-effects-221565?utm_medium=email&utm_campaign=Latest%20from%20The%20Conversation%20for%20February%2017-18-19&utm_content=Latest%20from%20The%20Conversation%20for%20February%2017-18-19+CID_7ecb0f9de-2822a9b84da770ba338257d&utm_source=campaign_monitor_ca&utm_term=Child%20poverty%20is%20on%20the%20rise%20in%20Canada%20putting%20over%201%20million%20kids%20at%20risk%20of%20life-long%20negative%20effects.

RAHMAN, WALI & ZEKERIYA NAS. 2013. "Employee Development and Turnover Intention: Theory Validation." *European Journal of Training and Development* 37(6): 564–79.

RAI, TRISHA & CAITLIN DUTKIEWICZ. 2022. "How to Navigate Pushback to Diversity, Equity, and Inclusion Efforts." *Gartner: Insights /Human Resources*, 10 May. Online: www.gartner.com/en/articles/how-to-navigate-pushback-to-diversity-equity-and-inclusion-efforts.

RAMIREZ, MARC. 2023. "Racism in Online Gaming is Rampant. The Toll on Youth Mental Health is Adding Up." *USA Today*, 3 September. Online: www.usatoday.com/story/news/nation/2023/09/03/online-gaming-racism-youth-extremism-mental-health/70721986007/?mc_cid=2e25dd9500&mc_eid=790e5cf131.

RANA, UDAY. 2024. "8 in 10 Black Canadians say They Still Face Discrimination at Work: Report." *Global News*, 5 February. Online: https://globalnews.ca/news/10273423/black-history-month-kpmg-survey-workplace/.

RAO, ANAND & EUAN CAMERON. 2018. "The Future of Artificial Intelligence Depends on Trust." *Strategy+Business (PriceWaterhouse-Cooper)*, 31 July. Online: www.strategy-business.com/article/The-Future-of-Artificial-Intelligence-Depends-on-Trust.

RASTELLI, DANY. 2018. "Bringing HR and AI Together." *HR Director*. Online: www.thehrdirector.com/features/artificial-intelligence/bringing-hr-ai-together/.

RAZA, ALI. 2022. "Being Black in School: Peel Students Open up about the Racism they Face in the Classroom." *CBC News*, 13 April. Online: www.cbc.ca/news/canada/toronto/peel-students-racism-panel-1.6408851.

RAZA, MUHAMMAD, RODERIC BEAUJOT, AND GEBREMARIAM WOLDEMICAEL. 2013. "Social Capital and Economic Integration of Visible Minority Immigrants in Canada." *Journal of International Migration and Integration*. 14: 263–85.

REALE-CHIN, DANIEL. 2023. "Majority of Racialized Canadian Employees have faced Workplace Racism during their Careers, Study Shows." *Globe and Mail*, 16 October. Online: www.theglobeandmail.com/business/article-majority-of-racialized-canadian-employees-have-faced-workplace-racism/.

REGISTERED NURSES' ASSOCIATION OF ONTARIO. 2022. "Black Nurses Task Force Report." February. Online: https://rnao.ca/media/2140/download?inline.

REICH, MICHAEL. 1978. "Who Benefits from Racism? The Distribution among Whites of Gains and Losses from Racial Inequality." *Journal of Human Resources* 13(4): 524–44.

REICH, MICHAEL. 1981. Racial Inequality: A Political-Economic Analysis. Princeton, NJ: Princeton University Press.

REITZ, JEFFREY. 2007. "Immigrant Employment Success in Canada, Part 1: Individual and Contextual Causes." *Journal of International Migration and Integration* 8, no. 1: 11–36.

REITZ, JEFFREY G., AND RUPA BANERJEE. 2007. "Racial Inequality, Social Cohesion and Policy Issues in Caanda." In *Belonging? Diversity, Recognition and Shared Citizenship in Canada*, edited by Keith Banting, Thomas J. Courchene, and F. Leslie Seidlle, 489–545. Montreal: Institute for Research on Public Policy.

RESTALLI, DANY. 2018. "Bringing HR and AI Together." *HR Director*, 30 July. Online: www.thehrdirector.com/features/artificial-intelligence/bringing-hr-ai-together/.

REYNOLDS, CHRISTOPHER. 2016. "Bloor West Village Rally Counters with a Celebration of Tolerance." *Toronto Star*, 26 June. Online: www.thestar.com/news/gta/bloor-west-village-rally-counters-racism-with-a-celebration-of-tolerance/article_2477a36d-3b0f-519f-abe5-4cd89398e901.html.

RIDGEWAY, C.L. 2019. "Understanding the nature of Status Inequality: Why is it Everywhere? Why Does It Matter?" In *Advances in Group Processes*, edited by S.R Thye and E.J. Lawler, 1–18. Leeds, UK: Emerald Publishing.

RIEDIGER, N. D. , O. KINGSON, A. MUDRYJ, K. L. FARQUHAR, K. A. SPENCE, K. VAGIANOS & M. SUH. 2019. "Diversity and Equity in Dietetics and Undergraduate Nutrition Education in Manitoba." *Canadian Journal of Dietetic Practice and Research* 80(1): 44–46.

RIKETTA, MICHAEL & ROLF VAN DICK. 2005. "Foci of Attachment in Organizations: A Meta-Analytic Comparison of the Strength and Correlates of Workgroup versus Organizational Identification and Commitment." *Journal of Vocational Behaviour* 67: 490–510.

RITTER, MOIRA. 2021. "A GB News Anchor Is Taking a Break – Just Two Weeks after the Channel's Debut." *CNN Business*, 25 June. Online: www.cnn.com/2021/06/25/media/gb-news-andrew-neil-break.

ROBERTS, JOANNE. 2022. "Manitoba: People of Colour Say Canadian Border Agents Discriminate against Them as They Return." *CBC News*, 16 September. Online: www.cbc.ca/news/canada/manitoba/racialized-travellers-border-security-1.6583899.

ROBERTS, MELANA. 2020 "Black Food Insecurity in Canada." *News and Blogs, Broadbent Institute*, 3 February. Online: www.broadbentinstitute.ca/black_food_insecurity_in_canada.

ROBINSON, GREG. 2017. "Internment of Japanese Canadians." *The Canadian Encyclopedia*, 15 February. Online: www.thecanadianencyclopedia.ca/en/article/internment-of-japanese-canadians.

ROBSON, DAVID. 2019. "The '3.5% Rule': How a Small Minority Can Change the World." *BBC*, 13 May. Online: www.bbc.com/future/article/20190513-it-only-takes-35-of-people-to-change-the-world.

RODRIGUEZ, JEREMIAH. 2021a. "COVID-19 Pandemic worsened Disparities for Ethnocultural Communities in Canada: Study." *CTV News*, 9 August. Online: www.ctvnews.ca/health/coronavirus/covid-19-pandemic-worsened-disparities-for-ethnocultural-communities-in-canada-study-1.5540007#:~:text=RACIALIZED%20PEOPLE%20BORE%20BRUNT%20OF%20PANDEMIC&text=During%20the%20first%20part%20of,higher%20concentrations%20of%20visible%20minorities.

RODRIGUEZ, JEREMIAH. 2021b. "'We Need to Call It Out': Canadian Athletes Say Racism toward Black Sports Stars Is a Problem Here Too." *CTV News*, 14 July. Online: www.ctvnews.ca/canada/we-need-to-call-it-out-canadian-athletes-say-racism-toward-black-sports-stars-is-a-problem-here-too-1.5508812.

ROYAL BANK OF CANADA. 2024. "Governance and Accountability of Diversity and Inclusion." Online: www.rbc.com/diversity-inclusion/governance-and-accountability/.

RYAN, TESS. 2019. "For Indigenous Women, the #MeToo Movement is a Deeper Fight Against Racism, Power Imbalance and Oppression." *The Conversation*, 27 October. Online: https://theconversation.com/for-indigenous-women-the-metoo-movement-is-a-deeper-fight-against-racism-power-and-oppression-124502.

SANTOS, SOFFIA FERREIRA. 2025. "What Is the 1798 Law That Trump Used to Deport Migrants?" *BBC News*, 21 March. Online: www.bbc.com/news/articles/cy871w21d3vo.

SASKATCHEWAN HUMAN RIGHTS COMMISSION. 2024a. “Employment Equity.” Online: https://saskatchewanhumanrights.ca/education-resources/employment-equity-program/.

SASKATCHEWAN HUMAN RIGHTS COMMISSION. 2024b. “Employment Equity Program Policy.” Online: https://saskatchewanhumanrights.ca/education-resources/equity-programs/employment-equity-program-policy/.

SAWCHUK, STEPHAN. 2021. “What Is Critical Race Theory, and Why Is It under Attack?” *Educational Week*, 18 May. Online: www.edweek.org/leadership/what-is-critical-race-theory-and-why-is-it-under-attack/2021/05.

SCASSA, TERESA. 2024. “AI, Human Rights, and Canada’s Proposed AI and Data Act.” *TeresaScassa*, 19 March. Online: www.teresascassa.ca/index.php?option=com_k2&view=item&id=380:ai-human-rights-and-canadas-proposed-ai-and-data-act&Itemid=80.

SCHAFER, J.A. 2002. “Spinning the Web of Hate: Web-based Hate Propagation by Extremist Organizations.” *Journal of Criminal Justice and Popular Culture* 9: 269–88.

SCHAFFER, BRYAN S. & CHRISTINE M. RIORDAN. 2013. “Relational Demography in Supervisor-Subordinate Dyads: An Examination of Discrimination and Exclusionary Treatment.” *Canadian Journal of Administrative Sciences* 30(1): 3–17. Online: https://doi.org/10.1002/cjas.1237.

SCHUAL, KEVIN, HAMZA SHABAN, SHELLY TAN MONIQUE WOO & NITASHA TIKU. 2022. “AI Can Now Create Images Out of Thin Air. See How It Works.” *Washington Post*, 20 September. Online: www.washingtonpost.com/technology/interactive/2022/ai-image-generator/.

SCHULTZ, VICKI. 1990. “Telling Stories About Women and Work: Judicial Interpretations of Sex Segregation in the Workplace in Title VII Case Raising the Lack of Interest Argument.” *Harvard Law Review* 103(8): 1749–1843. https://doi.org/10.2307/1341460.

SCHUMPETER, JOSEPH. 1943. Capitalism, Socialism and Democracy. London: Allen and Unwin.

SCOTT, J.L. 2020. “What You Should Know About Black Birders.” *The Conversation*, 2 June.

SCOTT, JACQUELINE L. & AMBIKA TENNETI. N.d. “Race and Nature in the City: Engaging Youth of Colour in Nature-Based Activities.” *Nature Canada*. Accessed 1 September 2023. Online: https://naturecanada.ca/wp-content/uploads/2021/04/Race-Nature-in-the-City-Report.pdf.

SENGUPTA, S.B. 2012. “An Overview of Succession Management: Contemporary Policies and Practices.” *Abhigyan* 30(1): n.p. Online: https://doi.org/10.1177/0970238520120101.

SHERIDAN, FIONA. 2013. "Prejudice against Women Leaders: Sex of Voice." In *Handbook of Research on Promoting Women's Careers*, edited by Susan Vinnicombe, Ronald J. Burke, Stacy Blake-Beard, and Lynda L. Moore, 269–88. Northampton, UK: Edward Elgar.

SHRIVES, PHILIP J. & NIAMH M. BRENNAN. 2015 (March). "A Typology for Exploring the Quality of Explanations for Non-Compliance with UK Corporate Governance Regulations." *British Accounting Review* 47(1): 85–99. Online: https://doi.org/10.1016/j.bar.2014.08.002.

SHUFELT, TIM. 2023. "Companies Keep Mum on ESG Intiatives as 'Greenhusing'Takes Off'Them" *Globe and Mail*, 18 August. Online: www.theglobeandmail.com/investing/markets/inside-the-market/article-companies-keep-mum-on-esg-initiatives-as-greenhushing-takes-off/.

SHUMAN, ERIC, ERIC KNOWLES & AMIT GOLDENBERG. 2023. "To Overcome Resistance to DEI, Understand What's Driving It." *Harvard Business Review: Diversity and Inclusion*, 1 March. Online: https://hbr.org/2023/03/to-overcome-resistance-to-dei-understand-whats-driving-it.

SIEGELMAN, PETER & JOHN J. DONOHUE III. 2024. "Studying the Iceberg from Its Tip: A Comparison of Published and Unpublished Employment Discrimination Cases." *Law and Society Review* 24(5): 1133–70. Online: https://doi.org/10.2307/3053565.

SIMPSON, LAURA. 2018. "Violent Victimization and Discrimination among Visible Minority Population in Canada, 2014." *Statistics Canada*, 12 April. Online: www150.statcan.gc.ca/n1/pub/85-002-x/2018001/article/54913-eng.htm.

SIU, BOBBY. 2017. Federal Equity Manual. Vols. 1 and 2. Toronto: Thomson Reuters.

SIU, BOBBY. 2021. *Opening Doors to Diversity in Leadership*. Toronto: Rotman School of Management, University of Toronto Press.

SMITH, ALANA & SHANNON PROUDFOOT. 2023. "Online Extremism on the Rise, RCMP Says." *Globe and Mail*, 18 December.

SMITH, ALLEN. 2025a. "How to Adjust Your DEI Initiatives under Trump's New Guidelines." *HR Daily Newsletter*, 28 January. Online: www.shrm.org/topics-tools/employment-law-compliance/how-to-adjust-dei-initiatives-under-trumps-new-guidelines.

SMITH, ALLEN. 2025b. "How Trump's EEOC, NLRB Firings could Impact Recent Labour Rulings." *HR Daily Newsletter*, 29 January. Online: www.shrm.org/topics-tools/employment-law-compliance/how-trumps-eeoc-nlrb-firings-could-impact-recent-labo.

SMITH, ALLEN. 2025c. "Judge Blocs Enforcement of DEI Orders as Applied to Companies," *HR Daily Newsletter*, 24 February. Online: www.shrm.org/topics-tools/employment-law-compliance/judge-blocks-enforcement-of-dei-orders-as-applied-to-companies.

SMITH, GARRY & CARL GRINDSTAFF. 1970. *Race and Sport in Canada.* Toronto: Centre for Sport Policy Studies, Department of Kinesiology and Physical Education, University of Toronto.

SMITH, RYAN A. 2002. "Race, Gender, and Authority in the Workplace: Theory and Research." *American Review of Sociology* 28: 509–42.

SOUISSI, TAKWA. 2021. "Islamophobia in Canada." *The Canadian Encyclopedia*, 13 July. Online: www.thecanadianencyclopedia.ca/en/article/Islamophobia.

SPIELER, CHRISTOF. 2020. "Racism Has Shaped Public Transit, and It's Riddled with Inequities." *Urban Edge, Kinder Institute for Urban Research, Rice University*, 24 August. Online: https://kinder.rice.edu/urbanedge/racism-has-shaped-public-transit-and-its-riddled-inequities.

SPITERI, SUZANNE. 2023. "What Can the Data Tell Us About Black Canadians and the Labour Market." *Labour Market Information Centre*, 1 February. Online: https://lmic-cimt.ca/part-3-what-can-the-data-tell-us-about-black-canadians-and-the-labour-market/.

STACKHOUSE, J. 2020. "Six Ways to Confront Bias in AI and How Canada Can Lead the Way." *RBC Borealis – Lectures*, 21 October. Online: https://rbcborealis.com/news/six-ways-confront-bias-ai-and-how-canada-can-lead-way/.

STANDING COMMITTEE ON CANADIAN HERITAGE. 2018. "Taking Action against Systemic Racism and Religious Discrimination including Islamophobia." Online: www.ourcommons.ca/DocumentViewer/en/42-1/CHPC/report-10.

STANDING SENATE COMMITTEE ON HUMAN RIGHTS. 2023. "Anti-Black Racism, Sexism and Systemic Discrimination in the Canadain Human Rights Commission." Online: https://sencanada.ca/en/.

STATISTICS CANADA. 2003. The Ethnic Diversity Survey: Portrait of a Multicultural Society. Catalogue no. 89-593-XIE. Ottawa: Statistics Canada. Online: www.hindawi.com/journals/usr/2012/385806/.

STATISTICS CANADA. 2020. "Impact of COVID-19 on Small Businesses in Canada. StatCan COVID-19: Data to Insights for a Better Canada." Online: www150.statcan.gc.ca/n1/pub/45-28-0001/2020001/article/00018-eng.htm.

STATISTICS CANADA. 2021 "Study: Indigenous Youth in Canada." 1 December. Online: www150.statcan.gc.ca/n1/daily-quotidien/211201/dq211201b-eng.htm.

STATISTICS CANADA. 2022a. "Average Employment Income Indicators, by Group Designated as Visible Minorities and Selected Sociodemographic Characteristics for the Population Aged 15 Years and Over I Private Households, 2006, 2011 and 2016." 17 May. Online: www150.statcan.gc.ca/t1/tbl1/en/tv.action?pid=4310006801.

STATISTICS CANADA. 2022b. "The Contribution of Pandemic Relief Benefits to the Incomes of Canadians in 2020." 3 August. Online: www12.statcan.gc.ca/census-recensement/2021/as-sa/98-200-X/2021005/98-200-X2021005-eng.cfm.

STATISTICS CANADA. 2022c. Employment Income Statistics by Visible Minority, Highest Level of Education, Immigrant Status and Income Year: Canada, Provinces and Territories, Census Metropolitan Areas and Census Agglomerations with Parts." 30 November. Online: www150.statcan.gc.ca/t1/tbl1/en/tv.action?pid=9810043901&pickMembers%5B0%5D=1.1&pickMembers%5B1%5D=2.1&pickMembers%5B2%5D=3.1&pickMembers%5B3%5D=4.1&pickMembers%5B4%5D=5.4&pickMembers%5B5%5D=6.2&pickMembers%5B6%5D=7.1.

STATISTICS CANADA. 2022d. "Homicide Trends in Canada, 2021." 21 November. Online: www150.statcan.gc.ca/n1/daily-quotidien/221121/dq221121a-eng.htm?indid=3435-1&indgeo=0.

STATISTICS CANADA. 2022e. "Housing Conditions Among First Nations People, Metis and Inuit in Canada from the 2021 Census." 21 September. Online: www12.statcan.gc.ca/census-recensement/2021/as-sa/98-200-X/2021007/98-200-X2021007-eng.cfm.

STATISTICS CANADA. 2022f. "Shelters for Victims of Abuse with Ties to Indigenous Communities or Organizations in Canada 2020/2021." 16 September. Online: www150.statcan.gc.ca/n1/pub/85-002-x/2022001/article/00014-eng.htm.

STATISTICS CANADA. 2023a. "Canadian Income Survey, 2021 (with Table 4 and Table 5)." *The Daily*, 2 May. Online: www150.statcan.gc.ca/n1/daily-quotidien/230502/dq230502a-eng.htm?CMP=mstatcan.

STATISTICS CANADA. 2023b. "Housing Conditions Among Racialized Groups: A Brief Overview." *The Daily*, 23 January. Online: www150.statcan.gc.ca/n1/daily-quotidien/230123/dq230123b-eng.htm.

STATISTICS CANADA. 2023c. "Labour Force Characteristics by Indigenous Groups and Educational Attainment." 6 January. Online: www150.statcan.gc.ca/t1/tbl1/en/tv.action?pid=1410035901.

STATISTICS CANADA. 2023d. "Labour Force Characteristics by Region and Detailed Indigenous Group." 6 January. Online: www150.statcan.gc.ca/t1/tbl1/en/tv.action?pid=1410036501.

STATISTICS CANADA. 2023e. "Labour Force Characteristics by Visible Minority Groups, Three-Month Moving Averages, Monthly, Unadjusted Seasonality." 5 May. Online: www150.statcan.gc.ca/t1/tbl1/en/tv.action?pid=1410037301.

STATISTICS CANADA. 2023f. "Labour Force Characteristics by Visible Minority Group, Three-Month Moving Averages, Monthly Unadjusted for

Seasonality." 1 December. Online: www150.statcan.gc.ca/t1/tbl1/en /cv.action?pid=1410037301.

STATISTICS CANADA. 2023g. "Labour Force Survey, October 2023." *The Daily*, 3 November. Online: www150.statcan.gc.ca/n1/daily-quotidien/231103/dq231103a-eng.htm.

STATISTICS CANADA. 2023h. "Representation of Women on Boards of Directors and Officer Positions, 2020." 29 May. Online: www150.statcan.gc.ca/n1/daily-quotidien/230529/dq230529b-eng.htm.

STATISTICS CANADA. 2023i. "Study: Childhood Factors Associated with High School Completion or Higher Education among Off-Reserve First Nations, Metis, and Inuit Children." *The Daily*, 6 April. Online: www150.statcan.gc.ca/n1/daily-quotidien/230406/dq230406b-eng.htm.

STATISTICS CANADA. 2023j. "Study: Housing Experiences and Well-Being Among First Nations People Living Off Reserve, Metis and Inuit, 2018." The Daily, 4 April. Online: www150.statcan.gc.ca/n1/daily-quotidien/230404/dq230404c-eng.htm.

STATISTICS CANADA. 2023k. "Survey of Household Spending, 2021." *The Daily*, 18 October. Online: www150.statcan.gc.ca/n1/daily-quotidien/231018/dq231018a-eng.htm?utm_source=mstatcan&utm_medium=eml&utm_campaign=statcan-statcan-mstatcan.

STATISTICS CANADA. 2023l. "Table 11-10-0093-01 *Poverty and Low-Income Statistics by Selected Demographic Characteristics*." 2 May. Online: www150.statcan.gc.ca/t1/tbl1/en/tv.action?pid=1110009301.

STATISTICS CANADA. 2024a. "Discrimination and Racism in Sports in Canada." *The Daily*, 4 March. Online: www150.statcan.gc.ca/n1 /daily-quotidien/240304/dq240304a-eng.htm?utm_source=mstatcan&utm_medium=eml&utm_campaign=statcan-statcan-mstatcan.

STATISTICS CANADA. 2024b. "Experience(s) of Discrimination, Reason(s) and Context(s) of Discrimination, 5 Years Before and Since the Beginning of Covid-10 Pandemic, by Groups Designated as Visible Minorities and Selected Sociodemographic Characteristics." 11 August. Table 43-10-0061-01. Online: www150.statcan.gc.ca/t1/tbl1/en/tv.action?pid=4310006101.

STATISTICS CANADA. 2024c. "Gender Results Framework: A New Data Table on Workplace Harassment." *The Daily*, 12 February. Online: www150.statcan.gc.ca/n1/daily-quotidien/240212/dq240212a-eng.htm?utm_source=mstatcan&utm_medium=eml&utm_campaign=statcan-statcan-mstatcan.

STATISTICS CANADA. 2024d. "Half of Racialized People have Experienced Discrimination or Unfair Treatment in the Past Five Years." *The Daily*, 16 May. Online: www150.statcan.gc.ca/n1/daily-quotidien/240516/dq240516b-eng.

htm?utm_source=mstatcan&utm_medium=eml&utm_campaign=statcan-statcan-mstatcan.

STATISTICS CANADA. 2024e. "Recent Immigrants Report Greater Difficulty Making Ends Meet and are Less Satisfied with their Amount of Free Time." 18 June. Online: www150.statcan.gc.ca/n1/daily-quotidien/240618/dq240618b-eng.htm?utm_source=mstatcan&utm_medium=eml&utm_campaign=statcan-statcan-mstatcan.

STATISTICS CANADA. 2025. "Impacts of Rising Prices on the Well-Being of Indigenous People, 2024." *The Daily*, 17 January. Online: www150.statcan.gc.ca/n1/daily-quotidien/250117/dq250117b-eng.htm.

STOKEL-WALKER. Chris, 2024. "Showing AI just 1000 Extra Images Reduced AI-Generated Stereotypes." *New Scientist*, 2 April. Online: www.newscientist.com/article/2425065-showing-ai-just-1000-extra-images-reduced-ai-generated-stereotypes/.

SU, SOPHIA & HYEONGSUK JIN. 2023. "Labour Market Outcomes of Indigenous Journey Persons in Canada." *Statistics Canada*, 13 March. Online: www150.statcan.gc.ca/n1/pub/81-595-m/81-595-m2022001-eng.htm.

SU, YVOONE. 2025. "Demonizing Foreign Students Sidesteps Solutions to Canada's Problems." *The Conversation*, 13 January. Online: www.yorku.ca/news/2025/01/13/demonizing-foreign-students-sidesteps-solutions-to-canadas-problems/.

SUBEDI, RAJENDRA, LAWSON GREENBERG & MARTIN TURCOTTE. 2020. "COVID-19 Mortality Rates in Canada's Ethnocultural Neighbourhoods." *Statistics Canada*, 28 October. Online: www150.statcan.gc.ca/n1/pub/45-28-0001/2020001/article/00079-eng.htm.

SUE, DERALD WING, CHRISTINA M. CAPDOILUPO. GINA C. TORINO, JENNIFTER M. BUCCERI, AISHA M.B. HOLDER, KEVIN L. NADAL & MARTA ESQUILIN. 2007. "Racial Microaggressions in *Everyday Life: Implications for Clinical Practice.*" *American Psychologist* 62(4): 271–86. Online: https://pubmed.ncbi.nlm.nih.gov/17516773/or https://doi.org/10.1037/0003-066x.62.4.271.

SUSTAIN ONTARIO. 2021. "New Research from PROOF and FoodShare on Food Insecurity and Anti-Black Racism." 29 October. https://sustainontario.com/2021/10/29/new-research-from-proof-and-foodshare-on-food-insecurity-and-anti-black-racism/#:~:text=PROOF%20and%20FoodShare%20have%20just,that%20lead%20to%20food%20insecurity.

SUTTON, DANIELLE. 2023. "Gender-Related Homicide of Women and Girls in Canada. Juristat". *Statistics Canada*, 5 April. Online: www150.statcan.gc.ca/n1/pub/85-002-x/2023001/article/00003-eng.htm.

TALAULICAR, AXEL & V. WERDER. 2008. "Patterns of Compliance with the German Corporate Governance Code." *Corporate Governance: An International Review* 16(4): 255–73.

TARASUK, VALERIE & ANDY MITCHELL. 2020. *Household Food Insecurity in Canada, 2017–2018*. Toronto: Research to Identify Policy Options to Reduce Food Insecurity (PROOF)." Online: https://proof.utoronto.ca/wp-content/uploads/2020/03/Household-Food-Insecurity-in-Canada-2017-2018-Full-Reportpdf.pdf.

TELUS. N.d. "Reconciliation Commitment." Accessed 3 October 2024. Online: https://assets.ctfassets.net/fltupc9ltp8m/7eMH2jA1q0Qasegx-Hx9SMM/a6c6037d3e8145564f0eed4b151bcd1a/EN_-_Accessible_-_TELUS_Reconciliation_Commitment.pdf.

TENOVE, CHRIS, HEIDI TWOREK & FENWICK MCKELVEY. 2018. "Tackling Online Hatred Requires Clear Government Guidelines." *Globe and Mail*, 12 November.

THOMPSON, DEBRA. 2023. "Affirmative Action Never Stood a Chance." *Globe and Mail*, 3 July.

THORPE-MOSCON, JENNIFER, ALIXANDRA POLLACK & OLUFEMI OLU-LAFE. 2019. Empowering Workplaces Combat Emptional Tax for People of Colour in Canada. Toronto: Catalyst. Online: www.catalyst.org/research/people-of-colour-in-canada/.

THURTON, DAVID. 2023. "Ottawa Says Human Rights Commission Discriminated against Its Black Employees." *CBC News*, 16 March. Online: www.cbc.ca/news/politics/canadian-human-rights-commission-black-racialized-1.6780794.

TJEPKEMA, MICHAEL, TANYA CHRISTIDIS, TOYIB OLANIYAN & JEREMIAH HWEE. 2023. "Mortality Inequalities of Black Adults in Canada." *Statistics Canada*, 15 February. Online: www150.statcan.gc.ca/n1/pub/82-003-x/2023002/article/00001-eng.htm.

TRADING ECONOMICS. 2024. "Canada Employed Persons." Online: https://tradingeconomics.com/canada/employed-persons.

TRAFFORD, MADISON. 2018. "Strategic Misrepresentation in Media during World War II." *Canadian Whites, Commando Comics*, 23 November. Online: https://cla.blog.torontomu.ca/strategic-japanese-misrepresentation-in-media-during-world-war-ii/#:~:text=The%20years%20surrounding%20World%20War,to%20incredible%20discrimination%20and%20mistreatment.

TRINH, JUDY. 2022. "Racism Blamed in Death of Man on Northern First Nation." *CTV National News*, 4 October. Online: www.ctvnews.ca/canada/racism-blamed-in-death-of-man-on-northern-ontario-first-nation-1.6090393.

TULLOCH, MICHAEL H. 2018. "Report of the Independent Street Checks Review." Online: www.ontario.ca/page/report-independent-street-checks-review.

TUNNEY, CATHARINE. 2021a. "Politics: Episodes of Racism, Harassment, Homophobia Recorded at Border Crossing." *CBC News*, 30 June. Online: www.cbc.ca/news/politics/cbsa-cornwall-akwesasne-1.6085999.

TUNNEY, CATHARINE. 2021b. "Politics: The Number of Misconduct Investigations of Border Officers Rose Last Year." *CBC News*, 6 June. Online: www.cbc.ca/news/politics/cbsa-terminations-misconduct-1.6048545.

TUPPER, HELEN & SARAH ELLIS. 2022. "Time to Reimagine Employee Retention." *Harvard Business Review*, 4 July. Online: https://hbr.org/2022/07/its-time-to-reimagine-employee-retention.

TUTTLE, MYRNA EL FAKHRY. 2022. "Racial Profiling in the Retail Industry." *Alberta Civil Liberty Research Centre, University of Calgary*, 20 July. Online: www.aclrc.com/blog/2022/7/20/racial-profiling-in-the-retail-industry.

TUTTON, MICHAEL. 2018. "More Than 100 Complaints of Racism, Rudeness against Canada Border Officers Were Founded Last Year." *National Post*, 4 September. Online: https://nationalpost.com/news/canada/travellers-complain-about-rude-disrespectful-canadian-border-officers.

UNIFOR. 2024a. "Constitution and Policies." Online: www.unifor.org/about-us/constitution-and-policies.

UNIFOR. 2024b. "Local Union Equity Fund." Online: www.unifor.org/resources/local-union-equity-fund.

URBANCOVA, HANN, HELENA CERMAKOVA & HANA VOSTROVSKA. 2016. "Diversity Management in the Workplace." *Acta Universitatis Agriculturae et Silviculturae Mendelaianae Brunensis* 64(3): 1086–92.

URBINATI, NADIA. 2019. "Political Theory of Populism." *Annual Review of Political Science* 22: 111–27. https://doi.org/10.1146/annurev-polisci-050317-070753.

US DEPARTMENT OF EDUCATION. 2025. "Press Release: US Department of Education Takes Action to Eliminate DEI." 23 January. Online: www.ed.gov/about/news/press-release/us-department-of-education-takes-action-eliminate-dei.

VALGAROSSON, VIKTOR, WILL JENNINGS, GERRY STOKER, HANNAH BUNTING, DANIEL DEVINE, LAWRENCE MCKAY, AND ANDREW KLASSEN. 2025. "A Crisis of Political Trust? Global Trends in Institutional Trust from 1958 to 2019." *British Journal of Political Science* 55: 1–41. Online: https://doi.org/10.1017/S0007123424000498.

VASWANI, MAMTA, ALINA SUTTER, NATALIA LAPSHINA & VICTORIA M. ESSA. 2023. "Discrimination Experienced by Immigrants, Racialized Individuals, and Indigenous Peoples in Small- and Mid-Sized Communities in Southwestern Ontario." *Canadian Review of Sociology* 60(1): 92–113. Online: https://onlinelibrary.wiley.com/doi/abs/10.1111/cars.12413 or https://doi.org/10.1111/cars.12413.

VELAZQUEZ, ANA I. et al. 2022. "Microaggressions, Bias, and Equity in the Workplace: Why Does It Matter, and What Can Oncologist Do?" *American Society of Clinical Oncology Educational Book*, 1 June. Online: https://ascopubs.org/doi/10.1200/EDBK_350691.

VIETEN, ULRIKE. 2016. "Contemporary Far-Right Racist Populism in Europe." *Journal of Intercultural Studies* 37(6): 533–40. Online: https://doi.org/10.1080/07256868.2016.1235099.

VUICIC, GEORGE G. 2019. "Looking Forward to 2020." 28 November. Online: https://hicksmorley.com/2019/11/28/incoming-legislative-changes-in-2020/.

VAN VULPEN, ERIK. N.d. "What Is Performance Management? The Complete Guide." *Academy to Innovate HR*. Accessed 15 December 2023. Online: www.aihr.com/blog/what-is-performance-management/#:~:text=Performance%20management%20examples,-HSBC&text=Employees%20can%20access%20an%20HR,productivity%20and%20facilitate%20continual%20growth.

WAGNER, ANDREA & ANNA BRIGEVICH. 2024. "Do You Know What Populism Is? Research Suggests Most Don't, but Some View It with Disdain Anyway." *The Conversation*, 3 December. Online: https://theconversation.com/do-you-know-what-populism-is-research-suggests-most-dont-but-some-view-it-with-disdain-anyway-244375.

WAMBACH, ABBY. 2025. "Why Protest Works – The 3.5% Rule with Erica Chenoweth." *We Can Do Hard Things*. Online: https://podcasts.apple.com/nz/podcast/why-protest-works-the-3-5-rule-with-erica-chenoweth/id1564530722?i=1000716270481.

WARD, LESTER F. 1921. Pure Sociology. New York: Macmillan.

WARUSZYNSKI, B., K. MACEACHERN & V. GIROUX-LALOND. 2019. Perceptions of Racism and Harassment among Visible Minority and Indigenous Members in the Defence Team. Ottawa: Defence Research and Development Canada. Online: www.canada.ca/content/dam/dnd-mdn/documents/reports/caf-retnetion-strategy/caf-retention-strategy-en-2022.pdf.

WEAVER, JACKSON. 2021. "How Kim's Convenience Showcases the Difficulties Faced by Diverse Creators." *CBC News*, 15 April. Online: www.cbc.ca/news/entertainment/kim-s-convenience-end-diverse-1.5988267.

WERHUN, CHERIE & APRIL PENNER. 2010. "The Effects of Stereotyping and Implicit Theory on Prejudice toward Aboriginal Canadians." *Journal Applied Social Psychology* 40(4): 899916.

WEYLAND, K. 2001. "Clarifying a Contested Concept: Populism in the Study of Latin American Politics." *Comparative Politics* 24: 11–22. Online: https://scholar.google.com/scholar_lookup?title=Clarifying+a+contested+concept%3A+populism+in+the+study+of+Latin+American+politics&author=K+Weyland&journal=Comp.+Politics&volume=24-&issue=1&pages=1-22&publication_year=2001&.

WHITE, JAMES D. 2022. "How to Build an Anti-Racist Company: A Playbook for Fostering Diversity, Equity, and Inclusion." *Harvard Business Review* (May–June): n.p. Online: https://hbr.org/2022/05/how-to-build-an-anti-racist-company.

WIESSNER, DANIEL. 2023. "Affirmative-Action Ruling could Place Target on U.S. Corporate Diversity Efforts: Experts." *Globe and Mail*, 1 July. Online: www.theglobeandmail.com/business/international-business/us-business/article-supreme-courts-affirmative-action-ruling-could-place-target-on-us/.

WILLIAMS, KEIZA. N.d. "Insights: A Guide to Communicate with Indigenous Audiences." *The Phoenix Group*. Accessed 8 December 2023. Online: https://thephoenixgroup.ca/insights/blog/a-guide-to-communicating-with-indigenous-audiences.

WILSON, GEORGE & VINCENT J. ROSCIGNO. 2020. "Race and Downward Mobility from Privileged Occupations: African America/White Dynamics across the Early Work-Career." *Social Science Research* 39(1): 67–77. Online: www.sciencedirect.com/science/article/abs/pii/S0049089X09000386 or https://doi.org/10.1016/.

WILSON, JIM. 2023. "3 in 4 Black Canadians say Racism at Work as a 'Serious Problem'." *Human Resources Director, HRD Canada*, 14 June. Online: www.hcamag.com/ca/specialization/diversity-inclusion/3-in-4-black-canadians-say-racism-at-work-a-serious-problem/449289.

WILSON-SMITH, CHRIS. 2024. "Business Brief: A Growing Backlash to DEI." *Globe and Mail*, 10 December. Online: www.theglobeandmail.com/business/article-business-brief-a-growing-backlash-to-dei/.

WINGFIELD, ADIA HARVEY. 2015. "Being Black – but Not too Black – in the Workplace." *The Atlantic*, 14 October. Online: www.theatlantic.com/business/archive/2015/10/being-black-work/409990.

WINGFIELD, ADIA HARVEY. 2023. "Culture That's More Inclusive for Black Employees." *Harvard Business Review*, 7 November. Online: https://hbr.org/2023/11/creating-an-organizational-culture-thats-more-inclusive-for-black-employees.

WOMEN COLLEGE HOSPITAL. 2023. *Indigenous Health*. Ganawishkadawe: Tending the Heart of the Fire. Online: https://indigenoushealth.womenscollegehospital.ca/.

WOMEN ON BOARDS. 2024. "More Men Than Women Joined Boards of Europe's Top Financial Service Firms Last Year." Online: https://womenonboards.net/WOB/WOB/News-and-Media/News_Stories/News-2024/Gender_balance_on_EU_boards.aspx#:~:text=The%20European%20Financial%20Services%20Boardroom,female%20representation%20on%20their%20boards.

WONG, JOEL, ANGELA HORN & SHITAO CHEN. 2013. "Perceived Masculinity: The Potential Influence of Race, Racial Essentialist Beliefs, and Stereotypes." *Psychology of Men and Masculinity* 14(4): 452–64.

WOOLF, MARIE. 2024. "Comparing People to Vermin, Excrement Could Prompt Hate-Speech Probe: Officials." *Globe and Mail*, 7 March.

YAP, MARGARET. 2010. "The Intersection of Gender and Race: Effects of the Incidence of Promotions." *Canadian Journal of Career Development* 9(2): 22–33.

YAP, MARGARET & ALISON M. KONRAD. 2009. "Gender and Racial Differentials in Promotions: Is there a Sticky Floor, a Mid-Level Bottleneck, or a Glass Ceiling." *Industrial Relations* 64(4): 593–619.

YOON, JENNIFER. 2018. "Canada's Diversity Not Reflected on the Silver Screen, Say Actors, Screenwriters of Colour." *CBC News*. 20 July. Online: www.cbc.ca/news/canada/montreal/canada-s-diversity-not-reflected-on-the-silver-screen-say-actors-screenwriters-of-colour-1.4745785.

YUEN, NANCY WANG, STACY L. SMITH, KATHERINE PIEPER, MARC CHOUEITI, KEVIN YAO & DANNA DINH. 2021. "The Prevalence and Portrayal of Asian and Pacific Islanders across 1,300 Popular Films." *USC Annenberg, Amazon Studios, and UTA Foundation*. May. Online: http://assets.uscannenberg.org/docs/aii_aapi-representation-across-films-2021-05-18.pdf.

YUKON CHILD AND YOUTH ADVOCACY OFFICE. 2023. "Launch of Review of Systemic Racism in Education." 27 March. Online: https://www.ycao.ca/post/launch-of-review-of-systemic-racism-in-education.

YUKON HUMAN RIGHTS COMMISSION. N.d. "2022–2023 Annual Report." Accessed 25 August 2024. Online: https://yukonhumanrights.ca/wp-content/uploads/2023/11/2022_2023AnnualReport_English_Final-compressed-1.pdf.

ZACK, NAOMI. 2023. "Political Racism and Populist Movements." In *Philosophy of Race*, edited by Vittorio Bufacchi, n.p. Cham, Switzerland: Palgrave Macmillan. Online: https://doi.org/10.1007/978-3-031-27374-2_12.

ZAJKO, MIKE. 2021. "Conservative AI and Social Inequity: Conceptualizing Alternatives to Bias through Social Theory." *AI and Society* 36: 1047–56. Online: https://link.springer.com/article/10.1007/S00146-021-01153-9.

ZETTELMEYER, FLORIAN & INHI CHO SUH. 2019. "How to Build Artificial Intelligence That Everyone Trust." *Kellogg Insight.* Online: https://insight.kellogg.northwestern.edu/article/how-to-build-artificial-intelligence-that-everyone-can-trust?utm_source=subscriber&utm_medium=email&utm_campaign=boomtrainmailer032019&bt_ee=PUSNc6kWSO3Sc%2F6z1%2FpxfrkEK%2BPhjGfUlkcoZNMbttr2vhyMHJi3nWz%2FyVD1xBhI&bt_ts=1551962857657.

ZIMONJIC, PETER. 2023. "Rise in Antisemitism, Islamophobic Threats Has Canadians 'Scared in Our Own Streets', PM Says." *CBC News*, 8 November. Online: www.cbc.ca/news/politics/trudeau-antisemitism-gaza-islamophobia-1.7022244.

Table of Statutes

Index

About the Author

Dr. Bobby Siu is an author of over ten books, including the *Federal Equity Manual* and *Developing Public Policy*. His *Opening Doors to Diversity in Leadership* was a finalist for the National Business Book Award. He is the co-editor of *Racial Profiling and Human Rights Policy in Canada*.

He is a management consultant and worked in the Government of Ontario with portfolios in public policy and program management in international education, human rights, equity, and skills development. He served as an expert witness on human rights cases for the Ontario Human Rights Commission and taught sociology and public policy at York University.